Marine Corps Generalship

For my father, Edgar F. Puryear, Sr. As a Marine in World War I, he received a bayonet wound in his leg and had a limp the rest of his life. He still wore his Marine Corps ring when I buried him at age 87.

# Marine Corps Generalship

Edgar F. Puryear, Jr.

*Foreword by*
*General Alfred M. Gray, Jr., USMC (Ret.)*

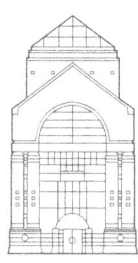

National Defense University Press
Washington, D.C.
2009

Published by Books Express Publishing
Copyright © Books Express, 2011
ISBN 978-1780390-42-0
To obtain further copies of this book please contact
info@books-express.com

# Contents

Foreword . . . . . . . . . . . . . . . . . . . . . . . . . . xi

Acknowledgments . . . . . . . . . . . . . . . . . . . . . xxi

Introduction . . . . . . . . . . . . . . . . . . . . . . . xxiii

**Chapter 1**
"Only One Officer Runs the Marine Corps":
The Role of the Commandant . . . . . . . . . . . . . . . . 1

**Chapter 2**
"General, Will You Do Me the Honor . . .":
Selection of the Commandant . . . . . . . . . . . . . . . . 9

**Chapter 3**
"Destiny Hangs by a Slender Thread":
Making the Decision to Join
the Marine Corps . . . . . . . . . . . . . . . . . . . . . . 71

**Chapter 4**
"Think of Yourself as the Institution":
Decisionmaking . . . . . . . . . . . . . . . . . . . . . . 133

**Chapter 5**
"You Have to Be Heard, and
You Have to Be Felt":
The Importance of Presence ............... 197

**Chapter 6**
"We Will Not Compromise on This":
Having the Character to Challenge .......... 231

**Chapter 7**
"Don't Ignore the Yesterdays of War":
The Importance of Reading ................ 269

**Chapter 8**
"As a Teacher Does a Scholar":
Mentorship. ............................. 291

**Chapter 9**
"Time with People Is Never Wasted":
Consideration ........................... 341

**Chapter 10**
"Authority and Responsibility Are Inseparable":
Accountability .......................... 381

**Chapter 11**
"Miracles Must Be Wrought if Victories
Are to Be Won":
Character and Leadership. ................. 443

**Chapter 12**
"The Marine Way of Life":
The Pattern for Success. .................. 469

Notes.................................497
About the Author .......................513

# Foreword

It is a rare privilege to prepare the foreword for this superb study on Marine Corps generalship. Dr. Edgar F. "Beau" Puryear is a renowned author and lecturer on military character and leadership. His previous books on Army, Navy, and Air Force flag and general officers have won wide acclaim from many distinguished military and civilian leaders. In many ways, this book is a unique history of our Marine Corps, as it tells the story of how many of our Commandants and other distinguished leaders met challenges in war, peace, and times of adversity. It also details the unusual role and responsibility that the Commandant has to our Nation and to our Corps of Marines.

There are many reasons why several general officers are not represented in this study, including availability of individuals for interview, lack of oral histories, and time and space constraints. Dr. Puryear has graciously consented to allow me to comment on some of these distinguished Marine general officers who are not included in this book:

- General George B. Crist, a brilliant officer and an expert in joint matters, who was our first Marine to lead a unified command when he was chosen to head U.S. Central Command in 1985.

- General Walter E. Boomer, whose leadership of the Marine Central Command and the I Marine Expeditionary Force in the Persian Gulf War of 1991 was superb. He later served with distinction as Assistant Commandant of the Marine Corps.

- General Thomas R. Morgan, who served as Assistant Commandant for both General Paul X. Kelley and myself from 1986 through 1988. A finalist in the 1987 Commandant selection process, Tom was an exceptional leader and a great team player with broad experience who can only be described as a class act.

- General John J. Sheehan, a consummate professional, who was the first non-Navy flag officer to command U.S. Atlantic Command and to serve as the Supreme Allied Commander, Atlantic for the North Atlantic Treaty Organization from 1994 to 1998. He was the leading contender to be the Vice Chairman of the Joint Chiefs of Staff but opted not to be considered by the President.

- General Joseph P. Hoar, who commanded U.S. Central Command from 1991 to 1994. Because of his leadership and broad knowledge of strategic matters, he received strong support from many corners to become Chairman of the Joint Chiefs of Staff in 1994.

- General Charles E. Wilhelm, whose major contributions to our special operations and low-intensity conflict policy were instrumental in elevating knowledge of this vital area within the Department of Defense. As the first Marine to command U.S. Southern Command, his oversight of military and defense policies throughout Latin America was superb and improved relations at a critical time.

- General Carlton W. Fulford, Jr., a great field Marine who was equally adept concerning joint and combined matters. He was the first Marine to be selected as Deputy Commander in Chief of U.S. European Command. He, too, was a finalist in the Commandant selection process because of his superb leadership and his breadth of experience in policy and military matters.

- General Joseph J. Went, a distinguished Marine aviator and a brilliant logistician, who made lasting contributions to our Corps. Well respected throughout the Department of Defense, Joe served as my Assistant Commandant from 1988 to 1990.

- General John J. Dailey, who served as Assistant Commandant during and after the Persian Gulf War with the highest distinction. His broad knowledge of air and ground matters and his total credibility within the joint arena and with the Department of Defense were priceless. A finalist for the role of Marine Commandant in 1991, General Dailey went on to a key assignment with the National Aeronautics and Space Administration.

- Generals Richard D. Hearney, Michael J. Williams, William L. Nyland, and Robert Magnus, who all served as Assistant Commandant with great skill and made innumerable contributions to the success of our Corps. Although their tours came after my retirement, I remain keenly aware of their accomplishments during critical times in our history.

There are additional general officers who should receive special recognition for their splendid service to our country and our Corps. Some who have been mentioned by other Commandants in this book are not mentioned here. For those who are serving on Active duty today, know that

I believe we have never been better led. You are the right people at the right time for this complex and dangerous time in our history.

Dr. Puryear has also asked me to make some comments on leadership based on my experiences and observations through the years. Since 1950, it has been my privilege to serve under and to personally know all the Commandants as well as some of the other "giants of the Corps," including Lieutenant General Lewis "Chesty" Puller, Lieutenant General Victor Krulak, General Lewis Walt, and General Ray Davis.

The great leaders that I have known or studied had, in their own way, similar traits that distinguish them from others. These leaders had broad professional knowledge of not just the military but also all other elements of national security, including political, economic, and social factors. They understood the value of training and education to include discipline, particularly self-discipline as essential to develop character, self-control, and effectiveness. A disciplined Marine was, in their eyes, a person who does what must be done.

The great ones had personal character that shone through in all decisions and judgments. They did what they thought was right, regardless of the consequences. They had a sense of fairness in dealing with people and more than a normal dose of common sense at all times. These leaders willingly shared their knowledge with others, and they took the time to teach, when appropriate. They had strong beliefs and a high moral code. "Service to God, Country, and Corps" was not just an expression, but a way of life.

Leadership by example and consideration of others were another hallmark of these distinguished generals. They understood the difference between authority and responsibility. They held themselves accountable for all that their commands did or failed to do, and they expected others to be responsible for their actions when appropriate.

These warriors were also fiercely loyal to their country and their Corps. They recognized that loyalty had to go both ways, and they never forgot those who had served well over the years. They were people who took great pride in their organizations and the people who made them elite. At the same time, they never sought personal credit for achievements, but rather saw to it that others were commended whenever possible.

They had a sense of humor, which they often used to put people at ease or to provide a steadying hand in times of confusion or hardship. Further, they had a knack for showing up at critical times to lend a reassuring presence.

The great commanders had courage, and they possessed the faculty for appearing unconcerned in the face of danger or grave uncertainty. They also were inquisitive by nature and were attentive listeners to others, regardless of rank or grade. They gave serious thought to the future and the preparations that would be required for various situations throughout the world. Their instructions and orders were clear and easy to understand, with a focus on what to do and not how to do it.

These traits and other human qualities made these generals inspirational leaders in their time. They also held one common belief that has been shared by all Commandants throughout the history of our illustrious Corps: they had an unbounded faith in their Marines and the Sailors who serve with them.

There may be as many definitions of leadership as there are authors or speakers on the subject. From my vantage point, there are three elements common to most definitions of the term. The first element encompasses the characteristics or traits possessed by the individual leader. The second element reflects the relationship between the leader and the followers. The third element, often somewhat neglected, is the effective utilization of the leadership process in the setting of goals and the time limits to accomplish them. Since I believe that leadership is more of an art than a science, this third element can be called "the art of getting things done." All three of these elements can be achieved by abiding by a simple credo: know your profession, know your people, and know yourself.

To know your profession requires a lifelong commitment to learning. In addition to undergoing rigorous training and education at all levels throughout your career, those who aspire to lead Marines at any level, lance corporal through general, must take every opportunity for self-study and improvement. There are many ways to accomplish this, such as thoughtful reading and taking part in the numerous continuing education programs available today. Modern technology continues to revolutionize training and educational opportunities and methods. Audio and visual technologies combined with computers and the Internet will continue to enhance the learning environment.

As Marine leaders grow and become more experienced, they assume larger responsibilities. In addition to being proficient in tactics and techniques, they must develop an understanding of military strategy and its role in national strategy. Marines operate and fight as an air/ground/logistics team under a single commander, so as a leader, you must be an expert in at least one of these areas and very knowledgeable in the others. The more senior you become as a staff noncommissioned officer or an officer, the more you will consider logistics, regardless of your occupational field. Further, it is never too early to learn about intelligence and how the system operates. No matter how complex the situation is, you must know the enemy, his capabilities, and his limitations. As one of our great warriors, General Ray Davis, used to say, "With good intelligence, I fought the enemy and not the terrain." Speaking of terrain, you would be well advised to learn all you can about military geography and practice its use. You must also understand combined arms and how to use fires from a variety of means as well as operating in the joint/combined and coalition arenas.

The United States remains a maritime nation. It is on those highways we call oceans that most of the goods and materials of commerce are moved for us and the rest of the free world as we know it. Marines are and will continue to be naval in character. Our expeditionary forces and our amphibious expertise will continue to play a vital role in maritime strategy execution. As the Nation's experts on coming from the sea, we must have a good grasp of naval operations to include air, surface, subsurface, and mine warfare, and naval special warfare capabilities.

Today and in the future, our Nation will continue to face dangerous challenges throughout the globe. Marines must renew efforts to understand the religions, cultures, languages, and thought processes of other people, as well as their needs. In other words, we must be able to see situations through their eyes and not just our own.

We must also understand other government agencies and the roles they play to support our national security interests. The interagency process as well as the roles of nongovernmental organizations are vital parts of any endeavor and require appropriate military support.

In review, there is much to learn and think about if you are a leader in the Nation's Corps of Marines. The aforementioned topics are by no means a complete list, but I hope they give you a flavor of the challenge. Of course, you can never learn all you need to know, and you shouldn't attempt to. More to the point, you make a grave error by acting like you do! A leader who has a fair idea of what he does not know and tries to broaden himself accordingly is on the right track.

People are the most important and precious resource you will ever have in the military profession or in any other institution. Hence, you must strive to know as much as possible about your people. Everything that a leader accomplishes is done through them. Taking care of people is the first responsibility of all leaders at every level. This obligation extends to their families and loved ones. This belief is an ingrained principle of Marine Corps leadership. It is the responsibility of the Commandant and the duty of all leaders to ensure that our people are stronger morally, mentally, and physically when they leave us than when they joined us.

Knowing yourself is perhaps the most difficult idea to master but is of the utmost importance in developing leadership ability. Leaders must be fully aware of their strengths and weaknesses. Know what you do not know, and focus on those areas that will expand your base of knowledge. You can learn much from junior officers and from enlisted men, who often have a startling grasp of topics and are often specialists in their own right. You will find them eager to share what they know, and they will respect you all the more for it.

In the book *The Conflicted Leader and Vantage Leadership*, which I had the opportunity to coauthor with Dr. Paul Otte (also a Marine), we applied our Marine Corps warfighting philosophy to examine leadership at every level and in every level of society. We brought leadership and warfighting together in our examination of military, business, government, education, and community institutions. We identified five characteristics of "higher levels of leadership," which we defined as seeing the possible over the probable; staying focused despite uncertainty; remaining conceptual in conflict; having commitment; and having a sense of presence. *Higher levels* does not refer to those in higher level positions, but rather includes all leaders who think at a higher level and as a result set higher goals for their profession, their people, and themselves. These leaders not only reach higher, but they also accomplish their goals in shorter timelines.

*Marine Corps Generalship* has many examples of these higher levels of leadership themes as well as the concepts embedded in the Marine Corps publication Fleet Marine Force Manual 1 (now titled Marine Corps Doctrinal Publication 1), *Warfighting*. These concepts of maneuver warfare are in reality a thought process built on the ideas of concentration, speed, surprise, boldness, friction, uncertainty, disorder, fluidity, philosophy of command, commander's intent, decisionmaking, focus of effort, shaping the situation, and mission tactics.

Envisioning the possible is closely linked to the maneuver thought process and exploiting or creating opportunities. Those whose focus is limited to the probable often employ attrition reasoning. The Marines have always been an opportunistic fighting force, and readiness to go with what they have in their toolkits is their forte. At the strategic level, one of the best examples of being ready to go with what you have was General Douglas MacArthur's use of the 1$^{st}$ Marine Division at Inchon during the Korean War. The South Koreans and their American allies had been pushed to the very tip of the Korean Peninsula by the onslaught of the invading North Koreans. MacArthur realized that he needed to strike hard and boldly to stop the invasion. In MacArthur's view, taking the time and effort required to reinforce the allied forces encircled at Pusan and then slogging northward would be extremely costly in time, men, and equipment, albeit the most probable course of action. He knew that the Navy/Marine Corps teams were experts at amphibious operations. Although Inchon presented an almost endless series of obstacles and the entire Joint Staff cautioned against such a precipitous move, MacArthur was determined to go with what he had. The North Koreans were stunned when the Marines, reinforced by Army units, seized Inchon and went on to liberate the South Korean capital of Seoul. Within months, the invaders were reeling all the way back to the Chinese border. By envisioning the possible, MacArthur had conducted one of the boldest and most successful maneuvers in American military history. This is a vivid example that an imperfect plan violently executed is often far better than waiting for perfect conditions.

As expeditionary forces prepared for any and all contingencies, Marines know well the uncertainties of potential conflict. They maintain their focus by applying maneuver concepts of speed, surprise, boldness, and concentration while building momentum. Instead of seeking certainty, Marine leaders have relied on fluidity and disorder to overcome friction and exploit opportunities. Recall early in World War II, when the United States was increasingly desperate to stop the Japanese advance toward Australia. On an obscure island named Guadalcanal, the 1st Marine Division, led by Major General A.A. Vandegrift, conducted the first amphibious operation of the war under circumstances fraught with uncertainty. Without sufficient air cover or supplies, Vandegrift's division fought tenaciously with focus and resolve. They never believed defeat was an option. Marines, Soldiers, and Sailors improvised by every means possible to defeat their enemy, and in the process, they proved to their nation that the Japanese war machine was not invincible. The Navy/Marine Corps team, again reinforced by the Army, had completely surprised the enemy, daringly seized the initiative, and at great sacrifice ended a long string of Japanese victories. In the 1st Marine Division, leadership stretched throughout the ranks, which, incredibly, included five future Commandants (Vandegrift, Clifton B. Cates, Randolph M. Pate, David M. Shoup, and Louis H. Wilson, Jr.) and numerous others who became legends.

Our warfighting philosophy provides broad concepts, and they require judgment in application. You cannot write a recipe for all situations, nor should you try. Doctrine itself should only be a guide; anything more defeats the whole purpose of having a thinking Marine Corps—one that always fights and operates in a smart way. Remaining conceptual relies on the critical concepts of philosophy of command, implicit communications, and commander's intent. Intent is the what, where, with whom, and why something needs to be done. It is the glue that holds it all together, and it must be thoroughly understood two echelons above and below in any command. Mission type orders and tactics tell people and units *what* to do and normally not *how* to do it, since that would restrict initiative.

Judgment is applied through decisionmaking. Dr. Puryear calls decisionmaking "the essence of leadership" and demonstrates through numerous examples how Marine leaders have applied their judgment. There is no decision—there is nothing worth seeking—that does not involve risk. Leaders must guard against the zero-defect mentality in all situations, as that is the antithesis of accepting risk in decisions. No one makes a mistake on purpose, and we must understand this. After all, it is a poor carpenter who doesn't hit his thumb once in a while, for he isn't driving many nails.

"Honor, courage, and commitment" is much more than a slogan in the Marine Corps; it is a way of life. A current recruiting commercial says, "We don't take applications—only commitments." Our Corps' ethos embodies just that: commitment!

As leaders grow to meet greater challenges, they will find that having more people requires more trust and commitment—and that must go both ways. In this regard, we must continue to treat our people the way we would like to be treated and develop the best in them. The American public may value Marines for what they see as their physical toughness, but Marines know it is our mental toughness, our values, our passion, our courage, and our resolve that get us over the hurdles when we are exhausted. That mental toughness comes from our commitment at every level from private to general.

Marines understand their sense of presence in both time and place. The Marine Corps was founded in 1775 and today, as in the past, when a recruit earns the title *Marine*, he or she inherits the past through our traditions, becomes accountable today for his or her actions and those of other Marines, and is responsible for the future of our Corps and our country. Achievement feeds on itself and fuels more achievement. These people remain the greatest thing we have ever had in our Corps, and leaders at every level must nourish them.

Although this book is about generals, permit me to say a few words about our young officers, staff noncommissioned officers, and the sergeants, corporals, and lance corporals who are performing so magnificently in the current conflicts in Afghanistan, Iraq, the Horn of Africa, the Philippines, and elsewhere around the globe. These Marines are fighting and winning against radical, unscrupulous enemies whose methods include terrorist tactics and ruthless murder of innocent people. Today, as in the past, small unit leadership is vital to mission success. These young warriors fully understand their commander's intent, their unit's role, the danger inherent to them, and their personal responsibilities to each other, our country, and our Corps. They operate far from home under intense scrutiny from a biased media against an enemy highly skilled in using propaganda to present a distorted view of events. Our generals and other senior officers also deserve enormous credit for providing the training environment and the framework within which these successes have been achieved. Marines, past and present, have always recognized that the backbone of the Corps is the noncommissioned officer.

On a personal note, I would like to thank all the Marines, as well as the civilian and military leadership throughout the Department of Defense, for the privilege of serving with you and learning from you throughout the years. Thanks, too, to Dr. Beau Puryear for his *Marine Corps Generalship* and the tireless research that he has put into it. In my judgment, he has hit a home run, and this effort should become a very special addition to our long and rich history.

For all Marine leaders: try to do as much good as you can, for as many people as you can, for as long as you can. Your reward will be very, very special.

For the Nation's Corps of Marines: take care of yourselves, take care of each other, may God bless you, and—Semper Fidelis.

General Alfred M. Gray, USMC (Ret.)
29th Commandant of the Marine Corps

# Acknowledgments

In researching and writing *Marine Corps Generalship*, I have been assisted by too many people to mention them all. This has truly been a team effort. Of greatest importance for the foundation of this work have been my personal interviews with 150 four-star generals and admirals from all the Services about how to lead successfully. These men represent the epitome of character; their selfless service to God and country has made others admire them, follow them, and believe in them. These exceptional men have never stopped serving and, unlike members of any other profession I know, have a never-ending commitment to the development of subsequent generations of young men and women who have chosen the military as their career.

When I decided to write *Marine Corps Generalship*, I met with Commandant Michael W. Hagee, USMC (2003–2006). He believed in the project and sent a letter to every retired and Active duty Marine officer of the rank of brigadier general through general, giving some background on me and requesting they provide me with their assistance. They have certainly done so.

I appreciate my association with National Defense University (NDU), where I served as scholar in residence, initially with NDU President Lieutenant General Ervin J. Rokke, USAF, from 1994 to 1997, and with NDU President Lieutenant General Frances C. Wilson, USMC, from 2006 to 2009.

Major General Donald R. Gardner, USMC (Ret.), President of the Marine Corps University, assigned me a reference librarian, Theresa Anthony, who provided me with research assistance, books, and copies of articles. I would telephone her when I needed something and normally received it within a day. Her assistance, along with that of the staff of the Library of the Marine Corps, moved the book along at a more rapid pace.

No author could have received better support from a publisher than the assistance provided by Colonel David H. Gurney, USMC (Ret.), Director of National Defense University Press. He has read and edited many drafts of *Marine Corps Generalship*, and it is a better book because of his comments. His colleague, Ms. Lisa M. Yambrick, provided extremely valuable input and did all the style and copy edit work.

I cannot thank Deborah L. Foster enough for her patience, speed, and efficiency in typing and editing for me *American Generalship: Character is Everything*; *American Admiralship: The Moral Imperatives of Naval Command*; and now *Marine Corps Generalship*. I could not have researched and written these books without her help. She typed, revised, and polished my work, all with remarkable speed.

Helen M. Slaven, my assistant for the last 34 years, has given me meaningful assistance in typing letters, editing, handling telephone calls, and relieving me of routine matters to permit me to focus my attention on research and writing.

My family collaborated in the making of this book as well, and I offer my thanks to each of them. I want to pay a special tribute to my wife and best friend for over 50 years, Agnes G. Puryear, for her support and belief in what I was doing and who was so patient with the extensive traveling involved and the many hours of research and writing on evenings and weekends. My son Beverly Spotswood "Chug" Puryear has offered a superb example of the character and leadership an individual needs to succeed in the business world. Special thanks to my son Edgar F. "Chip" Puryear III, who provided me with invaluable scholarly research in writing the book. My Soldier son, S. Braxton "Colt" Puryear, continues his selfless service to his country in the Virginia National Guard. And my Soldier son, Alfred A. "Cotton" Puryear, teacher, reporter, photographer, computer genius, and public affairs officer for the Virginia National Guard, offered editorial and computer skills and journalistic abilities that proved indispensable.

I want to especially express my gratitude to Brigadier General Philip J. Erdle, USAF (Ret.), for the opportunity to share ideas, his contagious enthusiasm, his character, his belief in this endeavor, but most of all, for his friendship over the past 40-plus years.

# Introduction

*Marine Corps Generalship* is a history of the Corps, developed around a study of the character and leadership of senior Marine Corps generals, their insights and thoughts on why they believe they were successful leaders, their analysis of the success of other senior Corps leaders, and how their leadership has contributed to winning wars and provided the high standard of preparation and readiness, particularly of the expeditionary force, that very likely has prevented many wars.

There are many thousands of books and articles written on leadership, and many autobiographies, memoirs, biographies, and military histories. What does *Marine Corps Generalship* have to offer the reader about leadership that has not already been said? The most important aspect of this book is its prevailing theme: the role of character in successful leadership within the American military. Character is a leadership quality that cannot be defined, it must be described; the descriptions of leaders and their words quoted herein give life and discernible meaning to the term. The personalities of these prominent and successful leaders in war and peace capture the elusive definition of true character.

After researching and writing on Army, Navy, and Air Force senior leaders, I now have had the opportunity to research and write *Marine Corps Generalship*, having personally interviewed retired Commandants Louis H. Wilson, Robert H. Barrow, Paul X. Kelley, Alfred M. Gray, Jr., Carl E. Mundy, Jr., Charles C. Krulak, James L. Jones, and Michael W. Hagee, as well as a number of other senior Corps generals.

Throughout its history, the Marine Corps has been blessed by the service of exceptional generals of great character and leadership, so selecting the generals to be discussed in this book was not an easy task. Concentrating on the Marine Corps Commandants was an obvious choice because of their stature, which is unequaled by that of the other Service chiefs. The Commandant has a more significant role and responsibility than those of the Chief of Naval Operations or the Chiefs of Staff of the Army and Air Force.

Choosing the Commandant and time period at which to start this study was really not so difficult—I decided upon Major General John A. Lejeune, Commandant from July 1, 1920, until March 4, 1929. He has been referred to as the "Father of the Modern Marine Corps," and his exceptional contributions have been long lasting and far reaching, which is clear to any student of the history of the Corps. Starting with General Lejeune, I cover many of the succeeding Commandants through General Michael W. Hagee.

It is not possible in a single book to cover all of the giants of the Corps, but I have selected in addition to the Commandants others who have made significant contributions. The selection in part was based upon the availability of resource material as well as their respective service to the Corps, and the suggestions of senior Corps leaders I interviewed. They include Lieutenant General Lewis B. "Chesty" Puller, one of the greatest legends of the Corps, the only Marine officer to be awarded five Navy Crosses; and Lieutenant General Victor H. Krulak, who was informed by the Secretary of the Navy and the Secretary of Defense that he was going to be Commandant, but politics intervened and it did not happen. Commandant Louis Wilson (1975–1979) said of Krulak: "He obviously has had much more influence than many Commandants of the Marine Corps. . . . In almost every incident as I look back, his gut feelings and his perspective were right on, he had great feelings for the future."

Major General Smedley D. Butler, another great legend of the Corps, was commissioned in May 1898 as a lieutenant at age 16, was awarded two Medals of Honor, and, as the senior general in the Corps, expected to succeed Major General Wendell Neville as Commandant in August 1930. It did not happen.

General Holland M. Smith, who probably made the most significant contribution to the development and implementation of amphibious warfare doctrine and was the third Marine in Corps history promoted to four stars, was recommended at one time by Commandant Thomas Holcomb to succeed him if he was forced to retire because of his age.

General Raymond G. Davis was awarded the Medal of Honor in the Korean War. Army General Creighton Abrams, who succeeded Army General William C. Westmoreland as top military commander in the Vietnam War, said of Davis, "Of the 50 or so division Commanders I have known in Vietnam, General Davis has no peer. He's the best."

General Lewis H. Walt, referred to as the "great grunt in the sky," was the senior Marine Corps officer in the Vietnam War for 2 years and was a strong contender to be selected as Commandant.

General Anthony Zinni served as Commander of United States Central Command and was highly respected for his knowledge of and wisdom on Middle East challenges.

This book is a compilation of the character and leadership of the giants from Corps history. You learn and grow from your personal experiences and study, but life is short and there will be limited personal experiences. Reading is important because one can grow through the experiences of those who have gone before you who achieved significant success and notoriety. Biography, in particular, is a catalyst for personal growth. This book speaks with much authority because of the direct input of the generals studied. Their insights will be part of the education and experiences from which the reader can learn about Marine Corps character and leadership, which will nurture and enhance their careers.

Throughout their careers, readers might well find themselves facing challenges similar to the ones these generals have faced and will find the elements and quality of their character and leadership worthy of emulation. Undoubtedly, some readers of *Marine Corps Generalship* will someday become Commandants and senior Corps leaders and can learn much that will benefit as their careers progress.

The special opportunity I have had interviewing the generals for this book, studying the careers of these great men—an experience that could be the envy of many who have such great love for the Corps, its rich heritage and its leaders—invoked tremendous admiration and reverence for them and the Marine Corps. Through my personal interviews, I could feel the strength in their character and personality and sense the deep love for the Marine Corps that permeated their careers, and as it did for all who knew them and who served with them, a strength that was contagiously generated through all ranks.

Part of the foundation for this study was my research and writing of four other books. *Nineteen Stars: A Study in Military Character and Leadership*, was a comparative study of the leadership of four of the most outstanding American Army generals of World War II: General of the Army George C. Marshall, Chief of Staff of the U.S. Army from 1939 to 1945; General of the Army Douglas MacArthur, Commander in Chief in the Far East; General of the Army Dwight D. Eisenhower, Supreme Commander of the Allied Forces in Europe; and General George S. Patton, Jr., commander of the U.S. Army I and II Corps in North Africa, the Seventh Army in Sicily, and the Third Army in Europe.

*American Generalship: Character is Everything*, was a study of the senior leadership of the U.S. Army and Air Force. For this research, I had personal interviews with over 100 Army and Air Force four-star generals, and read autobiographies, memoirs, biographies, military histories, diaries, correspondence, speeches, and articles in periodicals.

*American Admiralship: The Moral Imperatives of Naval Command*, compared leadership of the five-star fleet admirals of World War II,

William D. Leahy, Ernest King, Chester W. Nimitz, and William F. Halsey, and Chiefs of Naval Operations from after World War II, with personal interviews with seven of the living retired Chiefs of Naval Operations and many other four-star admirals.

*Stars in Flight: A Study of Air Force Character and Leadership*, was a comparative study of the first five Air Force Chiefs of Staff.

The objective of these four books is to focus on the insights of the senior leaders of the Army, Navy, and Air Force. The conclusion I reached in these studies is that the most important quality for these leaders is character.

It is so important to perpetuate the careers of the senior Marine Corps generals in this study for future generations to emulate so that their influence will never stop, and their character and leadership will live on.

Chapter 1

# "Only One Officer Runs the Marine Corps": The Role of the Commandant

Marine officers exist to care for and lead enlisted Marines. The Commandant of the Marine Corps is an officer who has, at a minimum, demonstrated excellence in leading Marines at every level of commissioned service. From small unit leadership as a company grade officer, lieutenants and captains have mastered one or more occupational specialties and were selected for greater responsibilities as field grade staff officers and commanders of larger organizations. At this level of professional development, Marines are expected to master the "whole Marine" concept of employing and orchestrating ground, aviation, and combat service support assets, as well as to understand the Service infrastructure dedicated to recruiting, training, and equipping Marines. When a Marine lieutenant colonel is considered for selection to colonel, a key precept guiding the promotion board is an assessment of whether the officer possesses the qualities required of a general officer. In this fashion, every Marine colonel has been prescreened for higher rank, and a more subjective process can be employed for the 3 percent of eligible colonels who receive a general's star. How a competent general officer ultimately rises to the pinnacle position of Commandant is closely related to the unique, patrician role that every Commandant must play.

In a *Marine Corps Gazette* article published in 1923, Major General John A. Lejeune wrote:

> The Marine Corps functions administratively under the command of the Commandant of the Corps. He is solely responsible to the Secretary of the Navy for the discipline and efficiency of the Corps.

I believe that one of the principal reasons for the efficiency of the Marine Corps is the fact that it has, in the Commandant, a single head, and that he is charged with the duty not only of building up its efficiency and of conducting its affairs economically, but also is regarded by all the officers and men as their natural protector and friend. As students of history, all of us must be convinced that unity of administrative control is as essential to success as is unity of command, that both are in accord with the principle of simplicity; and that, conversely, division of authority spells confusion, demoralization and disaster.[1]

## Responsibilities of the Commandant

In his appearance before the Senate Armed Services Committee on February 5, 1987, Commandant Paul X. Kelley highlighted his duties and responsibilities and placed his role into perspective as it compares to the other branches of the Armed Forces:

> Perhaps the proper place to start my opening remarks is to quote from the law as it defines my responsibilities while wearing my "hat" as the Senior Officer of my Service.
>
> Section 5042 of Title 10 states in part that under the authority, direction, and control of the Secretary of the Navy, Headquarters, Marine Corps, shall ... prepare for such employment of the Marine Corps, and for recruiting, organizing, supplying, equipping (including research and development), training, servicing, mobilizing, demobilizing, administering and maintaining of the Marine Corps.
>
> On the other hand, while wearing my "hat" as a member of the Joint Chiefs of Staff, I assist the Chairman in carrying out his functions, duties, and responsibilities. In this regard, the Chairman shall, as he considers appropriate, consult with and seek the advice of members of the Joint Chiefs of Staff. If, at any time, one either disagrees with the Chairman or desires to provide additional advice or opinions, the law provides that the Chairman must present his views up the chain-of-command.[2]

I discussed at length with General Kelley how he would distinguish the relative roles and responsibilities of the Commandant with those of the other Service chiefs. His response was intriguing: "There is goodness in smallness," obviously referring to the larger size of each of the other three Services.

I asked: "Is size a reason why you have the elitism and the high quality of leadership in the Marine Corps?"

He responded: "To an unquantifiable degree, but one can say with certainty that it helps. The other Services have large and fairly complex staffs. This, of course, often makes it difficult to move an action rapidly through their system. We don't have that problem. For example, when people speak of the Army system, they refer to the 'DA [Department of the Army] Staff'; for the Navy it's the 'OPNAV [Office of the Chief of Naval Operations] Staff'; and for the Air Force the 'Air Staff.' When they refer to the Marine Corps, it's 'the Commandant.' The end result is that there is never any doubt in the Marine Corps that the Commandant is both in charge and readily accessible.

"In this regard, let me give you another example. When I made the decision to replace the M16A1 rifle with the M16A2, I was concerned that there was insufficient coordination of my announcement with the Army. I called my old friend and Chief of Staff of the Army, General John Wickham, and told him of my decision and the fact that I would withhold any announcement until such time as he could determine whether or not he wanted to join me. He called me several weeks later and said that he couldn't move the system for an answer in a reasonable time.

"The Army has a top echelon who are all four-star equals in commands such as FORSCOM [U.S. Army Forces Command], TRADOC [U.S. Army Training and Doctrine Command], AMC [U.S. Army Materiel Command], and other parts of a large U.S. Army. These are all four-star guys. They have their bailiwicks, each with an independent organization. So the bureaucracy is very dense and hard to penetrate. The Army is a huge empire.

"If an action officer in the Marine Corps came to see me, and I had to make a decision on what he presented, I could make the decision that very day. That would be almost impossible in other Services, simply because of their size. The size of the Marine Corps makes it much easier to have a leadership style that is personal and very direct with the people who are executing the kinds of programs you want them to carry out.

"There were thirty-five four-star generals among all the Services when I was on active duty as Commandant, including the Combatant Commanders and the Service chiefs.

"The Army is the big green machine that can do things we can't, and we have things that they can't do. But the one thing that we can do that they can't involves rapid decisionmaking—I didn't have to coordinate with the other senior Marine generals. I could make a decision as Commandant and that was it."[3]

I asked Commandant Alfred M. Gray how he would distinguish the position of a Commandant from that of the Chiefs of Staff of the Army and Air Force or that of the Chief of Naval Operations (CNO).

"When the Commandant asks you to do something," he told me, "they're going to do it, and they're going to do it the best they know how.

"The big difference is that the Commandant commands support. The others carry titles like chief of staff and chief of naval operations that are more nuanced. With the Marine Corps, the families of Marines and the Sailors who serve with us really expect the Commandant to be personally responsible for their sons and daughters, husbands and wives. They want their Marines and Sailors to come home okay."[4]

Distinctions between the Marine Corps and civilian agencies have been drawn as well. After his retirement as Commandant, General Leonard F. Chapman, Jr., was left with free time to pursue his avid interest in golf, to spend time with his family, and to devote more attention to his ancestral farm on the Natchez Trace in Tennessee. Not content to rest on his laurels, he served as the Commissioner of the Immigration and Naturalization Service (INS) from 1973 to 1976. During a speech delivered to Marines at Quantico in the mid-1970s, he was asked how being head of INS compared with being Commandant. The general thought for a moment and said, "In the Marine Corps when I gave an order it was carried out. At INS it marks the beginning of negotiations."[5]

One of the clearest conclusions I reached in researching the role of the Commandant and how it differs from that of the other Service chiefs was precipitated by a comment made to me by Commandant Carl E. Mundy, Jr., on the relationship between Commandant Chapman and his Assistant Commandant General Lewis W. Walt, one of the truly great combat Marines. Walt happened to be a strong contender for Commandant at the time that Chapman was selected. I asked Mundy (who, as a major, was Walt's aide) whether Walt had any hard feelings toward Chapman for not being selected himself.

Mundy responded: "Never, not in any way. Lew Walt was probably the ultimate in loyalty. I can tell you that in any situation in which I ever saw him, the Commandant was the Commandant. If General Chapman said,

'Fall on a grenade,' I have no doubt but that the first man in line would have been Lew Walt."

I discussed with Commandant Mundy the distinction of the role of the Commandant vis-à-vis a Chief of Staff. He told me: "First is simply the word. *Commandant* suggests *command*. The staff of the Marine Corps is perceptibly in support of the Commandant rather than the Secretary of the Navy. The Navy, correspondingly, has suffered the problem of the various admirals on the staff trying to figure out if they work for the Service secretary or the CNO. Over time, the clout of various secretaries in the assignment and promotion of admirals has resulted in their often sensing that their 'bread is buttered' more by the secretary than the CNO, and their allegiance in some cases has been slanted toward the secretary. This has put more than a few CNOs in the position of trying to exercise direction of and receive the unqualified allegiance of aspiring admirals who seek to make their place in the sun with the secretary, rather than worrying too much about what the CNO might want. A Marine general's allegiance is to the Commandant.

"Finally, the dedication to the Corps and its chain of command to the Commandant is probably as much a matter of culture as anything else. In more than a few cases in our sister Services, loyalty is greater to community or color of beret than to Service. In the Corps, it is overwhelmingly the other way around. Thus, if selfless dedication to the Corps is the root foundation of being a Marine, it then follows naturally that devotion to the leader of that Corps—to the Commandant—is equally strong."[6]

I inquired of Commandant Charles C. Krulak: "What makes the Commandant different than other Service chiefs?"

He responded: "The answer is both simple yet complex. No Service chief is like the Commandant of the Marines. The Commandant of the Marine Corps is far more powerful than the Office of the Chief of Staff of the Army, Air Force, or the Chief of Naval Operations—quantum leaps more powerful. This is primarily because of our ethos and the way we are as Marines, our discipline, our belief in the chain of command, our absolute loyalty to the institution . . . no matter who the Commandant is. The position deserves the respect and honor. The simple fact is that we're smaller and word gets out quicker, and with more sting to it. And last, if not least, we don't have communities that are fiefdoms in their own right. Unlike the other Services, Marines are Marines first, not aviators, artillerymen, armor officers, logisticians, and the like. We have infantry, artillery, and tanks too—we just don't have those fiefdoms or multiple generals of the same rank as the Commandant within the Corps."

In my interview with Commandant James L. Jones, I inquired: "How does the position of Commandant differ from the other Service chiefs?"

"I believe," he said, "that the Marine Corps is first and foremost a society, not a bureaucracy. I think the Marine Corps should preserve the social aspect of its makeup above all else. The link between the Commandant and the newest private in the Marine Corps is real. It is palpable and we work on that, we work on socialization in the Marine Corps. We emphasize to officers how important it is that all Marines understand the rules of this society. We manage it that way, with the idea that we talk about people, not numbers. Despite the bureaucratic tendencies in the Marine Corps, the dominant characteristic is the social aspect of our brotherhood and sisterhood.

"I see the Army, Navy, and Air Force as very, very large bureaucracies within which are subcultures of societies: submariners, aviators, and surface warfare types. In the Army, you similarly have the Airborne Corps, armor, et cetera, so you have some socialization, but they are so big that it becomes kind of a confederated bureaucracy. However, the Marine Corps instills the concept that the first thing you are is a Marine, so whether you are wearing pilot wings or recon jump wings, whether you're an engineer or a communicator, you are first and foremost a United States Marine. That has a very powerful social context. To me, that is the essential difference between the Marine Corps and the other Services.

"But going back to the term *Commandant*, it is fair to say that the Commandant's stature is such that when he makes a decision, it filters down through the ranks. I think it is true today that the position of the Marine Corps Commandant is different than the other Service chiefs. The Commandant's control over his organization is unlike anything else for a few reasons. One has to do with size, another with the social aspect. Another factor is the way we educate our society. Finally, generally speaking historically, there are only two four-star generals wearing the Marine Corps uniform at any given time. The CNO, the Chief of Staff of the Army, and the Chief of Staff of the Air Force all have different ways of getting things done."[7]

General Krulak's statement on the role of the Commandant says it all: "Everybody understands it. Only one officer runs the Marine Corps; it's the Commandant."[8]

The selection of a Service chief is important for all the Services, but it is even more critical for the Commandant because of the strength and authority that he wields over the Marine Corps, which, for all the Commandants in this study, included the authority to appoint his lieutenant generals. Each Commandant has the opportunity to put his own personal stamp on the Corps: his philosophy of command and his vision for the future of the Corps.

General Krulak related to me: "The man who serves as Commandant through a four-year term wields enormous power and inspires almost mystic veneration. He is the leader of a warrior caste, the head of a multi-billion-dollar organization, and a member of the supreme military council of the land, the Joint Chiefs of Staff. There are, of course, institutional and other limits to what a Commandant can do, but an entity as old as the United States Marine Corps tends to march to the sound of its own drum. If the Commandant decides to do something, it gets done."

**Chapter 2**

# "General, Will You Do Me the Honor…": Selection of the Commandant

How is the Commandant selected? Not only is this little-known process different from that of other Service chiefs, but it also varies from Commandant to Commandant. There are numerous contextual elements in play, above and beyond the aptitudes of the individual candidates. The character requirements for a wartime Commandant might be seen as very different from those for one expected to rebuild or reform a Corps that is deployed and employed during both war and peace. Complicating this calculus are the chemistry and preexisting social relationships with the incumbent Commandant and the political decision-makers to whom he reports or provides advice. The pool of prospects from which the President can nominate can be extremely deep, to officers as junior as lieutenant colonel. From how far down the "lineal list" (known within the Corps as the "Blue Book") a new Commandant is selected may well reflect the confidence that the national command authority has in the ability of the institution to develop, promote, and nominate field grade and general officers for positions of great responsibility.

As one Commandant put it, the successful candidate must have "enough service in Washington to know what makes the wheels go around." But which factors are most important? Opinions vary and interact with the demands of the day. They include political connections, recommendations from serving and former Commandants, battlefield leadership experience, awards for combat valor, Naval Academy attendance, and personal quests for the role. A study of the process for selection of the Commandant provides great insight into the character and leadership of senior Marine Corps generals as well as into the evolution of the Marine Corps as an institution, as viewed by the senior general Marines themselves. A clear look at the process was provided by Commandant Robert H. Barrow (1979–1983), who went through it himself, participated in the selection of his successor, and observed the process for other Commandant selections.

Brigadier General Edwin H. Simmons, in his oral history interview of General Barrow, inquired: "I would like to ask you some questions about the selection process for Commandant. How does the selection process work? Who determines the next Commandant, and when did you first learn that you were being officially considered?"

General Barrow responded: "The selection process changes as personalities change. There is no fixed policy, but one way would have the Commandant of the Marine Corps informally or formally, probably both informally first and then formally later on, propose to the Secretary of the Navy his specific choice or some number of names in ranking order, and his personal recommendation obviously indicated.

"Then the Secretary of the Navy, who perhaps knows these officers, would discuss their qualifications in some detail with the Commandant, and then make his choice, which usually would be the Commandant's choice. Then it goes up to the Secretary of Defense, who, depending on who he is, gives a very brief interview, as if to say, 'I trust those in the Department of the Navy, the Commandant and the Assistant Commandant, making their selections.' Or he may interview the candidate in some detail.

"Then the nominee goes over to the White House. The President may or may not ask to see him, but once that's done and he makes his final decision, it's of course presented to the Congress as a nomination. Now, there are variations on this theme. I'm sure we've had Commandants who deferred the decision process to the Secretary of the Navy, saying, 'These three fellows are all equally qualified. I give you the choice.' It has also been not uncommon for friction to exist between the Secretary of the Navy and the Commandant. Secretaries have disagreed with the Commandant's choice and then went outside the Marine Corps to seek advice and counsel, probably even talking the situation over with the Chief of Naval Operations. Maybe even talking to the Chairman of the JCS [Joint Chiefs of Staff], and most assuredly in many cases talking to former Commandants or people that know the candidates that are being considered.

"I'm sure that influences sometimes come from the Congress to the President. Maybe not directly, but to those in the White House who would process the paperwork and could alert the President, people who have his ear. Perhaps the National Security Advisor would be an example of that, saying, 'It's about that time and we or I think very highly of General So-and-So.' I don't think anybody ever presumed to go beyond positive words that they feel highly about a particular candidate. I don't think you ought to nominate. That would be presumptuous."

"Sometimes," General Barrow said, "the selection process gets to be pretty torturous." A study of the selection process beginning with Commandant John Lejeune suggests that for some selections, this was an understatement.[1]

## Major General John A. Lejeune (July 1, 1920– March 4, 1929)

As a lieutenant colonel, John Lejeune was approached for the first time to be Commandant. He was commissioned in the Marine Corps in July 1890 and had only 23 years of Active duty service at the time. He reflected in his memoir:

> In the latter part of October 1913, I was greatly astonished by the receipt of a confidential letter from Rear Admiral Victor Blue, then the Chief of the Bureau of Navigation, and probably as close to the Secretary of the Navy as any officer of the Service. He stated, in substance, that Major General Biddle had applied for retirement, that Secretary Daniels was about to take up the question of the appointment of his successor, and that my name was among those under consideration by the Secretary. He further informed me that the Secretary wanted to see me and have a talk with me on the following Tuesday morning at ten o'clock and suggested that I come to his (Blue's) office and he would introduce me to the Secretary. I was duly presented to the Secretary and I had a half-hour personal interview with him.
>
> My youth and my rank—I was only a lieutenant colonel—militated against my appointment at that time, a fortunate circumstance for me, as had I received the appointment I would have missed the greatest experience of my life, and would not have been the commander of the immortal Second Division, AEF [American Expeditionary Force], during the World War.
>
> The officers most prominently mentioned as successors to General Biddle were Colonels [Littleton] Waller, [Lincoln] Karmany, and [George] Barnett, the last named being finally selected and appointed as of February 14, 1914.[2]

A significant assignment on the path to become Commandant for Lejeune was his selection for duty as Assistant to the Commandant of the Marine Corps, serving in that position until September 10, 1917. Lejeune recalled in his memoir:

> On January 2, 1915, I assumed the duty of the Assistant to the Commandant, relieving my classmate, Colonel Eli K. Cole, who had been assigned to that office by Major General Biddle. General Biddle recognized the need of a line officer of rank and experience to assist the Commandant in coordinating the various activities at Headquarters, especially with reference to matters pertaining to military training, military education, and equipment of troops, with their organization, distribution, and assembly at embarkation points for expeditionary duty.
>
> The assignment of officers and men to the various ships and stations, and the keeping of rosters for sea and foreign service, likewise required the personal attention of an assistant, while the necessity of preparing war plans, of itself alone, made it mandatory that the Commandant should have the assistance of an officer of the requisite military education and technical knowledge.
>
> To summarize briefly, the growth of the Corps in numbers and in importance, naturally, carried with it the creation and development of an organization at Headquarters, which would be able to assist the Commandant in administering its current affairs efficiently, and in making preparations to meet future eventualities successfully. In other words, an Executive Officer, or Chief of Staff, had become a necessity.
>
> Each day new problems came to me for solution and unaccustomed difficulties were encountered. To take intelligent action and to make sound decisions necessitated painstaking investigation and much thought.[3]

This assignment provided Lejeune with the opportunity to learn the responsibilities of the Commandant and exposed him to the workings in Washington and the key decisionmakers on personnel policies.

With the U.S. entry into World War I, Lejeune wanted out of Washington to see action in Europe. Before Barnett would let him go, he had to find a replacement as assistant to the Commandant. Lejeune suggested Lieutenant Colonel Charles G. Long, who "expressed his willingness to accept the detail":

> I then went again to General Barnett and told him I had found a relief and handed him Long's letter. He said, "Long is satisfactory to me, but I don't want you to go. If you are leaving because you feel that you want to be free to work for appointment as my successor as Commandant when my term expires next February, I am perfectly willing for you to stay here and do so." I thanked him, and then said, "General, I do not want to be Commandant during the war. I now have but one desire and that is to go to France, and I am asking now for transfer to duty with troops at Quantico solely for the reason that I want the opportunity to prepare myself for active service with the Marines in France." I further told him that, in my opinion, he ought to continue to serve as Commandant for the period of the war, as it would not be wise to make a change in such an important office in the midst of war.
>
> In a few days I was relieved by Lieutenant Colonel Long and was released from the heavy burden which I had carried for two years and eight months, and was able to spend four or five days with my family before going to Quantico.[4]

The selection of Lejeune as Barnett's successor after World War I was not without controversy. The rapport Lejeune had with Barnett began to deteriorate. The first indication he had of a changing relationship with Barnett was his exclusion from the original list of officials to review the parade of the Marine Fourth Brigade right after the war. Lejeune's biographer, Merrill L. Bartlett, noted, "The incident caused him to wonder if his professional and personal relationship [with Barnett] remained intact." Barnett assigned Lejeune on October 23, 1919, to again be the commanding general at Quantico.

The Secretary of the Navy from 1913 to 1921 was Josephus Daniels. "While the bond between Daniels and Lejeune grew stronger," Bartlett wrote, "the personal and professional relationship between the Secretary of the Navy and Commandant Barnett deteriorated rapidly." Lejeune was called to the Office of the Secretary of the Navy:

Charging Lejeune with strictest confidence, Daniels revealed that he intended to ask for Barnett's resignation as Commandant as soon as he had seen President Wilson and obtained his approval; moreover, Daniels intended to nominate Lejeune as the new Commandant of the Marine Corps. Stunned, Lejeune walked outside to his car to join Butler [Smedley D. Butler] for the return to Quantico. To his surprise and dismay, he learned that his earnest subordinate [Butler] already knew of the plan through his congressman father [Thomas S. Butler]. The plan—related to Lejeune "in strictest confidence"—began to take on characteristics of an unsavory cabal. The elder Butler encouraged Daniels, recommending Lejeune as the next Commandant in the strongest possible terms. Daniels, in turn, hoped for Smedley D. Butler to succeed Lejeune at the helm of the Corps—presumably after a single four-year term of office. Lejeune had expected to become the next Commandant of the Marine Corps, but not until Barnett's second term ended in 1922. A year after that, Barnett reached mandatory retirement age.[5]

Barnett had worked closely with Secretary Daniels over the year, particularly during Barnett's fight to increase the size of the Marine Corps. According to Lejeune's biographer, however, "in the process of arguing for more Marines, Barnett began to alienate Daniels." Merrill Bartlett further wrote of this matter:

> In the negotiations over requests for increases, Daniels supported Barnett, but always with a skeptical eye. Often, Barnett used the proposed legislation to argue for an increase in the number of general officers. In 1918, he and his political supporters raised the ante to dizzying heights.
>
> When the Senate Naval Affairs Committee considered appropriations for fiscal year 1919, Barnett's friends among the Republicans in the upper house attached a proviso calling for the promotion of the Commandant of the Marine Corps to the rank of lieutenant general and the elevation of the three principal staff officers to major general. Barnett claimed later to have had nothing to do with the genesis of the proposal. He denied vehemently that his supporters planned to prevent passage of the naval appropriations bill if legislation calling

for the promotions did not pass. Despite Barnett's disclaimer, he used all the political influence available to gain passage of legislation affecting the rank of Commandant of the Marine Corps. As Lejeune prepared to board his troopship for France, he received a telegram from Barnett asking for political support to ensure passage of the bill.[6]

Secretary Daniels was opposed to the Marine Corps promotions; the senior Navy officers expressed outrage over a plan that elevated the Commandant of the Marine Corps to the level of the Chief of Naval Operations and his principal staff officers to the level of bureau chiefs. In addition, a request for the promotions was attacked on the House floor by Congressman Thomas S. Butler. The most adverse aspect of this was an alleged lack of selflessness. Congressman Butler addressed his outrage in a letter to Assistant Secretary of the Navy Franklin D. Roosevelt, referring to the move by Barnett as "the selfishness of these men who are endeavoring to take care of themselves only."[7] This mention of selfishness hurt; selflessness was, and remains, an essential element of the character of a Marine leader.

Another cause of Daniels wanting to retire Barnett was a volatile relationship between Daniels and Barnett's wife. She was wealthy, had high social standing and many political contacts, and her social affairs in Washington circles were legendary. It was alleged that she all too often made Daniels the butt of her humor. Daniels laughed along with the other guests at jokes played on him, but the humor had a hollow ring to it. Mrs. Barnett's baiting of Daniels may have been a factor in the Secretary's decision to "oust" the twelfth Commandant. Daniels and Mrs. Barnett each called on political influence to prevail. Barnett did not succeed.

The conflict became unpleasant:

As the secretary and his protégé marched through the controversy created by Barnett's abrupt removal from the commandancy, the most painful encounter of all remained for Lejeune.

At 11:40 on 30 June 1920, Lejeune reported to Barnett's office at Headquarters Marine Corps. Both of the incumbent's aides-de-camp remembered the embarrassing and uncomfortable scene. Clifton B. Cates recalled that Barnett merely asked Lejeune why he failed to inform him of the plot. Lejeune replied lamely that "his hands were tied." Charles I. Murray remembered a more acerbic exchange in which Barnett ordered Lejeune to stand at attention in front of his desk. The outgoing Commandant delivered a stern tongue-lashing, charging his subordinate with disloyalty and unprofessional conduct and being a false friend. Once again, according to Murray, Lejeune repeated that "his hands were tied." At twelve o'clock, Barnett ordered an aide-de-camp to remove one star from his shoulders. The twelfth Commandant marched out of the office.

The former Secretary of the Navy took pains to calm Lejeune's fears and reminded him that his elevation to the commandancy had been on his merit alone. Despite Mrs. Barnett's revelation of material purporting the existence of a cabal to remove her husband from office, the overriding evidence suggests that the Machiavellian Daniels orchestrated the ouster himself.[8]

The controversy went back and forth for some time with Barnett's wife as the driving force. She made attempts to discredit Lejeune, but her efforts to stop his ascendance to Commandant failed.[9]

While the Marine Corps has always been rich in talented senior professional officers, it is frightening to think what a loss it would have been to the Corps had Lejeune not possessed the character, leadership, vision, and love of the Corps that he did. His contributions earned the tributes of many, and to countless Marines he is the "Father of the modern Marine Corps."

Lejeune was at the inauguration of President Warren Harding when:

I felt a hand on my shoulder. I turned and saw Mr. Denby [Edwin C. Denby], the new Secretary of the Navy, whose selection for that office had been announced a few days before. He was not a stranger to me by reputation, as he had enlisted in the Marine Corps upon entry of the United States in the World War and had been promoted grade by grade until he reached that of Major by the end of the war. I had known him personally, too, on the battlefield of Blanc Mont Ridge, where he called on me when that grim battle was at its height. He greeted me cordially on the portico of the Capitol and said, "General, will you do me the honor of serving as Commandant of the Marine Corps during my term of office as Secretary of the Navy?" I replied that I would do so gladly. He then told me to bring him my nomination for that office at nine o'clock the next morning. I did as directed and the paper, after being signed by President Harding, was transmitted to the Senate at noon and my appointment was at once confirmed by unanimous consent without being referred to a committee.

General Lejeune's term as Commandant ended after nearly 9 years on March 4, 1929. The selection of his successor was very straightforward. He recommended Major General Wendell Neville, who was Assistant Commandant from August 14, 1920, until July 11, 1923. Lejeune recalled:

> My interest in the great Corps in which I have served my country for nearly thirty-nine years will continue unabated, and I shall keep in close touch with its activities and with its officers and men not only during the remainder of my active service, but throughout the remaining years of my life as well.
>
> I also strongly recommended Major General Neville as my successor. He had served with me in the Second Division as the Commanding General of the 4th Brigade and on several other occasions, and it was my belief that his record was such as to make his appointment desirable. President Coolidge and Secretary Wilbur [Secretary of the Navy Curtis D. Wilbur] approved my recommendation, and he was at once nominated and confirmed by the Senate to take office on March 4th, after the inauguration of President Hoover. General Neville died on July 7, 1930, and was succeeded as Commandant by Brigadier General B. H. Fuller.[10]

Unfortunately, there are no autobiographies, memoirs, biographies, or oral histories on or about Commandants Wendell Neville (1929–1930), Ben H. Fuller (1930–1934), John H. Russell (1934–1936), or Thomas Holcomb (1936–1943), and thus their selections as Commandant cannot be developed as are those detailed in this book.

## General Alexander A. Vandegrift (January 1, 1944–December 31, 1947)

Vandegrift succeeded General Thomas Holcomb as Commandant on December 31, 1943. In his autobiography, *Once a Marine*, he addressed his relationship with Holcomb and his selection as Commandant:

Early in 1937 my education was cut short when unexpected orders recalled me to Washington to serve as military secretary to the new Commandant, General Thomas Holcomb. It may seem difficult to believe now, but such was the way we saw the world situation in 1937 that I figured this would be my last tour. I was a full colonel with twenty-six years of service and, like most of my contemporaries, planned to retire after thirty years.

Vandegrift reported to Major General Holcomb for duty, describing him:

General Holcomb's fifty-eight years included extensive expeditionary service and a brilliant combat record in France in 1918. He was well known throughout the Corps as an imaginative planner and administrator. He was a man of medium height and graying hair whose steel-rimmed glasses in no way hid the effect of piercing gray eyes, particularly if they were turned on you. A quiet firmness and a brain like a calculator caused many officers to regard the general as somewhat dour.[11]

With the war on in the Pacific, Vandegrift was a division commander. Holcomb traveled from Washington to visit and be briefed by him. Vandegrift recalled:

After dinner, he filled me in on the Washington scene and spoke of various developments both inside and outside the Corps. "You know, I turn sixty-four next year," he remarked. "If the President wishes me to stay on, I shall stay."

"I certainly hope that is the case," I told him. He studied me for a moment, then dropped a real bomb. "If he wishes me to retire, I am going to recommend you as my successor." Brushing aside my thanks he continued, "If he approves, I promise to keep you fully informed before you take over."

General Holcomb followed up on his promise to keep him fully informed to better prepare him for the challenges. Vandegrift commented, "Throughout this period, General Holcomb supplied me with the details of his office, quite often asking my concurrence in long-term officer assignments before he made them. He still intended to retire at the end of 1943 and was trying to figure out the best way to work me in, assuming the President appointed me the next Commandant."[12]

Vandegrift was not always Holcomb's first choice. Earlier, as he approached the mandatory retirement age of 62, Holcomb thought of Holland M. Smith to succeed him; it all hinged on whether Holcomb would be extended because of World War II, and if so, when. Holcomb himself wanted to be reappointed, but he had heard that the President was considering a certain colonel. Therefore, he wrote repeatedly to the Chief of Naval Operations urging that the colonel was unfit and asking that, if his own reappointment were unacceptable, Holland Smith be appointed instead: "Smith is splendidly equipped for the job. He is 58; has had enough service in Washington to know what makes the wheels go round; thoroughly understands the functioning of headquarters; has had FMF [Fleet Marine Force] service, and every variety of service known to the Corps; has a host of friends in the Navy."

There were three others whom Holcomb thought might be considered at that time, including Vandegrift, but, he said, there was "no reason to pass over a man like Smith just to get a younger man [meaning the rumor of a colonel being considered] . . . possibly the President will not ask my advice; in which case I am asking you to do your best to have Smith appointed."

In any event, Holcomb was reappointed for a 4-year term, which virtually destroyed any possibility that Smith would ever hold the top post in the Corps. When Holcomb's term expired, Smith would be too old for consideration as his successor. The appointment, however, left Smith available for field command and made it possible for him to lead the Marines in the coming drive across the Central Pacific in World War II.[13]

## General Clifton B. Cates (January 1, 1948–December 31, 1951)

General Vandegrift's term as Commandant ended on December 31, 1947, and he was succeeded by General Clifton B. Cates the next day. He was asked by his oral history interviewer Benis M. Frank, "When did you first know that you were going to be appointed as Commandant?"

*General Cates*: It was actually when President Truman told me, because I can say with all honesty that I never considered being Commandant. I never even thought about being Commandant. It never entered my mind.

*Frank:* There's always this element in the Marine Corps, I imagine, since the Marine Corps was founded. Always some pool of speculation as to who's going to be the next Commandant.

*General Cates:* Oh yes, there's always a lot of guessing but they're usually wrong.

*Frank:* Did you have any estimate or had you made some guesses as to who you thought was going to make it?

*General Cates:* As I remember, I really didn't give it too much consideration. Of course, with all due respect to General Vandegrift, who I think is a close friend of mine—I know I am to him—I don't think that he recommended me, or Shepherd either. I'm not sure of that, but I'm pretty sure that he was for General [Allen H.] Turnage. I actually do not know whether General Vandegrift ever contacted the President about it. At that time, the Secretary of the Navy was really a most important job and you might say that he carried a lot of weight, in fact in my opinion, practically all the weight. So one day I received a call from Secretary Sullivan [Secretary of the Navy John L. Sullivan] to be at his office at four o'clock on a certain date—I've forgotten when. When I appeared there, General Shepherd [Lemuel C. Shepherd, Jr.] was also there. I said, "Lem, what's this all about?" And he said, "I don't know." So we waited fifteen or twenty minutes and finally Secretary Sullivan burst out of his office in a hurry and said, "Come on, come on. Let's go, let's go." And he went out the door and we followed and got down to the car and I said, "Mr. Secretary, what is this?" He said, "We're going over to see President Truman and we're late." He said, "He's going to decide who's going to be Commandant. One of you is going to be Commandant." So that's the first we knew of it.

We went over and we first went in Charlie Ross's [Charles G. Ross, President Truman's press secretary] office and sat there for ten or fifteen minutes and finally some staff member of the President came out and said, "Cates, the President wants to see you." So I went in and he talked to me for a long time. He said in effect that he had to appoint the next Commandant and that "I really don't know anything about either of you but your records are practically identical. You both have been in World War I and World War II." And he said, "It's up to me to make the decision." He said, "I've had a lot of political pressure brought to bear on me to appoint a certain officer and I don't like it." I said, "Mr. President, they kind of insult your intelligence, don't they?" And he said, "They sure do."

So then after he dismissed me then Shepherd went in. He talked to him for quite a long time. Shepherd came out and Secretary Sullivan went back in. I said to Lem as we sat there, I said, "Lem, this is like a dog show. We're waiting to see who's going to get the prize." So after a few minutes we both went in and the President looked over at Lem and he said, "General,"—and I was just ready to reach out and shake Lem's hand, really I thought he was going to say you're going to be Commandant—he said, "It's all up to me to make the decision." He said, "It's all even practically. You're younger than he. Cates is senior to you on the seniority list." And he said, "You'll have your chance later." And he turned to me and said, "You're going to be Commandant."

*Frank:* What was your reaction?

*General Cates:* I really don't know. I know that, by the time I got back to Quantico and told my wife, I was doing a lot of thinking and wondered if I really wanted it![14]

## General Lemuel C. Shepherd, Jr. (January 1, 1952– December 31, 1956)

In his oral history, General Shepherd gave his account of the meeting he and General Cates had with President Truman: "General Cates was on duty at Quantico in command of the Marine Corps School when the question came up about the selection of a new Commandant. General Cates and I had been friends over many, many years, and frankly neither one of us particularly cottoned to having to become involved in the great responsibilities of the Commandant as the unification fight was going on at the time. Naturally we both would like to become Commandant, but neither of us made any unusual effort to do so.

"One morning we were both called to the Secretary of the Navy's office and had lunch with John Sullivan, who was Secretary of the Navy at the time. Both of our names had been sent to the Secretary with several others, and he in turn took our records to the President for his decision as to who would become the new Commandant. That afternoon Mr. Truman—I think this was a commendable thing for him to do—sent for Cates, me, and the Secretary of the Navy, to come to the White House. The President said, 'I have gone over both of your military records. You both have had distinguished careers. You both have approximately the same decorations. You both have performed the same types of duties. You're both, in my opinion, well qualified to become Commandant of your Corps.' Then he said, 'General Shepherd, I've been a military man myself, I've always believed in seniority. General Cates is senior to you, and he's older than you are. I'm going to make him Commandant this year, and I trust that I'll be able to have you follow him four years from now.' I think it was a very fine thing for the President of the United States to call us in and tell us personally why he had selected one over the other. And I might add that four years later, when I was out in the Pacific and General Cates' four years as Commandant were drawing to a close and he did not choose to be reappointed, General Cates went to the President and said, 'You recall, you promised General Shepherd that he would follow me when you appoint the next Commandant.' And that's what Truman did.

"We were on such friendly terms that when Cates and I were being considered to succeed Vandegrift, Cates called me on the telephone one day and said, 'Lem, if you're made Commandant, will you let me stay at Quantico?' [At that time in the history of the Marine Corps, the Commandant made all the general officer assignments and promotions, subject to the approval of the Secretary of the Navy.] I said, 'All right, Clifton, I will promise you that I will do so, I'll ask you, though, if you're made Commandant, to let me go to Quantico.' He said, 'I will,' and that's the way it was. When he became Commandant I went to Quantico. We both loved the station. I wish to emphasize again that I think General Cates is an outstanding officer, very fair in every respect and very considerate. Neither he nor I did any politicking to be made Commandant."

When asked by his interviewer whether some politicking was going on elsewhere, General Shepherd responded, "Well, I would rather not discuss that. No comment. Of course, both Cates and I were naturally anxious to be Commandant, and I was cognizant that some of my friends were putting pressure in various places, but I made no personal effort to promote my selection. When I was called back in, we'll say October, 1951, and told by the Secretary of the Navy that I would be made Commandant; I went back to the Fleet Marine Forces and began to make plans for who I would want on my staff at headquarters. [He selected then-Colonel Victor Krulak to be his military secretary.]

"Well, I was approached as to whether I would consider staying on [at the end of his 4 years], asked if I would consider a reappointment. I'm not at all sure that I would have been reappointed. I felt—and I still feel—that four years as Commandant, when you've given your best efforts to it, is long enough. I know in the olden days Commandants stayed on longer, but I think that after four years as Commandant you've just about expended all your efforts and ideas. It is a grueling life in Washington, fatiguing mentally and physically to every Commandant. At the end of four years, I was very glad to relinquish my duties to General Pate.

"I'm very grateful and shall always be grateful to General Cates for his cooperation with me, as was shown—when he proposed my name to Mr.

Truman for appointment as Commandant as his successor. We worked together in closest harmony until his final retirement two years later."[15]

## General Leonard F. Chapman (January 1, 1968– December 31, 1971)

General Chapman's selection as Commandant was a surprise, as he was only a two-star general at the time. Although the law permitted selection from commissioned officers ranking as low as lieutenant colonel, the Commandant normally was chosen from the group of three-star generals. Brigadier General Simmons asked Commandant Mundy about this in his oral history: "Word at the time had it that President Johnson could not choose between the two prime candidates, Generals [Lewis W.] Walt and [Victor H.] Krulak, so he picked a dark horse, General [Leonard F.] Chapman. Were you aware of this rumor?"

General Mundy said: "Oh, I was. I think that was fairly widely perceived throughout the Marine Corps in those days, because as part of that, there emerged the scandal that General Westmoreland [General William C. Westmoreland, USA] had recommended in his final fitness report on General Walt that he should be the Commandant, and how dare he intrude in the politics of the Commandant's selection and that sort of thing.

"But I know that Walt was a great favorite of President Johnson's. General Krulak was viewed by many to be the frontrunner, or at least a frontrunner. General Chapman had the grade of major general, and was something of a surprise. We had not focused on General Chapman as being a likely Commandant."[16]

It was quite clear that the Marine Corps did not want the other Services to get involved in the selection of their Commandant. General Westmoreland was Commander of the U.S. forces in Vietnam, and his authority in that position included Marine Corps forces in Vietnam. General Westmoreland reflected in his autobiography that when the tenure of Commandant Wallace M. Greene, Jr., was coming to an end:

> Although there was no question that since I was commander of all American military forces in Vietnam, the Marines were under my overall command, I had no wish to deal so abruptly with General Walt that I might precipitate an interservice imbroglio.
>
> Now, in 1966, I unwittingly got into the bad graces of some Marines and their ardent devotees in the press and Congress

when in writing Lew Walt's next-to-last efficiency report, I noted, as required, what I considered a logical next assignment for him. General Walt had served me loyally and had a genuine appeal to the men in the ranks. Knowing Lew Walt's ability, I could give him only the highest recommendation. When the question of General Greene's successor as Marine Corps Commandant developed as a spirited contest among three candidates—Walt, Krulak, and Chapman, all of whom I knew and respected—a newspaper article related that I had tried to intervene on Walt's behalf. Looking into the matter, I found it went back to that efficiency report in 1966 wherein I had indicated, without knowledge of whoever else might be considered, that General Walt was fully qualified to be Commandant of the Marine Corps. A telephone call to General Greene cleared it up.[17]

President Lyndon B. Johnson provided insight into his respect and admiration for Walt in his introduction for Walt's book, *Strange War, Strange Strategy*:

I remember well my first talk with General Walt about Vietnam. He had gone out in May 1965 to take command of Marine units that had landed in the northern part of South Vietnam to protect our airbases and other installations. A few months later their mission was expanded to include active combat against the Viet Cong and North Vietnamese who were threatening to take over the entire country by force.

In February 1966 General Walt returned to Washington for consultation. On the 25th of that month, he came to see me at the White House. I can still see him walking firmly across to my desk in the Oval Office—the square jaw and steady eyes; the shoulders broad as a fullback's; the straight back of the military professional; the strong, calloused hands of a man who likes to use them, and does. In every way, he was a "Marine's Marine," as they say in the Corps.

He told me a great many other things, too. He described the South Vietnamese Army—its strength and weaknesses. He talked with feeling and compassion about the Vietnamese people and what they were going through—the terror imposed by the communist forces; the pain they felt when their rice was confiscated and their sons were dragged away to fight; the torture and murders that were the penalty for failing to do what the Viet Cong demanded.

Here was a rugged Marine general fighting a tough and exhausting war. Yet he showed more real feeling, more sensitivity for the people who were its victims, than almost anyone I knew. Much of what he told me that day in the White House, and on numerous later occasions, is in these pages. But there is a great deal more.[18]

Brigadier General Simmons further inquired of Mundy: "Special legislation was soon passed, elevating the grade of the Assistant Commandant from lieutenant general to full general. Do you recall the circumstances of that legislation, and who was the prime mover?"

General Mundy replied: "Well, the prime mover—it was my perception, it was rumor, or it may have been fact, but it was the understanding that Lyndon Johnson had agreed that Lew Walt would not be the Commandant, but only under the circumstances that he be made a four-star general. So it was necessary then to achieve legislation that would authorize the Assistant Commandant to be a four-star, because he never had been before."[19]

It appeared that several senior naval officers were getting involved in choosing the successor of Commandant Louis H. Wilson. This prompted Wilson to seek a conference with the Chief of Naval Operations, Admiral James L. Holloway III, and ask him to tell his admirals to stay out of the selection process. This compounded the adverse reaction of Marines to General Westmoreland's recommendation that General Lewis Walt become Commandant.[20]

Interestingly, Lieutenant General Victor Krulak had been informed by both the Secretary of the Navy and the Secretary of Defense that *he* was going to be the next Commandant. I had the opportunity to discuss this with Krulak, and the matter was developed in detail in Krulak's oral history. Dr. John T. Mason, Jr., asked Krulak about the selection of Commandant Greene's successor. "Everybody," Krulak commented, "aspires to reach the peak of his profession and I was no different than any other. But, like anyone else, I suppose I have in my system that small leavening of hypocrisy that permits me to say that I didn't allow it to transcend my higher dedication.

"In 1962 or 1963, when they were groping about for the replacement for General Shoup, I was interviewed by the Secretary of the Navy along with several others and, when the interview concluded, he said some very encouraging things to me. I didn't particularly want to be Commandant at that time. I felt I had too long to go professionally, and that it would not be good because when you're finished with being Commandant you really ought to get out right away. That would have had me retiring at the age of about 55.

"General Shoup told me after this interview, when I went to report to him on it, that he fully expected to see me as Commandant in four years. 'Short of stubbing your professional toe,' as he put it, 'you must end up in this chair in four years.' Well, it was nice to hear the Commandant say that, nevertheless I went back about my business and spent the bulk of the remaining time as CGFMFPac [Commanding General, Fleet Marine Forces Pacific]. I had that job for four and a half years. Well, there was an awful lot of chattering—as there always is—about the next Commandant and I was just delighted to be so remote, as far away as I could get. I had more to do than I could manage.

"Then one day General Greene called and he made what I felt was a rather cryptic, but a revealing comment; he said, 'The Commandant's job is up for grabs, it's in the political arena completely, and I don't know what will happen.'

"Well, I won't burden you with further details, the record need only show that as far as I was concerned, I was far enough away from the political arena that I not only could not but would not (if I could) seek to influence it. But General Greene was very patient in describing to me what I felt was an almost disgraceful invasion of the executive, professional, and amateur, both in and out of uniform."

When asked, "What was the political furor?" he responded, "Pressure by the political sector, upon the President. Carried forward by an individual who had some relationship with a Congressman or a Senator or a member of the executive branch, on behalf of various people who were being considered, and General Greene kept me as informed as he could.

"I meanwhile, of course, migrated back and forth to Vietnam and attended to my duties. September, October, November passed and finally, as you know, it was announced that General Chapman was to be the next Commandant. I knew what I would do if I didn't get to be Commandant and that was to carry on in my then-present job as long as the Commandant wanted me to. But, when it came time to move, I would not stand in the way of someone whose star was in the ascendancy; after all, I was the senior permanent officer in the Marine Corps other than the Commandant. Despite my youth that was the fact of it, I was the senior permanent officer in the Marine Corps other than the Commandant. I had to step aside. When it became known to Mr. McNamara [Secretary of Defense Robert McNamara] that that was my intention, he called me and said, 'Please don't step aside until I talk to you because there are several jobs which I feel you might usefully fulfill.' And he mentioned one was CinCPac [Commander in Chief, Pacific], another was CinCSouth [Commander in Chief, South] (which would have been the first Marine to hold that position)."

Krulak's attitude about not becoming Commandant after being told he was going to was revealing of his remarkable character. He continued: "So ultimately, when it appeared to be a prudent time and a proper relief could be available, I realized it was time to retire. And I did it without any rancor. You might say that an individual would have a right to just a nickel's worth of bitterness having been told by the Commandant that the letter was signed, recommending that he be Commandant. But somehow I didn't. It may sound a little bit idealistic, but the truth of the matter is, that the Marines did a hell of a lot for me. When I became a second lieutenant, my real objective in life was to get to be a major so that I wouldn't have to wear puttees [leggings]. Well, I got a hell of a lot further than that. When I was sick or wounded they looked after me. I never had a bad job in all of my 34 plus years. I look back on it now as a most rewarding experience and I really ended up feeling in the Marine Corps' debt. That's the size of it."

When asked why the process got so political, Krulak responded: "Well, I'm not sure that I know. There were very strong emotions in the minds of some in civilian clothes and some in uniform with respect to me as an individual, I know.

"Well, there were some folks who didn't want me to be Commandant, I'm sure, because they felt I wasn't good enough, which is all right with me. The ones who were in uniform, and who became active campaigners, probably could be indicted for meddling. But after all, there are no laws that prevent them from going to their Congressmen. That's perfectly all right. But my comments on these aspects are sort of restrained because it's second-hand information. Nobody ever came to me and said, 'I don't want you to be Commandant,' or 'I want you to be Commandant and I'm going to go talk to the President.' No one ever said that to me. I had the very cleanest of consciences in this matter; I neither utilized nor sought influence. Of course, I'll go to my grave with a sense of satisfaction about that.

"I have a letter from a friend who was riding across the continent with President Johnson in his airplane and President Johnson said something to him about there being a very substantial conflict in terms of forces that were anxious to see Walt on the one hand and me on the other make Commandant, and so he took a fellow who embodied the best qualities of both of us [Krulak and Walt]."[21]

## General Robert E. Cushman, Jr. (January 1, 1972– June 30, 1975)

The tenure of General Leonard F. Chapman, Jr., ended on December 31, 1971. His successor was General Robert E. Cushman, Jr. He was asked by his oral history interviewer, Benis M. Frank: "When was your first intimation of being selected as the next Commandant?" General Cushman responded: "I think it was very late in the game because the Secretary of Defense [Melvin Laird] had said he didn't believe in lame ducks. Goddamn, that really caused me some problems. Laird told me in November that I was going to be the next Commandant, but I don't think that it was announced until, oh God, late in November. At that point, I immediately went over and started getting briefed. But, I was on duty in CIA [Central Intelligence Agency] until midnight of the 31st of December. In fact, I had to field several phone calls about problems. Then at midnight, I got a call and told the guy, 'I'm no longer here, you've got to call so and so.' You know, my next in line, the number three guy. It was time to start worrying about being Commandant."

Frank asked if Secretary Laird was the only person that General Cushman talked with. Cushman said: "There were some other people that were in the running. I thought Chaisson [Lieutenant General John R. Chaisson] was going to be Commandant. Ray Davis [General Raymond G. Davis] was sure he was going to be Commandant. Those were the two primary."

Cushman was asked about the chances of Lieutenant General William K. Jones, who was considered a strong contender for Commandant because of his brilliant career, rising to the rank of lieutenant colonel at the age of 27 during World War II. He responded: "He hoped for it, but he was out in Pearl Harbor and, of course, the guys right in town were Davis and Chaisson. I'm trying to think if there was anybody else. You know, some people think they are in the running, but they aren't. I think Jones thought he was in the running, but it turned out he wasn't."

Cushman was not interviewed in advance by the Secretary of Defense, nor did he know if the others had been interviewed: "I was sort of in left field while assigned to the CIA and out of the mainstream."

Seeking specifics, Frank asked: "Had you done any politicking for Commandant?" "Not particularly," Cushman said. "Well, yes, I did a little bit. I told Don Hughes [Lieutenant General James D. "Don" Hughes, military assistant to President Richard Nixon] and Rose Mary Woods [President Nixon's secretary], who were close to the President, and I told Bob Haldeman [White House chief of staff], and Wally Greene [General Wallace M. Greene, Jr.]. I told a couple of other people that I would be interested in being Commandant. I also told Chappy [Leonard F. Chapman, Jr.], who retired as Commandant on December 31, 1971, that I would be interested."

Then Frank asked: "Do you think there was any direct intercession on the part of the President to whom the Secretary of Defense makes the final recommendation?"

He replied: "I'd say this one came right from the top, yes. I think Mel Laird did not object—there would have been a big hassle. Previously, there was a hassle when Davis became Assistant Commandant, because my name was put in, too. Davis got the nod, but the Assistant Commandant decision was made at the SecDef [Secretary of Defense] level. Nixon stayed out of that one. There was a lot of consternation, and Chappy didn't like it, I'm sure.

"General Chapman had picked Davis to be Assistant Commandant and all of a sudden my name was in there holding up everything. Finally he said, 'Oh, the hell with this. I'll leave it in the hands of the civilians.' So, the civilians, SecDef primarily, I'm sure, put Davis in. Then later, when it came time for a new Commandant to be selected, I let a few people know, including the White House staff, that I was available so to speak, and that's all I did. I never talked to the President personally about it. I told Chappy that I wanted to be Commandant. I told him so he wouldn't think there was some skullduggery going on. I knew he wasn't recommending me. But I thought I'd better tell him because of the flap that had occurred before—when the Assistant Commandant was selected—I didn't want him to think something like that was starting again. As I say, I knew he wasn't going to recommend me for Commandant, I don't know who the hell he recommended, but it wasn't me. I was on pretty good terms with Chappy and always had been. We were classmates and we were at Headquarters at the same time. When I was G3 he was G4. We used to commiserate. He was a great favorite of Shoup's and

I was just the opposite. Occasionally, I'd commiserate with him on that. We had never served together until, by golly, we got to Headquarters. But of course, we were classmates, I'd known him."[22]

## General Louis H. Wilson (July 1, 1975–June 30, 1979)

The selection of a successor to General Robert E. Cushman, Jr., was controversial, and the events spilled over for public exposure and interest. In his oral history of Cushman, Benis M. Frank asked: "While events were going on in Southeast Asia, there were serious problems of a different sort at Headquarters Marine Corps. You were in your last year as Commandant and the selection process for the new Commandant had begun. Will you describe that process, please?"

Cushman responded: "I made my recommendation to Middendorf [Secretary of the Navy J. William Middendorf], who was out getting his own ideas from Officer's Club bars. He asked, 'Well, what do people think of your nominee?' And I said, 'Well, I'll take a sounding.' So, I sent out a letter to the general officers and I keyed it [inserted a code in the letter indexed to the recipient's region] to the area to see if the responses represented all the generals or didn't because my instructions were: 'You don't have to sign the letter if you don't want to, just let me know who you think would be a good candidate and your views will be between you and me.' I got each letter back personally, unopened, and made a tick mark by whatever name they had recommended which I wrote on a piece of paper and then destroyed their letters. Nobody has ever seen those letters but me because they were all destroyed. The sounding showed—I don't know what it was now—60–65 percent favored Anderson [General Earl E. Anderson] and number two was Lou Wilson [General Louis H. Wilson] and I guess there were a couple of other names. But the two people were Anderson and Wilson. I recommended 'Andy' Anderson and I was asked to provide a second name, so I provided Wilson's.

"Then somebody complained that the letters were keyed and I said, 'Well, I thought everybody did that,' not by name, but by area. Since they didn't have to sign their names it's nice to know that you got a response from Norfolk, represented everybody in Norfolk, or you got nothing from Norfolk. So, there was a big hue and cry over that, and I just told everybody it wasn't any of their damned business, it was private communication between me and my general officers. But I got hounded by—oh, what the hell was his name—he was Middendorf's undersecretary. He really was nasty about it and the complaint had been made so that several congressmen knew about it. They were raising hell. So, the end of it was nothing really, except I told a guy in the press that I thought it had been done before, and pressed to give a name, I made the mistake of mentioning Wally Greene. All hell broke loose, of course, and the next morning I said, 'I made a mistake,' because I had. I thought, due to some of our conversations, that it was true, but I certainly wasn't going to argue about it.

"I used to have former Commandants Wallace M. Greene, Jr., and Leonard F. Chapman, Jr., over to keep them abreast of what was going on and we'd have lunch and quite a lot of conversation and then they'd go down to the command center and get a briefing and go on home. My point is that I had lots of conversations with Wally and Chappy, so I made a doggone mistake and I had to eat crow, and I did. So, that was it. As it turned out, it was a hell of a mistake to key the damned things by location, but I hadn't given it much thought, not enough thought, obviously. If I had it to do over again, I wouldn't. It opens up the possibility of campaigning, opens up a politicking option. I don't think I would even have written the letter in the first place because I remember getting letters previously, from Shoup and by Wally Greene, which really encompassed the time I was a general. I don't think I ever got anything from Chappy. I might have, I can't remember now. But I did from Shoup and Greene."

Cushman's statement that he thought Commandant Greene had sent out keyed letters brought a vehement denial from Greene, who commented that he was "astounded by Cushman's remarks" and demanded a retraction, denying that he had never discussed such a thing with him, stating, "I'll take an oath on that. That's a pretty weak way for him to get out of it. . . . I suddenly appeared as the activator of this. It sounds like Watergate to me."

Cushman elaborated, "Well now, the Commandancy of the Marine Corps is sometimes compared to the Papacy with general officers forming the College of Cardinals. The general officers like to think they have a voice in deciding the selection of the next Commandant."

He summed up what he believed were the criteria for the selection process: "The selection of the Commandant is up to the President. A President who takes a strong, personal interest in the Marine Corps would have a lot to say about it, naturally. He might not even know some of the candidates and so forth. In my case, the President knew me personally and my record was supportive. In other cases, the Secretary of Defense may have a great say because he has an interest and knows somebody; witness Tom Gates [Thomas G. Gates, Jr., Secretary of Defense, 1959–1961, who advised President Eisenhower to select David Shoup]. Again, it could be the Secretary of the Navy who presumably would know practically all of the prospective general officers and would have the most say as people up above would simply take his recommendation, not personally knowing the other options or having any other inclinations. In all of this, the Commandant, of course, makes a recommendation, but if anybody up the chain of command disagrees with him, that's the end of that. In my case, I was disagreed with and was asked to submit a second nomination, so two names had to be forwarded. I said I didn't want to give two names, but I was forced to."

Cushman commented on the role of the Commandant: "There are three things you have to do. You have to get along with the Congress and be persuasive; and you have to get along with the civilian chain of command and be persuasive all the way along the line and you have to be able to function in the Joint Chiefs; and finally, you have to run the Marine Corps, which is the easiest part of it all. So, the civilian hierarchy has to consider whether you are competent to do all those things or not. And what other Marine generals might vote for, or even what the Commandant might recommend will not in every case go through. In addition, you always have personalities involved, sometimes politics are involved. I think we discussed a number of instances where that happened."[23]

In fact, many Marines of his day considered General Cushman himself to be the beneficiary, and possibly a perpetrator, of political cronyism. But political influence is a two-edged sword that can both help and hurt. On April 10, 1975, there was an article in the *Washington Post* concerning General Earl E. Anderson, Cushman's Assistant Commandant, and his aspiration to become Commandant. This article, entitled "Dispute Embroils Marines," exposed a controversy surrounding the selection of Commandant Cushman's successor.[24] The article alleged:

> The general officer corps of the U.S. Marines is wracked by controversy and some bitterness over allegations that the No. 2 Marine officer [meaning General Anderson] may have attempted to secretly code a letter from the Commandant's office soliciting private views of who should be the next Commandant.
>
> Top level Navy officials who have looked into the situation estimate that roughly half of the 70 Marine generals expressed some private concern that the forms they received from the Commandant's officer recently may have been deliberately typed in a fashion that would identify them and their views to other officers knowing the code.

Anderson has flatly denied any such activity and his boss, the Marine Corps Commandant, Gen. Robert E. Cushman, in an interview yesterday backed Anderson fully and suggested that some generals who didn't want Anderson as the new chief may be behind the allegations.

"If Gen. Anderson makes Commandant," Cushman said, "it would be tradition shattering. It would be the first time that an aviator, rather than a ground officer, made it. There is some undercover work going on that stems from that old rivalry. I'm convinced that's what's going on. I deplore it. I hate to see it."[25]

Cushman's oral history interviewer asked: "Did you know that even before the *Washington Post* articles that there was a widely held perception of the Marine Corps that you had either delegated control or lost control of the Marine Corps to General Anderson and that his nickname was 'Super Chief?'" He responded: "Nobody dared say that to me. I'd clobber him."

Things moved very quickly after the *Washington Post* articles. Less than a month after the scandal became public, it was announced that General Louis Wilson would become the next Commandant. Cushman illuminated the sequence of events that lead to his selection: "They just, you know, they picked Wilson and that was that." Commandant Cushman wanted to submit only a single name to succeed him and he submitted only General Anderson's. "I was told," he continued, "to come up with another name. I had to come up with another one, General Wilson, who was an old time comrade."

Cushman commanded a company in Wilson's battalion during much of World War II: "I got him his Medal of Honor. My relations with him were cordial, cordial. It was indicated to me by the Secretary—who was then Warner [Secretary of the Navy John W. Warner, 1972–1974] as I recall, not in writing but orally—that I ought to keep fresh blood flowing through the Marine Corps and that we needed some new lieutenant generals just as a matter of principle. Three-star generals did not ordinarily stay through the whole tour of the Commandant that made him. So, taking this guidance—which I didn't enjoy too much—FMFPac [Fleet Marine Forces, Pacific] and Quantico and Lou Wilson were all asked if they would step aside to get some new people in. Wilson refused. The other two did retire, but Wilson refused and said he wanted to become Commandant."[26]

Commandant Mundy, in his oral history, talked about Cushman: "He had served in an earlier assignment with Vice President Nixon, and it came time to select a Commandant, the odds-on favorites were others than Cushman. Suddenly Cushman popped out as the Commandant. So we were all rather surprised about that. And when I say 'we all,' you should understand that I was a lieutenant colonel in those days, just beginning to have the maturity to look at what we really want in the leadership of the Corps.

"Cushman's Assistant Commandant was a very ambitious man, a very talented man, General Earl E. Anderson, Assistant Commandant from 1972 to 1975. He was a very smart man, an aviator who wanted desperately to be the first aviator to become Commandant of the Marine Corps. That was very clear to everybody around."[27]

General Wilson gave his view on this in his oral history: "I was under pressure from the Commandant and senior officers at Headquarters Marine Corps to retire, suggestions that I should retire and forget my aspirations to the Commandancy. Many things were going on in Washington which I did not like. Nevertheless, I was far away in Hawaii. I knew from rumor that I was the target of unfounded allegations made by those trying to kill my chances to be Commandant. I did not mount a campaign for the job, although I was accused of that."[28]

Commandant Cushman decided to retire 6 months early. The public perception was that he reached this decision as a result of the embarrassment caused by the Anderson affair. Cushman was asked about the article: "The 6 May 1975 issue of *U.S. News and World Report* featured an article entitled, 'What's Wrong with the Marines?' It was probably triggered by the Anderson affair, but it also reflected growing criticism and doubts about the future of the Corps which reached a crescendo with the subsequent publication of the Brookings Institution study by Jeffrey Record and Martin Binkin entitled, 'Where Does the Marine Corps Go From Here?' Do you remember that?"

Cushman replied: "Well, yes. We knew about the study, it was in preparation for some time. As I recall, we had somebody that worked with them, you know, a Marine, in an assisting role trying to make sure that they put out something that was accurate. We knew that thing was coming out for a long time and we were trying to change its conclusion to something we thought was much more realistic."[29]

The *U.S. News and World Report* article is notable because it provides insight into the Marine Corps' problem that concerned Wilson. "What's Wrong with the Marines?" was written by Bem Price of the *U.S News and World Report* staff, himself a Marine for 12 years. To summarize his points, which were based on thorough research, he wrote that the quality of Marines serving on Active duty was in decline; the Corps was accepting more enlistments of high school dropouts to meet recruiting quotas; desertions were up; court-martial convictions were climbing; crime in the barracks was rampant; living conditions were worse than those of other Services; key equipment was in short supply; the Marines lacked the latest antitank missiles, even though such equipment was made available to Mideast nations; the Corps' own tank forces were approaching obsolescence; insufficient Navy transports were available to move Marine forces around; there were race problems; there were drug problems. With all these difficulties, reenlistments were down, and even career Marines were getting fed up and retiring. There were concerns over the Corps' future mission. There were signs that the stature of the Marine Corps as the Nation's elite fighting force was fading. There was considerable friction within the cadre of senior Marine generals.[30]

Was General Cushman retired early because of this controversy? An article in the *Washington Post* on May 6, 1975, announced in bold letters "2 Top Officers of Marines Ask to Retire":

> Rebuffed by civilian leaders, the two top officers of the Marine Corps have asked for early retirement, Pentagon sources said yesterday.
>
> Gen. Robert E. Cushman, Jr., Marine Commandant, and Gen. Earl E. Anderson, Assistant Commandant, have submitted letters asking for retirement July 1, the sources said. Secretary of the Navy J. William Middendorf II is expected to approve.
>
> The two generals acted less than a week after President Ford followed the recommendation of Secretary of Defense James R. Schlesinger and Middendorf and nominated Lt. Gen. Louis Wilson, a Medal of Honor winner, to succeed Cushman.
>
> Cushman, whose four-year term normally would end Dec. 31, supported Anderson to follow him as chief of the 196,000-member Marine Corps. Rarely has a Marine Commandant given up his post before finishing his full term.
>
> Cushman has told newsmen that he would lose about $300 a month in retirement pay if he stayed on beyond September

because of a technical quirk in the law. Anderson also would stand to lose the same amount, sources said.[31]

Was this statement in the press concerning retirement pay accurate? Cushman addressed this question in his oral history, saying that he would lose "a hell of a good sum because of the weird inversion between retired, Active duty, and the ceiling. And it was just topsy-turvy land, you know, absolutely no rhyme or reason to it except that Congress won't raise their pay and be criticized by the voters. So, of course, they go get more stamps and post allowance and stationery allowance and they're allowed to put that in their pockets [referring to fraud by certain Congressional representatives], so that's the way they raise their pay.

"In any event I told Secretary of Defense Schlesinger that I wanted to retire before the deadline, I think it was a September deadline, if you hadn't retired by then, you went into the next era, as I recall it. And he said, 'Okay,' and then in talking to him and saying I was going to get out in the fall in September, he said, 'Well, all the other chiefs change on the first of July,' which in those days was the fiscal year. So, I said, 'Well, it doesn't make any difference to me.' So, I went on out on 30 June. Well, of course, the fiscal year has since been changed to the 1st of October and I can't remember whether it was Rhodes or Towers or just who it was, somebody came up with an act of Congress that saved this pay inversion problem, at least for a while. So, that was the story of my getting out when I did. They asked me if I was going to get out, and of course, I said, 'No, no, I'm not going to get out.' But I'd already been doing the figuring and it was unbelievable the amount of money at risk. I just wasn't going to risk it, I knew there would be criticism, you know: 'After all these years you're going to worry about a little money?'"[32]

## General Robert H. Barrow (July 1, 1979–June 30, 1983)

General Robert H. Barrow became Commandant when General Louis H. Wilson ended his tour on June 30, 1979. Who were the contenders for the position? What role did Wilson, as the retiring Commandant, have in selecting his successor?

Brigadier General Edwin H. Simmons, in his interview for General Wilson's oral history, asked him: "On Thursday, 31 May 1979, you officiated at the retirement ceremony and parade of Lt. Gen. Larry Snowden, who had been your chief of staff for the second half of your tenure as the Commandant. We haven't had too much discussion of Larry earlier. Rumor has it that he and Bob Barrow were very close contenders to succeed you."

Wilson responded: "I think that is true. I had said to both of them along with General Tom Miller that I would take no active part in selecting my successor and that I thought there were numerous officers who were all fully capable of doing the job. I think that is particularly true of Bob, Larry, and Tom. They were the most senior, and probably the ones that were the most eligible.

"Larry Snowden is an officer of great ability, marvelous personality, wonderful family, articulate, dedicated, had been a tremendous Marine for 37 years and would have made a fine Commandant. The disadvantage for Larry is that he would have had to have a waiver because he would have been 62 before his four years were completed. I think that if there was any single disadvantage for Larry that probably was it. While this could have been overcome—as it presumably has been before—there was really no precedent that I could find, although I really did not search too thoroughly. Larry was interviewed, and I think that this is why he was not selected. For my part, he had certainly been a wonderful chief of staff, and I believe that I reflect the views of his subordinates in Washington that he had personality, ability, and all the attributes which made for a very strong working team."[33]

While General Wilson said he would play no active role in selecting his successor, a study of their professional relationship indicates that he had Barrow in mind and gave him assignments that groomed him to be Commandant. Certainly making him his Assistant Commandant near the end of his Commandancy gave Barrow considerable insight to the Washington scene; thus, he received considerable Washington exposure, and as Assistant Commandant, he sat in on almost all the conferences in Wilson's office and thus had the opportunity to be in on Wilson's key decisions as Commandant.

Another such assignment followed two incidents at Marine Recruit Training Depots: the death of a Marine in San Diego, and the drill instructor shooting of a recruit in the hand at Parris Island. "I was aware," Wilson said, "of the Ribbon Creek incident [the drowning death of 6 recruits at Parris Island in 1956] years before, of course. I could foresee that the Marine Corps was going to be on public trial again for these two unfortunate incidents." He assigned to Barrow the task of resolving these incidents, later stating, "I believe that experience assisted Bob Barrow in making him a superior Commandant."[34]

A significant factor in Barrow's selection was his exceptional performance in taking on some of the Marine Corps' greatest challenges of the time, among the most important being recruiting and basic training. Wilson promoted Major General Bob Barrow to lieutenant general on July 1, 1975.

He was coming from Parris Island, where he had been commanding general of the recruit depot. He brought with him some very definite ideas on recruiting and recruit training, which undoubtedly influenced the Commandant's decision to assign him as Deputy Chief of Staff for Manpower. It was a relatively short tour, for in October 1976, Wilson reassigned him to Norfolk as Commanding General, Fleet Marine Forces, Atlantic [FMFLant; now Marine Forces, Atlantic]. General Simmons commented that "the general perception was that Wilson was grooming him to be his successor."[35]

On July 1, 1978, Lieutenant General Robert H. Barrow was appointed Assistant Commandant and was promoted to general. That evening, Commandant Wilson had a dinner and a parade honoring him as the new Assistant Commandant.

"He had been in Washington," reflected General Wilson, "as Director of Personnel [Deputy Chief of Staff for Manpower] before he went to FMFLant. He returned to be the Assistant Commandant as I thought that he should be there when the time came for the selection of the new Commandant. He should have exposure along with the other lieutenant generals at that time, so all the potential candidates could be given a fair evaluation. There were a great number, at least four lieutenant generals, all fully capable of succeeding me the next year."[36]

Barrow's oral history interviewer asked him: "The public announcement was made on 18 April 1979 that President Jimmy Carter had nominated you for appointment as the 27th Commandant of the Marine Corps. Did President Carter personally inform you? If not, who did—if you recall?"

Barrow responded: "He did. Now, I'll be perfectly candid with you. There seems to have been two people that were thought of as contenders: Larry Snowden and myself. We're friends. I went to see him early on and I said, 'Larry, as with all these kinds of things, there will be people who will ascribe to me things about you that are not so, and probably vice versa, so I want you to know that my friendship for you and regard for you is constant and will remain so, and I intend not to engage in any kind of political activity.' Although that's been done in some of these. He gave me the same message back, and I am confident that the two of us lived up to that sort of gentleman's agreement to not let others play king makers for either one of us.

"So, I don't think either of us had any sponsorship by anyone. I don't know how far Larry got in the process, but I found myself seeing the Secretary of the Navy, who already knew me. Then I went to see the Secretary of Defense, and that didn't take very long, and then to my surprise, I ended up at the White House, and I do believe that I'm the only one that went to the White House. There may have been other contenders, but I think of Snowden as the primary one and I don't know that he got to the White House.

"I had what I would characterize as a pleasant visit with President Carter—and he's not an easy person to engage in conversation—but his manner and so forth was pleasant. He was interested in places I had served, and I gave him some of that, and we talked a little bit about the Marine Corps. There was kind of a lull. I remember mentioning what I knew about Georgia [Carter's home state] and gave some quotes from 'The Marshes of Glynn', that great piece of poetry, and told him about my time at Beaufort, South Carolina, where I came to love the low country which is also a part of coastal Georgia.

"So that warmed him up a little bit, and we continued to talk and he asked me a strange question. I thought it was strange. He asked me what my religion was. I figuratively swallowed hard because I'm an Episcopalian. I said so. Now, why do I feel strange about that? Well, Episcopalians have a bad reputation for being sort of—thinking themselves a cut above. I know that, but my family has been Episcopalian for generations and that's what we are, and that's what I am, and I knew he was what we'd call a hard shell Baptist. I didn't know how well that would sit with him, but he didn't show any reaction to it.

"It was really goodbye time. I stood up or he stood up first indicating the session was over, and I started towards the door thinking, 'Well, that's that.' And he said, 'General Barrow, I would like for you to be the next Commandant of the Marine Corps.' It was almost like catching me as I was getting ready to go out.

"I think Lou Wilson played it all very honestly. He and I are very good friends. We were friends before he was Commandant, during the time he was Commandant, while I was Commandant, and presently. He never told me, nor did I ask him what happened when I was selected to be Commandant. Not even after it was all over did I say to him, 'Well, Lou, how did it come about?'

"And to this day, I don't know if he went up with one, two, or three nominations, what he might have said, or how that part of it worked. That's unusual, because somehow it gets to be known and sometimes it even gets to be a little ugly, but that's the way it happened."

When asked what some of the salient points were that he made in his statement to the congressional committee, Barrow responded: "I talked about the fact that the Marine Corps was embarked on an era of getting better in areas of people and equipment, and the things that Lou Wilson had done for the Marine Corps which I thought were needed and were in fact well moved in the right direction, that I would continue to pursue those. I expressed my interest in people."

Barrow inherited a Corps that had obtained a high state of combat readiness for peacetime because of Wilson's leadership, but he also inherited a number of serious and nagging problems, including the key one of how to ease the impact of inflation on morale and modernization so that the highest quality personnel and materiel could be retained and obtained.

Commandant Barrow's oral history interviewer inquired: "On July 1, 1978, Commandant Wilson brought you back to Washington to serve as Assistant Commandant. This carried with it a promotion to four-star general and was regarded as a clear signal that you were General Wilson's choice to succeed him as Commandant the following July."

Barrow elaborated: "I must tell you that Lou and I were close friends. You always have a special feeling with someone when you think he has high regard for you. Whether it's well-founded or not, I always felt that Lou liked me, and I liked him for the kind of man he was. When you put that kind of combination together, a warm friendship is likely to be the result. We had so many things in common. We think about a lot of things alike: uncompromising standards about appearance, fitness, and conduct, good manners, people fulfilling their obligations as officers in terms of entertaining and dressing, and looking and acting the part of an officer. So we had a lot that we could just agree on; shared values, if you will, whatever.

"We're both Southerners, so we hit off. . . . one of us could fall back on some little anecdotal experience that would lighten the conversation—something that he remembers as a boy—which would probably make more sense to me than it might to someone else because I'm from the same part of the country and I would understand the little nuances of a story about the South, about some other experience, and vice versa. Anyway, we're friends.

"But I'll tell you in all candor, we never . . . I was never made to feel, by anything he said or anything else, that I was the heir apparent, that I was waiting to just simply take over. He had other people put in visible positions. General Snowden was then the chief of staff, which was always regarded as one of the top visible jobs in Washington. Les Brown, if you wanted to consider aviation—and why not—was made visible by being Commander of Marine Forces in the Pacific, a post that had produced Commandants in the past. General McClennon [Kenneth McClennon, Assistant Commandant, 1979–1981] had a number of admirers—I know Sam Jaskilka [Assistant Commandant, 1976–1979] thought the world of him, I do too for that matter—was the head of Manpower at Headquarters

Marine Corps having had a division command. He'd had his tickets punched, so to speak. So there were several contenders around.

"I thought of Larry Snowden as a very strong possibility. And there again, we had never served together in the same unit, but I have a lot of admiration for him and I think he for me. We're friends, and early on I went to his office and before I could even broach the subject. He was so quick to see what I was trying to say that he filled in all the missing pieces before I got to them, which to paraphrase was, 'We both know that each is being thought of and spoken of as a contender to relieve Lou Wilson. I want you to know that I will never, ever, say anything about you that would be considered a criticism or some effort to lessen your stature because you are seen as my competitor in this drill.' I said it better than that, but that is the thought that I was trying to express.

"And he fed right back to me—the same thing—so we kind of left there thinking, 'They say I'm a contender but if for some reason I don't get it, I ought to have great good feelings for the guy who does get it (assuming it's this fellow here I just talked with), the Marine Corps will be in great shape.' I think he may have thought that way too. I certainly felt that way about him. There was no rancor, none of this behind-the-back routine. We both laid it on the table."

General Barrow's assignments and his personal relationship with Wilson certainly groomed him: "I represented him in his absence at JCS [Joint Chiefs of Staff] and any of the other things that needed to be done at Headquarters. I made very few trips. I sat in with him on just about anything he was briefed on, routinely. I spent as much time in his office as I did in my own. If there was someone coming to visit, he would say on the squawk box, 'Bob, come on in. I think you'd like to hear this.' So I didn't miss anything. I can't think of hardly anything that I wasn't included on. What I'm trying to say is that I was not just a piece of dead wood sitting in another office because I didn't have a list of specifics that I was responsible for.

"Other than being the fellow who made the final decision, I participated in just about everything he participated in: going to the staff conference and going to that meeting, this briefing, the briefing coming to him, whatever, the only exception being that I didn't accompany him to the JCS. But when he was out of town, I went to the JCS alone as his representative. So that was the kind of the relationship that we had, and that's an answer to the question of whether I had specific duties or not.

"You can draw anything you want out of this, but before Lou would have a session with the staff or an individual, action officer, or whatever, we would usually sit and discuss it—and most assuredly afterward. He didn't need my counsel. We were comfortable together and he might have already made up his mind, but he might say, 'What did you think of that briefing?' and we could spend four or five minutes talking about it. This doesn't mean that I'm sitting there telling him things that are going to make him change his mind or anything else. We thought a lot alike, I suppose."[37]

## General Paul X. Kelley (July 1, 1983–June 30, 1987)

General Robert H. Barrow retired as Commandant on June 30, 1983, and was succeeded by General Paul X. Kelley on July 1, 1983. General Barrow's oral history interviewer asked him: "On 24 March, President Reagan announced his intention to nominate General Paul X. Kelley as your successor. This came as no surprise to anyone. General Kelley was then your Assistant Commandant and Chief of Staff, and widely regarded as the crown prince. Was this nomination as cut and dry as it appeared to be?"

Barrow responded: "Well, yes and no. When P.X. was promoted to three stars in conjunction with command of the Rapid Deployment Joint Task Force at Headquarters Marine Corps, seated on the front row was John Lehman, a businessman around DC in defense matters. But at the time, March 1983, John Lehman was the Secretary of the Navy. He had known P.X. a long time.

"So unlike some other experiences in which the Secretary might or might not know the prospective Commandant, one would assume that this early relationship was one of friendship—good acquaintanceship at least. He actually held down several challenges that gave him high visibility in the Pentagon, a particular requirement, in addition to his time down at the Rapid Deployment Joint Task Force. So he had already made a name for himself.

"He already had a good record. As you pointed out, he was Assistant Commandant. Qualified in every sense of the word to be Commandant. But it was difficult not to recognize that there were some other contenders. I'll give you one name, someone of whom I thought the world and still do: John Miller. A solid citizen, extremely well liked. He would have been a good Commandant.

"But without going into all the details, the process varies. Sometimes it gets to be pretty tortuous. Sometimes it involves a number of people, interviews, all kinds of things go on. But P.X., escaping all of that kind of business, received the appointment. And that's that."[38]

A study of Kelley's assignments and statements of his rating officers makes it clear that his record was outstanding throughout his career. From his early days as a company grade officer, it became apparent that Kelley was on a fast track. When he was a relatively new captain, Major General James P. Risely, his reporting senior for 3 years, wrote, "I consider him to be the #1 Captain I know." Upon transfer from the 2$^d$ Force Reconnaissance Company, where he was commanding officer, Brigadier General Leonard F. Chapman referred to him as "one of the two or three finest young officers I have ever known. . . . [he] has a brilliant future in the Corps." Major General Wood B. Kyle, commanding general of 3$^d$ Marine Division, wrote of Kelley while he was serving as the commanding officer of 2$^d$ Battalion for Marines in Vietnam (as the junior lieutenant colonel in the Marine Corps and while on temporary additional duty from the 1st Marine Air Wing), "Lieutenant Colonel Kelley was the most outstanding battalion commander in the 3$^d$ Marine Division (Reinforced) during this period of time." In addition, General Kyle recommended Kelley for the award of a Navy Cross (which was reduced to a Silver Star Medal by the commanding general, FMFPac) for his bravery during Operation Texas. For this tour of duty, he was subsequently selected from "below the zone" to the rank of colonel.

Later, Kelley returned to Vietnam, where he commanded the 1$^{st}$ Marine Regiment while a junior colonel. For this combat tour, Major General C.F. Widdecke, commanding general of the 1$^{st}$ Marine Division, wrote, "Colonel Kelley is the ideal regimental commander for the Marine Corps—young, selected below the zone for colonel, admired and respected by his officers and men, and fully qualified professionally." Subsequently, Vice Admiral Harry D. Train, Director of the Joint Staff, observed, "Colonel Kelley is the finest Marine it has been my privilege to know or serve with. I am fully confident that he will one day be Commandant of the Marine Corps." Kelley was the first Marine to be selected to the rank of brigadier general while actually serving on the Joint Staff. Lieutenant General T.C. Fegan observed of Kelley while he was serving as a general officer at the Marine Corps Development Command, "P.X. Kelley is an absolutely superb Marine who has the potential to be CMC [Commandant of the Marine Corps]." Finally, General Lewis W. Walt, the Assistant Commandant of the Marine Corps and one of its most highly regarded combat leaders, wrote of Kelley, "The finest Marine I have ever known."

In 1978, Major General Kelley was ordered to Headquarters, Marine Corps, for duty as Deputy Chief of Staff for Requirements and Programs. Serving with him as Deputy Chief of Staff for Manpower was Lieutenant General Richard H. Barrow, who subsequently became Assistant Commandant and eventually the 27$^{th}$ Commandant of the Marine Corps. In December 1979, 5 months after General Barrow became Commandant, he nominated Kelley as the first commander of the newly designated Rapid Deployment Joint Task Force (RDJTF). This was a unique four-Service command tasked with worldwide security responsibilities, excluding Europe. These responsibilities were soon limited to the Middle East. It was then that General Kelley believed that the RDJTF should be a separate unified command for this unstable region. After a bitter intra-Service battle, the Chairman of the Joint Chiefs of Staff and Service Chiefs voted for a transition to a subunified command under United States European Command, with the Commandant of the Marine Corps voting for one under United States Pacific Command. General Kelley convinced President Ronald Reagan, Defense Secretary Caspar Weinberger, and Members of Congress that it should be a totally separate unified command. On April 23, 1981, the Commander in Chief announced his decision: the RDJTF would become a separate unified command.

Shortly thereafter, General Barrow nominated General Kelley to be his Assistant Commandant and Chief of Staff, effective July 1, 1981. On March 17, 1983, General Barrow nominated him to be the 28th Commandant of the Marine Corps. During Kelley's confirmation hearing, Senator Sam Nunn (D–GA) remarked, "General Kelley is the greatest general I know." On June 26, 1983, with President Reagan presiding, General Barrow passed the Marine Corps colors to his successor. President Reagan later said that General Kelley was "one of America's most energetic, vibrant, and dedicated military men I have ever had the honor to know."

## General Alfred M. Gray, Jr. (July 1, 1987–June 30, 1991)

General Paul X. Kelley's tenure as Commandant ended June 30, 1987, and he was succeeded by General Alfred M. Gray, Jr., on July 1, 1987. This happened even though General Gray, as a three-star, had prepared and delivered his retirement letter to Secretary of the Navy John Lehman.

In a discussion with General Gray, he told me: "I put my letter in to retire because you've got to get nominated, you know, approved by Congress to retire as a three-star. It went over to Navy Secretary Lehman right away and he pigeonholed it, he didn't send it forward. And it stayed pigeonholed until James Webb became Secretary of the Navy on May 1, 1987.

"Secretary of Defense Caspar Weinberger liked General Tom Morgan because Morgan was really good in Washington. I was rooting for either Cheatham [Lieutenant General Ernest C. Cheatham] or Morgan, they were both good. People were asking me for some recommendations. Then they couldn't agree on the selection of the Commandant. A lot of retired Commandants got into it."

I asked General Gray how he felt about retired Commandants getting into the process. "I personally," he said, "don't think much of it, but they do it. Everybody has their own view, their own style.

"About seven weeks before my retirement at the end of June. I was out in the field as we had a big exercise at Camp Lejeune. Then, around the 7th of May, Webb called and asked, 'When are you coming to Washington?' I said, 'A matter of fact, I'm coming tomorrow. I'm going to Fort Meade for the annual Travis Trophy Award, which we [Gray's radio battalion] had won in 1966.' All the old winners go back for the annual awards ceremony. Webb told me, 'I've got some meetings, so come by and see me at 3:00.'

"We went up to Fort Meade in May 1987. We had the cell phone with us because there was a flap in Haiti and after the ceremony, instead of staying for lunch, I suggested that we skip lunch and go down to the Pentagon early. We could hide out in the bookstore or something. I wanted to be in that meeting with Mr. Webb and out of there as quickly as I could because I wanted to get back to Norfolk. I was worried about Haiti. So we're driving down the Baltimore-Washington Parkway at about a quarter to one with my aide, Major Mark DeForest. He was my aide in Norfolk. The phone rang and it was the three-star Air Force officer who worked for Secretary of Defense Weinberger.

"The message on the telephone was, 'Mr. Weinberger heard you were in town and he wondered if he'd get to see you.' I said, 'Yes, sure.' So he said, 'How about a quarter after one?' I said, 'Well, I think maybe we can make it. We'll get there as quick as we can.' So I actually saw Mr. Weinberger before Mr. Webb."

Obviously, Caspar Weinberger played a role in Gray's selection. "I went in and we had a great chat. To this day, I swear, he was not interviewing me. He knew me. He wanted to know about the other candidates and I gave them high marks: 'You can't go wrong with either of them and certainly the troops admire and respect Tom, Ernie, and D'Wayne.'

"Then Weinberger asked me, 'What should I tell the new Commandant?' I said, 'The new Commandant's got to get our act together. We've got to go back to what the Marine Corps is supposed to be all about.' Externally, we had a lot of fences to mend with Congress. A lot of people were upset with us. I know Congress was down on the Corps a little because of all the information that we had from legislative affairs and everything. Then he asked me about strategy, about NATO and other situations around Europe and the Middle East. We talked and then he said, 'Well, I know you haven't been in the Pacific very much, but tell me about the

Pacific.' Well, I didn't tell him that I lived out there for 22 years. I conversationally walked around the Pacific with him and that was it.

"Then I went down to see Secretary Webb and it was exactly the same kind of thought process, except that there was much more detail because Webb had been a Marine hero and in fact he knew a lot of Marines. In my opinion, I think that Secretary Webb favored Ernie Cheatham."

I asked Commandant Gray, "So Weinberger favored Morgan?" He answered, "I know that he liked Tom Morgan.

"General Robert H. Barrow was very supportive of Ernie Cheatham and Paul Kelley was very supportive of Tom Morgan, so you had all that going on. I returned to my command. Mr. Weinberger called me on Friday night, 16 June: 'It's all set. The President's approved you to be the next Commandant.' He did that and then Monday it was in the paper. At about 9:30 on Monday morning, Paul Kelley calls me up on the phone and said, 'Okay, it's you, congratulations. Can you come see me?' I said, 'How about Wednesday?' He said, 'Okay.' We spent about 10 or 12 hours together, just talking."

I discussed with General Gray his role in selecting his successor: "I understand that you put together five books of three-stars who were being considered. Did you rank order them in any way? Did you in any way indicate a preference?" "People talked to me about it," he said, "and I spoke to their strengths and weaknesses."

Then I told General Gray; "I've read a lot about this. One of the things I've read is that some people were opposed to General Mundy because they thought he would not continue the progress that you had made with the Marine Corps." He answered, "Right." I pressed Gray further: "Was that thought ever in your mind?" He responded: "Really it was no concern to me. Carl is a very good man, a superb Marine. I knew him well. He was one of my battalion commanders, one of my regimental commanders.

"By nature, he was a very deliberate decisionmaker, and that's probably good. There were some in the maneuver school and other schools of thought that didn't believe that he would be bold enough to keep moving this trend along. You know people, it's like anybody else in the public domain, some people admire you and some do not."

Then I asked: "But this fellow Bill Lind [a former legislative aide for the Armed Services to Senators Robert Taft, Jr., and Gary Hart], apparently he was writing letters. The history makes reference to some poison pen letters. Are you familiar with that?"

"No," he said, "that was before. I think he or somebody wrote a letter and one of Carl's friends got a hold of it and gave it to him. He then came to see me and I was concerned. I told Carl to forget about it and to press on!"

I told him: "General Mundy has made the comment to me, in one of my interviews, that you were tremendously helpful to him. Further, he believed that, of all the people that he worked with—Lew Walt, the whole bunch—it was you, more than any of them, that he had the greatest respect and admiration for. I mean, there are seven or eight places in his oral history where he makes a similar comment about you."

Gray responded: "Carl is a superb individual. Part of the problem was that Lind castigated a bunch of senior officers over time. Sometimes my fellow colleagues would criticize me about Lind. I said, 'The guy is trying, he spends his own money, he's got some ideas and, you know, wherever I've been I listen to people.'

I observed: "I was surprised that during World War II they did not extend Holcomb's tour as Commandant. They made Alexander A. Vandegrift Commandant. I would have thought in your case, in a time of war, particularly in view of the role you had in preparing Marine Forces for the war with Iraq in 1990, that they would have asked you to extend."

"They talked to me about it," he told me. "I would have been extended if the war hadn't ended. They had talked about that on both sides of the river and in the Pentagon. Also there was some discussion about becoming Vice Chairman of the Joint Chiefs of Staff. However, I discouraged this and said it was time to go. My waiver on age had already been granted in my case when I became commandant in 1987."

I then asked General Gray: "As you were developing in your career, did you aspire to become a Commandant?"

He responded: "I didn't have any intention of even being a general. I never really ever did anything that was oriented to get me promoted. I mean, I never thought about it. I took an inordinate number of risks as a young guy. I was a maverick, new ideas. I assumed lots of risks, combat and otherwise. An experienced Navy captain told me in 1957 that 'you are either going to be a Commandant or a career captain in the Marines the way you act.' I said, 'It's going to be the latter, I can promise you that.'"

He told me that he had spent 10 years as a captain. He humorously observed that Generals Wilson and Barrow were Southerners, "so I changed my address to South Jersey and starting walking and talking slower."

He continued: "You know, any success that may be attributed to me for whatever reason, well, there are two sides to that. One is that people made it happen and that I let them do it. The other part was I had strong backing from so many through the years.

"I knew a lot of senior generals at a very young age and they turned me loose. Whosoever turned me loose; they expected things to get done—and right. That's sort of the way it was."[39]

## General Carl E. Mundy, Jr. (July 1, 1991–June 30, 1995)

General Mundy was first approached about becoming Commandant as a two-star. He related: "It may be interesting to first review some background in the selection process of the 29th Commandant. In the mid-1980s, the Marine Corps senior leadership became the target for criticism by certain so-called 'military reformists' led by a former military affairs staffer to Senator Gary Hart, Bill Lind. And also by some mid-grade officers who shared Lind's views relative to a need for doctrinal change. A few years earlier, when he was commanding the Second Marine Division, General Al Gray had begun the doctrinal reformation of the Corps by embracing the principles of maneuver warfare and had thereby become favored by the reform activists. The other principal candidates were General Tom Morgan, the Assistant Commandant, and Lieutenant Generals D'Wayne Gray and Ernie Cheatham, all fine officers of solid reputation, but viewed by the reformists as more traditional than Al Gray. Somewhere between these camps was an advocacy—principally among a few active colonels and some retired generals—that the whole hierarchy of the Corps needed to be cleared, and a more junior candidate nominated—something of a repeat of the selection of Major General David Shoup to become the Commandant over all the eligible three-star officers some years earlier.

"About the time that the process of selecting the new Commandant began to take shape, Jim Webb, a distinguished Vietnam Marine veteran, and subsequently an Assistant Secretary of Defense, was nominated to become the Secretary of the Navy, with one of his earliest tasks being the selection of the next Commandant. Jim was of the same general age and lineage of a colonel, and may have shared—or at least been amenable to considering—some of the views of those who believed that 'deep selection' of a candidate to get fresh blood in the upper echelon was the way to go.

"As he was in the process of taking office as the Secretary of the Navy, together with a few other Headquarters generals, I received a call asking me to come over and talk with Mr. Webb. We talked for a couple of hours about where I thought the Corps should be going, what ideas I might have for change, what the various strengths of the candidates for Commandant were, to which constituencies they would appeal, and so forth. During the conversation, Webb surfaced the question of the feasibility of reaching down for a two-star, and I responded that to do so would, in my view, be destabilizing to the Corps. Dramatic actions like that might go over well in other Services, but the Corps would be better served by selecting from the ACMC [Assistant Commandant of the Marine Corps] and three-star ranks. We concluded the discussion without anything further of significance.

"In this same general timeframe, I received a call asking if my wife Linda and I would have dinner with Senator and Mrs. Howell Heflin of Alabama, a World War II Marine colonel, a close friend of former Commandant General Lou Wilson, and now Chairman of the Senate Judiciary Committee. We didn't know the Heflins, but we had a very pleasant 'get-to-know-you' dinner with them. Some time later, the man who had facilitated our meeting and dinner—also a World War II–era Marine—told me that the Senator had been informed that I was under consideration to become the Commandant, and wanted to get to know me. I told him that I appreciated the Senator's interest, but that I was well down the totem pole of seniority for such consideration.

"A few weeks later, I was on leave for some pre-season maintenance of our beach cottage in North Carolina and, our phone not yet being connected for the season, received a note delivered by our rental manager to call Colonel John Ripley, then the senior Marine at the Naval Academy, as soon as possible. John was a much admired friend, one of my former battalion commanders, and a close associate of Jim Webb. I went to a telephone booth at a shopping center in Cape Carteret, and called John, who informed me that Mr. Webb was fast approaching a decision on the Commandant, that he was leaning toward clearing out the hierarchy and nominating a two-star, and that I was the candidate of choice in that scenario. I recall saying, 'John, here I am standing in a phone booth beside a Piggly-Wiggly store being told that I may be the next Commandant of the Marine Corps!' John and I spoke for a few minutes more, and I reinforced with him what I had told Webb relative to what I considered would be a destabilizing act. Nonetheless, John advised, I was forewarned and should stand by.

"I returned to Washington from leave with a mixture of feelings about the direction things seemed to be shaping up. A few weeks later, a call came to me in quarters at night from another friend of long standing, a retired colonel with strong Pentagon connections whom I won't name because I believe he would prefer to remain anonymous. He advised me excitedly that the announcement was imminent, and that it's going to happen! The mixture of uncertainty continued until a few days later when the Secretary of Defense announced that Lieutenant General Al Gray's name was being forwarded to the White House to become the 29th Commandant.

"Whatever the sequence of events, or the accuracy of my friends' forecasts, I was relieved when the announcement was finally made because I continued then, as I do now, to believe that a two-star pick under other than extraordinary circumstances would have been destabilizing. And, as it seems to turn out more often than not with Commandants, Al Gray was the man for the four years that followed, and the Corps will reflect his contributions and stewardship in a long list of positive ways for a long time to come."

Four years later, as a three-star, Mundy again found himself in contention for Commandant. However, it almost didn't happen. As Mundy explained to me, General Gray had instituted a policy whereby three-star officers with 18 months in grade should turn in to him a letter offering to retire at the 2-year mark so as to provide the Commandant the option of continuing the officer beyond 2 years, or accepting his offer to retire in order to promote others. "I perpetuated his policy during my term," he told me, "because it was a fair way to deal with officers you might need to move on in order to bring up others to better meet the needs of the Corps, and to develop candidates to become four-stars. When I reached 18 months in grade, I asked some of my three-star counterparts whether or not they had sent in their letters. Some had, and some hadn't. 'Well, that's the Commandant's policy, and I'm going to write mine up and turn it in,' I told them. I began immediately to receive visits and calls from former Commandants and other active and retired senior officers all with the advice, 'Don't turn in your letter.' I thanked them, but responded that the Commandant had directed that we turn in letters and that was what I was going to do, and I did. A few months later, General Gray called down to tell me that I was going down to command Fleet Marine Forces, Atlantic, that summer to relieve Lieutenant General Ernie Cook—an exciting assignment. My offer to retire was never mentioned. A year later, however, after I had been nominated to become Commandant, I was informed that my letter had gone over from the Headquarters the previous year, but the Secretary had declined to approve it, saying, 'No, we're not going to retire him. I don't know whether he's the man or not, but I want him to be around next year when we make the choice of a new Commandant.'"

Mundy's oral historian, Brigadier General Edwin H. Simmons, noted: "On 22 April 1991, President Bush nominated you to be the next Commandant of the Marine Corps. When did you first learn that you were going to be nominated?"

General Mundy responded: "Well, you know officially, of course, when the Secretary of the Navy or Defense calls and says, 'I'm pleased to tell you that the President has nominated you.' Before that time, however, I doubt that there has ever been a nomination that hasn't carried with it a few months of rumors and speculation about who it's going to be. More than a few well-intended callers report that they have heard this or that and offer their best wishes, as though you were running an active campaign. The fact is that such calls and rumors become distracting and can also lead to the formation of 'camps' and stress within the upper ranks. Nonetheless, they are a fact of life.

"Under Secretary of the Navy Dan Howard was a very good friend of mine. Dan called me as the decision neared to say, 'It's beginning to shape up. Secretary Garrett [Secretary of the Navy Henry L. Garrett III] is coming down to the wire and I think you're going to be it.' So I had semi-official indications, I suppose, as early as the first of April that it looked like I was going to be the nominee. But, of course, going back to my experience four years earlier, you don't know until the While House announces such things.

"In mid-April, I was undergoing the Total Quality Leadership training [a spin-off of W.E. Deming's Total Quality Management system, popular at the time] that had been mandated for all senior officers in the Department of the Navy at the Naval Postgraduate School in Monterey, California. I checked into the hotel and went off to class, and a couple of days later, was besieged by calls—the first from Secretary of the Navy Larry Garrett, then General Colin Powell, and then General Al Gray—followed by dozens of others to tell me I had been nominated and to extend congratulations. The 'Please Return Call' notes continued to pile up, and while I tried valiantly to remain and complete the course, I finally gave up and thought, 'I may as well get out of here and go home,' because every time I sat down in class, someone would call me out to receive a call. So I left early and went back to Norfolk as the Commandant Designate."

General Mundy was asked, "Do you think you were General Gray's first choice to become Commandant? He said, "No, I don't. General Gray had been a mentor and one of the finest and most supportive teachers I've ever had. One could certainly say that in that sense he was a strong patron. I served under him as a battalion commander when he had the 4$^{th}$ Marines, as a regimental and MAU [Marine Amphibious Unit, now Marine Expeditionary Unit] commander when he had the 2$^{d}$ Marine Division, as a brigade commander when he was commander of Marine Forces, Atlantic, as his Operations Deputy when he was the Commandant, and for a short time, as one of his two Force commanders when I was at Marine Forces, Atlantic. He was a strong coach to me in most of those assignments and I have always admired and respected many of his professional qualities.

"That said, each of us comes, eventually, to the hard choice of who we believe is best suited to lead the Corps after us and when the time came for him to judge among the four or five of us who were eligible and to be considered, I believe he concluded that another candidate might be better suited. Those are reasonable assessments of a successor that any one of us makes."

I also asked Mundy: "Who do you think was General Gray's first choice?" He responded: "Lieutenant Generals Bob Milligan and Ernie Cook were probably the two leading preferences, although General Jack Dailey, the Assistant Commandant, Lieutenant General Norm Smith, and my Basic School classmate, Lieutenant General Joe Hoar, were also stellar officers, and had the ultimate choice been any one of them instead of me, the Corps would have been more than well served. However he may have ranked us, General Gray had developed a fine stable of candidates to succeed him, as I did four years later, I understand that he sent several—or perhaps all—of those names forward for consideration by the Secretary."

"So you believe the Secretary of the Navy was the key person in your selection?" I asked.

"Well, in those days, the Secretary ultimately made the choice of who went forward to the Secretary of Defense, and his choice may or may not have been in line with what the Commandant recommended. There were undoubtedly others who weighed heavily in influencing the final selection. I mentioned earlier that the Under Secretary of the Navy, Dan Howard, was definitely a friend and supporter, and I was also privileged to have the unsolicited, strong support of two extremely well thought of former Commandants—Generals Lou Wilson and Bob Barrow—along with a number of other four- and three-star retired Marine officers. I knew Colin Powell well, and we had good rapport. I had just finished a tour as Deputy Chief of Staff for Plans, Policies, and Operations, and in that capacity was also a known quantity to Secretary of Defense Cheney. Finally, as I related the story earlier, Senator Howell Heflin of Alabama, the very influential Chairman of the Senate Judiciary Committee, had taken note of me four years earlier. While I have no idea whether or not he lent active support, he was certainly in my corner. He subsequently introduced me when I went up for my confirmation hearing before the Senate Armed Services Committee.

"A point to be made," Mundy continued, "is that much of the support, especially by retired Marines, was behind the scenes and I was unaware of it until after the selection was made, and in some cases, several years afterward. It's safe to say that while a Secretary makes the final decision concerning whose name goes to the White House for nomination, there are a number of others who influence the decision."

But there were several interviews before the nomination was made. Mundy was interviewed, for example, by Defense Secretary Dick Cheney, who asked Mundy a question that made it clear that Mundy was not a "yes man." Cheney asked him, "What do you think of the MV–22?" because he had earlier cancelled the program. "I suppose," Mundy commented to me, "that this was something of a loyalty check to see I would answer something like 'I don't believe we should buy it.' But I didn't say that. I said, 'I understand the affordability issue, but I continue to think it's the aircraft for the future of the Marine Corps.'"

After the interview with Cheney, Mundy was called back to interview with General Powell. "The Chairman and I knew each pretty well so I would characterize the interview as a fairly 'softball' one. In that the Marine Corps had been directed by SecDef to reduce manning to 159,000 Marines, General Powell focused on that issue. I probably gave vague responses to his questions because while we knew that number was too low, we didn't have a firm foundation yet developed upon which to base convincing arguments for a higher number."

These interviews completed those conducted within the Defense Department, and soon thereafter Mundy's name was sent to the White House by Secretary Cheney as the choice to become Commandant. There was no subsequent interview by President Bush, who accepted Cheney's recommendation.

Mundy said, "The foregoing notwithstanding, the making of the 30th Commandant had its share of fractious circumstances. There was a certain amount of discreditation of me by a couple of younger general officers who favored other candidates, together with a small clique of 'reformists,' led by Bill Lind, whom I mentioned earlier. Lind had made some significant contributions to operational thinking in the Marine Corps, and in that sense, had been embraced by General Gray for his operational intellect. He was invited to participate in lectures and seminars in the schools at Quantico and published several articles in professional Marine Corps journals advocating the principles of maneuver warfare. However, he got a bit out of line by offering his views to younger officers as to which generals merited their trust. This became a matter of angry concern in the Corps, and as a result, Lind was made persona non grata at Quantico by the commanding general. During the run-up to selection of the Commandant, there were a few newspaper articles which obviously emanated from Lind or his supporters that sought to discredit some contenders and foremost among them, me. The most notable being a 'poison pen' letter over another signature, but unmistakably in 'Lind language' to Secretary Cheney advising him that if any other candidate among us—by name—other than Bob Milligan were selected, the many good initiatives instituted by General Gray would be reversed and the Corps would go straight downhill. Although we never discussed it, I have no doubt that Bob Milligan was as turned off by this trash as the rest of us.

"After copies of this defaming letter had been sent to me by a number of active and retired senior Marines who found it extremely offensive, unprofessional, and below the belt, I flew up from Norfolk with the letter in hand to see General Gray and said to him that whatever Lind's opinion of me, we certainly did not need a sensational, back-biting, character assassination campaign, and that I believed he was the only man who had any influence over Lind, and that I would encourage him to tell Lind to knock off his defamation campaign. General Gray had not seen the letter, and whether or not he subsequently made any connection with Lind, I don't know, but Lind and company were off the reservation. Their campaign lasted right up to the weekend in June before the change of command between General Gray and me with a 'Lind language' Sunday newspaper supplement entitled 'About Face for the Corps' in which the likelihood of me overturning all that General Gray had done and thereby taking the Corps back to the Dark Ages, was lamented.

"After my name had been announced by the White House, I received a call from Secretary Garrett asking me to come down to Cherry Point, North Carolina, to meet with him as he was returning from a west coast trip. I did so, and we had a very pleasant one-on-one conversation discussing policies and direction for a couple of hours. As we were concluding, I recall that the Secretary leaned on me heavily over the issues of the end strength of the Corps and the MV–22 aircraft—both of which were the subjects of specific direction by Secretary Cheney. The Marine Corps had—and later continued on my watch—to oppose these decisions, and Garrett reminded me in fairly explicit terms of the loyalty that was expected of a new Commandant. I listened, but was noncommittal, because I knew that these were critical issues for the Corps, and that we were likely going to continue to try to influence a reversal or modification of them in the best interests of the Corps. These issues—and particularly the end strength of the Corps—were to be among my greatest challenges and are characteristic of the fine line a Service chief must tread in being loyal not only to the orders and directions of his civilian superiors, but also being loyal to the Marines he commands and to their critical needs to remain a viable military Service."

But there is more to selection than the nomination of the President. The next hurdle is confirmation by the Senate. Mundy reflected, "The Senate confirmation process takes a lot of work. A thick stack of questions requiring a written response was sent to me a couple of weeks in advance of the Senate Hearing. By that time, I had chosen Colonel Pete Metzger to be my 'Military Secretary'—a historic Marine Corps title deriving from the British Royal Marines, that is the equivalent of 'Executive Assistant' elsewhere—and Pete had set up a small transition office at the Center for Naval Analyses near Washington with a clerk and a driver. I brought up Colonel Tom Wilkerson, at that time the Assistant G3 of II MEF [Second Marine Expeditionary Force] at Camp Lejeune, and a Washington-savvy officer, to assist me in the laborious process of answering the stack of questions. Most of these were policy questions. One that stands out in every case, however, and that is not often well understood by the public, who tend to believe that the uniformed military leaders answer only to their civilian superiors, is the certification both in writing, and in my case, orally during the subsequent in-person hearing, that when asked in testimony for 'your personal views,' that you will not simply recite the administration's line, but will promise to give your best professional military judgment. This occasionally puts a Service chief, in testimony, at odds with an administration position, but it is important to those who represent the people of the United States, that unvarnished military opinions be provided when sought. We eventually completed the questions and turned them in for analysis by the Senate Armed Services staff.

"In the same time frame, I spent a good amount of time in Washington up from Norfolk making calls on various members of Congress—principally on the Senate side, since they would be involved in the confirmation process. I knew a number of the key Senators, but enjoyed getting to know a number of others in the process. Finally, in mid-June, I appeared before the Senate Armed Services Committee for a hearing on my qualifications to serve. The hearing included both the nominee to become Chief of Staff of the Army, my good friend, General Gordon Sullivan, and me. By that stage of events, it was more pro forma than substantive, but there were several fairly specific questions dealing with the MV–22 aircraft and other significant issues.

"The hearing completed, I went back to Norfolk to begin the process of awaiting confirmation, and getting ready to turn over my command. We were still recovering forces from the Persian Gulf after the conclusion of Operation *Desert Storm*, and I was extremely busy. I tried to assist Linda with getting us ready to move, but as she had done on so many other occasions in the past, because I was gone so much of our last month or so in Norfolk, she shouldered the burden of packing us up again and getting ready for yet another in the long line of 34 household moves we made in my eventual 39 years of Active service."

I asked General Mundy: "You mentioned selecting Colonel Metzger to be your Military Secretary. How did you go about assembling the remainder of your staff in order to be able to begin functioning immediately when you assumed your post as Commandant?"

He responded: "Actually, I didn't go through much of a selection process. Colonel Metzger, who had worked for me at Headquarters before I left the previous summer to go down to Norfolk, let it be known that he would like to be the Military Secretary. He was a fine officer whom I had come to know well during our service together. At that time, there was a very strong undercurrent of concern in the officer corps that had come to be referred to as 'bubbaism.' In the often outspoken views of many mid-grade officers, to get a good assignment in those days, you had to be a 'bubba'—to know a general and be on his list of favorites. To send a signal, when I heard that Metzger had expressed a desire for the job, I simply walked down the hall to his office while in Headquarters one day, and said, 'I understand you want to be the MilSec,' to which he replied, 'Yes, I would.' I told him he had the job, and to get started putting the small transition staff I made mention of earlier together. He asked who I would like for my aides-de-camp, driver, et cetera, and I responded, 'You pick them.' So I really didn't have anything to do with selecting those who would serve on my personal staff because I wanted to begin with that to dispel the perception of 'bubbaism.' Colonel Tom Wilkerson, his assistance to me completed with the completion of the Senate Confirmation Questionnaire, returned to duty at Camp Lejeune, and when my two new aides showed up a few weeks later, I didn't know either of them."

I said to General Mundy: "You were a three-star when selected to become the Commandant. Were you promoted before you assumed command, or afterward?"

Mundy said: "My promotion was rather extraordinary. About a week before I was to assume command, I asked Colonel Metzger to investigate how I was supposed to be promoted. There had been no mention of it to me by anyone and we were getting close. The following day, Pete came in and said, 'We just got a call from the White House. President Bush is going to be unable to attend the change of command ceremony, but asked if you and Mrs. Mundy would be available to pay a call on him the morning before [the ceremony was to occur that evening]. He would like to promote you.' Of course, when you get an invitation like that, you don't dwell long on whether or not you're available! Of significance in the telling of this tale is that Pete Metzger had been Marine Corps aide to President Reagan, when George Bush was Vice President, and as I later came to realize, his ties into the White House were still strong. Although he denied it, I suspect that Pete may have set the occasion up with the President's Office.

"To make a long story short, Linda and I, together with our two Marine sons, Sam and Tim—both captains at the time—appeared at the White House at the appointed hour, and were shown into the President's office, where we were cordially received by President Bush. We sat and chatted pleasantly for a few minutes, until the President looked to his Marine aide, Major John Wissler, and said, 'Well, John, let's get on with this. How do we go about it?' Major Wissler asked us all to stand, read the appointment, and then President Bush administered the oath of office to me. Afterward, Major Wissler handed him the new four-star insignia, and the President gave one to Linda to pin on, while he pinned on the other. When he finished, characteristic of President Bush, he said, 'I hope I got that on right. I've never promoted anyone to four stars before'—to which I responded, 'Don't worry about it, Mr. President. I've never been promoted by a President before!' That's how the promotion came about. A very pleasant memory."

"Is that the way Commandants are usually promoted?" I asked.

"I imagine there may have been a time back in history when the President personally promoted somebody, but I haven't known of it before," Mundy replied. "I don't think there is a 'stock' procedure. It would seem that there is a standard operating procedure for such things, but recall that I had to set Colonel Metzger on an inquiry to find out how to get four stars on my shoulder before the change of command ceremony, so unless the incumbent Commandant or a secretary of something or other gets personally involved, I don't know who else would take the lead.

"Four years later, when Chuck Krulak was getting ready to relieve me, I arranged for President Clinton to promote him in the same fashion I had been. Chuck's father and mother were in town for the event, and the President also asked that Linda and I come along for a farewell call together with Krulak's promotion. Rather than the standard, presigned, framed commission which is ordinarily signed by the Service Secretary and handed to the promotee after the ceremony, I took Chuck's over with me, unsigned, and got the President to personally sign it on his desk, with all present, after administering the oath. President Clinton even penned a personal 'Good luck,' I believe. The certification of the commission, under the Secretary's—or in this case, President's—signature is ordinarily signed by the incumbent Commandant. However, I asked Chuck's father, Lieutenant General 'Brute' Krulak, to certify after the President had signed, instead of me. That was a 'first,' and ought to be a very special keepsake in the Krulak family for generations to come.

"But back to your original question, I'm unaware of anyone in recent times, at least, who was personally promoted by the President before I was given that privilege."

"Did your promotion to general also make you Commandant, or was there another ceremony for that?" I asked.

Mundy replied: "Well, there was the change of command ceremony which was conducted on the evening of June 28, although command did not officially change until July 1, inasmuch as General Gray's appointment was through June 30. However, because neither the Army or Air Force 'change command,' as do the Navy and Marine Corps, their chiefs of staff are ordinarily sworn into office by their Service Secretaries, or by the Secretary of Defense. That practice has expanded to all four DOD Services, so a few days after I had relieved General Gray, Secretary Cheney hosted a ceremony in his office for General Sullivan and me, where I was 'officially' sworn in as Commandant."

I inquired: "Did Secretary Cheney administer your oath of office?"

Mundy replied: "No. A few days earlier, the Secretary's office had called over to ask who I would like to have swear me in. They indicated that I could name anyone I wished who was authorized to administer the oath. A man I had admired for many years was my choice: General Leonard Chapman, the 24th Commandant of the Marine Corps. I had been aide-de-camp to the Assistant Commandant during General Chapman's tenure as Commandant, and had come to admire him as the epitome of a gentleman, Marine, and Commandant. He graciously accepted, and it was he who administered the oath of office to me. Just before me, General Sullivan had been sworn in by the Secretary of the Army, and as I stood looking into the crowd of attendees, I sensed a look of disappointment on Secretary Garrett's face. He never mentioned it, but at my first meeting with him in his office the following day, I told him that I hoped I had given no offense at not asking him to administer my oath. Although I believe I had, he was gracious enough to assure me that no offense was taken, and the matter never came up again."[40]

## General Charles C. Krulak (June 30, 1995–June 30, 1999)

General Mundy was succeeded by General Charles C. Krulak on June 30, 1995. Brigadier General Simmons, Mundy's oral history interviewer, asked about Krulak's selection: "General Krulak's nomination was no surprise and it lacked the controversy that often surrounds these selections. Still, there was some dissent and differing opinion. One handicapper listed the odds in the race as follows: Chuck Krulak, 60 percent probability, and Bob Johnston, 30 percent. Is that a fair appraisal?"

General Mundy responded, "Had I been asked to give odds, I would have probably put it more in the 40/40/20 framework. Let me go through the process to some degree.

"From my first month in office, I endeavored to develop a crop, a group of three-star officers that would afford good choices to those who select future Commandants—and that is usually someone other than the incumbent Commandant—from a stable of well-developed candidates. There may have been instances in our past where the Commandant's personal choice was selected to succeed him, but there have likely been far more in which the Commandant's favorite was not the choice.

"I wanted the civilians—those who ultimately make those decisions—to have more than just one or two choices. If possible, they would have five or six, so that if the chooser blindfolded himself and simply put a finger on any one of the candidates, the Corps would have a good Commandant. With some degree of pride—not necessarily because everything I was able to do in that regard was right—I believe I can say that the assignment process for generals over my tenure was successful in producing several well-qualified candidates. We did, in fact, emerge with about that number.

"Among those you have mentioned, Generals Krulak and Johnston were without question the two favored candidates in most minds. However, General Rich Hearney, the Assistant Commandant, was very strong, and was, perhaps, one of the best rounded four-star aviators we have had to contend for the position of Commandant. The Marine aviation community weighed in very heavily on his behalf and he had very strong support within the civilian echelons of the Defense Department. He was a superb officer in every respect.

"Lieutenant General Ron Christmas was not without consideration, and Charlie Wilhelm was also a name to be considered. Although very junior at that point, Lieutenant General Tony Zinni had also established superb credentials. Those five were probably the strongest contenders, with Krulak and Johnston leading the pack, but the others were certainly in the hunt right up to the decision point.

"I began the discussion of selection of my successor with Secretary Dalton in November 1994, reminding him that shortly after the first of the year, he would need to begin to focus on selecting the next Commandant. I told him that I would be there to help, but that I would not drive his thought process. I would provide him full details on all three- and four-star officers in the Corps, but I reminded him that technically, any colonel of the Corps or higher could be considered, and that David Shoup was selected from the two-star ranks.

"In the following weeks, I personally prepared a notebook with the photograph, official biography, and a one-page—no more, no less—summary of each candidate's qualifications. I used a specific format so that each candidate had the same summary. These, I personally wrote and edited—no staff input or assistance beyond their being typed up by my secretary, Gunnery Sergeant Ana Prada. I ensured that they were balanced and written in such a way as to give facts and judgments, but not implicitly convey a recommendation. I introduced the book with an overview of what, in my judgment, the Commandant was and should be. I later recovered the book from the Secretary, and it is in my personal papers.

"Shortly before Christmas, I delivered the book to Secretary Dalton and encouraged him to study it over the holidays. I recommended that he also interview each officer, and that for those he didn't know well, that he should make a point of getting to know them. 'Go down to Camp Lejeune and spend three or four days with Bob Johnston or go out and spend time with Chuck Krulak in Hawaii, or get Ron Christmas and go hunting with him at Quantico. But whatever you do, get to know the leadership of the Corps.'

"Dalton took that on board and began, in January when he returned from Christmas leave, to interview each officer in the book or to go to visit them in the field. I had also recommended that he should consult widely, including the former Commandants and some of the key retired generals. Bill Keys had just retired, along with Walt Boomer and Jack Dailey some years earlier. 'Go as broadly as you wish to get opinions from these people.' To my knowledge, he followed through pretty well on that. I had calls, for example, from Generals Chapman, Wilson, and Barrow that they had been contacted, and their views asked. I wanted him to get to all this early, because history suggests that the later the selection process, the more active the *Navy Times* becomes in beginning to write up that this guy or that one is favored, or flawed, and the closer you get, the more sensational the stories get. I advised that if he could get it done at least by the end of March, there would be time to get the nomination in the mill, through the Defense Department, and over to the White House. Even though it might mean 'lame-ducking' me to some degree, I wanted to encourage him to make the choice early—get the process done—and avoid the tension and divisiveness that occurs when constituencies or factions form, or somebody disruptive—like a Bill Lind—gets in the act. All of this is of no value to the Corps and can, as in my case, set a new Commandant off with stresses within the leadership to be patched up, and negative seeds sown that take time and energies away from far more important matters."

During a subsequent interview with me, General Mundy also offered the following: "I wanted, as best I could, to create conditions for a smooth transition from my tenure to that of my successor; one in which the direction and programs of the Corps could remain constant, rather than the usual pause and sometimes disruption that occurs when the transition isn't smooth. I wanted, also, to keep the senior leaders close together in order to avoid, as much as possible, the tensions that sometimes occur during 'the run for the roses.' I took a step in September 1994 that I intended to help the selection process for a new Commandant in the next year. I believe that it worked out fairly well.

"I held a symposium of generals each year in September, and following my last one in 1994, I assembled the Assistant Commandant, all three-stars, and select one- and two-stars who were clearly on their way up. I said to the ACMC and three-stars, 'One of you will be chosen to relieve me next summer, and whomever among you that it may be, I would like you to have a game plan developed with you, and some of the principal lieutenants, who will help you implement it as the architects.' With the ACMC coordinating, I charged them, over the next six months, to undertake a strategic vision study to determine what the course and speed of the Corps should be in the coming years, and the steps a new Commandant would need to take to maintain, or gain, momentum toward those goals. They were to come in—from wherever posted—for two days each month over the next six or so, to sit as a group, think about where we were, what needed to be done, and thereby chart the future. I told them that I would not be a participant; would receive no reports of their progress; and would not critique or review their end product. I wanted that to be up to the new Commandant-Designate, when he was chosen.

"My intent was two-fold, as I have alluded to earlier: first, to give my successor a blueprint upon which to commence his tenure—one that he and those who would help him implement it had designed; and second, to keep the principal contenders close and collaborating during the selection process. It's much more difficult to believe the innuendo and rumors that tend to fly around about who is better than who, et cetera, when you're collectively looking each other in the face for a couple of days each month.

The bottom line is that this process seemed to work, and I would like to believe it helped General Krulak and his leadership team step off together the following year.

"I relate this because I believe that whoever becomes the Commandant, it should be far less about him, the individual, than about the Corps, the institution. The smoother the wheels of the Corps can keep turning and the more cohesive its leadership during a transition, the better for Marines and the nation."

Mundy continued, in his interview with General Simmons: "In early February, the Secretary had his Marine aide notify me that he had done his homework and was ready to talk. I suggested that instead of my coming to his office, he come to mine—on Marine turf, if you will—and he agreed to do so. I had the aides—both his and mine—clear our calendars for a complete afternoon because I wanted him to have all the time he needed for discussion without the press of the next appointment. He came over on the appointed day, and I suggested he take off his coat and loosen his tie, if he wanted, so we could just talk. I also suggested that he do the talking, in effect debriefing his conclusions from his interviews and thought process, and that I would offer something only if he asked. That worked well. He started by telling me that he had come down to four candidates: Hearney, Johnston, Krulak, and Zinni. He then went through the book summarizing what his perceptions of each were—including those who had not made the first cut—and where he thought he was on each candidate. I worked hard at doing a lot of listening and nodding, but not much talking except when he asked me something factual. After a couple of hours, I asked him where he thought he had come down to, and he concluded, 'Hearney, Krulak, and Zinni.' I suggested that he walk through his analysis of each again, and at the end of that, it was clear that Krulak and Zinni were the two foremost in his mind. We had, by that time, spent about three hours in the process, and he said, 'Okay, let's go home tonight and both think about this and tomorrow morning, I will be in my office at 7:30. Why don't you meet me there at that time and we will sit down again and see if our minds are clear?' So we got back together the following morning at 7:30 and without any further discussion, he had concluded overnight that his choice was Chuck Krulak.

"All of the betting money six months before—even a year before—would have gone to Bob Johnston. Bob is one of the officers that I have admired longest and most in the Marine Corps. He has an immaculate record; he is perfect. He had executed Somalia to the applause of the President, was decorated by the President in the Rose Garden, and was riding a crest of admiration for being a superb Joint Task Force Commander. He had been Norm Schwarzkopf's chief of staff during the first Persian Gulf War and had great credentials in the joint community and with Colin Powell. However, after commanding I MEF, Bob came back to Washington to be Deputy Chief of Staff for Manpower, and while superb in the job for the Corps, he simply did not connect effectively with some of the key civilians in the Washington arena. When John Dalton began his search process, he commented to me, 'I really don't know Bob Johnston.' That's unfortunate, because those of us who know him know Bob to be not only a consummate professional, but also a fun-loving, exciting fellow, and his wife, Sandra, a delightful lady. Regrettably, however, Bob just didn't connect.

"Chuck probably had done more of what a Commandant does in his experiences at the Marine Corps Combat Development Command, in directing recruiting, in manpower management, and in having had both infantry, if you will, through the Assistant Division Commander level, but then the logistics track as Commanding General of a Force Service Support Group in combat as well. Chuck also had good OSD [Office of the Secretary of Defense] and White House Military Office credentials. And while I truly don't believe it was the deciding factor, Chuck was Naval Academy, and a classmate of John Dalton there, and had an absolutely splendid record throughout his career. Chuck's three-star job in the Washington area involved the Combat Development Process with lots of interface with the Navy and the Secretariat and the representation of the Corps in many, many Pentagon issues. He had broad and solid recognition in Washington and was a strong professional across the board.

"Rich Hearney, as I mentioned earlier, couldn't have been a stronger candidate. However, the Corps has not to date had an aviator Commandant, and there are many who believe that a ground officer is better qualified to exercise the broad range of command over what is fundamentally a ground combat organization which is supported by aviation. So while a superb officer in every respect, Rich probably suffered from that fact of life perception.

"Tony Zinni was very junior, and although Dalton was extremely high on him, I suspect that in the end, the Secretary concluded that Tony still had time ahead and was without question four-star material in waiting—which certainly turned out to be the case.

"So I think it was a combination of those factors, but in the final analysis, there were four fine officers who had 'made the cut' as of 3:30 the day before final selection and at that point, they were running pretty well neck-and-neck. By the end of the day, that had necked-down to two, and the following morning, it was apparent that the Secretary had settled on Chuck.

"The point of all this is that, had the nomination gone to any one of those four in the 3:30 'cut,' the Corps would have been well served, and that is the scenario I wanted from my first month as Commandant. I felt very good about the process and, as I told each of them at one time or another, 'If it's you, you will have nothing but support and hurrahs out of this particular Commandant!"[41]

General Krulak's tour before becoming Commandant of the Marine Corps was at Marine Forces, Pacific (MARFORPAC). Dr. David Crist, Krulak's oral history interviewer, asked him: "On 24 February 1994 General Mundy informed you that you had been slated for MARFORPAC. What do you recall of this? Did you know you were being contemplated for that position?"

Krulak responded, "Well, first off, it's important to know that at a three-star off-site held in California some months before, General Mundy had told me that I was going to MARFORLANT [Marine Forces Atlantic]. He even tasked me with some initiatives that he wanted to start at MARFORLANT. One of them was, in fact, to look at the viability of moving the LANT headquarters to Camp Lejeune. So I was going to LANT, not to PAC. Then I got a phone call from General Mundy saying, 'I changed my mind. I'm going to send you to MARFORPAC.' He did it because General Mundy is, in many ways, a very sentimental person. In the back of his mind was this idea of Chuck Krulak going back to his father's command. He felt this would be an emotional, sentimental, and historical event. At the same time, Lieutenant General Bill Keys, who was in some ways a mentor to me, had been talking to General Mundy. He told General Mundy not to send me to MARFORPAC. I think Bill Keys wanted me to be the Commandant, and he felt that MARFORPAC would be the kiss of death. We hadn't had a Commandant from PAC in 20 years. Lou Wilson was the last one. When I got the phone call from General Mundy, I went home and talked to Zandi and talked to my parents. Zandi was kind of focused to the east and now she had to be refocused to the west, but she's so talented that she was ready to go in any direction. My parents were ecstatic.

"I can't overemphasize the fact that I wasn't thinking of being the Commandant. I was a very junior three-star. I was deep-selected over 25 generals for three stars. So the idea that I was going to be the player for the Commandant was ridiculous. We had Hank Stackpole, Walt Boomer, and Bob Johnston, just to name a few. These were the people that I looked up to and believed would provide the next Commandant.

"I was excited about having the opportunity to command two-thirds of the operational Marine Corps and to hold the command my father once held. I went out to Hawaii fully anticipating to retire out of MARFORPAC. I called Bill Keys and told him to quit worrying about me. I told him that anyone who goes to a duty station because he thinks it might help his chances for promotion is not the kind of person we want in the Corps . . . certainly not the person we want to lead the Corps. I told him to quit worrying about it."[42]

Dr. Crist asked: "What do you recall about your confirmation?"

General Krulak responded: "The Commandant doesn't normally come from MARFORPAC. When I went out there, I literally did not go out there thinking I was going to be the Commandant. I thought that it was a signal that I wasn't going to be the Commandant. I was going out there to retire in the same position that my father had last occupied before his retirement. That's not bad; I was pretty excited about it! But when people said, 'Krulak is going to be the Commandant,' Krulak didn't think so."

Before becoming Commandant, Krulak was looking ahead and wanting to get his planning guidance written in time enough to release it at 0001 on 1 July. "One of the things that I got from my dad when I had gone and visited him was, 'Four years may seem like a long time, but in reality, it is very short. If you think of the Marine Corps as a big ocean-going vessel, and you're the CO of that vessel, and you say, right full rudder, you start that rudder turning, that ship doesn't turn for a long, long time. If it's a big oil tanker, it just takes forever to turn. That's the way the Marine Corps is. If you think that you can turn that culture on a dime, you're crazy. What you need to do is make every single decision that you're going to make of substance in the first year, because you will need the next three to institutionalize them.' I knew I was going to make the ship turn in many areas. I wanted it ready to go the minute I became Commandant. The actual minute that anybody becomes the Commandant is at 0001 on the 1st of July. The major challenge was to build the apparatus, my group, my transition team, in such a manner as to be able to achieve that goal."[43]

"Like I've said many times, Zandi and I went to MARFORPAC believing in our hearts and souls that we were not going to be the Commandant and the First Lady. We loved Hawaii and besides, anybody who seeks the Commandancy isn't the person who should be the Commandant."[44]

On March 14, 1995, at Mount Suribachi, Iwo Jima, Secretary Dalton announced Krulak's nomination as the 31st Commandant. Krulak said: "I think Mount Suribachi was chosen for a lot of reasons. One, obviously, was just the plain historical value to the Corps of this great island called Iwo

Jima, and the tremendous battle that took place there. I think that was a beautiful backdrop, too. We were in the midst of the 50$^{th}$ anniversary of the battle. It was even more special because a lot of the warriors who fought during the battle were there. Also, there was a great family connection in that my godfather, as we discussed, was H.M. Smith [General Holland M. Smith]. I think what Dalton was trying to do was tie the famous Secretary of the Navy Forrestal, standing next to Smith, pointing up on Suribachi, seeing the flag raised, and saying, 'The raising of the flag on Suribachi guarantees the Marine Corps for the next 500 years.' And fifty years later, the Secretary of the Navy is telling 'Howling Mad' Smith's godson, 'You are the Commandant.' So, there was all of that. I think that's kind of why this featured Suribachi and Iwo Jima.

"But again, although we were going there, there was not, in my mind, a defining sense that this was when it was going to happen. We only found out when we were actually circling Suribachi on a plane. The communicator came out of the front cabin with a yellow message that was given to Mundy. He looked at the message, gave it to my wife. My wife took the message, opened it up, started crying, and she handed it to me. The message read, 'The President of the United States announces that he has nominated General Charles C. Krulak.' When people ask, 'When did you find out?' I found out on that plane. It was very dramatic.

"I think General Mundy was honest in his desire to give General Hearney as ACMC and every one of his three-stars a shot at being Commandant. I don't think he set out to sponsor Bob Johnston, or Chuck Krulak, or Rich Hearney, or anybody. I think in his own mind, as he started looking at the potential candidates, that in all probability, he felt I would do the best job. They were great candidates. Tony Zinni, Charlie Wilhelm, Bob Johnston, Rich Hearney; they're really great. In my heart of hearts, I don't believe he ever reached the point of saying to the Secretary of the Navy, 'Here's the guy I think you ought to select.'

"Although I've mentioned this before, it's worth repeating, I had never served with Carl Mundy until I was a one-star general. And even when I was a one-star, I think I saw him a total of four times. This is not a case of 'bubbaism.'"[45]

General Krulak, in the interview process with the Secretary of the Navy for selection as Commandant, recalled: "When we talked about gays in the military, and I just said, 'No,' and if he had a problem with that, we ought to end the interview, because I would not support that, and I would be very vocal against it.

"I talked a little bit about Congressional relationships and how I thought that the Navy and the Marine Corps could improve in that area. We talked about the importance of the family. That as the Secretary of the Navy, he ought to be looking at the spouse, because the spouse was going to play a major role.

"Then he asked whom would I pick, if not me? I told him that, although he would probably run into some conflict from ground officers, I thought Rich Hearney would make a good Commandant and he would be the first aviator Commandant. If we were interested in doing a first, I know President Clinton is often interested in firsts, here's one he might want to think about. He said, 'Thank you very much,' and that was it. There was very little feedback from him. It was just one question after another.

"As I understand it, General Mundy provided to Secretary Dalton several nominations, as if each were the individual to be Commandant. In other words, he wrote up a series of people as if they were the candidate to be the nominee, then provided those to Secretary Dalton, then they talked through each one of those nominees. Secretary Dalton then did the interviews, and then I think he went down to Secretary of Defense [William] Perry, and to see Chairman Shalikashvili [General John Shalikashvili, USA]. They talked it over, and then they went to the President, and made a nomination there."

Crist asked: "You and Secretary Dalton were classmates at the Naval Academy. What was your relationship?"

"Dalton was at the Naval Academy when I went through," Krulak said, "but we had 24 companies divided into two regiments. I was in the first regiment; he was in the second. I rarely saw him."

General Krulak said he first heard he had been selected "around 1 to 3 March 1995, sometime in that timeframe. But, I learned long ago that until the President of the United States nominates you, all the rest is baloney. When people say, when did I find out, I found out on an aircraft right off Mount Suribachi. Although General Mundy had written me a letter saying congratulations, we're so proud of you prior to the actual nomination, I preferred to wait for the official nomination by the President. Let me tell you, the same thing had happened to my mother and father. My dad was told by the Secretary of the Navy, you're the next Commandant. It didn't happen."[46]

General Krulak devoted his adult life to the Marine Corps and because of his commitment to the Corps, he was confident of his abilities and "hit the ground running" when he became Commandant.

The relationship among the contenders when the Commandant is selected reveals their character. Krulak said: "We had great support from the leadership of the Corps, Rich Hearney and all the Deputy Commandants. They got on board and they made it happen. My sincere tip of the hat goes to those generals. You need to remember that the vast majority of them were competing to be the Commandant. All of a sudden one officer was selected and the rest immediately lined up and we all marched off in the same direction in a massive undertaking that was going to really stir the Corps up. They were with me the whole time. It was very positive.

"I think that's a real tribute and testimony to the way the Marine Corps thinks and behaves. Unlike any other Service, there is a Commandant. What the Commandant says is what we're going to do and we all get behind it. What is important is the institution. The day the Marine Corps has people who start thinking that they don't need to follow the head of the institution is the day we become like any other Service."[47]

For Lieutenant General Victor "Brute" Krulak, who never became Commandant despite being told by the Secretary of the Navy that he would be, the swearing-in of his son was a touching and sentimental scene. Chuck Krulak reflected: "That was done at the White House. In attendance were my wife, my mother, my father, my two sons, General Mundy, and Secretary Dalton. It was done in the Oval Office. The President had some very nice words to say about my father and myself. As we were preparing to put on the stars, my mother went into her purse and brought out a set of stars for the collar that apparently she had purchased years and years ago at the time they thought my father was going to be Commandant. As I indicated, he had been nominated by the Secretary of the Navy. She went out and got those stars, unbeknownst to him. When it came time to put on the collar insignia, my mother reached into her pocket and brought them out. It was a pretty emotional moment for my father. The ceremony was very nice, very short. What was important were the stars that had been purchased in 1968 for my father, and now his son wore them."

## General James L. Jones (July 1, 1999–January 17, 2003)

General Charles C. Krulak's tour as Commandant ended June 30, 1999, and he was succeeded by General James L. Jones on July 1, 1999. General Jones was 55 years old, a decorated Vietnam veteran with 32 years of service as a Marine. At the time of his appointment he was serving as Military Assistant to Secretary of Defense William S. Cohen. The best insight into General Jones' selection as Commandant is provided in the oral history of Commandant Krulak by Dr. David Crist. Krulak reflected: "We knew that on June 30,

1999, we were going to have a new Commandant. We didn't know who it was, but we knew that there was going to be one. So I set a couple of goals, one, to make sure that my generals knew that I knew I was leaving, and that they didn't need to walk on eggshells as we got closer to 30 June. Two, I wanted them to act like Marine generals. What I asked each of them, and later asked all of the generals in the Corps, was not to pick sides as to who was going to be the next Commandant. They could have their own favorite, and there was nothing wrong with that, but not to get caught up in badmouthing somebody else. If they got a phone call from somebody that asked what do you think about, for instance, Carl Fulford. They should have nothing but good things to say about him and all Marines. Tell the truth. If you happened to like one better, say my choice would be so and so. But in saying that, don't ever badmouth somebody else.

"Then I shared with them how I intended to help the Secretary of the Navy come to grips with who the next Commandant would be. Basically, I used the same pattern that General Mundy did. I provided to Secretary Danzig [Secretary of the Navy Richard Danzig] a list of those people whom I thought he ought to interview. I gave him a document that talked about each one of them from a comparative standpoint. I gave him all of that, and I encouraged him to interview everybody and to encourage the Secretary of Defense to interview everybody as well."

Dr. Crist inquired of General Krulak: "Did you have a recommendation on who the 32$^d$ Commandant should be?"

He responded: "This was a very strange run for the roses, so to speak, because I don't think there was any question in anybody's mind that the odds-on favorite was General Jones. My concern was that it would be unfair to General Jones and unfair to the Marine Corps as a whole if the Corps ever thought that there was only one option, and that the single option was Jim Jones. I shared this with the Secretary of the Navy and asked him to share it with the Secretary of Defense. It was because of that feeling that I thought it was necessary to identify and interview everyone who was a potential candidate. It all boiled down to [Peter] Pace, [Carlton] Fulford, Jones, [Martin] Steele, and [Terrance] Dake. They were the ones that I wrote up nomination packages for and gave to the Secretary of the Navy. He never asked me, okay, sit down and give me your recommendation because he basically knew what I thought about each one of them in the comparison papers that I put together and in my nomination packages. In addition, Mr. Danzig knew each of them very well. I then asked him to please ensure that the SecDef interview at least three. The four that I wanted him to interview were Pace, Fulford, Steele, and Jones.

"Danzig interviewed everybody. Danzig even spoke with people who weren't even in the running, like Frank Libutti, who had just made three stars. He literally called him on the phone. He said, 'I don't want to bring you all the way back from Okinawa, but could you talk to me about the candidates.'"[48]

In my interview with Jones, I asked him: "In your case, did they interview any other contender besides you?" He responded: "Oh, sure they did. Secretary of the Navy Danzig had multiple interviews; General Peter Pace was interviewed, and several others."[49]

I asked Jones: "Did you have any expectation you'd become Commandant?" He said: "No, not really." In fact, he almost retired after he had 20 years of service, thinking that "it might be a good time to leave because I have been a battalion commander," which he said "is really the best job in the Marine Corps, or at least I thought so."

A significant assignment in Jones' career was serving from August 1979 until July 1984 as Marine liaison officer to the U.S. Senate. Part of the Corps' greatest strength is the respect and admiration of Congress. The liaison assignment is normally a 3-year tour, sometimes 4, but it was 5 years for Jones because of the exceptional success he had with the Senate.

He was selected to be the military assistant to Secretary of Defense William S. Cohen on April 21, 1999. When asked why he was selected, Jones said: "That probably has more of a personal answer to it. When I was liaison officer to the Senate, I got to know Senator Cohen, and we maintained a relationship for quite a few years. We were roughly the same age, and we became good friends."[50] Secretary Cohen recommended Jones for the post of Commandant: "When I first met him, I truly sensed he was headed for greatness and would go on to achieve great things."[51]

## Conclusion

As the tenure of a Commandant's normal 4-year term draws to a close, rumors abound on the successor. General Krulak put this phenomenon into perspective and gave very sound advice, which, knowing the stature of the Commandant, was probably considered an order. He told his senior generals "not to pick sides as to who was going to be the next Commandant . . . to not get caught up in bad-mouthing somebody else . . . [that] they should have nothing but good to say about all Marines." The above studies are examples of the character of the senior generals and a very strong factor in perpetuating the "eliteness" of the Corps. The senior Marine leaders are a team and should, and normally do, pull together.

Chapter 3

# "Destiny Hangs by a Slender Thread": Making the Decision to Join the Marine Corps

The institution of the Marine Corps is a magnet for a certain kind of person. For many, the attraction is transient, and after a period of service, they return to civilian life, pursuing new careers with greater discipline, confidence, and focus than they had before. For others, the draw of the Corps only increases over time, inspiring an inordinate number of multigenerational Marine families. How did the most influential of career Marines come see the Corps as their calling, struggle to earn the title "Marine," and dedicate their lives to leading multiple generations of Leathernecks? The motivations and early experiences of these incipient Marine leaders prior to and upon entering the Corps are quite interesting. Their stories reveal much history as well as insight into the character, personality, and leadership of the officers who have exerted the greatest influence over the destinies of countless Marines, the future of the Corps, and of course, the very fate of the United States of America.

## Early Experiences of Future Commandants

### John A. Lejeune

Lejeune began his military career as a midshipman at the Naval Academy, class of 1888. In his memoir, *The Reminiscences of a Marine*, he expressed the thrill and adventure of a life of service to his country:

> For a number of years, my father had frequently discussed the possibility of my going to the United States Military Academy at West Point. He had acquired a very high opinion of that institution by reason of the sterling character and splendid

military ability displayed by the great military leaders on both sides in the Civil War. In fact, I was taught to revere them and above all to regard General Robert E. Lee as being the embodiment of the noblest qualities of which human nature is capable. General Lee's lofty character, as displayed in war under the humiliation of defeat, and in the years that followed the surrender at Appomattox, had a far-reaching and lasting effect on the soldiers of the Confederacy and on the generation of young men which succeeded them.

So it came about that when I had attained the required age, my father took steps to secure me an appointment. Our Congressman, Judge E. T. Lewis, informed him, however, that there was no vacancy at West Point, but that one had just occurred at the Naval Academy, and offered the appointment to me. I unhesitatingly accepted it because, after all, the chief reason for my willingness to go to West Point was to lift the heavy financial burden of my education from the shoulders of my parents.

It was early in April 1884 that I received notice of my appointment to the Naval Academy. I promptly resigned from the University of Virginia, being then near the end of the sophomore year, and went home, where I spent a month in self-preparation for the entrance examination and in association with the dear ones in the home in which there dwelt thrift, wisdom, unselfishness, love and, therefore, happiness.[1]

In *The Reminiscences of a Marine*, General Lejeune reflected on one of the cruises that were part of midshipman training that provided insight into his calling for a life of adventure and service to his country. Lejeune had a vivid recollection of the first ship he boarded:

The *Alliance* was beautifully decorated with flags and was spotlessly clean. The decks, the guns, the paintwork, the brass, the yards, the masts, the awnings and the rigging were immaculate, as were the sailors, the marines, and the officers in their resplendent uniforms. As we looked about us, taking count of everything we saw, we were thrilled through and through, especially when we turned our eyes towards our glorious flag flying to the breeze at the peak. We remained on board for an hour or two, visiting every part of the ship and watching the dancing on the quarterdeck.

On his tour of that ship, he saw his first Marine:

> I noticed that one of the officers was dressed in a different uniform from the others, wearing sky blue trousers instead of dark blue, and a braided blouse instead of a double-breasted frock coat carrying two rows of brass buttons. I asked the sailor who was acting as my guide who the officer was, and he replied that it was the Marine officer of the ship.

The Marine in question was Lieutenant George F. Elliott, who went on to become Commandant in 1903 and served in that position until 1910. "In after years," reflected Lejeune, "I came to know him well and had the honor of serving under his command."[2]

This experience of seeing the ship, the sailors, and most of all the Marines had a lasting impact on Lejeune's life and career:

> We went ashore with our minds filled with thoughts of the ship, the crew, the far-away ports they had visited, and the strange peoples they had seen, but somehow it never once occurred to me that the hand of fate was beckoning me to take the path which would lead me away from home across the trackless oceans and to far countries, but always under the inspiration and guidance of the beautiful flag—that symbol of the united nation which it would be my good fortune to serve, in calm or in storm, in peace or in war, during nearly all the remaining years of my life.[3]

The education and experience Lejeune received at the Naval Academy further strengthened his character, including his interest in serving his country, the development of which began in his home:

> Entrance to the Naval Academy, therefore, not only involved the beginning of a career, but the creation of new and lasting friendships as well. From both points of view, it marked the beginning of a new volume in one's life history, the ending of the individualistic conception of life, and the beginning of the life of service to the Government, our people, and the nation. Henceforth, while clinging with the strongest kind of sentimental attachment to the

locality in which I was born and bred, I became before all else, a citizen and a servant of America.

These thoughts were the product of gradual growth and development. They did not at once spring into being. In fact, my first thoughts, after taking the oath to support the Constitution and receiving instruction concerning the very practical things that I was to do, were to admit to myself that a "plebe" [freshman student] was a very humble and unimportant person who was lucky to be permitted to enter, even on sufferance, the sacred precincts of the Naval Academy where there dwelt the exalted personages known as "upperclassmen." Our first duty tended to increase the feeling of humility. It was to go to the Cadet Store and draw a great variety of necessary articles which we rolled up in a blanket and carried about a quarter of a mile to the USS *Santee*, an old sailing ship, which was fast in the mud alongside the dock and which was used as a temporary barracks or dormitory for the "plebes."[4]

On one of his lengthy cruises, Lejeune had an encounter that began his first mentorship:

Throughout the remainder of the twenty-five days in which we cruised before we entered the harbor of Portsmouth, New Hampshire, we enjoyed fine weather and had opportunity, especially in the night watches, to make the acquaintance of some of the "old salts" who constituted the crew. They were to us the most interesting human beings imaginable. They told us many remarkable stories of their adventures in far away parts of the world, and described their voyages on the Seven Seas. They were rough, seafaring men who had come in contact with the waifs and strays of humanity in the seaports of the world, but concealed in their bosoms were the tenderest and most generous of hearts and an innate refinement or whatever one might call it, which prevented them from telling us anything defiling. In fact, they always respected our youth and inexperience. I especially remember the captain of the forecastle. He was older than most, and a typical seaman of the old days. We often gathered about him in the evening watches to listen to his stories, which were interlarded, not with oaths, as might be supposed, but with sound advice. He described pitfalls that we should avoid and drew on his own experience to warn us against the harpies which were to be found ashore in seaport towns. His earnest face is before me as I write.[5]

My mind was filled with serious thoughts for a while, but I was young—just past twenty-one—physically powerful, and constitutionally lighthearted, so it was not surprising that my thoughts in time reverted to eager anticipation of the adventures ahead, or that my responsibilities should sit very lightly on my shoulders. In fact, I was filled with the joy of living. I am glad to say, however, that in a few years I began to realize that there was a serious side to life, that duty should come before pleasure, and that every man owed a debt to corps and country which it was his highest privilege to pay.[6]

I had my first experience of the most fascinating side of Navy life—the unexpected orders, the excitement, the hustling, bustling hurly-burly, the farewells to friends, the sudden departure—often for an unknown destination, and the speculation as to what it was all about and as to what was going to happen. It is events such as these which add the bright colors to pictures of life in the Navy and Marine Corps.

Youngsters on board felt they were like Crusaders of the olden time, and that on their shoulders rested the proud duty of protecting the interests of their country and of defending the lives and the liberty of the Samoans.[7]

Lejeune wrote of the excitement of the travel experiences, particularly a cruise to Hawaii, that was a large factor in deciding on a military career:

Our first port of call was Honolulu, the pearl in the "Paradise of the Pacific," as the Hawaiian Islands were then and still are called. We sailed under a cloudless sky the day of our arrival in the archipelago and at dawn we sighted Mauna Loa on the island of Hawaii at a distance of one hundred miles and later on, the great mountain mass of Oahu came into view. As we neared the southern coast of the island, we sighted Diamond Head, the beautiful, extinct volcano which appears to stand watchful guard over the approach to Honolulu from the east.

> It seems, somehow, to have almost a sacred significance to Hawaiians, who greet its appearance with shouts of joy in somewhat the same way as do Japanese travelers when Mount Fujiyama becomes visible to their straining eyes.
>
> As we rounded Diamond Head and approached the harbor entrance, an entrancing scene was spread out before our eyes. Lying at the foot of the great mountain bulwark was a lovely plain, dotted with houses all nestling in the midst of tropical foliage. It was our first glimpse of a foreign land and our first visit to the tropics, and we experienced a never to be forgotten thrill. I should have said a series of thrills, because, as the vista unfolded, the thrill was repeated over and over again, as indeed it was when we went ashore and saw close-up the unaccustomed scenes and heard the not to be understood chatter of the cosmopolitan population. The glamour of romance hung about these islands, had a potent and far-reaching influence on the whole of my after life.[8]

An incident occurred in Lejeune's first year at the Naval Academy that illustrated his character:

> I always received a great deal more than my fair share of attention from the upperclassmen. For this reason the other "plebes" in nearly all instances kept away from me and I was left to bear the brunt of my popularity alone. On one occasion, however, I looked up and there stood one of my classmates just as close to me as possible. He said, "I am going to stand by you. I like the color of your uniform" [meaning gray, reflecting his Confederate roots]. He was a young man of huge frame, powerful physique, and with a look of kindness, courage and affection shining in his fine blue eyes. He was Carlos Bonaparte Brittain, of the little mountain town of Pineville, Kentucky. From that moment we became fast friends, and my affection for him has continued unabated to this day. He died on board the Flagship of the Atlantic Fleet at Guantanamo Bay, Cuba, about seven years ago. He was then a Rear Admiral and the Chief of Staff of the Fleet. A nobler spirit than his I never have known.
>
> So much attention was paid me by the upperclassmen that it was observed by the officer in charge, and one evening an order was received on the *Santee* to send me under escort to

report to the office in charge. When my escort, Naval Cadet Harry G. Carpenter, a turn-back,[9] and I reached the New Quarters, we were ushered into the office. The officer said to me sternly, "I saw several upperclassmen surrounding you and apparently 'running' you just before supper formation, among them Mr. Griswold. I direct you to repeat to me in full just what they said to you." I replied that I didn't know Mr. Griswold. He then asked me if I could identify him. I stated in reply, with perfect truthfulness, that I could not identify any of the upperclassmen who had spoken to me, as there had been so many of them, and that I couldn't remember anything specific that any of them had said, but that nothing had been said which was humiliating to me, or to which I could properly take exception. This was the substance of the interview, which lasted some ten or fifteen minutes. On our way back to the *Santee,* Carpenter described it with a good many trimmings to several groups of upperclassmen that we met.

The incident passed from my mind until the following October, when, one evening, five or six members of the Class of '86 entered my room. They were in a fierce mood and gave every indication of being on a hazing expedition. They hadn't been on the practice cruise with us, their class—the second—having spent the summer at the Naval Academy, as was then the custom, and they had just returned from their September leave. Consequently, I had no recollection of ever having seen any of them before. The first question asked was my name. I answered, "Gabriel La Jeunnesse," which had been given me by a member of the same class. One of them—a six-footer—said, "Don't get funny, Mister. There isn't any plebe by that name. What is your real name?" I replied, "Lejeune, sir." He said, "Aren't you the plebe that the officer in charge, Lieutenant Manney, sent for last spring and asked if Mr. Griswold hadn't been 'running' you?" I answered that I was. He said, "I am Mr. Griswold," and turning to his classmates he said, "This plebe saved me from being court-martialed; he is my friend, and he is exempt from running or hazing by any member of the class of '86." They then wished me goodnight, left the room, and continued their activities at the expense of some of my less fortunate classmates living in nearby rooms.[10]

Returning from a midshipman cruise, Lejeune wrote:

At Annapolis we took off our coats and went to work. Hard study was essential, as we had lost our books in the shipwreck [Lejeune's ship, the *Vandalia*, was destroyed by a hurricane near Samoa during his first midshipman cruise] and did not replace them until we arrived at Annapolis.

Owing to the unexciting time we had enjoyed while on board the *Adams*, I was able to prepare a very complete and somewhat interesting cruise journal and navigation notes which included every conceivable kind of sight as well as a compass deviation table and dygogram. Then, too, my marks on the final examination were high, so that I materially improved my class standing, going up from twelfth place to sixth. This was very gratifying to me, as I thought that no doubt could exist as to my assignment to the Marine Corps, for which I had applied, naming the line of the Navy as my second choice.

I often have been asked for my reasons for applying for the Marine Corps, and this seems as good a place as any in which to record them. I arrived at my choice chiefly by a process of elimination. First of all, I promptly eliminated the Engineer Corps, because I had no bent for mechanical engineering. The choice between the line of the Navy and the Marine Corps was much more difficult to arrive at, and I gave much thought to the subject and weighed the pros and cons with great care. For instance, I liked going to sea occasionally, but not for the greater part of my life; I preferred the military to the naval side of my profession; I foresaw that the sail was doomed as a means of propulsion and the old-fashioned sailor would soon become extinct, replaced more and more by machinery. I realized that whatever ability I had lay in the direction of handling and controlling men, rather than in the direction of handling and controlling machinery. From my own standpoint, therefore, the Marine Corps seemed to possess more advantages and less disadvantages than did the other branches of the naval service, and I made my decision accordingly.[11]

Lejeune's experience as a midshipman at the Naval Academy, and his ability to stick out the austere, spartan life, is in itself a mark of his character; of the 90 plebes in Lejeune's freshman class, only 35 graduated with him in the class of 1888, with 5 resigning at graduation to enter civilian life.

While about to graduate from the Naval Academy, midshipman Lejeune had to fight to become a Marine. He wrote in his memoir:

> I returned to Annapolis after a two-day stay in Bel Air and found my classmate, George Hayward, at Mrs. Aspold's [a boarding house where he was staying]. After greeting me, he drew a long face and said in a very serious manner, "Gabe, I have bad news for you. The Academic Board has recommended your assignment to the Engineer Corps (Navy)." He could give me no information beyond the bald statement which I have just quoted.
>
> I was bitterly disappointed and intensely indignant, my indignation being stronger even than my disappointment, because I felt very keenly the sting of injustice. I had worked hard for six years and had succeeded in the belief that I was justly entitled to be assigned to the corps or branch which I had requested. My indignation was further stimulated by the fact that while my wishes had been completely ignored, the wishes of my juniors in class standing had, in nearly all instances, been granted.
>
> I, therefore, immediately came to the determination to do everything honorable in my power to overturn the decision of the Academic Board in my case. Hayward and I spent the evening discussing the subject and mapping out a campaign plan. I decided that, first of all, I would endeavor to induce the members of the Academic Board to change their decision, and early the next morning I called on my good friends, Lieutenant and Mrs. E.K. Moore, to obtain the benefit of their advice. They advised me to see Commander Asa Walker and Chief Engineer Milligan, two members of the Board, which I promptly did, and learned that Hayward's information was correct. I exhausted every argument I could think of in the endeavor to secure their support of a proposal to have the Board reconsider its action at a meeting to be held that day. I also told them that if the assignment were not changed, the action of the Board would be tantamount to forcing me out of

the Service, as I would resign as soon as I could find other employment in civil life.

They were non-committal and held out no hope of favorable action, but each advised me to see Professor Hendrickson, the head of the Department of Mathematics. Professor Hendrickson was a "fixture" at the Naval Academy, a man of great ability and force of character, and an exceedingly influential member of the Board. My interview with him was fruitless. He explained that Commodore Melville, the Engineer-in-Chief of the Navy, had insisted that all of the four Naval Cadets to be appointed to his Corps should not be chosen from the lower part of the class and, as there were twenty-four vacancies in the three branches to be filled, the Board had divided the upper twenty-four members of the class into four blocks, and had selected one from each block for the Engineer Corps. I had been selected from the upper block six. Evidently he was the author of the plan and was committed against making any changes in the assignments.

As a last resort, I called on the Superintendent, Captain W.T. Sampson. He listened to my plea attentively and then said calmly and dispassionately that the Board had made the appointment for the following reasons: first, they deemed it important to assign graduates of ability to the Engineer Corps; second, I was the only member of the upper block who had not applied for the Line as first choice; and third, because the Board considered that I stood too high in the class to be assigned to the Marine Corps. He further intimated that there was no probability that the Board would make any change in its action. I left his office depressed but more determined than ever to continue the fight until it was won.

I returned to my boarding house to get my baggage, intending to go at once to Washington, and there found a letter from Senator Randall Gibson of Louisiana, congratulating me on completing the six years' course so satisfactorily, stating that he wanted me to consider his home in Washington as a part of Louisiana, and insisting on my calling on him when I passed through Washington.

I immediately took the train for Washington, but upon arrival I went at once to the Navy Department to appeal to Commodore Ramsey, the Chief of the Bureau of Navigation (which then had the responsibility for personnel assignments as well as jurisdiction over the Naval Academy). I felt it to be incumbent upon me to conform to the Navy's code scrupulously by appealing to the next higher authority. My interview with him was of about the same tenor as that with the Superintendent. He expressed his personal sympathy for me, but stated that he could do nothing to assist me as the decision of the Academic Board was final and could not be altered even by the Secretary of the Navy. He added the advice not to attempt in any way to influence the Secretary on my behalf, as my efforts would prove unavailing and the only result would be to worry the Secretary.

I then called on Senator Chandler [William E. Chandler, Secretary of the Navy from 1882 to 1885 and Senator from New Hampshire from 1887 to 1889] and found my classmate, Stickney [Herman Osman Stickney, who rose to the rank of rear admiral], there. He had been found physically unfit for a commission by reason of defective eyesight, which he said had been brought on by hard study and was temporary in its nature. He desired assignment to the Engineer Corps, and in the conference between Senator "Sec" Chandler, Stickney, and myself, it was decided that Stickney would apply for appointment to fill the vacancy in the Engineer Corps for which I had cooperated with Senator Gibson, if necessary, in securing my assignment to the Marine Corps. Senator Chandler told me that he had already spoken to Senator Gibson concerning me, and advised me to call on him at once. This I did, and found him alone in his library. I spent the evening in conversation with him and found him to be a most delightful gentleman, and the most cultivated, intellectual, and interesting man I had hitherto known.

He listened patiently to the recital of my story and was indignant because of the arbitrary and unjust treatment of which he considered I had been the victim. He called up the Secretary of the Navy, Mr. Tracy [Benjamin F. Tracy], on the telephone and made an appointment to see him at the Navy Department at ten o'clock the next morning. He told me he felt certain that the Secretary, after hearing my case, would right the wrong which was in process of being done me. He then talked on many topics, among them his experiences in the Civil War and in politics, and his impressions of many noted men at home and abroad with whom he had been associated. I was fascinated and entranced and listened attentively until the clock struck eleven, when I reluctantly said goodnight and went to the rooms where several of my classmates had taken up their quarters, and where a bed was in readiness for me.

The next day, Lejeune took the issue to his U.S. Senator:

> I was at Senator Gibson's residence bright and early the next morning and accompanied him to the Navy Department. As soon as we entered the ante-room we were shown into the Secretary's office. The Senator introduced me to Secretary Tracy as a survivor of the Samoan hurricane and as a representative of his French-speaking Louisiana constituents. He then very briefly, but very forcibly, stated my case, and Mr. Tracy said: "The young man can have anything within my power to give him," and asked me what assignment I desired. I told him I wanted the Marine Corps. He rang for Commodore Ramsey, and when the latter came in, he said, "Commodore, I want this young man assigned to the Marine Corps." The Commodore made a note of the Secretary's directions and the interview was ended. I was very grateful and very jubilant.[12]

Lejeune was later selected to command the U.S. Army's $2^d$ Division as a major general during World War I, and he served as Commandant of the Marine Corps from July 1, 1920, to March 4, 1929. The growth, development, and professionalism of the Corps would have been quite different without this Commandant's vision, character, and leadership. The Marine Corps was an indisputable beneficiary of this giant of the Corps (Camp Lejeune, North Carolina, was named after him in recognition of his unique contributions). His determination to be a Marine was intrinsic to the character that made this leader notable throughout his professional career.

### Alexander A. Vandegrift

In his autobiography *Once a Marine*, Vandegrift reflected upon entering the Marine Corps:

Dr. Randolph (a prominent local physician) secured me an appointment to West Point, and with very hard studying I passed the mental examination. But up at Fort McHenry in Baltimore I failed the physical. The Army informed my father that I could still go to summer camp at West Point and if I then passed another physical, enter the fall class. But my mother, who didn't want me to go to West Point—or any other military school—persuaded him to send me to the University of Virginia. I did not know about this parental skullduggery until years later. At the time, I saw my mission as surviving the English, mathematics, German, and geology curriculum until I was twenty-one and could take the examination for an Army commission.

I spent two years at the University of Virginia before Cousin Charles [Charles C. Wertenbaker] took me to see our family friend, Senator [Thomas S.] Martin. The senator was sorry, but no Army examination was scheduled—on the other hand, the Secretary of the Navy had just asked him to nominate two persons to take the Marine Corps examination. Having never heard of the Marine Corps, I asked him what it was. The old gentleman leaned back in his swivel chair and said, "Son, if you go into the Marine Corps you will spend a large portion of your life fighting small wars in the southern American hemisphere." How right he was.

To prepare for the examination "prescribed by the President of the United States" and rumored to be difficult—only 57 out of 500 would be selected, a number that later earned for this particular class the nickname "the 57 Varieties"—I entered Swaveley, a Washington cram school designed to help such ignoramuses as myself. It was a fortunate move because there I learned to answer such questions as, "If you started at Chicago and traveled to Manila via the Suez Canal, name all the waters, all the countries, all the capes, and all the bays that you would pass on your course." In November came the examination at the Washington Marine Barracks. To be more precise, the Marine Barracks Band Hall, an old drafty building complete with musicians practicing in the balcony. To the accompaniment of horns, sousaphones, tubas, and fifes, we hopefuls began a spelling test which for some reason centered on medical terms such as *psoriasis, physiognomy, tonsillectomy,* and other horrors.

In three of the most ghastly days of my life, algebra followed spelling, then plane and solid geometry, trigonometry, English grammar, history, and geography. By the end of the week, the drums had taken over to help us through the geography exam. The final question was: "If you started at Chicago and traveled to Manila via the Suez Canal, name all the waters, all the countries, all the capes and all the bays that you would pass on your course."

I returned to Charlottesville to "sweat out" the examination results. Despite the vigorous schedule in Washington, I had seen enough guard mounts and parades at the Marine Barracks to know that I would never be satisfied with any other career. People in later years have asked what I regarded as the highlight of my life. Certainly one highlight occurred on December 20, 1908, when I learned that I had passed and would be commissioned in the Marine Corps. No matter that I wasn't too high in the class. I wasn't at the bottom and the important fact was to have passed.

On January 21, 1909, our prosecuting attorney, Mr. Gilmer, swore me in. The day after the ceremony I received a letter from the Secretary of War inviting me to take an examination for an Army commission—I replied to this rather smugly.

My new uniform was a beauty. At that time Marine officers—certainly second lieutenants—wore a dark-blue tunic frogged across the front, light-blue trousers with a bright red stripe down each leg, shiny black shoes, and a dark-blue hat with a little gold cord across the visor. Anxious to impress Grandfather Carson [Robert Carson Vandegrift, his paternal grandfather] I topped this with a long blue boat cloak, one side of which I casually threw over my shoulder to expose the red lining.[13]

Vandegrift was commissioned a second lieutenant in the Marine Corps in January 1909. In World War II, he was Commander of the Marine Division that conquered Guadalcanal, and he won the Medal of Honor for his heroic combat leadership. He went on to serve as Commandant of the Marine Corps from January 1, 1944, to December 31, 1947.

**Clifton B. Cates**

Cates attended high school at the Missouri Military Academy, where he was a four-letter man in sports—a path he would follow while studying law at the University of Tennessee, where he lettered in baseball and football. He played on the football team that achieved Tennessee's first winning season and its first win against Vanderbilt University, then considered a college powerhouse.

Cates' oral history interviewer, Benis M. Frank, asked him why he had entered the Marine Corps.

*General Cates*: I was getting ready to take the state bar examination and I happened to run into the son of the president of the University. And I asked him, "Has your dad had any calls for people going into the Service?" And he said, "Not that I know of." I said, "Well, if he does, put my name down."

About two weeks later I saw him and he said, "Dad has a letter from the Marine Corps wanting eight second lieutenant reservists. Do you want to apply?" And I said, "What in the hell is that outfit?" I really didn't know. I said, "Yes, put my name down." And that's the way it started.

*Frank*: That's where it started? That's very unusual—well, not so unusual because there were a number of people at that same time that came into the Marine Corps that had never heard about the Marine Corps.

*General Cates*: Oh, yes.

*Frank*: Where did you go immediately after you were commissioned? This was in 1917?

*General Cates*: Yes, it was in May 1917, and there's another kind of humorous story that I might tell. We were ordered to appear at the Marine Barracks in Washington for a physical examination on the 21st day of May. There were about, I'd say two hundred other college kids there, and we reported at nine o'clock. They said, come back this afternoon at one o'clock; come back tomorrow morning at nine o'clock; come back that afternoon at one o'clock. So that kept up for three days and we were all running out of money. In fact, we *had* run out and appointed a committee of three to go in to see the Commanding Officer. At that time, he was

Major Dick Williams and he was known as "Terrible Terry." So we went in and as the spokesman, I explained to him, "Major, we've been here three days now and we're all running out of money and if we can't get examined, we're going back home tonight." And he pounded the desk and said, "What the hell is this? Insubordination before you get into the Marine Corps? Get out of here!" So we got out, but as I went out, I said, "If we're not examined this afternoon, we're going back." So we were examined that afternoon.

*Frank*: What did he say after the examination, if you saw him?

*General Cates*: I don't think I saw him for a number of years, though later he got to be a very close friend of ours.

*Frank*:   After you were examined, I assume that you passed your examination.

*General Cates*: Oh, yes, and that was on May 24 as I remember. Then we returned back home and soon after, I was ordered to report for duty at Parris Island, South Carolina. I reported on 13 June 1917.

While at Parris Island, we took, of course, close order drill, bayonet training and rifle range marksmanship but, outside of the rifle range part, there wasn't any useful training. No extended order or anything else. And then, about the first of July, two weeks later, they gave us leave for five days and were then ordered to report in to Quantico, Virginia.

We reported to the Officers School at Quantico. That lasted approximately two months and on the 28th day of August, 1917, I was ordered to report to the 96th Company, Second Battalion, Sixth Marines. The company was organized that day.

*Frank*: At Quantico?

*General Cates*: Yes.

*Frank*: Had you gotten your uniforms while you were down at Parris Island?

*General Cates*: No, we hadn't. We ordered the uniforms after we passed our physical. We had a few of them but not many.

*Frank*: Had you been sworn in right after you passed your physical?

*General Cates*: Yes.

*Frank*: In other words, they knew immediately after they gave you the physical whether or not you had passed.

*General Cates*: Oh, yes.

*Frank*: Quantico was not much and was pretty rugged at that time, and I guess it was undergoing wartime expansion. Is that correct?

*General Cates*: Oh, yes, there was very little there. They were building the wooden barracks. Of course, there was lots of mud. We trained there for approximately four months, and General Thomas Holcomb, who was then a Major, was our Battalion Commander at that time. Then on—I think it was the 18th day of January—we departed for Philadelphia—the Second Battalion—and boarded the USS *Henderson* and sailed the next morning.

*Frank*: When you went through this officers' school up at Quantico before joining the 96th Marines, what did they teach you? What was part of the curriculum?

*General Cates*: I would say that at least half of it wasn't worth a "hoorah." For instance, I spent at least half of my time in trying to learn the semaphore and the Morse code, and what good was that for a second lieutenant? And, of course, we had lots of close order drill. We had some extended order drill and we dug trenches and we threw dummy grenades. Some of the training was good but a lot of it wasn't worth much.

*Frank*: There was no such thing as a command and staff course. Nothing about staff work?

*General Cates*: No. None at all.

*Frank*: Did you find, as you went on later in the Marine Corps, that this was something the Corps lacked?

*General Cates*: Oh, yes, definitely. I think, in view of the training that a Marine gets these days that, if we had such training during World War I, we wouldn't have lost one-third of our men. There was very little teamwork. You usually just got up, rushed in, fired, and there wasn't any covering fire, any maneuvering. You just got up and went forward.

*Frank*: Well, how about the staff work out in the field? If an officer wanted a report, did he just march back to where the battalion headquarters was?

*General Cates*: We used runners mostly, which was very unreliable. And we had telephones that didn't work. But you relied mostly on runners and semaphore. I must admit that we used quite a bit of semaphore. But the lieutenant didn't do the signaling, we had signalmen.

*Frank*: What was the voyage overseas like? What was the transport—the old USS *Henderson*?

*General Cates*: The old *Henderson* was rough as billy-hell. It was an exceedingly rough trip.

*Frank*: How long a trip was it over to France?

*General Cates*: I think it took us ten days.

*Frank*: What did you do aboard ship?

*General Cates*: Oh, stand watches—submarine watches. And they had classes and things to kill time. They even tried to teach us French.

*Frank*: What kind of classes did they have?

*General Cates*: Things like field fortifications, engineering.

*Frank*: When you were down at Quantico, were there any French instructors down there?

*General Cates*: I don't remember any French. We had some Scots.

*Frank*: You did have some Scots?

*General Cates*: Yes. And Canadians, but I don't remember any French.

*Frank*: These were veterans who had fought in France?

*General Cates*: Oh, yes. They had been in action and of course they scared us to death, particularly on the gas question. They said, "If you get one sniff of mustard gas, you'll die."

*Frank*: Was gas the main worry?

*General Cates*: Yes, I believe it was.

*Frank*: Were you gassed?

*General Cates*: Oh, yes. My company was wiped out with gas.

*Frank*: At Bouresches, wasn't it?

*General Cates*: No, it was a week later, near Belleau Wood.[14]

Cates led troops in combat as a platoon leader, a company commander, a battalion commander, a regimental commander, and as a division commander.[15] Appointed Commandant on January 1, 1948, he retired on December 31, 1951.

**Lemuel C. Shepherd, Jr.**

Shepherd did his undergraduate study at Virginia Military Institute (VMI). His oral history interviewer, Brigadier General Edwin H. Simmons, USMC (Ret.), asked Shepherd: "What influenced you to become a Marine officer upon graduation?" Shepherd replied: "During my Rat [freshman] year, I wasn't particularly interested in following a military life, but I got along all right. It was in my last year that I was at VMI, what they call the first class year, when I was rooming with three Norfolk boys. One was the first captain, the highest cadet office in the Corps. He was also president of the class and captain of the football team. His name was Oliver B. Booker. He had come to VMI with the definite purpose in mind of getting a commission in the Army. In those days, only one regular commission to the Army was given the whole graduating class, just one commission. This was long before the Reserves or anything like that. Several cadets were bucking for it, but my roommate Booker was the outstanding candidate. He was three years older than the rest of us so he had the edge on us because of his maturity. Another of my roommates was cadet Fielding Robinson, who subsequently became a Marine. The third one was Edward Cole, who was interested in going to the Army. I was the fourth one in this room of three cadet officers and I was just a private first class, because I'd gotten busted in my sophomore year for a firecracker episode on New Year's Eve and happened to be one of the few unfortunate ones that got caught.

"I really didn't care as I wasn't bucking for a commission. But, at the end of my second class year, at the commencement exercise, General George Barnett [Commandant, 1914–1920] came to VMI to make an address. He wore his blue uniform and he had a very snappy aide with him. The cadets had never seen Marines before in full dress uniform. George Barnett was a very distinguished officer, and when he made that address and reviewed the Cadet Corps, he impressed a lot of cadets.

"Well, the following year—I think it was about February of 1917—it became obvious that the United States was going to get into the war with Germany and the majority of my classmates began to think about getting a commission in the Army. By that time the Army had given ten appointments to VMI instead of the one and the Marine Corps had also given ten appointments, for members of the graduating class."

This was not the first time a VMI graduate had gone into the Marine Corps. According to Shepherd, "There had been one or two in 1916. I think there were several that came in that year during the build-up for the war. Prior to that, the only VMI graduate in the Marine Corps was General William P. Upshur, who was in the class of 1909. Perhaps there were several others whom I do not recall.

"But because General Barnett apparently had been very much impressed with VMI when he came to Lexington in June of 1916, the following fall, when the Marine Corps was given an increase in personnel, he assigned ten appointments to VMI. This was in November of 1916, before the United States declared war on Germany.

"Frankly speaking, there weren't many cadets who were interested in a regular commission in the Armed Services at that time, as most VMI students were taking engineering courses in preparation for a career in this field. About February 1917, though, when it appeared that the United States might become involved in World War I, a number of the graduating class requested commissions in the Army and Marine Corps. It was about this time that I became interested in applying for a commission in the Army. So during the latter part of March I went to see the Commandant, Colonel Hodges, and told him, 'I would like to apply for one of the Army commissions.' He said, 'I'm terribly sorry, Mr. Shepherd, I'd like very much to recommend you for a commission in the Army but, I just gave away the last one of the ten appointments to the Army a couple of days ago. We just don't have any more.' I said, 'What about the Marine Corps?' He replied, 'The ten Marine commissions we had were given out last November but all the Services are increasing their numbers and you might be able to get a commission in the Marine Corps.'

"My roommates and I talked it over, but I did nothing about it at the time. Coming from Norfolk, I knew that the Marines were part of the Navy and I liked the thought of serving aboard ship. When war was declared on the 7th of April, I said to my roommates, 'You know, we're going to war, we've got to do something about it,' so I typed up a letter requesting an appointment to the Marine Corps and went over to the Superintendent at one o'clock in the afternoon, to deliver it in person to General [Edward W.] Nichols. That was the only time a cadet could see the superintendent. I told General Nichols, 'I would like to apply for a commission in the Marine Corps, since there's no possibility of getting one in the Army because all the commissions have been given out. Although the ones the Marine Corps has offered also have to be filled, I know a couple of the cadets who have applied for them and I don't think they'll get through physically.' I happened to know that two of my classmates who applied for Marine commissions had certain physical defects so I said, 'I just don't think a couple of these cadets will pass the physical examination. Could I apply as an alternate?' General Nichols said, 'Yes, yes, I'd be very glad to recommend you to General Barnett as an alternate for one of the Marine Corps commissions.'

"Well, I went back to barracks and told my roommates what I'd done. Word got around and the next afternoon about ten of my classmates applied for Marine commissions. So General Nichols sent a telegram to the Commandant of the Marine Corps recommending us for commissions in the Marine Corps. This was, we'll say, about the 8$^{th}$ or the 9$^{th}$ of April. Shortly thereafter, we got an indication that we might receive an appointment. So we started scurrying around trying to get the birth certificates and letters of recommendation that you had to have. I think it was a birth certificate and two letters of recommendation. Mine arrived the day before we received orders to report immediately to the Commandant of the Marine Corps for examination.

"There were about a dozen of us. I didn't have any money, so I had to borrow the money to buy a ticket to go to Washington. We went down to Lynchburg where we learned that there was only one train leaving Lynchburg around midnight which arrived in Washington the next morning. Well, the train was crowded and we had to stand up all the way from Lynchburg to Washington, which was a pretty good piece. I was a young fellow then and could take it, but it was tiring standing up on this train for six hours. There were six or eight of us I think in the group. We arrived in Washington the next morning and went down on Pennsylvania Avenue to a hotel, rented a room, washed up and shaved and reported at nine o'clock to the Marine Barracks for examination. We reported to Colonel [Charles A.] Doyen, who was the commanding officer of the barracks at the time and was the president of the examining board. When we went before the board, we were told to report to the sick bay for a physical examination. We had a bull surgeon there by the name of [Lieutenant Commander Paul T.] Dessez, and they called him 'Bobo.' He was a distant cousin of General Dessez [Brigadier General Lester Dessez]. He was quite a big fellow.

"We went before the medical examining board, of which this old bull surgeon, Captain Dessen, was the senior member. He was a rough, gruff, old, and seagoing bull. After he looked us over he took our blood pressure and then said to me, 'Get down over there and stick up your ass. Have you ever had any piles?' I said, 'No, sir.' 'Turn around. Have you ever had a dose of clap?' 'No, sir.' 'You pass.'

"It was a pretty perfunctory examination. I was underweight because I think the minimum requirement was 135 for my height and I only weighed 123 pounds. I was on the track team and I was pretty thin in those days. After we finished our physical examination about noon, we reported before the examining board and Colonel Doyen said, 'Well, you young gentlemen have all passed your physical examinations. Your academic qualifications, of course, depend upon your graduation from VMI, which I assume you will do since you are in your last month of school. With those two qualifications, you're eligible for a commission in the Marine Corps. Now, the appointments which you will receive will be for regular commissions, probationary regular officer. But it will take some several months before your commissions as probationary regular officers are confirmed by the Senate. If you would like to be sworn in to the Reserves, then you'll be commissioned right away. I have orders to swear you in as officers in the Reserves if you so desire.' So we all said, 'Yes, sir, we want to be Reserve officers.' 'Hold up your hands.' When we did so we were all sworn in as second lieutenants in the Marine Corps Reserve on the 11$^{th}$ of April, 1917, just four days after war was declared.

"Well, that was moving fast. When we returned to VMI, we were all second lieutenants. It was an interesting experience to be a commissioned officer in the Marine Corps Reserve and still a cadet at VMI.

"Well, this was in the middle of April. About a week or ten days later, the superintendent of VMI, General Nichols, received a telegram from the Marine Corps stating, 'We'd like our second lieutenants to report to duty as soon as possible. If you can possibly graduate them ahead of time, rather than waiting till June 27$^{th}$, we'd like very much to have them report at once. We need their services.'

"So it was arranged to have the graduation ceremony on the 3$^d$ of May, 1917, for the ten officers of the Marine Corps. The Superintendent then decided to graduate the cadets who had received Army Reserve commissions, say, another ten in addition to the ten or twelve going into the Marine Corps. We were declared to have passed our studies and given full credit for our diplomas. On the 3$^d$ of May, 1917, we were graduated from VMI. The reason that date sticks in my mind is because it has had great significance to me. It was on the 3$^d$ of May, 1863, that Stonewall Jackson made his flank march at the Battle of Chancellorsville and attacked the Union Army, causing their withdrawal. The Battle of Chancellorsville was a great victory for the Confederacy. Just before the attack, when several

VMI men on his staff were standing with him, Stonewall Jackson remarked, 'I see that a number of my commanders are VMI men. VMI will be heard from today.' Stonewall Jackson had taught at VMI before the Civil War began. He was a local hero. His statue was on the parade ground, and he is buried in Lexington. From my cadet days, Stonewall Jackson was my great hero.

"It was on the 3$^d$ of May, 1863, when he said, 'VMI will be heard from today.' I've always felt VMI would be heard from from those of us who graduated on the 3$^d$ of May 1917, and went into the Services. After graduation exercises, I went home for several days, but didn't get any orders.

"After about a week, my classmate Fielding Robinson, who also lived in Norfolk and had been commissioned at the same time, and another classmate and close friend by the name of Charlie Nash, who lived in West Virginia, came home with me. We expected to leave immediately for Parris Island and decided to go to Washington to find out what was going on. So we got on the Washington boat, went up to Headquarters, Marine Corps, and called on Colonel Thomas Holcomb [Commandant, 1936–1943], the detail officer. When we told Colonel Holcomb the purpose of our visit he said, 'Well, I'm surprised that you haven't gotten orders. I can't understand why.' He called in the sergeant major, 'Write these young gentlemen orders immediately. Should have been done.' Apparently he didn't realize that we'd been graduated from VMI.

"So we walked out of Colonel Holcomb's office with orders in our hands to report to Parris Island, which we did on May 18$^{th}$ and were assigned to the Officer's School of Application [now the Basic School]. We reported to, I think it was Major Messersmith, the Commanding Officer of the School of Application. Well, first thing, before we got into the scholastic end of our Marine Corps education was to shoot on a rifle range. We had arrived on Saturday afternoon, I think it was, and on Monday morning we began our rifle range instruction. I think the course was two weeks. There was one weekend at Parris Island when I went over to Beaufort. The following weekend was May the 30$^{th}$, a holiday weekend. Several days before our group completed range instruction, Messersmith called all the young officers into his office. There were some thirty of us who had reported all together and he said, 'We've just gotten a request from the Commandant for volunteers for the Fifth Marines.' Well, I didn't know anything about the Fifth Marines, but I said, 'I'll volunteer.'

"Let's go back a moment. The Saturday afternoon we arrived at Parris Island on a tug which brought us over from Port Royal to the island, I met a number of my schoolmates on their way to Charleston to go to Santo

Domingo. We were all very envious. They were not classmates of mine at VMI, but friends who'd graduated from VMI the previous year and had been commissioned just prior to our group. It just happened that they were on their way to the tropics—Santo Domingo, Haiti, Nicaragua—they told us that was a good deal, 'Try to get there if you can.' We were very envious of our friends who were off for Santo Domingo.

"So when Messersmith called for volunteers, we thought, 'Well, maybe we can get out of here.' Parris Island was a deadly place—'Let's get out of here and go down to Santo Domingo along with our buddies.' Robinson, Nash, and I volunteered for duty with the Fifth Marines in Philadelphia. None of us knew where we were going, but we were glad to receive our orders and be on our way to join a regiment. My good friend Charlie Nash came home with me and we stopped in Norfolk en route to Philadelphia, and went to see our respective girls who lived there.

"I reported in at Philadelphia on the 5th of June. I remember being in Norfolk on the 30th of May, it sticks in my mind. We had a weekend in Norfolk on reporting to Headquarters at the Fifth Marines, we reported to the regiment and were assigned to the 2d Battalion commanded by Major Frederick M. Wise. Everything was in confusion. We lived in tents. Recruits and old-timers were coming in. They said, 'We're going on an expedition.' We didn't know where the hell we were going. We had no officers' uniforms and wore enlisted men's trousers. Our uniforms were supposed to have been delivered upon graduation, but since we had been graduated ahead of the scheduled time our tailor had not completed them. We just had to take what was issued to the men and put an officers' hat cord on our campaign hats. Second lieutenants wore no rank insignia in those days. Before we sailed, I was able to get my uniforms. The first night I stayed up all night long issuing uniforms to men joining the company. I was assigned to the 55th Company."[16]

Within 2 months after commissioning as a second lieutenant in the U.S. Marine Corps, in April 1918, Shepherd shipped to France and saw considerable action, being wounded twice at Belleau Wood. In March 1942, he assumed command of the 9th Marines, which became part of the 3d Division. As a brigadier general, he was assistant commander of the 1st Marine Division in the Cape Gloucester campaign in the Pacific, followed by the campaigns at Guadalcanal, Guam, and Okinawa. He later had a role in the planning of the Inchon landing in Korea in 1950. He served as Commandant of the Marine Corps from January 1, 1952, to December 31, 1955.

## David M. Shoup

When Shoup was asked how he first got started in the Marine Corps, he responded, "I was a student at DePaul University, where military training and ROTC [Reserve Officers Training Corps] was a requirement for two years. Then you could ask to take two more years, and during the third and fourth years of ROTC, you got paid 30 cents a day. The reason I took the third and fourth years of ROTC was simply an economic matter. The 30 cents a day, 9 dollars a month, paid my room rent. Otherwise, I would have never done it. Then, of course, you're subject to the Army's hocus-pocus of going to camps and all of that kind of stuff. After graduation, I was to go down to Camp Knox on active duty for two weeks. At the end of two weeks they kept continuing it two more weeks if I wanted to go, which I did. In the interim, just before college graduation, a representative from our class went to the national Scabbard and Blade, which was an honorary military fraternity, meeting in New Orleans. The principle speaker there was John A. Lejeune, Major General and Commandant of the Marine Corps. He gave the principle address and he said, 'If any of you young gentlemen have friends in your classes who are honor students that want to get in the Marine Corps, tell them to write me a personal letter.' Well, I took him at his word and went back to my room and I sat down and grabbed a piece of paper and wrote a personal letter to General Lejeune, head of the Marine Corps, and told him I'd like to get in the Marine Corps.

"While I was at Camp Knox, I got a telegram—which I still have. It directed me to go to Chicago at my expense and to take my diploma, my degree, and my birth certificate, to be considered for a commission in the Marine Corps. I went to my Army major and he said, 'Well, you're not supposed to get any time off when you're on these two-week duties, but I kind of envy you and if you leave a request for three days leave here and come back as you plan, I'll just tear it up.' I went to Chicago and met my father in Crawfordsville and got my degree and birth certificate and returned to Camp Knox, now Fort Knox. I finished that stint and another two weeks Active duty. In the meantime, I finally got some little word from Marine Corps headquarters, signed by General Lejeune, wanting me to fill out this or fill out that, which I did. It was always, will you please do this and will you please do that, and I did it. One day I got a letter which said that I had to swear an oath, so I told my mother. We went to the little hometown bank and I notarized the oath and I didn't pay much attention to what it was.

"Then some time later, I got this letter that said, 'You will report to Philadelphia Navy Yard.' I told my mother, 'This doesn't ask whether I want to or not, it says you will. Maybe I'd better see what this is all about.' I was given enough time to drive from Indiana to Philadelphia in a T-model Ford and I reported to Philadelphia. In the meantime, I had a commission in the Army Reserve and I also had a commission in the Marine Corps and I didn't know it. I didn't know they had overlapped. The day before I went to Chicago I was supposed to take an examination in calculus for a regular commission in the Army, but I went to Chicago instead and didn't take the exam and was commissioned in the Marine Corps. Then, of course, I wrote to the Army and resigned my commission in the Army Reserve.

"Up until I got to Philadelphia, I had been commissioned in the Army since May and here we were in September sometime, though I never saw a Marine. I never even saw a Marine uniform. It was many months later before I even had a Marine uniform. I went up to camp in New Hampshire to play football and to Parris Island, but I'd never seen a Marine uniform and I didn't have one. So that's how I now have in my possession a letter which acknowledges my resignation and I have an honorable discharge from the Army. A few years later, to my pleasure, I found out that the statue of limitations had run out, but that drawing a salary from two different jobs in the Federal Government at the same time was a criminal offense subject to five years in prison and a $5,000 fine. I read this when I was in Maryland aboard a battleship in 1920. After I read this in the regulations I found out from the lawyer on board that the statute of limitations had run out, so I was not even compelled to send back the duplicate money."[17]

Shoup was commissioned in the United States Marine Corps in July 1926. His attendance at the Basic School was interrupted by being sent to the 6th Marines at Trentsin in 1927, and upon his return he completed the Basic School, followed by assignments to San Diego, Pensacola, and Quantico. He assumed command of the 2d Marines just before the Tarawa operation in November 1943, and he was awarded the Medal of Honor for his extraordinary courage in that action. He then saw action in the Saipan and Tinian invasions.

President Dwight D. Eisenhower, on January 1, 1961, appointed Shoup Commandant of the Marine Corps, ahead of five more senior Marine generals. He retired in that position on December 31, 1963.

### Robert E. Cushman, Jr.

Cushman won an appointment to the Naval Academy in 1931 while still one semester shy of graduating from high school. He was only 16 years old and had to compete with classmates with prior college or military experience, some of whom were already as old as he would be upon graduation in 1935. He did exceptionally well at this level of competition, graduating tenth in a class of 442. As was so often the case, one of the most attractive aspects to Cushman was that the Marine Corps offered a regular commission, while the Navy only offered a Reserve commission.

Cushman was asked by his oral history interviewer, Benis M. Frank: "Why did you opt for the Marine Corps?"

"For rational reasons," he responded, "and well thought out. I would be much happier in my work as a Marine, even though it was difficult to find out what they did. I had read enough about it, and there were subjects pertaining to land warfare in the *Landing Force Manual*. I read all those assiduously. I felt I'd be happier and able to do better in the technical things that you had to do to be a Marine officer than those you did to be a naval officer. And as it turned out, I think I was right. The other reason, that I don't often tell, but sort of nailed it down, was that I overstayed my leave out in town one night, and came in—I should have been in at eight or something like that—at ten. The only way that I could get back in was to climb over the wall, which was surmounted with barbed wire. I threw over my uniform and started up the wall and as I got to the top—this is right behind the chapel—one of the Marines who walks around the chapel endlessly protecting John Paul Jones' bones took his rifle butt and held the wire apart so I could get through. I decided, 'That's my kind of outfit.' Any guy who will do that for me, he's alright. So, that just put the final nail in it."

Dr. Frank then asked: "You never had a Marine officer as a role model?"

"No," Cushman responded, "they were pretty scarce. We had a couple on duty as ordnance instructors, and then I went on a cruise—on a battleship—and there was a Marine officer aboard there. But they were all busy and harassed and didn't, I guess, see themselves as being in the recruiting business. The Marine Corps was very small and didn't look like it was going to get big. There just wasn't much exposure. In my first class [senior] year, they brought in a colonel who, I think, was I and I [Inspector-Instructor duty] from Baltimore or somewhere—because I don't think there was any billet for a colonel with the Marine detachment on the post—so he gave a talk and answered questions and that was about it. That was my total exposure. And I think he was kind of under wraps—the Navy in no way gave a damn about the Marine Corps in those days. It's much different now, there's been negotiated a proper percentage of all rankings in the class in making the determination as to which graduates could enter the Marine Corps. It's done fairly now. In those days, it was just the first 25 and that's it. Class standing enabled you to get a spot. That was the first 25 volunteers, and I was the first of these as I had the highest class standing. I went into the Marine Corps for those reasons and have been very happy ever since."

Frank inquired: "Did, as happened in other cases, the instructors or the tactical officers give you a hard time for choosing the Marine Corps?"

Cushman replied: "Yes. A number of them did, several, you know, in front of the class, gave me hell for picking the Marine Corps. I usually answered them respectfully but tartly. It didn't shake my convictions whatsoever.

"The Navy was, of course, somewhat different before World War II, and I just couldn't get up any great enthusiasm for being a member of the officer corps of the U.S. Navy. They had some good naval officers, no question about it, but their attitudes were really out of another century."

Cushman was in the class of 1935 at the Basic Course. "It was the first time," he reflected, "that anyone other than a handful of Naval Academy graduates plus a little handful of enlisted men had gone to Basic School during the Depression. We really had some fine officers because they only took in honor graduates and the ROTC cadet commanders and people like that—the athletes and class leaders into the Marine Corps. A lot of them also had opportunities to go into the Army, commissioned through ROTC, but they turned those down and came into the Marine Corps. We got so many honor graduates because if they went into the Army, they couldn't be assured of a regular commission and consequently, a full career."

Frank mentioned: "The other thing unusual about the class of '35 was that it was the class which provided two Commandants and more general officers than any other class in Marine Corps history [the other Commandant was Leonard F. Chapman, Jr.].

Cushman responded: "Yes, true. Partly because it was large, of course, but I think primarily because so many able men came in that year. In fact, there were so many able men that there were those who could easily compete and surpass general officers of other years. There just wasn't enough room to promote all those who were qualified to be general officers, in my opinion.

"In the Marine Corps, we had to do a two-year probationary tour, then take an exam at the end of those two years. But I didn't have to do it. They examined us on our record. So, almost everyone, as far as I know, withstood the probationary period, then they took an exam for class standing purposes. I guess we all got regular commissions—there may have been one or two who didn't."[18]

Cushman was commissioned a second lieutenant in the Marine Corps on June 6, 1935. After completing Basic School, he was assigned to the 4th Marines in Shanghai in February 1936. He saw considerable combat in the Pacific in World War II. In June 1944 as a lieutenant colonel, he was in the 1st Marine Division as commander of a battalion in the 11th Marine Regiment for the Peleliu operation in September 1944. Later, he commanded the 4th Battalion in the fight to conquer Okinawa. He was appointed Commandant of the Marine Corps on January 1, 1972, retiring from that position on June 30, 1975.

**Louis H. Wilson**

Commandant Wilson grew up in Brandon, Mississippi. Recalling his early life, he said: "Brandon in the 1920s and 1930s was similar to any small town in the south during the Depression. There probably were not over ten people in my class. When I started school, there were two grades in one room. It was, as I said, a typical small town. My earliest remembrances were probably during the days of the Depression, in 1929, when the banks closed and I had a goat-drawn wagon and sold vegetables to customers in the town, which was not over 300 or 400 people. I had chores to do: milking cows in the mornings and evenings and growing vegetables; things that were typical of a small town in the country for all youngsters in those days."

He went to high school in Brandon. "I think we had probably about 16 to 20 graduates," he remembered, "which was the largest class that Brandon had ever graduated, in 1937." General Wilson then went on to Millsaps College on a scholarship. The student body there was about 800. "It has a good reputation scholastically," General Wilson reflected, "not only in Mississippi, but in the south. It was then a liberal college as it is so considered now by a great many people who are conservative in the south. I doubt that it would be considered liberal from a national point of view, but from the point of Mississippi, it is still considered liberal. It is a Methodist school and still has a Methodist affiliation.

"I majored in economics in college," he said, "and was a member of the Pi Kappa Alpha fraternity. My grades were average. I certainly did not excel and did not apply myself really well. I suppose I was about in the middle of my class."

Brigadier General Edwin H. Simmons, USMC (Ret.), General Wilson's oral history interviewer, asked: "When did you first hear about, or learn about, the Marine Corps?"

"It must have been January of 1941 when a second lieutenant named Nathan Peters, who had graduated from Ole Miss a year before, in 1940, and was an honor ROTC graduate who was commissioned in the Marine Corps. He was assigned to recruiting duty in the colleges back in Mississippi. In those days, the Marine Corps took the honor graduates from the

ROTCs throughout the United States, and Peters was one of those in the class of 1940; in fact, he has returned and lives in Jackson now."

Simmons asked: "Did you know any World War I Marine Corps veterans?" General Wilson said: "No. I knew no Marines at all. In fact, I told Jane [at the time his fiancé and later his wife] this the day I joined the Marine Corps. It was the 16th of May, as I remember. We had gone over to the grill for a sandwich, and I said, 'I joined the Marine Corps today.' She said, 'What is that?' I said, 'Damned if I know, but I guess I will soon find out.'"

He was enlisted in the Marine Corps Reserve in May 1941, arrived at the Officer Candidates Class in Quantico on June 24, 1941, and was commissioned in November 1941.

"I rode overnight by train from Jackson," Wilson reflected. "I was assigned a berth according to my ticket, and there I met an increasing number of young men who got on the train at various stops, who I suspected might be destined for the same place. I met one of my earliest friends on the train, Royal 'Bubba' North, a graduate from Old Miss. He was already aboard when I got on in Brandon. I had heard of Bubba, who was a famous football player at Ole Miss, and I suspected who he was, but we did not really meet for a few miles. Then a third Mississippian came aboard. It was Hunter Cohern, also a famous football player, from Mississippi State. The three of us met in Meridian and as we proceeded on the Southern Railway and later the RF&P [Richmond, Fredericksburg, and Potomac Railroad], we met additional people who were obviously headed for the same place. We got off the train in early morning in Quantico and went to a barracks, which was the Officer Candidates School headquarters and living quarters."

Simmons inquired: "How long was that Officer Candidates class, and in general terms, what was the curriculum?"

Wilson replied: "Well, this was the third Officer Candidates class. The Marine Corps was just beginning these courses; remember, it was still before the war. We got there on the 25th or 26th of June and it lasted until about the middle of October. After completing the class, we were allowed to come home for ten days and then went back and were commissioned on the 1st of November, 1941.

"We had to clear an area where Russell School is located, called Flag Pole Hill, with machetes. Hardly a training session, but nevertheless, it had to be cleared and without the modern clearing equipment like bulldozers. There was no other way to learn the terrain. The Guadalcanal housing area in Quantico had not been purchased then and only the five thousand acres now comprising Quantico east of the old highway was all of the Quantico

Base that existed at that time. All of our training was done within that part of the reservation.

"Later on, we moved out to other areas such as the Manassas Battlefield. Various farmers would allow the instructors to bring the students on their farms to teach tactics. It was up to each instructor to seek out farmers who would allow them to bring second lieutenants to their farms in order to teach tactics. The instructors would go and get permission from the farmers, then go out, write the problem, and come back and have it printed and approved. Then the second lieutenants would go out to learn tactics."[19]

Wilson accepted a regular commission in the Marine Corps in April 1942. In combat to conquer Guam in July 1944, he was awarded the Medal of Honor for defending his position in a 10-hour battle against a banzai attack on July 25, 1944. He became the 26th Commandant on July 1, 1975, retiring from that position on June 30, 1979.

**Robert H. Barrow**

Like General Wilson, Robert H. Barrow was a southerner, growing up in rural Saint Francisville, Louisiana, where the prewar population was about 800. "Much of the time I recall there was during the Depression," he reflected. "Times were very difficult. . . . I grew up under what could be characterized as austere circumstances. Much of the food that was on the table was home grown. It was a very isolated, insulated kind of life, but a happy one, in that our parents were happy. . . . They were certainly good parents to all of us."

Barrow considered his upbringing a vital part of his character development: "Southerners in general have a very strong sense of place. My place for 41 years was the Marine Corps, and I have a strong sense about that. But then I also had this strong tie and good feel about where I came from. I'm not saying it's related to the fact that my family has been there in a somewhat prominent manner, so much as I grew up there and I liked it. The value of the community and whatnot is a value that I hold dear. I think most southerners have a strong sense of place, and I went back there in large part because of that."

After graduating from high school, he borrowed money and found jobs to work his way through Louisiana State University (LSU). He reflected: "LSU was one of the land-grant colleges that paid a lot of attention to the military aspects of that arrangement, and during the pre–World War II period, ranked along with Texas A&M and Clemson, as I recall. The ROTC there was very much a part of school life, and some of us stayed down in the stadiums which were built to house students. The infantry stayed in what was called the Pentagon, a building shaped like a pentagon. They were three stories and sectionalized three to a room, usually. I stayed in the Pentagon, Company A, infantry. I was the janitor, that is, responsible for removing the trash that came out of 12 rooms, 4 on each floor, and 3 floors.

"So my day consisted of rushing over to set up the eating arrangements and getting rid of that, then rushing back to get rid of the trash and clean up the passageway and staircases in the barracks. I had my classes scheduled so they started, I think, at nine o'clock. I had borrowed $150 and had a job hash-slinging which, with the janitor job, took care of all my expenses in going to school.

"I didn't think a major made a lot of difference, because I wanted to get an ROTC commission and hopefully become a regular Army officer. So I was in arts and science, doing the usual things. I took the placement tests which put me in the upper bracket. I had a good foundation in those schools in Saint Francisville. One of the things about a community like that, if you had to characterize it, was stability in every sense of the word. People didn't come and go. You didn't see many strangers—ever. People weren't uprooted. The teachers were the same—been there for years and years and years. Everyone knew everyone. There was a lot of stability. Good preparation for college. So I studied the arts and sciences curriculum, taking the usual courses for that program.

"I was vice president of the freshman class, having been talked into running for political office, if you can imagine. I was very much caught up in the ROTC, which was compulsory and was the most important thing to me. It was not a question of volunteering; everyone was required to participate for two years since it was a land-grant college. If you wanted, you went on beyond the two years.

"Then along came Pearl Harbor. When I went to LSU in 1939, the war was beginning to rage. That was one thing I kept up with and had an interest in, and all of the preliminary activity in Pearl Harbor. So when Pearl Harbor came, I was 19 years old. I had the strong impression that I needed to be involved. In most of the country, but especially down where I came from, the draft almost need not have been, because so many people rushed to the colors. So a lot of my friends who didn't go to college, and even some in college, enlisted in one Service or another. My oldest brother enlisted in the Navy. My second oldest brother was in South America. So I was very anxious to be a part of it somehow, but I also knew that if I stayed in school, I would have the prospect of getting a commission.

"So that, in combination with the Wake Island business, got me interested in the Marine Corps. There showed up on the LSU campus a Marine named Major Williamson. I think he was called 'Red' Williamson, a tall, fine-looking guy. He was there to recruit PLCs [Platoon Leaders Class; in the PLC program, candidates enlist for the purpose of officer training under the Uniform Code of Military Justice]. As I recollect, the promise was that I could become a commissioned officer in the Marine Corps quicker than I could if I stayed in the ROTC, something about early opportunity. I'm not sure what it was, but anyway, I signed up for the PLC. I don't know what waivers I had to get from the ROTC or anything else, but I enlisted in February 1942.

"I was in the PLC all the rest of that semester. This was one of the most difficult periods of my life, because while I was in something that had more appeal to me, I still wasn't happy, because the war was on and I was beginning to feel like a draft dodger, my friends for the most part, had enlisted. I can't remember any of my friends being drafted, they all enlisted.

"That summer, I worked to help defray the cost of school for my next year. This would be the summer of '42. When school started in the fall, I told people that I had enlisted in the Marine Corps in March of 1942. I left school at the end of the previous semester knowing full well that it was the same thing as enlisting in the Marine Corps, and that's exactly what happened. It was November, however, before they put me on a train to San Diego. So if you go to the roots of my Marine Corps career, I was a failed PLC candidate. I can reconcile that. Young and eager, I wanted to get in the war and didn't want to wait it out in ROTC. The happiest experience of my life was getting on the train to go to San Diego for Marine Corps boot training. If there was ever someone being in a situation that pleased him—I was like a duck to water—it was Bob Barrow going into the Marine Corps.

"I arrived in San Diego. It was about a three- or four-day train trip. I was in a platoon that was made up of about 50 percent from the Los Angeles area, many of whom were 'zoot suiters' [men who wore suits with tapered trousers and knee-length coats].

"The zoot suiters weren't bad. We were shocked at their exaggerated dress, but that, frankly, was about all there was to it. They were a bunch of peacocks with fine feathers and bravado, but they weren't anything like street gangs, not the ones I knew, anyway. The other half of that platoon was made up of Polish boys from Detroit, the Hamtramck area. So I was the only southerner, and I was called 'Louisiana' in my platoon by my fellow platoon members and by the two drill instructors.

"We had M1 rifles. There were a couple of people in my platoon who were retreads from Nicaragua. We used to talk about it. There were a couple of older ones in there also. I liked the military so much, when I was at LSU in the ROTC in my sophomore year, the biggest honor they could pay you was to make you platoon guide. I was the guide for my company and I liked and thrived on it. So when I got to recruit training, I had a little bit of a head start over the others, but I also had a lot of interest and enthusiasm in the things that they did, the drill and whatnot. So during the last couple of weeks of recruit training, the drill instructor used to order me to take the platoon to evening chow. There had to be some skill employed there, because the recruits converged on the mess hall from all directions. So I'd get a certain amount of harassment from the drill instructors, 'What are you doing over there, private? Get 'em out of here!' So I had to be skillful and tactical, too, in taking them to chow. That's how loose things were, and that's the way troop training was."

Barrow stayed on in San Diego as a drill instructor, as they were already using him for that since the noncommissioned officers (NCOs) were being shipped out. He commented on this: "I would expect that they were shipping out NCOs because, one, you didn't see many senior ones running around, and that made sense. I always say that I accepted being a drill instructor because they were hard up for drill instructors, and I was pretty good at drilling. Really, I was quite good at it and liked it. So, yes, I was kept there as a junior drill instructor. I was assigned to a staff sergeant who was an old-timer. He must have had 20 years then, I'm sure. His name was Mann, and he was a good man. I liked him very much. So the two of us were drill instructors for the next platoon that popped up. I only worked a couple of platoons before I left San Diego. So when I say I was a drill instructor, perhaps I am overstating it."

During his boot camp training, he recalled: "I was told, 'Barrow, go up to the depot headquarters for an interview, and to take some tests.' I don't recall who it was who passed the word, but it was not issued as an invitation; it was more or less a directive. It had to do with the application for officer training. I was interviewed by a Colonel Elmer Hall, who was the commanding officer of the recruit training part of that establishment. There was also a field sergeant major, as I recall, who had something to say to me. So I took some tests.

"The next thing I knew, I was told I was going to go to Officer Candidates School. We who had been selected that way—and they must have done it over several weeks and throughout the depot—were all segregated, moved over to some two-man tents that would be along the fence line closest to San Diego International Airport.

"I left San Diego to go to the 25th Officer Candidates Class in March of 1943 at Quantico, Virginia. I graduated from OCS fifth in a class of 236, so I did very well. I finished high enough that it put me in a position to get a regular commission. I was commissioned in the Marine Corps Reserve on 19 May 1943. Then I went into the 28th Reserve Officers Class.

"I would say the reason why was that, I tried as hard as Bob Barrow could, to do what needed to be done, to get a regular commission. I put out a lot of effort. I took to it. I had an early interest at LSU in the Marine Corps. I used to think, before I ever got a chance to go to Officer Candidates Class, 'I want to make this a career somehow.' I didn't even think that through to the fact that I'd be an officer. I just loved it. So when I got to Quantico, I took to everything there. I liked it very much."

He graduated from the 28th ROTC on July 27, 1943, and for his first assignment was sent to Marine Barracks Naval Ammunition Depot, New Orleans: "The people coming out of ROTC who were given regular commissions or who were prospects of getting regular commissions were those who finished up near the top of that class, however one measured it. Apparently, they were being sent, at least during that period of 1943, to the sea school and were seagoing. I reckon that in Washington there were a lot of senior officers, generals, and others, who believed—still believed—despite our great feelings about the Fleet Marine Forces, which were getting organized to fight the war already, that sea duty was for a regular officer. That's why, again if memory serves, we had a fair number of officers who became general officers, who, in World War II, were seagoing. Bob Bohn [Major General Robert D. Bohn] and Roy Geiger [General Roy S. Geiger] fall in that category."[20]

General Barrow saw combat in World War II, Korea, and Vietnam. He was selected as Commandant of the Marine Corps on July 1, 1979, retiring from that position on June 30, 1983.

**Paul X. Kelley**

In an interview with General Paul X. Kelley, I inquired: "What is it that attracted you to want to be a Marine?" He responded: "I graduated from high school in 1946. My father had died in World War II, and, although we lived rather comfortably, there was not enough money for me to go to college. So, having heard of the new GI Bill, I decided to enlist in the Marine Corps and then go to college. At this point I had no specific interest in the Marine Corps as a career.

"It was on the Friday before Labor Day weekend in 1946, which turned out to be important for my future. This was the era prior to computers. That afternoon, I took my oath to our Constitution and was placed in a holding pool for the start of my recruit training at Parris Island in October. I then went on a weekend holiday to Cape Cod. Upon my return, my sister told me that she had been looking for me all weekend to tell me that the Knights of Columbus had determined that I was to be the recipient of a full 4-year scholarship; tuition, books, room and board, at any Catholic college of my choice. So, here was my dilemma. I had already enlisted in the Marine Corps and now have been given the very education which I sought to embark upon after my enlistment. Fortune was on my side, however, since I had enlisted on a Friday, my official record of this enlistment would not be sent by U.S. Mail to Headquarters Marine Corps until Tuesday. It was still at the recruiting station. I was standing at the recruiting station door when it opened on Tuesday morning. I asked the recruiter if I could talk with the Officer-in-Charge, as I had a problem with my enlistment. A few minutes later, he ushered me into a major's office. I explained my problem to him and, without hesitation, he asked a sergeant to get my official record. I shall always remember his words as he tore up the record: 'Young man, my advice to you is to go to college and, when you do, I would appreciate it if you would take a look at the Marine Officer programs that may be available.'"

I commented: "Well, he must have really endeared you to the Marine Corps right then and there." Kelley said: "It certainly endeared me to the Recruiting Officer. He, through that one act of kindness, changed my life."

I asked: "And Villanova University had the Marine Corps program?" He responded: "No, they did not have one at the time of my arrival, but shortly thereafter, a Naval Reserve Officer Training Corps program did start, and that included a Marine Corps option. I received much more than a stipend. The Navy paid for tuition, books, and $50 per month, while the Knights of Columbus paid room and board. Upon graduation from college in June 1950, I was commissioned a second lieutenant in the Marine Corps and ordered to Quantico for the Basic School. My obligation at the time was 15 months. The Basic School back then was usually 9 months, but ours was cut short. If you recall, in June of 1950 the Korean War broke out.

"I did not get to Korea. One-half of our Basic Class went to Korea, and the other half went to the $2^d$ Marine Division at Camp Lejeune. It was in the $2^d$ Marine Division that I became an infantry platoon leader. During my time at Camp Lejeune, the $2^d$ Marine Division had a large number of Reserve officers who had been called up. Many were veterans of World War II. However, the majority of lieutenants were recent Basic School graduates."

I queried: "But as your career developed, why did you decide the Marine Corps was for you? What was there about the Marine Corps that made you want to stay in?" Kelley said: "Because it was and still is a very dedicated professional organization."[21]

Kelley was selected to be Commandant on July 1, 1983, retiring from that position on June 30, 1987.

**Alfred M. Gray, Jr.**

Gray enlisted in the Marine Corps in 1950, and upon completion of boot camp was assigned to the Amphibious Reconnaissance Platoon, Fleet Marine Force, Pacific, rising to the rank of sergeant. He was commissioned after graduating from the Officer Candidate Screening Course in April 1952.

I asked General Gray: "Why did you decide on the Marine Corps?" He told me: "I never really decided to make the Marine Corps a career. I just didn't decide to get out. I enlisted for all the right reasons and I got commissioned in 1952."[22] He became Commandant on July 1, 1987, retiring on June 30, 1991.

**Carl E. Mundy, Jr.**

General Mundy's earliest influence on becoming a Marine was his father: "My father always had great admiration for the Marines. When he was a young man, shortly after having left South Carolina to get a job in the 'big city,' he wound up in Philadelphia in the late 1920s as an assistant manager of a 5-and-10-cent store. After closing late one Saturday night, he was walking back to his rooming house and as he neared a bridge over the Schuylkill River, a couple of shadowy figures stepped in behind him. As he picked up his pace, they did, too. He told me that he always thought that in the morning, he would be found floating face down in the river with his wallet gone. As he approached the bridge, he heard voices, which turned out to be two Marines on their way back to the Philadelphia Navy Yard. He asked if he could walk along with them. They said, 'Sure,' and as he swung in step with them, the two trailing figures turned around and walked back in the direction they had come. My dad told me that story many times. He always believed he owed those two Marines his well-being, if not his life.

"I wanted to be a Marine when I was 6 years old. That was the year the Japanese attacked Pearl Harbor. I recall that Sunday, after church, the phone rang. My dad was a store manager in Cookeville, Tennessee, and the call was from his boss to tell him about the attack. He ended the conversation by saying, 'Mundy, I want you to go down to the store and throw every piece of Japanese junk we have in stock out!' After the phone call, Dad turned on our radio and we listened to the news reports for a few minutes. I had no idea where Pearl Harbor was, who the 'Japs' were, or what 'sinking the fleet' meant, but I knew from my mother and father's reaction that something bad had happened. After a short time, my dad said 'Come on, son,' and we got in the car and drove down to his store. It was closed, of course, but I still remember going into the stock room with him and watching as he threw out boxes of anything that had 'Made in Japan' printed on it.

"My dad was near the draft age limit when the war started, so he was never called. However, as the newsreels or papers brought the stories of the war to us, he would always ensure that he read me the articles or took me to the movies regularly—especially if there was anything playing about Marines or the other armed forces. For example, I saw 'Sergeant York' no fewer than 11 times. Alvin York lived near Cookeville, and I recall meeting him in my father's store one time. He was a short, fat, Tennessee farmer wearing a pair of overalls and a farmer's hat. If you ever wonder what a Medal of Honor recipient is not supposed to look like, Sergeant Alvin York would fill that bill for you. He was nothing like Gary Cooper! But his story was a tremendous influence on me. To this day, if it comes on television, I watch it.

"Then, of course, came Wake Island. As you know," he told Brigadier General Edwin H. Simmons, USMC (Ret.), his oral history interviewer, "Wake Island is still a haunting memory for me. I was stirred by all accounts of 'Send us more Japs.' Although they eventually surrendered, the Marines held out against heavy odds for a couple of weeks, but I was hooked for life by them. So I became, at the age of 6, in 1941, a Marine convert for life. I followed every battle of the war, whether it be the 'Battling Bastards of Bataan,' or the 'Battling Bastards of Bastogne,' but the Marines always had the greatest appeal. During the war, the Army sent soldiers up to middle Tennessee for maneuvers. I recall my best friend, Manson Henderson, and I standing by the railroad tracks watching as trainloads of tanks and trucks and Soldiers traveled through Cookeville. My mother made me a little fatigue uniform, as did Manson's mother, and my father made me a replica of a Thompson sub-machinegun, which I still have. It was made of wood because metal toys weren't available during the war. On Saturday nights, after my mother and other ladies in the town had spent all day making sandwiches and cakes, our family, with most others in Cookeville, would go down to the local armory, which was designated a USO.

Manson and I would 'stand guard' at the entrance as truckloads of muddy Soldiers came in from the field for a shower, clean clothes, and a dance with a local girl. We were awed and inspired by the Soldiers.

"The next week, as soon as school was out, we would rush home and grab our collections of miniature soldiers and airplanes and head into the woods to create a battleground. We would dig small trenches and bunkers and man them with the toy soldiers and then back off and toss acorns or pebbles at each other's defensive line or fly our P–38s or P–40s over on strafing and bombing missions.

"As an aside, Manson Henderson, whose older brother joined the Navy, always wanted to be a Sailor, but he retired many years later as a colonel after a distinguished career in the Army."

Mundy moved from Tennessee near the end of the war and graduated from Sidney Lanier High School in Montgomery, Alabama, in June 1953. That fall, he entered Alabama Polytechnic Institute, better known as Auburn. Simmons asked Mundy: "What made you decide to go to Auburn?"

Mundy responded: "Well, a chain of events. First, the war in Korea was going on while I was in high school. Some of my buddies decided to drop out at the end of our junior year and join the Marines. I wanted to do that, too, but my mother and father—neither of whom had had the opportunity to go to college, and in my Dad's case, even to finish high school—asked me to finish high school, and went on to say that they would like for me to attend college for at least one year, after which I could make my own choices. In my senior year of high school, I decided I wanted to go to The Citadel. My father was a South Carolinian, so we had some South Carolina ties. I applied for admission, but when the enrollment papers came back, the tuition costs were pretty high, and you also had to buy your uniforms your first year, as I recall. My parents were people of very modest means, and when we looked over the costs, we decided that The Citadel was just something the Mundy family couldn't afford. His business partner was an Auburn graduate, and he asked, 'Well, why don't you go to Auburn?' It was 60 miles up the road and, being a state-supported school, wasn't too expensive. I could hitchhike back and forth and work for my meals and dormitory room, which made it affordable. So that's how I wound up at Auburn: through default, if you will."

Simmons asked Mundy: "What were your career ambitions at this point? Had you decided what your major would be?" Mundy replied: "My objective was to go to college to meet my parents' wishes, and to get into the Marine Corps as quickly as I could by whatever means. I had no specific focus on a major beyond the foregoing. I figured that some sort of liberal arts was probably a better route to pursue to become a Marine, and I decided on business administration because that seemed to afford pretty good latitude in taking political science, history, English, and those sorts of courses that I thought would be of greater use to me. I eventually received a bachelor of science in business administration."

General Simmons asked: "Was ROTC compulsory?" Mundy replied: "Auburn was a land grant college and in those days, such institutions had compulsory ROTC for the first 2 years for all male students. The student population was about 8,500 when I was there, and with the entire freshman and sophomore classes being involved in ROTC, there were 4,000 or more cadets and midshipmen in the Army, Navy, and Air Force ROTC units.

"When I got to Auburn, I knew I wanted to get into the Marine Corps, and one day, I saw a Marine officer on campus, which surprised me because I had never seen a Marine officer before, and I wasn't smart enough to know that the Marines were involved with the Navy ROTC.

"He was a major, named Jim Gasser. In any case, I wandered up to him and said, 'Are you a Marine?' He said, 'Yes.' I asked, 'Are are you assigned here?' He said, 'Yes, I teach here in the Navy ROTC program.' I said, 'Well, I want to go into the Marine Corps.' He said, 'Navy ROTC is the route.' I said, 'No, I want nothing to do with the Navy. I want to be a Marine,' and abruptly walked off, uninformed, but also rather opposed to even considering anything other than the Marines. I went into the Army ROTC, because to me, land soldiers, the Army, were closer aligned with what I wanted to be, rather than Navy or Air Force."

Simmons asked: "What kind of uniforms did you get to wear, and how often did you wear them?" "Well," Mundy said, "in those days the uniform for freshmen and sophomores was the old Army OD, olive drab, which would have been an Ike jacket, the olive drab trousers, and overseas cap. The officers, or the upperclassmen, wore what we called 'Pinks and Greens,' which is the same cut as our Marine green uniform. It has a belted blouse and, in fact, was a very handsome uniform. In the spring and fall, we wore starched khaki uniforms. We wore them twice a week—Tuesdays and then to drill on Thursdays.

"I was an Armor ROTC cadet. They offered Armor, Artillery, and Signal Corps, but Armor seemed more like infantry to me, so that is what I opted for. I wound up on the drill team—called 'The Auburn Rifles'—because I had a fascination with all things military, and certainly with close order drill. Because we were a 'show outfit,' we wore white leggings and white helmets with a white cravat, and in the winter, we wore the 'Pinks and Greens' because it was a flashier uniform.

"In my sophomore year, I rose to be the commander of the Auburn Rifles, and was a cadet first lieutenant—the only officer in the second-year cadets. I had been to Marine Platoon Leaders Class training the summer between my freshman and sophomore years, and when I came back, the old Army sergeant at Auburn who oversaw our drill team apparently noted that I had definitely picked up something in my summer training, and made me the commander."

Simmons commented: "Your earliest Marine Corps record that I have seen is your application for the Platoon Leaders Class, which gives you a conditional enlistment date of 9 December 1953. You must have decided to get at least a Reserve commission in the Marine Corps as soon as you enrolled at Auburn."

Mundy responded: "As I mentioned earlier, I was determined to get into the Marine Corps as soon as possible. I recounted earlier having run into Major Gasser and talking about getting in the Corps. After I had waved off consideration of Navy ROTC, he later suggested to me, 'Well, the other program you can think about is the Platoon Leaders Class.' He told me further, that Captain Earl Litzenberg, Jr., who was then the Officer Selection Officer in Birmingham, would be coming to campus. When he came, I went down to meet him and he explained the PLC program to me, and also the fact that while in the program, I would be enlisted in the Marine Corps Reserve, and could attend drills with a Reserve unit in Montgomery. I really liked that idea because it would let me satisfy my itch to get into a Marine uniform, and it would also put me in a Marine commissioning program if I decided to stick it out at Auburn for more than a year. In the event I dropped out, the PLC program provided that my draft deferment would be rescinded, and I would be called to Active duty in the Corps, which would suit me just fine.

"I took the written test for the program, as I recall, standing in the basement storeroom of Brown Hall, which was the old ROTC building, and marking the test on a stack of cardboard boxes. Not very sophisticated, but I passed, and Litzenberg told me that the other qualifications are to be physically fit, and to achieve and maintain at least a C average.

"We finished the first academic quarter on the 8th of December, and I recall waiting outside the registrar's office for my grades. When they came out, I had achieved exactly a C—not a C plus, but just the required C. I then left directly with the transcript, hitchhiked over to Birmingham, and put myself up in some fleabag hotel overnight. I appeared in the basement of the post office in Birmingham the next morning, presented my grades, took my physical, and was administered the oath into the Marine Corps

Reserve and enrolled in the PLC program. Looking back, this was one of the most exciting days of my life!

"After being sworn in, I hitchhiked to Montgomery and home for the academic break. I recall proudly walking in when I got home that night and pulling out my brand new ID card, which proclaimed that I was a Private, U. S. Marine Corps Reserve. I still recall my mother, who was somewhat shocked by my having enlisted, saying to me, 'Now, son, you must take that back.' I guess either I, or my dad, were persuasive over the next couple of days because after that, she was always among my proudest supporters as a Marine.

"At the end of my freshman year a few months later, the war in Korea was winding down, college had turned out to be a pretty good deal, I had managed to get a Marine ID card in my wallet and had spent a summer at Quantico learning to be a Marine, so I decided to stick it out and finish at Auburn."

Simmons reflected: "I knew Jim Gasser, and you have mentioned Earl Litzenberg, who was Officer Selection Officer in Birmingham. Were these the only two Marine officers with whom you had contact on campus?"

Mundy replied: "No, there were two other notable ones. Vince Dooley, the famed Auburn quarterback, was 3 years ahead of me at Auburn. He was in the NROTC unit and was commissioned in the Marine Corps at the end of my freshman year. He returned to become a backfield coach after his 2 years on active duty and became my platoon commander in the Marine Corps Reserve. By then, because of the number of Auburn students who were in the Montgomery Reserve Unit, it had been decided to transfer one platoon from the company to Auburn, where it would hold its weekly drills, and First Lieutenant Dooley was assigned as platoon commander. He later, of course, became athletic director for the University of Georgia, but we maintained a distant association, and I had him to the Marine Corps Birthday Ball in Washington many years later when I was Commandant.

"The other officer of note was the Inspector-Instructor of the Marine Reserve Unit in Montgomery, then Captain Jim Wilkinson. Jim was a striking role model for an aspiring young Marine. A decade after I was commissioned, we would serve together in Khe Sanh, Vietnam: he, as the Commanding Officer of 1$^{st}$ Battalion, 26$^{th}$ Marines; and me as Executive Officer of the same regiment's 3$^{d}$ Battalion. After both our retirements, we wound up living one house apart on the mountain road where we both spend the summers."

Mundy concluded: "So, my becoming a Marine was not very complicated. I simply always wanted to be one, and I got my wish. As I was approaching retirement, a number of people would offer the thought, 'I'll bet you'll miss being the Commandant,' to which I replied, with honesty, 'I won't miss being the Commandant at all, but I'll miss getting up and looking at that Marine emblem on my lapels before I go to work each morning for the rest of my life.'"

When, in June 1957, Mundy received orders to active duty, he began a 38-year career that would culminate in his selection to be Commandant of the Corps.[23] He became Commandant on July 1, 1991, retiring from that position on June 30, 1995.

**Charles C. Krulak**

During an interview, I asked Commandant Krulak why he selected the Marine Corps. He told me: "Commandant Lemuel Shepherd was somebody that I saw a lot of. But probably one of the smartest, unsung heroes of the Marine Corps was a general by the name of Bobby [Robert E.] Hogaboom, who was famous for the Hogaboom Board [convened in 1956 to determine the optimum organization and composition of the Fleet Marine Force]. General Hogaboom was a dear friend of my father. His daughter, Gretchen Hogaboom, used to babysit for us, and we used to see the Hogabooms almost every weekend. Again, it's hard to think about specific instances where General Hogaboom made a difference. It's just that here is the forerunner of men like Lou Wilson or Robert Barrow. It was this gentleman who exuded the confidence of what a Marine general should be—tall, thin, good looking, with a great mind. He was just a real winner.

"Gerald C. Thomas—General Thomas—the first person I ever went hunting with. He took me into the woods overnight. I am not even sure how the trip was initiated. It just was a great time with a superb Marine general. To see him as human, and not as a general, not some automaton, that was really impressive.

"Colonel [Robert D.] Heinl used to come over to the house on my father's birthday and drink fish house punch (a very potent drink—just the fumes will put you under) and tell stories. From an early age, I knew all about the Marine Corps. I can remember asking questions about Korea and about World War II, and he'd just sit there and pick at the turkey and drink fish house punch and talk about Marine history.

"The Twinings. A great military family. General Twining was another extremely smart Marine who could easily have been a Commandant. All of the officers mentioned could have been Commandant. Just tremendous people. So they were coming in and out of our lives during the time of the Chowder Society [approximately a dozen officers, collectively known as the Chowder Society, helped defeat Armed Forces unification legislation in the House of Representatives; some of them also helped draft the National Security Act of 1947]. My dad would come home sometimes late at night and, when we'd wake up in the morning, there would be all these officers still working the issues that eventually resulted in the National Security Act of 1947 and the amendments to the Security Act in 1947 and 1952. They would work on these issues all night in our house.

"It's hard to remember any specific words of wisdom or, great input that changed my life. What I think was of most importance was just watching real professionals. They were absolutely selfless people. These officers had the chance to be Commandant. They didn't make it, but it didn't make any difference. They continued to serve their Corps. They were not afraid to take chances. They absolutely thought out of the box. They were not afraid of failure. When they did make a mistake, they admitted it. My father and General Shepherd had no problem saying, 'We were wrong on Inchon.' Today, we, as a Corps, look to the Inchon landing as one of the great moments in our history, but if you go to the books you'll see two of the key planners said, 'Don't do it,' and they were both Marines. I think that what I got out of the people that I grew up around was an understanding of what a professional is and how important it is to keep your hand on the touchstone of our Corps. Valor and values."

Dr. David Crist, General Krulak's oral history interviewer, asked him: "From an early age, did you have an interest in the Marine Corps? Did you know that was what you wanted to do?"

Krulak replied: "I think that the first time I really said, 'This looks like something I want to do,' was as a result of something my father did. I'm sure he had absolutely no inkling of the impact he had on me when he did it. He was in Korea, and for some reason he sent me a 1:50,000 map of a sector of Korea, and on it he annotated the Marine positions and the enemy positions, and explained that this had been a battle that Marines fought. He just sent it as kind of a souvenir for his son. Well, I took that map and I pretended like I was the Marine general and then I drew arrows and positions all over it as how I'd fight the enemy. I guess they were either Chinese or North Koreans. Then I sent it back to my dad. I was just a young boy. I was 8 years old, maybe 9. Well, my dad sent a letter back and said he got my map and he had studied what I had done, and he was really proud because he thought that I had a great scheme of maneuver. Well, I was thinking, 'I'm the next Clausewitz or Sun Tzu.' Here I am, 9 years old, and

I'm solving warfare problems by long-distance air mail! Now that I think back on it, it was a battle that had already been fought. He was just sending me something as a souvenir. But he took the time to critique what I had done, and instead of saying it was lousy, he said it was great. At that point, I thought maybe what I'm cut out to be is a United States Marine. So, that was the beginning of my desire to go into the Marine Corps.

"I went to a lot of schools and ended up at the Phillips Exeter Academy. They put me back a year because of the caliber of schools that I'd been going to as I grew up. Not that I hadn't gone to some good schools, but I'd also gone to some bad ones. They just thought it would be better if I went back a grade. So I repeated my sophomore year. After I finished my junior year, I had enough credits that I was only one class short of graduating. I was going to come back as a senior at Exeter, but really had very little to do, so at the end of my junior year I applied for several colleges, including the Naval Academy and Princeton. I got accepted to both of them. I received a nomination to the Naval Academy and was accepted. So I had an opportunity to go to Princeton or the Naval Academy. At Exeter, everybody was telling me to go to Princeton. That was the hot school at that time. It wasn't Harvard; it wasn't Yale. Princeton was the place to go. I remember turning down Princeton and accepting the Naval Academy. I went there because, by then, I had decided to be a Marine.

"Until my first class cruise at the Naval Academy, I was set on going into the Corps. I went on a diesel submarine, the USS *Bang*, SS–385. I loved it. It was the most remarkable event of my life at that time. I just fell in love with the wardroom. I fell in love with the camaraderie. Everybody ate at the same time in the wardroom. They played dice and cards, and had a great time. The officers were fine professionals, but were also very human and I felt that this is what 'a band of brothers' is really about. This is camaraderie.

"Well, at the end of the first half of the cruise, I remember getting off the submarine at New London, going to the end of the pier, calling up my father, and saying, 'Dad, I'm going submarines. I know I've always wanted to go Marine Corps, but I'll tell you, I just had the most unbelievable experience, and if you'd been there you'd approve of this. This is a good thing.' He said, 'Chuck, whatever you want to do. It sounds like a great thing. Go ahead and do it. You're going to love it. Put your heart into it. Don't worry about me; you're not disappointing me at all. I'm proud of you no matter what you do.'

"He never even tried to steer me into the Naval Academy. My dad never encouraged us to go to the Naval Academy. Both of my brothers went. Vic had to leave at the end of plebe summer for a medical problem, but both of them went. My other brother, Bill, graduated in 1962, and I graduated in '64. Although all of us went, we never felt any real pressure to go there from our dad.

"So, the next part of the cruise was on board the USS *Nautilus*, the first nuclear-powered submarine. Within 24 hours, I realized that this is not what I want and, unfortunately, that was what the submarine world was becoming. A very pristine environment; very, very cautious, highly intelligent officers; but none of the camaraderie I saw on the diesel sub. They were all a bunch of egghead nuclear physicists who were running a ship, and it didn't even seem like a warship. I realized that this was the future. The future is nuclear power, not diesel. So I decided to go Marine Corps. I called my dad back up and told him why and he said, 'Good call,' and I went into the Marine Corps, and that was it.

Dr. Crist asked: "Was there a Bulldog program or something similar to familiarize the midshipmen with the Marine Corps?" Krulak replied: "No, there was a period of time during your second class cruise where you went down to Little Creek to do some Marine things, but I stayed at the Naval Academy my second class summer as a member of what was called the plebe detail. I basically instructed the plebes, and I loved that. I did it my first class year, too, and I did it after graduation for a short period of time. So, I enjoyed the leadership challenge in working with the young plebes. I did not go to the Marine indoctrination. I didn't think I really needed it after living it for 20 plus years."[24]

Krulak was selected to succeed Commandant Mundy on June 30, 1995, serving in that position until he retired on June 30, 1999.

**James L. Jones**

In an interview with Commandant Jones, I asked him: "Why did you decide to go into the Marine Corps? Were you in ROTC at Georgetown University?" Jones was in the class of 1966, the School of Foreign Service.

*General Jones*: Actually, I wasn't. My father was a World War II Marine in the Pacific, and he was a Force Reconnaissance Marine.

*Dr. Puryear*: Was he a career Marine?

*General Jones*: No, he wasn't. He was a Marine literally for the span of the war, but he started as a second lieutenant and ended as a major, commanding the first Force Reconnaissance Company and battalion that the Marine Corps ever had.

*Dr. Puryear*: Which of the islands was he part of invading?

*General Jones*: He did reconnaissance on a number of islands. They operated off of a U.S. Navy submarine called the *Nautilus*. He did a lot of reconnaissance, and his brother was 3 years younger, but was the youngest battalion commander in the Marine Corps by virtue of surviving. He was on Guadalcanal and commanded a battalion at the ripe old age of 27. I want to add something about why I became a Marine because it wasn't just the family. In 1945, my father left the Marine Corps and got a job with International Harvester Company in Chicago. In 1947, the company sent him to Paris, France, and my family stayed in Europe until 1973. I spent all my formative years in Europe from '47 until '61, and I went to French schools. When you're raised overseas, you have a particular appreciation for your country. A lot of the things I saw as a young person were centered around what the American military had done to liberate postwar Europe, so I grew up with a very strong identity that I was an American—although I lived in a French environment. I was made to feel very proud, and every time I saw GIs, I was very proud of being an American—just like them.

My father embraced the small Marine contingent that was there, the Embassy Marines and the like. When NATO was there, of course, there were more Marines in the NATO Headquarters. So over the years, a lot of these folks influenced my life. So there was no question in my mind that I was going to join the Marine Corps voluntarily. I had no doubt. I had no notion that I was going to stay in and make it a career. That was completely unfathomable to me. So I did not join the Marine Corps with the idea of staying in, but just do what I thought was my duty as an American.

*Dr. Puryear*: During your Marine Corps career, did you ever consider leaving?

*General Jones*: Yes.

*Dr. Puryear*: When and why?

*General Jones*: The first one is humorous. It happened in Vietnam when I was convinced that majors were put on this earth to make lieutenants' lives miserable. I told one of our greatest Marine Corps generals, General Ray Davis, who asked me if I was going to make it a career, that I would stay in if I never had to be a major.

The second one was actually more serious and more troublesome because I was a company commander on Okinawa from '74 to '75 for 13 straight months, that's how we did unaccompanied tours in those days. Coupled with the fact that we really had a tough time—I wasn't sure whether I was in the foreign legion or the Marine Corps. There were many who should not have been wearing the Marine uniform, and we had drug problems, we had race problems, we had alcohol problems. We had gutted the staff NCO corps during Vietnam and made all the good ones temporary officers and they retired en masse when it came time to revert back to enlisted ranks.

The backbone of the Corps during those days was the second lieutenant. I was a captain, and between me, my XO and the four lieutenants I had, we ran Hotel Company, 2$^d$ Battalion, 9$^{th}$ Marines, Camp Schwab, Okinawa, and we did a good job, but it was a 20-hour-a-day job just to keep the troops under control. It was easily the hardest job I've ever had.

*Dr. Puryear*: Even more so than being Commandant?

*General Jones*: Yes. Being commandant is not hard. Being a company commander in 1974 was really hard. That was hard because you never knew what the troops were going to do next and trying to keep them focused and trying to make basic Marines out of them was very hard.

*Dr. Puryear*: That was the time then when you considered leaving?

*General Jones*: When I came back from Okinawa, I had left my wife with four kids under the age of 6. Our second-born child was severely handicapped, so for my wife it was like having triplets. It was a very hard year. Plus, just being exhausted at the end of the year from the mental effort of having to work with a company that turned out to be okay but wasn't really representative of what the Marine Corps ought to be. I never really understood as a junior officer why it was so hard to get rid of people who didn't want to be Marines. You could give them special court-martials, and they'd be back on active duty. You would try to discharge them and the discharge would not be approved at senior levels; it was quantity over quality, and it almost killed the Corps.

*Dr. Puryear*: General Henry Shelton, Chairman of the Joint Chiefs of Staff, had the same thing happen to him and he was ready to leave, but he was told things were going to get better, and for him, they did.

*General Jones*: Well, the same thing happened and I came back and I came to Washington and I saw the metamorphosis of the all-volunteer force. One thing led to the other and I'm sure glad I stayed, but it was a different Marine Corps in those days.

*Dr. Puryear*: How many tours in Vietnam did you do?

*General Jones*: One.

*Dr. Puryear*: And what was your responsibility?

*General Jones*: I was a platoon commander and a company commander. The last couple of months I was General Davis' aide; he was the division commander.[25]

Jones was selected to succeed Krulak as Commandant on June 30, 1999, and in 2003 became the first Marine to serve as Commander, Supreme Headquarters, Allied Command in Europe.

## Early Experiences of Other Influential Marines

### Lieutenant General Lewis B. "Chesty" Puller

In September 1917, Lewis Puller entered Virginia Military Institute. It was a spartan life, with no leave in the 10 months. He had no holiday for Thanksgiving or Christmas. The only break that the students had was from 2:00 pm to 5:00 pm on Saturdays and Sundays. Puller was more fortunate than most because he was related to Colonel George A. Derbyshire, the Commandant of Cadets at VMI, so he enjoyed a few lunches in his home.

Classes were held from 8:00 am until 4:00 pm, and then Puller had drill right after class. He had a mediocre academic year, standing 177th out of a class of 233 cadets. By subject, the breakdown is revealing: he was 200th in mathematics; 149th in English; 138th in German; 102d in history; and 89th in military science. But in the first year, Puller received no demerits—a remarkable achievement—and his leadership ability was recognized by his selection as cadet corporal, the highest rank possible for his year in the 4-year curriculum.

Puller was not happy at VMI. His biographer, Burke Davis, wrote:

> His chief disappointment was that they were soldiers without arms, for the rifles were taken by the Army as the war in Europe wore on, and ammunition had been too scarce for target practice. Lewis was impressed by the stern workings of the honor system, and developed a lifelong love for VMI and the town, but felt he had learned little of warfare.
>
> In the last days his cousin, Colonel Derbyshire, called Lewis in for a serious talk.
>
> "I hope you're coming back next year, Lewis."

"No, sir. I'm going to enlist in the Marines."

"Why?"

"Well, I'm not old enough to get a commission in the Army, and I can get one in the Marines right away. I don't want the war to end without me. I'm going with the rifles. If they need them, they need me, too."

"Lewis, I want you to promise me that you'll come back and get as much education as you can, when it's over."

"I hope I can, sir."

"All right, son. I know you've been disappointed with VMI in some ways, but I don't know what you expected. We can give you only the background to be an officer. Not even West Point can do any more. We'll get you as far as second lieutenant, and it's up to you to build on that. Good luck."

On June 27, the day after his twentieth birthday, Lewis took the train to Richmond and enlisted in the Marine Corps, bound for boot camp at Parris Island, South Carolina.[26]

Puller excelled in basic training and was selected for noncommissioned officers' school and for the drill instructors' course, but he was anxious to get into action in Europe in World War I. The war was winding down when he received orders to ship to France, but with the signing of the Armistice on November 11, 1918, his orders were cancelled. Instead, he was assigned to Officer Candidates School. Puller was determined to be a Marine. He commented, "I'm going to stay in the Corps, one way or another. I'm qualified for it. I don't know about civilian life."

Puller graduated in June 1918 and was commissioned on June 4, but on June 16, with the drastic reduction in the size of the Corps, he was discharged, having been a Marine officer for only 2 weeks. He reentered the Corps as an enlisted man. Still wanting to fight, he considered enlisting in the Polish-American army, which was recruiting a force on Long Island, New York, that was scheduled to go to Europe to assist in liberating the Poles.

On the way to Long Island to enlist, Puller stopped over in Washington. He saw Captain William H. Rupertus at Marine Headquarters, who asked Puller: "What are you boys doing?"

When they explained the plight of Poland and their plan to enlist, Rupertus countered: "If I were you, I'd go down to Haiti. You'll get commissions in the constabulary down there. They need men, and there's plenty of fighting. You'll see action and have some fun."

Puller and Muth went into a hallway and discussed the matter briefly, and though Puller still yearned for the battlefields of Poland, they agreed to sign for the *Gendarmerie d'Haiti*.

Lewis had a few more days at home, then found himself in Charleston, South Carolina, with Muth, boarding a transport for Haiti. He was barely twenty-one years old.[27]

Puller served brilliantly in the *Gendarmerie d'Haiti* and never gave up his desire to make a career of the Marine Corps. While he held the ranks of corporal and then sergeant in the Marine Corps, he was a lieutenant, then captain, in the *Gendarmie d'Haiti*. He served in Haiti for 5 years. He never gave up his quest for a commission in the Marine Corps or to make it his career.

There was a policy in the Marine Corps at that time of providing an opportunity for deserving NCOs to attend officer training school and earn a commission. Puller's brilliant record in combat in Haiti is a significant part of his legend as one of the greats of the Corps. He fought 40 battles during his years stationed in Haiti. He had certainly exhibited his combat leadership. Then-Colonel A. A. Vandegrift was Commander of the Department of the South and in 1922 selected Puller to be his adjutant. Vandegrift's responsibility as Commander was to lead 750 men covering half of Haiti's nearly 11,000 square miles, providing Puller a staff assignment where he learned the task of running such a large unit.

Vandegrift pushed hard for Puller to enter Officer Candidates School at Quantico, stating in a two-page letter of recommendation that Puller was "a man of sterling qualities and conscientious in the performance of his duties," and that he had "the ability to make an excellent officer." His academic record in trigonometry, geometry, history, geography and English had an overall average of only 78. In his military performance, however, he ranked second out of 17 NCOs in his class.

Puller was commissioned a second lieutenant on March 6, 1924, at the Marine Corps Barracks in Washington, DC, 7 years after he initially enlisted.

He commented to a friend, "I may not have had much else to go on, but I have some perseverance." How fortunate for the Corps and our country.[28]

### Major General Smedley D. Butler

Butler, a legend in the Corps, was commissioned a Marine Corps second lieutenant at the age of 16. He was a combat hero in campaigns and military expeditions beginning in 1898 in Cuba, the Philippines, China, Honduras, Panama, Nicaragua, Mexico, Haiti, France, and again in China in the late 1920s. Butler's career was highlighted by the award of two Medals of Honor. His first was earned in action at Veracruz in April 1914 for his courage in leading the Marines of the Panama battalion in an assault on the city. He earned his second Medal of Honor for action in Haiti in 1915, capturing the last rebel bastion, Fort Capois, on February 17, 1915.

In a book entitled *Old Gimlet Eye: The Adventures of Smedley D. Butler*, he described how he had entered the Marine Corps:

> When the *Maine* was blown up in Havana harbor, in February 1898, I was just sixteen. The excitement was intense. Headlines blazed across the papers. Crowds pushed and shoved around the bulletin boards. School seemed stupid and unnecessary.
>
> War was declared two months later and we boys thought our government exceedingly slow in avenging the death of our gallant American sailors. But here was the war at last, and we built bonfires and stamped around shouting "Remember the *Maine*, to Hell with Spain" and singing "We'll Hang General Weyler to a Sour Apple Tree."
>
> Enviously I watched volunteer companies marching gaily off to war to the tunes of "There'll Be a Hot Time in the Old Town Tonight" and "The Girl I Left Behind Me." I clenched my fists when I thought of those poor Cuban devils being starved and murdered by the beastly Spanish tyrants. I was determined to shoulder a rifle and help free little Cuba. It made no difference to me that the event was exaggerated. Cuba now seemed more important than all the Latin and history in the world.
>
> The 6th Pennsylvania Volunteers was recruiting a company in West Chester. I tried to join up, but was good-naturedly told to run along home. I couldn't even break into the Navy as an apprentice boy. Father refused to give his consent.

One night, as I was getting into bed, I heard him say to Mother in the next room: "Today Congress increased the Marine Corps by 24 second lieutenants and 2,000 men for the period of the war. The Marine Corps is a finely trained body of men. Too bad Smedley is so young. He seems determined to go."

The Marine Corps was little more than a name to me then, except that once I had seen a Marine officer flashing down the street in sky blue trousers with scarlet stripes. I had been much impressed with the handsome uniform. I knew I'd like to wear it. I tossed all night. In half-waking dreams I was charging up a hill at the head of my company, with sword drawn, bullets dropping around me.

Father's seal of approval on the Marine Corps settled it. The next morning I took Mother aside and told her I was going to be a Marine. "If thou doesn't come with me and give me thy permission, I'll hire a man to say he is my father. And I'll run away and enlist in some faraway regiment where I'm not known." [Butler was from a prominent Pennsylvania Quaker family.]

Mother sighed. "Let me think it over quietly today."

That evening she agreed to go with me on the first train leaving Philadelphia for Washington next day. Father knew nothing of our conspiracy. We started out at five o'clock. In the train Mother reached over and took my hand. I drew away. I was a man now and didn't want to be fondled in public. I've always hoped that my mother in her wisdom understood my lack of affection that morning.

In Washington, we went to the headquarters of the Marine Corps. Mother waited outside when I went into the office to introduce myself to Colonel Commandant Heywood. That fine old soldier looked at me quizzically.

"When I met your father the other day, he told me you were only sixteen."

"No, sir," I lied promptly, "that's my brother."

"How old are you, then?"

"I'm eighteen, sir."

His keen eyes twinkled. "Well, you're big enough, anyway. We'll take you."

The Colonel directed me across the parade ground to Sergeant Hector McDonald, a tall, swaybacked, weather-beaten old timer who was in charge of recruits.

While I was answering his questions I looked out of the window, and to my horror saw my father. His coattails were flying out behind him as he rushed wildly across the parade ground to the Commandant's office. Goodbye, war, now I'm in for a scene.

An orderly appeared at the door and said the Commandant wished to see me. I was quaking in my boots as I went to the office.

"Did thy mother give thee her permission?" my father demanded.

"Yes, sir."

"But thee is under age."

"Oh, there isn't any age limit now. Congress has never fixed one," I explained to my congressional father. [Butler's father was Thomas Stalker Butler, a Congressman for 31 years.] "Anyway, I've attended to that."

"How old did thee say thee was?"

"I told Colonel Heywood that I was eighteen, born on April 20, 1880."

Father smiled. "All right. If thee is determined to go, thee shall go, but don't add another year to thy age, my son. Thy mother and I weren't married until 1879."

The Adjutant and Inspector of our Corps at that time was Major George C. Reid, one of the gentlest and finest characters

I've ever known, not the least of his virtues was a military stride that I would have given a fortune to acquire. He had a keen sense of humor and took a great interest in me because of the way I had broken into the Marines. Major Reid's nephew, George, entered the Corps when I did. He is now a retired colonel, living in Cleveland.

The Major took George and me, one under each arm, and strolled over to Heiberger's uniform shop. With as much dignity as if he were outfitting Napoleon's grand marshals, he had us measured for two second lieutenant's uniforms.

Since we couldn't perform our full duties until we were properly garbed, George and I hung around Marine Corps headquarters, like two generals temporarily out of a job.

Our uniforms came at last. My heart thumped as I hurriedly pulled on the sky blue trousers with the gay red stripes down the seams, and buttoned myself snugly into the dark blue coat. The uniform was tight and covered with black braid. I looked thin and wasp-like, more as if I belonged to a boys' band than to a husky fighting corps. I was very much pleased with myself. I couldn't go home and parade down the streets of West Chester, so I did the next best thing. I had my picture taken.

Now that George Reid and I could dress like second lieutenants—no matter that we were so new we almost creaked—we were ordered to the Washington barracks for instruction. The school for officers was conducted by a wonderful old soldier, Sergeant Major Hayes. He had been in a Scottish regiment and had fought with Kitchener in the Sudan. After his discharge from the British army he came to America and joined up with the Marines.

Until the Spanish-American War, 2,000 men and officers constituted the total enrollment of the Marine Corps. Hayes, stationed at the Washington headquarters, enjoyed the distinction of being the one and only sergeant major for the whole Corps. His principal duty was to bring up young officers in the way they should go. He was getting on in years, but he was still a magnificent 250-pound specimen, built on heroic lines. He carried his 6 feet 3 inches as erect as a ramrod.

When we rose to recite our lessons, the Sergeant Major always stood up, too. Even though he was in charge of us, he never forgot for a moment the difference in our ranks, or that enlisted men never sit in the presence of officers. One rebuke from him cut to the quick. We all admired him so much that we didn't have the heart to disappoint him. He was one of the most perfect public servants I have ever met.

Those first 6 weeks of intensive training planted the seed of soldiering in me. And from that time on I never felt entirely happy away from the Marines.[29]

### General Holland M. "Howlin' Mad" Smith

General Holland M. Smith reflected in his memoir *Coral and Brass* why he decided upon the Marine Corps.

While I was at Auburn, the most momentous decision of my life was made. Had the decision gone otherwise, this book [his memoir] never would have been written.

Shortly after I entered the Polytechnic I was offered a nomination to take the examinations for entrance to the Naval Academy at Annapolis. Bored as I was by the pseudo-military air of Auburn—I still was an adventurous youngster, yearning to do and see things—I was attracted by the Navy. Therefore, when Congressman Henry D. Clayton, representing our congressional district, offered me the academy appointment, I was delighted. Why it was offered I learned later. My father was a prominent man and there was some question of his entering the race for Congress against Clayton. The Congressman got wind of this and suggested the appointment to the Naval Academy, which he knew I wanted, as a discreet bribe to head off Father's possible opposition.

I never accepted the appointment or even sat for the examination because my father and mother would not hear of it. They were both born during the Civil War period and they carried the mental scars of the conflict deep in their beings. They were still unreconstructed and would not permit me to accept an offer which, in their minds, would be a surrender to Yankee ideology.

Such an attitude would appear unreasonable today, but when I was a boy in the South these ideas were live, glowing embers of a fire that had not been extinguished, remnants of a pride that could yield but not surrender. Unforgettable associations helped preserve this attitude. It was in Montgomery, where my parents spent many years of their lives, that the congress of delegates from the seceding states adopted the Confederate constitution and inaugurated Jefferson Davis as president in 1861.

Destiny hangs by a slender thread. Instead of joining the Navy I became a Marine, following a brief and undistinguished flirtation with the law which convinced me I was not destined to become a John Marshall or an Oliver Wendell Holmes. In 1901, at my father's insistence, I entered the University of Alabama law school. My father had a comfortable practice and he figured his son would make a satisfactory partner, but I never had the slightest interest in law.

Two years at the University—except for my sprinting, which gained me campus popularity—were practically wasted and I barely graduated in 1903. After graduation, I entered my father's office and the firm became Smith and Smith, with the junior member disliking his job more intensely every day. I suffered a further impediment at a chance of a successful career. Acquaintances always introduced me as John Smith's son and this made me realize that as long as I practiced law I would only be John Smith's son. Like most young men, I had independent ambitions and they were far removed from the musty labyrinths of law.

My few appearances in court only emphasized my unfitness as a lawyer. The last time was in Montgomery, when I appeared as assistant to the County Solicitor in the prosecution of a Negro charged with attacking another Negro with a knife. I did what I considered a first-class piece of work and made (I thought) a fine argument. The judge looked at me pityingly and the defense lawyer rested his case and sat down, almost unable to believe that anybody could present a case as badly as

I did. The defendant was acquitted immediately and I walked out of the courtroom, vowing never to enter again.

That humiliating experience finally decided me: I would abandon law, which obviously was not my métier, and join the Army. This plan had been slowly forming in my restless mind ever since a youthful aversion to uniformed drudgery at Auburn started to wear off. My inclinations were definitely toward a military career and I had already worked up to first sergeant in a cavalry troop of the Alabama National Guard.

I was now 21 and ready to make something out of life that the law couldn't offer. My father was reluctant to see me desert the family profession but he didn't stand in my way when I announced my plans. Instead, he gave me his parental blessing and I went off to Washington to see our Congressman, Lieutenant Colonel Ariosto A. Wiley, who had served in the Army in Cuba during the Spanish-American War. Colonel Wiley heartily approved of my intentions but it was not easy to realize them. At the War Department, he introduced me to Secretary Mills, who was cordial and sympathetic, but wrecked my plans for an Army career by saying that no examinations for second lieutenants would be held until November 1905. That was more than a year away and I couldn't wait.

As we were leaving the War Department, Colonel Wiley, fully appreciating my disappointment, suddenly had an idea. "How would you like to join the Marines?" he asked. I know it sounds odd today but I answered, "What are the Marines?" Honestly, I didn't know. Nobody ever mentioned that branch of the service to me and even in my reading I never encountered the Corps. No attractive recruiting posters showing Marine life overseas plastered the country in the early years of this century.

Colonel Wiley explained to me the organization of the United States Marine Corps, its history and its functions. His little lecture on the street outside the War Department was the most convincing I have ever had. I am sorry I can't recall it exactly because it could be usefully incorporated in Marine archives as a gem of extemporaneous lucidity and conviction. His talk immediately won me over and we went to see Secretary of the Navy William H. Moody. Mr. Moody told me he was looking for some boys from the South to complete the proper geographical distribution of commissions in the Marine Corps and said he would give me a chance. I was overwhelmed and thanked him profusely.

In Washington, a school run by a Mr. Swaverly prepared candidates for Army, Navy, and Marine examinations. I enrolled in a class of about 40 young men studying for service careers. Looking back, I remember that among my classmates, who became lifelong friends, were Major General Ralph S. Keyser, Lieutenant Colonel Edward W. Sturdivant, Colonel Andrew B. Drum, Colonel Victor I. Morrison, Colonel David M. Randall, and Brigadier General M. E. Shearer, all stalwarts of the Marine Corps.

Examinations for entrance to the Corps were held in February, 1905, at the Marine Barracks in Washington, and I passed successfully. It was the proudest day of my life, even prouder than the day when, with Secretary of the Navy Forrestal standing at my side, I watched my men raise the Stars and Stripes on Suribachi, the climax of my years in service to my country. At last I was starting a career I felt would satisfy all my longings and ambitions.

I received a commission as second lieutenant and was assigned to the School of Application, known today as the Basic School, at the Marine Barracks, Annapolis, Maryland. Then came another proud day—the day I first wore my Marine uniform. At that time, the Corps uniform consisted of a dark blue blouse with elaborate frogs across the chest and braid around the hem. The pants were sky blue, with a broad red stripe running down. A blue cap completed the outfit. Afterwards, this uniform was discarded for one more practical, but I was deeply thrilled when I first wore it. To me, it represented admission to an old, honored, and distinguished company of men who had helped shape our country's history.

It was an intense, thrilling year at the School of Application. I began, as never before, to appreciate the qualities of my fellow men as we drilled on the parade ground, attended classes and studied or yarned far into the night.

At Auburn, he was exposed to his first Marine Corps mention: "In my class were 50 embryo Marine officers. The Commandant of the School was Colonel Lincoln Karmany, a magnificent man, the very embodiment of the ideal Marine officer. He had a long military record and was a strict disciplinarian, but he was essentially kind and sympathetic. We all left school inspired to emulate him."[30]

Smith was commissioned a second lieutenant on March 18, 1905, and was the third officer in the history of the Corps to retire as a four-star general.

## General Raymond G. Davis

Davis was selected for this study of Marine Corps generalship because of his combat leadership in three wars: World War II, Korea, and Vietnam. In World War II, he saw action in the Pacific theater at Guadalcanal and Peleliu. He fought as a member of the 1st Battalion, 7th Marines in Korea, and he commanded the 3d Marine Division in Vietnam.

Davis earned the Medal of Honor in Korea during the fight to break out of the Chosin Reservoir area. His battalion at that time was credited with saving a rifle company from annihilation and with opening a mountain pass so two trapped regiments could escape. It took 4 days of heavy, continuous fighting to accomplish this feat. Parts of Davis' citation read: "boldly led his battalion in the attack . . . and personally leading the assault groups in hand-to-hand encounters . . . led his battalion over three successive ridges in deep snow in continuous attacks . . . constantly inspiring and encouraging his men . . . his superb leadership, outstanding courage, and brilliant tactical ability." President Harry S. Truman presented him the award in a White House ceremony on November 24, 1952.

Perhaps the highest compliment was paid Davis by Army General Creighton W. Abrams, Jr., who commanded the U.S. Military Assistance Command in Vietnam from 1968 to 1972. General Abrams observed to General Leonard F. Chapman, Jr., during the Marine Commandant's visit to Vietnam, "Of the 50 or so division commanders I have known in Vietnam, General Davis has no peer. He's the best."

In his autobiography, General Davis wrote:

I was commissioned in the Army Reserve upon graduation. However, they had what they called the Thompson Act, where Reserve officers could serve on Active duty for a 5-year period, but with no assurance at all that you could continue in the Army. I obviously enjoyed my ROTC time; 3 years in high school and 4 at Tech. They had a Navy ROTC Unit at Tech, but I knew nothing about the Navy and didn't think about going into it. None of my immediate family had served in the military. I did have ancient relatives on both sides in the Civil War, one in Virginia and one from Indiana, as well as an uncle in World War I, but there were no service veterans in my immediate family.

My ROTC instructor, a friendly Army lieutenant colonel, told me that the Navy had a commission in the Marine Corps that represented regular Active duty of a more permanent nature. I went to meet with Captain Falwell, officer-in-charge of Tech's Naval ROTC unit, who described the program. They reviewed my A-plus grades in Army ROTC, interviewed me and many other candidates, and then I was selected as the Marine candidate from Georgia Tech's graduating class that year.

To be honest, I wasn't really sure what I was getting into, except that the Marines had a great reputation, and there had been a Marine or two around Georgia Tech at times. I had close friends in Navy ROTC who talked down the Corps by saying that it "had only two-star generals at the top," etc. I knew little about the Marines, but that "regular commission" on Active duty sounded good, so it was into the Corps for me.

My first face-to-face encounter with a Marine was at the Main Gate, Charleston Navy Yard, when I rode the bus over for my physical examination. Like most boxers and wrestlers in college, I was underweight (both sports strive to put their skills to work in the lowest weight class possible). My family doctor had prescribed beer and bananas, much to the horror of my teetotaling parents. At the bus stop in Augusta, I ate a sandwich which made me ill. In Charleston, I loaded up on water and bananas. Then I asked the doctors to weigh me first thing, but they refused. They gave me the usual bottle to fill, where I certainly lost some precious ounces before being weighed. I was finally passed, after the doctors accepted my story about losing my lunch because of the bad sandwich.

The next step was the classic one for all young incoming second lieutenants in those days. On to the Basic School for new lieutenants, which was then located at the Navy Yard, Philadelphia, Pennsylvania.[31]

Smith's Marine Corps career was brilliant, achieving the rank of general on March 12, 1971, when President Richard M. Nixon promoted him with his assignment as Assistant Commandant of the Marine Corps.

## Conclusion

General Holland M. "Howlin' Mad" Smith wrote in his autobiography *Coral and Brass*, "Destiny hangs by a slender thread." This comment could be applied to a great number of the Marine Corps generals in this study who nearly or actually were commissioned in the Army. It is also remarkable to note how many of them knew next to nothing about the Marine Corps when they signed up.

General Lejeune commented on his early years and of the eager anticipation of adventures ahead as a Marine: "I was filled with the joy of living . . . every man owed a debt to Corps and Country which it was his highest privilege to pay." Looking back on the comments in this chapter, it is clear how much each officer grew to love the Corps. They gave it their all and earned the heartfelt appreciation of a grateful Nation for their selfless contributions to Corps and country.

**Chapter 4**

# "Think of Yourself as the Institution": Decisionmaking

The position of command is a lonely one. At no time does a leader feel loneliness more deeply than when having to make a critical, high-level decision dealing with life and death, success and failure, victory and defeat. It is an overwhelming responsibility that few people desire and for which considerably fewer people are qualified. But making decisions is part of leadership; in time of war, the general who does not have the strength to make decisions and the judgment to be right a large percentage of the time does not remain long in a position of high command. Generals are human and are subject to the stresses and strains of the mind just as lesser beings are. Their mistakes can be counted in death and destruction, a responsibility that no sane person takes lightly.

Generals in time of war are faced daily with innumerable difficult and grave decisions. There are two points of caution, however, that need special emphasis. First, wartime commanders have had to make critical decisions, but seldom were these decisions based upon the kind of information that historians now have available for evaluation. A commander must act upon the facts available at decision time. Second, to one who has never been involved with making high-level decisions, the process looks easy. Those in lower echelons are mostly ignorant of the complexity of the commander's problems and become impatient when they receive a late or an unclear decision. It is easy to criticize but hard to do better if placed at a similar level of responsibility.

There is a third factor in high command decisionmaking. Normally, a wartime commander can select his key staff members, probably the most competent, dedicated, and strong professionals he knows. One cannot take the advice of such people lightly. When they are all opposed to a top general's conclusion, the decisionmaking process becomes far more difficult.

An understanding of the loneliness of command was provided by two Commandants, Thomas Holcomb and Alexander A. Vandegrift, who wrote in his memoir:

> On January 1, 1944, General Holcomb and I together with our families went over to Secretary Knox's office. After reading General Holcomb's retirement orders, including promotion to four stars, he read my appointment as Commandant of the Marine Corps.
>
> Back at Headquarters General Holcomb took his leave. When I accompanied him to the door he placed a hand on my shoulder and smiled. "Vandegrift, when I go out this door, I am placing twenty years on your shoulders and taking them off mine. You won't realize it at first, but you will finally learn what I mean." He nodded as if to confirm his thinking and continued, "You have a good many friends in the Corps. I only hope that when you turn your job over to a successor you have the same number. The Commandant does not make many new friends if he does his job well."
>
> I knew whereof he spoke, for any commander suffers similarly. I remembered an evening in Cuba back in the early thirties during some maneuver. Several of us dined with General Lyman, who afterward introduced the subject of retirement. He asked me where I planned to retire and I told him Charlottesville, Virginia.
>
> "Why there?" he demanded. "You should live in some place like La Jolla where you will be close to your service friends."
> "You are fortunate in having so many friends," I told him. "If upon retirement I have ten real friends I shall consider myself very lucky."
>
> I forgot about the incident until upon my return from the Pacific I dropped in to see him in the San Diego naval hospital. I found him ill and lonely. Reminding me of the evening's conversation in Cuba he said sadly, "How right you were in your estimate of the number of friends a man has after retirement."[1]

Commandant Paul X. Kelley revealed the emotion involved in decisionmaking:

> Unless a commander is human, he cannot understand the reactions of his men. If he is human, the pressure on him intensifies tremendously. The callous man has no mental struggle over jeopardizing the lives of 10,000 men; the human commander cannot avoid this struggle. It is constant and wearing, and yet necessary, for the men can sense the commander's difficulty. There are many ways in which he can show his interest in them and they respond, once they believe it is real. Then you get mutual confidence, the basis of real discipline.[2]

Commandant Carl E. Mundy addressed loneliness in his oral history: "The influences as Commandant, again, because of the loneliness of the position, and I do not mean that in a personal manner, but indeed, it is . . . you know, it is standing on top of the pyramid, and people who were your most confidential friends the day before you became the Commandant now call you 'Sir,' and you have assumed a different mantle. And I do not mean that they abandon you, but you have to work hard to make sure that people . . . do not become awed of what they think you are now and lose sight of the fact that you are not really any different than you were the day before you became the Commandant."[3]

But decisions have to be made all up and down the chain of command. How do you train Marines to make decisions in combat? Commandant Krulak addressed this: "If you're going to think in a chaotic battlefield, if you're going to have a strategic corporal, you're going to need to be able to make decisions almost instantaneously. We were looking for people who make instantaneous decisions that are of value where each decision has an impact. We started looking and the answer came up, the stock market. Traders have to make decisions. They may not be life and death, but they certainly are of value. How do the successful ones make the decision? How do they know when to decide? The only way to find that out was to go up and ask them; to try to get into their mindset and see whether there's any applicability to the Marine Corps.

"Well, what we found out is that successful traders basically saw fluctuations in prices and in the market in an almost cognitive thinking. They see and understand patterns. They've seen it so often, that when it gets to a point where they know what's happening, then they make their decision.

It's based on a pattern of recognition. Being able to sit back and say yes, I haven't seen this exact thing before, but I've certainly seen the pattern of it. That's the way that stock traders do it. They're in the pit, they're yelling and screaming, and they're doing it based on a sensing. The flip side of that for the military is that you can't always get into combat, so how are you going to prepare for it? Well, that drove the gaming that we're doing. For example, the squad leader, combat squad leader, you put them into scenarios time after time after time. They work their way through those scenarios, and sooner or later they become very effective.

"Why? Not because they know how to do each individual action but because they'd seen something like that before and can make a decision. That's why you find the team leader or the patrol leader in his eighth month in Vietnam far more effective than the one in the first month. Why? Because he's more experienced, he's seen more, and he can make instantaneous decisions at the right time based on not necessarily that exact event that's taking place, but on the pattern of that event. You don't have to go through the firefight to learn. You can learn through multiple training exercises that have to do with different types of firefights so that when you get to the real one you may not know the exact answer but you come pretty darn close because you've trained in so many scenarios. . . . this idea of trying to put them in multiple situations so that when the real one comes they'll at least have had some experience akin to what they are experiencing in combat.

"Decisionmakers are all up and down the line, from a private all the way up. A Marine makes decisions and some of them are important decisions. Everybody is a decisionmaker. Not everybody makes all decisions, but they have to make some decisions and the more experience you get in making decisions, the more capable you become at making decisions. So it's possible and frequently true in a bureaucracy that no decisions are made at lower levels because they aren't competent and they never become competent because they aren't permitted to make decisions, and so when . . . they are promoted to upper levels they aren't used to making decisions. So, after a while, in the upper levels they don't make decisions either because they're no longer competent to do so. And soon nobody can make decisions really, except the top man. This is what happens with centralized control. It's fatal in any military service because there always comes a time when the man on the spot, whoever he happens to be, whether he's a private, NCO, or flag officer, when the man on the spot is confronted with a situation in which he's got to make a decision. He's got to know he's got to make a decision. He's got to realize that it is a decisionmaking point and it goes through his mind in about half a second. So he's got to make a decision as best he can, qualified or not, he's got to make it, so he does. If he can't do it, then it's got to be made topside, some place up the line.

"More likely the situation will get out of hand right quickly. This is why you should have decisions made at the lowest possible level, nearly always. There are some decisions that should be reserved for the higher levels, but those should be known in advance. When a Marine is in the field, he's got a lot of decisions to make. Some of them are minor, but every once [in] a while one becomes very important and he might feel unqualified, he doesn't know quite what to do, but he's got to do something very fast. He can't wait for someone more senior, he must take action quickly. If he makes a decision not to make a decision, but calls on someone more senior, it can frequently be the wrong thing to do, where in the little time that he did have he could have saved the situation but he didn't, because he made the decision not to take the responsibility for it.

"A leader should push authority down. It's hard to do because lots of times I felt I could make a better decision than some of my subordinates. You might know the subject better, have had more experience, but not have the time to follow through, didn't know the detailed situation as well, and so the net result [was] you should try to keep as many decisions at the lowest levels possible. You will think if you had been in a subordinate's job, you could do a better job than the man who was there could do it. But, you weren't in that job and couldn't take over his job, and if you started to make decisions for a subordinate he or she would never improve. A subordinate would never be able to make good decisions if he kept bucking them up. You have to get rid of people who could not make decisions in their jobs, because you don't have time to make their decisions for them."[4]

Commandant Mundy commented on passing decisions down: "It is the difficulty of not making every decision yourself. Now, indeed we profess from the earliest stages of our leadership training to delegate responsibility, delegate authority, let the subordinates act, take responsibility for what they do but don't get in their way in trying to tell them specifically what to do. That is all good philosophy and it is all good in practice but indeed it is difficult to sit still and let others do it.

"In my case, when we get to reflecting on the past four years, to sit as the Commandant and to say, 'Ron, General Christmas runs Manpower for the Marine Corps,' and then you read an ALMAR that comes out and you say, 'Gosh, I don't know whether we should have done this or not, but then the lieutenant general leading Manpower for the Marine Corps did so let me turn my head and focus on something else.'

"Rarely do those come back to bite you, sometimes and I guess we will probably have the occasion to talk about at least one here later on. But for the most part you just have to adjust to realizing that you cannot make every decision in the Marine Corps. You have good people around you, let them run it."[5]

Commandant Krulak provided his thinking on tough decisions: "I'm an intuitive, feeling type of an individual and I have trouble in giving bad news. I have a difficult time saying to somebody, 'You're not doing what I want you to do,' or 'It's time for you to retire.' Those things are very difficult for me. An advisor said to me, 'Listen, you've got to quit thinking about yourself as an individual or even as the Commandant.' She said, 'You're the institution. When you take a stiff action against somebody, divorce yourself from saying it's you doing it. It isn't you, it's the institution. If you think of yourself as the institution, you'll always be able to do the right thing and it will be less painful than if you take it on as an individual act.' She turned out to be very sanguine in that area, because later on in my commandancy, I had to ask several general officers to leave the Marine Corps for numerous reasons, some of them because they didn't do the job or they did something they shouldn't have done. It became easier, because when I did it, I did it with the institution in mind and not thinking as an individual. She was very valuable."[6]

Risk is a significant factor in decisionmaking. General Ray Davis commented: "Well, risk taking is subject to a lot of definitions. As far as boldness is concerned and decisive action, there was never any question in my mind. If it was time to commit all of your forces with a minimum reserve in order to win a decisive battle, there was no hesitation. I guess the same thing applies a lot in peacetime. I was involved a great deal in the education and development effort in the Marine Corps. The bold ideas just had great appeal to me. Any boldness, of course, I guess by definition, involves some risk. Very many times there's not too much difference between receiving the medal and getting court-martialed. If you succeed you get a medal, if you lose you get court-martialed—that kind of attitude among many people."[7]

While a leader must carefully absorb all that he can before making a decision, he cannot procrastinate. Major General Lejeune, while commanding the 2[d] Division in France during World War I, described his plan for the St. Mihiel attack:

> This was the procedure followed in preparing the tentative plan of attack and the order for the battle of St. Mihiel, and for

other battles in which ample time was available. When the available time was short, it meant sleepless, hectic, and nerve-racking nights for the Division Commander and his staff in which hours seemed no longer than minutes and the hands flew around the face of the watch, for the element of time was then of crucial importance. In war, procrastination is a crime, and promptness is a handmaiden of victory.[8]

Similarly, Commandant Barrow said, "I have long believed that once a decision is made to do something, and you have a clear understanding of it, have done all the preliminary things to make it possible, then you must move out. . . . quick execution, move out. Rapidity of movement is almost like another principle of war." He has a caveat if there could be excessive casualties when carrying out a combat mission; then "there's some room for your judgment. . . . I will do what I think is best. If I'm right, it's going to be great. If I'm wrong, I'll pay the consequences."[9]

Three key case studies illustrate the critical decisions that reflect the character and leadership of Marine Corps senior officers: the development and implementation of amphibious warfare doctrine; the firing of U.S. Army division commander Major General Ralph Smith by Lieutenant General Holland M. Smith, USMC; and the development and acquisition of the MV–22 Osprey aircraft.

## Development and Implementation of Amphibious Warfare Doctrine

In 1915, British and Allied forces suffered a disastrous failure during the Gallipoli campaign, an amphibious operation by the British Navy to land a military force from the sea into Turkey, which was then allied with Germany. Its mission was to break the stalemate of trench warfare in Europe. This failure at Gallipoli established the conventional postwar wisdom that amphibious operations were difficult, if not impossible.

In *The U.S. Marines and Amphibious War: Its Theory and Its Practice in the Pacific*, Jeter A. Isely and Philip A. Crowl stated:

> In the first years of this century, technological improvements apparently strengthened the defender more than the attacker; this was most strongly felt in the fields of gunnery and airpower. It was believed that offshore mines, torpedoes, and land-based weapons would prevent naval gunfire support for the troops engaged in getting ashore.

The prominent British military historian B.H. Liddell Hart concurred with this observation, writing:

> A landing on a foreign coast in face of hostile troops has always been one of the most difficult operations of war. It has now become much more difficult, indeed almost impossible, because of the vulnerable target which a convoy of transports offers to the defender's air force as it approaches the shore. Even more vulnerable to air attack is the process of disembarkation in open boats.[10]

Why did the Gallipoli invasion fail? The reasons for its failure are important in the development of the Marine Corps amphibious warfare doctrine and implementation.

The British conducted the amphibious landing in the Gallipoli Peninsula of Turkey in the Dardanelles, with the mission of getting Turkey out of the war. It was a disastrous failure, but one in which the U.S. Marine Corps learned the importance of amphibious doctrine and implementation. "The British fiasco at Gallipoli," wrote Liddell Hart, "in 1915 seemed to confirm such fears, and many military writers concluded that crossing a hostile beach was no longer feasible." Alexander Kiralfy contended that the industrial revolution had given any guardian of the continent of Europe both superior defensive weapons and high land mobility. These would prevent operations against the coasts of Europe, and therefore that continent could best be entered by striking through the relatively backward areas of Asia. Liddell Hart was convinced that the great mobility and flexibility of airpower had weighted the scales heavily in favor of the defender.[11]

According to some scholars, the Gallipoli campaign failed for a number of reasons: debilitating errors in the poor overall planning and command; great confusion among the staff and soldiers who were to implement the plans (General Sir Dan Hamilton, the British Army Commander, did not keep his subordinates properly informed); inadequate planning for care and transport of the wounded (medical care was performed, not in the field of combat, but by the Royal Navy on board ships that proved to be inadequate for the proper care); inadequate plans for replacement troops; poor selection of the best landing beaches; loss of surprise through careless handling of the secrecy of the operation; the inexperience of the Allied troops in amphibious warfare; the failure to appreciate the adverse impact of the advice provided by some very able German generals on preparing the defense of the Gallipoli Peninsula;

lack of aggressiveness of certain Allied commanders, who lacked direct involvement in the frontline; ineffective naval gunfire support during the amphibious landing; and inadequate field artillery before landing and during the campaign.

A general sense of superiority was so prevalent at all levels within the Allied force from the high command down to the individual soldier that the Turks were simply written off as adversaries who were not up to the fighting prowess of the British, Australian, and New Zealand forces. The attitude of the British military leadership was one of overconfidence bordering on arrogance; the Allies vastly underestimated the fighting ability of the Turk forces. The Turks they faced at Gallipoli were the best trained and best led infantry divisions in the Ottoman Army; indeed, the Allies were up against the cream of the Turkish Army, which was able to fight the Allies on the grounds of its own choosing. The Turks sent their best troops, and it showed. In addition, the Turks had been working on the defense of the peninsula for over 30 years.

A significant factor was that the generation of senior British commanders responsible for the Gallipoli campaign were ill prepared and poorly trained to take the initiative, and some were unsuited for high command.

There were considerable failures in communications: messages were lost, misdirected, unclear, or misworded, and thus not understood. These mistakes on several occasions lost the taking of advantage or tactical opportunities. The landing on a beach designated "Y," for example, was comparably unopposed, but the opportunity to exploit this was lost because each of the two senior officers present considered that he was commanding officer, and they argued between themselves about what to do; thus, landing forces were left to stagnate while the arguing went on between the two.

There was widespread confusion because before the invasion was launched, the Allied army was scattered all over the Mediterranean; battalions were divided, transportation wagons were separated from their horses, guns separated from the ammunition, and artillery shells from their fuses. As the campaign unfolded, there was not enough ammunition, food, water, and appropriate clothing for the weather encountered.

One of the most significant errors was not understanding the need for air support for the landing force. British Army Commander General Sir Ian Hamilton requested air support from air commander Kitchener, who refused. Thus, there was no aerial bombing and no reconnaissance of the beaches for the landing forces that had to rely on field artillery for protection after the landing.

In the Gallipoli campaign, no one commander had the overall authority to accomplish the mission. Historian Robert Rhodes James in his study of the campaign pointed out that:

> Hamilton [the Allied troop commander] assumed that the operations to be undertaken by his Army were to be in conjunction with naval assault on the Dardanelles (a joint operation): deRobeck, the British naval commander, however, had made up his mind that his ships would not attack the forts until the Army occupied the Gallipoli Peninsula. Essentially this meant the senior Naval Commander was not going to pursue his primary mission any further, until the Army campaign for Gallipoli was won. Rarely was there complete accord between naval and army commanders on each of their respective duties and powers or who was in command of the overall operation over whom, when and where.

There was a monumental failure in intelligence gathering and dissemination by the British. Most significantly, the Allies did not consult a 2-year intelligence study by the British attaché to Turkey, Lieutenant Colonel Frederick Cunliffe-Owen. There was inadequate security about the campaign. Prior to the invasion, the British forces were getting mail from all over the Mediterranean that was addressed to the doctrinal: that is, the fact that the basic amphibious doctrines that carried Allied troops over every beachhead of World War II had been largely shaped—often in the face of uninterested or doubting military orthodoxy—by U.S. Marines, and mainly between 1922 and 1935.[12]

British historian and Major General John F.C. Fuller wrote: "The most important contribution of the United States Marines to the history of modern warfare rests in their having perfected the doctrine and techniques of amphibious warfare to such a degree as to be able to cross and secure a very energetically defended beach." It was this aspect of amphibious development that led Fuller, a brilliant and iconoclastic historian of that time, to conclude "that amphibious warfare had been 'revolutionized' by what was in all probability . . . the most far-reaching tactical innovation of the war."[13]

Lieutenant General Victor H. Krulak's book, *First to Fight: An Inside View of the U.S. Marine Corps*, is the best single text ever written by one who lived it as he did to provide an insight into the development and implementation of amphibious warfare doctrine. He followed the careers of visionary Marine Corps leaders who made significant contributions to the development of the doctrine, the training of the forces, and implementation in carrying out the doctrine in combat. General Krulak was perhaps the most important Marine assisting General Holland M. Smith, the preeminent contributor to the development of amphibious warfare doctrine, training the forces, securing the needed equipment, and leading them into combat in World War II.

There was considerable skepticism about whether there could ever be successful amphibious landings; mines, torpedoes, artillery placed behind pillboxes, and airpower were all barriers to prevent landing craft, troops, supplies, and weapons reaching shore.

Not all Marines were willing to accept that amphibious operations were impossible as portrayed by some military historians. The British mistakes in the Gallipoli campaign proved a gold mine of lessons for the Marine Corps in developing amphibious doctrine, and in a certain sense they learned the easy way—from someone else's war and mistakes.

A few of the Marine Corps leaders between the wars did not accept that amphibious landings were impossible. In *First to Fight*, Lieutenant General Krulak shed some light on those visionaries, what they learned, and how they passed lessons on to the Corps:

> After Gallipoli, the amphibious assault, never taken too seriously, was largely discounted. Offshore mines, beach obstacles, heavy artillery in fortified emplacements, integrated air defense, aircraft for both observation and attack were all seen as favoring the defense, making such an assault 'difficult, indeed almost impossible.'
>
> It is at this point that the Marine Corps entered the historical scene. In truth, however, both before and after Gallipoli only a very few Marines were convinced of the feasibility of amphibious assault operations or even interested in them—until the 1920s, there was no real institutional dedication in the Corps to the idea of an assault landing attack against organized defenses.

In Krulak's opinion, a minority of Marines were interested in seeing the Corps involved in the establishment and defense of naval base facilities overseas, a wholly defensive mission related to the needs of the U.S. Fleet. Many more of the senior leaders considered that their role was primarily expeditionary duty as colonial infantry—Haiti, China, Santo Domingo, Nicaragua—and they remained so oriented. Others who were convinced before World War I that the Corps' future lay primarily in service aboard ship and at naval stations favored expanding that important relationship with the Navy. Krulak continued:

> Only a few, a very few, visionaries were willing to attack the formidable conceptual, tactical, and material problems associated with the modern amphibious assault landing: how to get heavy equipment and weapons ashore through surf and across reefs: how to exercise command authority during the sensitive transition period; how to communicate effectively with ships and aircraft; how to cope with mines and beach obstacles; how to provide accurate, timely, and concentrated fire support for the assault forces; how to ensure that essential supplies were delivered ashore where and when needed; how to manage the evacuation of casualties seaward; and how to persuade the Navy to share its very limited resources in solving these problems. There was a hard core of Marines, who saw a future, despite the problems, for amphibious assault. They were resolute men, true pioneers. By no means military intellectuals in the image of Sun Tzu, Frederick the Great, Jomini, or Mahan, they were nevertheless capable of seeing the close relationship between the total exercise of sea power and the narrow issue of seizing a lodgment on a hostile shore against sophisticated opposition.[14]

One of the strongest and earliest supporters of the importance of amphibious warfare was General John A. Lejeune. He was a fighter for what he believed in for the Corps, a skilled diplomat in the Washington scene, and an in-depth military thinker. Because of his stature as Commandant and the respect he had within the military, his vision had a force that impacted the Marine Corps. Lejeune perceived the necessity of securing bases in the Pacific. He was disappointed, however, with the failure of Commandants Charles Heywood (1891–1903) and George Elliott (1903–1910) to grasp the relationship between the global needs of the Navy and the creation and defense of overseas naval bases. Their view, he believed, was that the century-old Marine Corps role of providing ships' guards and security for naval stations should still be foremost, that to commit Marine resources to advanced base force duty was an imprudent diffusion of effort. That group simply did not have the vision of the Marine Corps' future. In other words, they were the proponents of a retrospective philosophy that went back 100 years. Lejeune saw the Navy's need for advanced bases for coal and other logistical purposes as a cardinal factor in preparing to face the challenge of an imperialist Japan, and he was determined to get the Marines involved. He realized further that some day, somebody might have the unenviable task of capturing those logistics bases from a well-prepared enemy and defending them once captured. What would be a more logical organization to do the job than the Marines, with their traditional maritime orientation? World War II in the Pacific validated his vision.

In a 1915 lecture at the Naval War College, Lejeune told students that the ability not just to defend but also to seize those bases was a logical and critical Marine function in light of the Navy's growing strategic responsibilities. He saw the Corps as the first to set foot on hostile soil in order to seize, fortify, and hold a base. When he became Commandant, he stated clearly, "The maintenance, equipping, and training of its expeditionary force so that it will be in instant readiness to support the Fleet in time of war I deem to be . . . the most important Marine Corps duty in time of peace." He emphasized the importance and cooperation in working with the Navy in the seizure and defense of bases in the event of war.

In a 1923 article for the *Marine Corps Gazette* entitled "Peace Time Duties and War Time Mission in the Marine Corps," Lejeune wrote, "I have coupled these two together because in peace we must so construct our machine that it will function economically and efficiently when it is required to carry out the purpose for which it was created." The Marine Corps mission was succinctly stated in Lejeune's article:

> To support the United States Fleet and to aid the Navy in carrying out that part of the policy of the government which has been or may be assigned to it. In carrying out this mission, the Marine Corps is called on for the performance of many and varied duties. These may be classified as follows: (a) Detachments to guard and protect navy yards, naval bases, and other naval utilities, at home and abroad; (b) Guards for American legations in foreign countries, such guards being under the jurisdiction of the flag officer in command of the naval forces on the station; (c) Landing forces to protect American lives, rights and interests; (d) Forces of occupation to restore order and to maintain peace and tranquility in disturbed countries, as, for instance, Haiti and Santo Domingo; (e) Detachments for

Marine Corps administrative purposes, such as the recruiting service training stations, supply depots, etc.; (f) Aviation; (g) Marine Detachments for service on board the vessels of the Fleet; (h) Expeditionary forces for service with the Fleet in war.

It is not necessary to discuss all of these duties, and I will confine myself chiefly to the major war mission of the Marine Corps, which is to support the Fleet by supplying it with a highly trained, fully equipped expeditionary force for the minor shore operations which are necessary for the effective prosecution by the fleet of its major mission, which is to gain control of the sea and thereby open the sea lanes for the movement of the army overseas. These minor shore operations are numerous and varied in their nature. Probably the most important are the seizure and defense of temporary or advanced naval bases in the theatre of operations.

The training of an expeditionary force must be carried out so as to prepare the force to exercise a dual function: that of seizing a base and that of defending the base after seizure until relieved by the Army when the lines of communication have been made secure. The basic training embraces practical experience with the arms and equipment of the force and a study of the manner of its best employment. This should be followed and supplemented by actual experience with the fleet and actual embarkation and disembarkation under conditions as near actual war conditions as possible. This enables us to learn by experience how to handle our equipment and at the same time gives the Navy an opportunity to become familiar with the needs of the expeditionary force.

It must be understood that the Marine Expeditionary Force is as much an integral part of the Fleet as any other fighting unit and that all impedimenta, supplies, etc., must be transported by the Navy. Expeditionary forces should be considered as an integral part of the fighting line, and its equipment, material and personnel should be maintained in the same efficient condition as the component parts of the Fleet.

Cooperation between the landing force and the ships supporting must be complete. The responsibility in any campaign or adventure rests in its last analysis with the officer who commands, but his decision should be the result of mutual agreement with his subordinates rather than a compromise. History relates that the success of combined operations has often been jeopardized by the lack of unity of command. No such contingency can arise when the landing force consists of Marines, for we are part and parcel of the naval service—an integral part. A complete understanding of the respective missions of the Navy and the Marine Corps, and a familiarity with the respective functions of each organization, is bound to be conducive to best results. It is reasonable, for instance, to assume that an officer whose special training has been along certain defined military lines is better fitted for command on any duty coming within this category than one whose experience along the same line is not so extensive.

The seizure and occupation or distraction of enemy bases is another important function of the expeditionary force. On both flanks of a fleet crossing the Pacific are numerous islands suitable for utilization by an enemy for radio stations, aviation, submarine, or destroyer bases, etc. All should be mopped up as progress is made. Furthermore, the presence of an expeditionary force with the fleet would add greatly to the striking power of the Commander-in-Chief of the fleet.

One of the greatest disasters in history was the failure of the Gallipoli campaign in the World War. How different the result would probably have been if the British Mediterranean Fleet had been accompanied by an adequate expeditionary force when its first attack was made. By utilizing the principle of surprise it would have been comparatively easy to have seized the fortifications on Gallipoli Peninsula and then to have proceeded to clear the straits of mines, thereby permitting the fleet to enter the Golden Horn, to open sea communications with Russia, and to isolate all of Asiatic Turkey from contact with Bulgaria and the Central Powers.

The maintenance, equipping, and training of its expeditionary force so it will be in instant readiness to support the Fleet in the event of war, I deem to be the most important Marine

Corps duty in time of peace. It is with this end in view that this force has been concentrated, that it has held field exercises annually, that it is to take part in the winter maneuvers of the Fleet in the West Indies, and that the military and annual instruction of the officers of the Marine Corps has been developed and intensified even at the expense of some of its other activities.[15]

As a more junior officer, Vandegrift reported to Quantico in 1923 and described it as a "beehive" of activity:

Thanks to John A. Lejeune, Commandant since 1920, it housed the flourishing Marine Corps Schools consisting of a Field Officers Course, a Company Officers Course, and a Basic Course. In addition to teaching standard curriculums, instructors were worrying about the problems of what years later would be called the amphibious assault.

Lejeune's interest in amphibious development stemmed in part from the Versailles Treaty, which mandated the formerly held German islands in the Pacific to Japan. Both Navy and Marine planners now began to think in terms of a Pacific war against Japan. In 1921 one of Lejeune's most brilliant planners, Lieutenant Colonel Earl ("Pete") Ellis, wrote a remarkable 30,000-word thesis on the subject, which presciently began: "Japan is a World Power and her army and navy will doubtless be up to date as to training and material. Considering our consistent policy of nonaggression, she will probably initiate the war; which will indicate that, in her own mind, she believes that, considering her natural defensive position, she has sufficient military strength to defeat our fleet."[16]

A contemporary of Pete Ellis was Dion Williams, an 1881 Naval Academy graduate, who had been thinking about the amphibious problems since the turn of the century and who saw the horizons that would open up for the Corps were it to become the Nation's principal overseas expeditionary force. Because he believed strongly in the amphibious mission as supported by Ellis and Lejeune, Williams decided in 1923 while stationed at Quantico to prepare his unit (4th Marine Brigade) as an assault force, and because the senior Corps leaders were not that high on that mission, did so, according to Krulak, "at no small hazard to his own professional career."[17]

Williams lectured extensively to his troops on the history of amphibious warfare and had his troops practice actual landings on the Potomac River. He was in charge of the Fleet Exercise held in 1923–1924 on the island of Culebra in the West Indies.[18] The techniques used were those taught by Williams, and the commander of the landing was Brigadier General Eli Kelley Cole, who believed in Russell's strong advocacy of the amphibious mission for the Marine Corps. He was intensely interested in what went wrong in Gallipoli and why. The Cole force was composed of 1,781 men, and Williams, who commanded the defense, had about 1,600 men. It was a small operation, but a larger one than ever before taken by our country in peacetime.[19]

It did not go well, and General Cole was very displeased. He commented that "chaos reigned," with many of the same small mistakes made as had been made at Gallipoli. It was wrong to attempt the landing before dawn; there were insufficient boats to do the job; boat officers had not been informed of the designated landing beaches; no order was maintained among the boats carrying the landings made on the wrong beaches; the simulated naval bombardment would practically make no damages to artillery positions; the troop transports were badly loaded; there was no food for the first night; and medical stores had been stowed at the bottom of the holds and were almost completely inaccessible when needed.[20]

Thus, little progress seemed to have been made since 1915; what was learned "went practically unheeded until the 1930s."[21]

Another visionary of the Marine Corps mission in amphibious warfare was Colonel Robert H. Dunlap, who made a significant contribution with an article he published in the *Marine Corps Gazette* in September 1921, entitled "Lessons for the Marines from the Gallipoli Campaign." In his in-depth study of the campaign, he foresaw the future role of amphibious operations for the Marine Corps in World War II:

> The World War has unquestionably opened the eyes of the average soldier to the necessity for a detailed study of all matter pertaining to the planning of campaigns. This involves not only training methods essential to the production of a well-disciplined soldier, able to shoot a rifle with accuracy, but to the production of an organized body of soldiers capable of prosecuting the various phases of a campaign in a manner only possible where the lessons of like phases have been carefully studied, absorbed and applied in training.

This training should be designed to execute the plans against the most formidable of possible enemies and such training will also prepare us to meet enemies of lesser military strength, intelligence and morale. The Marine Corps is designated as that force which must accompany the Fleet in its advance into hostile waters, and there seize and hold a base or to prevent its possible use by the enemy.

It follows, therefore, in the preliminary phases of any campaign, excepting that of a purely defensive role; the Marine Corps must be trained and equipped for landing on hostile shores, often on open beaches and resist serious opposition.[22]

Dunlap summarized the problems the Marine Corps would confront in a war with a naval power: careful staff work in coordination with Army and naval staff officers to conduct landings on open beaches under fire; the need to plan for a continued supply by many of the forces landed; plans for the evacuation of the wounded; close coordination of naval gunfire with the movement of Marine forces once landed; the importance of following the gunfire with troops on the ground; weather conditions and tides; and proper loading of materials on ship (essentials are on top and in order of need).[23]

Dunlap developed a remarkable series of lectures propounding the idea that Gallipoli need not have been a disaster. He invited, but did not order, his officers to attend his Gallipoli lectures. Because of opposition to amphibious warfare, he delivered the talks in the post chapel at Quantico during the noon hour so that those leaders who still had little use for amphibious operations—led mainly by the base commander, Smedley Butler—could not criticize him for diverting his officers from their regular duties for frivolous purposes. Yet that was exactly the criticism leveled against him, giving further evidence of the deep schisms that existed among the Lejeune/Russell school of amphibious thought and those who still held, with former commandants Major General Charles Heywood and George Elliott, that the Marines' future lay in ships' detachments, and still others like Butler, who wanted an independent Marine Corps of colonial infantry, unfettered by the Navy. Cole's research was excellent, but his character in his fight, putting his career at risk, for amphibious doctrine warfare set him apart, particularly on how to proceed against the anti-amphibious group.[24]

Cole summarized the essence of his lectures in an article published in 1929 entitled "Joint Overseas Operations." Because of his vision, the long-range impact, and the audience he reached, the article merits quoting in some detail:

> In the event of a war in which our country is a belligerent, one of the most important duties of our naval service will be placing on hostile territory of military forces, and as the outcome of the war may well depend upon the efficiency with which such overseas operations are carried out, it is vitally necessary that the naval service have a thorough knowledge of the methods whereby unity of command and of effort are to be secured, of the duties it will be called upon to carry out in such operations, and a thorough appreciation of the difficulties of the operations. In order that the scope of the subject may be understood, the following definition of an overseas expedition is advanced: The movement overseas, including the embarkation at port of departure and debarkation at place of landing, under convoy and support of naval forces, of a military force having for its mission the seizure of a position on hostile territory from which further offensive operations may be undertaken.
>
> This definition is exact enough for the purpose, as under it there may be included operations incident to the advance overseas of our fleet, as well as operations involving a major effort, both military and naval, culminating in an invasion of enemy country.
>
> The geographic location of the United States, between two oceans, is such that in the event of a major war, for us to take the full offensive will require, with two exceptions in part, overseas expeditions.
>
> Amongst other requirements, the general naval policy is "to make war efficiency the object of all training and to maintain that efficiency during the entire period of peace;" "to develop and to organize the Navy for operations in any part of either ocean;" and "to maintain a Marine Corps of such strength that it will be able to adequately support the Navy . . . by the maintenance in readiness of an expeditionary force." The major war mission of the Marine Corps is to support the fleet by supplying it with a highly trained, fully equipped expeditionary force

for the minor shore operations which are necessary for the effective prosecution by the fleet of its major mission, which is to gain control of the seas.

If during the course of the naval campaign on the high seas the operations have to be carried on at a distance from home yards and bases, it will probably be necessary to seize and to occupy temporary bases from which the fleet can operate against the enemy fleet unhampered by a large train and to which the fighting ships can go to refuel, revictual, effect minor repairs, and, especially in the case of smaller craft such as destroyers and submarines, obtain necessary rest and recuperation for the crews. The establishment and maintenance of the shore defenses of such naval advanced bases is a war-time function of the Marine Corps, and requires that its forces be organized, equipped, and trained, ready to meet the contingency whenever it shall arise. Furthermore, the forces organized and trained for these duties must be ready to move with the fleet whenever the latter leaves its home bases for war-time service overseas.

The Navy will be ready before the Army, but as no military expedition will leave the shores of the United States until command of the sea has been gained by our naval forces, the naval service will have ample scope for its energy during the period concerned in searching out the enemy fleet and in establishing the necessary bases.

There is no operation in war that requires for its successful conclusion more thorough study, more careful planning, more complete preparation, more detailed staff work and more skillful execution on the part of all concerned, than does the seizure by a military force of a beach head on a hostile coast. Joint overseas operations may be divided into four main parts:

> (a) The preparation in home territory of the forces concerned, including plans of operation, mobilization, training, concentration of troops, ships, and supplies at ports of embarkation.

(b) The march overseas (in transports) including embarkation of troops and supplies in accordance with the tactical plan adopted for the landing.

(c) The debarkation, including the naval preparations therefore, the landing of the troops in tactical formation on the hostile coast, and the naval support during the landing.

(d) The securing of the beach or landing head with the subsequent advance inland up to the limits of naval support, i.e., effective gunfire.

Reasonable preparedness for possible wars includes the preparation of basic war plans, which are founded on thorough studies of the countries concerned, and which in their final form are presumed to have the approval of the chiefs of different executive departments concerned. On this general plan for the conduct of a war are founded the basic plans of the various services and executive departments concerned, and any operating plan must conform thereto; and, in the case of operations involving both military and naval forces, must, in addition, its final form, be in such shape that the specific tasks of, or parts assigned to, the different services are capable of execution, and that those tasks dovetail in and form a harmonious whole.

History shows that one of the most prolific causes for failure in overseas expeditions has been the inability or failure of the naval and military commanders concerned to work together harmoniously.[25]

Cole emphasized that there had to be coordination with the Navy to supply and operate all the needed vessels; to assemble the troops with all their necessary equipment and supplies at the port of embarkation; to load the transports in the ships provided by the Navy, particularly to ensure the loading of the supplies in reverse order of last in, first out; to watch the weather, winds, and tides; and to assist in getting needed medical attention to the wounded.

The Navy, he pointed out, must maintain the sea lines of communication; anticipate and prepare for enemy naval opposition; procure, man, and equip the vessels needed to transport the troops, equipment, and supplies; provide the ports for embarkation and debarkation; provide for the deployment into boats used for landing and operated by the Navy; deliver rifle and machinegun fire from the landing boats; conduct with the landing force operations beyond the beachhead; and cover the landing by minesweeping, gunfire, aircraft, and screening operations.

Then there was the challenge of coordinating with the Navy on the location for the landing; the nature of the beaches, sand, and rock; the tides; understanding that the Navy and landing force commanders will look at the problem of landing from different viewpoints; understanding the vital importance of the ability of the Navy to keep open sea lines of communication after the landing to assure an uninterrupted supply flow, provide, in his article in 1929, a broad outline of the various tasks and forcefully brings to attention the thousands of details involved in the preparation, and necessity that the details are so worked out as to result in a harmonious and successful plan with unity of command among the participating services.[26]

### Contributions of Commandant John H. Russell

General Lejeune had an understanding of the Navy that stemmed from his association with midshipmen in his years at the Naval Academy—friendships that continued with many Naval officers who rose in rank and responsibility as he did, which proved to be of great value to the Corps. His views were also held by Naval Academy graduates George Barnett, who preceded Lejeune as Commandant, and General John H. Russell, who was Commandant from 1934 to 1936.

Krulak commented that Russell "may well have exerted greater influence in rationalizing and regularizing the amphibious assault than any other single individual in the Corps. In 1910 he made the illuminating observation that when the fleet was operating at a distance from permanent bases it should carry with it 'a sufficient force and material for seizing and defending' an advanced base in the theater of operations."

In 1916, in the very first edition of the *Marine Corps Gazette*, Russell made an "eloquent—and almost heretical"—case for both the base defense and amphibious assault tasks as Marine Corps missions. As Assistant Commandant, he persuaded Commandant Ben H. Fuller and Navy leaders in Washington to accept as official his view that the amphibious assault function should be primary Marine Corps business and to adopt his conceptual creation, the Fleet Marine Force, as a Type Command of the Naval Operating Forces.[27]

Russell's most significant contribution was persuading Fuller that a formalized, written body of amphibious doctrine needed to be prepared by the Marines themselves, in great detail, to illustrate that the Marine Corps had a unique capability not shared by any other Service. What was produced because of his vision and drive was a remarkable document, a manual that provided the guidelines for amphibious warfare in World War II in the Pacific and in Europe. Some work had already been done on the subject as early as 1931. Russell's idea was to take these preliminary fragments and mass the total talent of the Marine Corps Schools in Quantico to prepare a manual. In 1933, the Schools at Quantico were made up of a Field Officers' School for majors and lieutenant colonels, some 15 students, and a Company Officers' School, 30 students in the rank of first lieutenant and captain. The study group was composed of 35 officers, staff, and students, who were directed to produce, in a single volume, a full exposure of everything involved in the amphibious assault that in any way affected the landing force. Russell's proposal was carried out. The mission to produce this document was given the highest priority. Marine Corps Schools classes were halted, and the total resources of the institution were directed toward developing the formal doctrine.

The role of the key leaders in accomplishing this project is fascinating. Brigadier General James C. Breckinridge was in charge of the project as Commandant of the officers' school system. But the driving force was Colonel Ellis Bell Miller, another of the unusual Marine Corps leaders. He was commissioned in 1903 and had service in Panama, Mexico, China, and the Philippines. Miller was described as intelligent, intellectual, perceptive, diligent, and thoroughly professional, and had all of the qualifications essential for the "pioneering job." He was demanding, intolerant of any dissent, and impatient with those who could not maintain his pace. "These traits," said Krulak, "may have kept him from advancing beyond the rank of colonel, but did not prevent him from producing a milestone document in the amphibious field."

First, the Marine officers involved in the study were thoroughly oriented on the errors of Gallipoli and given what little information there was on assault landing operations. Then, each one of them was instructed to set down his own thoughts concerning the sequence of events in an amphibious attack, from pre-embarkation through completion of the landing assault. These individual submissions were organized into topical categories by an intermediate committee and further reviewed by a steering committee, headed by Colonel Miller, which then created a chapter outline for the book.

After a critical review by a group of Fleet Marine Force officers, the chapter assignments were farmed out to writing committees, which based the content on the meager practical experience available and, probably more so, on their own reasoning and convictions.

Miller drove the group with apostolic fervor. He set deadlines and was merciless in his criticism. When all this was done, which took 7 months, he had produced a respectable product. He entitled it *Tentative Manual for Landing Operations, 1934*. It was not too well written, it was not handsomely printed, and it was bound with shoestring, but it was a beginning. There were 127,000 words of hard, doctrinal pronouncement on the seizure of an objective by amphibious assault. For the first time, the issues of air and naval gunfire support were addressed in detail. Likewise, principles of transport loading, debarkation procedures, and guidance for the ship-to-shore movement and the management of logistics at the beach line were treated in what still must be regarded as great detail.

But Miller was not content with the first draft of the *Tentative Manual* and was continuously updating, polishing, and refining it. It was accepted enthusiastically by the Fleet Marine Force for use in training, and it was adopted immediately as a tentative text in the Marine Corps Schools for its 1934–1935 term. It was also published by the Navy Department as the Manual for Naval Overseas Operations.

Over the next 2 years, a series of boards at Quantico—notably a group headed by Lieutenant Colonel Charles D. Barrett, "whose scholarly efforts and patient attention to detail resulted in a stronger and much more articulate document"—prepared revisions.

The *Tentative Manual* was groundbreaking work of the best sort, and it was received with enthusiasm in the Navy, which adopted it as official doctrine with minor alterations in 1938 as Fleet Training Publication No. 167, *Landing Operations Doctrine, U.S. Navy*. Three years later, the Army, whose interest in amphibious operations had been minimal, copied the manual lock, stock, and barrel, and published it as Field Manual 31-5. The manual guided the bulk of amphibious training in the immediate pre–World War II training period and governed every amphibious operation during the war.[28]

### Contributions of General Holland M. Smith

Of those visionaries who contributed to the development of amphibious warfare doctrine, it was General Holland M. Smith who was most responsible for the pre–World War II training and who commanded the earlier island invasions in the Pacific.

Holland M. Smith was commissioned in 1905 after graduation from Auburn and the University of Alabama Law School. Smith had followed the then-standard Marine pattern—service in the Philippines (where, incidentally, he led a company in the regiment commanded by Colonel Eli Kelley Cole), Nicaragua, Panama, China, Santo Domingo, and Cuba. Staff assignments in France in World War I were followed by a course at the Naval War College where, for the first time, the vigorous, straight-talking temperament appeared that later earned him the sobriquet "Howling Mad." He advanced his views regarding the importance of amphibious assault operations—and particularly the need for heavy naval gunfire and air support—with such logic and style as to acquire a reputation as a thinker and an eloquent speaker. Later, at the Field Officers' course at the Quantico Marine Corps Schools, he told his superiors that their curriculum was retrospective and gave them hard examples to prove his point. He was renowned as an outspoken pioneer and carried on correspondence with Commandant Russell, whom he admired and who was a strong advocate of amphibious warfare, complaining that war with Japan was clearly approaching and too little was being done in the Marines' amphibious training to meet the inevitable challenge.

Commandant Lemuel C. Shepherd, Jr., commented on Holland Smith: "He fought to establish the Marine Corps on a footing with the Navy, when we were getting pushed around by a staff officer on some naval staff. We are not an entity. We should be able to give orders and tell our troops where to go, what to do.

"I think he did a great deal of good in his fight for the Marine Corps. He was a fighter, with the Marine spirit in him. It was through him largely that we were able to finally establish our proper place in the Naval establishment, especially in the Pacific during World War II. In my opinion Holland Smith is one of the Marine Corps greats. . . . He was harassed terribly by the Army, and constantly fighting with the Navy. Smith fought for the Marine Corps, tooth and nail."[29]

General Smith's important leadership and character were recognized by the awarding of the Distinguished Service Medal, in the name of the President, by the Secretary of the Navy:

> Prior to our entry into the war and up to September 1943, Major General Smith was responsible for the operational training and combat readiness of various units comprising the

amphibious forces. By this capable performance of duty on both coasts of the United States he laid the groundwork for amphibious training of practically all American units, including at various times, the First and Third Marine Divisions, the First, Seventh, and Ninth Infantry Divisions of the Army, and numerous other Marine Corps and Army personnel.

As a brigadier general, Smith commanded the most significant prewar amphibious practice exercises in 1940 and 1941. Much was learned, and the lessons were important for the war in the Pacific in invading the Japanese-held islands. In all of the exercises, the deficiencies were made obvious: not enough navy transports, trucks, tanks, aircrafts, communications, anti-aircraft weapons, ammunition, combat uniforms. His position was that his Marines deserved the best of everything, and he was a very vocal fighter for all these deficiencies. He drove them unmercifully for the war he knew was coming with Japan.

### Lieutenant General Holland M. Smith and CNO Admiral Ernest J. King

In July 1943, Commandant Holcomb informed Smith he was being assigned to command Fifth Amphibious Corps, which had the mission for operating in the Pacific. A member of Holcomb's staff recalled the Commandant telling him: "The reason I am appointing Smith is that there's going to be a lot of trouble with the Navy over rights and prerogatives and such things and Holland is the only one I know who can sit at the table and pound it harder than any naval officer."[30]

An indication of the challenges he had with the senior naval personnel is provided by the contact with three of the key leaders, Chief of Naval Operations Admiral Ernest King, Admiral Raymond A. Spruance, and Vice Admiral Richmond Kelly Turner, who was given the name of "Terrible Turner" because of his strong position on his ideas.

Smith's character and leadership, his vision, his tenacity, his love of the Marines and stature were particularly impressive in his command relationships with Admiral King, who was the senior naval officer in the practice amphibious operation in the Caribbean before and during the early years of World War II in the Pacific. King supervised the exercise, named Fleet Landing Exercise 7, from the battleship *Texas*. Almost immediately, he found himself in conflict with General Holland M. Smith, who would not servilely allow the admiral to treat him in the autocratic fashion that King treated his staff and commanders:

The friction between the general and the admiral was in part about the area of command responsibility. King wanted to make decisions which Smith, always jealous of Marine prerogatives, considered within his own authority as troop commander. King wanted to choose the landing beaches himself and ignore Smith's long experience in amphibious training.

King, with no experience in amphibious operations, even objected to the use of the specialized term "beachhead," and demanded that the Marines use "beach" instead. Only after long and vehement argument, in which he told King that his choice of a landing beach ran counter to everything the junior Marine officers had been taught and would destroy their confidence in the high command, did Smith convince King to give up his idea.

Even after the problem of landing beaches was solved, the general and the admiral continued to grate upon each other. King caustically criticized Smith's tactical dispositions ashore and remarked confidently that he, too, had some military experience. As a student at the Naval Academy, he said, he had commanded a regiment of midshipmen. The general, who had spent thirty-five years in the study of land warfare, made no reply.[31]

By the end of the exercise, the two high officers could hardly treat each other with civility:

> By the time Smith left King's flagship at the close of the operation, he felt sure that he would be relieved of his command. He certainly was not a "yes man." He believed that he had acted properly and had done his job well, but that could have been little consolation. As the exercise ended, Smith was aboard a navy transport and received a letter by special boat from the Texas. His heart sank as he saw that it was from King. Knowing that he could not conceal the blow of his relief from those around him, he withdrew to the privacy of his cabin and opened the letter. King's message read in part: "I wish to express to you . . . my feeling of satisfaction that such well-trained troops, so well-commanded, are an integral part of the Atlantic fleet. . . . Well done!" There was also an obvious appreciation by King for the strength of Smith's

character as well as the vision and unparalleled knowledge of amphibious warfare.

"It was, in many ways," Smith later wrote, "the finest commendation I have ever received." It taught him, he said, that while King might be ruthlessly critical to one's face, he would not strike from behind, and he would recognize competent performance. Smith's troubles with King, however, were not yet at an end.[32]

As commander of Fifth Amphibious Corps, Smith was, along with King and Turner, under Admiral Raymond A. Spruance, Commander of the Fifth Fleet, in the chain of command. Spruance's Chief of Staff, Navy Captain Charles J. Moore, made the comment that Smith resented naval authority and was acutely sensitive to any imagined oversights or discrimination against his beloved Corps and would often overreact when he sensed an affront.

### General Holland M. Smith and Vice Admiral Richmond Kelly Turner

One of the primary failures of the Gallipoli campaign was a lack of unity of command. This had to be coordinated and developed between the Marines and Navy. There were often acrimonious arguments, particularly on when the command responsibility moved from the Navy to the Marine Corps. There was considerable trial and error before the issues were resolved. The primary resolution of command authority was between Vice Admiral Richmond Kelly Turner and Lieutenant General Holland M. Smith. The trouble was that Smith and Turner could not agree upon when control of the troops ashore should pass from the admiral to the general.

Captain Charles J. Moore said: "Holland Smith particularly complained about Kelly Turner. . . . I was trying to soothe him down, and Turner would come and complain about that blankety-blank Smith, couldn't get any cooperation out of him.

"After days of squabbling Moore came up with a solution on the amphibious command responsibility—that the landing force would remain under the control of the Navy commander until the troop commander informed him that he was ready to take command on the beach, with control passing to the Marine landing force commander."[33]

Holland Smith demanded what he thought his due, and believed he was not being properly supported by higher authority. Later, he told his aide that the Commandant told him that anything he could get in tactical command authority was fine, but that headquarters could give him no help. "When I realize how long I have fought all by myself with no help from anyone," he remarked, "I sometimes get disgusted and want to chuck the whole thing." He envisaged himself as single-handedly protecting the Marine Corps from the Navy. As he told his aide: "Nobody will fight the goddamned Navy but me. They don't know how or they haven't got the guts. They are all looking out for themselves. I have to do it all myself, because if I don't the Navy will run over us. (I remember the time when an ensign could spit in a colonel's face and all the colonel could do was laugh and beg his pardon.) The Navy would put their admirals on the beach and have them try to command the troops if they thought they could get away with it. But they know that if they tried I would knock their ears off. I've told them that no admiral would ever give a single order to any troops of mine in the beach and they know I mean business. . . . I told Turner once, 'I don't try to run your ships and you'd better by a goddamn sight lay off of my troops.'"[34]

As with Admiral King, Holland M. Smith's character prevailed in his work with the Navy. In July 1943, it was Turner who recommended to Admiral Nimitz to have Lieutenant General Smith as commander of the Fifth Amphibious Corps just as soon as possible. In October, Turner wrote to Commandant Thomas Holcomb that he had "asked Admiral King to order Holland Smith out here to take command of troops." To allay whatever fears the Commandant might have about placing two such volatile personalities in close proximity, Turner added: "Don't worry about the relationships between Holland Smith and myself. Necessarily, there are personal adjustments to be made, but they will be made, and I think we may be able, together, to start the ball rolling." Yet so stormy was their relationship that 20 years later, Smith obstinately refused to believe that Turner had recommended him until he was shown a copy of this letter.[35]

## Marine Corps-Navy Relations

Throughout the development of amphibious warfare, there is a continuing theme on the importance of the cooperation between the Marine Corps and the Navy. Why was amphibious warfare doctrine developed and coordinated between the Navy and the Marine Corps, rather than the Army? General Lejeune spelled that out as early as 1923 in an article in the *Marine Corps Gazette*:

> Before going to another branch of the subject, I deem it pertinent to add that there is the closest kind of liaison and cooperation

between Marine Corps Headquarters and the Bureaus and Offices of the Navy Department. There is no friction and the machine functions in high gear without any serious jolts or jars. We are working, so far as our abilities permit, for the welfare and upbuilding of the entire naval establishment and not in the interest of any clique or faction.[36]

In an article he published in the Naval Institute *Proceedings* in 1925, Lejeune continued to emphasize Navy-Marine Corps relations:

for a more complete and thorough coordination and cooperation between the fleet and the Marine Corps Expeditionary Forces, a coordination that can only be effected, if we are to secure the desired results, by frequent exercises of these forces on overseas maneuvers with the fleet. In order that such cooperation in plans and training and actual operations may secure the desired results it is necessary that every Marine from the general to the private must feel that he is of the Navy and in the Navy, and likewise that everyone in the Navy from the four-star admiral to the man before the mast must feel that the Marine is a part of the personnel of the fleet with a definite and clear-cut line of duties to perform in the general scheme of naval operations in peace and war.[37]

Major General Eli K. Cole, in an article in the *Marine Corps Gazette* entitled "Joint Overseas Operations," wrote:

History shows that one of the most prolific causes of failure in overseas expeditions has been the inability or failure of the naval and military commanders concerned to work together harmoniously. One thing that should be brought out is the absolute dependence of our overseas expeditions upon sea power.

The Marines are the logical solution of the problem presented for the personnel of the advance base forces. They are throughout their existence trained with the Navy. All except the new recruits have at one time or another served on naval vessels. They are well acquainted with the Navy methods and principles, an acquaintance acquired through experience. They have close and intimate acquaintance with the Navy personnel and are familiar with the Navy organization and methods of procedure. They have been accustomed during their military life to unity of control, and are able to fit easily and readily into the naval organization.[38]

Commandant Vandegrift concurred with General Lejeune on the importance of coordination between the Marine Corps and the Navy:

> I tried to explain the fantastic tactical demands levied by the amphibious assault and why we were able to meet them so effectively. To emphasize my statements I even penetrated the curtain of the future—as it turned out quite accurately: "Amphibious operations are highly specialized. Amid all the other requirements for employment of the peacetime forces under conditions of shortage of funds and personnel, only a specialized organization, closely integrated with the Navy, can be expected to continue efficient training and development in that type of operation after the war. In time of peace, the Fleet Marine Force would continue to be a laboratory for field tests of new equipment and for development of ideas on amphibious tactics, technique and material. In the event of another war requiring early employment if amphibious forces, the necessary striking force would be at hand, organized, equipped and trained."[39]

Lieutenant General Victor H. Krulak wrote in *First to Fight*:

> There is little that will sober a defender more surely than the knowledge that somewhere over the horizon lines a force of well-trained, well-equipped Marines in competently manned ships capable of delivering a stunning amphibious blow at a point and time of their own choosing. For the Marines, the maritime nature of the globe creates at once a grave responsibility and an elegant opportunity, and it makes a powerful statement of a truth the Corps must never, never forget: their future, as has their past, lies with the Navy.[40]

Colonel Rufus H. Lane published an article in the *Marine Corps Gazette* in 1923 entitled "The Mission and Doctrine of the Marine Corps," in which he emphasized that:

> there are no special troops of the Army that have the necessary training or knowledge of the operations in connection with the fleet, which are highly technical and complicated. The

troops engaged in them must operate from the sea itself and are during a large proportion of their time actually embarked on the sea. In order to discharge these functions, the troops must have a great deal of very careful and arduous training with the Navy itself if the best results are to be obtained. The officers and enlisted men of the Army have no opportunity for learning the methods of the Navy or of becoming intimately acquainted with its personnel. . . . Another consideration in regard to the employment of the Army for this purpose is the one of control. In a combined expedition of the kind under consideration, the employment of the Army would involve cooperation of organizations responsible to different departments, independent of each other. While elaborate attempts have been made by joint Army and Navy boards to establish rules governing the determination of control in cases of combined operations, no great success has yet been attained. . . . A further assignment by the Navy Regulations is the furnishing of such garrisons and expeditionary forces for duties beyond the seas as may be necessary. The character of duty of this kind pertains usually to infantry with artillery support, both of which are furnished by Marines. The special value of Marines for such duty is their great mobility, derived from the cooperation of the Navy. It is a matter of a few hours only to assemble Marines in the required number at a port, and to embark them on a naval vessel, often a battleship, in commission and in readiness. Marines only could be infiltered into a ship's crew for a voyage of many days. The common training of the sailor and Marine, and the introduction in the same principles, include a coordination and efficiency for expeditionary duty not otherwise attainable. . . . Many expeditions have been conducted by the Navy and the Marines with effective results. Cuba, Nicaragua, Panama, Haiti, and Santo Domingo have been objectives of such expeditions, and garrisons of Marines will be today found in some of them.[41]

### The Marine Corps, the Army, and Amphibious Training

There were no special troops in the Army prior to World War II with experience in amphibious warfare that had had the years of training and experience needed to perfect a doctrine for successful landing with a minimum of casualties. The Army had a lot to learn.

In February 1941, Fleet Landing Exercise 7, the joint operation of the Marine Corps and Navy, was held. Admiral Ernest H. King was Atlantic Fleet Commander and in overall charge of the operation. Three Army General Staff officers came down from Washington to observe the exercise. King's biographer commented:

> Shortly before the first full landing, three Army General Staff officers arrived from Washington as observers. King told them that they could occupy spare berths, mess in the wardroom of *Texas*, and have a boat available when they wished to go ashore, but King discovered that the Army observers regarded themselves as in a position to criticize the amphibious techniques of the far more experienced Marines. Creeping and walking normally precede an ability to run, and as it seemed to King that, so far as amphibious landings were concerned, the Marines had learned to walk and were beginning to get up speed, while the Army still had to master the art of creeping, he was both amused and annoyed by the attitude of these observers. Such a point of view was unintelligible to King, who saw every advantage in employing in amphibious operations a highly trained body of men, with experience of land fighting not only in France but in the Caribbean, Panama, and Central America, in preference to newly recruited troops fresh from farms, factories, stores, and offices.[42]

General of the Army Dwight D. Eisenhower initially did not appreciate the challenge of amphibious training, experience, and competence needed to land on the coast of North Africa, then on Normandy. In a postwar interview with *U.S. News and World Report*, he stated: "You know an amphibious landing is not a particularly difficult thing, but it's a touchy and delicate thing, and anything can go wrong."

General of the Army George C. Marshall acknowledged the importance of the need for trained and experienced troops in amphibious warfare. He commented in late 1943: "My military education and experience in the First World War has all been based on roads, rivers, and railroads. During the last two years, however, I have been acquiring an education based on oceans and I've had to learn all over again. Prior to the present war I never heard of any landing craft except a rubber boat. Now I think about little else."[43]

Fortunately, for the welfare of the World War II effort, the Marines shared their knowledge. That the U.S. Army was able so quickly to train troops for crossing beaches held by hostile nations is attributable to its own flexibility and leadership and, equally important, to the availability for its guidance of a sound body of amphibious doctrine previously drawn up by the U.S. Navy and the Marine Corps. For about two decades before the outbreak of the Second World War, the Marines had been establishing themselves as specialists in amphibious warfare. Thus, they were ready in 1940 with a cadre of officers who began indoctrinating Army troops in amphibious matters; and, more significantly, they provided a doctrine for amphibious operations which was drawn from Navy and Marine Corps publications and circularized as a U.S. Army field manual.

**Validation**

Major General Alexander A. Vandegrift commanded the mission to seize and defend Guadalcanal and Tulagi. He reflected in his memoir:

> Any one of us could have listed a hundred reasons why this operation would fail. In my case I had soldiered since 1909 and knew the rigors of jungle warfare from campaigns in Nicaragua, Mexico, and Haiti. I had seen the amphibious doctrine grow from General John A. Lejeune's first thoughts in the early twenties to General John Russell's Fleet Marine Force exercises in the early thirties. I had served as military secretary and later as assistant to the Commandant, General Thomas Holcomb, who continued to iron out the wrinkles in this demanding type of warfare.

He pointed out there was opposition to the development of amphibious warfare doctrine, and inferred that had he put forward his ideas at the more senior ranks he would have flunked:

> I knew only too well that if someone at Marine Corps Schools had answered a problem of this nature with the forces now at my disposal he would have failed the course. Bleak as was the picture, I did not think it hopeless. I realized and so did the other senior officers that it was going to be difficult, what Wellington after the battle of Waterloo called a "near-run thing." We didn't have much of anything, we didn't know what we

were going to hit, but we did know enough, in my opinion, to justify what military writers like to call a calculated risk. We knew that America needed a shot in the national arm.

The invasion of Tarawa was it.

Since December 7, 1941, our national heritage had yielded to a priceless humiliation. Half of our fleet still sat on the bottom of Pearl Harbor. The Philippines were gone, Guam and Wake had fallen, the Japanese were approaching Australia. What Admiral King saw, and what he jammed down the throats of the Joint Chiefs of Staff, was that just possibly the mighty Japanese had overextended. He saw that just possibly a strike by us could halt their eastward parade. The only weapon he held, the only weapon America held, was a woefully under-strength fleet and one woefully ill-equipped and partially trained Marine division.[44]

Soon after my arrival in America newspaper headlines screamed the news of the Tarawa assault to the nation. Our release of casualty figures quickly changed national pride to indignant gloom. A variety of factors, chiefly a hidden reef which prevented landing boats from reaching the beaches and an incredibly well dug-in and powerful enemy, exacted a heavy toll: well over 3,000 casualties in just over three days.

Most journalists did not realize that they had observed the first successful true amphibious assault of all time. At Tarawa we validated the principle of the amphibious assault, a tactic proclaimed impossible by many military experts. Of course it was costly—we all knew it would be, for war is costly. But hereafter the enemy could never know where or when we would strike. Hereafter no matter the strength of his bastion the enemy could never feel secure. This was the real lesson of Tarawa, this the public did not immediately realize.

I studied the reports more carefully because in Noumea Roy Geiger was looking already to his next operation, the assault of Guam, and I wanted to exact the most out of Tarawa, I wrote Holland Smith: "The people in your area will immediately have available to them the lessons to be learned from that show [Tarawa] as will also Harry Schmidt's outfit [4th Marine Division] who had observers there. . . . Could you have someone make a summary of the salient facts brought out by this show, as, for example, use or non-use of Alligator boats, and their effectiveness, gunfire, bombing, etc., and let me have it at an early date so that it can be gotten to Roy, as his planning will start almost immediately."

Holland replied, raising a key issue on who was to command:

We are now making up a summary of the salient facts established by the Gilberts show and we are forwarding you a copy in the near future. I have already requested Edson to send a copy of all orders issued by the 2$^d$ Division to Roy Geiger. . . . There is one definite point that I wish to stress: Where the hydrographical features are similar to the Gilberts only Alligators can land. Naval gunfire for the destruction of coast defense guns is a function of the Navy, but when the landing begins, the Landing Force Commander should have "the say" as to where, when, and what kind of fire he needs. When you receive my final report you will note things that must be corrected if we are to avoid disaster in the future. Only a military man with a background of experience and education can run the show on the beach and we must never surrender that thought.[45]

Vandegrift reflected:

We continued to receive considerable criticism of the casualties suffered at Tarawa. I found myself at odds with the official naval policy of downplaying what some persons seemed to believe a disaster. I felt that the American public should be told the truth—that the victory in war, just as victory in peace, sometimes has to be costly. When a censor wished to hold up photographs of dead Marines on the Tarawa beaches I refused to consider it. In my opinion the sooner the American people realized the sort of war we were fighting the better it would be all the way around. On December 15 old Senator Walsh telephoned me his concern over the national reaction. The senator was a good friend of the Marine Corps, and I welcomed the opportunity to spell out the problem in a letter to him: "A landing attack is recognized by all military experts as being the most difficult and costly of all forms of attack. Losses at Tarawa were heavy, and losses will be heavy in future attacks of this nature, the attackers being able to develop large forces ashore. Conversely, the attacker, having the initiative, is able to select the point of landing, and will, other things being equal, select a location which is least heavily defended. If he has achieved surprise, he can expect no serious resistance initially, and in turn endeavors to land. No one regrets the losses in such an attack more than does the Marine Corps itself. No one realizes more than does the Marine Corps that there is no royal road to Tokyo. We must steel our people to the same realization."[46]

## Lieutenant General Holland M. Smith, USMC, versus Major General Ralph Smith, USA

There is no more difficult decision for a commander than to relieve a senior general officer, particularly in combat, in time of war. On June 24, 1944, Major General Ralph Smith, the Army Commander of the 27th Division, was relieved of his command. The Corps commander of the Fifth Amphibious Corps, of which the 27th was a part, was Lieutenant General Holland M. Smith. It occurred while the United States was in the middle of its invasion of the island of Saipan, having landed on June 15, 1944.

The significance of this relief is discussed in detail in a superb scholarly study of Marine Corps combat operations in World War II, entitled *The U.S. Marines and Amphibious War: Its Theory and Its Practice in the Pacific*. Princeton University professors Jeter A. Isely and Philip A. Crowl addressed the controversy of the firing of Major General Ralph Smith:

> The inter-service dispute engendered at Saipan was not inconsequential. It resulted in the relief of a general officer of the United States Army, which though not unique in the history of World War II was certainly an unusual and alarming occurrence. It set off a train of charges and countercharges that were to strain Army and Marine Corps relations severely throughout the rest of the war and afterward. Hence, the facts of the case deserve careful attention, not only for their own sake but also for the light they throw on the difficulties inherent in joint operations involving more than one branch of the armed services.[47]

The 27th Army Division was a New York National Guard division ushered into Federal service in October 1940. It had been stationed in Hawaii for 20 months before the Saipan campaign and seeing any action as a full division. Three of the battalions, the 105th, 106th, and 165th, had seen rather small-scale action at Makin and Eniwetok. The 165th and 105th fought at Makin. Two battalions of the 106th fought at Eniwetok. The whole division as a unit, however, had never been in battle before Saipan. There had been allegations of problems with the poor leadership of the 27th Division in the invasion of Makin and Eniwetok, but its combat performance, in Holland Smith's opinion, got progressively worse in the Saipan battle.

The Army-Marine Corps controversy was far more important and much bigger than the principles, Lieutenant General Holland M. Smith and Major General Ralph Smith. It had repercussions of great magnitude during World War II that continued well after the war.

The issues will hereafter be discussed in detail, but in the way of an overview: the controversy reached to the highest level of who was to command the overall operations in the Pacific theater. The then-powerful Hearst newspaper chain had long been stirring controversy by arguing to have a single supreme commander, and wanted it to be General Douglas MacArthur. In an editorial in the Hearst *New York Journal-American* on July 17, 1944, a discussion of Ralph Smith's relief stated: "General MacArthur . . . should most certainly be Supreme Command of the Pacific Theatre NOW," arguing that there would be "an end of quarreling among rival commanders. . . . There would under his [MacArthur's] command be Fewer DEATHS."

The controversy of who should be the Supreme Commander in the Pacific had been ongoing since the beginning of the war, and the Smith versus Smith incident brought the matter to a head. If MacArthur were to become Supreme Commander in the Pacific, then Admiral Chester W. Nimitz would be subordinate to him. As the war in the Pacific progressed, President Franklin D. Roosevelt divided the Pacific into two areas, one under the command of MacArthur, the other Nimitz.

The comment of "fewer deaths" addressed the difference between the Marine Corps philosophy of combat tactics and that of the Army. The Marine Corps advocated a continuous, aggressive advance, swarming ahead, overrunning the enemy positions, bypassing the areas of greater resistance, not permitting those areas to slow the advance, then going back to mop up the last pockets of resistance. The Marine Corps believed that winning quickly ultimately resulted in fewer casualties. The Army in the Pacific theater believed in slower, more deliberate tactics. The different approaches, because of the relief of Ralph Smith, received a great deal of discussion as the controversy progressed, but the media did not really understand the complexity of fighting tactics in combat in the Pacific theater. Thus they were covering the controversy but were incorrect in so much of what they published and discussions that harmed the conduct of the war. The media did not point out, among other things, that the Marines took the beachhead and suffered the greatest losses in that part of the invasion, or that the Marine forces involved in Saipan were twice as large as the Army forces.

The Navy favored the Marine Corps doctrine because the forces moving rapidly on the ground reduced the time needed to keep their ships on station to support the forces ashore. A significant part of the defense of the Japanese mainland was the ring of islands in the Pacific. They defended the many islands through the use of surface ships, submarines, and later kamikaze pilots, to sink and damage the U.S. ships. Our ships were very vulnerable to attacks while unloading troops and supplies. With the threat of attacks by the Japanese Navy, U.S. ship commanders were justifiably anxious to unload and move out to minimize losses.[48]

The controversy, the most severe interservice dispute of the war, did great harm to interservice relations during and after World War II. General George C. Marshall, U.S. Army Chief of Staff, expressed concern as the controversy went on that the Saipan Army-Marine relationships had "deteriorated beyond healthy rivalry," and that the bad blood would develop to the point that it would infect future operations. Marshall suggested he and Admiral Ernest King should prevent this type of controversy from happening again in the future. Marshall instructed his commanders not to discuss the relief any further, desiring to minimize the adverse impact of the controversy on interservice relations.[49]

The invasion of Saipan was extremely important in the war in the Pacific. It was the major northern island in the Mariana Islands and was a significant military base for the Japanese in 1944. It was a small island, about 15 miles long and 7 miles wide. It was only 1,200 miles from the Japanese southern islands. Conquering it would breach the Japanese line of defense and would eliminate one of its strongest islands of defense of the homeland. It was decided to invade Saipan primarily to obtain naval bases and to establish an airfield and runways for the new B–29 long-range super bombers. Within 6 months after its capture there were two bomber fields, which provided a base for bombing Japanese cities. Not only did the capture of Saipan provide a base for the B–29s, it also denied the Japanese one of its major military installations in the area. The battle began on June 15, 1944, and on July 9, 1944, Saipan was declared secure.

It was a costly victory. Of the 71,000 troops that landed in the invasion, 3,150 were killed and 11,000 wounded. The Japanese were wiped out, losing 30,000 men.

Conquering Saipan was the beginning of the end of Japan's hope of resisting the U.S. advance. It broke Japan's inner defense line and destroyed the main bastions, thus opening the way to the U.S. forces to attack the Japanese home islands. With airbases on Saipan and other Mariana Islands, every important Japanese city was within the destructive range of U.S. Army Air Corps B–29 bombers.

Major General Ralph Smith was given the opportunity to improve the fighting ability of the 27th Division as the invasion of Saipan progressed. Even before his relief, he conceded that the 27th Division was not carrying its share of the load. Holland Smith requested that Army Major General Sanderford Jarman, who was scheduled to take charge of the occupation of Saipan after it was secured, call upon Ralph Smith to see if he could get the 27th Division to advance. He tried. Jarman reported that Ralph Smith "immediately replied that such was true: that he was in no way satisfied with what his regimental commanders had done during the day. . . . He further indicated to me that he was going to be present tomorrow, 24 June, with his division when it made its jump-off and he would personally see to it that the division went forward. He [Ralph Smith] thanked me for coming to see him and stated that if he didn't take his division forward tomorrow he should be relieved."

In more detail, Jarman reported that, on June 23, in a communication subsequently released:

> I found that General (Ralph) Smith had been up to the front lines all afternoon and was thoroughly familiar with the situation. I talked to General Smith and explained the situation as I saw it and that I felt from reports from the Corps Commander that his division was not carrying its full share. He immediately replied that such was true; that he was in no way satisfied with what his regimental commanders had done during the day and that he had been with them and had pointed out to them the situation. He further indicated to me that he was going to be present tomorrow, June 24, with this division when it made its jump-off and he would personally see to it that the division went forward. I explained my interest in the matter was that I was senior Army commander present and was anxious to see that the Army did its job as it should be done.

Jarman wished him luck, then returned to Holland Smith where he requested that Ralph Smith have one more chance to take his division forward. The corps commander replied that, if the division didn't make a proper advance the next day, he was going to ask Admiral Spruance for permission to relieve Ralph Smith.[50]

In the opinion of Holland Smith, the grounds for Ralph Smith's dismissal were primarily for not providing aggressive leadership when the situation demanded it. In addition, some of the battalion commanders were staying behind the front lines, preventing an efficient contact with its companies; and the division had an unfortunate policy of giving up at night ground gained during the day. Perhaps most of all, General Ralph Smith failed to relieve incompetent subordinates. The other charges were that on two occasions, Ralph Smith contravened Fifth Corps orders and on one occasion contravened an order to a unit that had been removed from his control; and that over a long period, the 27th was late in launching its part of the scheduled timing attack.

On the next day, June 24, Holland made the decision to relieve Ralph Smith. It was clear then that Holland Smith as Corps Commander had the authority to do so on his own, but he wisely decided to get the approval of Admiral Raymond A. Spruance. He met with Vice Admiral Kelly Turner, the officer in charge of the Navy's role in the amphibious operations in the Saipan campaign. Turner agreed with him, so the two of them proceeded to Spruance's flagship, the *Indianapolis*, and prepared to present their case, carrying with them with maps, supporting materials, and an official letter to Admiral Spruance. They then had the lengthy, soul-searching discussion that such a critical decision required.

The relief of Ralph Smith was described in detail in Admiral Spruance's biography. On the morning of June 24, 1944, Spruance's flagship *Indianapolis*, was:

> anchored in the transport area off Saipan to await Turner and Smith, who brought bad news: Holland Smith wanted to fire Major General Ralph C. Smith, the Army general commanding the 27th Infantry Division. He explained his drastic request. The 27th Division had failed to advance up the center of the island during the major assault the day before, imperiling the inboard flanks of the two Marine divisions moving up the east and west sides of the island. As a result the offensive was stalled. Smith felt that the Army division had failed him and

would continue to impede progress for the remainder of the Saipan campaign.

Ralph Smith had been in command for twenty months and had been unable to improve the division's fighting ability to Holland Smith's satisfaction. The Marine general, impatient and intolerant, now asked Spruance to replace Ralph Smith with Major General Sanderford Jarman, an Army officer then on Saipan, who would become the island commander when the island was secured. Jarman had agreed that the 27th's performance was unsatisfactory, and, according to Holland Smith, Jarman had vowed that he could make the division fight if he were given command.

Holland Smith thus forced Spruance to make a distasteful decision with potentially explosive repercussions. Although there was ample precedent for removing flag and general officers who failed in combat, such officers traditionally were relieved (discreetly if possible) by their own superiors within their own service. Spruance was contemplating the open firing of an Army general by a Navy admiral upon the recommendation of a Marine Corps general. The Army would be humiliated and infuriated. The Army-Marine Corps relationship, at best tenuous, could suddenly disintegrate into a permanent estrangement that would impair the future Pacific war effort. And giving Jarman command was no guarantee that the division would improve in the next few weeks' fighting on Saipan; its problems were too deeply ingrained to permit any immediate remedy.

Holland Smith was the commander responsible for the fighting ashore and presumably was best able to judge the ways and means necessary to seize Saipan. Furthermore, Kelly Turner supported Smith's recommendation. Yet all three officers, recognizing the gravity of the moment, groped about for a tactful way to fire Ralph Smith. They all liked him personally and knew they were about to ruin his career and reputation. Their discussion, according to Carl Moore, "bid fair to be rather endless." The chief of staff, hoping to end their soul-searching, drafted a terse, straightforward dispatch for Spruance's signature. All three parties read the draft, agreed with the wording, and Spruance signed the orders that relieved Ralph Smith and placed Jarman in command of the 27th Division.[51]

The order addressed to Holland Smith read, "You are authorized and directed to relieve Major General Ralph Smith from command of the Twenty-seventh Division, U.S. Army, and place Major General Jarman in command." General Smith's aide, Captain Mac Asbill, Jr., was given the job of delivering the relief order to Ralph Smith's headquarters. He did so and "turned around and got the hell out of there before he could read it."

In every discussion of the Smith versus Smith controversy, it was pointed out that a furor was caused by the actions of Army Lieutenant General Robert C. Richardson, Jr., and the damage he did to interservice relations. Holland Smith pointed out "that the whole incident of the relief of Ralph Smith might have well ended but for the uninvited visit and interference by Richardson to Saipan after the island had been declared secure, but while we were still mopping up."[52]

At the time of the relief of Major General Ralph Smith, Richardson was assigned to command Army forces, serving under Admiral Chester W. Nimitz in the central Pacific. In this capacity he was responsible for the administration, training, and supply of the Army units in the Pacific. He had no operational authority. He was not a combat commander.

Richardson was constantly very vocal in his opposition of having Holland Smith, a Marine, having operational control of the Army's 27th Division of which Ralph Smith was the Commander. He argued that there was no need for a corps headquarters to coordinate between the 27th Division and Vice Admiral Kelly Turner, with a Marine as Fifth Amphibious Corps Commander. He thought that eliminating Fifth Corps organization would mean there would not be a Marine general responsible for leading Army forces.

Richardson was unsuccessful in persuading Admiral Chester A. Nimitz, so he appealed to General George C. Marshall who supported Nimitz to keep the Fifth Amphibious Corps intact under Holland Smith. But Richardson continued his complaining, sending a secret memorandum addressed in bold letters: "FOR EYES OF ADMIRAL NIMITZ ALONE." Rather than sending it through normal channels, Richardson had it delivered by a special courier.[53]

He charged in his memorandum that the Marine Corps had no experience in commanding a corps, but, he said, the Army had many qualified to do so; that Holland Smith's staff was inexperienced and untrained; that Vice Admiral Richmond Kelly Turner, Commander, Joint

Expeditionary Forces, could handle the amphibious planning, loading and unloading the landings, so there would be no need to share these responsibilities; that the organization of Fifth Amphibious Corps was confusing; that it would be better if the Army would just deal with Turner. Richardson was upset that Holland Smith had successfully shot down a tactical plan for the assault on the Marshall Islands that was prepared by the Army division, and he, Richardson, had personally approved. Richardson summed up his position, recommending that Holland Smith should be limited to administration duties, and that in the future tactical operations should be handled by the Army.[54]

Nimitz sent the "Secret" memorandum on to Chief of Naval Operations Admiral Ernest King, who disagreed with Richardson quite emphatically. In his response to the report, King and Marine Corps Commandant A.A. Vandegrift emphasized that in amphibious operations, the Marines were far more experienced and had proven themselves in the invasions of Guadalcanal, Bougainville, Cape Gloucester, and the Gilbert Islands; that if Richardson found the command structure confusing it was because he was not experienced in amphibious operations; and that there was no more experienced leader in amphibious operations than Holland Smith.[55]

Holland Smith revealed his position on Richardson's actions in two letters he sent to Commandant Vandegrift, the first dated January 6, 1944:

> Ever since I have been out here, I realize that the Army is trying to take over this job, not that they have any particular objection to me, but they resent the fact the Marine officers are in command of the two Corps. The attitude of the Army generals who are assigned to my Corps is that "It won't be long until we are running the show." I have it from Army officers on my staff, that the Army is very resentful of their subordinate position in the Central and South Pacific. . . . the Army continually snipes at this Corps. They are determined to get command if it is humanly possible.[56]

The second letter is dated February 11, 1944:

> The Army is extremely jealous and is forever making false and specious claims. Both Bobby [Erskine, Corps Chief of Staff] and I are conscious of this and have leaned over backwards to assuage their feelings. The Army General in command of the division submitted an unsound plan and I pointed out the

unsoundness of the plan and insisted upon its being changed. I assure you that my conscience is wholly clear, but that I shall continue to exert every precaution to prevent any unfriendly feeling on the part of the Army.[57]

It was one thing for Richardson to fight for the status of the Army, but reprehensible to do so at the expense of Allied and U.S. interservice harmony in time of war. The controversy, unfortunately, filtered down to the troops. Anyone familiar with the mental frame of mind of soldiers in combat would not be surprised that ill will developed over this controversy between the Army soldiers and the Marines in the field. The Marines would land on the enemy beaches, suffering the heaviest losses to establish a beachhead and then move inland. The Army forces normally followed, suffering fewer losses in contrast. Not surprisingly, the soldiers of the 27th looked upon the relief of its commander as a slur upon the whole division.[58]

Spruance accepted the full responsibility for the decision to relieve Ralph Smith, but almost all the critical treatment in the press and histories refer to Holland Smith as really the person responsible for it. Spruance never backed off from his decision. In a personal letter to Admiral Nimitz, he stated: "The relief of Commander Ralph Smith from command of the 27th Division was regrettable but necessary. He has been in command of that division for a long time and cannot avoid being held responsible for its fighting efficiency or lack thereof."[59]

As pointed out by Holland Smith, the matter might have been less controversial if it were not for what Army Lieutenant General Richardson described as Holland Smith's "nemesis" for his Fifth Amphibious Corps.

Richardson further aggravated the controversy over the relief of Ralph Smith with an unfortunate inflammatory decision. He announced at a press conference that he had given Ralph Smith command of the 98th Army Infantry Division, then stationed in Hawaii; thus, it was Richardson who placed the firing into the national arena with its unfortunate consequences. It was an attempt to vindicate Ralph Smith and the Army, but was certainly an insult to Holland Smith and the Marine Corps. The press picked it up, and a July 20, 1944, article in the *New York Times* stated that Ralph Smith's relief was an ongoing argument about tactical methods, with the Marines favoring a rapid attack "even at a high cost of lives."[60]

The greatest factor in inflaming the interservice controversy between the Army and the Marine Corps was Richardson. He proceeded to establish a board of inquiry, named the Buckner Board after Army

Lieutenant General Simon Bolivar Buckner, Jr., its chairman. It was supposed to have two objectives: first, did Holland Smith have the authority to relieve Ralph Smith, and second, was his relief justified? The board met on July 4, 1944, and submitted its findings a month later.

It was clear before the board even began deliberation that Ralph Smith should not have been relieved, since Richardson gave Ralph Smith command of the 98th Army Division before the board even met. Richardson saw to it that the new command for Ralph Smith was made public. The composition of the board and its hearings violated every rule of fairness to Holland Smith. There were only Army officers on the board, composed of four generals of various ranks and the recorder, a lieutenant colonel. For the testimony, it interviewed only Army personnel; it examined only Army records; it viewed no Marine Corps documents; most of the statements were collected by Richardson during a visit to Saipan; there was no opportunity for the Marine Corps to present evidence or to cross-examine; there was no opportunity for rebuttal by the Marine Corps.[61]

One of the clear-cut decisions of even such a biased board was that Holland Smith as Fifth Corps Commander had the authority to release Ralph Smith. A second conclusion, not a surprise to anyone knowledgeable about the Buckner Board established and organized by Richardson, was that "the relief was ... unjustified, and the board recommended that Ralph Smith's official record on further commands be not adversely affected by his relief."

In summary, the board concluded that Holland Smith had full authority to relieve Ralph Smith; that Holland Smith was not fully informed regarding the conditions in the zone of the 27th Division when he issued orders relieving Ralph Smith; the relief of Ralph Smith was not justified by facts; and that Ralph Smith's official record or future commands should not be adversely affected by his relief.[62]

It would be appropriate to know what Holland Smith had to say about the controversy. In his memoir *Coral and Brass*, he addressed the matter of Ralph Smith:

> The whole incident might well have ended there but for the uninvited visit by Richardson to Saipan after the island had been declared secure, but while we were still mopping up. He arrived on July 12 and hardly had he set foot ashore where I was in command than he began making trouble. In flagrant violation of the oldest service customs, he began taking testimony for the Buckner Board, which he had convened at his

headquarters on Oahu, known throughout the Pacific as the "Pineapple Pentagon.' His purpose was to pass on my actions in relieving Ralph Smith.

"You had no right to relieve Ralph Smith," he told me. "The Twenty-seventh is one of the best-trained divisions in the Pacific. I trained it myself. You discriminated against the Army in favor of the Marines. I want you to know that you can't push the Army around the way you've been doing."

It was as much as I could do to contain myself as he continued with the old, familiar line.

"You and your Corps commander aren't as well qualified to lead large bodies of troops as general officers in the Army," he continued. "We've had more experience in handling troops than you've had and yet you dare," he almost screamed, "remove one of my Generals."

He next accused me of faulty technical decisions and indiscriminate sacrifice of lives. Apart from the fact that he was wrong, I was astounded by his impropriety in making such statements. A military command in battle carries with it the authority to conduct tactical operations according to the judgment of the commander. Results are the touchstone and success bears an automatic seal of approval. As long as you keep on fighting and winning, not even a superior in the chain of command is authorized to interfere. An officer outside the chain of command, such as Richardson, never possesses the right to meddle.

For a man with my explosive reputation, I must confess that I conducted myself with admirable restraint under this barrage when he said, "You Marines are nothing but a bunch of beach runners, anyway. What do you know about land warfare?"

To do Ralph Smith credit, I must say that his testimony was the most fair-minded of the lot. He repeatedly warned his inquisition that he had few if any records and was forced to rely on memory and, despite repeated openings offered him in Richardson's Star Chamber, he never once launched onto a diatribe or a sob story. Adversity, I think, became him well.

I have always deplored this incident as far too typical of the amount of top echelon time and effort expended in the Pacific on matters not pertaining to the winning of the war. Inter-Service disputes, given unmerited prominence, can grow into the greatest enemy of victory when they take priority over all other interests in the minds of Generals and Admirals. Equally deplorable is the effect upon the men who carry into peacetime the animosity thus engendered in wartime.[63]

Commandant Vandegrift commented on Holland Smith and on the Buckner report:

Furious at this obviously unfair attack, I told the Secretary of the Navy and Admiral King that I stood completely behind Holland, King did, too, but thought that in the best interest of fighting the war we should adopt a "no comment" policy. Logic forced me to agree, anyway for the time being, but I privately wrote Holland:

"Let me say right here that I think you showed more forbearance than I could possibly have shown under similar circumstances."[64]

Through all of this unfortunate controversy, in contrast to the board's composition and proceedings, Ralph Smith was remarkably honest and fair in his testimony. He was asked if he had ever had any disputes with Holland Smith: "No, I have always had a feeling of rather personal friendship for General Smith and rather felt that he entertained a friendly feeling for me." In oral testimony when he was asked why he thought Holland Smith had relieved him, he responded: "I am convinced in my own mind that he believed that the 27th Division was not pushing its advance as vigorously as it could." He wrote that Ralph Smith's decision "was based primarily on disappointment at what he believed to be a slow advance by Army troops against light enemy resistance."[65]

Norman Varnell Cooper made an in-depth study of who in the 27th Division was relieved after Ralph Smith and found that there were considerable command changes after Smith's departure. Nimitz's public relations officer told Robert Sherrod that 33 field grade officers were relieved. The division's historian admitted to only 19 such reliefs, 8 of which were allegedly for physical disability. Some of the reliefs, however, were of men in high positions. During his brief tenure, General Jarman relieved both the commanding officer (Colonel Ayers) and the executive officer of the 106th Regiment. The commander of the battalion left on Nafutan Point was reclassified so that he no longer directed operations. Another battalion commander was relieved for being unaggressive. At the battle's end, the colonel of the 105th Infantry, which had been hit by the great Banzai attack, was relieved for physical disability, according to the 27th Division historian. Holland Smith's diagnosis of his ailment, given at the time, was "he had the nervous jitters, was crying and taking on."[66]

This controversy was a terrible drain on the time and energy of the senior military decisionmakers in Washington. It should have been resolved without sending it up the chain of command. Marshall pushed such decisions back down, suggesting that the senior officer in the Pacific areas be instructed that "the prevention of such a state of affairs is squarely their own responsibility, as is also the task of remedying it should it be found to exist." That was certainly the message given clearly by Marshall to his Army commanders in the Pacific. Any officer who did not follow an order issued by Marshall did not last. As King astutely pointed out, the "controversy came at a time when we need all our energies to win the war."[67]

What became of the assignments of Holland Smith and Ralph Smith after Saipan? Tensions continued for a long time; to minimize further friction, changes in the command structure in the Pacific essentially assisted in calming the troubled waters. Richardson gave Ralph Smith command of the 98th Division on Hawaii. Shortly thereafter, he was recalled to Washington, then appointed military attaché to Paris. He retired without any further combat service.

There was no way the Navy or Marine Corps was going to transfer Holland Smith, one of the true heroes in the Pacific who had just won a great victory in Saipan. His situation was resolved by Commandant Vandegrift: "Toward the end of the Saipan campaign my long-awaited reorganization of the Pacific command took place. This made Holland commanding general of the new Fleet Marine Force Pacific. Harry Schmidt, a Marine, moved up to Fifth Corps command."[68]

Referring to the Ralph Smith relief, Nimitz biographer E.B. Potter wrote:

> This was one story Admiral Nimitz would have given a great deal to keep from public knowledge, but that was obviously impossible. People on various errands were constantly flying between Pearl Harbor and Saipan. General Ralph Smith had

been seen at Fort Shafter, Army headquarters on Oahu, where General Richardson, in high dudgeon, was organizing an Army board of inquiry headed by General Buckner to look into Smith's relief.

Richard Haller, of International News Service, went to see Commander Kenneth McArdle, assistant CinCPac public relations officer, and asked, "When are you going to release the fact that Ralph Smith has been relieved as commander of the 27th Division?"

McArdle replied that he had no official knowledge of any such relief and asked where Haller had heard the rumor.

"It's all over town," said Haller. "I heard it from one of the general's close friends."

McArdle, realizing that concealing the story had become impossible, added to the end of the communiqué on which he was working a straightforward paragraph reporting the relief, and took the communiqué to the chief of staff.

"No!" shouted McMorris when he came to the final paragraph, and he scratched it out.

"It's all over Honolulu," said McArdle.

"Who told 'em?"

"Fifty thousand men on Saipan know it. You can't keep a thing like that quiet."

"The answer is no," said McMorris with finality.

The time-honored, if slightly irregular, way around McMorris's frequent and definitive negatives was through the assistant chief of staff, now Captain Bernard L. ("Count") Austin, who had recently relieved Preston Mercer in that capacity. McArdle took the story to Austin and the latter agreed that it was a mistake to sit on it. Better publish the plain facts than have them leak out in some sensational form.

Austin went to Nimitz's office to discuss the situation with the boss. In ten minutes he was back.

"The answer is still no," he said. "The admiral is going to say nothing of the incident; the War Department can make such announcements as it cares to. You see, the admiral doesn't want to do anything to hurt Ralph Smith."

As McArdle had feared, the story "broke wrong" in the American press. One newspaper wrote: "Holland Smith, 'the butcher of Tarawa,' was again ruthlessly sending boys to certain slaughter." Others implied that Ralph Smith's soldiers simply refused to fight. The *San Francisco Examiner* accused the Marine Corps of incurring excessive casualties and called for unified command in the Pacific theater under General MacArthur, whose "difficult and hazardous military operations . . . have been successfully carried out with little loss of life in most cases." *Time* and *Life* came out with stories supporting Holland Smith. The *Time* article concluded: "When field commanders hesitate to remove subordinates for fear of inter-service contention, battles and lives will be needlessly lost."[69]

The Navy brass would have done well to have listened to Richard Haller and Commander Kenneth McArdle. It gave an opening to the powerful Hearst newspaper chain to continue pushing for General Douglas MacArthur to be the Supreme Commander of all the forces in the Pacific. The Hearst newspaper chain seized the firing incident and tried to use it "as a club with which to beat down those who opposed the selection of MacArthur."[70]

The first public notice of the incident came in Hearst's *San Francisco Examiner*, on July 8, 1944. Front-page headlines proclaimed: "Army General Relieved in Row over High Marine Losses." Inside headlines reiterated, "General Loses Command in Row; Objections to Huge Losses Cause." The report continued:

> Allegedly excessive loss of life attributed to Marine Corps impetuosity of attack has brought a breach between Marine and Army commanders in the Pacific.
>
> General Smith's opinion that the attacking aggressively should conserve lives to a greater extent is said to have been openly

> expressed when a late casualty report showed 1,289 Marine dead and only 185 Army dead in the same length of time.
>
> The difference between the two Generals Smith [began at Makin while] at the same time Marines, also under Holland Smith, took Tarawa at a heavy cost in casualties. Army casualties at Makin were relatively light.
>
> Major General Ralph Smith and other Army officers are reported to hold that lives could have been saved without damage to eventual victory. In the Tarawa, Kwajalein Atoll and Saipan actions had the Marine Command proceeded more deliberately and cautiously. . . .
>
> In the Kwajalein operation . . . casualties were light compared to Makin and Tarawa but the Marine losses were heavier than the Army's.

In his final paragraphs the reporter added two revealing statements: "The whole controversy . . . has been accentuated by placing a Marine general over Army generals. In the last war, there was strong feeling over the fact the Marines stole the headlines."[71]

A few days after the first article, Hearst's *New York Journal-American* editorialized that Americans were "shocked by the staggering casualties on Saipan." They were further shocked by the revelation that an Army general had insisted "that there was reckless and needless waste of American lives" and then this "advocate of more cautious tactics" had been relieved.

By this time, war correspondent Robert Sherrod, who so far had written nothing on the Smith versus Smith controversy, decided that Holland Smith should be defended. The correspondent was no stranger to combat himself. He had waded ashore the first morning at Tarawa and spent the day and night huddled behind the seawall with the Marines. Earlier he had made landings with the Army. In an article in *Time*, September 18, 1944, he wrote, correctly, that the relief of Ralph Smith "had nothing to do with tactics." The relief was because "he had long ago failed to get tough enough to remove incompetent subordinate officers." Sherrod added that the 27th Division was "bogged down," and that the men "lacked confidence in their officers" and "froze in their foxholes." The latter statement was unfortunate, as it seemed to imply that the men of the 27th Division were all cowards. Sherrod wrote later that he intended no such slur, and meant only that they were ineptly led.[72]

General Richardson asked Admiral Nimitz to have the Navy Department remove the stigma that the article attached to the 27th Division, and asked him to rescind Sherrod's standing to continue as a war correspondent. It became worse when Nimitz supported Richardson's request and wrote to Admiral King recommending the rescinding of Sherrod's credentials and forwarded the request of Richardson to King.

Nimitz's action embittered Holland Smith toward him. Holland Smith wrote to Commandant Vandegrift telling him that Admiral Spruance was "indignant" about the request. He informed Nimitz in writing and pointed out that several months before the first critical article appeared in the *San Francisco Examiner* on July 8, 1944, Ralph Smith had made a recording on which he spoke very favorably of his relationship with Holland Smith, saying that General Holland Smith told him, "Shells are a hell of a lot cheaper than men."[73]

By this time, the controversy had reached the Joint Chiefs of Staff, where Holland Smith had a very strong ally in Admiral King. After Saipan, King alluded to another controversial general whom he admired, Joseph Stilwell, when he remarked, "The trouble is that [Holland Smith] and Stilwell are alike: they both want to fight." When Nimitz's and Richardson's letters concerning Sherrod's *Time* article arrived, King forwarded them to General Marshall with a letter that left no doubt of his own position. He wrote that Holland Smith was willing to make a statement that the "personal bravery" of the men of the 27th Division was unquestioned. He pointed out, however, that Sherrod's articles had been properly submitted for review to both the War and Navy Departments and there were no grounds for rescinding Sherrod's credentials. He shared Nimitz's desire that the men of the 27th Division should not suffer unjust criticism because the relief of their commander "was found to be necessary." But, he added, he was much more concerned about General Richardson's unilateral investigation of the incident, involving as it did "joint command questions that were not within his province." King pointed out that the Buckner Board made "intemperate attacks on the personal character and professional competence" of Holland Smith while not allowing him "to hear the charges against him, or to testify, or to present evidence." Richardson's action, King concluded, was "improper and prejudicial to inter-service relations."[74]

King wrote to General Marshall that there were no grounds to take the credentials away from Sherrod, pointing out that Sherrod's articles passed the censorship of the War Department and Navy Department. He informed Marshall he did not like Richardson's one-sided investigation; the matter was outside Richardson's area of responsibility.

King sent a letter to Nimitz on November 8, 1944. King, apparently, was displeased by Nimitz's failure to take a stronger stand on the matter. Two days after his letter to Marshall, he sent Nimitz a sharp note stating that he agreed that the 27th Division should not be unjustly stigmatized, but he warned, "This matter appears to be heading toward blaming the whole affair on Holland Smith. I cannot tolerate an [sic] 'rectification' that tends to make it appear that the 27th Division was all that it should have been."[75]

How much could Holland Smith take? There was no tougher Marine in the history of the Corps, but it did get to him. He wrote to Commandant Vandegrift on October 11, 1944:

> At times I feel like saying my piece and pack up.... Richardson is on the rampage again and is requesting Nimitz to revoke Bob Sherrod's credentials. Apparently he believes anything Richardson tells him and what I say has little if any influence. Here I am in the midst of planning for an operation and I am harassed by Richardson and N. Ye Gods! I am disgusted ... Good God! I work my heart out, clean up the Marianas in good style and all I get is—Crap.

Then he added: "Read this and tear it up. [It was obviously not torn up.] It is all in the game but I don't like the rules."[76]

How much should a commander have to take from a cause driven more by Richardson's ego and his overzealous and inappropriate action rather than the support of effectively fighting the enemy? Smith's discouragement was reflected in his letter to the Commandant. He had earlier pointed out that in the action on the invasion and conquering the Japanese island of Kwajalein, where in Holland Smith's opinion that the Army was slow in advancing, he wrote to Commandant A.A. Vandegrift on February 4, 1944, commenting:

> The same Marine Corps spirit which has permitted us to survive for 150 years against hostile Army officers and two [e]x-navy presidents prevailed in the capture of Roi and Namur.... The 4th Division (Marine Corps) attacked with vigor and élan. Harry Schmidt was ashore on D-day at 1800 and actually had his CP set up before [his regimental commanders] had theirs. This is the real spirit....The slow progress [of the Army on Kwajalein] has tried my soul.[77]

It was a tough command decision that Holland Smith knew would be controversial. What went on in his mind as the scenario developed? He told Robert Sherrod, the war correspondent active in reporting the Saipan campaign:

> By God, I told him [Ralph Smith] to attack and he issued an order to hold. . . . I've got a duty to my country. I've lost 7,000 Marines. Can I afford to lose back what they've gained? To let my Marines die in vain? I know I'm sticking my neck out—the National Guard will be down my throat—but I did my duty.
>
> I don't care what they do to me. I'll be 63 years old next April and I'll retire any time after that. . . . My sun is setting. I'm just doing my duty as I see it. My conscience is clear.

Shortly afterward, in a handwritten letter to the Commandant, he said:

> My duty was clear. It is my belief substantiated by every Army officer here that he would never fight his division as it should be fought. . . . What happens to me matters little. My conscience and duty is [sic] clear.[78]

Returning to the subject 3 days later, he explained the situation in detail and added:

> Ralph Smith is a weak officer, incapable of handling men in battle, lacks offensive spirit, and tears would come into his eyes on the slightest provocation. My duty was clear. My action was approved by every Army officer with whom my staff or I discussed the situation . . . . I would have relieved Schmidt or Watson (both Marine commanders) under the same circumstances but God be praised they fought like true Marines.[79]

There is no better illustration of the character, leadership, and duty of a Marine Corps officer than the decision to relieve Army Major General Ralph Smith and face all the challenges it was destined to bring about. Certainly a part of his character was keeping his word to Admiral Spruance to not personally counter Richardson.

## Development and Acquisition of the MV-22 Osprey Aircraft

Commandant Vandegrift was a leader of great vision, and with the post–World War II prominence of the atomic bomb in U.S. military strategy, he realized the need to carefully review the future mission of the Marine Corps in such rapidly changing times. He wrote in his memoir:

> This was a necessary preliminary to probing the military curtain of the future. To better understand that future I wanted a definitive study made of our amphibious past. To this end we contracted with two bright Princeton historians, Jeter Isely and Philip Crowe [sic], to begin work on a book published some years later under the title *The U.S. Marines and Amphibious War*.
>
> I refused to share the atomic hysteria familiar to some ranking officers. The atomic bomb was not yet adapted for tactical employment, nor would this happen soon. Accordingly, I did not feel obliged to make a sudden, sharp change in our organizational profile.
>
> I did feel obliged to study the problem in all its complexity. For if we believed the basic mission of the Marine Corps would remain unchanged in an atomic age, we knew that the conditions surrounding this mission would change and change radically. The problem, in my mind, divided itself into three major considerations: how to reorganize the Fleet Marine Force to render its units less vulnerable to atomic warfare and at the same time retain the final assault concentration essential to success; how to decrease our reaction time or conversely, attain and maintain a preparedness by which a large unit could mount out in hours; and, how to put the atomic weapons of the future to our own best use.
>
> These and other problems I gave to O.P. Smith and Bill Twining at Marine Corps Schools for analysis by special study groups—*a procedure almost identical to that of the twenties when we went to work on basic amphibious doctrine*. Practically nothing was deemed too fanciful for consideration. We toyed with large troop-carrying airplanes as the assault vehicles of the future, and with troop-carrying submarines, and with helicopters then in their infancy. Eventually we decided upon

the helicopter for our major assault vehicle. Years would pass before Quantico developed what became as breathtaking a doctrine as our earlier 1934 effort. But the seed that grew with the years was planted then.[80]

As technology in weaponry moved forward after World War II, the Marine Corps decided it wanted to replace the helicopter with the MV–22.

There can be no more important decision by a military service than its selection of weapons systems to carry out its missions. The Marine Corps, after careful study, decided that the MV–22 Osprey was to be its workhorse of the future to perform its missions of transporting Marines and materiel from ship to shore, one of the missions that justifies the existence of the Corps. The MV–22 was given the name "Osprey" after a hovering and diving bird of prey of that name. The Marines believed the MV–22 would strongly enhance and maintain Marine Corps missions.

The MV–22 is a revolutionary design of aircraft with tilting engines that allow the aircraft to take off and land like a helicopter and fly like a conventional airplane at speeds of 300 miles per hour, while carrying 24 fully equipped infantrymen. Each wing tip has a large engine that drives a huge propeller. At takeoff, the engine nacelles are vertical so that the spinning propellers act as helicopter rotors pulling the plane aloft. Once the aircraft is in the air, the nacelles swivel to a horizontal position, which propels the aircraft forward. The nacelles then again can be rotated to the vertical position for a vertical landing. It is meant to be a replacement of the aging CH–46 troop-carrying helicopter, which is used to ferry Marines ashore. In addition to the Marine Corps mission, it would also be used by other services to enhance drug interdiction, humanitarian assistance, and civilian rescue capabilities. It can ferry troops longer distances than helicopters and can aerial refuel en route.

Understanding the leadership exercised by Marine Corps senior officers to overcome resistance to development of the MV–22 requires an analysis of the many entities involved over the last 30 years: the Marine Corps, Congress, the Department of Defense, the Secretary of Defense, contractors, and the media.

A foundation and overview for the Marine Corps' decision on its need for the Osprey are provided by the testimony by Commandant James L. Jones before the Senate Armed Services Committee on May 1, 2001. This statement addresses the aircraft's operational performance, mishaps and their investigations, challenges with Congress, the press, and competition among aircraft manufacturers:

It was over twenty years ago that the Marine Corps began to consider replacement options for its aging CH–46E Sea Knight and CH–53D Sea Stallion helicopters. Following a rigorous evaluation of future mission requirements, tilt-rotor technology was selected as the best option to achieve future needs for its promise to revolutionize our expeditionary capabilities. Since the early 1980s, various Government agencies and contractors have conducted seven major Cost and Operational Effectiveness Analyses. Each analysis validated the merit of tilt-rotor technology and concluded that the Osprey was potentially more cost and operationally effective than any existing alternative.

Over time, it became apparent that the enormous potential of tilt-rotor technology would allow the Marine Corps to greatly expand the scope of its combat operations. The Osprey would allow the Marine Corps, for the first time, to move away from traditional amphibious operations to more advanced, sea-based, expeditionary operations. At twice the speed, three times the payload, and five times the range, this aircraft significantly improves our operational reach and tactical flexibility. Furthermore, the Osprey dramatically increases our strategic agility with its capacity to self-deploy over 2,100 nautical miles with but one aerial refueling. Finally, tilt-rotor technology also has great potential for civilian application.

The Marine Corps' fleet of CH–46E and CH–53D helicopters began their service in the mid 1960s. At the end of their twenty-year initial projected service life, both began experiencing escalating maintenance costs; reduced reliability, availability and maintainability; and significant performance degradation. These challenges are even more pronounced today, as the average age of our CH–46E and CH–53D helicopters is over thirty years. These helicopters are old, their production lines are closed, parts are scarce, and their maintenance requirements exceed the bounds of reasonableness. They are truly "legacy systems" with numerous current and projected deficiencies: inadequate payload, range, and speed; and, no self-deployment or aerial refueling capability. Clearly, a capable replacement aircraft is required and long overdue.

The tilt-rotor, vertical/short takeoff and landing (V/STOL) Osprey is designed to replace our aging fleet of medium-lift helicopters and remedy their deficiencies while expanding our mission envelope. The MV–22 incorporates myriad advanced technologies: composite materials; fly-by-wire flight controls; digital cockpit; and a sophisticated airfoil design. The MV–22 can carry 24 combat-equipped Marines or one 1,700-pound single point external load. Its two 38-foot rotor systems and engine/transmission nacelles mounted on each wing tip allow it to operate like a helicopter for takeoff and landing. Once airborne, the nacelles rotate forward 90 degrees, converting the MV–22 into a high-speed, high-altitude, and fuel-efficient turbo-prop aircraft.

During the development of the MV–22 there were four serious accidents. It is a well-known fact that military aviation is an oftentimes hazardous undertaking. In 1954, the Department of Defense had its highest number of aviation accidents: 775. In the 1990s, thanks in part to technological advances the Department averaged about twenty aircraft accidents per year. However, the development of new aircraft retains inherent risk and, despite our best efforts, the MV–22 is not exempt from such risk. In the years of its development there have been four Class A mishaps, two involving the MV–22.

The first mishap of the MV–22 occurred on June 11, 1991, when Bell-Boeing Full Scale Development ship #5 crashed as a result of two out of three roll gyros being wired incorrectly. Essentially, the aircraft lost control due to reversed roll channel wiring. The second mishap occurred on July 20, 1992, as a result of an engine fire that spread through one of the nacelles and subjected the pylon-mounted drive shaft to high temperature exposure, causing it to fall. Consequently, the remaining good engine was unable to drive both prop-rotors and the resulting crash claimed seven lives. Tragically, there were nineteen fatalities in the third mishap that occurred on April 8, 2000. The cause of this accident has been primarily attributed to flying outside the flight envelope established for the MV–22 (250% above the Naval Air Training Operating Procedures Standardization limit). The most recent mishap occurred

December 11, 2000, near New River, North Carolina. A flight control hydraulic system failure was compounded by a flight control software anomaly, resulting in a crash and four fatalities. While acknowledging the tragic consequences of these mishaps, it is also important to recognize that none were the result of any failure of tilt-rotor technology.

The MV–22 has been described, by some, as an unsafe aircraft—a flawed hybrid, neither a good fixed wing aircraft nor a good helicopter. However, the facts show that the MV–22's safety record compares favorably with the safety records of most tactical aircraft in the Department of Defense at a similar time in their program life. The principal aircraft the MV–22 will replace, the CH–46 Sea Knight, had 44 mishaps during its first five years of service four decades ago. In the face of such enormous difficulties, adjustments in training methods, flight procedures, and maintenance were made.

The MV–22 has weathered over two decades of scrutiny. Seven major Cost and Operational Effectiveness Analysis studies have confirmed its viability and concluded that it is more cost-effective than any helicopter or any mix of conventional helicopter types. It is, in fact, the only practical alternative that meets the requirements of the Marine Corps. Other options offered no real advantages in cost savings avoidance, given the requirement. In fact, other options are accurately described as a "step back." A comparison of the capabilities of the MV–22 with those of the aircraft it will replace is illustrative.

The CH–46E has a crew of three, a payload of 12 combat troops or 4,000 pounds external, a cruise speed of 100 knots, and a combat radius of 75 nautical miles. By comparison, the MV–22 has a crew of three, a payload of 24 combat troops or 11,700 pounds (single point external), a cruise speed of 250 knots, and a combat radius of over 240 nautical miles. Additionally, it is capable of aerial refueling, "high speed" externals (10,000 pounds @ 227 knots), and it has an exceptionally large area of influence.

A thoughtful consideration of current and future threats, as well as the multitude of other demands for limited resources, leads me to the conclusion that the capabilities of the MV–22, which will enhance our national security, continue to justify the investment. We must understand that our armed forces help to protect and promote our national security through military forward presence operations that enable our Nation to project power and influence, and by maintaining the ability to conduct operations across the spectrum of conflict. Our men and women in uniform will always be the foundation for success in these endeavors. However, they will need superior equipment and weapons systems to prevail on the complex battlefields of the future. This really requires the Nation to leverage technology to not just do things better, but do things differently.

Maintaining our technological edge over future adversaries is fundamental to our Marine Corps success—the MV–22 significantly contributes to this requirement.

### The Role of the Office of the Secretary of Defense

The Office of the Secretary of Defense (OSD) has the responsibility for ensuring the defense and security of our country and our allies. Its role is to provide oversight to ensure effective allocation and efficient management of our resources consistent with administrative appropriateness for approval plans and program. The major entity with that responsibility in DOD is the Secretary of Defense and the section in the Office of Program Analysis and Evaluation (PA&E), which has the task of monitoring the cost and design of proposed weapons and weapons systems.

### Department of Defense

In 1991, the Pentagon comptroller of OSD, Sean O'Keefe, summed up his position: "The MV–22 may appear to be superior to existing helicopters, but our goal is to find ways of performing our most critical mission acceptably, at a funding level that does not draw excessively from our many other critical military missions."

The strongest opposition was from the Pentagon's Program Analysis and Evaluation office. When Richard Cheney became Secretary of Defense in the Bush administration, the influence of PA&E was fortified, and it renewed its effort to eliminate the MV–22. This gave Assistant Secretary of Defense for PA&E David Chu the opportunity to hit back at the military, arguing that it would be less expensive to update the CH–53E and VH–60. He maintained those aircraft could perform the same mission as the

MV–22 at one-half the cost, but the Marine Corps took the position that Chu's plan was more expensive, not less.

Cheney was persuaded by Chu's argument; he announced his intention to cancel the MV–22 in April 1989.[81] His reasoning was that it was too expensive; that the Cold War threat appeared to be diminishing; and that the defense budget needed to be cut in the expectation of a reduced threat to world peace.

Throughout Cheney's 4-year tenure as Secretary of Defense he made several attempts to cancel the MV–22, but each time he was overridden by Congress, which would not permit its cancellation. The project had bipartisan support. Why? First, because the Marine Corps made it clear it wanted and needed the MV–22. All Members of Congress need the support of their constituents. To get re-elected to Congress, it is necessary to obtain and maintain benefits for their respective congressional districts. The major benefit for constituents is jobs.

In addition, the proponents agreed that not only would the MV–22 improve the military's ability to perform its mission, but it also afforded possibilities to revolutionize domestic travel. The MV–22 could take off and land from a downtown or city helicopter pad, which promised to reduce the ever-increasing traffic activity at civilian airports. Previously inaccessible areas of the country could now be serviced. The existing major airports could expand their activity without need for the cost of constructing new runways.

The Marine Corps was prevented from lobbying—publicly—for the MV–22 because of its subordinate position to the Secretary of Defense. There were, however, subtle ways it could campaign for the MV–22. One Congressman, Representative James Bilbray, related: "I have never met a Marine yet from the pilot that is a second lieutenant . . . to some of the top people in the Marine Corps that did not whisper in my ear, 'The MV–22 is the plane we want.'"[82]

Congress was not convinced that there was really a cost-effective substitute for the MV–22. Attempts by OSD to search for alternatives were simply a delaying tactic. In addition, an Institute for Defense Analyses study concluded the MV–22 was the most cost-effective option to replace the aging Marine Corps helicopters.

Congress ultimately prevailed. OSD's recalcitrance aggravated Congress, which expanded its support. Congress was not going to be manipulated or denied.

The controversy over the MV–22 between DOD and Congress continued throughout Cheney's 4 years as Secretary of Defense. On July 2, 1992, an article in the *Washington Post* stated, "Cheney sounded his retreat in a meeting with 13 Members of Congress from Texas and Pennsylvania, home states of the manufacturers." Those who were present said Cheney agreed to spend $1.5 billion and test the first six production models but gave no assurances that the Bush administration would endorse full-scale production. Cheney also said he would continue to explore other alternatives.

The Marines were tenacious in fighting for the Osprey, maintaining that the (then) overall $37.3 billion price tag on the Osprey program would be well worth it because it would give them a revolutionary ability to attack rapidly over a far greater area. The Marine Corps considered the new plane "critical" to its ability to operate in the $21^{st}$ century. The Marines plan to replace all their current troop-carrying helicopters with the MV–22, acquiring about 360 of the aircraft over 10 years.

Because the MV–22 was still being put through tests, some mishap victims' family members were understandably upset and expressed that they were "guinea pigs." To this allegation, Commandant Jones responded: "These are certified airworthy aircraft. We didn't put people at risk. There is no such thing as human guinea pigs in this."[83]

The Air Force's retiring special operators commander, Lieutenant General Maxwell C. Bailey, said: "The fighting in Afghanistan proves there is a need for the MV–22 Osprey, despite the problems. . . . This war has definitely exposed the need for a MV–22."[84]

As accidents were reported, the press raised the prospect that these crashes would terminate the Osprey program. The Marine Corps continued to fight for it as its main combat workhorse of the future. Commandant Jones told reporters that he was confident that the Osprey would some day replace all military helicopters. Lieutenant General Fred McCorkle said in an interview after the accident that "for the Marine Corps, in spite of the crashes, it was essential to the mission. The Osprey is the fighting machine we need. The leadership of the Marine Corps, doesn't have any question about the safety and reliability of the Osprey. . . . Three years from now if you don't have an MV–22, you aren't going to be invited to the war."[85]

### The Allegation of False Maintenance Reporting

The Marine Corps as an institution is known for its character and integrity. This was carefully scrutinized in the development of the MV–22.

On January 12, 2001, the Marine Corps became aware of an allegation that had been made of false maintenance records on the MV–22. It goes without saying that if the maintenance records are falsified, there could be a safety problem with an aircraft that, if not revealed and corrected, could cause accidents, death, and inquiries. It would be criminal if such falsification was motivated to prevent the termination of the MV–22, an aircraft the Marine Corps wanted badly for its combat missions. Cancellation would also mean that billions of dollars would "go down the drain."

The allegation was made that the MV–22 squadron commander directed that maintenance action reports were to be edited to make "problems disappear." The objective was to falsify the maintenance records to improve the aircraft's performance rating. Incredibly, at an all-hands meeting of MV–22 personnel, the commanding officer told them: "We need to lie."

This allegation surfaced because one of the officers at that meeting taped the order given by the commander to submit false reports and sent copies of the tape to the news program "60 Minutes" and to the Secretary of the Navy. An immediate investigation of the allegation was made that resulted in reprimands for the commander and the aviation maintenance officer and forced overhauls in the MV–22 Osprey hydraulic and software system.

Of course, this allegation raised the question of whether the mishaps in April of 2000 and in December 2000 could have been prevented if there was an accurate reporting in the maintenance records. If an officer was responsible, there would be accountability. Depending upon the finding, he would be exonerated or take the consequences.

The Pentagon Inspector General conducted its own investigation. It concluded the alleged falsification of records had nothing to do with the accidents, and those officers responsible for falsifying the records were reprimanded.

The Marine Corps has a long history of battlefield innovation, with many of our military's most successful efforts coming in the field of maneuver. It was the Marine Corps that pioneered the military use of helicopters over 50 years ago, creating a new form of maneuver that significantly changed tactics having global impact. The Harrier and Osprey are similar innovations. The Osprey represents a major step in a new direction and the Marine Corps believes strongly that it is vital for the missions of tomorrow. An emerging fleet of MV–22s will ensure that our Marine Corps will continue to be ready for the missions in the 21$^{st}$ century. The MV–22 is the result of many years of research, development, and constant testing. The Marine Corps has never let up in its determination to have the MV–22 as its combat workhorse for assault support. There has been a constant concern in the development of the MV–22 for the safety and well being of Marines, present and future. General Jones said, "In the Marine Corps we do not love our machines, we love the people who use the machines and suffer loss of life. It is very painful for the entire Marine family."

Chapter 5

# "You Have to Be Heard, and You Have to Be Felt": The Importance of Presence

## Visiting

Despite distractions and preoccupations with many problems of great import, a leader must never lose touch with his troops and must maintain the closest contact with them through frequent visits with them.

General John A. Lejeune, as commander of the Army's 2$^d$ Division in France during World War I, made it part of his leadership style to visit the troops frequently. He recommended that:

> to be a really successful leader, a senior officer must avoid aloofness. He should not place himself on a pedestal and exercise command from a position far above the heads of his men, he must come down to the ground where they are struggling and *mingle with them as a friend and as a father*. A word or two of sympathy and of praise spoken to wounded men or to men exhausted from the stress of combat may change depression to exaltation and, being spread about among the men, may cause them to feel that their chief has their welfare at heart and that he is full of human sympathy for them.[1]

Before a battle, Lejeune would hold conferences with the regiments, battalions, and every commander, down to and including platoon leaders of the battalions who were to lead off the attack. He went to the front lines to observe the terrain over which they would be called to advance, just before dawn, on the crucial day of battle.

He visited each of his 12 battalions of the 2 infantry brigades, assembling the officers and men by companies around him, addressing them on their *esprit de corps*, and telling them of his confidence in them, saying he was certain that no enemy, however tenacious or courageous, could stop their advance. He would describe the immediate objectives to be attained and the associated strategies, the effects of victory, of their devotion to the cause for which they were fighting. He emphasized, "It matters but little what happens to us as individuals, the only things which really matter are the welfare of the great Division to which we belong and the speedy and decisive defeat of the enemy."[2]

Lejeune was a brigade commander before becoming commander of the Army's 2$^d$ Division. He described how his interaction gave him a feel for his troops:

> My conception of duty as commander of the 64$^{th}$ Brigade involved the gaining of the good will and the affection of the officers and men. I wanted to know them and I wanted them to know me. To accomplish this, I made personal visits to each regimental and battalion commander and impressed upon them that it was the desire of Brigade Headquarters to help them in the performance of their tasks in every appropriate way; that they should not hesitate to let us know their troubles or to ask us for what they needed; and that I wanted them to feel that I was their friend.
>
> I then visited each company, and when doing so, I not only questioned the company commanders concerning their mission, duties, and plans of defense, but I personally inspected the roller kitchens, observed the men at mess, and made inquiry regarding their food, their clothing, and their grievances. I also went into every front line position and in so doing, tramped untold miles through the trenches. I talked to groups of men informally, telling them that they were opposed by a wary foe who by reason of four years' war experience had acquired great skill in the profession of arms; that while Americans were by inheritance as brave as the bravest, it behooved them to acquire superior skill in war, and this could be done only by careful attention to their duties and by unremitting study and training.[3]

Visiting the troops was always a very emotional experience for him:

> My heart swelled with pride whenever I moved about among the men, which I did each day, sometimes in making informal

inspections, sometimes in presenting decorations, when I made an address, and at other times in attending horse shows, entertainments, religious services, boxing matches, and baseball or football games. As the Division Commander, I became somehow a symbol of the Division's *esprit* in the eyes of the men.

I felt myself to be the patriarch of the clan; every officer and man had his own place in my heart. It was a marvelous and never-to-be-forgotten companionship. Of priceless value to me now that I am growing old is the knowledge that I still retain the affection and the good will of the many thousand officers and men who served with the 2$^d$ Division during the period it was under my command.[4]

Lejeune reached out to his men with commendations. One of these read: "Owing to its world wide reputation for skill and valor, the 2$^d$ Division was selected by the Commander-in-Chief of the Allied Armies as his special reserve, and has been held in readiness to strike a swift and powerful blow at the vital point of the enemy's line. The hour to move forward has now come, and I am confident that our Division will pierce the enemy's line, and once more gloriously defeat the enemy."

Lejeune had several thoughts in mind when issuing this order. He knew that the junior officers and men had very little information about the general progress of the war, and in fact their knowledge was almost entirely confined to the happenings within their own units. He wished to make an appeal to their *esprit de corps*: "The order, I was told, had an excellent effect, as it caused each man to feel that he had learned something of the inner workings of the great machine, that he himself was an important part of it, and that the 2$^d$ Division would do its full share in helping to bring the war to a victorious end." His words reached beyond just the Americans:

It had an effect of some importance on the enemy. During the days and nights of constant fighting which ensued, the lines shifted back and forth, especially at night. One of the German prisoners, when captured, had in his possession the dispatch case of an American officer which he said he had picked up on the battlefield, and which contained a copy of the order. The prisoner said it had been translated and read aloud to the men of his company by a German soldier.[5]

Chesty Puller, winner of 5 Navy crosses, believed in visiting and, in particular, leading from the front. A veteran Marine sergeant, Red O'Neill, remembered for years Puller's early-morning instruction when he halted his troops in an exercise period: "Now, when this regiment goes into action, there will be platoon leaders in front of the platoons, and company commanders in front of the companies. The battalion commanders will be in front of the battalion—and your regimental commander [Puller] will be in front of all." It was not idle talk. It was part and parcel of his leadership style throughout his career as commander of a regiment in the First Marines; he began training them with characteristic thoroughness.

General Oliver Prince Smith, the assistant division commander, who came to observe Puller's work, arrived when Puller was off on a command post exercise, simulating an assault landing. Puller, taking only his staff and communications troops of the regiment, had crossed a bay near their camp to land on the far shore. Smith followed in search of Puller; he went in from the beach on foot and soon found the command posts of the two assault battalions, where their officers were waiting for developments. Puller was not to be seen. "He's up ahead," an officer said. Smith trudged inland. When he overtook Chesty, Smith laughed: "Lewis, don't you know that by the book you've got to have the regimental CP *behind* the battalion posts?"

"That's not the way I operate," Puller said. "If I'm not up here, my people will say, 'Where the hell is Puller?'"

What about the risks when visiting combat forces? When Smith had gone, Puller spoke to his staff: "I know you'll hear 'em say I'm a damned fool for exposing myself, and running along the front lines, and that I'm just a platoon leader at heart. I go up there because that's the only way a field commander can handle a force in combat. It was the reason Lee and Jackson exposed themselves so often in the War Between the States. I recommend it to you. It has nothing to do with bravery. I can feel fear as much as the next man. I just try to keep my mind on doing my duty."

A young officer spoke up: "But Colonel, you expose yourself like a private, and you're the most valuable man in the outfit."

"No officer's life is worth more than that of any man in his ranks," Puller said. "He may have more effect on the fighting, but if he does his duty, so far as I can see, he must be up front to see what is actually going on with his troops. They'd find a replacement for me soon enough if I got hit. I've never yet seen a Marine outfit fall apart for lack of any one man.

"I don't want to go up under the guns just for show. It's only the idiots and the green kids who think they're bulletproof. But if you don't show some courage, your officers won't show it either, and the kids will hang back. It's *that* kind of an outfit that always has trouble."[6]

Puller led many marches, pushing his troops to prepare for combat. One broiling day, he pushed them near the limit: "I want nobody to fall out today unless he falls on his face, unconscious. You're going to need every ounce of endurance you can build up, when you get into combat. Anyone who staggers to the roadside, and then sits down, will be court-martialed or surveyed out as medically unfit."

It was a 22-mile march, under an incredibly hot sun, over an asphalt highway. Many strong youngsters were felled, including Captain Regan Fuller, who was only 2 weeks out of bed from a shipboard appendectomy; Puller stopped by to congratulate him on his courage in keeping up for so long, for there were then only 2 miles to go. The going was tough, but Puller stayed with his troops. He asked no more of his men than he was willing to, and did, give.

One of his men was Private Gerald White who wrote in his diary: "Puller must have marched twice the distance we did, for all day long he kept marching up and down the column, jaunty as a bantam rooster, pipe clenched in his teeth, ever alert to see that men who were succumbing to the heat, exhaustion, or blisters were taken care of by corpsmen. Many times today I saw him take a BAR, machinegun, or mortar off the shoulder of some Marine whose fanny was dragging and carry it to give the poor guy some respite." Puller actually led from the front, the back, and the side.[7]

An hour or so after the start of the march, Corporal W.B. Winterberg said he was astonished to see Puller approaching: "He was running—and I don't mean walking—and he'd come back down that column, at least a mile and a half to see if I was still at the rear. Imagine an old bird like that. He ran back to the front, too. We all thought he was a wonderful son of a bitch."[8]

During the battle at Guadalcanal during World War II, a Marine in Puller's outfit commented, "The men needed to be in good shape. When, after weeks of attrition, his unit was down to 500 men, it was called upon to hold a line 2,000 yards long against a Jap division storming to capture Henderson Field. With three artillery battalions walking a barrage from 25 yards in front of the forward foxholes 1,000 yards into Jap territory and back again, Puller's Marines held against three bloody assaults when the Japs came in crying, 'Blood for the Emperor; Marines, you die!'"

As was his practice, Puller was with his men, leading and encouraging: "In the black night of pouring rain that was lit only by the flash of the guns, Puller moved from foxhole to foxhole, steadying his men, who fought the Japs with a strange, defiant battle cry of their own: 'To hell with the

Emperor! Blood for Franklin and Eleanor!'" Puller said they thought up this war cry themselves.

In the Korean War, Puller's visiting had a marvelous impact on his men's morale. With the fall of the next ridge, Hill 660, Cape Gloucester was made safe. Puller inserted himself into the final fighting though he had no battalion to command. Before the guns stopped, a staff officer from Division was spreading a new version of Puller's magic formula for handling men in battle: "I went up there in the heaviest of the action, when fire was flying all around us. Puller walked around the *outside* of the wire at Hill 660, and he stopped at every dugout to talk to some kid. He'd say, 'How's things going, old man?' just as if he'd come from next door to borrow a cup of sugar.

"Those kids thought it was the greatest thing that ever happened. You'd think he had been handing out thousand-dollar bills down the line, and that there was some place here to spend 'em.[9]

"Puller had found one demoralized boy sitting stonily in his hole, looking out with the telltale 'thousand-yard stare.' He muttered over and over: 'Colonel, we got to get the hell out of here.' Puller responded: 'That's no way to talk, old man.'

"Puller proceeded to lead the boy a few paces to the rear and sat with him for ten minutes or so: 'Look old man, I wanta go home, too. I'm not getting any younger. Hell, I'm forty-five years old, you know that? I got a family at home. I know this dump is no good, but neither of us is going home until we lick these bastards. We've got to help make our folks safe back home. I'll try to get you some hot chow up here, old man.'

"The boy went back to his hole with a brighter look in his eye."[10]

General Ray Davis commented that after Puller was badly wounded and insisted on staying with the fighting, his commander would not let him go into combat: "I was always convinced that Lewis Puller would not have survived had he not been crippled. You know, his old wound from Guadalcanal flared up and got him down where he couldn't walk. They were carrying him around on a stretcher. I was convinced that if he had been able to walk around the way he was prone to do, he was going to be killed."[11] Being awarded five Navy Crosses obviously meant repeated exposure to danger of being killed or wounded. While Puller may have appeared reckless in his supervision and exposure, he had a purpose.

During the Korean War, Puller's outfit moved forward with unrelenting aggression, and by leading from the front where the war was being fought, he was able to keep the forces moving in a coordinated fashion. "Puller's swift drive hurried adjoining forces in an effort to keep pace.

Captain Ray Stiles of Ridge's Battalion saw that the secret was not only in Puller's incisive orders: 'He gave us pride in some way I can't describe. All of us had heard hundreds of stories about him, and today, though we couldn't actually *see* him doing great things, he kept building up our morale higher and higher, just by being there.'

"When we were moving up, two companies from the adjoining battalions marched abreast and got a little mixed. One of the kids yelled: 'What outfit you with, Mac?' 'The Fifth Marines. How about you?' 'I got it better. I'm in Puller's.'

"The troops in the First thought of the Old Man before they thought of the regimental number."[12]

The effectiveness of Puller's presence up front in the fight was illustrated by an observation made during the landing of the Marines at Inchon in the Korean War: "Bill Ferrigno, the veteran who was field sergeant major, had a glimpse of the Colonel: 'It was like going through hell, passing down that Seoul street. And who should we pass in the middle of it but Chesty! It was so hot that I thought the grenades and ammunition we carried would explode. The flames almost met over our heads from the burning houses, but the Colonel didn't seem in the least concerned. *It gave us an extra push*.'" Puller knew the power of morale, and he recognized that a commanding officer is in the best position to maximize or undermine it.

Chesty Puller was known to be very, very tough. General Raymond G. Davis, a division commander in Vietnam, served under him in Korea. Davis was asked: "Was Puller as demanding of himself as he was of his Marines?" He responded: "I think so. He commanded the 1st Regiment of the 1st Marine Division at Peleliu, and I commanded the 1st Battalion of the 1st Regiment. He actually sought me out to take that battalion, even though I was a junior major. As a commander, he impressed me with his total effort to support the troops. Any time we got in trouble you could depend on him to get support, reinforcements, or whatever it took. Some people say he pressed too hard, but in my view he never pressed me or forced me. What he did was to support me, and I appreciated that."[13]

Davis commented on the lesson he learned from Puller on the importance of personally engaging the troops: "As a combat commander my first and total interest was in seeing that my units succeeded. I tried to be on the scene to ensure they were supported with reinforcements, increased firepower, or whatever was necessary to make sure they would win every skirmish. A group of Marines, properly supported with artillery and air power, will never fall back or give up. They will seize the objective if you support them."[14]

## General Alexander A. Vandegrift

Commandant Vandegrift clearly understood the importance of personal presence. As a young officer, he saw extensive combat in what are now known as the Banana Wars. Stationed in Haiti between the wars, he reflected in his memoir:

> Christian missionaries were devoting their lives to these people. Although a great many Haitians became sincere Christians, many more paid mere lip service and continued with their voodoo rites and beliefs. Still we unquestionably made progress in those years and though it was very hard work—on occasion I rode thirteen to fourteen hours a day—it was also rewarding.
>
> The duty also yielded numerous lessons. As division and later department commander I came to realize the importance of frequent inspections. If these are conducted properly, I know of nothing more beneficial to a command. The subordinate must be made to realize that no one is out to 'get' him but rather that an outside eye is often more observant than a local eye that sees the same perspective day in and day out.

Then and later, he preferred to avoid official channels whenever possible in inspection matters:

> On one occasion, I reprimanded a district commander by informal, private letter. He replied with a very pained personal letter and I replied by personal letter. I explained that these deficiencies had escaped his notice and there would be no problem if he would rectify them. I heard no more from him. On my next tour of his area I was gratified to see it cleaned up as it had never been before—nor did hard feelings result from the exchange.[15]

As a Commander of the 1st Marine Division in the Pacific in World War II, Vandegrift commented on his direct interaction with Marines:

> As soon as possible, I began an inspection of the perimeter. Although I purposely wore khaki to be recognized, I also wore a pith helmet [unarmored] because the steel helmet which I carried on my arm gave me a devil of a headache.

> In each sector I visited regimental headquarters, checked over the map situation, and went on to battalion headquarters and then down to companies and platoons, front lines and outposts. This way I talked to a lot of Marines, encouraging them to sound off and showing an interest in their problems. They were a salty lot, bronzed and lean, their dungarees practically in shreds. They held the enemy in terrible contempt. They laughed at Louie the Louse [a float plane that dropped flares] and Washing Machine Charlie [a lone Japanese aircraft flying around an area to keep the camp on guard] and even at the new long-range howitzers which they called "Pistol Pete." They joked about nearly everything but their humor didn't fool me. They were tired men. I wanted desperately to get them off the island [Guadalcanal]. They accepted their fate with marvelous equanimity.[16]

He pointed out another reason for the need to visit his troops:

> We listened to Tokyo Rose with considerably more amusement than to some of our own news broadcasts which tended to paint too black a picture of our situation on Guadalcanal. Defeatism is a terrible disease in a military organization. It can spread faster than dysentery or malaria. Because of that, I always tried to display confidence during my daily tours of the perimeter. When, for example, I saw an emplacement protected by only one or two strands of wire which was all that was available, I would say cheerfully, "That will hold anything they can throw against us."[17]

As a Division Commander on Guam, Vandegrift described the importance of Commandant Holcomb's presence:

> A few days later our cup brimmed over. Late on October 21 the Commandant of the Marine Corps, General Thomas Holcomb, flew in with several members of his staff. His visit put me in two minds. One, I looked forward to seeing him both because I could talk to him about many problems and because I knew he would inspire the troops as no one else could.

In the morning I took the party on a tour of the perimeter. I wanted the Commandant's reaction to my positions because I regarded him as the best tactician in the Marine Corps.[18]

During the Iwo Jima fighting I had wanted to get to the Pacific, not only to visit the wounded and the troops who were fighting so hard but also to see something of the largest operation yet mounted in the Pacific war—Okinawa, slated for April 1, 1945.

Much as I hated to admit it, my presence in the field could have yielded very little. I held the utmost confidence in my commanders or they would not have been there. In Washington, on the other hand, I had my job—at this particular time the perennial, seemingly endless Congressional hearings attendant to the next budget. On April 8, I finally shook free of the Capitol.

Field Harris, Assistant Commandant for Air, Jerry Thomas [Colonel Gerald Thomas, Operations and Training Officer], and I flew to the west coast, inspected installations in San Diego and San Francisco and proceeded to Honolulu. After conferring with General Holland Smith and his staff I flew to the island of Maui to visit the splendid 4$^{th}$ Marine Division, just returned from Iwo Jima, its fourth assault.

The Maui tour gave him a feel for the situation:

My gloom deepened at the sight of Cliff's [Clifton B. Cates] diminished division. Every inch the field commander, Cates tried to give me some idea of the fighting on those awful sands. As I talked to him and to many of his officers and men, I felt a terrible gratitude made the worse because no word of mine could express it properly and fully.

We flew on to the newly established Guam headquarters of Admiral Nimitz where I inspected Bobbie Erskine's 3$^d$ Division, also just recently returned from the Iwo Jima battle. I received a rude shock in Guam. To my consternation, Nimitz did not think I should visit Okinawa—my main reason for making the long trip. I thought I knew what was bothering him. It was the Saipan controversy and that was probably the main reason Holland Smith was sitting back in Pearl Harbor.

In Nimitz's mind, I concluded, a senior Marine general might upset the applecart of command relations by barging into Okinawa. I subtly tried to quiet his fears, but at the same time I let him know I intended to visit my Marines.

He countered with a suggestion to visit Iwo Jima. Recognizing a temporizing attitude and wanting to see the island anyway, I flew up the next day with Jerry and Field Harris. The commanding officer of the Army garrison unit showed us around. He had built a road up to Mount Suribachi, the elevation on the extreme left from where the enemy poured his lethal shower on the landing Marines. I later wrote General Holcomb: "I have had the privilege of going to Iwo and standing on Suribachi, and the terrain from there just beggars description. . . . I still don't see how they got ashore and having gotten ashore, I don't see how they stayed there."[19]

The wounded Marines always provided heart-wrenching scenes with his visits to the hospital. General Vandegrift recalled:

While the staffs worked out details, Bill [W.H. Rupertus, his aide] and I went below to see the wounded Marines. The pathetic sight of rows of helpless men, some of them only boys, brought home the crushing responsibility of command. Some of these Marines were in a bad way but the spirit they displayed deeply moved me and made me terribly proud. When I was satisfied that everything possible was being done for them, I returned topside.

**The Helicopter**

In the last 40 years, a revolutionary change has enabled commanders to visit their troops, to go by air to the scene of combat, to get to trouble spots quickly—the helicopter. General Lewis Walt, the senior Marine commander for 2 years in the Vietnam War, commented on this more efficient and rapid way of visiting and inspecting his troops: "To me, as a commander, the helicopter was one of the most significant differences of this war. Since Guadalcanal, as both a battalion and regimental commander in combat, I had chafed at my progressive isolation from the places where the battles were being fought. Modern warfare seemed to doom the commander to sit in some cubicle and fret out each bit of information that came in, hoping it was correct and not missing some small but vital fact.

"The helicopter ended this dismal restriction. Like the horse a century earlier, it lifted the commander above the tumult and let him see from place to place with comparative ease and safety. This new Pegasus allowed me not only to see what was going on, but also to know, first hand, what the men of my command were enduring, and to learn, assess, and share each unit's response to the circumstances of Vietnam." He made a comparison of pre– and post–World War II combat: "The incidents and men were strangely alike except for the dates, and it didn't even seem surprising when the United States Cavalry came to the rescue—only now they were riding in helicopters."[20]

General Ray Davis, whom Army General Creighton Abrams cited as the most outstanding of the 50 division leaders he had ever worked with, was asked: "How did you find out, throughout your career as an officer in the Marines, what was going on in the lower ranks? How the people felt? What the pulse of the enlisted Marine and Sailor was?"

Davis replied: "I guess it started in my early years even in college when I became a student of the history of Stonewall Jackson. I've collected things and studied and wrote some reports and made some presentations on Stonewall Jackson. The thing that impressed me most about him were reports of him on his horse going to the scene of the trouble. That pretty much describes my approach. Whether the trouble was in the barracks or something like a fire on a hill, I just had an urge to go there and confront whatever it was. This has led me to move right into the middle of every kind of situation imaginable and confront the people and talk to them. To get their views, I had a system of symposiums with junior officers that I established in various places ahead of them. Visiting troops in their barracks, never having an inspection without stopping and finding out where individuals were from, how they spend their liberty, what they're doing toward off-duty study, marriage, children, families, financial problems—this kind of thing. I suppose the answer to your question is direct contact with as many individuals as my time permitted, day, night, midnight, before reveille, or whenever there was an opportunity to come face to face and involve myself with individuals."

Could the troops and their commanders infer the visits as a lack of trust? Davis made a clear distinction between personal leadership and spying or disrupting the chain of command. "My interest was never of that sort," he said. "It was more like the inspector general who sits and listens directly to those in the lowest echelon and their views and their complaints, primarily. My objective was to get at the facts right down at the lowest levels. I've attended many staff meetings at various command levels, participated in discussions when I could, commended those that were good, condemned those that were not. Again, this idea of a direct approach and going to the scene of the action, more or less seemed to succeed."[21]

Then Davis was asked: "What was the reaction from your staff, junior officers, the enlisted people, the NCOs? Did they appreciate this? How did they generally react?"

"Well," he said, "you run into two or three things. Those who are having problems tend to resent the commander's direct insertion into their area. On the other hand, it gave the junior officers a chance to display their wares, for example. There were times when some mighty good things were unearthed and they were rewarded for it. I never tried to use this to undercut the commanders. This happens in a lot of situations where a commander gets too involved in the details of management."[22]

General Davis elaborated on the use he made of the helicopter. "Sometimes," he said, "there was no way for the commander to get there. But in this age of the helicopter, you'd know where the problem is and you could go there and successfully influence it. You could talk to people on the radio and so forth all you want, but you are not going to get a precise indication of what's going on and what you could do about it without going there. That's the thing that takes commanders to the scene of the action.

"I don't mean you seek out a rifle company in the middle of a firefight and go sit down on top of a company commander. But you could go up and see where it is and what it is and get to a nearby place and sit down and talk with his adjacent units or his battalion commander and so forth and see what you could do to influence it.

"Sometimes there is a conflict; maybe you've got three companies going at once, with reports coming in all reading exactly the same. But you get out there, you see that one is much more serious than the other, and therefore you can shift the artillery resources and the air resources and the other things to the most serious place. That is, to me, the essential part of command."[23]

### General Robert H. Barrow

As a regimental commander in Vietnam, Commandant Barrow provided his personal insight into General Ray Davis' approach to direct leadership: "General Davis was the right man for that particular kind of situation. I don't know how to describe it other than to say he almost seemed to have a kind of sixth sense about the enemy, and while a kind of pleasant, mild-mannered man in many respects, he was also one of the most aggressive personalities you have ever encountered, sort of a bulldog determination. He would visit me virtually every day, and he didn't operate in the conventional, by-the-book fashion. He would come and sit in front of a map board that I had, and he would stare at it and stare at it. Maybe nothing was said between us for several minutes. Then he would get up and, with his hand, gesture to an area, and he'd say, 'You know, we ought to take a look at that.' I knew him well enough to realize that this was his five-paragraph order [commander's guidance for an operation]. I didn't need any more than that. He left it up to me as to what size force, how to develop the situation, whatever, but he wanted that area pretty well covered to make sure that there was no enemy or enemy caches in it. So from a simple thing like that, I could turn to my S3 and tell him what I wanted, and he would refine it and would go out to whatever forces we had to work with, one or two or three battalions, and away we would go."[24]

Barrow stated that the helicopter provided an excellent perspective for getting the feel for the area of combat. He related: "You know, when we worked on those tactical and operational manuals at Quantico, one of the things we came up with was that the helicopter gave us a whole new dimension. Some of us later proved in Vietnam that you could leave your operating base—in this case, ships at sea—and go some distance inland where you were least expected to be.

"General Davis had a practice of putting all lieutenant colonels and above in his helicopter to give them a different view of what they were doing. He made daily helicopter visits to all the units, sometimes dropping down to the level of companies. It gave him a great chance to get a good look at the terrain and the friendly situation. I spent about three days doing that with him—much more than most— much of the time spent in helicopters and in his quarters talking about what his expectations were."[25]

Commandant Barrow also did a considerable amount of supervision. If he could not be somewhere in person, he was on the telephone. "Every week," he said, "I would call the CG of a Marine Corps base or some unit. I know at first they were probably alarmed. When someone would say, 'The Commandant of the Marine Corps is on the phone,' usually he's the bearer of bad news. I'd just say, 'Well, I just thought I'd give you a call and see how things are going down in Albany, Georgia.' Well, I think that's important. You can always find time to do it. I practiced that during my four years as Commandant. I'm not suggesting that I didn't miss some weeks here and there, and it's certainly true that I'm not a big person on the telephone by the way."[26]

Barrow's philosophy on inspections, to get a feel for any situation requiring a decision, was that he "found out a great deal in poking around the Marine Corps and I guess I'm old-fashioned. When I entered, there was a school of thought that held that if you kept a clean barracks, you were a squared-away good unit, and the people who ran it had good morale and a sense of responsibility. So to the extent I could, I poked around—inspected bases. Sometimes bases didn't know I was going to inspect them, and still under those circumstances you would expect that they would be in ship-shape condition.

"The area of concern that this addresses is that in the minds of some commanders, when the Corps went to the motel type of living arrangement that gave to the individual or the two or three that were in such facilities, some sort of privacy rights that they did not enjoy in an open squad bed. If you walked into an open squad bed, every bunk and foot locker and wall locker looked just the same and squared away. You did it routinely. One of the big advances is you could do it quickly. You could walk down one row and come back the other, and inside of five minutes you just inspected maybe 40 people in the squad bay.

"When the Marines transitioned to motel-like quarters and did away with the barracks, you still had every obligation and responsibility to, sometimes unannounced even, go through the rooms and see if they are tearing up the place, or doing things that they shouldn't be doing in those facilities. And so in my looking around, I found that some of them were being abused. They were nailing things in the wall and just not taking care of it."[27]

"I always trace success and failure to individual Marines. I guess I'll never turn that subject loose. I am pleased that people are so much a key to our distinctiveness and our ability to do whatever has to be done for mission accomplishment. As a Marine officer, I kept a steady hand of interest in the people part of things."[28]

General Krulak told his oral history interviewer his philosophy on supervision in detail: "I guess the most important thing was to talk to individual Marines. I took one trip after another, not just to the operational forces but also to Marine Corps Recruit Depot in Parris Island for events like the Crucible [the final stressful exercise immediately before graduation that bestows the right to be called "Marine"]. It might be of value to know that when I finally finished my travels we had gone about 750,000 miles. That's a long, long way."[29]

Earlier Commandants revealed that they visited their troops extensively to get a feel for the situation and did things that reached to the lowest ranking Marine to confirm expectations on the commander's intent and his objective. General Krulak did something unique that was very effective in reaching every Marine in his command.

"Let me talk a bit," he said, "about some of the things that I would like young officers to know. Very similar to when I became Commandant, I had taken the time before I became CO of 3/3 to write down a planning guidance, the first expression of a new Commander's intent. On the day I assumed command, during the actual change of command ceremony, I had officers placing on the pillow of each one of my Marines a letter from me, whether they were a private or a captain. Every single member of that battalion got a personal letter from their battalion commander saying, 'Here's who I am, here's what you can expect from me, here's what I expect from you as Marine, here's what I expect from our battalion. We're in this thing together. You're going to be seeing a lot of me. I'm not spying on you. I'm with you.' And I then laid out the goals."

In June 1992, Brigadier General Charles C. Krulak was selected to serve as Commanding General, Marine Corps Combat Development Command (MCCDC), a three-star position. His marching orders from Commandant Carl E. Mundy were to "go down and make MCCDC work. In order to make MCCDC work, you had to bring to MCCDC the sense that they were going to be the change agents for the Marine Corps. MCCDC was going to become, once again, the soul of the Marine Corps. More than a crossroads. The place where the Marine Corps looked for doctrinal solutions, for manpower solutions, for organizational solutions, educational solutions, Marines would look toward the soul of the Corps, which is MCCDC."

Krulak developed a plan to immediately reach every member of his command, starting with his officers: "The first day at work I brought all of the officers at Quantico into the base theater. I explained to them the vision for MCCDC, and that they had an unbelievable opportunity to be a part of something very special. They were about to see the officer strength of the Marine Corps Combat Development Command increase by a third, and that MCCDC was going to really be a vibrant place. Instead of saying, 'Oh, this is Sleepy Hollow. Let's go out and play golf,' MCCDC was really going to be a fast moving train, and that I wanted them to get on board. Then I dismissed all of the officers but the colonels, and asked them to move to the front of the theater. They came down to the front row, and I said, 'You all are the Senate of the Marine Corps. You are like the senators. This train that I mentioned is rolling down the tracks, and by tomorrow it'll be going 50 miles an hour. The day after tomorrow, it's going to be going 90 miles an hour. You're either going to be on the train or not. There will be no harm and no foul if, in the next 24 hours, you drop me a note that says: one, 'I'd like to retire,' or two, 'I'd like PCS orders.' I promise you, you can either retire or you can take the PCS orders and I will do everything in my power to get you to the duty station you want to go to. But you need to understand that there is no place in Quantico for a colonel who is unwilling to work as hard as a PFC, a staff sergeant, a captain at the Basic School, or a major at AWS or Command and Staff. I'm going to expect that you will be leaders. I'm not going to get in your way. You're going to have an unbelievable opportunity. But if you are tired, if you are at the end of your career and Quantico was the place you were coming to take off your pack, then this will be pure misery for you. So you've got 24 hours. Give me your resignations if that's what you want, your retirement if that's what you want, or your request for orders."

Beyond calling a meeting for his officers, he had a very clear way of making it known to all he meant business: "The next morning at 0630, I went out to the main gate in Quantico, Virginia, and waved traffic with the troops on the gate and stayed there till 0830 in the morning. That afternoon, starting at 1600, I went to the back gate and waved cars out and watched, and I did that for the next week. Every morning and every evening, and it got to the point that you would see cars making U-turns to get to the other gate because they didn't want to be seen leaving MCCDC early. Finally, people realized that this little guy is serious. The train is going. Some left, some retired, but most stayed and were magnificent. These colonels really got on board and did superb jobs. The bar was set high and they all got over the bar."

Earlier in his career as a battalion commander, he described the way he reached out to the troops in the command: "On the day of my assumption of command, I asked my battalion sergeant major—a superb Marine by the name of Pete Ross—to pick me up a pair of coveralls. Then, on the first day of my command, Sergeant Major Ross and I showed up at the battalion motor pool at 0600. There were only one or two Marines at the motor pool at 0600. They wouldn't let us in. I finally said, 'Look, I'm the new Battalion Commander.' They couldn't believe it. After I repeated myself, they let me in. Using much of the knowledge I gained at Leavenworth in the course entitled 'Logistics for Commanders,' I began to inspect our rolling stock. By about 0700, I probably had 10 lance corporals and below following me and Sergeant Major Ross around, probably thinking we were crazy. By 0730 we had several staff NCOs, the motor transport officer of the battalion, and the S4 [logistics officer] of the battalion and the maintenance management officer of the battalion watching the Battalion Commander literally going through every bit of rolling stock. We were down there from about 0700 until around 1400 in the afternoon and inspected every single vehicle, every trailer, everything. By about 0830, the word was out throughout that battalion that the Battalion Commander was down there in coveralls, by this time filthy dirty, along with the Battalion Sergeant Major, pulling PM [preventive maintenance] and inspections on all the vehicles. From then on, the stage was set for what I wrote in my letter to them about 'being with you and around the area.' From then on, we would go to the armories, go out in the field, et cetera, trying to get morale up, and the troops just loved it."[30]

General Krulak would often visit part of his command unannounced. Dr. Crist asked him: "On 6 May you made an unannounced visit to the Fourth Marine Corps Recruiting District in Harrisburg, Pennsylvania. Was there a specific reason, or was this part of your 'kicking boxes' mode that you like so much?"

General Krulak replied: "It was part of 'kicking boxes' but it raises a pretty good issue and that's the concept of unannounced visits. I did that a lot. As an example, on this visit, I sent my driver up to Harrisburg the day before. He drove a four-wheel drive vehicle up there with no military plates on it. He reconnoitered where the District Headquarters was. He then met us at the airport outside of Harrisburg where we flew in. We had flown out of Washington at about 0600. So we showed up bright and early at the District Headquarters. There was no requirement for the Marines to hold a field day [thorough house-cleaning] because the Commandant was coming or to get briefings ready for the Commandant or to paint rocks because the Commandant was coming. What they got was their Commandant's visit, unannounced and unexpected. They got the opportunity to talk with their Commandant without having to get all prepared. As a matter of fact, the District Director wasn't even there. He was in Washington meeting with Recruiting Command. So it was just a great opportunity. We did these unannounced visits all the time.

"My first unannounced visit was to Cherry Point. We started to fly in and my pilot was afraid that they would know who we were. I said to just tell them you're a C–130 needing fuel. So they did. They told the tower that it was a C–130 and we landed the Gulf Stream and taxied right up to one of the AV–8 hangars and the door came down and I jumped out and spent the whole day talking to Marines, officers and enlisted. The Second Wing Commander and the Group 14 Commander and the VMA Squadron Commander had no idea I was on the ground for about 45 minutes. They knew who I was as soon I hit the ground but I was moving so fast they had trouble finding me. The point was not to harass my officers but to ensure that nobody had to prepare for my visit. I'd get a chance to see them and it would be without all of the hoopla that goes with a Commandant's visit.

"I remember a visit to Barstow [Marine Corps Logistics Base Barstow, California]. I sent the driver out. He had to land in Orange County where he rented a vehicle. We then flew into this little airport outside of Barstow and as we drove through the gate at about 0730, I looked over to my left and there was a parade deck and it was filled with Marines. They were having a practice parade for a change of command. Just about every Marine at Barstow was out on that parade deck. We parked behind this formation and I just walked up through the formation towards the commander and his staff. I got about halfway through between the commander and his staff and the formation and the sergeant major of Barstow yelled, 'What the hell are you doing on the parade deck? Get out of here!' I just kept on walking and all of a sudden they realized that there were four stars on my shoulder. We stopped the parade practice and got everybody around and I was able to talk for about an hour to the officers, staff, and NCOs and enlisted Marines of Barstow. It was great and it was very beneficial. These are just a few examples of what I did all throughout my commandancy."

Dr. Crist continued: "In addition to avoiding wasting Marines' time by 'painting rocks,' did you do this as a way of gaining a real sense of what was really going on in the Corps?"

General Krulak said, "Yes. That was the whole point. I could see it the way it really was. It was real valuable. I think an important part to note is that I never discovered, in all of that time, anything that really disturbed me. They were out there doing what Marines do, doing exactly what the Commandant would have wanted them to do. It reinforced my belief that the Corps was on the right track and the Fleet Marine Force and others were doing just what they should be doing. It was very positive. Additionally, it gave Marines stories to tell, which is also good for the Marine Corps. It is good to have a lance corporal be able to say, 'I was sitting at my desk and all of a sudden the Commandant of the Marine Corps came walking in and we spent five minutes talking about how hard it was to get brake shoes ordered for the motor pool!'"

Dr. Crist continued: "These stories are legendary in the Marine Corps. I've heard a number of them preparing for this. I notice in schedules, especially toward the latter half of your commandancy, almost half your time down was set aside for 'kicking boxes.' That's what it actually said in the calendar."

General Krulak replied: "Yes. I didn't feel I needed command briefs or dog and pony shows, or demonstrations. I just don't think the Commandant needs that. The Commandant has a pretty good idea what's happening in the command. What is valuable to a Commandant is the opportunity to talk to the young officers, talk to the staff noncommissioned officers, talk to the colonels, the commanders and talk to the troops. The best way to do that is to do it in their spaces, on their time.

"Another lesson of importance," he continued, "is when you have the opportunity, tell your people the 'why' of your actions. There will be times when you will demand instantaneous obedience. If your Marines know you to be a person who explains why you're going to do something when you have the time, then, when the time comes that you tell them to move, they're going to move because they know if you had the time you'd tell them. You need to be able to articulate in very clear terms, not just to your officers, but more importantly to your staff NCOs and to your NCOs, what it is you want them to do. In the maneuver sense, we call it commander's intent. It cannot be articulated in pure militaristic terms. It must make sense to the corporal. It has got to be an intent that is understood by the people who are going to have to execute it. In the 21$^{st}$ century, there are the strategic corporal and the strategic lieutenant.

"Motivating Marines is not a magic trick. Motivating Marines and motivating people to do what you want them to do is basically the same as it's always been. You set the example. You're not asking them to do anything that you aren't willing to do. They see you standing tall with them. I'm reading a book called *The Gates of Fire* right now, the Battle of Thermopylae and the Spartan king Leonidas. He's out there. Every single time the Spartans fought, he was there with them. This was a king. That still needs to be part of our ethos. That's why no matter how much you talk about technology and ability to have perfect battlefield awareness, sooner or later, the leadership had better be out there with the troops so that the Marines know that their leadership is with them.

"Well, any trip is always great. I mean, that's when I was happiest. After four years as Commandant, traveling 750,000 miles to talk with officers and Marines, could I see a difference? Absolutely. They all could tell me about making Marines and winning battles and why this was important. They understood why we were doing what we were doing. I think they knew I loved them. Without any question, they knew I loved them. When we left Futenma, it was a remarkable scene. We were leaving at—I think it was 0800 or 0900. We got there a little early. By the time I left, as I was walking out, there were over 1,000 Marines, lance corporals and corporals and staff NCOs and junior officers, all just standing there, had just come out, and Lord knows where they had come from, but literally they covered the whole tarmac. They were not there in any official capacity. They just wanted to be there to say goodbye. It was very emotional. We stayed there for probably an extra 90 minutes, spent an hour and a half taking pictures, individual pictures with Marines, and I gave out every coin I had. When we left, they were cheering. I think that they understood the effort that was put out over four years, and they were just appreciative of it, just like they were appreciative of P.X. and Al Gray and Carl Mundy. You know, you're so busy as Commandant that you don't understand that they are appreciative until the very end, and then it comes home."[31]

## "Feel" or "Sixth Sense"

General Anthony "Tony" Zinni provided an example of an important feel he developed while supervising combat in Vietnam: "One especially vital type of tactical knowledge is what we might call the 'sense' of a firefight. That is, the sense from sound and visual cues of what is actually happening when the bullets are flying. Closely allied to that is a sense of what you have to do to respond and act. These can only be learned from experience. Though I had a lot of operational experiences from the beginning of my time with the Vietnamese Marines, it took about three months into my tour before I was at a level of competency where I had a real 'sense of a firefight.'

"At first, when there was shooting, it was a cacophony of sounds to me. I didn't know what was going on. I had no idea whether I was in World War III or a small firefight. At the beginning I wasn't even sure which direction the firing was coming from.

"But by the end of three months, I could tell which kinds of weapons were firing, where they were firing from, and about how far away they were. I could also get a pretty good sense of what was happening by the way the firing was taking place. Was somebody just taking potshots? Or was the firing building up to a larger engagement? Was the enemy going to stand and hold in place (with all the implications of that)? Or were they simply going to engage us and then try to move away?

"By three months, I could quickly process situations like these with just a few sensings."[32]

Zinni was a company commander in the 2$^d$ Marine Division in 1971 where he served as a general's aide, an assignment he strongly resisted, but he soon realized that such duty was important to the continuation of the growth in his feel or sixth sense and assisting his senior officers with their feel. He wrote in his book *Battle Ready*:

Not long before the end of one of our Caribbean deployments, my battalion commander called me to his office at our camp on Vieques Island [a U.S. Navy bombing range in Puerto Rico] and handed me a message from the division commander, Major General Fred Haynes. Haynes was asking for nominees from each battalion to be his aide-de-camp. The last line of the message directed that our battalion's nominee be me.

"Do you know anything about this?" my battalion commander asked. "Why are we the only battalion with a directed nomination?"

"I'm as much in the dark about this as you are, sir," I told him. "I definitely do not want the job." It was a staff job, and I never wanted staff jobs.

"Okay, then. I'll tell him that," the CO said, and sent a message back to the commanding general stating that I declined the nomination.

I forgot all about this thing and went back to the field with my company.

Two weeks later, as our ship docked at Morehead City, North Carolina, to off-load our battalion landing team, I was greeted by an officer from the division staff who told me I was to immediately get in the staff car waiting at the bottom of the brow and proceed to the division commander's office to report to General Haynes.

"I can't do that," I said to him. "I have to get my company back to Camp Lejeune and settled back into our barracks."

"That's an order," he laughed.

So I let my battalion commander know where I was headed, took off for the division headquarters, and nervously entered the general's office. Haynes was a tall, distinguished-looking Texan, an Iwo Jima veteran, who was considered one of the most brilliant men in the Marine Corps. At his invitation, I took a seat.

After asking me about the deployment and how things were going, he explained what he was looking for in the job. "I want my senior aide to be my operational aide," he explained. "I'll have the junior aide, a lieutenant, to handle all the social requirements, the proper uniforms, and all that kind of business. For my operational aide I want an advisor, somebody who's been in the pits whom I can trust. I want a guy that knows what the hell goes on in a division, knows abut training and operations, and who's been in combat. I want someone who the junior officers and NCOs of the division will honestly talk to, who'll be my point of contact with them, and who can tell me what they're thinking and their perspective on what we need to improve. When we go out in the field and see what's out there, I want a guy savvy enough to say, 'What you're seeing there, General, is not good,' because he knows it's not . . . I'm removed from that. That's years ago, in my past. Now I get screened and filtered. If I talk to colonels and other generals, I get good information, but it doesn't come from the ranks. I want my operational aide to give me that sense.

"I've already interviewed all the nominees," he went on, "but waited to make my decision until you returned and I could interview you." He then read to me the list of other nominees.

"Sir, I know most of them, and you couldn't pick a finer group of captains. I'm sure you'd be satisfied with one of those guys."

Then he looked at me. "You know, Captain, the message from your CO is very interesting. It seems that you're the only nominee who does not want the job."

"I don't feel that I'm really aide material," I told him; and I meant it. You always think of an aide as a tall, bullet-headed, poster Marine. And here I was, a short, squat Italian guy, rough around the edges, and he's a better than six-foot-tall Texan—a golf-playing gentleman. (A little later, when I told him I didn't play golf, I thought I'd put the final nail in the coffin.)

By then he was smiling at me . . . just playing with me. "I take it that's just because you want to stay on as a rifle company commander," he said. "This I can understand. You don't have anything against being my aide, do you?"

"Certainly not," I said, thinking, "Shit, I hope I haven't insulted him"—the last thing on my mind.

"Well, I understand you don't want the job. I've had some tremendously talented captains who are interested and who've interviewed for it; and I appreciate your coming by. I didn't want to make the decision until I interviewed all the candidates."

This kind of confused me because I didn't think I was a candidate. I thought the message from my CO had killed that. But because I thought there might have been a misunderstanding, I said, "Well, I appreciate your interest, sir. But, no, I really don't want the job, and you have some fine officers there."

"I do; and I also understand your position; and we'll go ahead and make a decision."

"Thank you, sir, for the understanding," I said, and left.

When I got back to the battalion area, I went to my CO's office and told him everything was okay. It all seemed to be just a formality the general needed to go through so he could say he had interviewed all the nominees. But when I arrived back at my company area, there was a call waiting as I walked in. It was my CO. He'd just received a call from General Haynes. I was selected as the aide and was ordered to report for duty the next day.

It was obvious that Major General Haynes had made up his mind before he met me. Later, I found out why. He had prepared a list of eight or nine criteria—most of them fairly obvious, like commanding a company in Vietnam in combat, attendance at the career-level school for captains [amphibious warfare school], and commanding a company in the $2^d$ Marine Division. As luck would have it, I came out as the only guy in the division who met every one of the criteria.

Meanwhile, his current aide (I didn't know him well) had talked to other people who had mentioned my name; and when they matched these recommendations up with the other thing, he seems to have fixed on me.

I spent a year as the aide to two generals—first to General Haynes; and after he got orders to Korea, I became the aide to Brigadier General Jake Poillion, who'd been Haynes's assistant division commander. When Haynes left, Poillion was fleeted up [succeeded to command as the second in command] as the CG and told it was just an interim appointment; a major general would be coming down the track very shortly. In fact, the interim turned out to be six or seven months. Later when the major general did finally come down, he started making noises like he was going to keep me in place, too. So I had to really fight to get out of the job.

Though in many ways my tour as aide was a valuable experience, I never really enjoyed it; my original reasons for not wanting it remained valid. Still, I was fortunate to work for generals who were interested in my views and were highly respected leaders. And the experience exposed me to a different level of perception than I was used to. Problems I'd been sure I had absolute answers to when I commanded a company got a lot less simple. I came to realize that there was a great deal I didn't know and had to learn.

When you're down at the company level, you see things in black and white; you don't have a broader view. I'd see all kinds of things wrong in the weapons ranges, for instance, and it seemed obvious to me: "These ranges should be better. They're shabby. They need serious maintenance and renovation. This is what we're all about, and we're letting it go to hell."

Well, all of a sudden I was seeing things from a general's point of view, looking at the budget he has to work with, looking at all the alternatives, realizing he has to give some things up. Now suddenly, I was forced to realize that my "absolute answers" were not as absolute as I'd thought. And I came to appreciate that a lot of the choices generals had to make did not come out of a lack of interest or failure to care. It was a matter of priorities. It was a matter of other competing realities that you don't have a sense of when you're down at the company level.³³

Having a feel for the complexities of supervision was critical in the Marine Corps relationship with the civilian community. Zinni had this experience during his tours in Okinawa in the 1970s and 1980s. He commented on this opportunity: "These two commands came with a third responsibility—maintaining relationships with the local Okinawan community. The district included a number of small towns and villages and the major town, Kin, adjoining the camp.

"Operational command of the camp gave me the fascinating and new experience of running what was in effect a small city, while my connection with the local community added to the diverse cultural experiences I've always enjoyed and taught me a great deal about the art of negotiations, and cross-cultural communications. This would come in handy many times in the future.

"In Oriental cultures, form and politeness can be more important than our preferred 'in-your-face' direct responses. Orientals see these as insulting.

"My Civil Affairs officer, a local Okinawan, taught me a great deal about customs and procedures necessary to be effective in that community. I also tried to pick up a little of the language—not just Japanese but the local Okinawan. I rehearsed speeches in front of the 'mama-sans' who worked at the camp as laundry workers and housekeepers.

"The more experience you've got, the larger is your inventory of pattern analysis that allows you to pick up on what you need to know; you can make a solid decision based on a very few key indicators, rather than having to try to mentally process a complex or even chaotic set of inputs. After I'd had sufficient experiences of firefights, I was able to process one or two indicators fairly quickly and come up with a satisfactory course of action.

"I have to add that the kind of sensing I'm talking about is not just a matter of experience. It also involves understanding what you were sensing. There's a strong analytical component, involving reading, research, and applied intelligence. If you don't have a background of knowledge and understanding that allows you to appreciate these 'sensings,' you might undergo these experiences and miss everything they're trying to offer you. For example: Now that I know I'm hearing an AK–47 and not an M–16, I need to judge from the pattern of firing whether this is somebody who's just taking a couple of random shots and moving away or somebody who's hanging in there in a fixed position and plans to stay."³⁴

"Supervision is worthless if it's not based on experience. If I could find someone that claims to have a sixth sense with no military experience and telling me to do things, I wouldn't trust it.

"But if I'm with somebody who's had a tremendous amount of experience, and I don't mean necessarily actual experience, it could be virtual experience, it could be that this person is well-versed, deep in his or her profession, has been through exercise and training and education, has been around the world, has commanded at different levels, has been in different cultures. And if someone like that says I have a sense that this is cultural—what I read into that is not intuitiveness. I read that they have this tremendous bank of experience that allows them to see things. They see trends. They see things that they have seen before, they're able to draw from one or two different experiences and put them together to see a pattern. And this sort of pattern recognition is what I really believe the most effective decision makers call upon."[35]

In an interview with Commandant James L. Jones, I pointed out that General Eisenhower made the comment that you've got to have a feel for the troops and you do that through supervision. I asked Jones: "What is your procedure now, your routine, as Commandant as far as supervision? Every top general I've interviewed claims he has a feel or sixth sense of knowing what to do and when to do it. Do you?"

General Jones responded: "Somebody told me the other day that in two years I've set a record in terms of travel. I don't know whether that's true or not, but I'm going to check it. But clearly, the thing you have to do is keep in touch. My analysis of this job is that there's two distinct worlds I have to deal in. Maybe three but I'll narrow it to two for this discussion. One is inside the Beltway, Washington, DC, the Pentagon, the White House, the Congress, and the media. The whole business end of the Marine Corps is literally inside the Beltway. We have a campaign term for that, we call it "the battle of the Beltway." You have to be able to fight there and you have to know what the rules of engagement are and everything else, and you have to have a plan.

"The other part is the rest of the Marine Corps outside of the Beltway and that metric is completely different. It is based on what they expect leaders to do and be and you can only be effective if you're seen. You have to be more than just seen, you have to be heard, and you have to be felt. I really don't have a set approach. It kind of depends on where we go."

I asked him: "What's your procedure at Camp Lejeune?" He replied: "Well, if I go to Lejeune, I will try to have at least one session with a large number of troops. If I have to do it in three different increments, that's okay, too. In other words, if you can't get them all together, we'll do it two or three times.

"In the beginning, my standard pitch was to cover the guidance that I wrote on the day that I assumed command of the Marine Corps. I put out a conceptual, philosophical direction for the Corps. But I probably worked harder on that than I did on anything else. I deliberately didn't set objectives, but rather philosophical goals for how we should do things. Everything I do goes back to that document, even today. At the end of each year, we ask if we need to write an addendum to that document."[36]

## Showmanship

As a leader supervises in war and peace, showmanship is one of the most effective military leadership techniques. It has a significant role in permitting the leader to reach all levels of his command. Showmanship depends upon being seen and recognized by the troops and is of particular importance in combat.

Commandant Wilson was asked what he considered his most significant success in his tenure as Commandant. He responded: "I suppose that the high points of my career were when I was CG, Fleet Marine Forces Pacific, and was appointed Commandant. I am convinced that our readiness has improved. I believe we improved the quality of the Corps with the help of a great many people. The recruiting service did an outstanding job under the most difficult of circumstances.

"I believe we improved the standards of conduct of the Corps which includes the appearance, grooming standards, and weight control. I can almost spot a Marine anywhere. His pride, bearing, and alertness are marks he cannot hide. Marines are proud of this. We had some complaints during the period when the long hair was popular in Zumwalt's years in the Navy, but this had largely dissipated, even the sailors are ashamed. So I believe these are my highlights of my tour."[37]

Endorsing Commandant Wilson's comment about the hallmarks identifying a Marine was President Lyndon B. Johnson, who said of General Lew Walt, the senior Marine Commander in Vietnam for 2 years: "In February 1966 General Walt returned to Washington for consultation. On the 25th of that month, he came to see me at the White House. I can still see him walking firmly across to my desk in the Oval Office—the square jaw and steady eyes; the shoulders broad as a fullback's; the straight back of the military professional; the strong, calloused hands of a man who likes to use them, and does. In every way, he was a 'Marine's Marine,' as they say in the Corps."[38]

## Uniform and Appearance

The uniform is a critical part of leadership and showmanship. Commandant Lejeune offered his thoughts on the Marine uniform in discussing discipline:

> Discipline consists in securing the voluntary cooperation of subordinates, thereby reducing the number of infractions of the laws and regulations to a minimum; by laying down the doctrine that the true test of the existence of a high state of discipline in a military organization is found in its cheerful and satisfactory performance of duty under all service conditions; and by reminding officers that a happy and contented detachment is usually a well-disciplined detachment.

> It is accepted wisdom that well-dressed soldiers are usually well-behaved soldiers. This thought led to the restoration to the Marine Corps of the blue uniform, to the successful endeavor to induce American manufacturers to produce a khaki cloth of high grade both as to texture and dye, and to improvements in the design and the cut of all articles of uniform.[39]

Lejeune's high standards governing the wear of the uniform have continued in the Marine Corps to this day. It is a vital part of the stature of the Corps and something that sets the Marine Corps apart from the other Services and why the Corps is considered "elite."

Commandant Carl E. Mundy had some amusing reflections on the importance of the Marine Corps uniform: "When we went to the wooly-pully sweater in the Marine Corps we adopted the green British model of that and that is fine. It is a very practical piece of gear because it keeps you warm and it looks good and it is more casual, easier to work in uniform but in the early phases we authorized that throughout the Marine Corps. Here you had a Marine on recruiting duty running around with his modified blue uniform, his blue trousers, his khaki shirt, his white cover and this rather fundamentally ugly green sweater. Well, we knocked that off so now the recruiters had no sweater, they had no alternative except to put on their all-weather coat, their raincoat, the pewter-colored coat that General Barrow had brought in.

"So as I would go around the country, I would show up and even though it would be a bright sunny day and everybody else might be walking around in business suits were it a little chilly the recruiter had no alternative but to put on his trench coat. Getting in and out of cars and walking around town, it just looked rather illogical to have to be wearing a trench coat when everybody else was not and it was not raining.

"So, anyway, to make a long story short I started looking around. The Army of course had a black sweater, the Navy had gotten a blue sweater. Everybody had sweaters by that time.

"I got one of the Army sweaters which was black/navy blue if you choose to call it that and we tried various variations with it. We put red and gold chevrons on it, we had a black shirt from the Navy or navy blue shirt and put that on and used a dark tie and what not and it really was a fairly good looking uniform. The good aspect of it was that you could then wear a sweater and shirt combination that would be the same color combination as the dark blue blouse which is very uncomfortable to wear, sharp looking uniform but it is not something to wear except when you are doing parades, but you would have consistency in the uniform and it looked good and it went with the uniform.

"At any rate, I put together a package on it. Got photographs of a sharp young sergeant made with these various variations and sent it off with a recommendation that this be considered by the Uniform Board. I got a very quick reply which probably was signed 'Simmons' as I note at that time. Got a quick reply back saying that this just was not a good idea. I do not even remember what it said but anyway it was an impractical thing to do.

"So, anyway, I filed that away and one of my successors along the line, Brigadier General Gary Brown, again brought it out and sent it forth and tried to do something with it. Again it came back as an illogical idea."[40]

When Mundy became Commandant, he continued his desire to have a better and more appropriate uniform for the recruiters: "When I became the Commandant, guess what—I pulled it out early on and sent in and it was a wonderful idea. We tested the blue sweater. We adopted the blue sweater. It is very popular with the recruiters today. I wish we had been able to afford the shirt and the tie because fundamentally going back to my days on sea duty and proud as I am of Marine Corps uniforms, I do not think anybody would go out and buy a set of sky blue trousers and put on a khaki shirt with green chevrons on it and a white hat and wear it around."[41]

Commandant Mundy had an appreciation for the role that a uniform can have: "I would note only for the record that I have long had a fascination with boat cloaks, which probably by the time someone gets around to reading this oral history we will note they will ask what a boat cloak is and no one will know because it is a fading piece of uniform equipment. But it is grand. It is elegant. It is beautiful. And anyway, so I wore my boat cloak to the inauguration and, of course, drew a great deal of derision from General Powell and my Air Force counterpart and so on as to, you know, my fuzzy velvet collar and the rich, red lining. It is a very flashy piece of uniform to wear."[42]

Attention to detail for the appearance of Marines was important, particularly in ceremonial support of events in the public domain. Commandant Barrow commented on the appearance of the Marine Corps color guard: "Well, this is one of my quirks. It seems like a nitpicky sort of thing, but to have seen on television or in person for many, many years, not only the Marine Corps, but all the other people who have color guards, some of the strangest looking formations you could possibly imagine.

"Someone who looked like he was 5'2", standing next to someone who was 6'4". And it just looked like you threw it together at the last minute. So I don't think anything is sharper looking than not only a properly uniformed color guard carrying the national and organization colors correctly, but that they be sized so that you have a uniformly sized color guard. Call it a quirk, but that's the genesis of this particular letter."[43]

He was again asked about this matter in a later white letter. He responded: "Here we go again. I turned to the next white letter, and see I'm still obsessed with the idea of uniformity in color guards. And I'm saying I find it necessary to address the subject again. I hate to say it, but this initiative in time became fruitless, because after I left it lapsed back into mismanaged color guards. It still drives me up the wall."[44]

The great pride the Marine Corps has in its uniform is part of the pride and showmanship. Not maintaining a proper uniform or being under the influence of alcohol while in uniform could result in court martial. Vandegrift recalled:

> Shortly before I arrived in San Diego, a senior Marine officer known to me from Haiti gave a dinner party followed by a dance at the Coronado Hotel. This officer discourteously served drinks in his home even though he knew that his senior guest, General Butler [Major General Smedley Butler], disapproved. When Butler arrived, the host pressed a drink on him, which he refused.
>
> That was all right, but later at the dance when the host, now very intoxicated, disgraced his uniform, Butler ordered him escorted from the premises. The next day, with the full concurrence of the Navy district commander, Rear Admiral Robertson, he preferred

a court-martial charge—indeed, the admiral told Butler that if he did not so charge him he, the admiral, would.

Local papers and certain national papers picked up the story, in most cases telling a lopsided anti-Butler version. The court-martial found the officer guilty and sentenced him to a loss of a few numbers in grade. He was transferred to San Francisco and lost his life a few months later in an automobile accident, thus reviving the story.[45]

Vandegrift provided an interesting reflection on haircuts in his memoirs:

> Upon reporting to Quantico in the summer of 1933, I returned to a changed and changing Marine Corps. A long-delayed building program had given Quantico new quarters, brick dormitories and even an airfield. It was still the dual home of the Marine Corps Schools and the East Coast Expeditionary Force, the latter commanded by Brigadier General Charles H. Lyman, to whom I reported as personnel officer or S1.
>
> General Lyman stood over six feet. An intelligent, courteous, and immaculately dressed general, he was one of the most handsome officers in the Corps. He also possessed several idiosyncrasies, one of which centered on haircuts. In his early days he carried a small ruler and if a head of hair rose beyond its dimensions the owner suffered along with the company commander and company barber. The troops for this reason reversed his initials to come out with 'Haircut Charlie.' He rightfully deplored Marines walking about with their hands in their pockets—if he caught this the Marine had his pockets stitched together.[46]

Certainly, haircuts stand out in the appearance of a military man and the stature of his service. During the tenure of Admiral Zumwalt as Chief of Naval Operations, one of his famous Navy-wide "Z-gram" memos relaxed considerably the standards of appearance. Specifically, Z–57 ordered that "styles of hair, beards, sideburns and civilian clothing" be liberalized. The Sailors took advantage of this, resulting in beards and particularly longer hair.

The Marine Corps reaction was expressed by General Raymond G. Davis: "I traveled around some of that time and it was a Marine detachment.

I found without exception that every Marine, every Marine in every detachment, seized this as an opportunity to get his hair cut shorter, make himself cleaner, stand taller, be a better Marine so that he was a man apart from what he saw going on in the Navy. Almost universal among Marines serving with Navy units. To them it was just a challenge to not be a part of what they saw and to lean over the other way entirely."

General Davis concluded that the relaxing of standards by the Navy assisted Marine Corps recruiting: "The whole approach in the Marine Corps at the top was all those people are going in that direction, we'll head in the other direction and invite people who want to go our way to join us. This was successful. We found that among the American youth there were great numbers of people that wanted to go the other way and they saw us as leaders in that direction. And this was deliberate on our part, to tighten up, to restate our standards and enforce them.

"As I see it, there's only room for a certain number of elite forces in any group of forces. The elite force has to be the one that's different, the one that's a challenge to its members. As soon as you reduce these challenges and the requirements that the fellow has to meet and accomplish in order to be a member, then you've diminished the quality of the fellow who wants to compete. So I don't think you can have a Marine Corps which by definition is an elite force without having these kinds of standards that require a different kind of man or woman to step forward and say, 'I want to try to do that.'"[47]

There was a purpose in short haircuts beside grooming—health. It even provided some humor, according to Puller's biographer: "Lieutenant Lew Devine saw Puller on deck one day after Puller had come from the barber with a shaven skull. Devine laughed, and the Colonel laughed, too.

"'It's the only time I ever got away with laughing at a superior officer,' Devine said. 'He had dignity and common sense enough to realize he looked funny, and he didn't chew me out, as any other officer would have.'

"Devine did not realize that Puller was following one of his strict orders—that all troops should keep scalps cut short to avoid the menace of lice. When an Army health team visited his troops to lecture on the threat of disease from lice and other pests, Puller introduced them: 'I want you to pay close attention and do as they say. I know how to write your parents and tell 'em you've been killed in battle for your country—but damned if I can write and say you were done in by a buggering louse.' The troops howled with laughter."[48]

I asked Commandant James L. Jones about leadership and the aversion of top successful Marines to "yes men," and how he created an atmosphere that encouraged his people to challenge him during the process of decisionmaking.

General Jones said, "By watching my own reactions. You get people to do that if you're willing to hear bad news as well as good. You have to be, I think, open-minded but you have to create an atmosphere of comfort. And I think the more senior you are, the more important it is to do that. I find that most of what I do is consensus building. If you want something to last and if it's important to the institution, you need to make sure that you can get as much 'volume' as you can. You step down from office, your successor will come in and it will disappear.

"So you can drive this train and people will follow it. To me, the right balance is to know when you have to drive the train and know when you need to build consensus."[49]

General of the Army Dwight D. Eisenhower, commanding almost 2 million in the invasion of France during World War II, said, "A leader must never lose touch with the 'feel' of his troops," which required "frequent visits to the troops. . . . Visits by the high command can scarcely be overestimated in terms of soldiers' morale." Visiting gives the soldier "a sense of gratification whenever he sees very high rank in the vicinity," and the "visits improve the efficiency when men are encouraged to speak to their supervisors," and "encourages speaking to openly express their idea on how to do things better."

All the senior Marine Corps leaders in this study believed they had that feel or sixth sense; if they did not, they would not have achieved the rank of general. But is it a God-given talent, or can it be developed? This study establishes that it can be developed. The consensus of over 150 four-star generals of all Services is that experience and study are the keys, knowledge that is stored in a leader's mind, then when suddenly faced with a decision, a button is pushed in your mind and out comes the right answer. Feel is based first of all on knowledge that is developed by working hard and studying as a young officer, and continuing studying throughout one's military career. It requires an interest in people, having an understanding of men, with experience having a key role. What might be called intuition or gut reaction, described by Chairman of the Joint Chiefs of Staff General John M. Shalikashvili, is "a feeling in the part of my stomach when things are right, or they're not right, which comes from confidence after you have done things often enough—experience."

**Chapter 6**

# "We Will Not Compromise on This": Having the Character to Challenge

The leadership climate that has been cultivated within the Marine Corps rewards audacity and independent thought as essential elements of combat leadership. However, audacious generalship is not reckless, nor should it be defined or described solely in juxtaposition with foreign enemies. In fact, Marines exhibit loyal opposition and the character to challenge ideas in war and peace, in garrison and in the field. It is a notable, defining characteristic of Marines that sets them apart from military professionals in any but the smallest, most elite organizations. Examples of audacity, conviction, and intolerance of sycophants in the course of relations with friends and allies are legion, and some of the associated confrontations are legendary. An enduring characteristic of Marine generalship is undeniably the character to challenge.

## Combat

General John A. Lejeune wrote about his experience commanding the Army's 2d Infantry Division in World War I that:

> a division commander must stand ready to fight for his men, even at the risk of offending higher commanders. The knowledge that in him they have a champion who is willing to go to the mat, if necessary, to protect them from injustice, to see that they are not imposed upon, and to insist that their creature comforts are looked out for, will cause them to redouble their efforts to gratify him, to give all their strength and all their power to carry out his will, and to do more than is humanly

possible to defeat the enemy. It is indeed true that in war the spiritual is to the material as three or even four is to one.

Lejeune's memoir of that command experience includes details of an incident when he had to challenge higher authority:

> One evening—I think it was November 18th—I overheard the officer on watch at Headquarters talking over the telephone in the next room. I gathered from his replies that instructions for an immediate march were being given him. I went into the office and asked him what it was all about. He said, "The Corps is giving orders for the Division to march tomorrow morning." I took the receiver from him and said, "This is General Lejeune speaking; what are the orders for the Second Division?" The reply came, "The Second Division is to march south tomorrow morning to Dun-sur-Meuse, and on the following day it will cross the river there and march north to Stenay, preliminary to jumping off from that place on November 17." I said, "Who is speaking?" The voice replied, "Clark of Emerson."
>
> It was Lieutenant Colonel Clark, representing the Third Corps, the code word for that Corps being "Emerson." He explained that Marshal Foch had directed that the troops jump off from Stenay, which made it necessary for the Second Division to march to Dun-sur-Meuse (a distance of nearly forty kilometers) in order to cross the Meuse and then back to Stenay (about twenty kilometers), as all the bridges north of Dun-sur-Meuse were down.
>
> I told him that we had already rebuilt the bridge at Pouilly and could cross there. He explained that the instructions forbade passing through the German lines, which would be necessary in order to reach Stenay if we crossed at Pouilly. I suggested that the bridge at Stenay be repaired, and offered to do the work ourselves if the material were furnished. I then told him my persistence was due to the exhausted and weakened condition of the troops and to the necessity of reequipping and reclothing them, which could not be done while they were on the march. He answered that he was without authority to make any changes in the orders, but was simply repeating them to me as they were given to him by higher authority.

I then asked that the matter be taken up with the appropriate officer with the view of obtaining a modification of the orders. He said that all the higher officers were asleep and he did not care to wake them. I replied, "It is better to wake up one General than to have twenty-five thousand sick and exhausted men march sixty kilometers, and I will do so myself." He then said he would deliver my message.

In a few minutes he called back, saying that he was directed to inform me that the bridge at Stenay would be repaired, that the march to Dun-sur-Meuse would not take place, and that the march to Stenay could be made on the afternoon of November 16th.

I have given the details of this conversation not with any intent to criticize a loyal and faithful officer, but in order to illustrate the importance of sometimes being rather determined and persistent when necessary to protect the welfare of the officers and men under one's command.[1]

Anyone who has ever been in combat has, at one time or another, encountered staff behind the lines, handing down orders not appropriate to the situation of the troops on the front lines. Those behind the lines do not have a "feel" for the fluid and changing nature of a combat situation.

Chesty Puller did not hesitate to use his own judgment when orders were unrealistic. During the Banana Wars:

A troubling affair developed at headquarters in Jinotega. A new battalion commander had arrived from the States, who was a vigorous take-charge type, but inexperienced. He issued to then Lieutenant Chesty Puller a series of naive and wasteful orders, because he had no feel for combat in that area. One day when his company was at the village of Corinto Finca, about fifteen miles from Jinotega, Puller received an order from the new major that a bandit force was reported in a hill town some thirty miles south of his Company's position. Puller was ordered to march to this town and destroy the enemy.

It was a mandatory order and Puller put his men on the trail, using an old hunter's device he learned from his childhood, and it cut directly across the circle in which Puller expected his quarry to move. He had gone only a few miles when he learned from natives that the bandits they were after had departed the town, and were circling to Puller's left on a wide arc. He immediately turned, and at a crossing of the Tuma River, Puller found that he was only one day behind the bandits.

His Company followed for several days, until it caught the rebels on a hill in open country, attacked and overran their camp killing or capturing those who did not flee. They killed about fifty wounded animals on the scene, and went back to headquarters with a string of eighty-two captured horses and mules with pack saddles. The new major watched the victorious patrol along with the animals. Puller was obviously very successful, but the only comment from his commander was: "Why did you disobey my orders? You should have gone directly south as I told you."

He responded: "If I'd done that, you'd never have got these animals, and I'd never have seen the bandits. They'd still be tearing up the countryside. I always carry out orders implicitly, and if I had not found the enemy, I would have marched south before coming back in. Since we were successful, it seems to me it didn't matter whether I carried out the letter of the order."

The Major studied Puller's face, hesitated, and nodded in dismissal.[2]

Puller had strong feelings about the staff in combat. While recovering from a wound in a field hospital in the Pacific during World War II, he was visited by Lieutenant Colonel Russell P. Reeder, Jr., who had been sent by General George C. Marshall to evaluate the fighting against Japan.

They talked at length, and one of Puller's strongest comments was that "the staffs are twice as large as they should be. The regimental staff is too large. I have five staff officers in the battalion and I could get along with less." But he also blasted some of his superiors: "Calling commanding officers from the front lines back to battalion and regimental command posts to ask, 'How are things going?' is *awful.*"[3] He believed they should lead from the front and it would not normally be necessary to pull him away from his troops.

After securing Guadalcanal, the First Marine Division troops under Major General Archer A. Vandegrift needed medical attention and rest, particularly since they had over 500 severe cases of malaria. He and his staff concluded that Melbourne, Australia, was the best locale for his troops to quickly restore their health and return for assignment to future combat missions.

Movement of the division there required the approval of General of the Army Douglas MacArthur since it was in the part of the Pacific over which he had authority. MacArthur authorized the transfer, but placed a restriction that would have made it prohibitive:

> No transportation facilities are available in the Southwest Pacific Area to effect the move which will have to be carried out by shipping made available from the South Pacific area. . . . the already overburdened railroad facilities of Australia cannot cope with such a movement without jeopardizing operations upon which our forces are now engaged.

Melbourne was where Vandegrift wanted his troops to go, so he went around MacArthur. Vandegrift said that asked Admiral William F. Halsey for help: "I knew how he was hurting for ships, but I was not surprised at his instant reply: he was arranging for all further troops coming from Guadalcanal to disembark in Melbourne and was sending the *West Point* to move the Marines now in the Brisbane camp to Melbourne." Vandegrift said that General MacArthur later congratulated him for standing his ground.

Vandegrift reflected in his memoir of Melbourne:

> We could not have been in better hands. Having had little contact with military units, the people of Melbourne opened their hearts and homes to us. Melbourne is a perfectly beautiful city enhanced by a cool climate—all that it had to offer was offered to us. In addition, the Army maintained a nearby base hospital staffed with medical units from Cleveland, Ohio, a splendid group of professionals who made our return to health their primary concern.

> These doctors really proved a godsend. When I was standing on the docks to watch the first contingents of Col Amor LeRoy Sims' 7th Marines disembark, a British colonel remarked, "I was in charge of a base in the Middle East and saw thousands of men come through on the way to rest areas. None appeared

as tired and worn as your men." The commanding officer of the Cleveland unit said to me a little later, "Had I room, I would suggest we send this whole regiment to the hospital. Lord knows they look as if they need it."

Shortly after we settled in Melbourne, General Holcomb ordered me and Jerry Thomas back to Washington for conferences. Before leaving, I flew to Port Moresby to pay a courtesy call on General MacArthur. I was certain that I had annoyed him in the process of getting the division transferred to Melbourne, so I was agreeably surprised when he greeted me with a smile and outstretched hand, telling me, "You were dead right in taking your division to Melbourne."[4]

There were times when General Holland M. Smith, particularly while commanding amphibious invasions, had almost violent confrontations with his Navy counterpart in the Pacific during World War II. Admiral Kelly Turner was referred to as "Terrible Turner" for good reason. One such controversy was over where to land during the Tinian Island invasion:

> There were two choices: the White Beaches on the north end of the island, just across from Saipan, or the Red and Green Beaches near Tinian Town in the southwest. General Holland Smith's staff had prepared—and he had approved—a plan for landings across the northern White Beaches. The valuable intelligence learned in the air reconnaissance of Tinian during the Saipan operation reinforced the Marines' belief that those beaches should be used. They reasoned that a landing there could be covered by artillery on Saipan. Land-based guns could lay down a curtain of fire behind the beaches, thus minimizing enemy opposition. The Tinian Town beaches, on the other hand, were beyond the range of guns on Saipan, and a landing there would derive no benefit from their tremendous firepower. In addition, the enemy apparently expected a landing at Tinian Town. The beaches there were heavily defended and fortified, and attacking them would be costly. The assault troops, the 2$^d$ and 4$^{th}$ Marine Divisions, were already weary and depleted by the battle for Saipan, and Smith wanted, if possible, to spare them another assault on a fortified beach.[5]

Admiral Turner believed the northern beaches were not strongly fortified because the Japanese considered them unsuitable due to terrain obstacles, and therefore an unlikely approach. Admiral Kelly Turner agreed with the Japanese assessment. These differences between the senior Navy and Marine commanders resulted in one of the bitterest arguments that Smith and Turner ever had.

Turner's main objection to the northern beaches was that they were too narrow. Previously, a division commander had expected to land on beaches from 1,000 yards to a mile in length, with several routes of egress leading inland. At Tinian, the proposal was to land 2 divisions on beaches measuring a total of about 400 yards, flanked by cliffs from 3 to 10 feet in height, with few routes inland. Never had such a large force landed on such constricted beaches. Turner was afraid that even if the troops were not hemmed in, adequate supplies could not be landed rapidly enough on such a narrow beach. In addition, the admiral thought that an advance down the length of the island would be too time consuming. (Holland Smith was not alone in his desire for speed.)[6]

Smith's key staff officer for the planning was Rear Admiral Harry W. Hill. Smith's staff, knowing Turner's preference for the other beaches, tried to present their plan to Turner, who refused even to listen and gave Smith's staff firm orders to stop all planning for such a landing on the northern beach. In vain, Hill pled with Turner to defer a final decision until a reconnaissance could be made. Not accepting orders to stop, Hill ordered part of his staff to continue planning for a landing on the northern beaches while the rest studied Tinian Town.

Smith's staff tried to reason with Turner, but he would not listen, and again ordered Smith's staff in a very positive manner to stop all northern beach planning and to "issue my plan for Tinian Town landing."[7]

Holland Smith got into the argument to convince Turner to use the northern White Beaches. Shortly after Saipan was secured, Turner came ashore and visited General Smith's command post to discuss the coming operation. Smith's aide, Captain Mac Asbill, Jr., overheard the conversation from the next room and recorded it:

"The formalities were few. After pouring himself a drink on the General's invitation, the Admiral came right to the point. 'Holland,' he roared in his most authoritative tone, 'You are not going to land on White Beaches. I won't land you there.'

"'Oh yes you will,' replied the General, 'You'll land me any goddamned place I tell you to. I'm the one who makes the tactical plans around here. All you have to do is tell me whether or not you can put my troops ashore there.'

"'Well, I'm telling you now it can't be done. It's absolutely impossible.'

"'How do you know it's impossible? You haven't studied the beaches thoroughly. You're just so goddamned scared that some of your boats will get hurt that you've closed your mind to it. You don't know a goddamned thing about it.' The general was getting in his old defiant mood.

"'Why, those beaches are too narrow to land one division over, much less two,' the Admiral replied, equally vehement. 'You might get the troops on the beach if you're lucky, but even then you couldn't get enough supplies ashore to keep them fighting. Besides, the hydrographic conditions are bad.'

"'How do you know they're bad?' answered Smith. 'You haven't looked at them, have you?'

"'No, I haven't looked at them, and neither have you. I can tell from the photographs that they're bad.'

"'Aw, you can't tell a goddamned thing from those photographs, Kelly. I intend to send my recon company over there at night and find out definitely what the beaches are like. Then we'll know.'

"At this point the argument began to get rougher. The natural heat of the conflict was abetted to a certain extent by the liquor. Turner mistakenly—he should have known better from previous experience—tried to bluff General Smith. 'Why those goddamned people can't find out anything. They don't know what to look for. They're just a bunch of Marines. How can they judge beach conditions? People will laugh at you, Holland, if you keep on talking about this idea. They'll think you're just a stupid old bastard.'

"To have taken this tack was a grave mistake; a tactical error. Smith came back at him with both barrels: 'Why you old son of a bitch, I know a goddamned sight more about it than you do. These recon people are better at this than anything you've got. They've had plenty of experience and they've proved themselves before. You don't want them to go over there because you're afraid I'll be right. Why don't you keep an open mind on the subject until we can find out about it definitely?'

"'Because I know you're just wasting time and effort. You have a bunch of goddamned dummies on your staff and you've let them talk you into this.'

"'Well, I know some people in the Navy who aren't so goddamned smart, too, and I could name a lot of them right on your staff.' The conversation had long ago overstepped the limits of propriety.

"Turner finally bellowed. 'Well I'm tired of talking about it. You're not going to land there and that's that.'

"General Smith replied slowly, 'Oh yes I am. You ought to know by now that you can't bluff me, Kelly. You've tried it plenty of times before and you've never succeeded yet, and you never will. You know goddamned well that it's my business and none of yours to say where we'll land. That's a tactical matter to be decided by the landing force commander. If my recon company comes back and says we can land there, we're going to land there. And if you say you won't put us ashore I'll fight you all the way. I'll take it up with [Admiral Raymond A.] Spruance, and if necessary with [Admiral Chester W.] Nimitz. Now just put that down in your goddamned book.'

"Turner . . . left, still muttering his disapproval. Whether from the whiskey or from the heat of the argument he staggered out of the house, climbed in a jeep and returned to his ship. The General walked around repeating to himself, 'I guess that will show that goddamned fellow that he can't come over here and bluff me. I'll fight him the whole goddamned way and he knows it, too.'"[8]

Shortly thereafter, on the nights of July 10 and 11, a Marine reconnaissance company and Navy underwater demolition teams explored the White Beaches and reported that they were usable. The proponents of those beaches were then thoroughly convinced.[9]

By July 12, with the landing less than 2 weeks away, the decision still had not been made, and Turner called a conference, at which Spruance was present, to settle the matter. General Smith attended with his chief of staff, Brigadier General Graves B. Erskine and Colonel Robert E. Hogaboom, his operations officer. He and his staff expected a knock-down fight and were prepared with every detail of their plan. With Spruance listening in his quiet way, Turner asked first for the Marines' view and then for Admiral Hill's. When both had spoken in favor of the White Beaches, Turner announced dramatically that he, too, now favored the northern beaches. All hands were amazed by this revelation, even Spruance who, according to his biographer, was happy to have been spared the task of overruling Turner.[10]

While commanding the 1st Marine Division during the Korean War, Chesty Puller had a confrontation with Air Force General Earle E. Partridge, the senior officer in charge of air operations, on the issue of Air Force close air support for the combatants: "One day General Partridge, the senior air officer in Korea, came in to our little field. He got out of his plane and his first words to me were, 'I came up to see what all this damned bellyaching from the Marines was about. How about this close air support?'

"I asked him into my office and told our tactical air people to get General Partridge's headquarters by radio—they were back at Taegu. The men tried for fifteen minutes and couldn't raise an answer. Then I asked them to try by telephone. No answer.

"General Partridge was losing his temper. He said, 'What the hell you trying to pull on me, Puller?' I told him this was what we went through every day when we wanted air support. I asked him to look over some of our log books and note the elapsed time between our calls for air and the arrival of planes. He found that they took from one to five days to get there.

"Then I tried to explain about air power from the viewpoint of a fighting man on the ground, and that air targets were usually targets of opportunity, so far as we were concerned, and that if they weren't hit within a short time, these targets disappeared.

"Partridge went out of there without saying goodbye, though he had been drinking Marine coffee and smoking Marine cigarettes. I guess we just didn't see eye to eye."[11]

Puller challenged Partridge and received the close air support he needed.

An excellent example of challenging a senior officer during combat in Korea was offered by Major General Lemuel Shepherd:

"In my opinion, Rear Admiral James H. Doyle [commander of one of the gunships] was a first rate naval officer. What—in my opinion—made him great occurred during the landing at Inchon. Somebody had called for an air strike—or maybe it was for naval gunfire—on some spot. I had received a message saying that our troops were on this spot. He'd just given the order to put gunfire down there. I went to him and I said, 'Admiral, don't do that, the Marines are right there.'

"His face turned as white as a sheet. You normally don't tell an Admiral in command of his ship, 'Don't do that.' And he said, 'All right. I won't.' I told that story to Admiral [Arthur W.] Radford before his conference of officers in his briefing room, and I said, 'To me that was one of the greatest actions of a Naval Officer that I've ever known to have countermanded his order.' Doyle was standing on the bridge during the battle and he'd given an order, everyone was jumping around to expedite it. When I said, 'Admiral, for God's sake don't do that!' he immediately countermanded the order without question. In my book Doyle will always be a great Naval Officer."[12]

When the United States was evacuating its forces from Saigon in the Vietnam War, Lieutenant General Louis H. Wilson was the Fleet Marine Force Pacific Commander. He tolerated no interference with protecting his Marines. "The Seventh Fleet commander frankly panicked in commanding the evacuation," he recalled. "I was horrified, at 3:00 in the morning, when I heard his message in the CinCPac [Commander in

Chief, Pacific Command] Command Center that pilots had flown more than their allocated hours and they must stop flying.

"I sent word back immediately that under no conditions was he to give such an order and that the Marine pilots were to fly long enough to evacuate the Marines, no matter how much longer it took, and that I did not ever want to hear such a message again or would prefer charges against him. I was aware that I really had no authority to give such a message to the Seventh Fleet Commander, who was indeed the operational commander at the time.

"But nevertheless, I could not, under any conditions, allow the Seventh Fleet commander to interfere with what I considered a primary duty of the Marines, to evacuate the Marines, no matter what the regulations said. I was prepared to take whatever heat was necessary including being relieved of command if necessary."[13]

The stature of the Marine Corps and its position with the other Services continued to steadily grow, but the Corps had grown into the habit of fighting hard for its standing. Commandant Robert H. Barrow was confronted with a continuing dispute with the U.S. Air Force over the command and control of Marine Corps tactical aviation operations ashore.

Barrow commented on this controversy: "It's not that the Marines want to go off by themselves and fight their own war. It has to do with who is going to control Marine aviation, and so when we talk about the integrity of the Marine Air-Ground Task Force, we don't mean that we're looking for our own special piece of real estate, it's just that since World War II there has been an institutional determination on the part of the Air Force to gain operational control of Marine air.

"The argument about control of Marine air was most evident in this particular set of exercises and in the Korean Peninsula in general, and it goes something like this: the Air Force fundamentally believes that there should be centralized control of all aviation assets and when anybody brings them into the theater where they are the dominant air service, the air component commander is to be the overall commander, for tasking and determining what they're going to do, how many sorties, where, what kind, et cetera, and the Marines have always been sort of hanging from their fingernails to make sure that they preserve authority over their organic air assets while at the same time recognizing that they would provide support in general. They never were able to get it pinned down in writing, so to speak. It almost always had to be an ad hoc thing agreed to. It turned on the personality of the commanders. It was something that came up almost every year. . . . we were going to be independent as all get out about what we would and wouldn't do and we left the message about as clearly as I think it had ever been stated about how the Marines regarded their air component, that it was like flying artillery and all those arguments we've talked about, and it didn't mean that we wouldn't work with them, but you cannot just take our air away from us."

The subject was brought up in the Joint Chiefs of Staff (JCS) meeting when Barrow was Commandant: "Quite clearly, Lou Allen followed the Air Force line. He was a friend of mine serving as Chief of Staff of the Air Force and I liked him very much. He was a very taciturn, quiet sort of fellow, even brilliant. He was a physicist and more. But he followed the Air Force line, you know: if Marines come in the theater, they're going to have to give up their air. So, we sought a JCS document to get this doctrinally squared away. I had some sharp people in Marine Corps headquarters, both down in the Division of Aviation and in Plans, who fought with their Air Force counterparts, dug in their heels, and worked the problem. We worked it to the point that I had a special meeting with Lou Allen, and I said, 'I'm interested in avoiding acrimony. This thing is almost getting out of hand. I would not like to see you and me at some sort of loggerheads over this thing in the JCS, and you need to know that, whereas I'm a student and admirer and practitioner of compromise on a lot of things, *we will not compromise on this one*. So, do you want to be reasonable and yield to our desires on the subject, or do you want to go to the mat? We're going to go all the way and I'll take it up to the Secretary of Defense and even to the White House if necessary. I would like to avoid bloodshed. I would hate to see us get into a real acrimonious division on the subject in JCS, because then maybe we would have to drag the Secretary of Defense into it.'"

The controversy was resolved when the issue came up at Barrow's insistence in a meeting for a decision by the JCS. "There were months of not talking about it," he said, "months of it being an issue; most of the time it being put off, because nobody wanted to handle it.

"The chairman didn't want to have to deal with it. He knew the emotions about it. I'm talking about Dave Jones [General David C. Jones, USAF] who was chairman. This was one of his last acts as a matter of fact. This all sort of came about just before Dave Jones left.

"I don't think Lou Allen was personally terribly interested in the issue. He was not the traditional Air Force general in a sense. He was a technician. He had done a lot of duty in areas other than flying airplanes. But he supported his people, who were of a mind to take up this thing one more time to get control of the Marine air. So Lou Allen took a hard line. I had a one-on-one meeting with him. I told him that I knew how he felt.

"But probably my main purpose in talking to him was to let him know the deep-seated conviction that I held personally, and which was also representative of all Marines that this was a sacred asset, like 'flying artillery' as far as Marines was concerned. He just could not let anything happen to the control by the Air Force of that asset by letting someone else do it. I told him I would fight with great determination; take it as far as I could take if it had to be taken that far. He listened, but I didn't give one inch. But he at least knew that he was in for a fight. I didn't expect him to say, 'Oh, well, I'll give up if you are going to take that kind of position.'"

But the JCS finally hit the issue head on. Barrow summed up the resolution by stating of the written doctrine by JCS: "The first sentence tells it all, 'The Marine Air-Ground Task Force commander will retain operational control of his organic air assets.' That was a victory for us."[14]

There can be professional risks in not being a "yes man." As a captain, Commandant Charles C. Krulak had such an experience in Vietnam. The G3 of his division was Colonel William E. Barrineau. "A great, great guy, but a very hard man," he said. "I was a watch officer down in the Combat Operations Center, which was underground. One day I was getting ready to get off watch and there had been a hell of a fight up along the DMZ where a fire support base had received some incoming that hit one of the ammo bunkers and blew sky high. It literally blew the top off of the mountain. I'm down there just turning over the watch to my relief when Colonel Barrineau and the division commander came down. The map showed where this fire support base was and the location of the nearest infantry company. They were afraid that the NVA were going to follow up with an infantry attack on this fire support base. We had an artillery unit that had been hit hard by the explosion. We also had an infantry unit somewhat distant from the hilltop where the artillery unit was located. The discussion was between the Commanding General, Colonel Barrineau, and my boss, who was a lieutenant colonel (and a comptroller by trade). The General asked, 'Can this infantry unit get there in time?' It was bad weather and with a low-lying fog they couldn't get helicopters in. Krulak's boss answered, 'There's no way we'll be able to get that company up to that fire support base because of the jungle.' He noted that it was triple canopy jungle and that the company was never going to be able to get through it.

"I'm sitting there, listening to the exchange. At that point, I looked up and saw where the friendly infantry unit was. Then I looked at where the artillery fire support base was and I said, 'Sir, excuse me.' Colonel Barrineau looked over and he said, 'What's up, skipper?' I said, 'Well, I've operated in that area. There's a high speed trail that goes right from that company position up to that fire support base. They can make it in 45 minutes if they push.' My boss disagreed, saying 'Sir, that's not correct. This is heavy jungle. I flew over it just the other day and I'm telling you this is thick jungle. They're not going to be able to get in.' I said, 'General, with all due respect to the lieutenant colonel, there's a big difference between flying over it and walking under that canopy. There's a high speed trail and they can make it.'

"At that time the CG turned to Col Barrineau and said get a hold of that company and move them immediately up to the fire support base. The general and Colonel Barrineau then did an about face and walked out of the Combat Operations Center leaving me with the lieutenant colonel. He chewed my butt. He said, 'You humiliated me. You made me look bad!'

"My [combat] wounds had healed and I was leaving to go back to 3/3. The OpsO wrote me a fitness report. Gave me a 'be glad to have in combat.' Be glad to have! [In a fitness report, placing a check in this mediocre endorsement block could be a career-ender for an officer, especially in wartime.] It went up to Colonel Barrineau and he signed off on it as the reviewing officer. I'm sure he didn't even look at it. . . . he probably signed hundreds of fitreps. I didn't know that I was given a 'be glad to have' report. I got back to Washington and it's now 1970. I'm at the Naval Academy. Somebody tells me I should go down to HQMC and check my record book. So I go down and check my record book. And here's this fitness report that says, 'be glad to have in combat.' I said, 'This is not too good.'

"I was down at Quantico at the club and Colonel Barrineau was there. So I went up to him that time and said, 'Sir, did you know that I got a "be glad to have" from Lieutenant Colonel [blank]'— and I won't mention his name. Barrineau said, 'No way, no way.' I said, 'Yes sir. You signed off on it.' He said, 'Well, send it down to me and I'll fix that for you.' So I went home and I thought about it for a while. And I thought, no, I'm not going to go down there and get this damn thing changed. One, that's what the lieutenant colonel thought. For whatever reason, that's what he thought. Two, the colonel signed it. I'm not going to have him change it a year later. Also, in the back of my mind, was the issue of getting 'special compensation' because I was General Krulak's son. I said to myself, no way.

"To this day, you can break open my microfiche and you can see the 'be glad to have' is still in my OQR. It turns out the lieutenant colonel was medically retired from the Marine Corps for mental problems. So there were multiple ways I could have gotten rid of that 'be glad to have' report, but I just never chose to do it. Eventually, it became a great point of pride that the Commandant got a 'be glad to have' fitness report.

"What was really interesting is I ended up being deep-selected to major with that 'be glad to have' in there. Every time I got career counseling or anything like that, people always looked at that report and asked, 'How the hell did you get promoted with that report in your OQR?'"[15]

## Marine Membership in the Joint Chiefs of Staff

There were many occasions when the senior Marines were not "yes men" when fighting for policies that were important to the stature of the Corps. An action by Commandant Wilson significantly enhanced that stature: the Marine Corps Commandant becoming a full member of the Joint Chiefs of Staff.

General Wilson provided insight into the workings in Washington and was asked about this development by his oral history interviewer: "On the 20$^{th}$ of October 1978, something very important to the Marine Corps happened: HR–10929, the DOD appropriations bill, was signed into law by President Carter. The bill contained an amendment to Section 141, Title 10 of the United States Code, which gave the Commandant of the Marine Corps full membership in the Joint Chiefs of Staff. This was a status to which we had aspired for many years. On 3 May 1978, you received a routine memorandum from the office of the Chairman of the JCS, stating that on Thursday 4 May, General 'Dutch' Kerwin, Vice Chief of Staff for the Army, would be the acting chairman of the JCS because the other Service chiefs were going to be out of town. You were going to be in town, and as senior officer present, you took exception to General Kerwin being named the acting chairman. I believe you telephoned General David Jones, who was acting chairman at that time because of General Brown's illness."

General Wilson responded: "Yes, I did. I will give you my best recollection of this. . . . Where I use the word 'I,' it should be understood that I am not trying to receive personal credit. However, I felt that this incident might be the catalyst I was waiting for. I had the right contacts at the right time and I determined to pursue it rather vigorously. With that background, I'll try to relate as best I can the circumstances.

"When I became Commandant, my long-range plan was that in my fourth year of office, if Senator Stennis [John C. Stennis, D–MS] were still chairman of the Armed Services Committee, and if I still had friends in the House, that I would try to have the law changed to make the Commandant a full member of the JCS. The reason why I was waiting for my fourth year, was to make it clear that it was not self-seeking for me personally, rather I was doing it for the Corps and for my successors.

"On the date that you mentioned, I was incensed that . . . the Vice Chief of Staff of the Army would be the Acting Chairman while I would be counted as a junior member of the JCS. I called Dave Jones and Bill Smith, who was his assistant, and told them that I was upset about it and I would like for them to justify why I could not be the Chairman. Within a couple of days, I had a call from Dave, who said that he had discussed the problem with his lawyers and they said there is no way for one who is not a member of an organization to become the 'acting' head of the organization. Dave, in his usual manner said, 'Now, of course, Lou, you have to understand that I would very much like for you to be the Chairman. You're perfectly capable of this, but the law is the law.'

"I said, 'Fine. Thank you very much. I'll take it from there.' So with that, I determined upon a course of action. First I talked to Bob Wilson, the ranking minority member of the House Armed Services Committee, and requested his advice. It is to Bob that I owe the suggestion which I followed. He said, 'The Authorization Bill has passed the House but if you can get the Senate to come up with a clause in the Authorization Bill which would make the Commandant a member of the JCS, I believe that I can get the House to agree with it.'

"With this promise I went to Senator Stennis, and told him that it would mean a great deal to me for the Commandant to become a full member of the JCS, that I would like to have it happen on my watch, and needed his active support and experience. He was enthusiastic. I told him that I could get the bill introduced by Senator Dewey Bartlett and asked if he, as the floor manager of the Authorization Bill, would recognize Dewey at the proper time. He said, 'Yes, you talk to Bartlett. I'll talk to him and we can work it out.' I talked to Dewey, who was delighted to comply. He called me back in the afternoon and said that he had talked to Sam Nunn and Sam was more than willing to second it and sponsor it from the Democratic side, Bartlett being a Republican.

"I then went to see Senator Stennis and he said, 'Yes, alright. I will do it.' He said, 'There are ways and means of doing these things. I will recognize Senator Bartlett as one of the last speakers of the day. When senators get tired they are not as apt to be as controversial as they may be earlier.' He said, 'I don't think anybody is going to resist it. On the other hand, it really is not germane to the Authorization Bill and there may be an objection to it.' He added, 'I must say to you that I have been very strict in not having peripheral issues brought into the Authorization Bill which frankly, this is. But I will do it for you.'

"Naturally, I was very pleased. We both chatted with Bartlett about our plans. The Marine Corps JAG drew up a recommendation for the bill.

I then began to lobby in earnest. I talked to Bob Wilson, Mr. [Melvin] Price, Sam Stratton, and several other of the ranking members of the House Armed Services Committee, none of whom disagreed with it, saying that they believed they could get it through in conference if the Senate passed it without controversy.

"The day of the bill, Senator Stennis called and said, 'Now Louis, what is this that I told you about the bill?' He said, 'Dewey Bartlett has been in here and I didn't quite remember that I said it that way.' I repeated our plans to him and he said, 'Well, that's what Bartlett is saying, but it's not very germane, and I must say that I'm a little reluctant to bring it up.' I said to him, 'Senator Stennis, this means very much to me and I would deeply appreciate it if you would do it, and I will be very disappointed if you do not do this.' 'Well,' he said, 'I can't promise you, but I will see about it.' I had the feeling that he had forgotten it but, to his everlasting credit, he came through.

"I had a debrief from the Legislative Assistant, Al Brewster, that Senator Stennis when the time came, late in the afternoon, before he recognized Senator Bartlett, made an impassioned speech on the floor for about five minutes in which he unerringly brought up all of the problems which the Marine Corps had experienced during about 25 years, his years in the Senate. These were problems when the Marines had little authority but had performed magnificently. He said, 'I recognize that it may not be germane, but nevertheless, this is the time to make the Commandant a full member that he should have been 25 years ago. The Marine Corp has not had the opportunity in the past to express themselves and I think this bill should be passed tonight.' And indeed it was passed without a single vote against it.

"No one knew of what I was doing. I had kept this very quiet. I did tell—not ask—tell the Secretary of the Navy the day before what I was doing and requested his confidence. I had not said a word to anybody in the Department of Defense about it, or to my fellow members of the JCS. Well, the next morning, this came as quite a blow in the halls of the Pentagon when it was discovered that the Senate had passed a bill which made the Commandant a member of the JCS. Harold Brown said that he was appalled that something that was this important had gone through without any discussion whatsoever and he knew I was behind it.

"Nevertheless, the die was cast and the Senate had passed it. It was the talk of the day in the halls of the Pentagon. I had a call from the Chairman, who said that he was quite surprised that this had been done without his knowledge and that he was sorry that I had not discussed this with him. I pointed out that I had told him in July when he had said to me that he could not make me the Chairman because of the law, that I had said, 'Very well, Dave. The ball is in my court.' He said, 'Yes,' that he had remembered that. I said, 'Well, I had taken the ball and this is my serve. Stand up and be counted. If you don't want the Commandant as a member of the JCS, I suggest you call Senator Stennis and tell him so.' He said, 'Why, you know I can't do that. But you have used your influence with Senator Stennis to get this through.' I said, 'I did it without any malice whatsoever, but nevertheless, stand up and be counted. Are you for us or are you against us?'

"I really thought that they would make an effort to fight it, the Army particularly. But the CNO, I must say (at that time it was Admiral Tom Hayward), was very supportive. I understand that the Army and the Air Force were upset and frustrated, but none of them were willing to stand up and openly criticize the Commandant's full membership. I have no indication that there was an organized effort to try to get it deleted in the House. It went to the Conference Committee, with the ranking members of the House Armed Services Committee present, and it passed without dissent. I was feeling pretty good, when lo and behold, the President vetoed the bill because a nuclear carrier was authorized and therefore it caused the whole bill to be vetoed.

"I was then discouraged because I thought that this would have been an excellent time for our opponents to dissect the bill, piece by piece. Led by the Department of Defense and the other Service chiefs, they could take out or try to resist our part of the bill along with the nuclear carrier. But fortunately, this did not occur. They chose not to resist and so, when the bill went back to the conference, after the deletion of the carrier, it was passed and the President signed it. I was given a plaque on the day the President signed it by the JCS members and welcomed as a full-fledged member of the JCS. I believe they were sincere.

"In fact, the Armed Forces Policy Council met the very next day. Secretary Brown congratulated 'the Marine Corps for the high prestige it has in Congress which permitted such a potentially controversial bill to go through in such a smooth manner.' So that is how it came about. I believe that future generations of Marines will benefit from the fact that the Congress was finally able to have the Commandant take his rightful place as a full member of the JCS."[16]

### Gays in the Military

Gays in the military have received considerable attention in the last two decades. General Barrow related an incident that occurred during his Commandancy that the newspapers played up following an alleged confrontation between Marines and a group of homosexuals. General Barrow said, "I've forgotten when this particular event happened, but this type of thing has happened more than once on my watch. There was a fray, a brouhaha down in southeast Washington involving Marines who were readily identifiable by their short haircuts, military bearing, and physical fitness, all of this and their youth. They were involved in a fight with some homosexuals in which the homosexuals came up on the short end of the stick.

"The papers picked it up and I guess my reaction was interpreted as being very supportive of my Marines. I certainly didn't say that homosexuals by their very nature should be good targets for folks like Marines. I don't even believe that, much less say it, but I was supportive to such a degree that some people inferred that I thought it was not such a bad thing to have happened. Such interpretations happen.

"So, I got one of these messages passed down through the chain of command that the White House would like for the Marines to cease and desist seeking confrontation with homosexuals, 'put them back in their cage' sort of message. I can't remember the text of it, and it was a verbal thing so I had nothing in writing, and I don't know who in the White House it came from, but I don't think a staffer would just presume to say it without it having come from maybe the President because it was also in the *Washington Post*.

"That admonition or charge, whatever one chooses to call it, didn't go any farther than me. There comes a time when you get such messages which you don't push down the chain of command until some squad leader asks, 'What am I supposed to do with that?' So, I was the final recipient of that particular concern."

Allowing open homosexuality in the military was an issue that the Marine Corps strenuously opposed. General Edwin Simmons, General Mundy's oral history interviewer, commented: "The Department of Defense issued new regulations codifying the 'don't ask, don't tell, and don't pursue' policy toward homosexuals in the Services. The new regulations would take effect 5 February 1994. Despite your defensive statements, it seems to me that you were losing on all fronts."

General Mundy replied: "Well, I do not really think so. As we discussed earlier, it was the conviction of the Chiefs at the time that while we understood that this was a political concession, one the President had to make in light of his campaign promises. We all felt that the revised policy, as we earlier discussed it, was as tight, arguably, in fact, tighter, than had been the former policy which was simply 'are you or aren't you?' After that, it was rather loose as to what the specifics were. We thought that we had a pretty tight policy.

"And, as I mentioned earlier, statistically under two percent of the discharges that we had had for other than normal active service expiration were for homosexuality. So it simply was not a problem within the Armed Services at that time, except among gay rights groups who were seeking to use the military to advance their cause in general. The military made a convenient whipping boy, if you will. If the barrier had been broken in the military and Servicemen could proclaim, 'Yes, I am gay, but I am going to be a Soldier or a Marine or an Airman,' then what could you deny in our society to gays?' So I think that the military was a natural penetration point. But, we felt that the policy was acceptable and to this day I still believe it is."[17]

General Krulak addressed this: "There was absolutely no question which Service chief took the point, bore the torch, and carried his shield for the barring of gays in the military. It was the 30th Commandant of the United States Marine Corps, General Mundy. Although General Mundy was at odds with his Commander-in-Chief, he was at odds in a very professional manner."

General Mundy said: "Well, that's very nicely written [referring to Krulak's statement in his oral history]. It's an attribution to a very tense and difficult time, because it pitted me, as a serving officer, against the Commander-in-Chief, and that is a very difficult position. However, open homosexuality in the Armed Forces was simply something not consistent with good order and discipline, and for that matter, something contrary to the law.

"Interestingly, however, I think that if anything, that experience, tense as it was, may have helped establish a unique relationship between President Clinton and me. He came over to National Defense University to announce the 'Don't Ask, Don't Tell' policy—a term, incidentally, with which I never agreed because it did not convey the true fact of the policy, or the law. Although the President was visibly ill at ease at standing before an audience of military officers to make his announcement, he made a special effort after his remarks to walk over to me and to stand and talk with me about it. He didn't do that with any other of the Chiefs who were there. For the rest of my tenure, to include the day I made my final call on him the day before I retired, the rapport between the President and me, and for that matter, between the Clintons and the Mundys, was something of a special one. I believe it may have rested, in part, on the fact that I was candid in my opposition to what he attempted to do, but that I never defamed the President or anyone around him, but rather, stood on my convictions and, more importantly, on the convictions of the Marine Corps.

"It was very clear to me from Marines and the parents of Marines that they expected the Commandant to go down in flames on this one, and uncomfortable as it got from time to time, I was prepared to do just that because it was what the institution—the Corps—expected of its leader."[18]

## Establishment of Rapid Deployment Joint Task Force

A controversial issue was the establishment of a Rapid Deployment Joint Task Force (RDJTF) and whether its headquarters would be located in Europe or the United States.

Simmons asked Barrow: "General Kelley is cited as being in favor of the RDJTF becoming a brand new geographic combatant command and that, of course, is what it eventually became. Any comment on that?"

Barrow responded: "That was his position, but he was very quiet about it because he was working for the Chairman of the JCS, who he recognized to have a lot of emotional feelings on the subject. He was not about to stick his head up and say, 'I don't agree with any of you, the Commandant or the rest.' So, whereas, those were his views, if they were expressed at all, they were done only when asked in a special kind of way. This whole issue was most unfortunate because, in some respects, my relationship with the Chief of Naval Operations wasn't as good thereafter, which is unfortunate.

"From my point of view, I think it was one of the best things that ever happened to the JCS. It showed to those who were interested that these weren't a bunch of guys who sat around and had to agree on everything or that they had no idea. In other words, if we can't all agree, then we have no position. This was the way they were viewed by a lot of people anyway, and many viewed them as seeking unanimity to the point where you went down to the lowest commonly held view on a subject, which meant it was pat by the time it was presented.

"We not only had our session which made it public on Capitol Hill, but in the tank [the Pentagon's JCS Conference Room], we met with Cap Weinberger and Frank Carlucci, his Deputy Secretary of Defense, and I was given a chance to express my convictions. I had it all wired as to what I believed, and the rest of them spoke in favor of the European command solution. Cap listened to all of it, and ended up with the decision that it be a command established down in Tampa, Florida."[19]

Colonel Charles C. Krulak related in his oral history: "My best friend, Tom Draude, went to the National War College with me. While we were there, the Commandant of the Marine Corps established a new policy that everybody who graduated from the War College had to go to a staff billet—everyone. It didn't make any difference how long the officer had been out of the FMF. You had to go to a staff billet. Well, I had been out of the FMF for the last part of being a major and a part of my time as lieutenant colonel and it was obvious to me that I was going to spend my entire 'lieutenant colonelcy' out of the FMF. That was personally of concern, but nowhere near as much concern as I looked at my classmates and saw that many of them had not been in the FMF since they were captains. I felt this was wrong.

"So Tom Draude and I decided to do something about it, and we wrote a letter to the Commandant of the Marine Corps saying that we thought this is a bad move and here's why. We laid it out in great detail. In order to ensure that it did not look like we were doing this for our own benefit, we waited until our orders were cut and we had the orders in hand. As soon as we had the orders cut and in hand, we submitted the letter to Lieutenant General D'Wayne Gray who was the head of Personnel Management Division. He called up and said, 'You two guys are crazy. You're cutting your throats. This is the Commandant's policy. Who are you to challenge the Commandant's policy? And secondly,' he said, 'this is going to look bad because obviously you're one of the people affected.' And we said, 'No, it shouldn't look bad. We've got our orders. We're executing.' Our household goods have already gone to Hawaii. We said, 'We're trying to do this for those people who will follow on after us.' We heard nothing from the Commandant, so about six months after getting to FMFPac, I called back to Lieutenant General D'Wayne Gray, and said, 'Sir, what was the Commandant's response to our letter?' And he says, 'You mean the letter that's in my desk drawer?' He had not sent it.

Krulak's oral history interviewer asked: "Did he agree with you, do you think?"

Krulak responded: "Yes, because the policy eventually changed. Our point was that if these officers are in fact the best lieutenant colonels we've got, don't our young Marines deserve to be led by the best lieutenant colonels in the Marine Corps?

"I had no idea that I was going to the G5 when I first got to FMFPac. What was very interesting is that Tom Draude went to the G3. I went to the G5. And we were the first two top level school graduates to arrive at FMFPac in years. It was in many ways a sleepy hollow when we got there and, by the time we left, it was pretty vibrant, not just because of us but because more top level school graduates started showing up and a lot of energy was developed."[20]

## Standing Up to Other Services and Organizations

Commandant Krulak provided an example of not being deterred from "telling it the way it is," hitting a crisis incident head-on by defying the advice of Defense Department officials. One of the first challenges Krulak had as Commandant was the arrest and trial of three Servicemen (two of whom were Marines) in Okinawa for the abduction and rape of a Japanese girl on September 4, 1995. They ended up getting convicted and sentenced to 6 ½ years on March 6, 1996. Later that year, U.S. and Japanese officials signed an agreement to reduce the size of the American military on Okinawa and to eventually turn over some additional acreage.

Krulak made an unscheduled trip to Okinawa on October 3, 1995, to assess the impact of this trial on the Marines' and DOD's status in Okinawa and to personally try to mitigate the consequences of this unfortunate incident. General Krulak recalled: "I made the statement that it was going to be a defining moment in not just the Marine Corps, but the entire U.S. relationship with Japan and more importantly with Okinawa. This rape had given [Okinawa] Governor Ota all he needed to achieve some sort of attention or recognition by the Government of Japan. I think what people fail to understand is that before this rape, the Okinawa government and the people of Okinawa were looked at with little respect by the people on mainland Japan. As a matter of fact, they looked at Okinawans as something less than Japanese. That came as a result of World War II and how the Japanese treated the Okinawan people during that war. Up until the rape, the Government of Japan kept Okinawa at arm's length. Although Governor Ota had been complaining about the U.S. presence on Okinawa for some time, it was not until the rape that he was able to leverage the anger of the Okinawan people to finally get the Japanese government focused on what he called the 'Okinawan problem': the great preponderance of military presence there.

"It was a defining moment because it caused a couple of things to happen. All of them turned out to be fairly positive. It caused the U.S. and the Japanese to step back a few paces. It caused the U.S. and Japanese to reevaluate what each one of them brought to the mutual treaty. It caused a great deal of dialogue between the U.S. State and Defense officials and their Japanese counterparts. Eventually, it brought about a redefinition of the military and State Department relationship with the Government of Japan. The mutual defense treaty that was signed after the rape was a far more important document than existed before the rape, it made clear how and what we could expect from the Japanese government in case of conflict in Asia, whether it was Korea or China or another location. The bottom line was the rape had a major impact on DOD, DOS, USMC, and the overall U.S. relationships with Japan.

"When the rape took place, I felt it was going to be a defining moment and I went to the Undersecretary of Defense for Policy, specifically in the area of Asian policy, and asked permission to go to Okinawa because I felt that it had to be done. Action had to be taken immediately or people would think we weren't serious. I was told no, you can't go, that it was a bad idea. Things were so volatile over there that it would cause things to get worse, not better. I then went down and saw the Deputy Secretary of Defense, who also encouraged me not to go. I then went to the Secretary of Defense, Secretary Perry, who also understood the Asian mind. I said, 'Look, we need to get over there right away at the highest levels and show our regret at this terrible tragedy and to offer our condolences.' He agreed. I took a second flight crew and had them fly to Alaska. Once I got the approval, I boarded a plane, our Gulfstream, and flew up to Alaska. There I changed the flight crew and continued on to Okinawa, arriving at MCAS Futenma at sometime shortly after 7:00 in the morning, that would have been 3 October 1995.

"I had sent instructions to the MEF commander that I wanted to talk to every single Marine and sailor in III MEF. I hit the deck and I immediately walked down the flight line to a helicopter hangar where there was a squadron of Marines, some 150 people. I turned to the III MEF commander and said, 'You've got to be kidding me! I want to talk to every single Marine in this MEF. If I do it in 150-person groups, I'm going to be here forever. I don't have that much time. I've got one day to do this, so I want you to get the Marines in theaters and gymnasiums, every single Marine in the MEF. I'm going to talk for 35 minutes, to the minute. I'm just now beginning with this one little tiny group. You've got 35 minutes to change whatever you're going to do and start packing people into wherever you can get them.' They did that.

"In that one day, I gave twenty-one 35-minute speeches. By the end, I was taking throat lozenges like they were going out of style and pumping liquid. I could barely talk. But I spoke to every Marine in that MEF and ended up with my last address to every hospital corpsman at the Navy hospital in Okinawa. In those twenty-one talks, I spoke at every camp in theaters and chapels, in gymnasiums. With me was Sergeant Major of the Marine Corps Gary Lee. At the end, I literally staggered back to the Awasi house and lay down for 30 minutes, and then flew nonstop back to Washington, again going through Alaska, where I picked up new aircrew. That trip was affectionately called the 'trip from hell' for the rest of my commandancy! It was an unbelievable effort from all those who were involved in arranging the trip.

"The Okinawan and Japanese government officials were flabbergasted that we would make a trip like that. It probably saved the day, or we would have been in deep trouble. Less than three days later, the Chairman of the Joint Chiefs of Staff of the Japanese Self Defense Force—the equivalent our CJCS, General John Shalikashvili—came to the United States. I asked General Shali if I could meet with this Japanese general. I met him in our liaison office located in the joint staff area. Before the Commandant's office was relocated to the Pentagon itself, we only had a liaison office. That office was located down in the joint staff area of the Pentagon. I asked to meet the Japanese Chairman down there. I dressed in my blues with medals and sat in the office. When the general arrived, he was escorted in, I stood up, came around the desk and he shook my hand and appeared very friendly. I stopped him and I said, 'I asked you to come down here and I got dressed up in my dress uniform to officially offer my personal apology for the tragedy that took place in Okinawa. I want you to know that I say this as the Commandant of the Marine Corps, the institution that those two Marines belong to, that I take it as my personal failure and wanted you to know that.' I basically gave up face to the Chairman of the Japanese Self Defense Force. He was flabbergasted that a United States military officer would go to that length. From then on, the relationship between the Japanese Self Defense Force, the Marine Corps, and the Japanese Minister of Defense and their Foreign Ministry really took a turn for the better in that we were given the benefit of the doubt all the way through. We then went and turned the Marines over to the police, and opened up everything to the public. The Marines eventually received 6 ½-year sentences.

"The bottom line is my own experience with the Asian mindset drove much of what I did during that timeframe to include going all the way to the Secretary of Defense to get permission to fly over there. My formal apology to the senior ranking military officer in the Japanese Self Defense Force was also a result of understanding the Asian mind after all my time in the Pacific."

Dr. Crist asked what the State Department's reaction was to not only his trip over there, but also to his formal apology. He responded: "As it turns out, they were very appreciative. After all was said and done, they said I did the right thing."[21]

There was another particular occasion when the Marine Corps stood up to the Navy's attempt to obtain the Marine Corps Recruit Depot in San Diego. General Vandegrift was Commandant at the time. He reflected:

> I learned of a Navy attempt to acquire our San Diego recruit
> depot, the argument being that we had sufficient land at both

Camp Elliott [15 miles northeast of San Diego] and Camp Pendleton to relocate. The Navy had wanted this property for some years since it sat adjacent to their naval training center and held some excellent buildings and family quarters.

The Marine Corps was in a more subordinate position vis-à-vis the Navy than it is today, but Vandegrift would not be intimidated when looking out for the Corps. He related:

> I opposed any such transfer. I believed it essential to have our recruit training physically separated from organizational training. Our recruit depots ran on a unique concept that a man was not a Marine until he graduated. Only then could he wear the globe-and-anchor emblem of dress blues and until he earned these privileges he would remain isolated from organizational Marines.
>
> Tradition also entered. Marines had built the San Diego base from nothing. I told Admiral [Frederick J.] Horne, deputy chief of naval operations, "You are going to have a terrible revulsion of feeling from Marines if you let your people grab that depot. The area was salt flats when we acquired it. Marine officers and men and their families worked with wheelbarrows building it to a base. I was there myself when Smedley Butler started the tree program."
>
> Admiral Horne received my argument sympathetically, but the project snowballed in spite of him. In February Mr. Knox [Frank Knox, Secretary of the Navy] called a conference on it, but by then I was prepared. Realizing that after the war we would have to yield some of our west coast land, I decided to yield now if forced. Sure enough, the Navy representatives told their heartrending story about lack of space. Turning pointedly to me, Mr. Knox allowed something must be done. I told him I wished to be fair. Realizing the pitiful plight of the Navy I wanted to offer them Camp Elliott, which easily held 12,000 men. The Navy representatives nearly died. They wanted Camp Elliott like they wanted a barren island. Mr. Knox, however, beamed and told them to accept such a generous offer gratefully. Events justified my logic—the Marine Corps still holds the San Diego and Pendleton bases.[22]

During World War II in the Pacific theater, the Marine Corps answered to the Navy for planning and afloat combat operations. General Archer A. Vandegrift made his position very clear from the start as Commandant in his relationship with CNO Admiral Ernest King, recalling in his memoir:

> As Commandant I was responsible for the administration, training, and readiness of these forces to Secretary of the Navy Knox and to Admiral Ernest King, commander of the United States fleet. I had known Knox for years and dealt quite amiably with him. Poor health increasingly caused him to turn the job over to James Forrestal, one of the smartest men in our government. Forrestal's integrity was unquestionable, his easy grasp of the most complex problems almost unbelievable. I don't remember our ever exchanging a cross word in the many years of our close relationship. I know I respected him as I respected few men in this world.
>
> Ernest King was something else again. Although I had met him in prewar years, neither I nor many people ever knew him. His was a formidable reputation, juniors liked to say he shaved with a blowtorch and they raised him to almost demigod status. Probably because the Marine Corps boasted its unique brand of toughness, I wasn't much concerned about his reputation. Upon paying my first call on him as Commandant I felt that we should understand each other, so before taking my leave I said, "Admiral, I want to tell you what I have always told seniors when reporting for duty. If one of your decisions is, in my opinion, going to affect the Marine Corps adversely, I shall feel it my duty to explain our position on the subject, no matter how disagreeable this may be. If you disagree, expect to keep right on explaining until such time as you make a final decision. If I do not agree with that, I will try to work with it anyway. I say this, sir, because if you want a rubber stamp you can go to the nearest Kresge (a five and dime) store and buy one for twenty-five cents."
>
> King stared at me a moment, then abruptly nodded his head, a characteristic gesture. In any event, I worked more closely with his deputy chief, Admiral Horne, his chief of staff,

Admiral Edwards, and his planner, Admiral Savvy Cooke. On a few matters I was forced to go to him and I generally won my point.[23]

Similarly, the strength and character of Marine Corps Commandants in their relationships with Chiefs of Naval Operations revealed that they certainly were not "yes men." General Clifton B. Cates, Commandant from 1948 to 1951, is a case in point. Admiral Forrest Sherman became CNO in 1949, and Cates had been Commandant for a year. Cates was brutally candid in his opinion of Sherman: "Forrest Sherman, our CNO, certainly is no friend of ours. For the record, I would like to say something in regard to him. When they were going to make the appointment, Secretary of the Navy Mathews [Frances P. Mathews, 1949–1951] and I would talk, and I recommended Admiral Arthur W. Radford, USN [who was selected as Chairman of the Joint Chiefs of Staff, serving 1953 to 1957] very strongly at that time. In fact, the day that Forrest Sherman was appointed, I sat next to the Secretary in a briefing of some kind and I showed him an article that was in the *Christian Science Monitor* that more or less attacked Forrest Sherman. And I said, 'That's the way I feel about him.' So he read the article at this conference, turned it over and looked at it and handed it back to me. That afternoon Forrest Sherman was appointed. So as soon as he came in, I went over and paid a call on him and I told him, 'Admiral, I want to tell you very plainly, you were not my candidate for CNO.' And I said, 'I know that you have been more or less thumbs down on the Marines. I don't know why. But I want to tell you that I'll support you.' And he said, 'Well, I'll support you, too.'"

General Cates continued: "He did, you know. After that, he was kind of lukewarm, but I must say that as far as I know, he played fair and square. But I think actually me telling him very plainly that he was not my candidate and I wasn't for him might have had some effect."[24]

Marines of a more junior rank were also very honest and candid with senior officers in the Navy. As a Lieutenant Colonel, Charles Cooper was considered for duty as an aide. He wasn't pleased with the idea:

> I had been nominated as the Marine aide for Admiral McDonald [Admiral David L. McDonald, CNO, 1963–1969]. The Admiral asked for a ground officer with operations and command experience, though a Marine aviator usually filled the billet—a carryover from the old days when the Marine aide also served as the admiral's pilot. It was a lieutenant colonel's billet.

We went up to the upper deck, where the VIP suite was, and knocked on the door. Admiral McDonald personally greeted us. He was my height, slim and handsome. "Mrs. Mac'" as he later referred to his wife, was a beautiful, charming lady. I was sun-tanned and lean from my exercise and field time, but that $24 suit didn't do a thing for me. Nevertheless, they made me comfortable, and the interview started. He asked about my family and their health, about my education, and about my financial condition. I told him we were down to one more car payment, and we had $1,000 in a Navy Federal Credit account. I owed no money and we were better off now than we'd been at any time since we married.

Then he asked me if I would like to work for him as a Marine aide. I had to be honest, but I wasn't dumb. I told him that it didn't matter whether I wanted to work for him or not. The Commandant had ordered me to report for this interview: if the Admiral saw fit to take me on I would promise to give him my very best shot. Then I paused briefly and said that I didn't play bridge or golf, but I supposed I could learn if I had to.

The Admiral seemed puzzled. "What do you mean it doesn't matter whether you want to or not? I asked you if you wanted to!" I repeated that I was ready to do whatever he would like for me to do. To be perfectly honest, I had never aspired to be an aide, but since the Commandant of the Marine Corps chose me for his interview I realized it was important. "It's entirely up to you, Admiral." He shook his head and said something about "You Marines sure are different." On the other hand, he said, he appreciated my honesty. I told him I was honored to have been considered and pleased to have met both of them. He told me he would have to think it over but he would let me know shortly. Commander Barney Martin, USN, asked me to wait in the hall while he spoke with the McDonalds. He came out shortly and shook my hand, saying, "I think you've got yourself a job, but he wants to sleep on it."

I received orders in a few days to report within ten days of detachment to the Chief of Naval Operations as OP–006, Marine Aide and Aviation Advisor. The CNO had hired himself a ground pounder: he wanted a field Marine. He told me later that one of my jobs was to make him a little smarter about the Marine Corps. He only knew the aviation side and realized that he had a lot to learn. He said later that he chose me more because I told him honestly how I felt about being an aide than for any other reason. He had once been an aide himself. He hadn't wanted to be one either, but he learned from it and knew that I would, too. He was right.

The day before I reported to Admiral McDonald for work in the Pentagon, I checked in with my administrative parent unit at Headquarters, Marine Corps. At that time, General David M. Shoup was Commandant of the Marine Corps. His Chief of Staff was Lieutenant General Wallace Greene, who had left instructions for me to report to him.

General Greene spent almost an hour with me and impressed me with the fact that I wasn't being sent over to some "fop" job in the Pentagon. First, in the strictest confidence, he explained to me that General Shoup had been totally at odds with the Navy's senior leadership since early in his term, three and a half years ago, when he learned that Admiral Arleigh Burke had been recording a very personal, sensitive, private discussion they were having in his office. After Burke's departure, things had not gone much better with his successor, Admiral George W. Anderson [CNO, 1961–1963]. Shoup was feisty anyway and difficult to work with, but General Greene told me that he personally hoped to improve this communication gap by working more closely with Admiral McDonald.

These are my observations. President Eisenhower had appointed General Shoup to be Commandant when he was a middle-grade major general, passing over all of the Corps' senior leadership. Ike was looking for an "independent thinker" and he found one in Shoup. Shoup also became close to John F. Kennedy after he was elected President. Shoup ran the Marine Corps with a handful of his generals, and treated the rest of the Corps' generals with contempt. He did not trust the Navy, and felt that the admirals in charge took his loyalty for granted.

General Greene wanted me to understand the undercurrents I'd be swimming in. He charged me with giving the CNO my very best, and added that whether things worked out with the CNO or not (some people fire aides almost on a whim), I had a good record and the Marine Corps would take care of me. His final remark was: "Your loyalty is to your boss, but you can serve the Corps well by being the best Marine aide he could ever have."

A few months later, General Greene, who had graduated from the Naval Academy a few years behind Admiral McDonald, became Commandant of the Marine Corps. Despite some disagreements, he and the CNO maintained an open and continuous dialog during my tour. I was happy to become a somewhat unusual conduit for this relationship.[25]

The Marine Corps is highly respected in the eyes of the other Services, Congress, and the American people. This stature is due in no small part to the predilection of Marine Corps officers to challenge a senior if he didn't show proper respect to them, because such conduct was an affront, not only to Marine officers, but to the Corps itself. Commandant Vandegrift provided an amusing anecdote concerning an incident with a senior Army officer. One of the truly great Army field commanders in the Pacific theater in World War II was General Walter Krueger, who rose from private through every rank to four stars, and he had a well-deserved reputation for toughness. He became Commander of Sixth Army operating in the Pacific, to which Vandegrift's Marine division became attached. Vandegrift reflected on his initial meeting:

> General Walter Krueger flew down to witness our early amphibious exercises. A soldier of the old school, Krueger was a real Spartan, sparing of praise. I was more than pleased when he made several compliments on the appearance and attitude of Marine officers and men and the appearance of our camp sites which he inspected with a highly trained, critical eye. Naturally, he had to find fault with something. His time came when I took him to my combined quarters and command post, a perfectly beautiful country house belonging to the American representative of the McCormick Harvester Company. Looking over the ivy-covered walls and the pleasant

interior, Krueger growled, "Well, Vandegrift, you certainly are doing very well by yourself here."

I promptly answered, "I certainly am, sir. You are older than I am, General, and of course you are senior. But five dollars will get you twenty-five that you haven't been as uncomfortable for so much of your career as I have. I don't need to practice it. I can take it when it comes, but when there is no need, I don't want either me or my men to be miserable." Much to my relief he laughed.[26]

As an action officer, Marine Colonel Charles Cooper was not intimated by Army Lieutenant General Walter Woolwine. Cooper reflected in his memoir:

The director's billet called for a three-star general or a vice admiral, and there were two deputy billets that called for two-star officers. My first director was Air Force Lieutenant General O'Keefe, a very decent man, who was rebuffed by higher authority when he tried to reduce his commissioned officer strength by 25 percent.

The next director was a tall, aggressive three-star general from the Army, Walter Woolwine, an interesting man. Early in his tour I had to brief him on a subject I had been shepherding for more than six months. I had prepared a message dealing with the matter for him to release, and it was on his desk before I entered his office. We had not met before. When I knocked and entered General Woolwine's office, he started his conversation with me by asking, "Are you the idiot that wrote this stupid message?"

While it would be impossible to remember the exact words that followed, that day is still very clear in my mind. I took a deep breath, looked him directly in the eye, and responded. "General Woolwine, we have never met before. I'm Colonel C.G. Cooper, U.S. Marine Corps, but you already know that. I am not an idiot and don't accept being called one, and that message is a product of about six months of hard work by a lot of competent people. Your predecessor and I worked on the draft together about a month ago. It has been fully staffed in the Joint arena and has both State and Treasury concurrence.

If you want to discuss any specific portion of the message I'll be glad to answer you, *but first I demand that you apologize for what you called me when I entered your office!*" At the time I never gave a second's thought to the consequences of my response. Even now, I still feel that it was the correct one. Apparently General Woolwine did, too.

His reaction was to pour a cup of coffee, point to a nearby chair, and ask me to sit down. He offered me the coffee, apologized, and said that he deserved what I had said. He did have a question or rather a comment on the message, which I answered quickly. There was a pause in the conversation while he signed the message and handed it to me. I rose, stood in front of his desk and said, "Is that all, Sir?" He nodded his head and I about-faced. We were to work together for another year and a half and become rather close professionally. He was a good man and a friend to this day, but his proclivity to bully, to test the mettle of an action officer, had given us a most uncertain start.[27]

When Lieutenant Chesty Puller attended the U.S. Army Infantry School at Fort Benning, he had a confrontation with one of his instructors, then-Major Omar N. Bradley, who made the mistake of pushing Puller too far. He encountered Puller's candor during a field exercise. As Puller recalled it: "One morning my section had a map problem, and we rode out to the area on horseback, left the mounts with horseholders, and walked through the problem. We walked about eight miles through woods, mapping defensive positions, and then waited for the horseholders on the other side of the woods. We had a long wait, and Major Bradley suggested that we wait in a field of sedge, where the sun would keep us warm. While we were there he began kidding me: 'Mr. Puller, while we're here, explain just why the Marine Corps sends its officers to this great Army school.'

"I said, 'Major, I've been here four months, and I still don't understand why the Commandant sends us.'

"Several students sniggered, but Major Bradley was vexed and kept it up. 'This school is on the division level. You Marines never command more than a platoon. I don't see why you come.'

"I asked him if he'd heard of the Second Army Division, and he said he had. I reminded him that it did most of its fighting in Europe under General Lejeune, a Marine, and he said he knew that.

"The students were laughing by then, but the Major kept pressing me, and I finally said, 'Major, I'll tell you something Lord Nelson is supposed to have said—that before a British naval officer can aspire to high command, he must first know the duties of seaman. So I say that Marine officers are fit for high command because they not only know the duties of a platoon leader, but have commanded platoons in combat. It doesn't happen in every Service.'

"The students all laughed, Major Bradley laid off me, and we soon got back on the horses and left."

"A fellow Marine who witnessed this asked Marine Captain Oliver Prince Smith: 'How many like that do you have in the Marine Corps?'

"Smith smiled: 'Just the one,' he said, 'just the one.'"[28]

There were other times when Puller had to be more restrained in his candor. Davis describes a discussion in the presence of Puller's division commander in Korea, Major General Oliver Prince Smith:

> Puller and Smith worked well together. Smith's detached, but relentless, methods of making war combined with Puller's drive to make the Division highly effective. Smith understood Puller and only occasionally tried to restrain him.
>
> Once the staff of the Division dined with the X Corps staff after a Chinese attack had driven U.S. Army and ROK units from their fronts, leaving the Marines with both flanks exposed. A Corps staff officer spoke to Puller: "Didn't you fellows know that all units were ordered to withdraw in the face of strong enemy pressure?"
>
> "I knew of no such order," Puller said. "It took this Division fourteen hundred casualties and eleven days of hard fighting to reach that position. If I'd known we were going to withdraw the first time the Chinese turned and yelled *Boo* at us I'd never have moved an inch. If I were commanding, I wouldn't be looking for units to pull back—I'd be forcing those people who pulled back to fight their way into position."
>
> In the silence which fell around the table Smith gave Puller a warning boot on the shin and the exchange was ended.[29]

The Marine Commandant's rapport with his immediate civilian boss, the Secretary of the Navy, is often critical to success in looking out for the

Corps and its readiness to fulfill its mission. In his last few days as Commandant, in preparation for relinquishing command of the Corps, General Mundy recalled: "I made a number of final calls around town with the SecDef, Secretary Dalton, General Shalikashvili, and a variety of others with whom I had worked closely during my tenure, both on the Hill and in the Pentagon. All of those were 'back pat' types of meetings. My successor had been named, and I was simply 'checking out.'

"Among all those I called on, the only one who asked for my views was John Dalton. As Secretary of the Navy—even though I always introduced him as 'Secretary of the Marine Corps'—John and I had had our moments of tension and disagreement, but we always remained on good terms. The fact is that there is an inherent built-in friction between a senior military professional who is intensely devoted to his Service and a civilian political appointee given authority to oversee that Service for three or four years. That relationship abounds with opportunities for stress and strain, but in the best interests of his Service, the uniformed officer must work carefully to ensure that a positive relationship exists. John and his delightful wife, Margaret, were both 'Southern to the core,' and from the outset of his tenure, we hit it off personally. The Daltons had two sons, the eldest of whom became a Navy officer, and the youngest, a Marine officer. As a result, John was truly devoted to both Services in his Department.

"When I made my final call on him, Secretary Dalton asked for my assessment—not only of himself—but of his staff. I admired that, and I gave my views as candidly as I could. I gave him some plusses, but I also told him that he was ill served by his General Counsel—a New York prosecutor who had made his way politically to become General Counsel of the Navy. I was candid with him in my expressed belief that in personnel matters, his General Counsel did not represent him well, and the advice he received ran counter to the best interests of the Department. The General Counsel, in my judgment, should advise the Secretary on those broad contractual and industrial problems that have to do with such matters as shipbuilding, corporate lawsuits, cost overruns, failures of aircraft engines or ship design, or what have you. However, on Dalton's watch, this prosecutor had also become the foremost voice in personnel issues for the Department. The result was that on more than a few occasions, Dalton was counseled and persuaded by his General Counsel to take personnel action completely at odds with that recommended to him by me. The Counsel was a civilian. He came from a civilian prosecutorial background, and he and his staff had a completely different focus than a military officer. If Dalton had a weakness, it was that he tended on virtually every issue to take the position of his civilian counsel rather than that of his uniformed Service Chief who had 38 years experience in dealing with such matters, and that created enormous tensions between us from time to time."[30]

Again, there is a risk in not being a "yes man." General Holland Smith, never a "yes man," stood up to Admiral Nimitz and Army Lieutenant General Richardson in asking for the relief of Army Major General Ralph Smith, but he paid a price for it: "An officer of long acquaintance visited him one day. Smith showed him the fitness report he had just received for April–July 1944. Nimitz had marked Smith only 'Fair' in loyalty. He was furious. Just furious! . . . It hit him where he lived."[31] What to Admiral Nimitz was a lack of loyalty was to Holland M. Smith character and leadership, which was responsible in achieving a great success in developing operations of amphibious doctrine that were so successful in the Pacific theater during World War II.

## Conclusion

General Anthony Zinni told me: "In the Marine Corps, we make the most detailed and specifically significant demands on our people in terms of iron discipline and precise standards. Yet all of the Services, we probably have the greatest tolerance for mavericks and outside-the-box thinkers. In other military Services, if you don't fit the usual pattern, you rarely succeed. You punch all the right tickets, and you move up. In the Marines, you're much more likely to find people who succeed who don't fit the usual pattern.

"This means also that we are encouraged to speak out . . . to let it all hang out, no matter whose ox gets gored. Outside the Marine Corps, I have a reputation for being outspoken. This has always sort of surprised me, because within the Corps being outspoken is the expectation. This also means that we are an institution where people are judged on their performance and not their opinions."[32]

No commander, certainly not one who has responsibility for momentous decisions, wants a staff to say what they think he wants to hear. A senior officer in the decisionmaking process wants subordinates to do what they believe to be right, and to have the guts to stand up to him, preferably in private, if they perceive that the senior officer is wrong. Commanders must work hard to create an atmosphere in which those serving will disagree with them. An effective decisionmaker, when challenged during the decisionmaking process, never holds it against the person who disagrees with him. Some of the ideas may change a critical decision. The right atmosphere will create a more productive, efficient, and wiser decision and will raise staff morale by making junior commanders and staff feel they are a part of the process.

Rank and experience can give validity to decisions, but just as often they stifle contrary opinions from subordinates. The ideas and decisions of seniors are not sacrosanct. They sometimes may not seem to be the best, but a subordinate might not know all the factors that were considered. A subordinate might have an uneasy feeling that something is not quite right, but not have enough data to confront someone senior. He should still bring up his doubts.

The institutional bias against being a "yes man" is revealed in full glory when Marines rise to the position of Commandant. From the beginning of the Republic, the intent of the founding fathers for civilian control of the Armed Forces has been fundamental to the Nation's democratic process and tradition. But executive civilian control of the Armed Forces does not prevent the candid testimony of our military chiefs before congressional committees.

There is constant tension among senior Marine leaders not be "yes men" yet remain loyal to the President as Commander-in-Chief, particularly on matters of budget. It is a scenario that has to be faced each year. The President's budget goes to Congress for the input, adjustment, and approval. But a Service chief must understand that the Commander-in-Chief of the Armed Forces must weigh the views of many advisors. There are the needs and demands of each of the Services, each competing for the requirements they deem necessary. In addition, of course, there are commitments to our allies, as well as the domestic and political needs of our country. We are a wealthy nation, the wealthiest in the world, but our resources never meet demand.

A senior officer, when advising the President or a Service secretary, owes it to the country to stick to his guns and give his best advice. But he will be of little value if he has not done his homework and will lose credibility if his advice is not well grounded. When he believes he is right, he must always stand up for what he believes. It is the height of disloyalty to do otherwise.

A Commandant is selected on the basis of his character and professional competence. No Commander-in-Chief with the tremendous responsibility for military decisions requiring the advice and counsel of his military chiefs should disregard their advice, but when leaders differ on the decisions, the military must be prepared to uphold and defend its decision.

It is appropriate to end this chapter as it began, with the wisdom of Commandant John A. Lejeune. Throughout his Marine Corps career, Commandant Lejeune was never a "yes man." He had certain objectives he wanted to accomplish for which he fought hard:

> To secure sufficient appropriations to keep [the Corps] in an efficient condition and provide for housing, clothing and feeding its personnel properly; to retain its status as the Navy's expeditionary force in peace and in war; to build up Marine Corps aviation as a vitally important element of the expeditionary force; to erect at Quantico permanent buildings to replace the temporary wartime structures; to recreate the Reserve as a constituent part of the war time strength of the Marine Corps; and to secure the enactment of a law providing for a modified form of promotion by selection, combined with an annual, automatic elimination of a certain percentage of non-selected officers.

> The fight for every one of these objectives, except the last, was won, as was the fight for a great many less important objectives. I was fortunate, too, in being able to gain my objectives without the creation of ill feeling. If I made any enemies, I am not aware of the fact; rather do my memory and my heart tell me that I made a host of friends.

Chapter 7

# "Don't Ignore the Yesterdays of War": The Importance of Reading

To speak of the importance of reading is to speak of the importance of experience. In the profession of military art, experience errors can produce consequences of unsurpassed severity, including the loss of state sovereignty and mass destruction. The impact of human conflict has inspired thinkers to observe, chronicle, and analyze military operations and attendant strategies throughout the ages, from Sun Tzu to Thucydides, Clausewitz, Mahan, and beyond. The study of both ancient and contemporary campaigns equips military professionals at all levels of experience to avoid pitfalls, repeat successful strategies, and even innovate when technology or other contextual elements make the historically inadvisable practical for the first time. First-hand experience is time-consuming, risky, and increasingly expensive; reading is therefore indispensible to excellence in Marine Generalship.

The Marine Corps has had a professional reading program for decades, but it received new impetus during the tenure of Commandant Al Gray, who had a vision for Marines and their professional development. In the beginning of his Commandancy, Gray designed an updated Marine Corps professional reading program to enhance every Marine's understanding of the art and science of war. In the May 1989 issue of the *Quantico Sentry*, he explained the value of professional military education: "The stakes are too high and our profession too complex to allow the dabbler or less than the fully committed, to pursue a commitment that will be less than rewarding to the individual and/or the Corps."

Gray said, "Success in battle depends on many things, some of which we will not fully control. However, the state of preparedness of our Marines (physical, intellectual, psychological, and operational) is in our hands. The study of our profession through selected readings will assist each Marine's efforts to achieve operational competence and to better understand the nature of our 'calling' as leaders of Marines."

Commandant Gray believed that reading books on "all wars and conflicts," the three levels of war, and major battlefield functions would allow Marines to gain knowledge and understanding of war, which in turn would enhance their ability to make timely and sound decisions.

According to Commandant Michael W. Hagee, "Warfighting excellence demands that our Marines not only maintain physical endurance and technical proficiency, but, just as importantly, they also continue to develop intellectual adaptability along with effective problem solving skills."

All-Marine Message 007/05 announced an updated Marine Corps professional reading program—the first step in reinvigorating a key element of Marine professional military education, according to General Hagee. The revised program maintains an emphasis on warfighting and is designed to instill wisdom and judgment.

In November 2006, a panel of retired and Active duty military personnel met to update the professional reading program, formally known as the Commandant's Reading List. "There were 112 separate books on its required reading list: 45 books on the enlisted reading list and 83 books on the officer reading list," according to Colonel Jeffery Bearor, Training and Education Command's Chief of Staff. "There are 16 books shared between the enlisted and officer lists." The panel concluded that revisions were necessary to reinvigorate the program. They noted that the strategic environment is ever-changing and will become progressively more complex and challenging.

General Hagee approved the revised program, seeing it as a clear continuation of Gray's reading program designed to promote lifelong learning. He recognized that full implementation of this goal, however, would require a new sense of ownership and creative inspiration. He wrote:

> All Marines must develop a disciplined approach to studying, thinking, and discussing our profession, fully fostering a higher level of shared competency within our Corps. In addition, we will not achieve continuous improvement in warfighting proficiency without guided professional growth and a sense of comradeship that only leaders at all levels can instill. The revised reading list has a number of books assigned to multiple ranks and provides a starting point for these goals. The selected books will facilitate a common understanding, stimulate intellectual curiosity, and enhance unit cohesion.[1]

But a reading list is not enough. The readings become more meaningful when discussed with others. General Donald Gardner, USMC (Ret.), president of the Marine Corps University, points out:

> While the individual books give Marines historically-based information that emphasizes warfighting, the discussion of the readings among Marines that follows, properly contextualizes the works and place them in the proper perspective. The group discussions serve to encourage critical thinking skills, create an environment where ideas are introduced and debated, promote higher levels of professional understanding, and raise the intellectual bar of the individual Marine. Those who lack sufficient understanding of the lessons learned in the various works would gain greater comprehension by listening to their peers discuss the material in a manner that they can easily grasp. This approach fosters both unit cohesion and intellectual development, whereas the prior programs only seemed to increase an individual Marine's knowledge of a particular topic. One of the key components in emphasizing a discussion-focused program is selecting appropriate works that are both timeless and relevant to today's geostrategic environment.
>
> In addition to classical works, the program now contains contemporary works that emphasize terrorism and the Middle East, such as *The Arab Mind*, *From Beirut to Jerusalem*, and *Terrorism Today*. Both sets of books encompass broad topics and are timeless in application. Furthermore, works such as *The Face of Battle*, *This Kind of War*, *Rifleman Dodd*, and others are found on both enlisted and officer lists because these books apply across the board and demonstrate sound lessons on basic leadership for all Marines. It is important to note that the works in the program are not set in stone. While all of the selections are essentially timeless and formative in relation to their academic standing, the program will not remain stagnant in terms of its composition. Marine Corps University now manages the Professional Reading Program and will establish a Board to make recommendations concerning what material will best meet the program's enduring objectives in the future.

> The senior leadership chose to attack the stagnation of the reading program at a crucial time in our Corps' history. By placing this program at the forefront of his agenda, General Hagee insisted upon high intellectual standards during a time that requires mental agility and analytical versatility. Dialogue and discussion groups can facilitate the critical-thinking skills that are necessary for the professional growth and creativity of Marines, regardless of rank or background. Today's warfare continually demands flexibility and split-second decisionmaking skills from Marines at all levels. Thus, the Professional Reading Program serves as a mechanism to develop the individual Marine's intellectual framework and tactical calculations. The future of our Corps continues to depend on strong leadership and a prodigious pursuit of lifelong learning. This program seeks to encourage all Marines to become creative thinkers in an age where the individual Marine is faced with constant battlefield dilemmas.[2]

What books did the senior Corps leadership read, and what role did reading have in the development of their character and leadership? General Holland M. Smith reflected about his college studies in his memoir *Coral and Brass*:

> While my grades were not very high at Auburn, I did well in history. Before I went to Auburn, I had fallen under the magic of Napoleon's genius and read everything about him I could get my hands on. In Seale [Smith's hometown], I had to buy books out of my allowance and consequently my reading was limited. Furthermore, my father strongly disapproved of this hero worship and promptly confiscated any book he found dealing with Napoleon. To counteract what I considered an unreasonable prejudice, I took to hiding my books under the house which stood off the ground.
>
> At Auburn things were different. The college had an excellent library and I read everything it offered on Napoleon, to the detriment of other studies. Napoleon's character fascinated me, his prowess awed me, and his rapid marches and countermarches across the map of Europe, defeating one adversary

> after another, implanted in my mind military principles that served me well later.
>
> The trait that counted most heavily in my youthful assessment of Napoleon was his offensive spirit. Inevitably, later in my life the halo I had envisioned around his head began to tarnish when I appreciated the tyrant, the unscrupulous plotter, the enemy of freedom he became. It never occurred to me at that time that years later I would be wearing the Croix de Guerre awarded me by the French Government for fighting to save the land of Napoleon from her traditional enemy.[3]

Smith certainly demonstrated some of Napoleon's offensive spirit in leading the amphibious operations in the Pacific in World War II.

Commandant Archer A. Vandegrift grew up in Charlottesville, Virginia, home of Thomas Jefferson. He wrote in his autobiography *Once a Marine*:

> My interest in history was growing in those years. Monticello, Thomas Jefferson's home, stood a stone's throw away; every surrounding hamlet and terrain feature had played a part in either the Revolutionary or the Civil War. But mostly I learned from reading. I was a keen G.A. Henty fan. Henty wrote dozens of books about a young British subaltern and I read them all. I fought with this fellow in India and in Canada and in the Boer War and on the Peninsula and in the Orange wars—every place a British soldier ever fired a shot. I was also fond of [Charles] Lever's stories about Charles O'Malley, an orderly to an Irish Fusilier captain in the Peninsular War. Much to my disgust, for every one of these my father forced me to read a standard classic, usually Scott, Thackeray, or Dickens. But I was and am incorrigible and still prefer Lever's books to Mr. Dickens' best.
>
> This being only thirty years after the Civil War, Charlottesville abounded in military experiences. From as long as I can remember, Grandfather Carson told me stories about his campaigns. He was a very impressive man and I listened carefully to his tales. He was also very devout. A Baptist deacon, he said prayers before breakfast; if you missed these, you missed breakfast. He held few men in awe, but those few he treated

mighty respectfully—he always prayed to "the God of Abraham, Isaac, Jacob, Robert E. Lee, and Stonewall Jackson." Thanks to reading, and to Grandfather Carson, a military career early claimed my ambition.

Vandegrift was stationed at Portsmouth Navy Yard in 1910 and was strongly influenced by one of the senior officers:

> Major [Henry] Leonard had made his name in the Boxer Rebellion in China where, in rescuing a young officer named Smedley Butler during the Tientsin fighting, he lost an arm. He was still an impressive figure of a man and was a fine Marine. Major Leonard insisted that his officers know military theory as well as practice. Under his tutelage I read twenty-three standard military texts including *On War* and *Stonewall Jackson's Life and Campaigns*. I not only read them but wrote an essay on each which he corrected in discussion periods. His instruction proved a wonderful extension of my childhood interest in military writing; under him I gained and retained a strong interest in military history.[4]

Commandant Barrow described how in his early life, family funds were limited. "It was a difficult time, but we were brought up right. I mean by that values, a sense of morality, our church attendance, our reading. One of my chores, as a child, everyone had some chore, one of mine was cleaning the globes of the kerosene lamps, filling the lamps with kerosene, making sure I didn't overfill them. Sometimes I would read quite late at night, my parents thought I had gone to bed. They would go to bed early and then they'd say, 'Now, you go ahead and go to bed.' They may have gone to bed at 9:00 and expected that I'd go to bed at 10:00, but I would read until the kerosene ran out. That might be 12:00 or 1:00 at night. Often I read in bed until the lamp started sputtering. I knew I had about a minute before it went out.

"One of the things that probably did more than any other single thing to prepare me for the future was an insatiable appetite of the written word. I read. I read every day. Some of my favorite books in the early period of my life were not very heavy, but were kind of fun to read, the usual things like *Robinson Crusoe* and *Swiss Family Robinson*. I used to read a lot of Zane Grey. I know he's not a foremost writer, but he was appealing to a youngster in the country. A lot of fantasizing takes place when you read those kinds of things.

I read a lot. I read all of Mark Twain's books, *Life on the Mississippi* and his other books. We happened to have a lot of books at home. I read most of them, some of the titles I can't recall, but books were available. I didn't have much choice sometimes, so I read whatever was there.

"My interest from very early on was in military history. I remember as a young child, I used to practice writing my name with different titles and ranks associated with it. When I was 15 or so, I sent off to West Point for a catalog, brochures, etc., and would have liked an appointment to a military school, but I was discouraged in that. If you recall, in those days politics had an awful lot to do with it, and my family was not right politically."

As Commandant, Barrow commented on his Chief of Staff, George Crist, and one of the reasons for their compatibility was Crist's extensive reading: "I had a close association with him and he assisted me in various capacities in future years. I came to admire him enormously, his intellect, his aggressiveness. He is a very dynamic officer. He leaves no stones unturned. He is a doer, an achiever, a self-starter, and extremely well read, knowledgeable about a lot of subjects; he has had a lot of experience."[5]

Of all the generals in this study, the most widely read was Commandant Gray. I asked him: "How many books are in your library? It is clear to me the perception and depth of our most outstanding military leaders comes from reading. Also, an important thing is not just reading military books, but also reading literature, fiction."

General Gray responded: "I've never been too big a fictional guy other than for books like *The Red Badge of Courage*. Historical novels I read, such as *The Deerslayer*, and other adventure books. My dad had some good books. I read books when I was young. Most of what I read is nonfiction. I think that reading helps you see other viewpoints, broadening your horizon. My reading was designed to help me understand the mores, cultures, and languages of other people, other regions. A lack of knowledge of these is a big weakness of our country."

I asked: "A brand new second lieutenant comes to see you. He's eager and wants to learn and grow; he wants to read. What are the books you would recommend?"

Gray answered: "I read a lot about guerrilla warfare because I thought those were the kind of wars that we were going to be involved in. I still think that's good advice. The Marine Corps put one out, for example, which was a compilation on war. There were some articles on guerrilla wars in the *Marine Corps Gazette* and how to fight in them. Osgood's books on warfare are fascinating, very detailed, very rich. I emphasize the importance of books on insurgency, guerrillas, and counterinsurgency.

"There are several pretty good books on leadership; start with the Bible, including *Battles of the Bible*. Pick one of those. I think there are great leadership examples going back to before Frederick the Great and Clausewitz. There certainly are great leadership examples out of Chinese and Japanese military classics. I read Grant's autobiography and all the biographies of the Civil War generals. I read the Bruce Catton books, his three volumes about the Civil War, the three volumes of Shelby Foote's book on the Civil War and of Dr. Douglas Southall Freeman.

"I think *Warfighting* is the best leadership book around. The more you read it, the more you can see how it applies to life. Even when I was an enlisted Marine, when I was on a submarine, I did a lot of reading. The books I collected were oriented mainly on what I thought would be useful. I always had a footlocker or two of books. I had a bookshelf on just the Mideast and Turkey. Also I read a lot about naval warfare.

"I think with my background I wasn't very smart. I had to do a lot of reading and a lot of thinking. A number of times in my young career, I was thrown into assignments which were very technical. I did a lot of studying of electronics and antennas and a whole bunch of other technical things. I was always very interested in reading as much as I could about areas that we may operate in. I just made a pretty disciplined habit of reading a lot through the years.

"When I went to Okinawa as a colonel, I did a lot of reading on war and the international scene. I always did my share of reading when on deployments. I spent four months in northern Norway and Denmark and Germany in '76 and then Turkey in '77. I was able to read on that assignment. When I went on board ship and I'd be gone for a long time, I would read everything I could find on the Mideast and wherever we might go. The Soviet Union, of course, was very high."

General Gray recalled a wartime experience where reading helped him. "In June 1967 in Vietnam, a young officer said to me, 'Come here, quick, look.' I looked out there and as far as the eye could see were Vietnamese refugees streaming out of North Vietnam coming down to the bridge and coming into South Vietnam. 'I said no, don't let them in. Make every effort to stop them.' I had read a little bit about this type of situation in studying military history. We all knew what happened in Korea when the refugees came down but many were disguised as refugees, but we knew they were North Korean soldiers. We stopped them. They had civilian clothes on and underneath they had their guns.

"I spent a lot of time in the library when I was stationed in the Philippines and in Thailand. There was a pretty good library at Clark Air Force

Base. I read everything there was available to read about Vietnam and Indochina then. This was like 1958 to 1961. We were gone four months at a time and I read Alan Hammer's book on the struggle for Indochina and Bernard Falls' books as well as Southeast Asia history. It was part of my technical profession and current mission to know all about them. So there weren't really many surprises for me during my two tours in Southeast Asia and south Vietnam.

"I used to read a lot of biographies, even before I came in the Marines. I read all the major biographies, about World War II and that type of thing. I remember reading about Marshall Tito in Yugoslavia. I read the autobiography of General of the Army Omar N. Bradley, all of the well-known World War II books. I was always interested in history and the social sciences.

"I read the four-volume biography on General of the Army George C. Marshall, *Reminiscences* by Douglas MacArthur. I read *Lee's Lieutenants* by Dr. Douglas Southall Freeman, the four-volume biography of General Robert E. Lee. I didn't read to memorize a lot of battles and dates. I read to see if I could understand the situation and what was done and what could have been done differently to get better results. I read everything there was about Genghis Khan through the years. I read all the Samuel Eliot Morison books (seventeen volumes), entitled *The History of the Navy in World War II*, some of his other books, too, the *American Republic*.

"I have books that are marked, 'First Lieutenant A.M. Gray.' So I guess I started building my library early on. I was always very interested in reading as much as I could about areas where we may operate. So I just made a pretty disciplined habit of reading a lot through the years. From Vietnam on, I've had the habit of immersing myself in the people and cultures of the countries where I've been stationed. I met frequently with people from other nations and areas, both individuals and groups, which provided additional insights into understanding the situation."[6]

Burke Davis' biography of Chesty Puller described how he developed an extensive interest in reading:

> Lewis learned to read early and devoured books on war and warriors that might have been beyond his youthful grasp but for his impassioned interest in military life. He read G.A. Henty's adventure novels with a relish he seemed to lose in the schoolroom.
>
> There were pictures of great Confederate soldiers in the Puller home—Lee and Jackson in particular. But there were older

heroes, too, from Caesar to Gustavus Adolphus. When his mother first read to him of Genghis Khan, Lewis was so smitten that on his next trip to Richmond he bought a book about the Mongol conqueror.

Mrs. Puller managed well on a limited income; she insisted upon the best education within her means for the four children, occasionally with vehemence. Once when his school proposed dropping Latin from the curriculum, she organized a parental posse and had the subject retained. Lewis was grateful, but not for considerations of pure scholarship. His efforts at translating Caesar made him impatient for the true message of the soldier-author, and when he bought a "pony" in Richmond, he was so fascinated by the narrative of war that he devoured it in one night. It opened a new world for him and began a lifelong career of serious military reading.[7]

Puller read widely in school beyond what was expected in his classes and homework. Burke Davis related:

The young athlete was not a star student and had little interest in English or mathematics, but never neglected his own reading. One day when he misbehaved in school his teacher, Rose Althizer, challenged Lewis: "Young man, get your books and go home. I can stand no more of you today."

"You mean all of 'em?"

"I certainly do." She was astonished to see him pull more than two dozen books from his small desk and stagger out with a double armful—none of them textbooks.[8]

One of Puller's instructors at recruit training camp was flabbergasted at his intellectual depth and knowledge of military history:

"Hell, he gives me an inferiority complex. I've read some, but that kid knows von Clausewitz backwards—and guys I never heard of, by the dozens. He's some kid. This stuff is like a religion with him. He takes in all this stuff about the Huns and their atrocities. He hates 'em like sin."[9]

As his career progressed the reading had application to combat:

Puller's military reading bore fruit in the jungle fighting; he conducted experiments with the aid of Brunot and Calixe. He told the lieutenants: "In the Boer War, the English found that they killed few enemies when they lay on high ground, and the Boers were low. They always shot overhead. Men usually fire too high on such ground."[10]

In combat in World War II in the Guadalcanal Campaign, Puller's pocket had his old, jungle-stained copy of Caesar's *Gallic Wars* which he had now carried for more than twenty years. He always followed Caesar's policy of fortifying his camp every night. It saved a lot of lives.[11]

Puller was surprised to find that Japanese soldiers were avid readers. One evening, Puller's interpreter brought him a translation of the diary taken from the Japanese major he had shot on Mount Austen. He found he was a veteran in many campaigns and was surprised to learn he had been a student of great military leaders, like Genghis Khan, even Civil War generals such as Lee, Jackson, and Grant. Puller learned about the Japanese military thinking. The captured officer had written: "The Americans amaze me, I never violate the principles of warfare, and they never obey them. We never move without an advance guard, but when we attack Americans, it is always the main body we meet. We Japanese take advantage of the country; the Americans use great machines to clear the jungle."[12]

Fighting on the Pacific island of Pavavu, Puller still found time to read a new volume of Douglas Freeman's *Lee's Lieutenants*, which his wife had sent for his birthday.

In retirement, Puller continued his love of reading. His wife commented that he read scores of new military books, especially those on World War II, the Civil War, and Korea. She said that he could recall battles and officers and units going back to Hannibal and Frederick the Great. He was so very fond of Stonewall Jackson that he read and reread Henderson's *Life of Stonewall Jackson*. While in combat in the Korean War, he had lost his copy of that book, which was dirty and worn on every page, much of it underlined, with Jackson's mottoes, such as "Never take counsel of your fears," copied in margins and on flyleaves. It was so worn from constant study that it was held with bicycle tape. A Marine officer found it in Puller's command van in Korea and, knowing how much it meant, returned it to him.[13]

His widow recalled that he followed Napoleon's recipe for proficiency in the military art: to study and reflect upon the campaigns of the great captains, such as Hannibal, Turenne, Saxe, Frederick the Great, Gustavus Adolphus, and Charles XII, and Lee, Jackson, Forrest, Sherman, and Grant in the Civil War. She also recollected that in retirement he loved to read beside the fireplace with a nice fire burning. He'd sit there for hours, reading and smoking his pipe.[14]

Others learned from Puller's reading. General Ray Davis, in his autobiography, pointed out a book that he learned a great deal from:

> When I was asked how I knew what to do in the crunch situations I met in my first infantry command at Peleliu, I not only gave credit to Chesty's teachings; and from his reading, noting how in World War I, the Army's Infantry School in Georgia had gone to great pains to publish *Infantry in Battle*, mostly stories of smaller units in all kinds of situations, what happened, and how they responded, thus learning something about what combat is all about. Clausewitz called it "the fog of war." There are so many things that you wouldn't believe could happen, but they do happen. Thus, listening to those like Puller who had experienced combat, plus the detailed study of others' experiences by reading, that's all you have to go on until you get your own experience.
>
> I very dutifully studied in great detail the *Infantry in Battle* book, you know, which described infantry operations in World War I.[15]

When I was in ROTC at Georgia Tech in the 1930s, I did a presentation on Stonewall Jackson's valley campaigns in the Civil War. The thing that impressed me about Jackson was his mobility: he would mount his horse and ride to the sound of the guns. I thought of that in Vietnam when we finally got enough helicopters. The division commander could mount his horse, so to speak, and ride to the sound of the guns. The Army provided me with a super-powered helicopter so I could operate in those mountains with safety. I would fly out to firebases and forward units in the field every day.[16]

General Anthony Zinni counts reading as a key factor in his brilliant Marine Corps career. "When I was a child," he said, "my father made sure we had every periodical, news magazine, everything in our house. We always had *Time*, *Newsweek*, you know, some of the magazines that don't exist anymore. I was fascinated by them.

"I've done a lot of teaching in the Marine Corps. I spent a lot of time on instructor duty, and I think that that requires not only study, but it requires your ability to present things; and you've got to work on that."

Zinni believes that reading has been the single most significant factor in his intellectual leadership and career development. "When I'm about to get into something, I do a lot of reading. I'm doing work for the Philippines now. I was asked by the State Department to work with the Moral Islamic Liberation Fund. Well, I'll read five or six books. When I first was told I was going to CENTCOM, I read 50 books on Arab culture, you know, Islamic culture, and that sort of thing. It has always been my approach, as soon as I get involved, either I get fascinated by something or I get a mission to do something.

"I try to immerse myself in the subject and try to get my hands on—not only books now, but audiotapes and things that I can do in the car, books on tape. They make it much more efficient.

"When I was a young officer, a second lieutenant platoon commander, I had a company commander. His name was Charlie Sampson. Charlie was kind of a brash, outspoken company commander. I think the battalion commander in many ways didn't like him, because he knew more than the battalion commander. I was always impressed with the fact that nobody ever took Charlie on. I mean, he was the most respected guy amongst his peers and seniors, and when he spoke everybody listened.

"One time I asked him, 'You know, people don't mess with you, Charlie. I mean, when you say something.' He told me: 'Let me give you a piece of advice.' In his office he had all of these bookshelves, and all of these manuals and military history and all sorts of professional reading. And he said, 'See those shelves,' he said, 'I know every page, every word, in all of those.' Sampson gave words of wisdom to his students: 'My piece of advice to you as a young officer,' he said, '*Read, read, read*. If you're the most knowledgeable guy in the room, if you're the guy that has done his homework, if you're the guy that technically is the most proficient because he has strived to do that, you'll always be the most respected.'

"Then he said, 'More importantly, this is the best service you can give your troops—to have that professional knowledge and in-depth understanding—it just opens up so much.'

"Mornings are my best time to read, and even now I get up very early, 5:00, and that's when I like to read the newspapers. I like to do any reading that requires especially a lot of concentration. You want to be at your best to do it.

"I try to do it all along the day. I would keep books maybe by my bedstand that whenever I have a moment, I would grab a book to read, would read a few pages or a chapter or something like that.

"You have to legitimize reading. If a young officer says, 'I'm going to go out today at lunchtime and run three miles,' oh, everybody salutes him. If he says, 'I'm going to go out and read a book,' you have to legitimize that.

"General Gray was one of my mentors, maybe the most significant mentor I had. He was a reader. What I liked about General Gray was, his reading wasn't just about people. To him reading was a requirement he imposed on all of us, and he legitimized the reading. I mean, he made it acceptable to read.

"General Gray did several things. First of all, he put out a Commandant's reading list. This was required reading. . . . The list was highly selective; it had to be put together by a board of prominent and very competent people and it was focused. You didn't have to read all of these books. For example, as a lieutenant colonel, here is the book you should be reading this month; then the book you should read next month.

"The second thing he did was to encourage reading. At the Marine Corps University, I created an atmosphere that you would receive a book, read it and then exchange it for another. We started to give books as awards, not letter openers.

"Then, General Gray did much the same as you were describing Marshall had done. He encouraged groups to get together, after hours, to discuss what they had read. Especially in that period of time, it became sort of a renaissance. These are late '70s throughout the '80s, early '90s. I encouraged discussion of the operational art. We talked about warfare and the concept of that opposed to attrition warfare. So there was a real renaissance taking place and how we thought about the operational art.

"The discussion groups were coming together to discuss reading, controversial readings, coming out with new ideas on concepts of operations. It not only became the popular thing to do, it became necessary and required. Pretty soon, among your peers and others, if you weren't well read, it became clearly evident. You have trouble keeping pace with those that were well read. It was an expectation that was driven from the bottom up, because then the lieutenants were reading.

"So when the lieutenants come up and say, 'Sir, I've just read Liddell Hart (and other military historians), and I wonder what you think about this comparative analysis of something that you've said,' well, if you don't have a clue, you know, you lose a tremendous amount of respect."

I asked Zinni: "In your career, were there any particular books that you found where you'd reflect on that book or that experience as far as your decisionmaking and your career development?"

He responded by referring to a book on Vietnam War experiences of Australian officers called *In Good Company*, which he read after Vietnam. "But it was the best book I read on Vietnam, it was straightforward, and talked about mistakes. Wasn't inflated, it really captured the environment and the nature of what we were doing. I read all Bernard Falls' books. I read a lot of books on insurgency and the nature of insurgency, as a junior officer.

"I obviously read the military classics, you know, books to improve operational skills, like Rommel's book of the First World War infantry attacks. I read Clausewitz and Liddell Hart, whose books were basic, then a lot of technical books. I'm fascinated by tactics and techniques. I used to teach scouting and patrol, and so I used to absorb books written by—you know, for example, a Royal Marine that was fighting an insurgency in Malaya. We talked about jungle techniques, that sort of thing. So I was always fascinated by those sorts of things, too.

"I think, you know, later in life like now I read more books on cultures, on societies, because, I mean, to understand some of these problems now, you're really got to understand the people, their culture, their society."

I asked General Zinni: "You're pretty well known for emphasizing the importance of reading for a successful career. Can you tell me how you motivated your young Marines, even older Marines, to read? Do you have specific subjects that you would recommend?"

"I'm a big believer in education. I don't believe that education is just for the schoolhouse. Every unit that I've ever commanded I felt that one of my obligations as a commander was educational. I used to run extensive officer schools, NCO schools in my commands. I pulled my officers away two days a week for officer school and my NCOs almost the same.

"As part of all that came—not only the teaching—but going through the kind of mental exercise and things that helped develop people better, and the reading requirement. And, of course, we were blessed when General Gray came in as Commandant of the Marine Corps, he emphasized this at the service level and we had, you know, the Commandant's reading list and other things.

"But you know the kind of thing I emphasize is obviously the professional reading of military history. Books on strategic operational issues. I really emphasize the importance of understanding cultures. International issues, on decisionmaking. There's a lot of books and I've done a lot of work consulting after retirement on decisionmaking, how it's done and what the processes are, the organization, information technology. Those are the kinds of things that I believe help people.

"It taught my subordinates to handle situations better. I always believed that as a leader, whether you're an NCO or an officer, you're basically a problem solver."

I asked Zinni: "When did you personally learn the importance of reading?

"I think when I came back from Vietnam, my first tour. I went to the Marine Corps Basic School where we taught second lieutenants, so I was in my first true position as an educator.

"I had two things that played on this. One was my obligation as a teacher to understand what the hell I was talking about, and I was surrounded by a number of people who encouraged reading and understanding in great depth.

"The second one was Vietnam. I had just come from this experience. I realized there was a lot to learn in this business we didn't understand. I mean this was an insurgency, this was a strange culture. So I wanted to know as much about that as possible, not only from the operational and tactical mind, but who the Vietnamese were, what their history was. I didn't feel we had the depth of understanding.

"That began, I think, my interest in really learning as much about military history, about cultures, about the conflicts we were involved in, and about our responsibilities. At that time, too, we were going through a number of social changes in the military. I mean there was the race issue, drugs, women in the military, so these were social and cultural issues that you have to understand had a greater depth than I felt we were equipped for, so required a lot more education and therefore reading.[17]

"Back when I commanded D Company, a fellow captain and company commander, my friend Jack Sheehan, had bragged a lot about his great battalion commander. Jack's commander really knew the stuff the gung-ho younger officers were living and breathing and spending every spare moment talking about—landing plans, tactics, small units, patrol formations, weapons employment, all of that stuff. He'd had a long stretch in Vietnam, five or six years, and his operational skills were legendary; and like all the best leaders, he'd read everything. Not only that, he was one of the few senior officers who actually liked to sit down and talk tactics and hold forth on his own with the junior guys. His name was Al Gray."

General Zinni recalled how his friend Jack Sheehan happened to introduce him to General Gray: "'Hey, how about coming to dinner?' Jack said to me. 'You and I can hook up with Colonel Gray—sort of like a guys' night at the club.'

"'Sure,' I said. I knew something about Gray; it was hard not to at Lejeune. He was a legend. The troops loved him, and he was truly great with the enlisted Marines. He himself had come up through the ranks and never lost that connection. Later, as the aide, I learned that he was held in equally high regard by the generals.

"So I met Al Gray at the officers' club at Camp Lejeune with Jack Sheehan. When he walked in, the first thing that impressed me was how down to earth he was. He talked to us, not down to us (he was not patronizing). But what really impressed me was how much he was really into the operational stuff. 'He knew his shit,' as the troops would put it. He had the same sort of fire that I had. No matter what came up for discussion, he had an informed and pointed opinion about it. I had seen this kind of fascination for tactics and war fighting in only a very few senior officers. I was really impressed. Of course, I hoped I'd have a chance to see him again and take our discussions further."[18]

I discussed reading with Commandant Mundy: "How did you do scholastically in high school and college; any favorite subjects?"

General Mundy responded: "History and English were always my forte, I guess. I enjoyed history, not the rote memorization of what year was the Declaration of Independence signed or something like that, but more the events of history rather than the dates of history, because so much of our education in those days, as you will recall, you could pass if you could memorize five things. But I enjoyed history." He had an intense interest in studying General Robert E. Lee.[19]

Commandant Gray summed it up: "The stakes are too high and our profession complex to allow the dabbler or less fully committed to pursue a commitment that will be less than rewarding to the individual and/or the Corps. . . . Success in battle depends on many things. . . . The study of our profession through selected readings will assist in each Marine's efforts to achieve operational competence and to better understand the nature of our 'calling' as leaders of Marines. . . . Warfighting excellence demands that our Marines . . . continue to develop intellectual adaptability with effective problem solving skills."[20]

Every senior Marine Corps general I interviewed had read and studied *Lee's Lieutenants: A Study in Command,* by Dr. Douglas Southall Freeman; almost all also had read his four-volume definitive biography of General Robert E. Lee. They cherished these books, and most still had them in their personal library. No other books equal the impact of Dr. Freeman's on the education and development of the leadership and character of our military leaders.

Dr. Freeman was a remarkable man. His self-discipline was staggering. He held simultaneously two careers, one as a military historian and another as a journalist, and excelled in both of them. In addition to editing the *Richmond News-Leader,* he gave two daily radio broadcasts. His editorials were read and highly regarded throughout the country. His four-volume definitive of General Robert E. Lee represented 20 years of research. It won a Pulitzer Prize and established him forever as a premiere military historian.

Dr. Freeman, always humble, related a conversation he had with Fleet Admiral Chester W. Nimitz, USN (Ret.), Commander of the Naval Forces in the Pacific in World War II. Dr. Freeman recalled, "Nimitz said to me one time, 'Ah, Doctor, you never will know how grateful I am to you,' and he mentioned one of my books that he had read at Guam while he was in command there. I said, 'How is that, Admiral?' 'Well,' he replied, 'every night after I had finished my duties I would go to bed and turn on the light and I would read for about half an hour of some of General Lee's problems in dealing with his subordinates. Then I would go peacefully to sleep, because I would reason then that General Lee's problems of command were infinitely greater than mine were, and that I had a far easier time with my subordinates than he had with his.' I said, 'Admiral, you never were more mistaken in your life; what put you to sleep was not peace of mind—it was my style.'"[21]

I inquired of Commandant Gray what books he read, and he told me, among others, "I read *Lee's Lieutenants* by Dr. Douglas Southall Freeman, and the four-volume biography of General Robert E. Lee. . . . I didn't read to memorize a lot of battles and dates. I read to see if I could understand the situation and what was done and what could have been done differently to get better results."[22]

Commandant Mundy was a student of Freeman's books. In his oral history, he reflected, "In my senior year, I took a course entitled 'Great Leaders of History.' We each had to select a figure of history that was a leader. I took Robert E. Lee and studied him closely. And I can recall that the thing that I suppose struck me about Lee, not only his military genius, his ability to direct the Army, but the term 'noblesse oblige' was used in describing him and his calling, if you will. That always struck me.

"But I still have, in fact, tucked away somewhere back in one of the boxes at home, I have a folder on Robert E. Lee by senior Carl Mundy, Jr., at Auburn. And that course stuck with me. Lee stuck with me."[23]

In a speech at the Naval War College, Dr. Freeman told the audience, "You can't know too much if you're going to be a successful leader. Know the yesterdays . . . don't ignore the yesterdays of war in your study of today and of tomorrow." This was a theme he emphasized in all his presentations to military audiences. He certainly provided the opportunity for learning about "the yesterdays" in his classic works.

After interviewing more than 150 four-star generals over a 40-year period, I concluded that those who were avid readers were superior in depth and perception to those who were not readers. Their interest in reading biography and military naval history had a role in the development of their character and leadership abilities, but so did their interest in the works of Socrates, Plato, Aristotle, and Shakespeare. As youths they all read the adventure books of such authors as Sir Walter Scott, Rudyard Kipling, and James Fenimore Cooper, which sparked their interest in the adventures of a military career. While these men were warriors, their love of reading and wide-ranging tastes—including poetry—showed them to be sensitive and caring individuals as well.

There is a message of value to the young military officer on the importance of reading and building a professional library in citing the influence it had on the leaders discussed here. William Lyon Phelps, a professor at Yale University for over 40 years who had a library of over 6,000 books, made a radio broadcast on April 6, 1933, on the importance of reading and building one's own library. Part of this speech is worthy of quoting here:

> The habit of reading is one of the greatest resources of mankind; and we enjoy reading books that belong to us much more than if they are borrowed. A borrowed book is like a guest in the house; it must be treated with punctiliousness, with a certain considerate formality. You must see that it sustains no damage; it must not suffer while under your roof. You cannot leave it carelessly, you cannot mark it, you cannot turn down the pages, and you cannot use it familiarly. And then, someday, although this is seldom done, you really ought to return it.

But your own books belong to you; you treat them with that affectionate intimacy that annihilates formality. Books are for use, not for show; you should own no book that you are afraid to mark up or afraid to place on the table, wide open and face down. A good reason for marking favorite passages in books is that this practice enables you to remember easily the significant sayings, to refer to them quickly, and then in later years, it is like visiting a forest where you once blazed a trail. You have the pleasure of going over the old ground, and recalling both the intellectual scenery and your own earlier self.

Everyone should begin collecting a private library in youth; the instinct of private property, which is fundamental in human beings, can here be cultivated with every advantage and no evils. One should have one's own bookshelves, which should not have doors, glass windows, or keys; they should be free and accessible to the hand as well as to the eye. The best of mural decorations is books; they are more varied in color and appearance than any wallpaper, they are more attractive in design, and they have the prime advantage of being separate personalities, so that if you sit alone in the room in the firelight, you are surrounded with intimate friends. The knowledge that they are there in plain view is both stimulating and refreshing. You do not have to read them all.

There are, of course, no friends like living, breathing, corporeal men and women; my devotion to reading has never made me a recluse. How could it? Books are of the people, by the people, for the people. Literature is the immortal part of history; it is the best and most enduring part of personality. But book friends have this advantage over living friends, you can enjoy the most truly aristocratic society in the world whenever you want it. The great dead are beyond our physical reach, and the great living are usually almost as inaccessible: as for our personal friends and acquaintances, we cannot always see them. Perchance they are asleep, or away on a journey. But in a private library, you can at any moment converse with Socrates or Shakespeare or Carlyle or Dumas or Dickens or Shaw or Barrie or Galsworthy. And there is no doubt that in these books you see these men at their best. They wrote for you. They "laid themselves out," they did their ultimate best to entertain you, to make a favorable impression. You are as necessary to them as an audience is to an actor, only instead of seeing them masked, you look into their inmost heart of hearts.

Chapter 8

# "As a Teacher Does a Scholar": Mentorship

When asked how to develop as a decisionmaker, General Dwight Eisenhower said: "Be around people making decisions." The generals in this study who have achieved top positions in the Marine Corps were around decisionmakers who served as their mentors, and they in turn mentored the generation that ultimately succeeded them.

The Marine Corps University *Users Guide to Marine Corps Values* defines *mentoring* as "a formal or informal program that links junior Marines with more experienced Marines for the purposes of career development and professional growth, through sharing knowledge and insights that have been learned through the years." A *mentor* is defined as "a senior Marine who voluntarily undertakes to coach, advise, and guide a younger Marine in order to enhance technical/leadership skills and intellectual/professional development," and a *mentee* is "a junior Marine who voluntarily accepts tutelage from a more senior Marine for the purpose of enhancing skills and professional development."

Mentoring is not a new concept to the Marine Corps as it emphasizes the importance of passing on professional knowledge to those who are led. General Lejeune described imparting that knowledge "as a teacher does a scholar."

The concept of mentoring has widely differing connotations in its role in leadership development. The positive meaning of mentorship is to improve leadership, growth, and professional development. There is a thirst to learn from the wisdom and camaraderie of senior officers or experienced NCOs. Mentorship is an investment in the future leadership of the Corps; it should improve morale and retention. Seniors should expose juniors to the decisionmaking process, thus preparing them for future responsibility and encouraging their empowerment through the opportunity to make decisions at the lower level as they progress in rank and responsibility.

To some, mentorship has negative aspects, particularly if it is perceived as favoritism, special treatment, cronyism, or what Commandant

Carl E. Mundy, Jr., calls "bubbaism." The mentorship should not give the appearance of familiarity or undue informality; it should be open and above board.

The criterion for identifying whom to mentor is potential. Senior leaders are obligated to select and grow the most promising leaders. The mentor must set the right example and live the core values of the Corps. He must be aware that mentorship should be the legacy of every truly committed and dedicated professional leader: that through his mentorship, he left his organization better than when he took command.

Commandant John Lejeune had many mentors in his career, but arguably, the most influential was General John J. Pershing. General Lejeune began a long-term association with Pershing when they were both stationed in the Philippines in 1907. It was a fortuitous relationship impacting considerably on Lejeune's career:

> General John J. Pershing, Mrs. Pershing and their children were at Camp John Hay, also then Major General and Mrs. James G. Harbord, and many other Army people. I first came to know General and Mrs. Pershing at Baguio. Mrs. Pershing was extremely charming and attractive, and the Pershing home was a delightful place to visit.[1]

Lejeune wrote of his continued association with Pershing and Army General James Harbord, who briefly commanded the 2$^d$ Infantry Division during World War I:

> Early in the morning of July 28, 1917, General Harbord sent for me. He had just returned from a twenty-four-hour conference with General Pershing at Chaumont. He looked very grave as he told me that he had orders to assume command at once of the Services of Supply of the American Expeditionary Force as the relief of Major General Kernan, and that General Pershing had instructed him to turn over to me the command of the 2$^d$ Division inasmuch as I was the senior Brigadier on duty with it.
>
> [That] I was surprised is putting it far too mildly. I was stunned. To become suddenly the commander of a division after only a brief experience as commander of a brigade in a quiet sector, especially of a division with such a remarkable combat record as the 2$^d$ Division had, and one whose ranks

were filled with officers and men who had already gained fame in battle, brought to me the fullest realization of the responsibility which rested upon me, the keenest sense of my own lack of experience, the most earnest and solemn determination to dedicate myself wholly to the sacred duty which had come to me, and the resolution to seek always the guidance of Almighty God, knowing full well that only by His help could I hope to achieve success as a division commander.

At noon on July 28th, General Harbord invited the senior officers on the Division to luncheon at the château where he was sojourning, and after luncheon he told them of his orders, of the deep sorrow he felt on leaving the Division, of his good wishes for it as a whole, and of his affection for the officers and men. It was a very impressive scene and one I remember most vividly.

He then introduced me to them as his successor, making the kindest of references to me. Each of these officers congratulated me heartily and said that while they deeply regretted General Harbord's departure, they were glad I had been selected as his successor, and pledged me their loyal support. I was deeply touched, especially when Brigadier General Ely (an Army officer), next in rank to me, said in his emphatic way, "I have known General Lejeune for years and I know of no one I would rather have succeed General Harbord." It is a matter of the greatest pride to me that the good will between the Army officers of the Division and myself—which began that day—continued unbroken until the end of our service together.[2]

Lejeune recounts a Naval officer who served as an example very early in his career during the Spanish-American War:

A day or two after our arrival in Key West, Rear Admiral John C. Watson came on board with Captain Chester and it was announced that he had selected the USS *Cincinnati* as his temporary flagship. He had no staff with him, consequently it fell to my lot to act as a member of his staff during his stay on board. I shall never forget my introduction to my new duties. It was late in the evening when Captain Chester sent for me and told me that he was acting as Chief of Staff, and that the Admiral wanted me to serve as his Flag Secretary for a few days.

> I felt it to be a very great honor to be selected to assist the Admiral and to be taken into his confidence. He was a courtly gentleman of the old school and an officer of distinguished record, having established an outstanding reputation for efficiency and courage while serving as the Executive Officer of Farragut's flagship, the USS *Hartford*, during the Civil War, especially in the famous battle of Mobile Bay, the occasion of Farragut's often quoted "Damn the torpedoes."
>
> Captain Chester took me into his cabin and after I had reported to the Admiral for duty, he invited me to sit down. It was a very interesting and inspiring evening that I spent with those two gallant gentlemen. I had never before met Admiral Watson, although, of course, he was well known by reputation to every officer of the naval service, and I was deeply impressed by his courtesy, his kindness and his simplicity—qualities which I have learned to be the attributes of true greatness. He and Captain Chester were lifelong friends and it was delightful to listen to their intimate, personal conversation and to obtain there from an insight into their characters. Their love of country and their pride in the Navy were the dominant notes in their utterances.³

Commandant Thomas Holcomb recognized potential in A.A. Vandegrift and closely mentored him, playing a role in his selection as a commander in World War II and later as Commandant. General Holcomb was a worthy mentor with 58 years' experience, including extensive expeditionary service and a brilliant combat record in France in 1918.

Holcomb's mentorship was detailed clearly by Vandegrift in his memoir:

> Early in 1937, my education was cut short when unexpected orders recalled me to Washington to serve as military secretary to the new Commandant, General Thomas Holcomb. It may seem difficult to believe now, but such was the way we saw the world situation in 1937 that I figured this would be my last tour. I was a full colonel with twenty-six years of service and, like most of my contemporaries, planned to retire after thirty years.
>
> In 1937, Marine Corps Headquarters occupied a wing in the Navy Building on Constitution Avenue. Here, I reported to Major General Holcomb for duty.

> [Holcomb] was well known throughout the Corps as an imaginative planner and administrator. He was a man of medium height and graying hair whose steel-rimmed glasses in no way hid the effect of piercing gray eyes, particularly if they were turned on you. A quiet firmness and a brain like a calculating machine cause many officers to regard the general as somewhat dour. Having known Holcomb in China and Quantico, I sensed that this briskness concealed a considerable amount of warmth and humility—and I was correct.[4]

> I spent most of December at General Holcomb's elbow, being read onto the numerous problems of his office. Fortunately, prewar duty at Headquarters prepared me to handle some of them. General Holcomb also had been most cooperative in keeping me informed of his major policy and personnel decisions during the past year or more. As a result, I quite rapidly oriented myself, benefiting also from the Secretary of the Navy's daily conference. After my Pacific duty this struck me as a strange kind of life.

It was a tough job. He wrote to General Roy Geiger: "Things are about as hectic as you told me I would find them: and many times have I longed, even in this brief space of time, for the peaceful calm of a bombing raid on Bougainville."[5]

Another giant of the Corps, Major General Smedley Butler, also mentored Vandegrift, who recalled:

> I learned a great many things in Nicaragua. Most important was the value of leadership as demonstrated by Smedley Butler. He impressed not by words but by action. He was a fighter in the fullest sense of the word—at one point in the campaign he was terribly ill of malaria and yet with a 104-degree temperature he not only held on but carried on.[6]

> It was decided to send me to the Army's Command and General Staff School at Fort Leavenworth; my orders were in the mill when Smedley Butler telephoned. Without offering details, he wondered if he could persuade me to forego the new assignment and come out as his operations officer (at Marine Barracks, San Diego). He made it clear that he needed me, but said he would request me only if I wished to come. Much as I wanted

to go to Leavenworth, I, of course, agreed and within a week was headed west. Back in 1921, a series of mail robberies had finally caused the Postmaster General to ask the President for Marine mail guards. With 2,300 Marines on the job the robberies immediately ceased and the crisis passed. Now in October 1926, the mail robberies again began. This time the Postmaster General promptly asked for and received 2,500 Marines. The bulk of them formed into the Eastern Mail Guards commanded by Logan Feland at Quantico with the remainder—nearly the entire 4th Regiment—forming the Western Mail Guards commanded by Smedley Butler with headquarters in San Francisco. I accompanied Butler as his operations officer with additional duties as battalion commander.

Our mission was to furnish armed guards both in mail cars hauling large money shipments and in certain post offices concerned with handling large sums of money. Our routes included all the western states as far east as North Dakota, Colorado, and El Paso, Texas, some 40,000 miles of railroads plus 28 major post offices. We armed our people with .45 automatic pistols, 12-gauge riot shotguns, and Thompson submachine guns. We publicized both their armament and Butler's personal orders, those once given by Spartan mothers to their sons: "Come back with your shields or upon them." The bandits disappeared as rapidly as they had struck and never did return.

The guard duty earned the Corps many new friends in the western states. In my frequent tours of inspection I was particularly impressed at the attitude of average townsfolk toward the Marines. More than once our men were practically dragged off the streets into private homes and clubs where they received every possible courtesy and, I am pleased to say, replied in kind. Once the crisis ended Postmaster General New cited us: "Efficiency and courtesy were combined to a degree that could not but evoke a wholesome respect for the Marine Corps, that fine arm of the Service which by reason of its training may be utilized in any character of emergency."[7]

General George Barnett mentored a young Marine who went on to become Commandant—Clifton B. Cates. After his exceptional combat performance in France in World War I, Cates returned to the United States. He reminisced: "A rather odd thing happened the day after my company was demobilized there at the Marine Barracks. I had no idea—I had never thought about staying in the Marine Corps. So I submitted my resignation and was at the Barracks that afternoon and I was walking around the compound when I saw General Barnett coming down the sidewalk. He was then Commandant. I looked for some place to duck, but I couldn't. So I saluted and he returned the salute and said, 'Young man, I understand you are resigning.' And I gulped a few times and said, 'Yes, sir.' He said, 'How would you like to have two months' leave and then make your mind up?' And I said, 'Well, that's certainly fair enough, General.' He said, 'All right. Withdraw your resignation; put your leave slips in tomorrow morning.' So I did. I hadn't been home ten days when I was ready to get back again."

Cates had never met the General before, but evidently Barnett knew of Cates. Cates' oral history interviewer asked him: "You were his aide for a period of about six or seven months, is that right?"

Cates replied: "Yes, I was his aide and also an aide at the White House to President Wilson. Then, as you know, General Lejeune came in as Commandant and Barnett was ordered out to the Department of the Pacific in San Francisco. I was appointed as Aide to the Commandant, so I held over for maybe three or four weeks as Aide to General Lejeune. In the meantime, when Barnett was ordered to the Department he asked if I would like to go with him as his aide. I told him I was planning on being married and I knew it wasn't the custom in those days to have married aides. He said that would be fine; 'I know your wife-to-be. I want you to get married and come out with me.' I said I wasn't going to be married for about a couple of months. He asked, 'Why?' I said, 'Well, I don't have the money.' He said, 'Hell, I'll lend you the money.' So then I went out and I was aide to him for a year and a half out there."[8]

In his oral history, Lemuel C. Shepherd, Jr., recalled returning to France in September 1919 for duty in connection with the preparation of relief maps of the battlefields over which the 4th Brigade of Marines had fought. The Brigade Chief of Staff, then Major Charles D. Barrett, headed the effort. Shepherd said: "I returned to the States. Barrett was the Brigade Chief of Staff and I served directly under him so I had the opportunity to become well acquainted with him and learned to admire his fine qualities and able mind. Just to show you how the man's brain worked, he had a forward thinking concept about history. He said, 'Belleau Woods is the greatest battle in which the Marines have participated in a long time. We should make a relief map of this battlefield.' You know he was a great cartographer. That was his specialty. I mean he was an expert in topography which he had taught at the Marine Corps Schools. He said, 'I think we ought to go back to Belleau Woods and make a relief map of the area for historical purposes.' In those days there weren't but two relief maps in the United States, one up at Gettysburg and—I forget where the other one was.[9]

"Because Barrett considered Belleau Woods 'the greatest battle the Marine Corps has ever participated in,' he told me: 'If I can arrange to return to France to make a map of Belleau Woods, would you like to go with me?' Since I had studied Civil Engineering at college [Virginia Military Institute] and was well versed in topography, I told Barrett I would like to go with him. Barrett obtained authority to carry out his proposal to make a relief map of Belleau Woods. Upon the disbandment of the Brigade at Quantico we organized a mapping detachment consisting of four officers who were familiar with map making and six enlisted men to be rodmen and automobile drivers. We obtained transits, drawing boards and other engineering equipment from the Marine Corps School and within two weeks we sailed back to France."[10]

What was extremely meaningful to Shepherd's career is that he learned about amphibious operations and was exposed to the most important leaders in planning and implementation. Shepherd commented further: "He [Barrett] wanted somebody to help him and I was fortunate to have the opportunity to do so. I earned my staff pay in those days, but I learned a lot about amphibious warfare operations.

"In my opinion Charlie Barrett was, with all due respect to General Holcomb, whom I admire, the officer who contributed more than anyone else in the Marine Corps toward the broad concept of amphibious operations. You may not agree with me, and I admit my opinion may be influenced by my great devotion to Charlie Barrett. I knew him personally and discussed amphibious doctrine with him on many occasions. He was closer to me than my father. I mean professionally. My father was a doctor in Norfolk, and I seldom saw him when I was a boy because he was practicing medicine night and day. But I grew to know Charlie Barrett intimately especially when we went back to France together after the war to make a relief map of the Belleau Woods.[11]

"It was while I was assigned to the France Map Detachment that I came to know Major Barrett intimately and learned to admire his outstanding character and professional ability. We became close friends. Some years later I was a student in the senior class of the Marine Corps School while he was an instructor. Barrett had just come back from the *Ecole d'Guerre* in France and was well versed in modern warfare. He was an enthusiastic supporter of the amphibious concept. I recall his discussing sending reconnaissance patrols ashore from a submarine. He said: 'Now we send out patrols when we are engaged in combat ashore to determine the strength and location of the enemy.' He once said to me, 'Why can't we send patrols off a submarine to make a reconnaissance of the hostile shore line and locate the enemy's defenses?' This was the concept, which was often followed during World War II, of making a reconnaissance of the beaches before a landing was made. This is an example of Barrett's forward thinking on amphibious operations for which I believe historians should give him full credit.

"Maybe Ellis [Lieutenant Colonel Pete Ellis] was the first Marine to foresee the need for the development of amphibious operations to be employed in the Pacific in the event of war with Japan. But Barrett, in my opinion, was the officer who contributed more than anyone else to the development envisioned by Ellis insofar as the doctrine and employment of troops in a landing operation is concerned; without detracting from General Holcomb or General Holland Smith who later carried out the tactical and logistical procedures formulated in the Marine Corps School while Barrett was an instructor.

"Our friendship continued throughout the years and it gave me great pleasure to serve as one of his regimental commanders when he became commanding general of the Third Marine Division during the early part of World War II."[12]

The expertise Shepherd developed in amphibious combat operations before and during the war continued to influence his career. He recalled: "General Vandegrift changed my orders and I went up to headquarters on a special assignment for several months. . . . About the first of March, General Vandegrift called me into his office and said, 'I have a request from Admiral Ralph Davis at Norfolk to form a troop training unit on the East Coast similar to the one he commanded on the West Coast during World War II. I'm going to send you down there. I want to bring you back here as Assistant Commandant, but I've got to get this organization straightened out. Davis insists he wants an officer well versed in amphibious operations. I'm going to send you down there for some months 'til you get that going, then I'll bring you back up here to headquarters.'"[13]

Commandant Shepherd described other opportunities he enjoyed early in his career: "I was rather surprised I was appointed aide-de-camp to the Commandant of the Marine Corps (and was simultaneously aide at the White House). I'd never sought such an assignment, but as it turned out, I found this duty most interesting and I believe beneficial to my subsequent Marine Corps career.

"On December 20, 1920, I reported to the Commandant of the Marine Corps, who at that time was Major General John Archer Lejeune. The following February I was appointed one of the junior aides at the White House. At that time, President Woodrow Wilson was still in office. There were only four aides: the President's military aide and three White House aides, one from the Army, Navy, and Marine Corps. I was the Marine aide. My first duty as White House aide was to accompany Vice President and Mrs. Marshall on the east porch of the Capitol when President Harding was sworn in.

"During the next two years I was personally very close to General Lejeune, whom I consider one of the finest Commandants we've ever had in the Marine Corps. General Lejeune was a very easy person to work for. He was a very able officer, with the outstanding reputation as commander of the 2$^d$ Army Division, of which the Marine Brigade formed a part in France during the latter part of the war. It was a great privilege for me, a young captain of three years service, to be associated with an officer of his caliber.

"I especially enjoyed my morning rides with General Lejeune. He rode horseback every morning. The horses were delivered to the Commandant's house. The general, Captain Craig, who was serving as one of the aides, and I rode through the southeast part of Washington, where the National Museum and Smithsonian Institute are located and then around Hains Point, arriving at Headquarters Marine Corps which was then on Constitution Avenue in the old Navy Building exactly at 9 o'clock, after a nice morning's canter."[14]

Shepherd was mentored by another Commandant. "I was ordered to the Marine Barracks in 1934. General John H. Russell was Commandant at the time and he was unhappy with the way things were being run at the barracks. I remember being called in by General Russell and he said, 'Now, I want this place straightened out. Make a military garrison of this post. It's the oldest post in the Corps and it should be the best.' He gave me a free hand to do more or less as I wished."

Shepherd's performance in this responsibility gave him considerable exposure to the entire Marine Corps; his enduring contribution is what has become known as the "8$^{th}$ and I" ceremonies. "It was during this period that in order to smarten the men up as General Russell had told me to do, I started having a parade and guard mount every morning. In addition we held an afternoon parade once a week and invited guests to be present at this formation. These parades were the forerunner of the ones held at the

Marine Barracks today. Of course they have been modified and improved, but the basic ceremony, less the silent drill, we didn't do in those days, is the same ceremony we conducted every morning. We were doing the old squads right drill which was prescribed, before World War II. This was in '34 to '36. The old type of squad drill was good disciplinary training for both officers and men. I also turned out the Marine Band for our morning formal guard mounting.

"In addition, I was registrar of the Marine Corps Institute which I found to be an interesting job. My organization conducted correspondence courses to improve the education of enlisted men. I also built up this activity to a marked degree during this period that I was assigned to Warm Springs in command of a guard for President Roosevelt when he went down there each fall.

"The President had received many threatening letters. The 'Little White House' was unprotected and there was a possibility of assassination. The Secret Service couldn't handle it all, so Colonel Stallings, the Chief of the Secret Service, requested a detachment of Marines to assist in the President's protection. The Commandant ordered me to organize a company of selected Marines to go to Warm Springs for this duty during the fall of 1935. It gave me an opportunity to meet and get to know President Franklin Delano Roosevelt quite well, and I found him a most agreeable person to work for. We covered his activities every day. We had sentries around the 'Little White House.' He spent a great deal of time on an enclosed glassed-in porch in the rear, which was just 150 feet from where there was a wooded hill, so it was an excellent spot for anyone who wished to assassinate the President to get a shot at him. They couldn't have missed.

"President Roosevelt swam every morning. We provided an escort for him at the pool. It was a difficult task, as the President didn't want us in his hair all the time. We had to remain in the distance, more or less out of his sight, but still we were responsible for the protection of the President. I'm telling you, when we finally put him on the train for his return to Washington I heaved a great sigh of relief. I took it very seriously—the responsibility for the safety of the President of the United States was on my hands.

"After two years at the Marine Barracks, I wished to improve myself professionally so I asked General Russell to send me to the Naval War College, which he kindly did. I was in Newport for a year in 1936 to 1937. In June 1937, on the request of General R.P. Williams, I was ordered to Quantico to command the 2d Battalion 5th Marines."[15]

On October 17, 1946, Shepherd became Assistant Commandant under Alexander A. Vandegrift. "I was ordered to headquarters to become Assistant Commandant. . . . It was during this period that Vandegrift directed I was both Chief of Staff and Assistant Commandant. This was significant since as the Assistant to the Commandant I had the authority to make decisions in the name of the Commandant."[16]

As World War II developed, Shepherd was frustrated with his stateside assignment. In time of war, a Marine wants to be in the fight. But to prepare troops for combat, it is critical that the very best officers are responsible for their training. So, as one of the most qualified Marines, he was involved in training. Shepherd reflected: "I was at the Marine Corps School as Assistant Commandant when the United States entered World War II. Naturally, I was most anxious to get into it, especially when the 2$^d$ Division went to Iceland. I was hoping very much to be assigned to a combat organization. General Holcomb was the Commandant of the Marine Corps then. I'd served with General Holcomb in the 4$^{th}$ Marine Brigade in France during World War I and knew him personally. When he came down to Quantico for the graduation of the Marine Corps School in June of 1942, I waited for a proper moment when we were alone together and said, 'Couldn't you send me out, General? I am most anxious to join a combat organization and get into the war.' General Holcomb's reply was, 'Listen, Shepherd, you're going to stay here in the Marine Corps School where you are needed to train these young officers whether you like it or not.' That's how far I got. But he didn't forget it, and some months later, in the spring of 1943, I was ordered to Camp Elliott in California to organize and command the 9$^{th}$ Marine Regiment."[17]

Serving with the Commandant, one of the most important experiences he had was meeting Lieutenant Colonel Earl Hancock "Pete" Ellis, who was referred to as the "Father of Marine strategy in the Pacific." He was very close to General Lejeune, and Shepherd was in on many of their meetings and learned a great deal about the threat of Japan. "I remember him [Ellis] going in to see the Commandant from time to time, but at the time, I didn't realize his foresightedness about the Pacific. Of course, we all knew that the Pacific probably would be our next battlefield with the Japanese as our enemies. But I didn't know at that time that Ellis was a great student of amphibious warfare."[18]

Mentorship is also provided by civilians serving their country. One advantage that Commandant Shepherd had in his career was meeting informally and socially with members of President Dwight D. Eisenhower's cabinet: Charles Wilson, who became Eisenhower's Secretary of Defense, Bob Stevens (Secretary of the Army), Harold Talbot (Secretary of the Air Force), and Bob Anderson (Secretary of the Navy). "I had gotten to know them well. We'd been wining and dining together. I had the advantage of knowing them personally before I came to Washington.... I could go into any one of their offices and immediately be recognized and warmly greeted.... As Commandant I could talk to them man to man.

"As a result of this working relationship, General Order No. 10 was placed into effect. General Order No. 10 gave us independent status from the Navy. We were able to accomplish many things which we wouldn't perhaps have been able to have done otherwise."[19]

General Louis H. Wilson recalls being selected to be an aide to the President of the United States when he was a captain: "As it turned out I had been ordered to be an aide to the President. When I reported for duty, Colonel Kendall, who was then the commanding officer of the Barracks, said, 'Well, I am certainly glad to see you, Major. We have been waiting a couple of months. The very idea . . . young officers these days, captains (I was a captain, then) are even getting married. I'm certainly glad to see you.'

"Then I lowered the boom, telling him: 'I got married on my way.' And I thought he was going to kill me." But Wilson still had the recognition offered by assignment in Washington. So since I was already there he had no choice but to keep me. We stayed two years.

"Since I could not be a Presidential aide, because they couldn't be married, I was assigned at that time to be the commanding officer of the barracks detachment which is now the Ceremonial Guard Company, and later on was the dean of the MCI."[20]

Following Wilson's promotion to Brigadier General in November 1966, he was assigned to Headquarters Marine Corps as Legislative Assistant to the Commandant of the Marine Corps. General Wilson reflected on a lesson learned while serving as the legislative representative to Commandant Wallace M. Greene, Jr., and later, Commandant Leonard F. Chapman, Jr.

General Simmons asked Wilson, in his oral history: "Do you have any recollection of the styles employed by those two Commandants in addressing congressional affairs?

"Yes," General Wilson said. "General Greene, being the very meticulous and thorough individual that he is, had a massive amount of notes. He would practice a technique, which I later used to good advantage. He would have notes in a file box manned by his military assistant and when a question would be asked of him, he would drop his right hand down and at the same time begin to answer the question. The military assistant, who was very familiar with the cards, would find the card with the appropriate answer and hand it to him, very much like a surgeon is handed his instruments. He would then glance at it and refresh his memory. A very good technique that I used, not nearly as effectively as General Greene, but one which I thought was a fine idea.

"This tour was a marvelous preparation for my relations with the Congress. As I look back, this was the best preparation that I had for one of the most difficult jobs of being the Commandant. I felt comfortable on the Hill; and knew a great many of the Senators and Congressmen from my days as the Marine Corps legislative representative."[21]

In 1943, Lieutenant Robert Barrow was stationed at the Naval Administration Depot in New Orleans: "Going to the Naval Administration Depot, New Orleans was not a bad experience for me. I didn't stay too long, and I had this unusual commanding officer who had an unusual interest in me. . . . The thing I remember most about that experience was that I arrived right after the new CO arrived, who had been picked to 'straighten things out.' He was an old-timer who, at that time, in the summer of 1943 had 35 years' experience in the Marine Corps, and he was a major. His name was Herbert S. Keinling. He was about 6'4" and stood very straight, had a hawk nose, and he was a forbidding-looking character, stern. He was a product of a lot of wartime experience in the Banana Wars and considerable peacetime experiences. He was knowledgeable in all of those things that a young officer would not be knowledgeable in, so he was a source of learning. He took it upon himself, since I was the only regular officer assigned, that he would be my personal tutor.

"I was present for all of his office hours, and he had them every day. That was a great learning experience, because he was so skilled in understanding human nature, and he'd heard it all, that he could tell easily when someone was trying to pull a fast one on him.

"Herbert S. Keinling had enlisted in the Marine Corps under an assumed name of Frank Kennedy. I'm not sure why he felt compelled to take on an assumed name, but I saw all of this because part of his tutelage of me was also to show me his records.

"After he'd been a sergeant and had about six or seven years under the assumed name of Frank Kennedy, he was offered a commission. He had to reveal his true identity I suppose, or he felt compelled to, so then he became himself again, Herbert S. Keinling. That made quite an impression on me. I learned things good and bad out of it, impressions of both."

Commandant Barrow received his earliest training in guerrilla warfare and learned about Asia and the Asian culture with his experience in World War II: "I believe it was early 1944. I was a regular officer, having earned my commission at Quantico. I only mention that because I was picked to be a volunteer for the China duty. I think there was some thought that this duty would be so unusual and attractive to the infantry that maybe a regular should be offered the opportunity to volunteer for it. I wasn't picked for any Chinese language skills or any prior knowledge of China.

"I reckon I was picked because somebody thought, well, he's a regular officer, and maybe he should have this kind of unusual experience. In any case, I was volunteered for China duty.

"There was a great deal of mystery and appeal about China. We had heard about China Marines and things in China. So it wasn't too difficult for me to say, 'Yeah, I'll go to China,' without any knowledge or understanding of what the duty was all about. So I volunteered to go 'to China.' That's all I knew.

"I was going to go over there and work with the Chinese guerrillas. I will never forget this man in Washington, the Commander of the Navy, talking to me, a young lieutenant. I was eager to do just about anything. He looked across the desk at me and his eyes squinted a little bit, and he said, 'Lieutenant, are you prepared to live in caves and diet on fish heads and rice?'

"Well, in retrospect that's kind of ridiculous. He didn't know any more about the environment than I did. But being naïve and enthusiastic, I responded resoundingly, 'Yes, Sir!' I really didn't know what we were actually getting to beyond the fact that we were going to China and work with Chinese guerrillas. I got no training in the six weeks I was in Washington, and I doubt that there was any kind of training that was available. Nobody even gave me any little brief language preparation or environmental studies or anything.

"It's true that we trained, but to some extent we also were trained. That is, the Chinese needed skills, particularly those who hadn't served with any army, which was the case with most of them, the basic skills of how to handle weapons, and basic tactics, and how to employ them.

"But then, there were things like field crafts. How to get along in the country and how to move and things like that, that we had to learn. So it was an unusual learning experience. I learned an awful lot about, and still to this day have a high respect for, the capability of the Chinese, the civilian, farmer if you will, to endure all kinds of hardships and to do so much under adverse circumstances."

Barrow commented that as a commander in Vietnam, he often looked back to his experience in China: "I'm speaking of, for example, the movement of supplies. That is why in Vietnam, and even in Korea, I felt that I had a better understanding of what the Oriental capability was to move things at night, than anybody else, because I saw them do it.

"They can mass thousands of people. We think you have to move things by truck, train, boat, and rail. If you get thousands of coolies, each carrying 80 or 100 pounds, you can move enormous amounts of things, which is what was done in Vietnam. It was done in Korea."

His interviewer asked: "Is there any other thing that you recall that you looked back on, reflected upon from your experience in China that served you well in Vietnam?"

"The one thing that stands out," Barrow said, "my perception, if I may say, my very accurate perception of the individual capabilities, the capabilities of the individual Chinese or you could almost say any Oriental, to do things.

"The point is, as a young officer, being out there conducting independent kind of operations, without any direction; I had no radio, so I didn't get any data, weekly or monthly instructions as to what I was to do next; it was largely my initiative. My initiative plus what cooperation I could get from my Chinese counterparts, which in itself was a learning experience, to find one who would cooperate.

"So in a sense, my time in China contributed rather substantially to my development as a Marine officer. . . . I had the opportunity to be responsible in terms of the mission to be performed, in a large area to be covered, and the wherewithal to do it."[22]

Sometimes mentorship is provided by assignments, particularly when a promising officer is pulled out of an assignment that was not sufficiently challenging or commensurate with the officer's ability and potential. Barrow describes one such incident in his oral history. It was 1950 and Barrow was a captain stationed at Camp Lejeune. At the time there was considerable dissatisfaction with the marksmanship of the Marines: "Apparently, up at the 2[d] Marine Division Headquarters they deduced that training needed to be done differently. 'We're going to put out there, at the rifle range, a detachment of people who are going to be sufficient in numbers to provide coaches for every guy that comes out to re-qualify. We're going to have an officer in charge of that elite detail and it's going to be done right.'

"They were going around and finding the best in the entire 2[d] Marine Division to be coaches, and they cast about looking for the officer in charge. I'm told that General Hart came back to the CP and among his briefings he was told, 'This is all set to go and we have picked an officer down at 2[d] Marines.' He asked, 'Who is he?' and was told 'Captain Barrow. We think he would do a good job.'

"I will forever be grateful to General Hart. I'm not suggesting he knew me that well, but he knew something—he is supposed to have said about assigning me: 'No, you're not. For two reasons. One, he's a super company commander, doing a good job, and we should leave him there.

But I'm going to tell you something else, I happen to know that he's a bachelor. Being a bachelor at Camp Lejeune, at Paradise Point, is bad enough. But how would you like to be a bachelor out at the rifle range?'

"Well, I didn't have a car in those days and being a bachelor at the rifle range would, indeed, have been absolutely deadly. So I didn't get that assignment." It seems Barrow was saved for greater leadership responsibilities.

Barrow went on: "The third point that he couldn't have predicted was that, in taking my name off, I then kept my company and went to Korea with them. Otherwise, I could have been kept there and then locked in, like for maybe two or three years. 'Don't move him because he knows the ropes and so forth, and so forth.' And I may have missed a career altogether."[23]

One of Commandant Kelley's key inspirations was Major General John A. Lejeune. Commandant Kelley related: "When one speaks of leaders within a Corps which prides itself on leadership, the name Lejeune is without equal.

"As Commandant I lived in a very special home in Washington, a historic residence known as 'The Commandant's House.' First occupied in 1806 by our third Commandant, Lieutenant Colonel Franklin Wharton, it has been the home of every subsequent holder of that office. In this magnificent, federal-style house hang the portraits of 26 of our 28 Commandants.

"One of the first things I did upon taking occupancy of this house last July was to relocate the portrait of General Lejeune to the wall overlooking my desk in the library. I did this for a very special reason. I hoped that the Marine in this portrait would help to provide the inner strength, the inspiration, and the leadership necessary to continue the proud and distinguished legacy passed to me by my forebearers. There have been only 27 other Marines who have occupied the Office of the Commandant in over two centuries. The wisdom of my decision to relocate this portrait did not take long to materialize.

"At one o'clock in the morning of 23 October 1983, a date which I shall forever remember, I received the first notification that there had been a massive explosion of undetermined origin in the building which housed the headquarters elements of the 1st Battalion, 8th Marines, in Beirut; a building where I had stood only two weeks earlier to award 14 Purple Hearts to brave young Marines who had shed their life's blood for their Country and their Corps. The initial assessment indicated that there could be over 200 dead.

"As I sat in the unlit library I experienced shock and disbelief. A short time later I received another phone call, this time from our Commander-in-Chief. As I listened to his sincere and heartfelt words of condolence, the only light in the room was from the button on my telephone—a glint, which in otherwise total darkness, shone up upon John A. Lejeune. With the President of the United States providing me comfort in this hour of need, and General Lejeune looking down upon me from above, I silently asked these two great leaders for their prayers that I would have the strength, the courage, and the wisdom to guide our Corps and our Marines through the worst peacetime tragedy in our history."[24]

General Mundy's oral history provides considerable detail of his assignment to serve as one of General Lewis H. Walt's aides as a major. Mundy's interviewer asked: "General Walt gave you four fitness reports, each one better than the last. The last three were straight 'outstanding' with correspondingly complimentary remarks. Do you recall any mentoring or counseling that General Walt might have given you?"

Mundy replied: "General Walt would go anywhere and speak to any group because he truly was passionate in the belief that we were winning in Vietnam. That it was a winnable war, that the North Vietnamese were a people without a just cause and the South Vietnamese truly relied upon, trusted, and believed that the United States would win for them. So he was passionate on that.

"I viewed General Walt's function as really, more the administration's uniformed advocate for the war in Vietnam than any degree of focus that he put on or was involved in being the Assistant Commandant of the Marine Corps. That is not to say that he abdicated his duties, he had many. We would get requests from the White House or from Congress. General Chapman liked to see him go out [Walt was Assistant Commandant under Commandant Leonard F. Chapman, Jr.], so we traveled an enormous amount of the time.

"A typical trip would be going out to Andrews [Air Force Base] and get in the airplane, brief him, on how long a trip it was, precisely who was going to meet him at the airport and what he would do when he got there, and whether or not be there would be press there. You had better be right, because if the person you had told him was going to meet him was not there, whatever the circumstances, it was fine, it was no problem at all until you got to the hotel, and you paid the price, or if the assistant mayor showed up and not the mayor. There was a price to be paid by the aide.

"But General Walt's mentoring or counseling was routinely fairly harsh. In other words, you learned by getting something thrown at you. Rarely did he sit you down and say, 'Let me talk to you about your future and where you're going.'

"Now, I knew—it was a love-hate relationship, I guess, because I knew he thought well of me. I have always been of the conviction that you don't need a lot of counseling. You know if you're doing well or not, and you know when you are meeting the mark, and when you finish doing something, somebody doesn't have to tell you that they are real pleased, and that makes you feel good. But I knew that I was doing well, and I knew that I was serving him well. I think Lew Walt was a fish out of water. He was a Chesty Puller-type or a Lou Diamond or something. He was happiest on the battlefield.

"But when I say love-hate, I admired him, I thought a lot of him. He was an idol in my view. But at the same time, I, and I know my successor, [Curtis G.] Gene Arnold, we spent many anguished hours ourselves, trying to grit our teeth enough just to tell this man to stick it in his ear, we were through, we quit, because he was very hard to work for. It was probably more in the form of—I remember vividly his favorite saying: 'Don't assume the prerogatives of the commanding general.'

"My dad was a great admirer of his. My dad would write, and General Walt would always write back and tell him what an absolutely superb son I was. I think Lois Parham [Walt's secretary] probably wrote those letters; I didn't write letters back to my dad. But anyway, he thought well of me, so I am not surprised that he rated me well. But his mentoring was a painful experience."

Mundy was asked: "What do you think you learned from this tour near the apex of the Marine Corps?" He replied: "Well, Vietnam, being at III MAF, probably was my first introduction to general officer command and decisionmaking. But there, I was well removed from it. In this assignment, I was able to learn a little bit about the mechanics of Washington and how the Headquarters staff worked. I didn't really learn much about JCS or about the relationship between the Secretary of the Navy and the Marine Corps. But I did come to understand the Headquarters.

"Our title was not aide-de-camp, it was administrative assistant, so the administrative assistant was thrust into more in the Headquarters than just being the bag carrier, the aide. I came to know the Headquarters. I read a lot of P–4s from generals. I understood how the generals were maneuvered. In those days it seemed to me that the generals really didn't like each other very much, and there seemed to be cliques all around the place. The way you would get rid of a general would be—instead of just calling him in and saying, 'I'd like for you to go,' you would give him some intolerable assignment that you knew he wasn't going to take, and he would get out.

"I think the relationship—General Chapman, of course, was very formal and rather aloof—that's not snobbish, but General Chapman was the Commandant. I did not perceive that there was a great deal of interface.

I perceived, as I said earlier, that there was a tremendous loyalty on General Walt's part toward General Chapman. He would do anything. The Commandant spoke, and it was law."[25]

Major Mundy left his assignment with General Walt on July 30, 1969, and he recalled: "I went off to Command and Staff College from there. One seeks, I think, or I sought at least, not to be labeled as 'General Walt's aide.' So I think you try and shed those trappings as quickly as you can. But I saw him on a couple of occasions.

"I was still working on the book [*Strange War, Strange Strategy*], when General Walt's fourth star was approved by the Senate and he was going to be promoted. He called me down one day and said, 'I want you to come back in as the aide,' because the aide that he had, Gene Arnold, about whom we have spoken earlier, didn't work out. I think Gene was a splendid aide, but he was not the man for Lew Walt. But anyway, he said, 'I want Major Arnold to go to Command and Staff College and I want you to come back in as the aide,' and I did.

"When I got there he said, 'Now I'm going to be promoted to four stars and I rate a lieutenant colonel. So you go down and see who is available.' I went down to the Personnel Department, to Brigadier General Lou Wilson, as a matter of fact, and told him I needed him to find out what lieutenant colonels were coming in. He gave me a list and I saw that Lieutenant Colonel P.X. Kelley was coming out of the Air War College. I asked General Walt, 'How about P.X. Kelley?' He said, 'Great, get him.'"[26]

"So we had a lot of humor about that over the years. Even P.X. Kelley, who—if there was ever a halo in the Marine Corps, P.X. Kelley must have worn it most of his career—and was certainly held in high esteem by General Walt. But P.X. will tell you tales of forgetting the general's white cover on a trip or something, and how painful it could be.

"So at any rate, those were my reliefs. Yes, I left the Headquarters, having had a pretty exciting tour, and having learned a lot about functioning at the senior level.

"I was surprised about going to Command and Staff College as a student. As I mentioned to you, General Walt had said to me, 'Send Arnold to Command and Staff College and you come down and be the aide.' So it was fairly short notice that he said, 'You have been here about a year and a half. I don't want to keep you around here too long, where would you like to go?' I said, 'I would like Command and Staff College.' He said, 'Go down and tell them to assign you to Command and Staff.' So even though the class had already been made up, I was a late add-on. I think I only had about a month's notice. But I was pleased and excited. It was a good tour."[27]

Commandant Alfred Gray was another significant mentor for General Mundy. Asked if he thought he was Gray's first choice for Commandant, Mundy replied: "No, I don't. General Gray had been mentor and certainly one of the best teachers that I've ever had, and Lord knows he has been a patron in that sense. I served under him as a battalion commander when he had the 4th Marines, I served under him as a regimental commander when he had the 2d Division, as a MAU commander for exercises, as a brigade commander when he was FMFLant, as his Operations Deputy when he was the Commandant. So we certainly had a long linkage together and I have always known and admired him and respected him for his tremendous professionalism.

"That said, we are completely different personalities. And General Gray, I think what he had sought to achieve in the Marine Corps was an operational orientation. He wanted gunslingers. He wanted tobacco chewers. That was his image of a Marine. I think that very frankly, I believe that General Gray's first two preferred candidates would have been either General Bob Milligan who had an equal tenure of service with General Gray, or Ernie Cook, with me coming in, at best, as a third.

"We would all have people that we would think more of than others. I think that General Gray sought to continue the operational focus that he himself saw, and if you will, the revolution in military affairs in the Marine Corps. Milligan was the man most like him in thinking and in operational orientation.

"But he [Gray] has been, during my tenure as the Commandant, and certainly to this day, no one has been more supportive, when times were tough, he would give me a call or come to see me or offer advice when it was sought. General Gray has been a very strong supporter."[28]

"When I was a lieutenant general at Headquarters and General Al Gray became the Commandant, I remember that I had just come up from Little Creek and I was certainly on the, I guess one would say, on the Gray team. . . . I mean, he had been my division commander, he had been my force commander. I learned an awful lot from him. I was certainly a Gray admirer and a Gray advocate, and I was delighted when he became the Commandant.

"But, at any rate, Gray established a policy which I perpetuated, and I thought and still do think is a good one. And that is, that in order to keep the blood flowing in the senior ranks, when you were appointed to lieutenant general, that you should, 18 months thereafter, submit your letter indicating your willingness to retire, and that would give him [the Commandant] the flexibility to say, 'No, stay,' or, 'No, I've got another assignment,' or what have you, or to say, 'Yes, thank you, I need for you to step aside so someone else can move up.' So, I understood the policy, and I respected it, and I still think it is a good one."[29]

"Now, the other aspect of it was, remember, if you will, that the Gray era ended with a really bubbling-hot feeling of 'bubbaism.' That was the term used.

"People would talk about the 'bubbas.' If you were one of the 'bubbas,' you got to do this. If you were one of the general's 'bubbas' you were going to command a battalion or you were going to command a regiment. If you were not, you were going to be the G4 or the G2. You might get something, but not if you did not know him. There probably is some unfairness in this, because we all have confidants and lieutenants that we like to lean upon.

"But there was a feeling that there were 'bubbas' that belonged to the Commandant. There was a feeling, also, of great depression to many very fine officers. That when, for example, you get a set of orders to the 2$^d$ Marine Division, that you would say, 'Oh, my gosh, I don't know General Simmons,' and so there was this quick rush to go down and try to curry favor with the division commander, begging him, in effect, for a good job."

Mentorship is not synonymous with favoritism. General Mundy commented that in his own career he had "a sense of accomplishment that I have earned my regiment or I have earned my battalion commands and regimental commands.

"But, that being as it may, the three-stars were fairly strongly convinced that we needed to do something to get quality commanders in.

"I sought to behead the monster by saying, 'Well, okay, in the future it will be a selection board up here comprised of generals that will sit around and determine who is going to go to a command, and then we will let the commanding generals have some latitude in assigning them, but we will determine who is going to command.'

"I think the overall effect of the selection board process is healthy, in the sense of the leadership of the units. It may still be a little bit unhealthy; in the sense of, what do you do if you have been tremendously successful and you do not screen for command. It is a tremendous morale shock."[30]

General Mundy was asked whether the troops realized there was no "bubbaism" during his Commandancy: "How did this filter down to the troops?"

General Mundy answered: "Well, it was an objective assessment. In other words, when a board selects, you are inclined to agree or not because you're on the list or not. I think people generally accept that you had a body of your peers, or seniors in most cases, who have sat and looked over your record and have collectively decided merit, rather than all of us saying he knows General So and So. He's going to get a command. You better bet that. He used to date the General's daughter. You know that sort of thing. That's bubbaism.

"No policy is ever perfect in perception. People that are screened are very happy with it. The guys that aren't screened, you know can find fault with the system. 'If I could get down there and get a battalion, I'd show them. I know I can be a good battalion commander.' And there's some truth there. Undoubtedly, there are some nuggets that don't get the opportunity."[31]

Mundy benefitted from being assigned to General John Cox on the Prepositioning Plans Working Group. "I did not know General Cox well. I knew who he was, but he was in aviation when he was promoted, I think, and I didn't know him well. I thought a lot of him.

"He was a stickler for details. John Cox was really 'in the weeds' on everything that went on, because he wanted to know. But, there was no such thing as giving him a briefing and saying, 'Don't worry about this part. I know it will work and we'll move on from here.' He wanted to know every detail."[32]

Commandant Charles C. Krulak was raised in a Marine Corps family and his most important mentor was his father, Lieutenant General Victor "Brute" Krulak, one of the giants of the Corps. He said of this experience: "I was blessed to come in as the Commandant with something that nobody else had ever had. I grew up in the Corps. People like General Shepherd and Chesty Puller used to sit around my breakfast table. My godfather was 'Howlin' Mad' Smith.

"Even at a young age, I knew that something very important was going on. Growing up, I saw what my Dad did at the educational center and in special ops. I came into this position with much more than a varied 30-year career. At the other end of the phone, I had my Dad. Whenever I had a question I could always go back and ask, 'Why are we at this position? What do you think we ought to do?'"[33]

But being "Brute" Krulak's son also had some challenges. He reflected: "From a personal standpoint, it was the beginning of an understanding that I was 'Brute' Krulak's son and that this was not always going to be a good thing. People either loved my father or they hated him. I mean, there was no in-between. For every one that I met who loved him, there were those who hated him. Now it's totally different because they recognize what a wonderful person he was, what a brilliant man he was, and what he did for the Corps. But he was also a very, very abrasive, tough cookie, and so he stepped on a lot of people's toes. It's the first time I had to deal with being the Brute's son and all that entailed. People saying, 'Well, he's got that because he's Krulak's son,' or, 'We're not going to let him have it because it'll look like favoritism.' I always felt like I was walking this fine line between I don't want to be his son, but I'm proud of him. I didn't want to get the crap, but I also didn't want to get the benefits either. I just wanted to be Chuck Krulak. That's what I wanted.

"The beauty of Vietnam coming as quickly as it did was that it allowed me to be Chuck Krulak. I mean, your dad can't be out in the foxhole—your dad couldn't be out on patrol. The fact that I was in infantry battalions during both of my tours and I never served above the battalion level, it showed that I was not ducking anything, and the fact that I was wounded twice and the fact that both of my brothers were over there and, every one of us was decorated, I think did a lot to mitigate against any sense that I or my brothers received any special treatment.

"Then, obviously, he retired in '68, which was only four years after I became a Marine officer, so I was able to get out from underneath his shadow. It was interesting that there were other Marine generals' sons who came in my basic class with me. Len Chapman, Buzz Buse, Pete Van Ryzin. There were several Marine generals' sons there. So, I wasn't the only one suffering. I'll tell you that."[34]

Many years after Vietnam, Krulak was assigned to be the Battle Management Command and Control Communications Officer for the Strategic Defense Initiative. After he had endured several awkward interviews and was convinced this was not an appropriate assignment for his talents, he had a final interview. He recalled a discussion with a senior civilian member of the Defense Department that changed his perspective.

"My final interview was with Don Latham. Don Latham should have been a Marine. He was the Assistant Secretary of Defense for Command, Control and Communications and Intelligence for over seven years; longer than any $C^3I$ in the history of the business. Brilliant man, hard driving, very tough, very, very sharp. I went in to see him, sat down, and by that time, I had reached a frustration level regarding my fit into this organization and I said, 'I don't want to take up your time. You're an important man and I don't want to take your time. I don't think there's a fit. I've interviewed with Dr. Bertapelli; I've interviewed with Dr. Quinn. What they're talking about is something that is not in my portfolio of talent.'

"Don Latham immediately sat me down and said, 'Listen, General Kelley says that you're the man for the job I'm thinking about and he is very high on you. That's good enough for me. What I want you to be is the

Battle Management Command and Control Communications Officer for the Strategic Defense Initiative, Star Wars.'

"I said, 'Pardon me?'

"He said, 'I want you to be the expert on the battle management $C^3$ for Star Wars.'

"'You have got the wrong man. I could no more do that than be a nuclear physicist.'

"He described to me that it would be battle management. It would be conducted outside the Earth's atmosphere. It would be done from satellites. And he explained this unbelievably complex capability that the country was trying to put up.

"I just said, 'You've got the wrong man.'

"He replied, 'You missed the whole point, Colonel. Quit telling me that I've got the wrong man. That's my decision, not yours. What I want you to do is be Napoleon's corporal. I want you to come in and tell me if the common sense equation doesn't fit with what you're hearing from General Abramson.'

"Lieutenant General Abramson was in charge of the Strategic Defense Initiative. So for the next several months I went to every single meeting that General Abramson had and would come back and report personally to Mr. Latham about what I felt vis-à-vis the Strategic Defense Initiative. Very interesting, very interesting time; very rarely saw Dr. Bertapelli or Dr. Quinn. It was all one-on-one with Don Latham.

"Then a big event took place that had a major impact on my career. Don Latham was a bachelor and he was dating a young woman who was interested in reptiles. She was a scientist and so Latham called me in one day and said, 'Look, what can you tell me about crocodiles and alligators in Vietnam and in China?' I said, 'Well, I don't know what I can tell you. Why?' He said, 'Well, I'm dating this girl. I want to impress her. I want to put together a little package and then I'd like to take her to the Smithsonian and take her through some of the displays there as kind of a date.'

"I said that I'd look into it. I literally put together a book report on reptiles in Asia. Typical Marine, you're asked to do something by your boss and you do it. Then I called up the Smithsonian. I said, 'Look, I'd like to do something special. Is there a way to have a special tour for the Assistant Secretary of Defense for Command, Control and Communications and Intelligence and a young lady after hours?' They said yes. So when I gave Mr. Latham the report, he loved it.

"Next thing I know, he brings me up to his front office. I said goodbye to Dr. Bertapelli, I said goodbye to Dr. Quinn. At that very moment in time, the Department of Defense was reorganizing itself by establishing an acquisition czar, the Under Secretary of Defense for Acquisition.

"Deputy Secretary of Defense asked Don Latham, because of his experience in the Pentagon, to help put together that organization. So he went full time down to an office right beside the Under Secretary of Defense's office and he took me down there to help put this new organization together. I worked almost 18 hours a day, seven days a week for Mr. Latham in that position. We just worked ourselves to death, but in the end, we built the whole office of the Under Secretary of Defense for Acquisition to include all the acquisition plans, the infrastructure; it was a tremendous, tremendous undertaking.

"While this was going, Mr. Latham was very friendly with the people over in the White House. There was a problem with an Army officer who was a deputy to the White House Military Office. He got caught up with an integrity problem and was fired. The White House was looking for an officer to take that job. There was no Marine anywhere in the White House or the National Security Council because of the issue with Ollie North. There was a sense that it was time to bring a Marine back into the White House.

"The request came in to the Department of Defense. Mr. Latham called the new Commandant, General Al Gray, and said, 'What do you think about Colonel Chuck Krulak going over to the White House?' I knew nothing about it. General Gray said 'Yes,' and so Don Latham recommended my name to Mr. Rhett Dawson who headed the administration for the Reagan White House. That began my time at the White House. As you can tell, it was a very interesting year for me in the Pentagon. I went from not even having a job coming out of Hawaii to a year later being in the White House."[35]

Commandant Carl Mundy also had a key role in mentoring Chuck Krulak and expressed his appreciation for his ability: "If you have Chuck Krulak around, you very rarely want for information. He is on top of everything. I called him lightheartedly the 'whirling dervish,' because we had a joke going around down there, at least between myself and the Chief of Staff, that no matter where you went at Camp Lejeune, General Krulak would come out from behind a bush, he was always there.

"He had been the Assistant Division Commander and had just moved over to the Force Service Support Group [FSSG]. Characteristic of him, tremendously knowledgeable, professional, and a quick study; he's the type of individual that when he was given command of the Force Service Support Group, within two or three weeks he knew more about it than just about anybody there.

"So, as it turned out, as far as the man to deploy the II MEF forces to the Gulf, we could not have had a better man in position than Chuck Krulak. He really knew his business, he knew logistics and was a tremendous leader as well, with his orientation on families, and looking after our families was certainly my own philosophy. But I think within the $2^d$ FSSG, among all the elements there we talked about, they had the strongest family support program as well."[36]

I inquired of General Jones: "Who were your mentors in the Marine Corps, those who helped develop your character and leadership on active duty?"

He replied: "Well, the first two I give particular credit to are my father and my uncle, my father's younger brother. He retired as a lieutenant general in the Marine Corps. His last boss was Admiral McCain, Navy CINCPAC and my uncle was commanding general of Marine Forces Pacific. My uncle was 27 years old as a lieutenant colonel, at the time a commander on Guadalcanal, and was awarded the Navy Cross, Silver Star, Purple Heart, Bronze Star, and the whole shooting match. He retired as a three-star in 1973. I was commissioned in '67, so from '67 to '73, I was in uniform with my uncle who was very much a big part of my life."

I asked: "What influence did he have on your development? You were just a first lieutenant then?"

Jones responded: "I was a first lieutenant and General [Raymond G.] Davis came out to the field to visit $3^d$ Marine Division. I think I had about 60 days to go on my tour and he asked me if I would be his aide. I said yes and it turned out to be one of the most illuminating experiences of my life because he was arguably the most highly decorated officer, Medal of Honor, everything, every combat decoration the Marine Corps has, and a man who is of absolute calm and dignity and poise under any imaginable conditions. I learned an awful lot from him.

"I learned from him the importance of being able to project a sense of calm in the face of crisis. The worse a situation got, the calmer he got, and that projected across all of the subordinates. The old man never lost his cool; he really was calm under fire. That's an important attribute, I think, for leaders to be able to convey that sense when things are really going bad, you somehow can turn it into a success if you're willing to persevere and lead your subordinates. He never did panic."

When asked what some of the positions were that Davis was in where he might have been so challenged and ordinary people might have panicked, Jones responded: "Well, I think the everyday command decisions. In Vietnam he was a general that led from the front; he was out each day in an unarmed helicopter going up the DMZ visiting every single unit. It didn't matter whether people were advising us not to land. He was going to see the troops and get a sense, a feel."[37]

Chesty Puller mentored officers and enlisted men of all the Services. One in particular was General Lewis H. Walt, who saw combat in two wars and was the senior Marine Corps officer in the Vietnam War. Historically, the Marines had only one four-star general. The first four-star Marine general, other than the Commandant, was Walt when he was selected as Assistant Commandant in 1969. General Walt said of Puller's mentorship: "Puller was my company commander, and to me was the epitome of Marine Corps training—he gave us everything hard. At every break in the field, though he drove us until our tongues were hanging out, men still gathered around him. He told us tales about fighting in Haiti and Nicaragua, of his patrols living off the land, and fighting natives—all his experiences, not just guff. Every tale had some point.

"Being under Puller in Basic School did more for me than anything I experienced until I got to Guadalcanal. He taught us the use of terrain like a master, how to use the tiniest bit of cover to our advantage. Ground form really meant something when he explained it. He taught us to use the bayonet with all the tricks of close-in fighting. You couldn't mistake it, he knew the stuff cold."[38]

E.B. Potter gave insight into Puller's relationship and resulting mentorship with Admiral Chester W. Nimitz in his biography of the admiral. Potter wrote of an incident when one of the Marines in Puller's detachment was "taken to mast," an Article 32 hearing under the Uniform Code of Military Justice before the Commanding Officer of USS *Augusta*, Captain Chester W. Nimitz, USN, in 1934:

> At another mast, one of Marine Lieutenant Lewis Puller's men was called up. On such occasions the accused division officer stood beside his man and usually opened with a good word for him, such as, 'Captain, this man, who has been accused of such-and-such, has done a good job. He's a reliable man aboard ship. He sometimes gets into trouble ashore, but generally he behaves himself and is a credit to the ship.'
>
> Puller's man was charged with being asleep on watch. Captain Nimitz asked if Puller had any comment. To the surprise of Nimitz and everyone else, Puller shot back, 'I certainly do, Captain. Get rid of the son of a bitch. He's not a Marine if he

goes to sleep on watch. I never want to see him again.' This reply, so utterly contrary to the usual pattern, left Captain Nimitz little choice but to court-martial the man.

Lieutenant Puller was USS *Augusta*'s third Marine commander during Nimitz's command, the other two having been dismissed as unsatisfactory. He won the approval of Nimitz, who reported, 'The work of Lieutenant Puller on board this vessel has been excellent.'[39]

Ray Davis commented on Puller's ship duty in his autobiography:

At the same time that I was serving aboard USS *Portland*, Captain Chesty Puller was Commander of the Marine Detachment on a nearby battleship [the USS *Augusta*, the flagship under the command of Chester W. Nimitz]. Fortunately, I met him ashore on liberty on more than one occasion, whereupon my mentor provided me with further professional guidance, building on the Basic School Company Commander-Officer Student relationship from the preceding year in Philadelphia.

Naturally, as you would expect, Chesty's was the best detachment afloat. When we were ashore on liberty, he always had a word of encouragement or advice. Once he said: 'It's been years since we've had a war. Might be years before another, so you are being judged in your peacetime roles: perfection in drill, in dress, in bearing, in demeanor, shooting, self-improvement. *But more than anything else, by the performance of your Marines.*' Those words formed another key lesson learned for me, which was that whatever success I might have in the Corps would be totally dependent on how well I could motivate and lead the men who served with me. I would suggest this as a great lesson no matter what walk of life one may follow.

I might add that Puller did have a great advantage: His detachment was on a senior flag ship, and he was able to convince his admiral to give him the pick of all Marines joining the force since the senior flag ship should always have the best detachment. Chesty chose all one size—tall, trim Marines with good records, etc. Perfection was the name of the game with Chesty, and he never missed a trick.

Puller summed it up for me thusly. 'Every waking hour Marines are to be schooled and trained, challenged and tested, corrected and encouraged, with perfection as the goal!' Then and there, perfection in every United States Marine Corps task became my goal![40]

The comment was made to General Davis: "So, in many ways, for individuals such as yourself, being in the right place at the right time combined with having the initiative and the drive, the ability, is almost necessary to get ahead."

Davis replied: "Yes. To really move out you have to have that. Another great fortune I felt I had was on two or three key occasions I was involved with an outstanding leader of some characteristics that I could see and realize how they could promote success. Started out early with Lewis Puller in his regiment in World War II, then I went to Korea with Litzenberg, who was a different kind but also one of our greats. Exposed to Lew Walt and a number of others who, through the years it seemed, not only to be at the right time and the right place, but also be involved with some of the key history makers in their role. It's also a people-input then.

"It's hard to put my finger on one individual who most affected my career. Certainly Chesty Puller, Litzenberg, Nickerson, and Walt were four outstanding ones. Then, in Vietnam I had exposure to some outstanding Army people. Stilwell, out in Korea. Bill Rosson, who was Army commander in the Pacific. Abrams, of course, down in Saigon, spent an awful lot of time up in my area and gave me a lot of guidance and also a lot of examples of the kind of leadership it takes to get things done.

"To me a Marine is a highly individual personality who is able to subdue or to mold himself into a team effort. In other words, it's a team effort of a lot of highly individualistic efforts. That, to me, has been the secret of the Marine Corps. I don't think anybody ever, in my career, tried to put people into a precise shape or form. Sure you have rules because these rules are what hold the unit together. But I think the key to the Marine Corps has been taking these individuals who have great spirit and great desire and determination on their own and convince them that the best way to get what they want accomplished is through a unity of effort, a combination of themselves into a team."[41]

General Raymond G. Davis was another who benefited from the mentorship of Lewis "Chesty" Puller as a student in the Officer's Basic Course. His comments echo General Walt's recollections: "Lewie, I guess, if you have to look back and see the road markers along the way that turns you in the right direction, you have to think of Lewie Puller. He was a great inspiration. Of all those that you've mentioned, I don't know of any other who had a course of instruction where the students would ask him to continue through the lunch hour, and he was just that kind of a guy. He would walk in, have his lesson plan—I guess that they had to have a lesson plan to suit their superiors—but Captain Puller would put his lesson plan up on the lectern and pick up the cue stick that they used for a pointer. He would refer to about three words out of the lesson plan and the rest of it was right down to the nitty-gritty of the wars that he had been in, the kind of things that make or break people, what's right and what's wrong.

"As far as running a troop organization is concerned, particularly in the lower levels, I don't think that he had any peers. He was teaching tactics. Primarily small wars. He was also our tactical instructor or whatever it was that ran the drill. He operated one of the two companies, and helped us get our uniforms. You had to pass the Puller inspection for your uniform and if there was any room in there to breathe, it was too loose!

"One lieutenant came out and said one time that he had his uniform made down in Philadelphia, at Jacob Reed's, and Puller told him, 'You go down there and tell old man Jacob or old man Reed or whoever in the hell is in charge that I said that that uniform is not going to pass.' This was his approach to most of our uniform problems. But he got us fitted out and in regulation attire, and taught us great, great troop inspections and drill. He was a perfectionist in his way.[42]

"The thing I remember, too, about him was that he lived there in quarters in the Navy Yard, in a big house, Captain Puller and Mrs. Puller were as nice and gracious as they could be. But if you had a dance or anything at the club, the real gentleman and ladies' man of the whole crowd was Lewie Puller. He was a perfect host, dancer, conversationalist, taking care of everybody, and gracious, and totally different character, a true Southern gentleman when he was required to be.

"I ran into him many times. Later, he and I went to sea duty; he was in one of the nearby battleships, I was in a cruiser. During World War II, I had a special weapons unit and he had the 1$^{st}$ Marines, at the time we were loading up to go up to Cape Gloucester for the New Britain operation. My unit being in support, had been attached out to the regiments for the voyage so I was personally in a stay-behind status. So I went to Colonel Puller.

"I walked in and he remembered me and said, 'Hi old man. How are you? What can I do for you?' and I said, 'I'm looking for a ride,' and explained my situation. All my units were up there and they were going to the war and there were a lot of things that needed to be taken care of. There were equipment problems and so forth. I told him I could contribute more up there than I could back here. He says, 'Well, I'll tell you, old man. Anybody who wants to go to war, they can go as far as I'm concerned.' He turned to an assistant and said, 'You put Davis on the roster. We'll take him.'

"So that's how I got to Cape Gloucester. While we were up there (he was initially the exec of 1st Marines) he got command of the regiment, and when he had a vacancy for a battalion commander and I asked him for that job and got it. I got transferred from special weapons, which, as you know, was antitank and antiaircraft, over to infantry through my personal relationship with General Puller and his acceptance of my desire to get involved with that part of the war."[43]

Davis saw combat in Korea in significant leadership positions. It was truly tough: "To show you how bad it was, even though we came ashore 'in reserve'—probably because our commander had been relieved and I was the newest battalion commander—the second day ashore I was assigned a mission of the central thrust up to the north of the island, in the worst of the defended territory, and we went to work on it. One historian said we expended more eleven-inch battleship shells in one night than ever were expended before, trying to break up this enemy defensive system and keep them off us during the night. After three days of this deadly fighting, we had enough success to please Chesty Puller as he came forward. He then recommended me for the Navy Cross.

"Puller was impressed as he was carried up there on his stretcher—he had a flare-up of a bad wound he sustained as Commander of 7th Regiment's 1st Battalion on Guadalcanal and could not walk—and he could see that this was a near untenable position with fire coming from three directions, but one where we held on to our gains. The situation was desperate, and we held on. While he was there Puller saw the bandage on my knee, he pulled it off, and told me that it was not bad enough to be evacuated. He was aware that they had wanted to haul me off to the hospital ship, but that I wouldn't go. He almost smiled at that."[44]

As an instructor at Quantico, Davis mentored many Marines. He had a reading program, like the one of Lieutenant Colonel George C. Marshall when he was Commandant of the Infantry School at Fort Benning. "If you appear long enough in front of bright, hard charging youngsters they are going to ask you hard questions, and that was my scheme. I found no one reluctant to ask questions. Later I instituted programs of having each unit in Quantico select one or two young lieutenants out of their organization to come with their wives to an evening discussion session in the library at

Breckenridge Hall. There we sat around having cookies and coffee in a very formal fashion. I presented my general views on Marine Corps policies and conducted a two- or three-hour discussion with them, provoking them and drawing them out. Later we conducted a like program for the captains, then the majors. We had some complaints about not doing it for the lieutenant colonels, but we just did not get around to it before my departure. This was one of the origins of exposing ideas and communicating with people through key select groups of junior officers and their wives. There were other similar programs developed through the Corps. I think that input from them in the development of the total team and family effort is one of the keys to our continuing success as a Military Service."[45]

Lieutenant General Victor "Brute" Krulak was a significant mentor for Davis. General Ray Davis, who received the Medal of Honor for his service in Korea, wrote of a sequence of events following the withdrawal from Chosin: "Aboard ship, I drafted a recommendation for the award of the Medal of Honor to Colonel Homer L. Litzenberg, since I felt that his was the main effort in extricating our forces from the Chosin threat. He said: 'No! It was an All Hands effort! But here is one thing that will fly!'

"He handed me a draft with my name on it. That was my first hint that 1st Battalion, 7th Marines had earned for me a recommendation for the Medal of Honor! I was speechless as he insisted 'Don't you agree?'

"These original papers were lost in a Division Headquarters fire, but were reconstructed a year later, largely through the personal efforts of General V.H. 'Brute' Krulak."[46]

### Mentorship by Noncommissioned Officers

Newly commissioned officers have much to learn from tough, talented noncommissioned officers who really know the territory. Why should an NCO take orders from you? What do you bring to the game? Put aside the fact that you are an officer and he is not; what do you have to offer? Are you more experienced? Do you know the job better? What do you have that he hasn't got more of? It is never too soon to start thinking about how you would answer those questions. The officer will probably have a better education, but that does not mean he is better than the NCOs. What each officer must do is earn the respect of his NCO, and do it quickly.

I asked Commandant James L. Jones: "Who were your mentors and what did you learn from them?"

"They weren't all generals. As a matter of fact, they weren't all officers. Some of them were sergeants. I learned a lot from a platoon sergeant named Staff Sergeant Reynolds in Vietnam. He was one of the finest combat Marines and natural leaders I've ever been around."[47]

Commandant Lejeune recounted insights he developed early in his career on a training cruise while a midshipman at the Naval Academy:

> Our voyage to Honolulu was uneventful and the days were spent in stationing and training the crew. It fell to my lot to command the 6-inch pivot gun which was mounted on the forecastle. It was manned by Marines, and for the first time in my career I came into close relationship with the enlisted men of that branch of the Service. The Marine detachment was divided, the major part being detailed as sharpshooters and the remainder as the gun crew. The Marine officer, First Lieutenant F.E. Sutton, preferred to command the sharpshooter group.
>
> He gave me sound advice on how to handle Marines and emphasized the importance of giving orders to the Sergeant who acted as gun captain rather than to the individual men, and then to hold him responsible for the execution of the orders. I found that this sound military system worked most satisfactorily and that the gun's crew soon functioned like clockwork. This system, I learned after years, was the foundation on which the efficiency of the Marine Corps was built, and its result was the development of a reliable, trustworthy and faithful corps of noncommissioned officers. No doubt my experiences with the Marines on the USS *Vandalia* had something to do with the decision which I ultimately made to apply for commission in the Marine Corps at the end of my six years' course as a Naval Cadet.[48]
>
> Upon reporting at the Marine Barracks, Navy Yard, Norfolk, I took up the routine of duty. The quality of the men was astonishingly good under the circumstances. Although a large majority was foreign-born, many never having been naturalized, they were nevertheless intensely loyal to the Marine Corps and to the flag under which they served. It mattered not whether they were American-born citizens, or immigrants from the Emerald Isle, the states of the German Empire, or other Old World nations, they always stood ready to defend Corps and Country against all their enemies and opposers

whomsoever and they were worthy of the motto of their Corps—*Semper Fidelis*. At various times, I learned much of the practical side of the duties of a Marine officer, especially relating to handling men, form such splendid old-timers as First Sergeants John Rice (English), Richard Evans (American), Barchewitz (German), and Daniel Reardon (Irish), and Sergeant Major John Quick (American). Perhaps of all the Marines I ever knew, Quick approached most nearly the perfect type of noncommissioned officer. A calm, forceful, intelligent, loyal and courageous man, he was. I never knew him to raise his voice, lose his temper, or use profane language, and yet he exacted and obtained prompt and explicit obedience from all persons subject to his orders.[49]

Vandegrift recounted similar experiences in his memoir:

Upon recall to Guantanamo Bay I met Lieutenant Colonel John A. Lejeune for the first time. He looked very much as he later appeared in life and pictures, the same lock of dark hair draped over his forehead to give him a striking resemblance to Napoleon.

Under separate orders I now shipped to Panama to join Major Smedley D. Butler's battalion. Everyone in the Marine Corps at this time had heard of Smedley Butler just as nearly everyone in America was to hear of him before his career ended prematurely. To officers and men he formed an almost legendary figure, the hero of the Boxer Rebellion and famous throughout the Corps for his drive, determination and intelligence.

I reported to Bas Obispo or Camp Elliott, his headquarters, with considerable trepidation. I found him dressed in spotless khaki. He was under medium height, weighed probably about 130 pounds, and inclined toward a round-shouldered posture that defied a correct fit of uniform. He was most courteous but there was no missing the scrutiny of his searching deep-set eyes, his most prominent facial feature other than his beak nose. He assigned me to Company D, commanded by Captain John Hughes.

Captain Hughes also received me courteously, gave me the afternoon off to get settled, and ordered me to report at 7:00

A.M. for drill. The next morning I observed Captain Hughes drill the company for some time. He then ordered me to take over. I explained that I had not seen the new Navy manual which he was obviously using and he said, 'Very well, this is Friday. On Monday morning you will be prepared to drill this company.' On Monday morning I drilled the company to his satisfaction.

A few weeks later Captain Hughes called me to his office. 'Vandegrift, the end of the month is coming up. I want you to prepare the company payroll and muster roll. When you have finished bring them to me for signature.'

In those days the muster roll and payroll were made out in long hand with no erasures allowed on any page—in all, a tedious but exacting task for anyone. Fortunately, the First Sergeant Slingloff, took me aside. 'If the lieutenant pleases, the captain is never in the office in the afternoons. I would suggest we work on this job in the afternoons.'

We started the next day with the muster roll. First Sergeant Slingloff said, 'Arnold, John J.,' and I wrote, 'Arnold, John J.' When in doubt I asked him how to spell a name. For days this routine continued until finally I took the completed reports to Captain Hughes. He glanced at them and signed them. 'Well done, Vandegrift. You will never have to make them out again.'[50]

Commandant A.A. Vandegrift learned from other NCOs. He wrote in his memoir:

Non-commissioned officers provided another healthy influence on my education. My chief tutor was First Sergeant Barney from his close-cropped gray hair and clipped gray mustache to the mirror shine on his shoes. Having learned that I enjoyed good music he often asked me to his quarters where an early model Victrola with a big horn played a splendid variety of classical Red Seal records. He told wonderful stories about what he called the "old" Marine Corps. While serving in the Army early in life he was a member of the detail that captured Chief Sitting Bull, and I guess there wasn't much of anything he missed in his career. I certainly was flattered to have him as a friend, and I learned an enormous amount from him.

Quartermaster Sergeant John Edwards was another fine instructor and friend and so was Gunnery Sergeant Lattimer. Lattimer had fought in the Philippine Insurrection, a campaign etched on his face by the broad scar of a bolo. I met him on my second tour of OD [officer of the day] duty when, investigating a racket out by the guardhouse, I found him confronting a drunken Marine. To my question of what was going on he replied, "If the lieutenant pleases, the sergeant of the guard will handle this." Fortunately I had sense enough to please, and the racket soon ceased. Next morning Lattimer hauled a very subdued private before Colonel Kane, who awarded him five days' bread and water. The experience taught me that many activities in the Marine Corps must be handled by non-commissioned officers.

Both noncoms and men were an interesting lot. Generally uneducated in the formal sense, they were powerfully wise in the ways of the world. For the most part the noncoms were older because at the time you often served a four-year cruise before making corporal and such was discipline that stripes vanished easier than they came. Most of them wore mustaches, a few beards, and all but the most recent recruits featured lurid tattoos with the same aplomb that many of us today wear campaign ribbons. The majority of men drank, and since a private's pay amounted to $14.80 a month he was usually broke long before pay call. Because he didn't have much money he depended on his own merits for entertainment which is why I suppose the ranks bred such incredible characters. The things they said and did were normally funny as the devil even though on occasion they misbehaved badly. But outstanding in their character, I believe, was an intense loyalty and I shall never forget how much they wanted to help a new lieutenant.[51]

The most important NCO to a commander is the sergeant major. Commandant Robert H. Barrow told me: "I can't say enough about the importance of the sergeant major. I think each commander, be he a battalion commander or the Commandant, would use his sergeant major as an extension of his eyes and ears to help him, very conservatively in some areas, and very vigorously in others.

"The relationship of a commander with the NCO depends upon the chemistry between the two. I've seen some sergeants major and COs who looked like they didn't belong together, and you wondered why that situation continued to exist. Counting my time as Commandant, I had command responsibility, about twelve years of my fourteen years as a general officer. I had an array of sergeants major over those years.

"My Sergeant Major as Commandant was Leland Crawford. Crawford was picked by the selection committee that most recent Commandants have used in looking at some number of sergeant major prospects and narrowing it down to some four or five that they would suggest that the Commandant himself interview in person, which I did.

"Crawford, whom I had not known, was interviewed by me. I just liked him. I selected him from the three finalists; and I picked a jewel. A West Virginian, out of the coal fields, limited education, not a high school graduate who in many ways murdered the King's English, rough, but soft on the inside where it counted, with people, young Marines. He hated to see a young Marine wronged in any way, shape, or form.

"He had a devoted following of senior staff in the field with other sergeants major. They thought he walked on water; the smooth, polished ones forgiving of his gruffness and poor English and all of that. He could go someplace and talk to the troops, again in sort of rough terms, with maybe a little humor, yes, poor English, but they ate it up. I could see it.

"So I leaned on him for a lot of these little things, specific incidents. He had his ear to the ground, and his own tentacles out there working. He had absolute free access to see me. All he had to do was just walk in the door. He could just walk in. Routinely, at least once a week, and it might be just a simple thing like talking about a trip.

"If we went on a trip, he would go his way and I would go mine. We probably wouldn't meet until we were back on the airplane, and then we would compare notes so to speak. Very often they would fit. It was a good command, everybody was doing his duty, and interested in what he's doing, happy. Or, maybe a little bit of the other.

"He was just remarkable, an interesting personality. The Sergeant Major was on the job historically with the Commandant for two years. I liked him so much I did something I probably shouldn't have done, but I asked him to stay beyond two years. He, being the kind of fellow he was, wouldn't have said, "No, I've had enough." He stayed.

"So, he had what amounted to an unaccompanied tour with me for four years and I admire him tremendously. I'm not sure how we were perceived in the Marine Corps, but from my perception, I thought we had a nice harmonious relationship. We saw things alike. He could bring problems to me that perhaps no one else could; and I could be confident that he wasn't being superficial. He wasn't flying off the handle at something that irritated him. He would've looked into it, and if he brought it to me as a problem, it was a legitimate one, and it was also one he couldn't have done anything about 'cause he would have not brought it to me if he could solve it himself. I can't begin to tell you how many of those kinds of situations he did solve. Anyway, he was the Sergeant Major of the Marine Corps at the time. He was a very handsome, impressive looking man and had a great deal of presence, and he and his wife made a very impressive combination.

"Let me give you a little anecdote. We were in Perth, Australia the summer of '82. I wanted to see the NTPS [near-term prepositioned ship] partially unloaded to see if we had indeed acquired the capability that was as advertised; and furthermore, the WestPac Marine Expeditionary Unit was conducting an exercise north of Perth; and an A–6 squadron was coming in from Iwakuni, Japan, exercising with the Australians and doing some support of the MEU. So, there were really three things going on, not all tied together.

"The NTPS unloaded at III MAU, which is a port near Perth, and it was as advertised. We went to see the MEU both ashore and aboard ship. I remember talking to all of the officers in the ward room, and Crawford got a number of the enlisted people who were still aboard ship down in the hangar deck, and talked to them. I'm not saying that I never talked to troops. I did, but it was very easy in many instances where we were limited by time to have him talk and take questions. He was a master at knowing the details about pay and re-enlistment bonuses and all those things. He knew them backwards and forwards, so some kid would raise his hand and ask a question which I couldn't have answered, but he had the answer.

"That night Patty and I were in our hotel in Perth, which incidentally is a pretty city. It reminds me of San Diego 50 years ago. And the evening news came on and this Aussie voice with film footage along with it said, 'And the head of the United States Marine Corps is telling his troops on no uncertain terms about what's expected of them,' or words to that effect. So, Patty and I both whipped our heads around and here's a picture of Crawford standing on a table in his typical dramatic fashion! We both laughed. I remember saying to her, 'I don't resent that one bit,' because if he had had the opportunities of education, et cetera, he probably could be head of the

Marine Corps because he has it in his heart, the kinds of things one would want in a senior leader."[52]

Commandant Gray's policy, often at a dinner and at other meetings when the Sergeant Major was present, was to ask him to stand and Commandant Gray would tell all who were present, "That's the guy who really runs the Marine Corps." Gray's Sergeant Major was David W. Sommers. General Gray described Sommers' role in giving him the feel for what was going on with the troops because more than any other NCO, he had the most intimate contact with the troops and had the responsibility of advising the Commandant on financial arrangements, training, family housing, dependent schooling, child care centers, on all issues involving the combat readiness and the quality of life for the troops.

Sergeant Major Sommers was jumped over many more senior NCOs. A group of senior officer and NCO Marines screened 150 of the most senior NCOs, reducing the list to 25, which was narrowed to 5, out of which General Gray selected Sommers.

Sommers had served with him in two different assignments and knew what he thought General Gray's policy was to move the Corps forward, that he should not be afraid to make a decision, and should have as a guideline, "What is the best thing to do for our country and the Corps?"

Gray spelled out his policy to Sommers to assist him as Commandant: Follow what has been proven to be the Marine Corps' successful ideas; be a spokesman for the Corps' philosophy; travel with the Commandant to see what needs to be done for the welfare of the Marines; and have his own agenda and move forward with it. The relationship became even closer when Gray moved the Sergeant Major's office immediately next to his.

After each trip Commandant Gray met with Sommers to compare notes on what he found. During his tenure as Commandant, Gray believed he and Sommers probably talked to all of the Marines on Active duty.[53]

In discussing the role of the NCO, Commandant Kelley said: "In retrospect, I sincerely believe that one of the wisest and most meaningful decisions I made during my tenure as the 28th Commandant was to insist upon an accelerated passage of command responsibility for the leadership of the Staff NCO Academy at Quantico from commissioned officers to the Staff NCOs themselves. In that same vein, many of the finest officers with whom I served in combat were, in fact, permanent Staff NCOs with temporary commissions. It can be easily said that it isn't always just rank that delivers performance—more often than not it is a combination of knowledge, leadership, courage, and experience. As a group, the NCOs and Staff NCOs I served with in the fledgling 2$^d$ Force Reconnaissance

Company were the most influential in my future career. Capable of independent thought and action, they were smart, tough and decisive. Above all, they were loved and respected by their subordinates. Twice each year I would have the company conduct a comprehensive reconnaissance exercise wherein the NCOs and Staff NCOs would assume company and platoon leadership billets while the officers were down in the ranks with the 'troops.' As Marines traditionally do, the NCOs and Staff NCOs 'reached beyond their grasp,' and performed in the highest traditions of their Corps. Let me simply say that it would be difficult, if not impossible, to single out one NCO or Staff NCO who had more influence than others on my career. Suffice it to say, my respect for them during 37 years as a Marine was and is deep and abiding. Given the proper respect, authority, and responsibility, they will never let you down!"[54]

Commandant Mundy was strongly influenced by NCOs: "The impact of non-commissioned officers during my career was continuous. It began with my Drill Instructor. He taught me what it was to be a Marine. To this day—with many other names along the way forgotten—I can still tell you his name: Sergeant Tall. That the impressions and name recognition of one man with whom I was associated for a relatively short period of time still lingers with me after fifty-two years is a testament to his impact on my development.

"There were so many others along the way. When I was assigned to independent duty as an Officer Selection Officer just after having been promoted to captain, I faced the new challenge of recruiting without prior experience. My first year was framed by an extraordinary mission of recruiting officer candidates only for flight training—no ground applicants—and double the usual quota, as well. I was to learn that recruiting and qualifying future pilots is tough under any circumstance, but to be given twice the usual number seemed mission impossible. My boss—a couple of hundred miles away at District Headquarters—called me in to tell me that he doubted we would make it that year, but to give it all I had trying. My recruiting team included a Navy Chief Corpsman and two Marine sergeants. Staff Sergeant Bill Weaver was my NCO in Charge. When I returned from Atlanta with the news that our boss expected we would fail, Weaver said, 'Aw, Sir; we're not going to do that.' He took me under his wing that first year, schooled me, prodded me, and at the end of the year, we not only achieved, but exceeded our assigned quota, and emerged tops in the District. Bill Weaver accomplished that while I learned from him.

"Angel Carrasco was a young Mexican who made it across the Rio Grande River, and was later picked up by the authorities in South Texas. As he took pride in describing himself in later years, he was a 'Wetback—pachuco haircut, switchblade knife, and all.' Taken to court, the judge offered him jail or the Marine Corps, and he chose the latter. I met him when I assumed command of Second Battalion, Fourth Marines in Okinawa in 1973. He was a company First Sergeant. We were in the midst of extraordinary racial tensions in those days with gang riots and assaults by Marines of one ethnic group or another on other Marines almost nightly occurrences. There were enormous pressures from higher echelons, and commanders were measured almost totally on the number of incidents in the command, rather than any other measure of effectiveness. In the midst of all this, one company stood out from all others in the Division as a role model—even to the extent that at the end of their tours, First Sergeant Carrasco and his company commander were brought to a Division staff meeting to brief the staff on how to run a company under the extraordinarily trying conditions of the times. Throughout my year of command, we became fast friends, and on 'unofficial occasions,' even though not the Battalion Sergeant Major, Carrasco would quietly coach me on how to deal with various problems. His favorite saying was, 'Sir, you just got to remember that we own all the balls and bats in this game. It ain't their game; it's ours.' More than anyone else, he inspired enormous confidence in me and other officers and NCOs in the battalion in dealing with toughest leadership challenges I ever faced.

"Eight years later, when I was given command of the Second Marines, Carrasco was the Regimental Sergeant Major. He continued to coach me on more than one occasion. His favorite technique when some policy or practice was not going well, was to walk into my office first thing in the morning with two cups of coffee, close the door, and in his special way, begin with 'Colonel, you're really screwing up bad.' I would stop whatever I was doing and say, 'O.K., Sergeant Major, tell me what now.' He would lay out whatever the issue was, and I recall no occasion on which he wasn't right, and whatever it was I was 'screwing up,' I reversed course on. Carrasco had enormous influence on my leadership development, even in the senior years of my career.

"As Commandant, my Sergeant Major of the Marine Corps was Gene Overstreet—one of the most positive and enthusiastic men with whom I ever worked. Like Weaver and Carrasco, he continued to coach me when I needed it, and quietly shaped my thinking and approach to leadership and problem solving throughout our four final years together. Among his strongest qualities, in a profession being shaped today by the sometimes incongruence of 'Jointness,' was that even though he was the highest ranking NCO in the Marine Corps, and dealt with senior uniformed and civilian Defense officials and members of Congress on a daily basis, he continued to understand, adhere to, and take pride in the role of being a good sergeant. I never observed him in a situation in which an officer of any grade was made to feel inferior, or was treated with less than the respect that any good NCO would exhibit—even when coaching and teaching. I fear that today's policies are tending to blur that longstanding and critical role by confusing senior NCOs and petty officers as to who they are and what their longstanding role has been. When an illogical joint policy that equates a senior enlisted advisor to a three-star officer in matters of protocol comes out, and imitating subordinate policies and practices cause senior pay grade NCOs and petty officers to become uncertain of their positions and authority vis-à-vis officers in the chain of command, the military profession is headed in the wrong direction. We are moving toward creation of a generation of officers who are confounded by such policies and practices, and of senior NCOs whose focus is more on their seating priority and prerogatives than their professional role, and who worry more about whether they are being paid due respect by officers they consider subordinate, than whether or not they are earning that respect as 'good sergeants' like Tall, Weaver, Carrasco, Overstreet and a hundred others in my career did."

In his oral history, General Mundy related an incident and a lesson learned from his NCO: "In those days, generals rode in their staff cars with the small car, or boat, flag fluttering from the right fender—a grand symbol, which I personally hated to see go away, but it pretty much has. Anyway, when the Assistant Division Commander would come to visit, his car—usually with the driver still inside—would sit outside the facility announcing to the world with the fender flag that a general was inside. One day, I received a call from the ADC's aide with a little more frantic than usual note in his voice telling me that the ADC would like to see me right away. I went up to the Headquarters and was shown in promptly. Brigadier General Hopkins was sitting sternly behind his desk and, without pause, said to me, 'I was at your regimental mess hall at noon today and when I came out to get in my car, my flag had been stolen. I expect the flag to be returned by tomorrow noon.' I expressed appropriate concern, and assured him that I would look into this transgression right away. I then returned to my regimental CP, called in Angel Carrasco, my Sergeant Major, explained the problem and concluded by saying, 'Sergeant Major, this is sergeant's business, not officer's. Find the flag!'

"The next morning at 0700, the door to my office opened, and there was Carrasco with two cups of coffee. He came in, closed the door, and said, in his inevitable manner, 'Hey, Colonel, we need to talk about this flag thing.'

"There followed one of the most humorously poignant outpourings a Sergeant Major could make. 'Colonel,' he said, 'just imagine that you're a PFC in the barracks, and every day or so you look out after chow, and here's this shiny car that the general rides in, and it's got this flag on it. The general comes in, and he's not really interested much in what you're eating; he just goes back and looks around for something that don't matter much and then gives some corporal a ration over it. You watch this go on, and then you and your buddies begin to formulate a plan. You plan how a couple of you will keep watch and then, at just the right time, you, the chosen one, make a run for the car, grab the flag, and probably run all the way into the woods on the other side of the mess hall and dive in a ditch for cover. After a while, your buddies give you the all clear signal and you come out. You're a hero in your platoon; you captured the general's flag! Colonel, we wouldn't want to take that away from that kid, whoever he is; and Colonel, the ADC's gonna look real bad if we go shaking down the regiment to try and find the general's flag. If he can't hold onto his flag, how's he gonna look?'

"I had a hard time keeping a straight face, but finally said, 'O.K., Sergeant Major; I've got it.' He left and I drove up to the division CP and went in to see Hopkins. He had mellowed a bit from the day before, and I gave him the same thrust as the Sergeant Major had laid on me: 'Somebody's going to look bad if we go shaking down a regiment because the general lost his flag.' Joe Hopkins looked at me across his desk for what seemed like ten minutes, and then said, 'That'll be all, Colonel.' I left and never heard another word about the flag from him."

Mundy's story continues after he was promoted to brigadier general and was to move on to his next assignment: "The last battalion I visited was my old one, 2/4, my 'fourth battalion of the Second Marines.' My old regimental executive Nick Schreiber had moved down to command the battalion, and after my brief remarks to them, I started to walk away. Nick said, 'Just a minute, Colonel; the battalion has something to give you.' His Sergeant Major walked up and gave me a box, which I opened, and there was a framed one-star flag with a brass plate under it wishing me well from 'The Magnificent Bastards' of 2/4. I started bubbling with thanks, and then it hit me. 'Nick,' I said, 'Where did this flag come from?'

"His response was sober and direct: 'Sir, we did not touch the car!' The one-star flag is, to this day, displayed proudly among my most meaningful memorabilia, as the first gift I received upon becoming a general, and as a testament to the undying spirit and humor of young—and not-so-young—Marines!!"[55]

General Charles Krulak described the role of the NCO as a mentor in his career: "I commanded the 2$^d$ Platoon of G/2/1 and I was blessed to have as my Platoon Sergeant a staff sergeant by the name of Robert E. Clemens. Clemens had been awarded the Silver Star in Korea and he had what looked like 50 rows of ribbons. I thought to myself, 'I've died and gone to heaven. I've got the world's greatest Platoon Sergeant.' In fact, he was phenomenal.

"In those days and hopefully continuing on today, it was in the mind of that platoon sergeant that his job was to make 'his lieutenant' the best in the battalion and the best in the regiment. Staff Sergeant Clemens really worked hard with me. He had poor material work with, but he did a hell of a job.

"As we prepared to go to Vietnam, I was sent to a couple of schools, one of them was Embarkation School, which was the first sensing of logistics that I received, and it was a real 'eye opener.' Then, I went to the Counter-Guerrilla Warfare School, where one of the instructors was a gunnery sergeant by the name of Jimmy E. Howard, who went on to receive a Medal of Honor and is famous on Howard's Hill. From the day I reported in to the Counter-Guerrilla Warfare School, for some reason or another, he always called me 'little fellow.' He never called me lieutenant; he never called me Mr. Krulak. He always called me 'little fellow.' To this day—I was a general and he was a Medal of Honor recipient. Before he died, he still used to call me 'the little fellow.' But those are the types of staff NCOs that I was blessed to be around. I mean, you always talk about the officers you were around. Well, SNCOs like Clemens and Jimmy Howard really gave me an idea of what it was to be a staff NCO."[56]

Chesty Puller took great pride in his ability as a rifleman and was quite an expert marksman, but found he could still learn. Puller's biographer wrote:

> He considered himself a good shot, had for five years been rated an Expert Rifleman, and was thus nettled when a veteran sergeant suggested that he teach him to shoot.
>
> 'I know how to shoot, Sergeant.'
>
> 'I can give you enough pointers in two weeks to raise your score twenty points.'

Puller became the sergeant's pupil, shooting when targets became vacant during the training, and shot an average of two bandoleers daily. He improved rapidly, and brought his record score from 306 to 326, of a possible 350. For years he qualified as expert with both rifle and pistol, and when a rifle team was sent from Pearl Harbor to a competition in San Diego in 1928, Puller was a member.[57]

Burke Davis writes of a somewhat humorous lesson Chesty Puller learned on a different range:

> Puller was tossed headlong into the mysteries of artillery, assigned to the Tenth Regiment at Quantico. He confessed to his new commander an almost total ignorance of the big guns. The captain waved airily.
>
> 'I'll give you a first lesson.' He sketched a triangle, turned to answer a telephone and left the drawing incomplete. When he returned to Puller, he said: 'Lieutenant, I have permission to begin my leave now. The battalion will begin thirty days of training to prepare for the interservice firing at Camp Meade next month.' The commander picked up his cap and halted at the door: 'By the way, you'll have to fire a battery problem next Wednesday. God help you.' He disappeared.
>
> Puller conferred with his first sergeant, who told him that other junior officers would be of no help, but that the enlisted men and non-commissioned officers were experts.
>
> Lewis spent the noon hour in a gun shed, sweating under the direction of one Bernoski, a gunnery sergeant, who interpreted the sheets of the battalion schedule for the next month, day by day, and then put him to work: 'Here are the textbook references you will need, sir. You can study those every night, and keep ahead of the men. And now, if the Lieutenant pleases, I can show him the insides of the 75.'
>
> Puller tore down and reassembled the big gun for five hours, learning the parts and nomenclature, reciting them until he was intimate with the secrets of the weapon and its shells. He spent the weekend studying for Monday's firing, and when the battery

began blasting, felt somewhat at home. On Wednesday, he fired for a critical audience which included the post commander, General Kelly Cole; Colonel Moses, the regimental commander; and Major Freddie Erskine, the battalion commander.

The artillery of the time used the No. 2 gun of a battery as a base, with the three others firing parallel to it. The base gun was corrected after three rounds if necessary, and other guns adjusted to conform.

Sergeant Bernoski gave Puller final advice: 'Sir, just leave it all to us. Good gunners are supposed to be right on target. General Cole and the Colonel will be watching. Their eyesight ain't too good, sir. Now, after the this shot, no matter where we're hitting, if you'll just crack loose right away with a salvo from the whole battery, turn and salute the officers and yell like hell, 'Sir, I'm right on target!' then we'll get away with it. They'll never know the difference.'

The battery followed instructions, and in the roar of the guns Puller went through Bernoski's paces. The senior officers were pleased. To Lewis, it was evidence that the Corps was in fact operated by its senior noncoms and that too few officers knew the basic details of their trade.[58]

General Raymond G. Davis, who was commander of the 3ᵈ Marine Division in Quang Tri Province in Vietnam, learned a lesson in leadership from a first sergeant in his very first assignment. "We had no field units before our expansion in World War II. As non–Naval Academy graduates, most of us were sent to sea for our first tour. About 40 Marines were aboard my first ship, the USS *Portland* (CA–33), a heavy cruiser. The first lesson I learned came when the first sergeant lined up the Marines and introduced me to each one. We reached the end of the line and I asked, 'Top, could I have a copy of your list of Marines?' He said, 'Sir, it's all right here in my head.' So I picked up on the idea."

Davis was asked in an interview: "Looking back over your years of military service, did you seek to cultivate a leadership style and follow through with that vision during your career?" He replied: "It impressed me when I went to sea duty and saw the commitment of the first sergeant in knowing each one of his troops. Everywhere I went I tried to be fully aware of the individuals in my outfit. This generated a leadership style that paid off heavily."[59]

In his book *Cheers and Tears: A Marine's Story of Combat in Peace and War,* Lieutenant General Charles Cooper gave an excellent example of the role of his NCO in bringing the Eighth Replacement Draft's Composite Company up to speed. Cooper begins with a description of how the Company was formed of prisoners who had been offered conditional pardons:

> A prisoner who had one of the sought-after skills and was serving a sentence for a non-violent crime would be offered a conditional pardon. The condition, of course, was that he serve an honorable tour in combat. If he did so, the condition would be removed and the offense expunged from the Marine's record. All of the brigs on the west coast had been combed for the needed occupational specialties: the men this process had found formed the Eighth Replacement Draft's Composite Company for transportation to Korea and assignment to combat duty.
>
> This particular company contained radio operators, cryptologists, surveyors, aviation metalsmiths, legal clerks, artillery fire controllers, armorers, and many other hard-to-find specialties. They had been gathered together the previous day, formed into platoons, issued equipment, and assigned spaces in the barracks. Unfortunately, they had also been paid $50 each and given access to the enlisted Marines' club adjacent to their barracks. There was no doubt that they had enjoyed themselves for either $50 worth or the evening, whichever ran out first. The result of all this fun and frolic was mine at 1030 the next morning.
>
> As I approached the barracks, I saw more than 200 Marines on the grass plot out front, sitting or lying in ranks with rifles and packs at their sides. Some were asleep. Others appeared to be unconscious. The odor of secondhand beer was overpowering. The odor got worse when it was joined by that of recently emptied stomachs. All I could think was, 'My God, this is the Marine barracks,' the NCO of the company saw me, saluted, and walked over to introduce himself. He was the company first sergeant: at six feet, four inches he was an impressive-looking individual. He reported that he had cleared out the barracks and that his four platoon sergeants would join us shortly. Looking around, he smiled and said something to the

effect that, 'I thought you might want to inspect the company, sir. It's not in very good shape.' He was right . . . more than right. And this ragtag collection of misfits was scheduled to board ship the next day.

We hadn't studied anything like this at Annapolis, and Colonel Shoup's finishing school for third lieutenants had featured combat training, not training in the art of shepherding drunks. Nevertheless, it was obvious that something had to be done and done quickly. The first sergeant's suggestion that I inspect the company was an excellent start. He was a true professional: although our association with the replacement draft was to be relatively brief, I came to rely on his judgment, and in a very real way, his tutelage. We discussed possible courses of action while waiting for the platoon sergeants to join us. We made some quick decisions and, when the platoon sergeants arrived, issued the orders.

There was no specific authority for us to do what we did. It made sense to the sergeants, and it seemed like the right thing to do at the time. Besides, as long as what is contemplated is not illegal, it is usually better to ask for forgiveness rather than permission. First, the platoon sergeants forcefully aroused the troops, getting them all on their feet, at the position of attention, some more so than others, and prepared the company for inspection. The first sergeant told the troops that I would inspect each man and that when I halted in front of them, each was to state his name, rank, and military specialty. Since they were all privates, the rank business was not really necessary. It did, however, remind them of their status in the eyes of the Marine Corps. Besides beginning the process of pulling these less-than-sober yardbirds back to the paths of righteousness.[60]

Not every Marine will achieve flag rank, and normally there is only one Commandant every four years. There are varying degrees of leadership ability, but the goal of mentorship is to assist every Marine leader in achieving the best with the abilities he and she has. General Mundy summarized, "Mentorship is another leadership tool that can benefit both the individual Marine and the organization and is consistent with the strategies for achieving one of the goals outlined in our vision of the future—to utilize fully the talents of our people."

I want to close this chapter with a moving and sensitive reflection of Smedley Butler as a 16-year-old Marine Corps lieutenant on the impact of his first NCO:

> We were ordered to the Washington barracks for instruction. The school for officers was conducted by a wonderful old soldier, Sergeant Major Hayes. He had been in a Scottish regiment and had fought with Kitchener in the Sudan. After his discharge from the British army he came to America and joined up with the Marines.
>
> Until the Spanish-American War, two thousand men and officers constituted the total enrollment of the Marine Corps. Hayes, stationed at the Washington headquarters, enjoyed the distinction of being the one and only sergeant major for the whole Corps. His principal duty was to bring up young officers in the way they should go. He was getting on in years, but he was still a magnificent two hundred fifty pound specimen, built on heroic lines. He carried his six feet three inches as erect as a ramrod.
>
> When we rose to recite our lessons, the Sergeant Major always stood up, too. Even though he was in charge of us, he never forgot for a moment the difference in our ranks, or that enlisted men never sit in the presence of officers. One rebuke from him cut to the quick.
>
> We all admired him so much that we didn't have the heart to disappoint him. He was one of the most perfect public servants I have ever met.
>
> Those first six weeks of intensive training planted the seed of soldiering in me. And from that time on, I never felt entirely happy away from Marines.[61]

Chapter 9

# "Time with People Is Never Wasted": Consideration

I asked over 150 four-stars and 2 five-stars, "How do you lead men in such a way that they die for you in combat and work twenty hours a day in time of peace for weeks and sometimes months, if necessary, to resolve a certain crisis or problem?" Their answers were nearly identical: the successful leader must first set the example and show his devotion to a life of service to God and country; second, he must show consideration for the people serving with and under him.

In general, consideration as a leadership trait means that the welfare of the leader's subordinates rises above his personal responsibilities. The leader who is "tough but fair" seldom is considerate. He does what the regulations require, and the regulations are mute when it comes to a leader sacrificing his own time or privileges to go beyond the official requirements of his duties toward his subordinates. For a commander to provide aid, comfort, and benefits to his subordinates simply to conform with regulation is not consideration. There must be some aspect of giving or self-sacrifice on his part. The standard for the importance of caring for troops was embodied in the Marine Corps as dogma, first appearing in the 1921 Marine Corps Manual, written by Commandant John A. Lejeune:

> The relation between officer and enlisted men should in no sense be that of superior and inferior nor that of master and servant, but rather that of teacher and scholar. In fact, it should partake of the nature of the relation between father and son, to the extent that officers, especially commanding officers, are responsible for the physical, mental and moral welfare, as well as the discipline and military training of the young men under their command who are serving the nation in the Corps.

What is expected of a Marine in regard to looking out for the physical, mental, and moral welfare of the troops? This question will be given life and meaning as developed through the careers of the leaders in this study. To obtain insight and a feel for taking care of troops, I cite some considerate thoughts and deeds performed by some of the giants of the Marine Corps that illustrate the importance of the individual.

As a captain, Commandant Lewis H. Wilson cited in his oral history an incident when he challenged a full colonel, his battalion commander, on behalf of one of his Marines. It could have had serious repercussions for Wilson, but in hindsight, he even saw humor in the incident. He related in his oral history: "A woman Marine was married to a warrant officer who was under arrest. A corporal was assigned to guard his room. The battalion executive officer [XO] found this warrant officer drunk and charged the corporal with dereliction of duty for permitting the warrant officer to have liquor in his room. The XO went in before the commanding officer to make the charge and I accompanied him. I stood up in the corporal's defense, saying that it was unfair because the warrant officer's wife was also an officer and the corporal didn't have any orders to shake her down when she visited her husband. Therefore, if he [the warrant officer] was drunk, she could have very well brought the liquor in. So the battalion commander said, 'Fine, I agree with you.' The XO came out and looked at me and shook his finger in front of my face. He said, 'Captain, when I want a corporal locked up, I don't want some damn young captain standing up contradicting me. You better look out here because you're in trouble from now on.'

"Well, that was the day I got the letter from my sister telling me of my orders to the Marine Barracks in Washington. That commanding officer told me, 'I can spring you from this if you don't want to go.' I said, 'I want to go.'"

General Holland M. Smith, as V Corps Commander in the Pacific during the Saipan invasion, was solicitous of the welfare of his men. When he inspected subordinate units, he always instructed his orderly to mingle with the enlisted men and listen for complaints and problems, and he saw that remedial action was taken. At times, he had to intercede at the highest command level. A typical incident, according to his aide, was an occasion when Marines on an advanced island base had no tent decks [wooden planking to cover dirt floors], and Admiral Nimitz was sending several shiploads of furniture to the naval headquarters in that area. Smith learned of this and said, "Boy, if you get your furniture before my Marines get their tent decks, there's going to be all hell to pay. I can promise you that." He got the wood for his tent decks for his men.[1]

General Oliver P. Smith was the commander of the 1st Marine Division during the Korean conflict in 1950. His biographer wrote:

> He never forgot his most important weapon was the individual rifleman, and he had the knack of obtaining the best his troops had to give by setting an example of confidence and faith in their ability to succeed. His style of leadership developed from his strong character and an inherent optimism that tempered everything he did. He radiated confidence and a sensitivity to the men under his command, and the troops responded in kind.[2]

An example was provided by an incident with Major General Oliver Prince Smith, commander of the 1st Marine Division during the withdrawal from the Chosin Reservoir operation. The I Corps commander was Major General Edward "Ned" Almond, USA. Almond came to his CP to discuss the situation with him. At this conference, Smith related: "He [Almond] authorized me to burn or destroy equipment or supplies, stating that I would be re-supplied by air drop as I withdrew." Smith would not do this. "I told him that my movements would be governed by my ability to evacuate the wounded, that I would have to fight my way back and could not afford to discard equipment and that therefore I intended to bring out the bulk of my equipment." The Marine Corps has always given first consideration to the welfare of the wounded, and because frugality was so necessary in time of peace, Marines were not in the habit of abandoning precious warfighting equipment.[3]

A vital part of Marine Corps leadership is the important duty of communicating with the families of the wounded and especially those families whose loved ones died in combat or training. Commandant Archer A. Vandegrift provided in his memoir sound advice of value to all Marine leaders regarding concern for Marines and their families:

> I hastened to try to make the worth of these operations known to the public by speaking whenever possible. It seemed to me that Americans were entitled to learn as much as we could tell them of the conduct of these campaigns and the reason for heavy casualties. Besides speaking frequently, I never refused the call of a gold-star mother, one whose child has been killed

in combat, and I paid close attention to incoming correspondence on this sad subject, answering each letter as it arrived.

Sometimes, particularly in combat, this was difficult. Vandegrift provided an example of a letter to the mother of a Marine killed in Guam; he did not back off from the fact that it was he who "got him [her son] into the Marine Corps" and "got him sent to the combat zone." He wrote to her:

> On my return from the Pacific, I received and read your very wonderful letter which I appreciate more than words can tell. I knew, of course, that your son had been killed and had been worrying about it as I remembered it was I who got him into the Marine Corps and got him sent to the combat zone when by all rules of the game he should have been doing something else.
>
> Yes, you are right, the Marine Corps has suffered a loss equal to that of yours, and the country also has suffered a loss in that had he been spared, his work in chemistry would have done much for the country. I feel relieved to know that he was killed doing what he wanted to do, serving his country in one of the finest divisions that we have; that he was killed in taking from the Japanese the first piece of American territory that has been regained.

Vandegrift recalled:

> In my mind this time-consuming task was vital to humanity and was clearly a task for every officer whose men died or were wounded for him, the Corps and country. I wrote one of my division commanders on the subject:
>
> It [the writing of such letters] may seem rather trivial, but it is just the not doing of such trivialities that has tended to give the Marine Corps a name for callousness as shown by the letter I am enclosing with this. About a month ago, I was down in Atlanta and I saw a Mr. _____ whose son was killed in Guam. . . . I talked to him for about thirty minutes and he is the first parent who has lost someone that I was unable to show that the Marine Corps was not callous to the death of their people. He was very courteous but was firmly convinced that whereas I thought he would have been informed and that

the commanding officer of his son would have written to him it had not happened. I am also enclosing with this copy of a memorandum that was sent out by air mail requesting that the commanding officer of [this man] write a letter to the father and mother. Will you please see personally that this is done and right away. If it is not a practice in [your division] for the commanding officers of the lower units such as companies and battalions to write such letter, I think it is a good idea that it be started. . . . This is not something one cares to get out an order about but it is something that the junior unit commanders should in all decency want to do.

Vandegrift continued, "I could not have felt more strongly about this subject." One day an aide, Buddy Masters, came to him:

"General," he said, "I am worried about your eyesight, which is getting worse. You read all day here in the office and then you take a couple hundred Purple Heart certificates home, sign them at night, and read some more. I have found a way to ease this."

"How?"

"The other day over at Navy I saw a new machine bought for the Secretary. It writes his signature automatically, and it only costs a few hundred dollars."

"Save the money," I told him. "If those boys can get wounded, I can find time to sign my name on their Purple Hearts." Leaders are incredibly busy during combat, but no commander should use this as a reason for not writing.[4]

Chesty Puller was sensitive to the importance of this and personally wrote his own letters for each Marine lost in combat under his command. In the Guadalcanal campaign, Puller wrote letters to all wounded men from his outfit who had been evacuated to hospitals or home. Captain Zach Cox got one of these letters from Puller while stationed in port:

The officers and men of the First Battalion, Seventh Marines, recall with pride the part that you played in our successes against the enemy until you received your injury in action.

> They employ this medium to express their appreciation for the part you played while you were here, wish you a speedy recovery and hope that when you return to further action, it will be in the same outfit.
>
> They further assure you that until you return and thereafter until the enemy is destroyed, they will continue the fight with ever-increasing vigor and determination.[5]

Writing letters to family members of Marines killed in action requires careful, sensitive thought to mitigate the grief in the tragedy of losing a loved one. Major General Oliver Prince Smith's biographer provided an excellent example of sensitivity for the family of a Marine:

> Major General John Marston, then Commander of Forces in Iceland informed Lieutenant Colonel Oliver Smith on 7 January 1942 that his promotion to full colonel had been approved. The general awarded the promotion at a ceremony in which the other officers in the battalion presented him with new collar insignia, a colonel's eagles. The joy of being promoted must have been overshadowed by the sad duty two days later of burying the first member of the American forces to die in Iceland, in a cemetery overlooking a seaplane anchorage. A Sergeant Pickins had been stabbed during a party for sergeants, and it was Smith's duty to write the parents. The cemetery might have been beautiful in the summer with green grass and the blue water beyond, but the aspect certainly was bleak when we buried Pickins. "When I wrote the mother I did not have the heart to describe the weather in connection with the funeral. I told her what the cemetery would look like in the summer."[6]

The importance of personal letters cannot be overstated. Secretary of Defense Donald H. Rumsfeld was reminded of this during Operation *Iraqi Freedom*. He created a furor when it was announced in the press on December 19, 2004, that he did not personally sign the condolence letters to the families of soldiers killed in Iraq, but rather his signature was signed by a machine. It deeply hurt the family members who had received his letters, one of whom said, "When Baghdad insurgents killed Army Specialist Irving Medina last November, the condolence message from Pentagon Chief Donald Rumsfeld just added to his family's pain. The signature on the letter was done by a machine. As somebody who fought in the war and lost a loved one, I felt a lot of anger. . . . Rumsfeld has relinquished this sacred duty to a signature device rather than signing the sad documents himself." Another father bitterly commented that he thought it was a shame that the Secretary of Defense could keep his squash schedule but could not find the time to sign his dead son's letter. The *Stars and Stripes* newspaper quoted families of the dead who were insulted that Rumsfeld had not signed the letters himself.

Secretary Rumsfeld did not try to cover up or deny the machine signatures accusation. In a statement provided to *Stars and Stripes*, which is broadly read throughout the military, Rumsfeld said: "I wrote and approved the now more than 1,000 letters sent to family members and next of kin of each of the Servicemen and women killed in military action. While I have not individually signed each one, in the interest of ensuring expeditious contact with grieving family members, I have directed that in the future I sign each letter."

Allegations were made that President Bush did the same on similar letters sent to the family members and next of kin of Servicemen and women killed in military action, but a White House spokesman emphatically stated that President Bush signed each letter himself.

For the troops, receiving mail from home is always important for their morale and well being. Vandegrift commented that he was concerned during World War II about the slow delivery of mail from home. He sent a dispatch to General Holcomb [Commandant at the time] about the delay, which he followed up on. "In Pearl Harbor, Admiral Chester W. Nimitz showed it to him and asked his opinion—he gave it and King [Chief of Naval Operations Ernest King] approved the dispatch and returned it to Halsey [Admiral William "Bull" Halsey, Battle Group Commander]."

Vandegrift reflected:

Besides doing us all a world of good on Guadalcanal, the Commandant's visit resulted in a significant improvement in mail delivery. Coincidental with his arrival on the island came the first V-letter. Colonel Bill Twining looked at it closely, pondered and observed, "I don't see why it is any easier to send a *little* envelope through the mail than a *big* one."

"I don't either," I agreed, "and I'm damned if I understand why the Navy takes so long to get any size envelope here from the States." Back in Washington, Commandant Holcomb remembered this complaint and discussed it with Admiral King. They finally learned that the Navy in San Francisco was keeping ship movements so secret that no one gave the schedule to the fleet post office, thus the mail was often held up for long periods. King changed this to our considerable benefit.[7]

In World War II, Vandegrift made a point, while fighting in the jungle, to constantly visit his troops. With the adverse impact of malaria on fighting efficiency, he showed his concern for the health of his troops and realized the importance of rotating the forces. Vandegrift reflected, "In the South Pacific theater, one of our greatest problems is malaria. Such is the perniciousness of this disease that we will have to plan to replace the fighting units and send them back to a nonmalarious country for rehabilitation. I feel that units should be evacuated after a given length of time to a cooler climate and built up, and that these rehabilitation areas should have as much thought given to them as training camps in the vicinity of a theater of operations for staging-in processes."[8]

Lejeune learned early in his career from superiors who did not take proper care of their Marines. He related that during a Navy ship tour that:

> our month there was very unpleasant, as we lived under the strictest sanitary regulations. There was no liberty for the crew, no leave ashore after sunset for officers, practically no drills on board, no harbor water used for scrubbing decks, no pulling boats used, no laundry sent ashore. In fact, we ran the gamut of 'don'ts.' Nowadays, all is different in the tropics. We have learned by experience that exercise, occupation, and recreation are just as necessary for good health and contentment in the tropics as they are in the temperate zones, and that night air may be enjoyed by strangers as well as natives without injurious effects.[9]

General Ray Davis added a new aspect of consideration for the troops, in their physical training:

> In addition to the leadership requirements of the various schools in Quantico, I fortunately spent much time in the field observing and commenting on the tactics and techniques taught. I was impressed with what the Commandant, General Chapman, had caused to be done in Quantico. I am still sold on the Physical Fitness Academy. Perhaps it could be done on

a lesser scale, but we always needed a fountainhead place for developing and then closely monitoring ideas on achieving relative perfection in physical fitness. I'll never forget those days when we ruined a lot of Marine knees from duckwalk contests [an exercise where recruits were required to walk in a squatting position], and the like. We need true professionals in this important part of the education and training of all our Marines, from the youngest to the oldest.[10]

He saw to it that duckwalk contests ended.

Along with food, nothing is more important for their health and welfare than for the soldiers' gear to be warm and dry. One of the most fascinating examples of caring was a meeting Commandant Charles E. Krulak had with Congressman Patrick Kennedy of Rhode Island after his selection as Commandant: "It turned out to be a really important call for the individual Marine. I went to see Patrick Kennedy, absolutely not what you'd call a military type of individual. He's interested in the military, but not in the warfighting part; far more interested in the personnel issues. We talked for a little bit. Then, like they all do, he said, 'Okay, now, what can I do for the Marine Corps?'

"I remember at that point in time, just as clear as day, a memory of me back in March standing on a pier in Pohang, Korea, after I had been nominated to be the Commandant. It was cold. It was about 33 degrees and raining. I had a lance corporal on my left and a PFC on my right. We were standing there in our typical Marine foul-weather gear, in our field jacket, my cover on my head, all the starch out of my cover, water pouring down over the brim of my utility cover, running down my nose and my chin. My jacket was soaked. These two Marines next to me, one on each side, were soaked. I knew in their minds they were saying, 'What the hell are we doing? We are standing here with a three-star general designated to be the next Commandant.' We were all standing out in the rain getting soaked!

"So when Pat Kennedy said, 'What do you need,' I said, 'I'll tell you what I'd like for my Marines—some Gore-Tex rain gear.' He replied, 'What?' I said, 'Well, I got to tell you . . .' and I related the story to him. He looked at me and said, 'General, you've got it. I will ensure you have $10 million in this year's budget for Gore-Tex rain gear.' I walked out of his office. My Office of Legislative Affairs liaison at that time was a general by the name of Mike Ryan. The House liaison officer was a colonel by the name of John F. Sattler who went on to become brigadier general, and he'll go higher. They both looked at me and said, 'Are you crazy? Sir, you're going to be the Commandant. When they ask you a question like that, tell them V–22, AAAV.' I said, 'I'm sorry, but it's what I thought of,' and it turned out to be one of the best things that ever happened. First off, the word got around Capitol Hill quicker than anybody could imagine that the Commandant of the Marine Corps was asked what the Corps needed and he gave a $10 million figure for something to take care of the troops. I'm telling you, from that day, for the next four years, we averaged $30 million for personal equipment for the troops. We got Gore-Tex rain gear. We got the 'bivy' sacks. We got the new load bearing system. We got the boots. All of that because this naïve Chuck Krulak was stupid enough to ask for a $10 million item instead of a $100 million one. But it turned out to be a good thing, so we've equipped the Marine Corps with a lot of individual equipment based on that one call. Not real important in the overall history of the Marine Corps, but it does go to show that sometimes if you aren't an insider politically but your heart tells you what to say, it may turn out to be a good deal."[11]

Consideration was certainly something John Lejeune practiced. He reflected that while traveling with President Calvin Coolidge after World War I:

> Whenever the train stopped anywhere, the President sent for me to join him on the rear platform of his private car. At St. Louis, a man in the crowd came up close to speak to me, saying he was determined to have a word with me as he had served in the 2d Division overseas and had never forgotten seeing me one day during the battle of the Meuse-Argonne, when he was one of a group of men who were lying down on the ground, having halted for a brief rest. As I drove up in my car, they rose to salute me, and I said to them, "Sit down, men. It is more important for tired men to rest than for the Division Commander to be saluted."[12]

As a lieutenant, Clifton B. Cates was the most decorated Marine officer in World War I. One particular incident illustrated his concern for the well being of his men. He related that his troops "hadn't been paid for over two months. And at the time, I remember I had ninety-six hundred francs left. Ninety-six hundred was almost a thousand dollars. So I said to this gunnery sergeant who was with me, 'Ben, I know the men haven't got any money and they are going to give them liberty this afternoon and night.' And I said, 'Here's fifty francs for each man.' That was about nine dollars. I said, 'Give each man fifty francs.' Well, my reputation was made from then on. They never forgot it. It gave them enough money to go out and have a good dinner, and go to a show if they wanted."[13]

Commandant Lewis Wilson remembered well the consideration that was given to him as a young captain. When his regiment was going into combat to take Guadalcanal, he recalled, "I had a hernia operation in New Zealand. General Lemuel Shepherd was regimental commander and he was kind enough to come to the hospital to see me and I told him that unfortunately, it didn't look like I was going to get to go with the regiment. So he made arrangements for me to be taken aboard ship in a stretcher. Those days, if you had a hernia operation, you couldn't even sit up in bed for two weeks instead of getting up now, being forced up, in two hours, which has happened to me two times since then. And so, I was taken aboard in a stretcher on the ship to go to Guadalcanal and didn't have to climb the cargo nets. But I was able to be up and around soon after that. I was so afraid I would miss the trip with the regiment, but he was kind enough to intercede."[14] Wilson was received the Medal of Honor for his role in that battle. This incident was the beginning of his brilliant combat record—a large factor in his rising to the top of the Marine Corps.

Lieutenant General Charles Cooper, as a junior officer recovering from wounds he received in combat in Korea, never forgot the consideration he observed on the part of Lieutenant General Lemuel Shepherd:

> One of the most beloved leaders in the entire history of the Marine Corps was the Commanding General, Fleet Marine Force, Pacific at the time of our arrival in Hawaii. Lieutenant General Lemuel C. Shepherd, later to become Commandant of the Marine Corps, had his headquarters at Pearl Harbor on the island of Oahu. A legendary hero from World War II, and a driving force in the successful Inchon amphibious landing in 1950, he was the image of a warrior/gentleman, with his cultured manners and Virginia accent. All Marines knew who he was.
>
> About 3:00 AM I was sitting on the bed clad only in my pajamas and my newest body cast with the large stomach hole. Something made me look over toward the door of the room. Standing there alone in the doorway was a three-star Marine general. We all tried to stand up, but we waved us down immediately. This wonderful caring leader had come down to visit with us, talk about our outfits and our battle experiences, and

tell us how proud he was of us. He told me he had been wounded as a platoon commander in the Fifth Marines during the battle for Belleau Wood in 1918. He asked each of us when and where we'd been wounded and checked a list he had to verify our names. He pinned a second Purple Heart on my pajamas that night, and stayed with us while we had an early breakfast of fresh scrambled eggs and sausage. When he left, one of the troops summed up our mutual feelings: "Old Lem Shepherd, he really cares about his troops, doesn't he?"[15]

The Marine Corps Commandant's House has a special aura to Marines. On one occasion President William Clinton attended a social function at the Commandant's House, which was preceded by a reception. Commandant Carl E. Mundy recalled, "We had a receiving line in the garden. I had specifically structured the guests that night because I wanted to impress the President with the Marines. So, of course, we had the general officers which I did routinely anyway." But what was special on Mundy's part was his having representatives of more junior officers out of the Basic School. "I also wanted," he said, "captains, majors, and lieutenant colonels, and some NCOs, because I wanted him to come to meet a lot of Marines and to feel very comfortable and to identify with Marines." It was incredibly exciting to those younger officers and NCOs. Mundy continued: "So it was a very, very successful gathering. The Clintons are warm and gracious people. I would venture to say that no one who wanted a picture taken with the President walked away without a picture that night, to include my own children."[16]

Commandant Mundy was asked by the editors of the book *Four Stars*: "I vividly remember, General, when General Lew Walt visited Albuquerque some twenty years ago and he was on active duty as the Assistant Commandant in uniform. I will never forget. He got off the plane and there, among the people greeting him, was a young staff sergeant; and the first person that he greeted was that staff sergeant, with a hug. Is such a show of affection between general and sergeant alien to the Marine Corps of the '90s and beyond?"

"Absolutely not," responded Mundy. "General Walt was the 'squad leader in the sky,' the 'three-star grunt,' and all those sorts of characterizations that derived. And he was a great combat leader and he had great compassion for the troops. Now troops can be colonels and troops can be sergeants or privates. But he had great compassion. I think that each of us, as we become older and more senior or longer serving, each of us feels an increasing affection for the people below us. So the affection between senior officers today and between those junior to us grows over time."[17]

Mundy's response illustrates the relationship that Lejeune called for in the annual birthday message: "The relation between officer and enlisted men should in no sense be that of superior and inferior nor that of master and servant, but rather that of teacher and scholar. In fact it should partake of the nature of the relation between father and son."

General Ray Davis gave an illustration of how he protected the enlisted men from being taken advantage of by civilian merchants when stationed in Okinawa. He wrote in his memoir:

> On Okinawa we kept a number of Chinese tailors busy—their headquarters was Hong Kong—buying clothing, civilian and military, for ourselves and our family: shirts, suits, jackets, coats, dresses. We also collected artifacts of all varieties. Two happenings are noteworthy: We discovered that one of the shirt makers was giving a special price for seniors while charging the younger Marines more. We invited the owner out to our Headquarters and confronted him with our findings. He was "directed" to charge one price to all Marines or be "blackballed." He complied readily and the word spread throughout the business community in Okinawa. We found no further such practices.[18]

Chesty Puller had a well-earned reputation for toughness, but there are many examples of his sensitivity and caring. Major Robert H. Barrow reflected on a time when he had to return to the United States because of his father's serious illness: "My next stop in getting transportation and what not was the regiment. The regimental commander, Colonel Puller, knew that I was in the regimental area, so he sent for me and said, 'I understand you can't get out until tomorrow, anyway, so you go ahead and bunk down here with me.' So I spent my last night in Korea with Chesty Puller, regimental commander. To his credit, I think he sensed my deep concern and worry about my father and felt, somehow, that he could maybe take my mind off of that by having me there in his tent and having conversation. So we spent a very long time talking, just the two of us. Not so much about Korea but about the Marine Corps and some of his past experiences. I must say that, to some extent, he did take my mind off of my worries."[19]

On one of many hard marches for his troops to prepare for combat, Puller had a Private White, who went AWOL briefly for one day to climb a mountain and find the overgrown grave of Robert Louis Stevenson. White wrote of Puller's unexpected kindness to him and to a boy he caught asleep on guard duty at an ammunition dump. Puller shook the boy awake: "Old man, it's dangerous to pull a trick like this. Suppose Captain Rogers had caught you. He'd have made a big fuss, and then I'd have to court-martial you and slap you in the brig. Maybe that's what I should do—but I'll give you another chance. Pretty soon, now, we'll be fighting for keeps, and you'll stay awake, or risk the lives of every one of us. You understand me?"

"'Yes, sir, Major.'"[20]

Puller took command of the Second Marine Division in July 1954. One of his first discoveries on the base was that there were staggering numbers of courts martial. He called in his sergeant major for an explanation:

"Well, sir. It's the beer. They don't allow beer in the enlisted men's clubs at noon, and the men have been stepping across the streets to the civilian beer joints. The MPs pick 'em up."

Puller solved the problem within seconds: "'Tell the clubs to serve beer at noon and let me hear no more of this foolishness. You just make sure we have no drunkenness. We've got more to do than hold courts.' The problem of absenteeism disappeared. He also canceled orders requiring Marines to wear dress uniforms to baseball games and other sporting events, ending more gripes and discomfort."[21]

Safety of the troops is important in peacetime. Commandant Barrow was alarmed with the number of Marines killed or injured in automobiles and motorcycle accidents. He told me: "We had a lot of 18- to 25-year-olds behind the wheel of vehicles and potential for serious traffic accidents, and we had them. I hated to see this.

"I wrote a letter saying two Marines a week were being killed in motor vehicle accidents. I couldn't say you can't drive your car or motorcycle, but I could have repeated classes on the dangers of bad driving or driving under adverse weather conditions or while they've drunk too much to drive." The important thing was that the problem was recognized and Barrow did something about it.[22] Accidents were reduced considerably.

Ray Davis, as a junior officer, was on his way home from Korea, and he took a troop train. Army military police were in charge of the military personnel on the train. Davis related:

> One of these train cars was assigned to officers with our men in two connecting cars—all combat veterans. The young Military Policemen hassled the troops unnecessarily, in my view, and were disrespectful to the officers. After they refused to

listen to reason and challenged me to do anything about it, I wired ahead and had them relieved at the next stop.[23]

Marine leadership does not tolerate mistreatment. As a captain, Charles Cooper was incensed when he learned a Marine was mistreated, and he acted decisively to correct it:

> When we arrived at Camp Lejeune, just a few days before Christmas, we were fortunate to find off-base rental housing available immediately. The summer cottage on the banks of Bogue Sound seemed idyllic to a new family such as ours. All of our neighbors were Marine officers who commuted to either Camp Lejeune or Cherry Point.
>
> I was assigned to the Barracks Military Police Company as its executive officer. My tour with the MPs was short, but several interesting things happened to me. First, I was defense counsel on dozens of special court martial cases, mostly those of Marines who had been absent without proper authority (AWOL), but also a few more serious cases. A new military justice system, the Uniform Code of Military Justice, had gone into effect in June of 1951, and I got a crash course in its many complexities.
>
> Second, the provost marshal was short one officer in his CID [Criminal Investigation Division] office. After my efforts as a defense counsel had resulted in a large number of acquittals, the PM had me removed from the courtroom and assigned to full-time work in CID. The talent working in MP Company was impressive. They were all Marine Reservists who had been recalled. Our senior night desk sergeant, a black master sergeant, was a PhD and president of a black university in West Virginia. The head of CID had been chief of detectives in the Chicago Police Department. And so on.
>
> One day soon after I'd joined CID, Major Cruise, our provost marshal, called me into his office. He had just received a phone call from an anonymous member of the Jacksonville Police Department telling him that he ought to send someone to the city jail. A Marine officer was locked up there, and he was in bad shape. The provost marshal didn't have the sort of relationship

with the Jacksonville Police Department that would allow him to make a direct phone call to the chief of police about a matter like this, so he sent me out to pay a surprise visit. He wanted a return phone call ASAP.

I walked into the jail unannounced, accompanied by a large gunnery sergeant, a former Virginia highway patrolman. I told the jailer that I had come to see the officer they had in custody, right now! He mumbled something, and my "gunny" stood face to face with him and said, "Where is he?" He escorted us to the officer's cell. The officer was a Reserve major who had been charged with driving under the influence and resisting arrest, but someone had beaten him into a bloody pulp. We could hardly distinguish the features of his face, and he had not had any medical treatment. I turned and strode back to the desk, picked up the phone, and called Major Cruise. He told me to stay where I was: he was on the way.

The officer's story, later verified by others, was that he indeed had been intoxicated. He had run a red light and the local police pulled him over. When he had reached for his driver's license, the two policemen threw him against his car and beat him senseless. Most of his front teeth were gone, his nose was flattened, and he had cuts over both eyes. We demanded custody of him and delivered him to the naval hospital on base.

After the major had been treated and sewn up, he gave us a complete statement of his travails. With his statement in hand, Major Cruise and I proceeded to the office of the Commanding General, Major General Ray Robinson, USMC. There I learned that this wasn't the first incident of this type: there had been all too many. General Robinson had made calls on the mayor, warning him, and had threatened to take unusual and drastic action if the authorities failed to get the rogue police under control. They had failed to do so. This was the "straw," apparently. While we were still in his office, he summoned his staff judge advocate and told him, "I've had enough of this crap. Let's do it. Declare the city of Jacksonville off limits to all military personnel and their dependents. We'll make those bastards crawl!"

The restrictions lasted just eight days and served its purpose—in spades. The merchants went ballistic and applied the proper pressure. Before the order was lifted, the chief of police and a third of his officers had been fired. The county sheriff fired three senior deputies, and the attorney general of the state paid a visit to Camp Lejeune, dispatched by the governor to help us in our conflict with the local authorities. The governor wanted to put a quick lid on this tempest. He and his attorney general did just that. They proved most helpful.[24]

A Marine leader particularly doesn't tolerate any mistreatment of a Marine by a Marine. Commandant Charles Krulak was asked to comment on "blood winging," which was a policy of pushing the jump wings that were awarded into the bare skin of the Marine. It was painful and it caused bleeding.

In early February 1997, the blood winging incident was exposed. The incident had occurred earlier, and the report on the television show *20/20* made it public. While it happened six years earlier, the ramifications of it were on Krulak's watch.

He commented on this: "It was a real, real tough time for me and for the Marine Corps. It was a tough time for me because many Marines didn't understand why I was so angry. It was difficult, because I didn't feel like I had a whole lot of support up and down the chain because people thought, well, this has been going on for years. I tried to tell them, no, we haven't done it for years. The first type of that kind of macho hazing probably started in 1965, '66, '67 when we started getting the lowest IQ category of testing, 'mental group four' recruits and you couldn't get them to do anything. You couldn't instruct them. You couldn't motivate them. People started using other methods.

"My father commanded a parachute battalion in World War II. I think there were only about five people who were still alive in his parachute battalion. He called me the night this played. He said, 'Chuck, I just got a phone call from five members of my battalion. All of them had seen this thing on TV and were flabbergasted and just could not understand. When did Marine parachuters start beating Marine parachuters? It was a disgrace.' It was interesting that the old Corps recognized how dangerous this was, but the new Corps had trouble.

"On February 4 1997, I sent an open letter to the Corps. In it I stated that this has been a tough couple of days for all of us. It's not over. There will be more to come. My concern, like yours, is for the institution. I appreciate the calls and messages regarding my own personal well being. Believe me, I'm in the fight. This issue of how we as Marines treat each other has been the core of our efforts in the area of making Marines. Each of us has committed to the concept that there is no room for treating Marines in any manner other than with respect and dignity. We've been banging on that since 1 July 1995. My predecessor hit it hard before his departure. The fact that this event, the 'winging,' took place in September of 1991 meant nothing to the American people. The fact that it involved the Marine Corps meant everything. They expected us to set the highest of standards and to maintain those standards, and to hold accountable those who do not. Toward the end of that open letter, I said, 'These actions are anathema to our core values of honor, courage, and commitment, and those who cannot live these basic moral tenets do not deserve to wear the Eagle, Globe, and Anchor. I will not allow them to tarnish the sacred trust between you and one of America's most dependable steadfast institutions . . . the United States Marine Corps.'"

Krulak saw to it that it stopped, "but my head is not in the sand. We know our rules and understand the Marine Corps policy on hazing. We know that our Marines understand that it is not tolerated. We also know that there are Marines who are willing to disregard that policy because of some misguided sense of tradition or macho-ness. Those Marines must either change their thinking or leave the Corps. There is no gray area. The treatment of Marines in any manner other than with dignity or respect: sexual harassment, discrimination, hazing, will not be tolerated. Those who violate this basic foundation of our Corps must be held accountable, no matter what the rank, no matter how much the time in, no matter how good they are in military skills. Do I think we're nearing the point when the Corps will quickly disappear? No. Do I think that the publicity we receive from situations such as this and others in the recent past draw on reservoir of good faith that our countrymen and women place in us? Yes. They will continue to support us as long as they see us as an institution that is trying to set and meet what my father called high, almost spiritual, standards. As my father stated in his famous quote: 'We exist today—we flourish today—not because of what we know we are, or what we know we can do, but because of what the grassroots of our country believes we are and believes we can do.'

"We are doing that now. We must continue to do that. This is what transformation is all about. This is what cohesion is all about. This is what winning battles is all about. We must not lose sight of where we are going. We all need to articulate how making Marines and winning battles fits into the concept of a Corps of Marines that belongs to the American people.

1991 is not 1997. We have new Marines, new NCOs, new staff NCOs, new commanders and new commanding generals. We have a Corps that is moving out at flank speed toward the 21$^{st}$ century with a well-defined goal in sight. I have total faith in my officers and the Marine Corps under their charge. We just need to reiterate to all Marines that our standards are unwavering and that we will not bend to the actions of a few.

"The end result of that was bringing an Article 32 against everybody involved in blood winging and holding them accountable. Every time another incident comes up, hold those involved accountable. Marines left the Corps because of it. People had trouble understanding why I was upset. Again, reading my father's quote: 'We exist today, we flourish today,' and you understand how important standards are in the Marine Corps, you'll understand how blood winging could have been a disaster. It was bad enough. But it could have been really bad. By getting out in front of it, by going on TV, by expressing disgust with it, the American people stuck with their Corps.

"Like the rape [of a Japanese girl by several Marines in Okinawa]. We stood up to the media. We told it like it was. We opened up all this for a look by the American people and by being open and honest they realized that we are going to keep our standards."[25]

Holland M. Smith was very sensitive to protecting his people. When one day his orderly was unavoidably late for pay call, having been on an errand for the general, the payroll officer brushed aside the enlisted man's explanation, upbraided him severely, and told him that if he were late again, he would not be paid. When Smith heard of it, he sent for the officer and kept him waiting outside his office for 4 hours before emphatically pointing out the error of his ways. In telling this story afterward, the orderly added, "He'd look out for the Marine Corps the same way he'd look out for me."[26]

One day when Smith and his aide were visiting an officers' club, their driver, a sergeant, inadvertently entered the officers' locker room to comb his hair. A Navy commander discovered him and, after giving him a severe verbal reprimand, bitterly complained to the general's aide that the sergeant had invaded the officers' privacy. When the general was informed, he called the commander aside and "turned the air blue," roaring: "Who in the hell are you to say that he shouldn't go in there? I suppose just because he's a sergeant he's not supposed to comb his hair. Well, let me tell you something, that's a good boy—all my people are good people. They go out and fight and die while you sit here on your ass and look for something to complain about. That sergeant sleeps in the same house with me, he eats the same food; he's just as good a man as you or I. If you say one more word to him, you'll have to fight me over it—and don't you forget it!"[27]

The Post Exchange is important to the quality of life for Marines. When Colonel Barrow was stationed in Okinawa, he was concerned that the Marines were not given proper treatment: "We did not have our own PX on Okinawa. We had a Marine Corps exchange in Iwakuni. Marine exchanges, in my judgment, were the best, maybe because we were a smaller Service and we could be very attentive to it and put good people in there. But we didn't have our own exchange on Okinawa. We had some kind of exchange facility in each of our camps, and we had an enormous exchange at Fort Buckner, and we had an enormous exchange at Kadena. All of this was the Army-Air Force Exchange Service, run by an Army Colonel with an enormous staff on Okinawa. Historically, that whole approach to the Marine presence was, 'You guys need a little toothpaste and shaving cream and that's it. So that's about what we have up in these camps. If you're serious about buying anything, you'll have to come down to Kadena or Buckner.' Now, I've overstated it for emphasis; there was more to it than that. The attitude toward the Corps was 'whereas you are the big population, and wherever you shop, you have to come down to Kadena and Buckner, you've been big spenders, unlike the rest of us out here, who have families, who have responsibilities for spending our money for food and things for our children. You Marines are all out here unaccompanied, so you have fat wallets. You buy a lot of stereo gear and all that sort of stuff. But we're not going to give you very much back for your recreation.'"

Barrow refused to tolerate Marines being treated in this way: "I will not belabor this, but I got my teeth into that situation, and it was a wonderful experience, of how to bring these characters to heel, if you will, who were arrogant about their relationship with the Marines, the Marines that they were responsible to serve."

"It's the most impersonal, cold, could-care-less kind of an arrangement. If we get that way in the Marine Corps exchanges, somebody needs to, as we say, kick rear ends and take names. I didn't mean to get off on that, but I use that as an example of opportunity to do things. I learned a lot."[28]

General Barrow was sensitive to providing other needs of Marines. During his tenure as Commandant, a McDonald's restaurant opened at Camp Pendleton. It was the first fast-food enterprise at a U.S. military base. Barrow commented: "Well, we have a number of them now. It's not all McDonald's. But someone seems to be represented on every major base. At first blush it might seem like an unacceptable thing, an intrusion into a purely military environment. But the facts are they are who we are. They attract the young Americans to eat in those establishments, so you know they do it well. If the young man wants a McDonald's hamburger, I think it is only right to let him be able *to walk* someplace to get it, as opposed to trying to get in the car and drive way off base to get it. So I think it's a plus overall. It was one more example of how troop life was changing and improving in all of the Armed Services."[29]

Payday for the troops is an important part of a Marine's life and is a heavy responsibility for the officer in charge of his unit. Commandant Barrow as a company commander described payday: "A pay table with a blanket, a .45, and the exact amount of money. You, as company commander, paid your Marine. It was a very personal thing. You not only paid him, but payday gave you an additional opportunity to look at him and say something to him. Something maybe encouraging or something to remind him of some obligation or responsibility. 'Remember, you have a new car'—maybe not new, but an old one. 'Don't forget to make those payments on that vehicle.' Just a little comment."[30]

Enlisted personnel frequently had financial problems. "One solution," Barrow concluded, "was the direct deposit of net pay to a checking account. I think this has reached a happy conclusion, but it took some doing, because we had people who liked to get their pay in hand. They want to see that they are getting what they think they should be getting. They wanted cash to do with it what they want to. Many of them don't even have bank accounts. That's one reason why this was hard to get off the ground. They live from payday to payday.

"Only about 7 percent of the Marine Corps, in the beginning, had checking accounts, but it's close to 100 percent today, both in terms of persuading people to do it, and growing acceptance of it by other Marines, having more young Marines getting used to a checkbook and having a banking account. But we lost a personal touch when the check went into the bank."

Often, other problems needed attention from a thoughtful commander. Barrow saw to it that centralization of pay administration and personnel administration happened: "It was an effort to try to do something about the chronic problem of people being underpaid, not paid on time, et cetera. All the things about travel pay and household movement pay. It's a complicated issue and was subject to being sloppily done sometimes, and it was recognized that it wasn't perfect and let's try to make it better.

"We had an initiative working. I don't know if it's mentioned in here or not, but to tighten up personnel administration and pay administration, so that they are really kind of tied in both, even the location. You know the dispersion office was over on the other side of town, I brought them together which was efficient and convenient for the troops."[31] It was an incredibly considerate move for the troops.

A man who wants to be a Marine is one who wants to fight for his country. It has always been what the Marine Corps is about. Men didn't join to pull KP duty, peeling potatoes and washing mess hall dishes, but those chores had to be done by someone. Commandant Krulak established a policy of outsourcingo these jobs, contracting civilians to do the KP duties and cooking for the mess, which also saved money and freed Marines to fight.[32]

The Marine Corps was also sensitive to the care and welfare of civilians. President Lyndon B. Johnson commented on a meeting he had with Lieutenant General Lew Walt when he was the senior Marine General serving in Vietnam, a position he held for 2 years.

"We talked for nearly 2 hours," Johnson related. "He told me in crisp detail what was happening, how things looked, how our men were doing in a kind of war some people had argued they never could fight effectively. He told me a great many other things, too. He described the South Vietnamese Army—its strength and weaknesses. Above all, he talked with feeling and compassion for the Vietnamese people and what they were going through—the terror imposed by the communist forces; the pain they felt when their rice was confiscated and their sons were dragged away to fight; the torture and murders that were the penalty for failing to do what the Viet Cong demanded.

"He also told me what his Marines and our other fighting men were doing to help the people. They were building schools and dispensaries in nearby villages. Medical corpsmen were going out during their off-duty hours to give inoculations against disease, to treat the festering sores of young and old, and to relieve the pain and the suffering. Many young Marines were living in villages with local defense forces, helping to protect the people against the terror and taxation of a ruthless, demanding enemy.

"Here was a rugged Marine general fighting a tough and exhausting war. Yet he showed more real feeling, more sensitivity for the people who were its victims, than almost anyone I knew. Much of what he told me that day in the White House, and on numerous later occasions, is in these pages. But there is a great deal more."

Why? Walt put this into perspective:

The war is among the people, and it is allegiance or control of the people that is at the root of the conflict. It is all-important not to forget the people, as sometimes happens; and to try to see our actions through the eyes of the people.

Our soldiers, sailors, Marines, and airmen now returning from Vietnam need to make no apologies for having largely stamped out terrorism and pushed back the invading hordes of communism. They can be proud of the millions of refugees to whom they have given shelter, the civilian millions whom they have fed and clothed and provided with medical care, the young generation to whom they have given an opportunity to be educated for life in a free society.

We had half a million men in Vietnam at the peak of our military effort. They battled an enemy of freedom, and at the same time battled disease and privation, desolation, and despair. Their victories have less to do with "body counts" than with security and a helping hand given a suffering and deprived people. Happiness, health, and hope, food and shelter for millions, hospitals, orphanages, and schooling for children, have been the fruits of their labor. We can be proud, not ashamed, of our young Americans.

The care was provided to enemy soldiers even though the Communists were guilty of unlimited terror, the slaughter of tens of thousands—teachers, priests, police officers, local leaders and their families—kidnapped even larger numbers during the past fifteen years. He deliberately hurls rockets and firebombs at random into crowded cities, movie theaters, schools, markets. He has committed crimes with calculated savagery, such as public beheadings, disembowelings, and maiming of innocent victims.

In contrast, the U.S. forces had an instinct geared to compassion, restraint, and sympathetic caring for the people in Vietnam. Our Marines shared the victories and defeat, suffering with them, wanting to provide a better life—to give them dignity. So much was accomplished through the U.S. Civic Action Program.[33]

General Walt gave a specific illustration of Marines providing attention to captured Vietnamese soldiers:

> One day, Thiet and five others were ambushed by the American Marines as they were leaving a village laden down with confiscated rice. Three of his friends were killed and two wounded and captured, but Thiet was in the rear and escaped to a nearby cave. From there, he watched his two wounded comrades bandaged by the Marines, saw them offered cigarettes and water. Thiet thought of the lectures he had received on how the Americans tortured and killed his people and starved and brutalized the peasants, and he thought on what he and his comrades had been required to do because they were soldiers of the National Liberation Front, of the Vietnamese people they had killed and the rice they had taken from the poor people and the school they had blown up.[34]

Major General Oliver Prince Smith was the division commander of the Main Marine Corps in the battle at the Chosin reservoir. He became concerned about the welfare of one of the female reporters. Smith's biography stated:

> The news correspondents had not been aware of the potential story at the Chosin reservoir until the Yudam-ni breakout by the Fifth and Seventh Regimental Combat Teams (RCTs). When they finally understood what was taking place, it became one of the most heavily reported stories of the Korean War. On 5 December, several correspondents, including Charlie Moors of UP, Macbeth of the Associated Press, Edward L. Keyes Beach from *Time*, and Marguerite Higgins of the *New York Herald-Tribune* arrived to report on developing events. The presence of Miss Higgins at such an exposed position prompted General Smith to issue instructions to get her out of Hagaru-ri, regardless of her pleading to stay and "go out with the troops."
>
> Marguerite Higgins found a chilly reception whenever she appeared at the center of activity during the breakout from the Chosin reservoir area. She came in by plane on 7 December and was met by Puller, who immediately assigned an officer to her with precise orders to see that she was put on the last plane out of the area. Miss Higgins appealed to General Smith for

help in the matter. She told him that she wanted to walk out with the men, because it was a terrific story and she thought that she had a right to tell it. Smith told her, "There are a lot of good Marines who are getting frostbite, and if you march down with these Marines you probably will get frostbitten, and then somebody is going to have to take care of you. I am sure these Marines will see that you are taken care of, but we haven't got men for that kind of business."

On 9 December General Shepherd visited Smith with the intention of staying overnight, but Smith insisted that he leave on the last flight out of Koto-ri. He did so, with Marguerite Higgins as a fellow passenger. The plane was hit by ground fire but got safely airborne.

Higgins later wrote a book about her experiences in Korea, noting that "General Smith had a strong seizure of chivalry that afternoon and insisted that the walkout was too dangerous." As Smith's aide Captain Sexton recalled decades later, "Smith firmly directed Colonel Puller to see that she was personally escorted to the next plane and flown out of the area. This mission was accomplished with firmness, amid loud protests and profanities from the female passenger."[35]

General Krulak gave a superbly insightful description of the Marines for civilians. One of his contributions to Corps strategy in combat is what he named the three-block war: "The three-block war is the concept that in a moment in time a Marine will find himself with a young child in his hands and wrap that child in swaddling clothes, feed it, care for it and it's called 'humanitarian assistance.' We do that all the time. We did it in Mogadishu, we're doing it in Kosovo. At the next moment in time, that same Marine will be placed in the position where's he's got his hands outstretched, he's got a weapon with him, and he's keeping two warring factions apart, and it's called 'peacekeeping.' We're doing that right now in Kosovo. At the third moment in time you'll find that same Marine involved in mid-intensity, highly lethal combat.

"The best example I can give is the Marine who a week ago was at Camp Hope in Albania taking care of refugees. The next moment that same Marine is in Kosovo at a roadblock trying to keep the peace between the Serbs and the KLA. The next moment, that same Marine is taking fire from a bunch of snipers up in a building. Now, you say well, sniper fire, that's not mid-intensity conflict. Well, it may not be mid-intensity to Chuck Krulak, but let me tell you something, to the kid that's getting fired at and returning fire, it's mid-intensity conflict. He's gone from humanitarian assistance to combat in a very short period of time, and more importantly, he will move back and forth between these various states of conflict. It really takes a special kind of Marine to be able to do that."[36]

Brigadier General Raymond A. Davis was stationed in Okinawa as Assistant Division Commander of the 3d Marine Division. He related an incident when one of the civilian businessmen had a serious problem:

> One Chinese merchant with whom I dealt extensively came to my office in great distress saying that his license had been canceled by senior U.S. authorities and he could not find out why. My inquiries brought no information other than that customs problems were involved. I asked our security/counterintelligence units to explore the problem through their special channels. It turned out that the merchant allegedly had been caught up in a "sting" operation. There were photos of him purchasing items in Hong Kong, flying these items to Okinawa, hauling them to his shop without customs declarations or duties. His license was canceled but he was not told why so as to protect the ongoing sting. But the merchant was innocent. The items photographed were actually some which had been purchased in Hong Kong by a senior U.S. official on Guam who had flown them to Okinawa and had asked the merchant to pick them up at the airport for modification and refinishing. I obtained a letter confirming this; the license was cleared. The Chinese merchant was very relieved, most grateful, but greatly mystified. He felt that I had "saved his life" and made many efforts to favor me with gifts. When I returned home I discovered that some artifacts which I had refused to accept had been surreptitiously packed in my personal effects shipments at the time of my departure from Okinawa.

The significant impact and appreciation was further made known to him when 5 years later, his son Miles, a Marine lieutenant, saw his father's photo on the walls of this merchant's store, and made himself known to the merchant. "The old man became very emotional and wanted to reward Miles with a gift. Instead Miles ordered a set of fine furniture made by the merchant, which he paid for, but feels to this day that a lot of extra care went into its construction."[37]

General Anthony Zinni was stationed in Vietnam and embedded with the Vietnamese Marines. He showed his consideration for the Vietnamese civilians:

> Zinni's tour in Vietnam was not confined to military operations. Along with his Vietnamese Marine companions he lived much of the time with ordinary Vietnamese in their villages and hamlets. Vietnam had a quartering law that required the people to allow troops operating in their area to move into their houses. This was not the burden on the people that it might seem. The Marines didn't take a place over and throw people out of their houses. They treated the local people with respect, paying for their food and helping with the village chores. The country-bred troops especially enjoyed helping out with the familiar tasks, which reminded them of their own homes.[38]

Consideration and caring for the welfare of the troops are a vital part of the Marine Corps' successful leadership but also part of the contact and conduct with the defeated enemy. Major General John A. Lejeune and the 2$^d$ Army Division were responsible for the occupation of Germany after World War I. In his memoir, Lejeune described his postwar responsibilities:

> Edicts were the supreme laws and as such took precedence over their own laws. The security, the comfort, the welfare and the supremacy of the army of occupation were always the first consideration. No abuse or mistreatment of the inhabitants by the troops was permitted. In consequence of this system we lived side by side with the civil population during the long period before the signing of the peace treaty without any serious disturbances or disorders, and, I believe, left behind us when we departed for home a reputation for justice, honor, and fairness that has never been excelled by any army of occupation in the history of the world.[39]

The consideration of leaders goes beyond their own troops when looking after prisoners of war. As the fighting for Saipan in the Pacific was progressing, Lieutenant General Holland M. Smith's biographer wrote:

> In the midst of planning and fighting the battle, Smith never lost his concern for people. The day he came ashore, as he

walked down the beach, he came upon a Marine sentry guarding a barbed wire enclosure which held a half dozen or so Japanese prisoners. The prisoners, obviously thirsty and hungry, sat exposed to the broiling sun. Smith summoned the officer in charge and ordered him to provide the Japanese with shade, water, and food. Later, he returned to see that he been obeyed. A staff officer, surprised at his action since the situation was very tense and desperate fighting was in progress only a mile or so away, asked him about it. "Goddamn it, Bobby," he replied, "we're supposed to be Christians! And we have to act like Christians! We're not Japanese and we've got to act like what we are."

Later in the operation the general visited a rough, crude field hospital in which some Japanese, as well as Americans, were being treated. Many of the wounded were in terrible condition, suffering from open wounds infested with maggots. Smith's aide observed that "whether it was a Japanese or an American, it affected General Smith very deeply.... he felt a great compassion."[40]

Commandant Lemuel C. Shepherd, Jr., reflected on an experience he had in the occupation of Japan after that country's defeat in World War II. His oral history interviewer asked Shepherd: "How do you account for the fact that now today Japan is one of our closest allies?"

Shepherd responded: "Well, we licked them so badly that I think we took all the sting out of them, for a while, anyhow, and they are very nice to us, for they know where their bread is buttered. I recall an incident when General Nagano surrendered to me. I demanded he surrender his sword at Tsingtao. He laid his sword down, as the symbol of his defeat. It was a symbol, because the Japanese samurai sword is something they prize and treasure highly. And his staff was required to do the same thing. But he wrote me a letter on the day of the surrender, in which he said, 'I hope that you treasure this sword with honor and respect, because it has always been carried in the cause of virtue. It has been in my family 350 years, and it's my most prized possession, and I hope you won't just throw it into the heap with the others, to be disposed of.'

"I was so touched by this letter that I was all for giving this sword back to him. My staff said, 'Oh, you can't do that, General. That's a symbol. If you give it back to him, he'll think, *Oh, well, these Americans are too kind.* You have to be forceful with him.'

"So I wrote him a letter saying that his sword would always be treasured as a symbol of his service and his family and the fine courageous fight that the Japanese had put up, that although we were enemies in this war, we had fought on the same side in World War I. He was a professional soldier and I was a professional soldier. I had great respect for my adversary.

"When years later, Admiral Nimitz returned Admiral Tojo's sword, I thought I should do the same thing. I know how much General Nagano treasured his sword. So I wrote a letter to him during the Korean War. General Willoughby, MacArthur's G2, had a list of all Japanese officers, so I was able to get Nagano's address. He lived on the Inland Sea. I said, 'Years have passed since you surrendered your sword to me. Our countries have become friends. I know how you treasured your sword, and although I have given it to a museum, I would like to get it back from the museum and return it to you personally.'

"I received a letter from him saying, 'I am now an old man. I recall very vividly my surrender to you, and your kindness to me upon my surrender. But I surrendered that sword to you as a soldier. I cannot take it back.'"[41]

Charles Cooper, as a unit commander in the Vietnam War, rhetorically asked, "Who were the enemy to these brave young troopers in the field? They were faceless and always threatening. During the day, any male of military age that the trooper spotted was a target. And he had to suspect even the women and children he came across. Every trooper had heard tales of the 8- or 10-year-old girl that got one of our troopers to approach her by pointing to a body on the ground then pulled a wire that activated a claymore mine, killing the Marine. I marveled that the Marines and their Navy corpsmen could show compassion to wounded civilians or even the relatively rare captured enemy soldier when treating their injuries."[42]

The visit by a senior officer is very demanding in time, with considerable effort required for preparation such as requirements for the Marines to hold field day because the Commandant was coming or get briefings ready, or to "paint rocks." Commandant Krulak was different. He reflected: "What they got was their Commandant seeing them, unannounced and unexpected. We did these unannounced visits all the time.[43]

"My first unannounced visit was to Cherry Point. We started to fly in and my pilot was afraid that they would know who we were. I said to just tell them you're a C–130 needing fuel. So they did. They told the tower that it was a C–130 and we landed the Gulf Stream and taxied right up to one of the AV–8 hangars and the door came down and I jumped out and spent the whole day talking to Marines, officers and enlisted. The Second Wing Commander and the Group 14 Commander and the VMA

Squadron Commander had no idea I was on the ground for about 45 minutes. They knew who I was as soon as I hit the ground but I was moving so fast they had trouble finding me. The point was not to harass my officers but to ensure that nobody had to prepare for my visit. I'd get a chance to see them and it would be without all of the hoopla that goes with a Commandant's visit."[44]

Major General Oliver Prince Smith was sensitive and caring. On December 13, 1950, memorial services were held at Hungnam Cemetery in Korea for those lost when the Division broke out from the Chosin Reservoir; Catholic, Jewish, and Protestant chaplains participated. Smith's biographer wrote:

> Amidst the rows of white crosses and Stars of David, the plaintive notes of "Taps" echoed across the windswept plain. Major General Oliver Prince Smith, more than anyone else, knew how high the cost had been. Two days later he returned alone to the sanctity of the cemetery to pay a final tribute to those who had paid the supreme sacrifice and would remain forever young. Smith's sad eyes reflected the strong emotions that he kept to himself while he bid a final farewell to the best of American manhood. He then boarded the USS *Bayfield* and left Hungnam, leaving an enduring legacy that will be studied and honored for as long as mankind admires those qualities that allow the human spirit to rise above all expectations.[45]

In his relationship with his men, Puller was unpretentious and very down to earth, and he fit in with his troops without any inappropriate familiarity. His biographer Burke Davis gave an example of his caring for his men:

> Captain Regan Fuller, USMC, who was serving under Puller at the time, kept an increasingly close watch on Puller: "He became more concerned for the men being killed and wounded as it grew worse, I saw his eyes puddle up many a time, but he would have died rather than have any of us think that he could weep for his men, or anything else. He never lost control."

> Puller frequently sent the men to the nearby river to bathe, with riflemen on constant guard. The jungle itch had become serious and was weaving red welts over the bodies of men; they were ordered to wash as often as possible.

The colonel washed in the river with the troops, too, and Regan Fuller noticed that even when he washed his uniforms he stripped with the enlisted men in the river. A common touch the men liked, Fuller said. Though a few of the Clausewitz-type officers in the rear ranks snickered behind his back, his men knew he was real, that he never put on an act, and they loved him.[46]

General Krulak was asked what he recalled about the crash of an aircraft that killed 14 Marines: "It was a terrible, terrible tragedy. We were involved in a joint and combined exercise. I'm not sure what the name of it was, but it was with the British and the Dutch. I can remember getting called at home and told that we had lost two helicopters and fourteen Marines, plus one Army soldier. A Huey Cobra doing close air support and escort duty at night, ran into the CH–46 and took it out of the air. One of the great stories, which occasionally come out of tragedies like these, was of a young captain by the name of Chuck Johnson. He was the copilot of the CH–46. He was crushed in the crash and they didn't think he was going to live. His parents, who were very strong Christians, had a whole bunch of people praying for this young officer. He pulled through and is flying today.

"The death of those Marines added a lot to my cards. When I became the Commandant, I made a 5x8 card for the spouse of each Marine killed in training-related accidents. I would use these cards when I called the families and tried to call each family once a month. Unfortunately, most of these were aircraft accidents or mishaps. Sadly, I had to get a large number of cards as a result of this accident because we lost so many Marines. It was a very tragic time and a very sad time. I was heartened and warmed by the number of fellow members of the military of other Services who wrote or called and expressed their regret, but it was a sad time."[47]

How does a commander who cares deeply for his Marines handle the loss of troops? General Tony Zinni expressed his sorrow at losing any of his Marines:

> In one night helicopter training event, we had a helo crash at sea and lost a number of Marines. This was not the first time I'd seen a fatal training accident, and it wasn't the last. Despite all of our best efforts, shit happens. Yet, each time I've been torn by the loss of some great Marines. Peacetime training deaths in your unit are, in many ways, far more difficult to deal with than combat deaths. After a memorial service the next

day and an extensive air and sea search, we resumed the training. Though I knew this was difficult for young men to understand (and it was hard for me as well!), I felt I had to send a message that we had to immediately get our minds back into our training. I knew the demands of combat don't give us the luxury of grieving for long.[48]

Situations where there is a gross lack of consideration emphasize its importance even more. Holland M. Smith had a bitter experience with this as a junior officer. Smith was assigned, after his tour in Nicaragua, to the Marine Barracks, Annapolis. His first child was born that spring of 1910, and Smith and his family lived in government quarters at the naval base. Housing was limited, and according to military custom, senior officers had first claim on what was available. If a senior officer wanted for himself the house in which a junior was living, he could require him to move, or "rank him out of quarters." During the summer of 1910, a Marine officer who was slightly senior to Smith arrived at Annapolis and requested that Smith vacate his quarters. Both Smith and his infant son were ill in bed at the time, and his son's condition was critical. Smith asked for a delay, but the senior officer was adamant and insisted upon his removal. Smith complied—and within days the Smiths' first-born son was dead. Thirty-five years later, although he omitted this incident from his autobiography, Smith remained bitter. "That officer is dead now," he told a friend, "and burning in hell."[49]

Sometimes a commander is so dependent upon a subordinate that he does not permit leave. But leave is important to the morale, health, and mental well being of Marines. General Barrow commented on this: "A senior's attitude toward leave has a direct bearing on job satisfaction and motivation. It is of no satisfaction to an individual that he is doing this job so well that he cannot be spared to take leave. Leave which is given begrudgingly is offensive to the individual taking leave and the Marine who acts for him while he is absent. Commanders and seniors should encourage, even insist, that their Marines take leave. Among other things, it is a challenge and vote of confidence for the Marine who has to fill in for the Marine on leave."[50]

I asked General Zinni: "What role would you say consideration has in successful leadership?" He responded: "Well, I think when you deal with subordinates, it's important not to talk down to them. They really appreciate the fact that you treat them with respect.

"You're not only accessible and approachable, but you care about what they think, what they have to say, what their problems are. That you acknowledge that you are a part of a special organization. They're as much paid up members of that organization as you are. I mean, everybody gets one chit.

"There are moments in my life when it has hit home to me the awesomeness of this responsibility. There are the obvious times in combat when you see it, you see heroism, bravery, camaraderie, and all of that.

"I remember I was on a ship, and my company was going to the Caribbean. I had just finished eating the evening meal, and I went out on deck to get a little sea air. One of my Marines was out there, a PFC—an African-American Marine—named Washington. I went up to him next to the railing where he was out standing. I struck up a conversation, 'Good evening.' 'Good evening, sir.' I said, 'PFC Washington, I just wanted to tell you how proud I am of you. You are a remarkable Marine.' He was; he was a meritorious PFC. He did everything exceptionally well. He was very highly motivated and dedicated.

"I thought that when you tell someone you're proud of them, it really means a lot. He looked at me and he said, 'You know something, sir, you're the closest thing I have to a father. I have no father. I really have no family. Things were pretty tough, then I went into the Marine Corps. I had no family life or any institutions like school or church growing up.' So the Marine Corps became his life. Here I was his company commander, and he said, 'You're my father.'

"With that we said good evening. I went into my stateroom and I thought, I'm responsible for their lives and everything else, but for many of them you are their father, you are their parental figure. They put their lives in your hands. They want from you what you give to your own kids—acknowledgement, discipline. They expect you to discipline them, you are someone who cares about their welfare and well being and what happens to them. You've got to express that."[51]

A comment by General Paul X. Kelley about the individual puts it into perspective. He told me: "I have a philosophy which I have lived by for 29 years as a Marine Corps officer: 0800 to 1630 is people time—you can always catch up on what you thought was essential paperwork during the evenings or on weekends—but, once neglected, you will find it difficult, if not impossible, to catch up on people. Being accessible demands time—but there isn't a better way to spend your time. Time with people is never wasted!

"We Marines have a time-honored tradition which, to me, symbolizes the way we should always think about those who serve under us—in the field our officers always eat their rations *after* the men. In this one, often inconspicuous act, we tell the world that we as a military Service have the well being of our troops foremost in our thoughts and actions. To be totally successful, then, we must apply the same sound philosophy in every act and deed relating to those in our charge."

General Kelley possessed a great sensitivity to his Marines. Each Marine, to him, was special and different. He commented, "Don't be a martinet who hides behind his rank and authority to lead. True leaders are respected, never feared; true leaders are compassionate, never abusive; true leaders express their views articulately and, when required, forcefully, but never in demeaning, abusive, or four-letter language. A Marine officer who abuses his authority is an absolute coward, for he resorts to fear when he is unable to earn respect.

"I recently heard a story of a young rifle company commander in the Fleet Marine Force, whose company had the lowest rate of unauthorized absences in his division. When asked by a senior officer for the secret to his success, he replied: 'It's simple, every time one of these birds goes over the hill, I immediately start the paperwork moving to throw him out of the corps.'

"Just for the record, were that young company commander working for me, he would be seeking employment elsewhere in short order. The day we establish hard and fast policies, which dramatically alter the lives of young Marines without taking into consideration the circumstances surrounding each case, we have taken the people equation out of our Corps. While there will be some who will misunderstand what I just said, and others who will wrongfully accuse me of being soft on those who go U.A. [unauthorized absence], let me say that I suspect in the history of our Corps there have been hundreds of young Marines who gallantly gave their lives for their country who may have been U.A. a time or two."[52]

General Kelley shared with me one of the most moving accounts of consideration and caring I have ever been told: "An important part of your job is to build quality. With this in mind, there are bound to be occasions when that young Marine entrusted to your care will stumble and perhaps fall. It's easy to leave him lying in the gutter, but a bit more difficult to pick him up, dust him off, and point him in the right direction. You may find that a little concern applied at the right moment could produce a heck of a fine young Marine and American.

"One serious question we should all ask of ourselves when a young Marine is in serious trouble: Why? Where did *we* let him down? Did he have a problem and nobody to turn to? Remember, every malcontent was at one time a very proud Marine—in the case of our enlisted men, each and every one was extremely proud that day he graduated from either Parris Island or San Diego; that day, after weeks of arduous training, that he, for the first time, wore the 'eagle, globe, and anchor' and was called Marine. The question we leaders must address head-on is: 'What happened to that young Marine between then and now?'

"Sometimes the answer is simple—more often than not it's complex.

"In this regard, I'm reminded of a young black lance corporal who worked for me in Vietnam. The answer to his problem, as it turned out, was relatively simple. Let's call him Lance Corporal Jones. It seems that Jones had a reputation for being a malcontent. One day as I was walking up a path to my bunker, I noted Jones cutting grass nearby. I made it a point to engage him in a conversation, asked him where he was from, and he told me Philadelphia. When I told him that I had graduated from Villanova, he informed me that he had attended the Philadelphia Conservatory of Music for 12 years. Needless to say, this took me back somewhat, and I then asked him what was his specialty, and he replied, 'The violin.' I tried to determine whether or not he believed that a layoff of over a year would have any effect on his playing ability. He really didn't know, but he did know that his mother and father had worked and toiled to buy him a quality violin, and he wasn't about to subject it to the hazards of Vietnam. That night I approached the Division Special Services Officer to ask when he might be going to Hong Kong to buy recreational equipment, which he did from time to time. When he gave me the date, I asked a favor: 'Will you buy me a violin?' You can imagine the look on his face, and I eased his concern by telling him that every regimental commander in the corps needed a violin. In any event, a beautiful violin, together with a pitch pipe, appeared on my field desk the following week. It was then that I experienced a sinking feeling in the pit of my stomach—did Lance Corporal Jones really play the violin, or had I been given a con job? And, if he didn't, what was I going to do with a magnificent violin in the middle of Vietnam?

"With some degree of justifiable nervousness, I sent for Jones, and when he reported in front of my desk I asked: 'Lance Corporal Jones, last week you told me that you played the violin, is that correct?' He replied in the affirmative, and I then said: 'Turn around and play me a tune.' When he saw the violin, the tears streamed down his face, and my fears were put to rest when he tucked his new violin under his chin and his left hand went expertly to the strings—he was a real violinist! He played at our church services each Sunday, and at gatherings we had at our enlisted club. He became one of the most popular young Marines in our camp, and I am pleased to footnote this story with the fact that he became a superb individual in every way. The moral of the story is that there was something very important lacking in his life, and once his need was satisfied, he was well on his way to bigger and better things. Now I'm not suggesting that the Marine Corps rush out to buy 190,000 violins and that will solve all of our problems, but I am suggesting that by knowing your Marines, we will all have a better Corps."⁵³

One of the most appreciated acts of consideration was performed when Colonel Kelley in Vietnam. He was constantly visiting his troops who, in combat, were hot, dirty, tired, and living on "meals ready to eat." Chaplain of the Marine Corps Eli Takesian, USN, told me: "During his tenure with the 1ˢᵗ Marines, the last ground combat organization to leave Vietnam, Colonel Kelley was affectionately known as 'The Good Humor Man From the Sky.' Whenever he flew out to visit regimental units operating in the field, he was armed with containers of ice cream, cases of Coke, and hot chow."⁵⁴

Anyone who has ever been in a parade is aware of the difficulties, particularly in hot and humid weather, made all the worse by long-winded speeches, even worse when read out loud to them. Charles Osgood in his book, *Osgood on Speaking*, paid a significant tribute to General Kelley in his consideration for the troops. Osgood wrote:

> When General P.X. Kelley retired as Commandant of the U.S. Marine Corps, there was a ceremony at Fort Myer, honoring him and Army Chief of Staff General John Wickham, Jr., who was also retiring after a long and distinguished military career. It was a muggy June afternoon. Vice President George Bush and Secretary of Defense Caspar Weinberger were there. Both the U.S. Army Band and the U.S. Marine Band played. There was a nineteen-gun salute. General Kelley had written a dandy stem winder of a speech, criticizing Congress and the news media, and he meant every word he wrote. However, as temperatures climbed into the nineties, several soldiers on the field in dress uniform collapsed in the heat and humidity. So General Kelley, taking pity on the troops, discarded the text and simply said, "There is no prouder commander than the Commandant of the Marine Corps, and I salute you. Carry on."⁵⁵

General P.X. Kelley commented on the importance of the individual: "Despite what scholars, academics, media, and other pundits may profess from the comfort of their air-conditioned offices—where they have never smelled a sweat-soaked infantryman, and wouldn't like it if they did—battles are won by people—brave and patriotic people. When we talk of tolls of war and the influence of technology, I pray that we never forget that machines do not have a heart—they do not have a soul—and they are not very patriotic. When they quit, they quit—and no whit of man can command or inspire them to go on. But, a young Marine—with his boots firmly planted on his objective—does have a heart—does have a soul—is very patriotic—and will never, ever, quit his country, his Corps, or his fellow Marines."[56]

Commandant Alfred Gray put the role of consideration into perspective in his book *Warfighting*, one of the best books on leadership ever written:

> Because war is a clash between opposing human wills, the human dimension is central in war. It is the human dimension which infuses war with its intangible moral factors. War is shaped by human nature and is subject to the complexities, inconsistencies, and peculiarities which characterize human behavior. Since war is an act of violence based on irreconcilable disagreement, it will invariably inflame and be shaped by human emotions.
>
> War is an extreme trial of moral and physical strength and stamina. Any view of the nature of war would hardly be accurate or complete without consideration of the effects of danger, fear, exhaustion, and privation on the men who must do the fighting. However, these effects vary greatly from case to case. Individuals and peoples react differently to the stress of war; an act that may break the will of one enemy may only serve to stiffen the resolve of another.
>
> No degree of technological development or scientific calculation will overcome the human dimension in war. Any doctrine which attempts to reduce warfare to ratios of forces, weapons, and equipment neglects the impact of the human will on the conduct of war and is therefore inherently false.[57]

Gray summarized his philosophy in my interview with him: "You should do as much good as you can, for as many people as you can, for as long as you can."

In his more than 8 years as Commandant, Lejeune had certain objectives he wanted to accomplish, and he made it clear that they could be accomplished because of his character, without making enemies:

> [To] secure sufficient appropriations to keep [the Corps] in an efficient condition and provide for housing, clothing, and

feeding its personnel properly; to retain its status as the Navy's expeditionary force in peace and in war; to build up Marine Corps aviation as a vitally important element of the expeditionary force; to erect at Quantico permanent buildings to replace the temporary wartime structures; to recreate the Reserve as a constituent part of the war time strength of the Marine Corps; and to secure the enactment of a law providing for a modified form of promotion by selection, combined with an annual, automatic elimination of a certain percentage of non-selected officers.

The fight for every one of these objectives, except the last, was won, as was the fight for a great many less important objectives. I was fortunate, too, in being able to gain my objectives without the creation of ill feeling. If I made any enemies, I am not aware of the fact; rather do my memory and my heart tell me that I made a host of friends. Men prefer a considerate and courteous "No" to a curt and discourteous "Yes." It was made the invariable rule at my Headquarters that all telephone calls be answered politely, that all callers be received courteously, and that all letters be replied to promptly and in a friendly manner.[58]

This practice is still emphasized in Marine Corps units everywhere.

Lejeune had a policy of being available to listen to Marines of all ranks. He wrote an incident that surfaced from letters:

> It was a bleak, cold, and rainy evening when we reached Les Islettes. Headquarters was located in a large, old-fashioned residence, and at eight o'clock I went to my room, where a blazing fire had been built to take off the chill. Presently Captain Nelson told me that a Private Marine wanted to see me, and I told him to let him come in. My pity was aroused when I saw him. He was a mere boy, very tired and suffering from a bad cough. I made him sit down by the fire to dry his wet clothes and asked him what I could do for him.
>
> He said he had letters for me which had been given him when he left the United States, and which he now handed me. They were from officers I knew who asked me to keep an eye on the youngster and told me that he was actually only sixteen,

although eighteen was the age he gave when he enlisted. In response to my questions, he said that his name was Frazier; that he was from Philadelphia; that he had arrived in France in August; and that he had joined the Division a week or two before the battle of St. Mihiel. I then asked, "Why didn't you bring me these letters before?" He said that he was afraid that I might keep him at Division Headquarters and cause him to lose the opportunity of going into battle with his platoon. I then said, "Why do you bring them to me now?" He answered, "All my buddies were killed or wounded at Blanc Mont and I am worn out from the forced marches. I saw you drive by us on the road today, so I got permission from our Captain to bring letters to you."

I called Captain Nelson and told him to see that the boy got a hot supper, a bath, and a cot with mattress, sheets, and blankets to sleep on; and I gave Frazier a note for Colonel Lee in which I asked that he be transferred to Regimental Headquarters for duty so that he could be under shelter, as his youth and his sickness made him unfit to undergo further exposure to the elements.

Several years afterwards, a gentleman called on me at my office in Washington and, introducing himself as Mr. Frazier, recalled to my mind the incident I have just related which he had learned about from his son. He thanked me earnestly, saying that in all probability I had saved the boy from an attack of pneumonia and perhaps death, and that his service in the Marine Corps had made a man of him, so much so that he was then seriously at work in college studying medicine.

I have told this story to illustrate that fact that when my thoughts turn backward as they have been doing since I began to write my reminiscences, the memory of the little deeds of kindness which I have been able to do for a fellow human being stand out preeminent among the events of my life, and afford me more gratification and more pleasure than does the memory of any contacts I have had with great men, or any prominence I may have achieved. That this is the case with most men during their declining years, I believe to be true, and this statement is recorded here for the benefit of the young men and women who may chance to read these lines.[59]

Lejeune described an incident as commander of the 2$^d$ Division in combat in France about his challenging an order from his higher headquarters to embark upon a 40-kilometer march just after the war. His troops were exhausted from a long-endured fight that ended the war. He wrote:

> A Division Commander must stand ready to fight for his men, even at the risk of offending higher authority. The knowledge that in him they have a champion who is willing to go to the mat, if necessary to protect them from injustice . . . to insist that their creature comforts be looked out for, will cause them to redouble their efforts to gratify him, to give all their strength and all their power to carry out his will, and to do more than is humanly possible to defeat the enemy. It is indeed true that in war the spiritual is to the material as three or even four to one.

The above insights into the role of consideration in the leadership of the Marine Corps generals in this study answer the question, "How do you inspire the people who work with and for you to give their all—to get the most out of his people, often more than they themselves realize?" In every position, a commander's troops will want to know how much you care for them more than they will ever care how much you know.

First, a leader who is dedicated to serving God and country is an inspiration and a role model to follow; he has a contagious leadership quality. Second, the hallmark of a leader is one who has respect and admiration for people, which is engendered through caring about them and showing genuine consideration. This fosters confidence and loyalty and raises morale. In the commander's personal humanity lies his ultimate strength.

Chapter 10

# "Authority and Responsibility Are Inseparable": Accountability

It is important to distinguish between accountability and blame. Assessing accountability implies examining events to determine what can be learned from them; but to fix blame is merely to pass on to someone else the responsibility for mistakes, to find a scapegoat. If an investigation is channeled to find someone to blame or is designed to cover up mistakes, there will be no accountability, and no lessons will be learned. Leaders must learn from mistakes; they owe that to those whose lives are destroyed by tragedies such as those discussed in this chapter.

General A.A. Vandegrift learned early about a senior officer accepting responsibility. As a Marine lieutenant in 1913, he was involved in a confrontation in Vera Cruz, Mexico. Vandegrift recounted the story in his memoir:

> When Moffett [Commander of the USS *Chester*] received news of the landing at Vera Cruz he ordered full steam south, an effort that strained about every seam in USS *Chester*. We reached the port that night. Without lights, Moffett conned USS *Chester* into the inner harbor, a piece of seamanship that drew praise from even Admiral Cradock, commanding the British fleet there.

In darkness, Vandegrift disembarked with his platoon and went into position for the morning assault. They hit some heavy street fighting but pushed on until it secured the town that day, his platoon suffering no casualties. With the battle over they moved to the railroad depot where his men slept in the roundhouse and the officers in boxcars.

General Vandegrift's memoir continues:

> Shortly after we were settled, I was ordered to establish an outpost line of standing trenches on the sand dunes west of

the city. This is not the easiest task but it was vastly simplified when an alert gunnery sergeant indicated a deserted house off to our right. We were tearing it down when an irate Mexican approached and through an interpreter complained that we were dismantling his house. To get him off my neck I scribbled a note stating the circumstances, signed it, and gave it to him.

Some months later, I received a letter from the Claims Commission demanding an explanation of why I destroyed a Mexican house claimed at 5,000 pesos. My explanation was returned disapproved as were a second and a third. In a desperate attempt to save 5,000 pesos I asked to see Colonel Lejeune who commanded the regiment.

I was quite relieved at Lejeune's reaction. To my halting story, Lejeune asked, "What are you worried about?" I responded, "About paying five thousand pesos which I don't have." Lejeune continued, "Who told you to build those sanding trenches?" My answer was, "You did, sir."

Lejeune said, "It is therefore my responsibility and I shall take care of it." Noting my relief, he added, "Let this be a lesson to you. Never sign your name to a foolish paper when you don't have to."[1]

Commandant Carl E. Mundy gave the eulogy in remembrance of Commandant Louis Hugh Wilson, Jr., one of the true giants of the Corps. At the memorial service in the Old Chapel at Fort Myer, Virginia, on July 19, 2005, Mundy reflected: "Three years after I graduated from the Basic School at Quantico, I was ordered back to become an instructor. I reported to the Adjutant, who informed me that the Commanding Officer was absent for a few days, but would return the following week. He advised, further, that it was the colonel's policy to address all newly forming companies of lieutenants on the first day of training, which would occur, coincidentally, on the day of his return, and that I should be there.

"At 0700 on the prescribed day, I mustered with a half-dozen instructors and a couple of hundred new lieutenants in the outdoor classroom just in front of the headquarters building. Precisely at 0715, the front door opened and a tall, rangy, all-business-looking colonel walked out. We were called to attention, then put at ease and given our seats.

"The colonel spoke for probably no more than eight to ten minutes, citing what was to be accomplished and what was expected of the lieutenants in the next six months. He concluded by saying: 'While you're here, you'll find many things that are wrong . . . that are not to your liking . . . not the way you would do them . . . and you'll find yourselves talking about how *they* ought to change this or that . . . and how *they* just don't understand the problem. When you have those thoughts or discussions,' he went on, 'I want you to remember: I . . . am *they*!'

"He stood looking at us for probably no more than five seconds, which seemed like minutes. Not a head turned; not an eye blinked, and I'm sure two hundred second-lieutenant minds were working in unison to figure out how they could go through twenty-six weeks of training without ever once uttering the word *they*!

"This was my first association with then Colonel Louis Wilson. Like a few others, the 'I am they' assertion became pure 'Wilsonian' over the years, and like me, I suspect that many here this morning have heard it on more than one occasion. It contained a little humor, but it also characterized the man as the leader he was: 'I am in command; I'm responsible; I give the orders.' It sent a clear message on his position on accountability."[2]

In an oral history interview in 1992, General Robert H. Barrow recalled the critical problem of drug use in the military. On January 20, 1981, Commandant Barrow announced that the urinalysis test results he ordered from drug testing laboratories would be used in disciplinary proceedings involving Marines accused of drug use. He followed this with ALMAR–246 issued on February 1, 1981, in which he launched a concentrated campaign to eliminate the use of illegal drugs in the Corps. The language of the order was simple, beginning with: "The distribution, possession, or use of illegal drugs is not tolerated in the United States Marine Corps." He ordered further that all Marines were subject to random urinalysis testing.

"I considered," Barrow continued, "this to be a subject of great magnitude. It was an issue in which I involved myself personally as much as any other thing I did as Commandant.

"I'll give you a little bit of history. If we looked at the drug scene in the country, we knew that the drug problem was bad, as it still remains, and much of that problem simply moved into the Marine Corps when we brought people in, some of whom had been on drugs and continued to be on drugs after they came in, despite the fact they wouldn't have access to them while they were going through recruit training.

"It was a problem that just sort of fed on itself. I made a bad assumption during my first couple of years that, yes, we had drug usage, but our commanders, leaders at all levels were aware of it and working the problem; and we were doing about as well as we could do and though it wasn't by any means good enough it wasn't all that bad."[3]

Then a few things happened that made General Barrow aware that drug use was a significant problem. A survey of the military revealed a very high percentage of people were involved in drug use. About that time, General Barrow was visiting Marine Corps military installations. At Camp Pendleton, he asked the Commanding General of the 1st Marine Division to arrange for him to talk to captains from the infantry and artillery. He requested to meet with captains because they were the officers who were closest to the problem who also had some maturity as officers. He met with a group of 10 or 12 of the best of the officers of that rank.

General Barrow commented: "I was absolutely floored to see there were generally two attitudes among them. One characterized as apathy: 'It's terrible, but there isn't anything we can do about it. It's a reflection of society and there's no tool, nothing that's available to make us do better.' Secondly, a lesser number also had the belief that, 'As long as these fellows perform well during their work day, that's all we ask of them. What they do after hours is their own business.' Which is a terrible way to look at it.

"I did more questioning, asked many more questions, did more looking, did more listening, and I came to the conclusion that the only way to address it was to put the full authority, the power if you will, of the Commandant's office in a very personalized way behind this thing.

"I started with my sergeant majors who had some good skills in straight talk to the troops. They knew how to do that. We blanketed the Marine Corps. We didn't have time for me to talk to everybody, so my sergeant majors talked to the bulk of the enlisted, particularly the NCOs and staff NCOs. I talked to the officers. I remember the figure, I gave 17 talks to theaters full of officers in every major command in the Marine Corps.

"I began by not fussing at them, not taking them to task. I began with an admission. It went something like, 'Who is responsible for our serious drug problem in the Marine Corps?' That was my lead-in comment. Then I would say, 'You are looking at him.' Not a bad technique to make your own admission that you're largely responsible, and I guess I was the guy that was responsible for it being as bad as it was.

"That made them all kind of sit up. 'Well, he didn't come here to fuss at us. He came here to say that he's part of the problem and now let's get with it.'

"I said, 'We're going to give you the tools to fight this, but you must fight it. For example, we used to excuse ourselves about peer pressure, that people used drugs out of peer pressure.' And I used to ask the question, 'Well, there are two kinds of peer pressure: good peer pressure and bad peer pressure. What you've just said is that we have more bad guys than good guys. Where are the good guys, who I still believe to be in the majority, exercising their good peer pressure?' What we ought to seek to have in all of this, is a sense of pride about being Marines; and a recognition that it's mutually exclusive to say, 'I'm a Marine and still use drugs.' The two are just not consistent. We are looking for the day when everybody is so proud to be a Marine, and a great deal of that pride comes from being in an environment in which there are no drugs, that the users of drugs are the exception, not the rule.

"With drug testing, an excited and energized leadership, emphasis on good peer pressure, the emphasis on 'you can't be a Marine and be a druggy, too,' we just busted our butts working the problem—with success.

"It didn't just happen. A lot of hard work went into it. Now, we have indeed, and have for some time, reached the point where people are in a drug-free environment and don't want to accept or tolerate some fellow that's fooling with it. They became quick to identify him and have him thrown out, or punished, or both. I think that's a dramatic achievement, and I'm not saying I did it. I said I had a hand in doing it. It was done by the people who were close to the problem; and what the people up above did was give them the tools, the encouragement to do it, and the backing to do it."[4]

## The Beirut Tragedy

One of the greatest tragedies in our peacetime history occurred on October 23, 1983, when an 18-ton truck, which had been rebuilt in Iran and was carrying explosives equal to 18,000 pounds of TNT, smashed at high speed into the steel reinforced concrete building at Beirut International Airport that housed the headquarters element of Marine Battalion Landing Team (BLT) 1/8 and exploded, killing 241 Americans, of whom 220 were U.S. Marines. The Commandant of the Marine Corps at the time of the attack, General P.X. Kelley, had been in office less than 4 months before the terrorist attack.

Returning to Washington from Augusta, Georgia, President Reagan immediately dispatched Commandant Kelley to Beirut to inspect the scene and make recommendations on how to provide better protection for his Marines. Kelley remarked to the press before taking off on this mission: "I've been a Marine all of my adult life. Yesterday, I have to say to you in all sincerity and honesty, was the hardest day of my life." He defined his mission in going to Beirut. "It is," he said, "what any Commander would do as a Marine, that's to go and pay my personal respects to our dead, visit with those who have been seriously injured, and also to visit with those who will remain. I would simply ask that all Americans this evening, with bended knee, thank God that this country of ours can still produce young Americans who are willing to lay down their lives for free men everywhere."[5]

As soon as General Kelley returned from Beirut, he recommended to Secretary of Defense Caspar W. Weinberger that an investigative body should be convened. On November 7, 1983, Weinberger appointed a commission that had as its mandate to address how the Department of Defense intended to deal with the accountability for the heavy loss of life, and to make recommendations to prevent it from happening again.

An interview with Marine Corps Chaplain Eli Takesian provided a moving insight into the character and leadership of General Kelley. "My first opportunity," commented Chaplain Takesian, "to meet with the Commandant took place a few days later, after he had returned from Beirut. It was at the Pentagon helicopter pad. We shared an embrace and with tears in his eyes he said, '*Eli, I have just lost 241 sons.*' Minutes later, he and his party, including me, departed for the U.S. Air Force Base in Dover, Delaware, to greet and honor the first planeload of our fallen comrades.

"In a cold and drafty aircraft hangar, the Commandant addressed grieving families that had so suddenly lost loved ones. He underscored the quality, vitality and importance of these superb troops whose lives were unexpectedly taken by terrorists; and then, looking down the line of flag-draped caskets, he asked, 'Lord, where do we get such men?' During moments that were emotionally wrenching, draining, and spiritually consoling, General Kelley met with members of each family and, together, they shared their mutual, heartfelt grief."[6]

There were two investigations of the Beirut tragedy: one by Congress and a second by the Department of Defense referred to as the Long Commission, headed by Admiral Robert L.J. Long, USN (Ret.). Commission members traveled to Lebanon, Israel, Spain, Germany, Italy, and the United Kingdom and interviewed over 125 witnesses, ranging from national policymakers to Lebanese Armed Forces. They reviewed extensive documentation from Washington agencies, including the Department of State, Central Intelligence Agency, National Security Council, and the Federal Bureau of Investigation, as well as all echelons of the operational chain of command and certain elements of the Department of the Navy administrative chain of command.

The congressional hearing began a day and a half after General Kelley's visit to the Marines in Beirut, 8 days after the bombing. General Kelley's testimony before the congressional investigators on November 1, 1983, was based upon the facts known at that time: two of the Marine sentries were killed; the truck drove over a sewer pipe filled with cement that had been placed as an obstacle to impede any possible threat; the sentries' M–16 rifles were loaded; the estimated speed of the truck was 60 miles per hour. As the investigation of the attack progressed, better information was obtained and these "facts" changed. It was learned that there were not pipes filled with cement to impede a truck; the sentries were not killed, and their rifles were not loaded; and that the truck's speed was between 25 and 50 miles per hour.

Because of the differences in the facts revealed, the investigations were protracted. A congressional subcommittee conducted its own investigation, with some members accusing General Kelley of presenting testimony that was "often inaccurate, misleading, and erroneous."[7]

General Kelley was angered by the allegations made against himself and the Corps, and he didn't hide it. The first week after the tragedy was one that would test to an extraordinary degree the leadership, loyalty, emotions, endurance, and values of the Commandant.

The "tentative nature" of the evidence he presented is made clear in some of his responses: "I ask for your patience while I try to tell a story of what we think, at this time happened. . . . For the past week we have been groping at straws, asking ourselves the agonizing questions as to how this could have happened. For all of us it has been a week full of haunting speculation."

On one occasion, he responded: "My remarks, sir, are based on historical facts as I know them at this time, and the purpose and objective of the Long Commission is to learn the details.

"The inquiry to determine the facts in an atmosphere which is conducive to a proper inquiry . . . [that] there will be a complete and thorough examination of this awful tragedy. I would hope that our patience would be sufficient to await the Board's findings." At one point, Kelley stated: "I am making an assumption. . . I did not conduct an investigation."

Finally, he told the commission: "Why don't we let the Long Commission do its job, Sir, instead of speculating on that type of micro-detail? We have to separate the facts, and that is why I applaud Congressman Nichols [William Nichols, D–AL] and his group and also our group that we will have under the Secretary of Defense [Long Commission]. That is essential to our process."[8]

Rarely in Washington has there ever been such a quick and emphatic response from senior elected officials as there was to defend General Kelley against the allegations that he presented "inaccurate, misleading, and erroneous" testimony. Secretary of Defense Weinberger addressed the misinformation allegation in a press statement upon the release of the Long Commission on December 23, 1983:

> I have conveyed to the President my concern regarding recent statements that imply that General P.X. Kelley may have intentionally misled the American People in his testimony before the House Armed Services Committee. That simply is not so. General Kelley was placed in a very difficult position immediately following the attack. There was a lack of solid information concerning the situation in Lebanon at the time. When he was called to testify, General Kelley attempted to be as forthcoming as possible in making available to the Congress all of the information he had received. He did so knowing that the details were incomplete but believing that the Congress and the public had the right to all of the information then available. He noted repeatedly in his testimony that his information was not complete and advised the Committee that it was subject to change as more facts became known. Indeed, it was General Kelley who recommended that I appoint a Commission to investigate the bombing. General Kelley is an outstanding officer and is a credit to the United States Marine Corps. I have every confidence is General Kelley and in his professional abilities.[9]

The Secretary also made it clear there was no coverup in the investigation and conclusions of the Long Commission: "Our action in appointing the Long Commission and the thorough, candid nature of the Commission's report underscores our commitment to a full and frank appraisal of this tragedy. We have the highest commitment to the security of our troops in Lebanon. We appreciate your Committee's deep interest, and we shall review your report with care."[10]

General Kelley gave his own position on the misinformation in a letter dated January 10, 1984, to Congressman Nichols: "As the Commandant of the Marine Corps, I sincerely regret that any early information or testimony provided by me or any other Marine concerning the precise details of the attack was not ultimately supported by evidence. I can assure you that all information provided by Marines concerning this tragedy was the best and most complete that we had at the time. I know I need not tell you of my personal and professional respect for the Congress of the United States. In the future, as in the past, I shall provide testimony which is as honest and forthright as humanly possible.

"In closing, let me say what we all have recognized: that this tragedy was of such immense proportions as to stagger the imagination and outrage the civilized world. Given the circumstances of you investigation, I share with the members of your Subcommittee the considerable emotional strain of their task. The period since 23 October has been one of great stress for all of us."[11]

Chaplain Takesian related one of the conversations he had with General Kelley as the inquiries and investigations developed: "He shared with me an off-camera meeting with two senior members of the House of Representatives. When they suggested that the two Marine commanders in Beirut be court-martialed as soon as possible, 'to get this all behind us,' his refusal was adamant. Appalled, General Kelley informed them that, as a United States Marine, he had taken an oath to support and defend the Constitution, which includes the right to due process.

"The Commandant and I met frequently during that long ordeal, most often in private. I shall always remember one particular morning when, speaking with his usual candor, the General said: 'Eli, I've spent many years of my Marine Corps career here in Washington, and have a lot of respect and admiration for politicians on both sides of the aisle. Several of them have given me invaluable advice and counsel on how the Marine Corps should deal with this, the worst tragedy in its entire peacetime history. However, some others have jumped the gun and are looking for a quick and easy way out. One suggestion, which I find particularly offensive, is that I should become less visible and let responsibility roll down hill. I've always lived by the principle that authority and ultimate responsibility are inseparable. The law gives me the authority of the Commandant and, therefore, I have certain inherent responsibilities. First and foremost, *to obviate any suspicion of a cover-up*. I have, as you know, requested an independent investigation to determine the facts.'

"On another occasion, General Kelley addressed the matter of sweeping dirt under the rug. I vividly recall his words: 'Marines would never expect, or want, their Commandant to lie to them or to lie for them. Therefore, I will not lie to my Marines, to the President of the United States, to Congress, or to the American people!'"[12]

The Long Commission's investigation lasted 7 weeks and included two visits by the commission to Beirut. It examined the mission, rules of engagement, responsiveness of the chain of command, intelligence support, security measures in place before and after the attack, the attack itself, and the adequacy of casualty handling procedures to include offers of assistance from our allies and friends. The Pentagon report authored by Admiral Robert Long recommended "that the Secretary of Defense take whatever administrative or disciplinary action he deems appropriate," citing the failure of the USCINCEUR operational chain of command to monitor and supervise effectively the security measures and procedures employed by the U.S. Multi-National Force (USMNF) on October 23.

The report went on to say, "The Commission concludes that the security measures in effect in the MAU compound were neither commensurate with the increasing level of threat confronting the USMNF nor sufficient to preclude catastrophic losses such as those that were suffered on the morning of 23 October 1983.... The decision to billet approximately one-quarter of the BLT in a single structure contributed to the catastrophic loss of life.

"Based on our findings, the Commission concluded that the BLT commander must take responsibility for the concentration of approximately 350 members of his command in the BLT Headquarters building, thereby providing a lucrative target for attack. Further, the BLT commander modified prescribed alert procedures, thereby degrading security of the compound."[13]

After studying the Long Commission report, President Ronald Reagan spent a weekend with his national security advisor and staff. In his statement on the report at the White House on December 27, 1983, President Reagan commented:

> I have soberly considered the Commission's word about accountability and responsibility of authorities up and down the chain of command. Everywhere, more should be done to anticipate and prepare for a dramatic terrorist assault. We have to come to grips with the fact that today's terrorists are better armed and financed, they are more sophisticated, they're possessed by a fanatical intensity that individuals of a democratic society can only barely comprehend. I do not believe, therefore, that the local commanders on the ground, men who have already suffered quite enough, should be punished for not fully comprehending the nature of today's terrorist threat. If there is to be blame, it properly rests here, in this office and

with this President and I accept responsibility for the bad as well as the good.[14]

This comment is even more significant from the perspective President Reagan shared years later in his autobiography, when referring to the successful military intervention on the island of Grenada and then to the terrorist act at Beirut International Airport, both of which took place during the week of October 23, 1983: "But if that week produced one of the highest of the high points in my eight years in the presidency, the bombing of the Marine barracks in Beirut had produced the lowest of the low."[15]

One of the finest tributes to the character of General Kelley was in an editorial in the *Las Vegas Sun* on December 21, 1983, written by former Nevada Governor Mike O'Callighan:

> Following the killing of 220 Marines by an unprecedented terrorist attack on their Beirut compound, the word was out in Washington that politicians wanted some military heads.
>
> If U.S. Marine Corps Commandant Paul X. Kelley would return from his Beirut inspection tour and offer up a couple of field officers for sacrifice, he would be given a clean bill of health. The heavy loss of life, during what politicians refuse to accept as a war, demanded that somebody be punished publicly. Swift punishment of a couple of military officers would allow the politicians to spend more time campaigning for the 1984 elections and also have clear consciences to comfortably celebrate Thanksgiving, Christmas, and New Year's.
>
> P.X. Kelley, a Marine's Marine, went to Beirut and returned with a full report. He didn't bring back the head of Colonel Timothy Geraghty, the U.S. Marine Commander in Beirut, nor did he blame any individual for what had happened. He reported to Congress the facts and problems he saw as a skilled combat military commander with 33 years of invaluable experience.
>
> P.X. Kelley refused to offer up Tim Geraghty on the political altar of Congress. That's why today Kelley is being hit with the political garbage he knew was coming when he refused to play politics or make excuses. That's why Kelley is Kelley; and every Marine knows their Commandant will never leave him behind if he is dead or wounded.[16]

Commandant Kelley was a fighter. In this crisis, in a tragedy of losing 220 Marines, should he be fired, particularly if the politicians and media were looking for a scapegoat? Kelley was indignant when asked if he would resign in the wake of the unprecedented peacetime catastrophe at the Beirut airport.

"Absolutely not," he told a visitor at Marine Corps headquarters in Arlington. "Why should I? What purpose would it serve? You should see the letters I have received—over 150—some of them from families of victims." One of the most meaningful was from the father of a Marine who was killed:

Dear General Kelley:

I wish to express my sincerest appreciation for the great effort you and the Marine Corps put forth so that October 23rd would not pass without our Marines being properly remembered. We all thank you and your Marines from the bottom of our hearts.

My son, Corporal Michael C. Sauls, was a third-generation Marine when he was killed in Beirut. It was a special honor for my mother, Michael's grandmother, to be escorted so gallantly by your Marines. That must have reminded her of her husband, her son and her grandson. We are all grateful for the kind, efficient, and respectful treatment we received while visiting Camp Lejeune.

When in the past year I've heard discouraging talk of blame and charges of possible incompetence, I wish I could shield your ears and the ears of other Commanders from such talk. But, I realize I can't and I want to apologize for my more critical fellow citizens. They don't understand that Marine Commanders need not be reminded of their responsibilities.

I would like to express to you and the other Commanders on behalf of that segment of us, who the press chooses not to search out, that we hold no feelings of blame for you, the Marine Corps, or the President. We know our sons were doing their duty as it was handed to them and we are very proud of them and their service. We want nothing to mar the remembrance of their sacrifice or your future.

You said, "We in the Marine Corps are family," and I believe we are, and if we are, I lost a son, but the Marine Corps lost 241. Sir, I grieve for you. We will never forget your kind thoughtfulness in our loss.

With the greatest respect and kindest regards from a former Marine.

Henry C. Sauls, Jr.[17]

General Kelley stressed, "I will not resign. In fact, I'll invite you to my retirement parade on 30 June 1987."

General Kelley said, "There is responsibility implicit in command. I am responsible for the conduct of every Marine—even though we are not technically responsible." By refusing to take an easy way out, or to protect himself, or to victimize others by seeking scapegoats, the 28th Commandant remained steadfast and faithful in caring for his Corps of Marines.

## The V–22 Aircraft Accidents

In an interview I had with Commandant James L. Jones, I asked if he agreed with the maxim, "Fix the problem, not the blame." He responded: "I absolutely subscribe to that philosophy. I do believe in accountability, and I also believe that whoever is the senior guy should stand up and hold himself accountable."[18]

Just as General Kelley had a tragic loss of Marines, so did General Jones. "The hardest times for me as Commandant," he told me, "were the V–22 crashes which killed the Marines who were aboard."[19] There were two such incidents during General Jones' tenure as Commandant.

When asked to comment on the tragedy before Congress or the media, General Jones told one interviewer, "I didn't try to pass the blame off on someone else. I did what was expected when I appeared before the Senate and the House to explain how it could have happened. It was definitely the lowest part in my tour as Commandant. The irony of it is that, by law, Service chiefs are not supposed to be involved in the acquisition process. In other words, we are supposed to identify our requirements and the acquisition community decides on how to field the equipment. They give it to you and you say, 'Thank you very much.'

"I believe strongly in this concept and have believed in it my entire Marine Corps career. When the time comes on your watch, whether you are a platoon commander, company commander, battalion commander, whatever command you have the responsibility for and if something goes wrong, you have to stand up and be recognized."[20]

## The Controversial Marriage Policy

Commandant Carl E. Mundy, Jr., was asked in his oral history interview: "The 11th of August [1993] was not necessarily a happy day for you. SecDef Aspin took you to task for a directive you had issued that would have barred the enlistment of married recruits after 1995. Would you review that issue for us?"

General Mundy answered: "As the new Chairman of the Joint Chiefs, General Shalikashvili, was being announced at a press conference in the Rose Garden, the first question asked of the President after he had made the announcement was, 'Mr. President, the Marines have announced that they are not going to take married people anymore. What do you think of that?' The President responded, 'Why, I am astounded.' So the marriage policy really did not get off to a very good start at the outset.

"The background on the marriage policy goes back a number of years. During General Gray's tenure, and indeed even before that time, all of us who had been commanding in the field realized that for a force comprised of young Americans that we drive very hard, keep away from home most of the time, and place great demands upon, youthful marriage is difficult. When you have a young man who is married and living in a trailer park somewhere, in some cases to a 14- or 16-year-old wife—a reality not recognized in the newspapers—who has come from the hills of Kentucky to go to Camp Lejeune or Oceanside to live with a young man who is on the demands of a high tempo training and operational schedule; that is just not a stable marriage. And when we take him away, within two days after he is gone, in comes a Red Cross telegram that says: 'Wife cannot cope,' and he has to go home on emergency leave. He is a loss to his unit; in effect, a casualty. So we had a tremendous drain on the effectiveness of deployed units because of these unstable marriages.

"Even in routine garrison training it was a real problem and every junior leader, staff NCO and company grade officer was telling us, 'I spend more time as a sergeant or lieutenant dealing with the problems of three or four of my young married people than I do leading my platoon and teaching it how to maneuver in the field.'"[21]

Over time, the Headquarters staff looked at this problem extensively. Mundy attended several meetings. General Walt Boomer, his Assistant Commandant, wanted to personally take the problem and run with it and did so from the standpoint of developing a position. That decision called for reducing the relatively small number of married enlistees and developing a counseling program on marriage for all young enlistees to make them aware of the difficulties of youthful marriage in the Corps.

Mundy continued: "The staff put together a package from the Manpower Department and came forth with an all-Marine message [ALMAR] that laid out the position. The last line stated: 'We [USMC Headquarters] will work toward the eventuality, in 1995, of eliminating the 5 percent of recruits that we were taking who were married before enlistment.'

"Our intent was to bring in the recruits, provide them counseling on the demands of service in the Corps and on the need for maturity and stability during their extended periods of absence. Thereafter, there was no restriction on their right to marry. We just wanted them to be responsibly aware of the difficulties before the fact. That was the policy."[22]

General Mundy was traveling when the staffing package came to the Office of the Commandant. As he recalled: "The routing sheet was appropriately initialed by my Military Secretary, but thereafter, erroneously returned to the Manpower Department instead of being held for my review, approval, and initial. The staff officer in Manpower, having received the package with an initial apparently did not take note of whose initial, and assuming it had been approved, released the ALMAR.

"When I returned to my office, General Boomer was waiting for me to tell me, 'We have a firestorm brewing on our marriage policy.' To which I responded, 'What marriage policy?' He replied, 'The one promulgated in the ALMAR.' And I responded, 'What ALMAR?' I had not seen the draft ALMAR; and had I, I would have undertaken to broach the subject with SecNav and/or SecDef before promulgating the policy. However, the water was over the dam.

"All this occurred about 1600 in the afternoon. Secretary Dalton was traveling to give a speech in San Francisco that day. I had a call placed to him and told him, 'Mr. Secretary, you're about to go before an audience, and possibly the press, and it's likely that you'll be asked about the Marines' new marriage policy. So, let me bring you up to speed on what our policy seeks to do.'

"After briefing him, Dalton responded, 'I want to be supportive, but I believe we really need to sit down and review this. Is there a way the message can be pulled back until we have time to work on it together?'

"I responded that we could, and should, do that and that I would recall the ALMAR, pending our review.

"Because Secretary Dalton was out of town and the press was heating up on the issue, I thought it wise also to call the Secretary of Defense, and so I placed a call to his office.

"The Secretary was out but his Military Assistant, General John Jumper, said, 'Boy! We're really getting a lot of interest on this, and the White House wants to know what's going on.'

"I responded, 'Tell them that I will be glad to come over—or send someone over—to explain the policy. Tell them also that Secretary Dalton and I have discussed the issue, and that I have recalled the ALMAR in order to more thoroughly review the policy.'"

At about 2100 that evening, General Jumper called Mundy back, telling him, "Secretary Aspin needs to say that he told you to recall the message."

"After a brief discussion, I said, 'Okay.'

"It was clear that the Secretary was under great pressure and needed, politically, to show that he was in charge. Thus, the press the following day carried the story that SecDef had directed the Marine Corps to rescind the policy, and so the 'heat' remained on me and the Secretary got to ride off on a white horse."

The following morning, the Joint Chiefs were to meet with Secretary Aspin.

Mundy recalled: "When I arrived, General Powell and my Service counterparts all took delight in prodding me good-naturedly. Each of us had 'been over the barrel' over something or other from time to time, and the camaraderie among those of us during my watch was such that we almost always reached out to give a counterpart support when one of us was taking Washington flak. I recall that one of my counterparts had even pulled off his wedding ring 'so Mundy wouldn't come after me!' which, of course, brought a laugh. When Secretary Aspin came in, he came over and put an arm around my shoulder and punched me lightly in the ribs.

"Secretary Dalton, however, turned out to be a bit 'hotter under the collar.' He was out of town when all this took place, and became quite upset when he learned that Secretary Aspin was getting political credit for giving the Marine Corps a slap instead of him, the Secretary of the Navy.

"Dalton sent word through his Marine aide that the Secretary would be landing at Andrews Air Force Base outside Washington at 2200 that night, and he wanted me on hand to meet him. I was there when his plane landed, and we proceeded directly into the VIP Lounge, where we sat down and he read me the riot act. 'I'm the Secretary of the Navy, and you had no business going around me to the Secretary of Defense,' was his thesis.

"I responded, 'Well, Mr. Secretary, you are right under normal circumstances, but you were out of town, and since you're new to town, let me tell you that when the press begins throwing cordwood on the fire and the White House gets excited, it's action time. In your absence, I had to inform SecDef so he could handle it with the White House.'"[23]

The following day, there was a Pentagon press conference on the subject of the Marine Corps policy, and Mundy took it to try and explain what the Corps was trying to address with the policy. After his opening statement, a reporter asked, "I'm told by a reliable source that you didn't see the ALMAR before it was sent out."

Mundy didn't look for someone to blame. He responded, "Look, I'm the Commandant of the Marine Corps, and I'm responsible for what goes on in the Corps. Hang this one around my neck! A leader takes responsibility for what his organization does, and I wasn't about to get up and be seen to lay blame on one of my staff officers for an honest mistake in judgment, or even a blunder."

Mundy continued, "So that's the saga of the 'Marriage Policy.' I certainly took a lot of heat in the press during the episode, but I also got a lot of support from inside the Corps, from moms and dads around the country, and from members of Congress, like Congressman Ike Skelton, who called to say that he was ready to hold hearings on the subject of the difficulties inflicted on the services by youthful, immature marriages. He was dissuaded, however, by Secretary Aspin's directive that the matter be the subject of a study by OSD to determine whether or not it was a problem. As one might imagine in so tender a subject as marriage, a few months later, the study conducted by some think tank concluded that there was no problem. Unfortunately, the researchers never apparently got around to talking to the young leaders who had then—and now—to deal with the day-to-day problems at the small unit level.

"An ending to this saga that should not go unrecorded occurred at the White House Christmas reception a few months before I retired. Preceding that event, President and Mrs. Clinton had traveled to China a few months earlier, and on their return had stopped for a couple of days rest and recuperation at the Marine Corps Base at Kanehoe Bay, Hawaii. While there, Mrs. Clinton visited some of the child care centers and met and lunched with a number of the Marine wives. As was the procedure at the Clinton's Christmas receptions, guests were greeted and photographed with the President and First Lady in front of a beautifully decorated Christmas tree. As my wife and I moved across the room when our turn came, Mrs. Clinton took a few steps toward me, grasped my arm, and said, 'You know, you had a point on that marriage policy. There are a great many young wives out there who are having real difficulties without their husbands being around.' The President added, 'You took a lot of heat on that, and maybe we ought to reopen the issue.' It being Christmas, my response was light. I said, 'Mr. President, that's a great idea. This time, you suggest the ban, and I'll be in direct support!'

"That is the overlong saga of the ill-fated marriage policy. As a matter of fact, the policy we sought to put in place in 1993 was subsequently quietly implemented by the Corps, and is, I hope, helping with the problem of immature marriages in the Corps today. We are today doing everything that that ALMAR set out to do in terms of counseling and the education programs and everything else except not taking that very small five percent of enlisted. We could have managed that down if we chose to."[24]

In closing, Mundy elaborated on his comments to the press conference when he was challenged about the premature release of the ALMAR: "You take responsibility for what your organization does and you don't try and abdicate that by saying, 'Some lieutenant did it and it's not my fault.' The lieutenant is one of your officers. Throughout my career, every time that I kicked one into the grand stands, I never really needed to be told. You know, you know when you've screwed up. You don't have to have somebody counsel you and say, 'You didn't do this well.' You know it and it hurts very badly. But I never got in trouble by walking into a boss and saying, 'Sir, I didn't do this one too well and I learned from it,' nor did I ever get anything other than you know, occasionally, a 'Goddamn, Mundy, I don't see how you could have done that but get out of here and get on with it.'

"So I was never hurt, I'll put it in that sense, other than internally in my own self being, by the mistakes that I made along the way when I'd admit it."[25]

### Allegations of Racism

During his tenure as Commandant, General Mundy had a second challenge that received considerable attention. It provides insight into his acceptance of accountability and provides lessons learned, particularly on how to handle the media.

On October 31, 1993, General Mundy was a guest on the CBS News program *60 Minutes*. The actual interview with Leslie Stahl had been held in the Office of the Commandant on August 26, 1993. As background, there had been allegations of minority racism and a lack of promotions for minority officers in the Marine Corps. In response to allegations that blacks were discriminated against in promotions, General Mundy was quoted as stating that in the Marine Officers Basic School, whites outperform minorities in just about every category and specifically that, "In some key military skills, we find that the minority officers do not shoot as well . . . don't swim as well and when you give them a compass and send them across the terrain in a night navigation exercise, they don't do as well at that sort of thing."[26]

This issue requires further discussion to understand its ramifications. First, why was General Mundy interviewed? Second, what can future Marine leaders in positions of responsibility learn from it?

Mundy's oral history interviewer asked: "On the afternoon of 13 July, you had an office visit by Brigadier General Les Palm and Colonel John Shotwell who apparently convinced you that you should submit to an interview by *60 Minutes*, the CBS news magazine. What was the purpose of this interview, and why were Brigadier General Palm and Colonel Shotwell persuasive that this was to the advantage of the Marine Corps?"

General Mundy responded: "Brigadier General Palm was at that time the Director of Manpower, Plans, and Policy and thereby more or less oversaw the policies that applied to minorities, as well as to all personnel situations in the Marine Corps. Colonel Shotwell was Director of Public Affairs. We had been approached some several months earlier by *60 Minutes* based on complaints from a minority officer, a captain, who claimed to represent a group of disgruntled minority officers.

"Although it never turned out to be much of a group movement, there were at least some who apparently shared the complaining officer's concerns and *60 Minutes* picked up on the group idea. The complainant was a black officer, and is today a major. He had been passed over for promotion and his assertion was that as he looked at promotion statistics, the success rate for non-minorities was significantly out of proportion to minorities and he was right. That said, there were reasons behind some of the statistics.

"*60 Minutes* decided to take the issue on. The Staff recommended, and I concurred, that Brigadier General Palm, as the cognizant Headquarters staff officer, was the appropriate interviewee. He was subsequently interviewed by Leslie Stahl, and the bottom line is that the interview had not come off well, and many of the challenges to Marine Corps fairness had gone unanswered, or had not come across clearly.

"My Public Affairs people, not only Colonel Shotwell, but principally, Lieutenant Colonel Robin Higgins, who was really overseeing this effort, came to me to advise that, 'We are not going to fare well at all in this interview. We need to put you in the game. The only way that *60 Minutes* will agree to a re-interview is with you. They are not going to do it with anybody else.' After consideration of their points, I said, 'Okay, put me in the game,' and we set upon the briefings and discussions necessary to give me the details necessary for the interview.

"At this point, it's important to point out that the addressal of the problem of disproportionate statistics in the screening and promotion of minority officers was a long-term effort that had been going on at the Headquarters well before interest by *60 Minutes.*

"Shortly after I became Commandant, I sat down with Lieutenant General Terry Cooper, the Deputy Chief of Staff for Manpower, and Brigadier General Charles Krulak, the Director of Personnel, and told them that I wanted to explore all options possible to expand opportunities for women, consistent with those places in the Corps where they could or could not be assigned—ground combat, for example—and that I wanted also to redouble our efforts at getting a foothold into minority officer recruitment, and retention.

"When I was an Officer Selection Officer as a captain, we had essentially the same dilemmas in getting quality minority officer applicants—principally, African-Americans—to apply for the Marine Corps, as well as retaining them in the Corps after we had recruited them. Over the years, the Corps had done a number of studies, and tried a number of techniques, but we continued to face the dilemma of retention of quality minority officers.

"My intent was that we get away from the notion that the Marine Corps was seeking to oppress or prevent opportunity for anybody, and to gain insight into whatever factors were causing this. At the same time, I wanted to ensure that we upheld the demanding standards that have long characterized Marine officers.

"The Manpower Department undertook a study, under the oversight of a Quality Management Board, to gather and analyze statistics, and to determine, as best we could, the reasons behind the statistics. This takes time, and the study had been going on for a year or more before the *60 Minutes* evolution came to pass. The network relayed that they had received complaints from some minority officers; that they knew we had initiated a study to determine reasons; and those two facts, together, formed the basis for the *60 Minutes* request for interview."

The interview from which excerpts were taken for the actual program that aired, General Mundy said, "was two and a half hours long, and the lesson learned from that, is never give a taped, two-and-a-half-hour interview to an interviewer who is approaching the issue with an already negative point of view. The theme that *60 Minutes* came in with was that the Marine Corps was a racist institution, which was proved by statistics, and by the complaint of the small group of officers who had approached them. They maintained that Marine Corps screening and training policies at

OCS and the Basic School were conscientiously designed to be discriminatory, and that our promotion boards were clearly rigged because we did not promote at a balanced rate.

"It's important to note, also, that as they were setting up for the interview, *60 Minutes* asked that there be no duplicate taping of the interview by the Marine Corps, because to do so would result in technical interference in the quality of production. My staff acquiesced, and from that, we learned another valuable lesson: Never give an on-tape controversial interview without duplicate backup.

"Leslie Stahl was a delightful lady, and we had a warm conversation before taping started. It was my impression then, and now, that she came with no biased position, but it became clear that the *60 Minutes* producer did. As the interview progressed, I felt good about the way it seemed to go. I had really done my homework and had answers for every question. That, perhaps, was one of the reasons the interview took so long, because Leslie Stahl would pose a *60 Minutes* scripted thesis and question, and I would say, 'Let me explain to you.' I would then offer an explanation of the statistics or circumstances alleged, after which Leslie would frequently say to her producer, 'O.K., let's stop the cameras. Where do we go from here?' and her producer would then suggest a different approach or question. In hindsight, we should have stopped the interview after a certain period, but my staff and I were so anxious to provide complete and well-reasoned answers to the complexities of the issue that we continued for two-and-one-half hours.

"As a result of the foregoing, *60 Minutes* came out of the interview with a couple of hours of footage which was clipped down to two or three minutes on-air. The result was a piece that was far from fair or balanced. I was seen on the air to give answers to questions that had been cut from elsewhere in the interview, or which was simply a 'sound bite' from a lengthy response to a complex question. It was truly a 'cut and paste' job.

"To be sure, there were some blunders on our part in not controlling the interview better, but its worst impact was that the way it was pasted together and presented cast the Commandant of the Marine Corps as coming across in a demeaning way about some truly fine Marines. I doubt *60 Minutes* had any understanding of the terribly demoralizing impact of their production on an institution that believes in its leader, and he in those of all colors who comprise it.

"As a somewhat 'light' ending to what was not at all a 'light' moment for me, the day following the airing of the *60 Minutes* fabricated segment, I received a call from a greatly admired friend, General Colin Powell. Colin was, by then, retired and on a book writing and speaking circuit. Characteristic of this good friend and fine leader who had never failed to give me his support when I needed it, he opened with, 'Carl, I'm sitting here in a swanky, high-rise hotel in Palm Beach, Florida, waiting to give a speech tonight. I just wanted to call and tell you that I can shoot, and I can navigate—but I can't swim worth a damn! However, I'm going straight down to the pool and start learning how!' That was his way of lightening what he knew was a heavy burden of stress brought on by this fabrication. He followed by saying, 'I wish you had given me a call before you went on *60 Minutes*. I'd have told you not to get within a mile of them!'"[27]

## Vietnam: The Shooting of Civilians

During the Vietnam War, the mass media brought into every American home the bloodiness, tragedy, confusion, and horror of an insurgency war in brief television clips, an extensive volume of newsprint, and a considerable number of biased and partisan books. It was a struggle for the average citizen to sort out the extensive information being disseminated, and this created a crisis in public confidence, more so at the time than in any previous war in the 20th century.

What was the truth? What was the influence of the media in shaping our nation's thinking and its impact on our national policy in the Vietnam War? What can be learned from the experiences of our combat leaders?

The military became the focal point of what developed into press antagonism toward the administration. The media criticism of our involvement in Vietnam was initially not informative to the American people, so suspicion of the government developed, and the secrecy encouraged "exposé reporting." The government's apparent inability to respond to the hostile press contributed to a major psychological victory for the enemy. The credibility of the administration and, therefore, our military deteriorated as the war progressed. Many Americans did not believe the government was telling the entire truth.

It reached the point where reporters giving negative coverage were accused by the military and civilians of siding with the enemy and being disloyal to our country in a time of crisis; that the news media were too interested in reporting failures; and, in the case of the Tet offensive in particular, not emphasizing the heroism of our military, reporting the battle not as a decisive defeat militarily for the Vietcong, but as a victory for them. The press was not addressing clear communist failures and was portraying the Vietnamese as nice guys who were victimized by U.S. military. In the opinion of the administration, the media provided aid, comfort, and encouragement to Ho Chi Minh. The press coverage of the Tet offensive portrayed it as if it was a U.S. loss, which it was not, and unfortunately was an adverse turning point in the Vietnam War.

On February 28, 1970, there was considerable press coverage on allegations that 5 enlisted Marines had killed 16 Vietnamese civilians, 5 women and 11 children, in the village of Sonthang, on February 19, 1970. It is important to discuss this incident in detail because of the lessons that can be learned from it on handling the media for future commanders who will undoubtedly face similar crises.

To better understand the significance of the allegations and put the incident into perspective, it is appropriate to review an earlier incident in Vietnam referred to as My Lai, the lessons learned, and the contrast on how the Marine Corps handled its incident so successfully.

A serious and alarming allegation had been made on March 29, 1969, by former soldier Ron Ridenour when he wrote to several Congressmen and high-level government officials that, in March 1968, war crimes occurred in the Vietnam village of My Lai. The charge was that Charlie Company of the American Division's 11th Infantry Brigade massacred numerous Vietnamese civilians, primarily women, children, and old men.

When General William C. Westmoreland, the Chief of Staff of the Army, learned of this, he ordered an immediate investigation. It was necessary in this incident to determine exactly what happened and who was involved.ABrote General Westmoreland:

> Almost as deplorable as the events alleged was the possibility that officers of the 11th Brigade and the American Division had either covered up the incident or failed to make a comprehensive investigation. The developing evidence in the criminal investigation and in indications of command dereliction led Secretary of the Army Resor and me to arrange for an additional formal inquiry into the adequacy of the criminal investigation and the possible suppression of information. When I learned that some members of President Nixon's administration wanted to whitewash any possible negligence within the chain of command, I threatened through a White House official to exercise my prerogative as a member of the Joint Chiefs of Staff to go personally to the President and object. I squelched any further pressure for whitewash.[28]

Westmoreland appointed Lieutenant General Ray Peers to head the board of inquiry because:

> he had a reputation throughout the Army for objectivity and fairness . . . and had also been a division commander in Vietnam and thus was thoroughly familiar with conditions; he had never had jurisdiction over any activity in Quang Ngai province. Because he had entered the Army through ROTC at the University of California at Los Angeles, there could be no presumption that ties among brother officers from West Point would be involved. As a result of evidence developed by the Peers board, charges were brought against twelve officers, primarily involving dereliction of duty in suppressing information and failing to obey lawful regulations. These included the former Americal Division commander, General Koster, who at the time of the investigation was Superintendent of the Military Academy. Lest any findings reflect adversely on the Academy, he requested relief from that post. . . . Something had to be remiss in the Americal Division's chain of command if anything as reprehensible and colossal as the My Lai massacre occurred without some responsible official either knowing or at least suspecting.[29]

General Koster, as commander of the Americal Division, had ordered an investigation, but Westmoreland believed that he made a basic error in assigning the investigation to the commander of the responsible unit. As matters developed, Koster was only censured. General Peers thought that this proposed action against Koster was "a travesty of justice and would establish a precedent that would be difficult for the Army to live down. . . . I felt the matter should have been adjudicated in a duly appointed court martial, which would have served the best interests of General Koster, the Army and the nation." Field-grade officers were asking why top officers got off with dismissal of charges whereas the lower grades were subjected to courts-martial.[30]

The investigation resulted in charges against four officers and nine enlisted men and ultimately with trials of two officers and three enlisted men. In the criminal proceedings, all but the platoon leader were in one way or another exonerated, but First Lieutenant William L. Cally, Jr., was charged with the murder of more than 100 civilians. On March 29, 1971, he was convicted personally with the murder of at least 22. He was sentenced to dismissal from the Army and confinement at hard labor for life, but the sentence was later reduced by judicial review to 20 years. After General Westmoreland's retirement, the Secretary of the Army reduced it to 10 years, a decision sustained by President Nixon. Cally was later released on parole.[31]

The investigation thoroughly studied whether General Westmoreland should have been guilty and exonerated him. It was certainly not a "whitewash" of Westmoreland. All one has to do is read General Peers' report to understand that he sought the truth and showed no favoritism to the Army Chief of Staff. The importance in the Cally case in fixing the blame was to ensure that this type of incident never happened again.

The Marine Corps had an incident involving the death of civilians and handled it quite differently. Lieutenant General Charles Cooper, who at the time of this incident was a Lieutenant Colonel and the battalion commander of the accused Marine patrol, related the events: "At night I slept in the operations center bunker. I had a cot in there. I stayed awake as long as I could with two radios in each ear of different frequencies to listen to what was going on in the field."[32]

On February 19, 1970, an incident came to his attention that he found disturbing and suspicious. "Early in the evening, a message from B Company reported that their patrol had established a hasty ambush and encountered a column of fifteen or twenty VC. The patrol reported killing six male soldiers and one female. The details were very sketchy and immediately aroused my concern. I told the S3 to ask for more information and to ask specifically about enemy weapons. Lieutenant Ambort said he would get more info when the patrol returned. He called later to say they had one captured weapon, an SKS rifle. I was not convinced that the report was an accurate one and asked for the serial number of the rifle. In a few minutes a response came in with a number. I told Ron Ambort we would be at his position early the next morning, and that I'd want to see the rifle and talk to the members of the patrol.

"This was the beginning of an investigation into what I've termed a tragic 'incident.' It is a good example of both the irony and the heartbreak produced by this strange war we were fighting. I am describing it carefully, because some dedicated Marine historians have become so mesmerized by the 'laws of war' that their historical accounts of what a handful of young, bitter, frightened Marines were facing became more idealistic than realistic, in my opinion.

"The next morning, after I learned about the incident, Major Theer and I proceeded to the B Company position by helicopter. As they produced a rifle, I remembered that they had reported a captured rifle earlier that week.

I asked if this was the same one. The answer was a less-than-convincing 'negative.' I remained skeptical but didn't press the point further.

"Then I was surprised to learn that this had been an all-volunteer patrol. The commander of the second platoon, Lieutenant Carney, had asked for volunteers. Here in front of me were the five very junior Marines who had stepped forward. The patrol leader was a machinegunner, Lance Corporal Herrod, who had arrived recently from the Third Division. Machinegunners do not normally lead patrols of this type. The five did not know each other well and had never worked closely together. None of the experienced NCOs had gone out with them.

"One of the five had just joined our battalion from the Third Reconnaissance Battalion. His rifle had a shortened barrel, a folding stock, and a recon-style silencer on the muzzle. Another member, a black Marine, had joined the battalion less than two weeks earlier. To me, this tossed-together patrol appeared to represent a breakdown in professionalism.

"I was convinced that B Company's patrol report was false, and I wanted to check out the area in question. Soon after that, a small Marine patrol visited the hamlet of Son Thang and made a startling discovery. Only 500 yards from B Company's position they found the bodies of 16 women and children. There were spent shell casings all over the place. Although it looked awfully bad initially, I did remember that B Company had had a firefight in this area the previous day and had lost a Marine in the ambush. These people could be victims of that battle. But my instincts told me that wasn't the case. After discussing it briefly with Dick Theer, I told him to have B Company return to the base area. And I ordered Lieutenant Grant to collect all the available information, take pictures of the remains, and then bury them in the hamlet before returning. He was also to identify and describe the location of each of the bodies.

"B Company came in early the next morning. I called for Ron Ambort and his five Marines to report to me personally in my hootch. I wanted to see them as a group: to tell them what we knew about their actions, and that we knew they had submitted false official reports. They all started to blurt out their stories, but I stopped them and warned them of their rights. I told them that this was very serious business, and that there would undoubtedly be trials to sort out what had happened. I added that I would ask the Commanding General to have them tried before combat-experienced Marine officers, and that I intended to offer my own testimony about the battlefield environment we were facing in Que Son Valley. I told them that my S3, Major Theer, would be the initial investigating officer, and he would be the next person to talk to them. This was the last occasion on which I talked to the five Marines as a group. In the next day or so, they were sent to pretrial confinement in the III MAF brig.

"After the enlisted men left, I informed Ron Ambort that I was deeply disappointed in him, and that he would be relieved of his command the following day. He had not realized the full extent of the tragedy until I laid out what the S2 patrol had unearthed. He had been protecting his troops, but now he was crushed to realize the gravity of what occurred. The facts weren't all in by any means, but the picture was filling in rapidly.

"I had watched their trauma from close up. On the one hand, they had seen artillery and airstrikes destroy hamlets from which they had received fire and where Marines had died. Artillery and airstrikes are impersonal weapons and are not directed at individuals. Troops use personal weapons to disable individual enemies. They are expected to be discerning and they must be responsible. But who is the enemy when a child has just helped spring an ambush on your platoon—an ambush that killed your platoon sergeant, who was also your good friend? This was a very tough call. The four trials showed how touchy it was: they convicted two of the men and acquitted two others.

"Late that afternoon, the patrol returned after carrying out its grisly orders. I had John Curnutt join us as Dick Theer and I debriefed the entire patrol and viewed the photos. Lieutenant Grant was a thorough and responsible officer. He had a topnotch SNCO assistant, and they both gave us a complete account of what they had discovered. After dismissing them, I picked up the land line telephone to talk to Colonel Codispoti, my regimental commander, at LZ Baldy. I told him there'd been a very significant happening, something that required me to fly to his headquarters that night to report it. Without being specific, I strongly suggested he call General Wheeler and ask him to send his Assistant Division Commander, Brigadier General Bill Doehler, to Baldy to receive my brief also. I simply stated it was that important.

"Colonel Codispoti accepted my recommendations. He offered to request a helo for me, and we set a time. I asked that only he, his XO, and General Doehler attend my brief. Again, he acquiesced. Then, as later, in this most difficult situation for a battlefield commander, my superiors at all levels were supportive and cooperative.

"I spent about an hour briefing them on the situation, the battlefield circumstances, B Company's background, and a bit on the five very inexperienced Marines that had been sent out. There were few questions. I gave the Polaroid photos to General Doehler and spent about half an hour writing out in longhand what I had briefed them on.

"Later that evening, after returning to FSB Ross, I received a phone call from General Wheeler. I had worked for General Wheeler in the Second Division. We had a close relationship. He had all the facts currently available and didn't press me for more information. He told me he was going to report the incident up the line.[33] He said, 'Charlie, we've got to get this out to the media.'

"I said, 'I agree totally.'

"General Wheeler asked, 'How do you think we can do it?'

"I said, 'Well, I think you've got to look at how many members of the press we should take.' We agreed on a group of 25 to 30.

"But, I said, 'I think about a maximum number would be about 30 that we can handle. You can put them in a big helicopter. I would like to have them come down about mid-morning or later and I personally will brief them. The ground rules are that they should not feel that they will be able to run around our fire base and talk to anybody.'

"They will see everything. I will escort them and I'll show them with these 20-power binoculars we have. They can look at the area where the battle was, or this incident. I will take them down at a little dugout we have and I'll answer all their questions and tell them about it, everything that I can."

The media arrived exactly on schedule. There were about 20 of them, including a woman from a European wire service. All were carrying cameras, including several of the bulky TV shoulder cameras. The III MAF press officer with them handed Cooper a list. Every major news gathering agency was present, including international wire services and radio. They were escorted into an underground briefing bunker with a large area map displayed.

Cooper introduced himself asking each of them to briefly stand up and do the same. Some of the top U.S. correspondents were present.

"I got in there and they had everybody from the *New York Times*, *Washington Post*, ABC, CBS. I think Ron Nesson who later became a White House press aide was one of the correspondents there. But there was one major network that wasn't there. I think maybe it was NBC. We had Reuters, *London Times*.[34]

"I told them that we had discovered the bodies of 16 women and children in a hamlet near the fire base. We had reason to believe that a patrol of five Marines from B Company that was in the vicinity the previous evening could be responsible. The matter was under investigation, so names of individuals would not be available. I continued with a description of the type of warfare we were conducting in this hotly contested area. I depicted the area as 'Indian country,' a free-fire zone from which all friendly families had been removed by the South Vietnamese government, and noted that many of the hostiles we encountered daily were women and even children. I cited the several recent incidents involving B Company.

"I told them basically that this was a hard-pressed battalion. We were right in a free-fire zone and we were right astride the main route of the enemy, and we had taken some pretty good hits. I told them that B Company was a proud, aggressive, and tough fighting unit that had suffered heavy casualties in recent fighting. Then I spent some time discussing the 'fog of war' that had prevailed in this valley since I had assumed command slightly over a month ago.

"When I got through of course, I briefed them on the map and I took them up and showed them the little rocky knoll that went up about 30 feet. I took them up to the top of that and I said, 'Keep your head down.' Whether by design or not, the area for the briefing was an 'eye-opener.'

"About the time I said, 'Keep your head down,' we received machine-gun fire. It was long range but it was spreading all over the place. You know where it was coming from? That damn village, that little hamlet. I returned mortar fire. The media was watching this return fire we were putting out shooting at the place I was talking about.

"The briefing went well. There were good questions to which I responded calmly—until one reporter really raised my hackles. He referred to the incident as a 'mini My Lai' and I exploded. I asked him to stand up. I noted that we had some civilian deaths that concerned me deeply as they always did. These men could not be labeled guilty until all the facts were in and they had undergone a trial, if that were to become necessary. 'To equate this with My Lai burns a hole in my britches! We called you in two days after the incident. We're trying to get on top of a situation that we discovered just hours after it occurred. We're being honest, frank, and professional about the entire matter. This is no My Lai, and you'd better find a better synonym if you want to write or talk about the proud Marines of this fighting battalion. We've got problems aplenty, but we deal with them! We don't hide them or cover them up. This is a nasty war. It isn't neat and tidy, but we are responsible for what we do or don't do. I don't shrink from that.' The reporter apologized."[35]

So much can be learned from the way Cooper handled this incident. He answered questions, then went outside the bunker where there were TV cameras. Two of them taped him and it was on the major networks. His briefing was on the evening news all over the world after that.

"Within 24 hours the story and my face were on the front pages of newspapers all over the country and abroad. Clippings that my family and friends saved showed me that the reporting had been accurate and free of innuendo. The media did not render any judgment in advance, but 1/7 wasn't to escape media scrutiny for the rest of my tour. The ordeal just beginning would not be pleasant, but the much-maligned press always treated us fairly and factually, as we had them." Extensive coverage was to last for more than 6 months.

"Basically, that media briefing that I gave was probably the best thing we could ever do. I told the reporters: 'Anytime that you want to come back, if you want to get your boots muddy, I'll arrange that. I'll get you out with the rifle company. If you want to go with me into the field, I'll take you. I don't want a big gaggle and I don't want a camera running around. You can take some still pictures but I don't want any TV cameras.'

"They would come up to my hut and talk to me for an hour or so about my concept and tactics and so forth. We had quite a turnaround.

"The media became kind of embedded. Of course, they covered these courts-martial like it was one of these trials out in California. The last court-martial, the one where I had gone home and came back, in this little court-martial room, you know."

The best testimonial of his leadership in handling this incident with character and professionalism was his account that "the day I left to get on my 'freedom bird' to come home the second time, a delegation of reporters from the press center came out to send me off.

"There must have been 25 or 30 of them. They wanted to shake my hand and tell me how they admired me and respected me. They put a lei around my neck. I want to tell you what the lei was. It was about eight canteens tied together with bandoliers. You know the cloth frame that holds the bullets.

"They had scotch, rum, gin, and vodka. They told me, 'Please offer this to the stewardess on the plane and serve it to the troops.' There were some very sentimental people there telling me goodbye. With a great sigh of relief that the whole thing was over I flew off."[36]

When asked why he had once said that he was "the perfect guy to have this tragedy happen to," Lieutenant General Cooper offered, "I was a student in the Army War College in 1969. I had written my thesis on the role of the press in Vietnam and its influence on the war. General Westmoreland had returned from Vietnam and was appointed Army Chief of Staff. He spoke to our War College class. In his presentation he asked some of us to look into the role of the press and asked for a studied analysis of it since it exerted so much influence on the war. I'm not sure My Lai had happened. I guess it had. I was the only guy that decided to take the mission and to do it, by myself. There were five Army classmates who went together and formed a group to research the issue and all five wrote in a joint thesis together. I took off on my own and I think I wrote a real good paper.

"I had really studied this issue. My conclusion in my thesis was that as long as you were honest and professional, you would be square with them, as long, of course, as it didn't endanger security. My thesis was hard on General Westmoreland on the way his command worked with the press."

A significant tribute to General Cooper in the way he handled this incident surprised him. "I received a letter," he told me, "handwritten, from General Westmoreland stating he wished to hell he had read my thesis before he took command."

Cooper handled this potentially explosive incident remarkably well, and his example provides a lesson from which Marine leaders of all ranks can benefit.

## The Ribbon Creek Incident: The Drowning of Six Recruits

On April 6, 1956, six Marine recruits drowned while trying to cross a river during a late-night forced march as a result of the actions of Drill Instructor (DI) Staff Sergeant Matthew C. McKeon. The men were in Platoon 71, Third Recruit Battalion, Parris Island, South Carolina. The platoon was 5½ weeks into boot camp training, and McKeon was not pleased with their progress. He had tried the normal training approaches, so he decided on a more drastic training step: a night march through Ribbon Creek, a foul-smelling, chilly creek with mud varying from inches to a foot deep, and shoulder-high grass infested with unmerciful biting sand fleas.

The incident immediately received overwhelming attention in the media throughout the country. It presented a crisis. It had the potential to challenge and change the Marine Corps method of recruit training. If not properly handled, the entire Marine Corps could be in jeopardy. For years, Members of Congress had received numerous allegations and complaints of abuse in Marine recruit training, and this incident might bring about a congressional investigation, a public hearing, and a requirement to change recruit training methods, something Marine Headquarters wanted to avert.

There are two books that cover this incident that have been thoroughly researched. In *The Ribbon Creek Incident* by John C. Stevens III, the bibliography includes personal and telephone interviews with 29 members of Platoon 71; 18 personal and telephone interviews with persons who had knowledge of and insight into the tragedy; 20 books and articles; and 18 newspaper articles. In addition, Stevens also had the benefit of obtaining insights and answers from giants of the Corps who were knowledgeable about the incident: General Wallace M. Greene, Jr., General Merrill H. Twining, and Lieutenant General Henry W. Buse, Jr., among others.

*The U.S. Marine Corps in Crisis*, a dissertation by Keith Fleming that was later published as a book, had archival documents and private papers as primary sources. The sources included the General Wallace M. Greene, Jr., file at the Marine Corps Historical Center.

The Ribbon Creek incident exposed the entire country to alleged and real abuses of Marine Corps recruit training. Colonel Mitchell Paige, a Medal of Honor recipient, provided a vivid description of his experience in boot camp as recruits were marched to a sandy area infested with the sand fleas: "With our arms and necks exposed, since we could only wear an undershirt, the thousands of sand fleas were all over us, in our nostrils, eyes, ears, and hair. [The drill instructor, Corporal] Webb paced back and forth around us, pounding the palm of his hand with a stick screaming, 'If you move a muscle, I'll kill you.'"[37]

The objective of this type of training was to weed out those recruits who could not take it—better to test the recruits through this intense, high-stress challenge before actual combat where a Marine's action, or inaction, involved life and death; to understand the importance of discipline—the immediate, instinctive obedience to orders; and to develop cohesiveness and camaraderie among the troops by going through this ordeal together, realizing "the one thing he is likely to value more highly than his life [is] his reputation as a man among men."[38]

The Marine Corps recruit training has traditionally been known for its toughness, but some of these kinds of abuses were out of hand. It had been proven in past years of recruit training that disciplined, proud Marines could be developed without this oppressive treatment. How, when, and why did such abuses develop? Was there a need for the accountability of senior leaders?

In his book, Keith Fleming expanded on the environment of the Marine Corps at the time of the abuses in recruit training which failed to provide the best potential for successful training:

> Other bases, following orders from Headquarters Marine Corps, had to transfer prospective DIs to Parris Island. The quality of these varied. Most commands tended to keep their best men and use Parris Island as a dumping ground for lower-quality NCOs. In one class at the DI school, almost 30 percent failed to complete the abbreviated course. Inevitably, as it had in World War II, the depot turned to the pool of

recent recruit graduates to fill half its input of new drill instructors. The average age of these new DIs was 19 years.

The Korean War brought an increase in the amount of hazing and use of profanity. Recruits caught chewing gum marched with wads of gum stuck to their noses. Any recruit apprehended eating an unauthorized candy bar carried it in his hand for the rest of the day.

Those who lost their footlocker keys had to sew their spare keys to their caps, and thereafter open the box without removing the caps from their heads. Drill instructors also resorted to more severe punishments, ranging from jerking a recruit's cap down over his chin to a swift kick in the seat of the pants. Tom Bartlett, a *Leatherneck* magazine correspondent who went through Parris Island in 1952, wrote, "I remember being thumped on the gourd [i.e., being hit on the head], and for two days I had a size ten and a half double-E boot imprinted on the soft flab of my posterior."[39]

Lieutenant General Greene describes the DIs' recruit training in Ribbon Creek during this period: "Various forms of hazing and corporal punishment gradually crept into the system and eventually became common as the training load required the use of more and more recent recruit graduates as drill instructors. These young, inexperienced Marines had trouble asserting themselves with new recruits their own age. They relied upon their fists and heavy doses of profanity to gain ascendancy over recruits who could not hit back. The traditional practice of giving DIs great leeway and relatively little supervision, combined with supervision by officers and senior NCOs who themselves were relatively new to the Marine Corps, contributed to the increase in hazing and corporal punishment. Many drill instructors, too inexperienced to know enough to fill the hours with productive training, spent considerable time hazing their trainees."[40]

According to Fleming:

The drill instructors could get away with using such methods because the training system traditionally involved little officer supervision. Thus, while the duties of the DIs were exceedingly onerous, those of the officers decidedly were not. Parris Island became, for officers, a quiet backwater, a peaceful interlude after years of hard service in two wars. They and their families enjoyed comfortable housing located near the river and shaded by enormous live oak trees festooned with Spanish moss. The base had an excellent golf course and the nearby tidal estuaries and Atlantic Ocean offered superb fishing. Hunting in coastal Carolina was just as good.[41]

The quiet backwaters of any institution do not attract the ambitious. Parris Island, in the years after the Korean War, became a favorite duty station for officers on their "twilight cruises" at the end of their careers. Younger, more ambitious officers tended to seek assignments elsewhere. When Major General Joseph C. Burger took over the base in January 1956, he found that, with some notable exceptions, his staff was merely average in professional quality. Further, while the depot rated only one warrant officer, there were as many as twelve assigned. Lieutenants were rare on Parris Island. Burger recognized the problem but had not made his final decision about a recommendation to the Commandant when the Ribbon Creek incident occurred. Inertia, inability, or lack of desire to correct fundamental problems had crept into the training system.[42]

Another indicator of the officer problem was that the little supervision the DIs did receive came primarily during normal working hours. At night, the officer of the day supposedly kept an eye on what went on in the recruit training areas. It was not enough; even General Burger realized a lot of abuses went on at night at Parris Island that never came to light.[43]

The low level of the officer supervision did more than permit abuses; it also affected the quality of Marines who became drill instructors at Parris Island. Little supervision resulted in little recognition for superior performance. "When you turn out a good platoon, they don't say anything," said Staff Sergeant Trope in *Life*, "and when you don't, they yell 'why?'"

The depot, under these conditions, became equivalent to Siberia in the minds of many capable, ambitious Marine NCOs who were potential drill instructors. Too many of the best enlisted Marines, like the officers, sought assignments elsewhere. Parris

Island made do with what it could get, and too many of these were misfits wore chevrons.[44]

During the mid 1950s, there were few charges of abuse, and rarely was there a conviction of DIs accused. Why were there not charges, trials, and convictions when the abuses did surface? Fleming wrote:

> Such refusals to testify took on additional significance as the rate of maltreatment spiraled upward, yet courts-martial continued to convict only the very worst offenders. Only nine of these came to trial in the fifteen months prior to the Ribbon Creek incident. The courts convicted only six. An example of those convicted was the case of a sergeant found guilty of hitting a recruit in the stomach nineteen times on his nineteenth birthday, kicking another in the stomach, beating a third with a swagger stick, and jumping on the stomach of a fourth recruit. During the trial, witnesses testified that the sergeant hoisted himself in the air by grabbing the tops of two bunks and then "mule-kicked" a recruit in the chest. The court acquitted the man of six other charges.[45]

> By January 1956, when Major General Joseph C. Burger took command at Parris Island, the level of corporal punishment and other abuses in the recruit training battalions had reached near explosive levels. Unfortunately, it was precisely at this point that the restraining pressure of command leadership lessened both on the Marine Corps in general and on Parris Island in particular. The new Commandant of the Marine Corps, General Randolph McCall Pate, who took office on January 1, 1956, was a more passive leader than his predecessors. He did not immediately establish the firm grasp of command over the Marine Corps. As a consequence, Burger came to Parris Island with no sense of urgency; three months later he had yet to "dig in his spurs." His light hand was insufficient for such a volatile situation. The element of "inevitable" disaster awaited merely a time, a situation, and a place.[46]

What about the leadership at the top? The observation Fleming made about Commandant Randolph McCall Pate in *Marine Corps in Crisis* provides an important insight into his leadership and to inquire how well the leadership handled this incident:

Early Monday morning, April 9, 1956 [three days after the drowning]. Most senior officers were at their desks. However, General Randolph McCall Pate, the new Commandant of the Marine Corps, was visiting his alma mater, the Virginia Military Institute, in Lexington, Virginia, to give a speech.

When his staff reached him in Lexington, Pate immediately decided he had to go to Parris Island. He gave orders for the inspector-general of the Marine Corps, Brigadier General Carson A. Roberts, to join him there. Pate later said he went to Parris Island to see the depot officers properly handled the incident and to ensure that such a thing could never happen again. However, the effect of his direct involvement was to draw even greater media attention to the tragedy.

Such abrupt decisions and actions were typical of Pate's performance while Commandant and made him probably the most controversial holder of that office in the twentieth century. General Pate was more attuned to the quiet pre-World War II garrison years than the hectic Cold War of the 1950s. He was more interested in appearances than substance. As Commandant he spent as little time as possible in Washington, preferring instead the honors and deference Marine commands gave a visiting Commandant. His erratic behavior and judgment caused many of his closest associates to worry about the state of his physical and mental health.

Probable illness aside, there were other reasons Pate was not popular as Commandant. Retired Brigadier General Samuel R. Shaw described Pate as an intelligent officer with fine ideas but few firm convictions about what the Marine Corps was or should be. His convictions always had been those of his boss, a trait that helped to further his career as a staff officer. However, as Commandant, a position requiring strong convictions based upon much previous thinking, Pate was beyond his depth. As a result, he was far more passive and a creature of his staff than his predecessors had been.

Fortunately for the Marine Corps, as this tragedy reached the media the Corps could call on Colonel James D. Hittle, who for the previous three years had served as legislative assistant at Marine Corps Headquarters. In carrying out his responsibilities he had established a superb rapport with the key congressional leaders. His boss, Lieutenant General Vernon E. Megee, Chief of Staff of Marine Corps Headquarters, upon learning of the incident contacted Hittle, telling him, "Please come down to my office," and upon reporting told him there was a tragedy at Parris Island where some Marine recruits were drowned because of a "drill instructor's mistake."

Hittle requested of Headquarters that he be given time to alert the key members of Congress before any press conference was held to provide him the opportunity to first inform the powerful members of Congress and ask them to refrain from making public statements, other than they were waiting to be more fully informed of the details of the incident. Because of his stature and rapport, he was given an immediate audience with the influential members of Congress, most importantly with Representative Carl Vinson, Chairman of the House Armed Forces Committee, and with Representative Dewey Short. In the Senate, Leverett Saltonstall and Richard B. Russell. He was successful in persuading these legislators from making any immediate statements to the press.

Unfortunately, while Hittle was coordinating with congressional members, Marine Corps Headquarters drafted a news brief that was released over the telephone, stating: "Six Marines are missing from the Marine Recruit Depot at Parris Island, South Carolina following a night training exercise conducted last evening."

It was poor judgment and resulted in an absolute disaster—it did not identify the platoon number, alarming thousands of families. Parris Island and Washington Headquarters were inundated with concerned family members desperate to know if their sons were alright. The delay in holding a more detailed press release made editors throughout the country suspicious that the Marine Corps was trying to hide something.

When Commandant Pate gave his press conference he deviated from a thoughtfully and carefully prepared press statement. When he was asked by a reporter if McKeon had violated any regulations, he answered, "It would appear so." This was premature. It prejudged the incident and McKeon's actions before a thorough investigation. Pate's comment was essentially accusing McKeon of manslaughter.

The incident did not go away. For help, Headquarters called upon Major General Merrill B. Twining, then in command at the recruit training at Camp Pendleton, California, who proceeded to make a thorough investigation. He found among the records thousands of earlier letters from Congressmen pertaining to complaints of abuses at the recruit training camps, but no real effort had been made to correct the problems. If Congress decided to take action to stop the abuses it could jeopardize Marine Corps recruit training which had graduated so many exceptional Marines.

Burger's testimony seemed to be advancing an excuse, that "it didn't happen on my watch," at the same time that Twining's draft statement contained a straightforward acceptance of Marine Corps responsibility.

Twining convinced Pate of the need to re-establish confidence of the American public opinion of Marine Corps training methods. The essence of Twining's advice was being straightforward and the Marine Corps Headquarters accepting the responsibility, and assumes that it would restructure recruit training.

When the House Armed Forces Committee scheduled a hearing, the Marine Corps' rapport was so remarkable that Representative Carl Vinson, Committee Chairman, requested that "the Commandant come over ahead of the hearing for an hour and we'll go over this thing." Pate did so and they carefully went over the statement.

Incredibly, Vinson was so much a friend of the Corps and so appreciative of General Twining's findings that when he met with Hittle on 1 May, he turned to him with a friendly laugh and said: "I'm going to have to say something about this. You go on out, get together with Bob [Robert W. Smart, chief counsel for the committee] and Russ, and you write up my remarks right now of what my reaction is going to be after I hear this thing."

Pate gave his prepared statement and Vinson appreciated the Marine Corps' admission of problems at Parris Island, stating: "During my 42 years in the Congress, this is the first time within my memory that the senior officer of any Armed Service has had the courage to state in public session that his service could be deficient in some respect." Vinson concluded by saying he believed the Marine Corps should have time to put its own house in order before the committee decided whether a congressional investigation was warranted.

After Vinson finished his statement, he opened the floor to questions. Other members of the committee asked a few innocuous questions before they agreed to give the Marine Corps time to correct the problems at Parris Island. The chairman then instructed Pate to report back to the committee before the end of that session of Congress, at which time they would decide whether to investigate.

Convinced the Marine Corps would do its own house cleaning, the House Armed Forces Committee announced it would wait until it received the Marine Corps report before deciding if it would have its own investigation.[47]

Staff Sergeant Matthew McKeon was a native of Massachusetts, 32 years of age, and not new to the military. He had previous military service of 10 years, during World War II in the Navy on the *Essex*, an aircraft carrier. After he was honorably discharged from the Navy, he enlisted in the Marine Corps in 1948, and served as a platoon sergeant, seeing action in the Korean War as part of a machinegun platoon of the 1st Marine Division. He was married, and he and his wife were devout Catholics and active in their church. They had two children and were expecting a third when the Ribbon Creek incident occurred. It was considered to be a stable marriage.

McKeon graduated from drill instructors school on February 3, 1956. His performance in the course was above average. There were 90 students that entered the class; 55 graduated and he stood 14th in the class, with a course average of 84.9 percent. He was assigned to Company A, 3d Recruit Training Battalion, with Platoon 71, on February 23, 1956. Because he was not the senior NCO with the platoon, he was given the night and weekend duty in addition to the daytime responsibilities, a very demanding schedule. He was personally plagued with health problems, a bad back that frequently caused him severe pain, and it was alleged it resulted on occasions in him being short-tempered and irritable.

There was suspicion that McKeon might not receive a fair trial and might be given all the blame for the tragedy. An informal committee of prominent trial lawyers was put together in New York City to assist in the McKeon defense. It was organized by two New York State Supreme Court judges, James M. McCally and Walter A. Lynch. In the group were a number of very able trial attorneys who had a record of a strong commitment to protect civil rights. They were concerned it would be a modern Dreyfus trial.[48]

As it developed, one of the attorneys who answered the call was Emile Zola Berman, the son of Jewish Russian immigrant parents whose legal career was committed to the cause of civil rights. Coincidentally, Berman was named after Emile Zola, a prominent author who was openly critical of the poor defense for Captain Alfred Dreyfus against the French Army's allegations of his spying for the Germans in World War I. Captain Dreyfus was framed and made a scapegoat for a corrupt French military hierarchy. After many years of fighting to prove his innocence, Dreyfus was ultimately exonerated, but not until he had been through hell while incarcerated on the dreaded Devil's Island. Receiving a call from Justice McNally, Berman responded: "I'll not only join the Committee, I'll try the case."[49]

Berman was described as a brilliant, successful trial attorney; always prepared and exceptional in his trial presentation and the analysis of his cases. In addition, he possessed a magnetic personality and courtly manners. Surprisingly, and fortunately, as the trial developed, while vigorously defending McKeon, he was essentially an asset to the Marine Corps.

Berman was no stranger to the military. He had an exceptional record of service in World War II, enlisting in the Army Air Corps in 1942 at the age of 40. He was an intelligence officer who, though not rated, flew many hazardous missions in carrying out his responsibilities, receiving the Distinguished Flying Cross and rising to the rank of lieutenant colonel by the end of the war.[50]

Fleming described Berman's trial strategy:

As McKeon's chief defense counsel, Berman approached the trial in a manner that gave his side the initiative. By keeping himself one step ahead of the prosecution, he managed to control events from the very beginning. He managed to do so because the Marine Corps, including its prosecuting officer, took a narrow view that the courtroom trial was only one step in a complex legal process. The latter included the various forms of automatic review of the court-martial verdict and sentence required by the Uniform Code of Military Justice. Berman also perceived that public opinion could be as important in the ultimate resolution of McKeon's case as the evidence presented in court.

Berman began his orchestration of McKeon's defense the day after he became the chief defense counsel. He appeared on Dave Garroway's nationally televised *Today* show. Berman announced during the interview that he had been retained without any agreement regarding a fee, a statement likely to help shift public opinion in favor of the defense. He raised the Dreyfus analogy by saying he was defending McKeon out of a feeling that there were broader issues involved above the mere fact of the drownings. Berman continued that he wanted to ensure that these issues were adequately presented in court.

Berman's appearance on the *Today* show was an astute act of pretrial stagecraft. The analogy to the Dreyfus case was weak, yet the mere mention of that famous case would ensure that the Marine Corps bent over backward to ensure a fair trial. In addition, his on-camera statement about wider issues being involved served to tap the wellspring of Marine Corps paranoia. Prosecutor Lieutenant Colonel Duane Faw, the legal officer at Parris Island, saw the statement as a preview of Berman's tactics in the forthcoming trial. Faw expected Berman to attempt to shift the blame from McKeon to the Marine Corps itself, to put the institution on trial. Faw was not the only one who took this view. A few days later, on May 1, General Pate's statement before the House Armed Services Committee also contained the declaration that "the Marine Corps was on trial." Then, Berman took it one step further.

Berman was able to persuade Commandant Pate to testify, having met him privately during the course of the trials to discuss the possibility of his testifying. Berman was asked how he achieved this, and he responded: "I told the general that it was the only way to get himself and the Marine Corps out of this jam."

When Pate's staff learned of this, they thought it not a good idea, but were unsuccessful in changing Pate's mind. On August 1, the twelfth day of the trial, Pate entered the courtroom, went up to McKeon, and shook his hand, telling him: "I am here to help you in every legal way. Good luck to you, boy." Pate then proceeded to the witness chair to testify.[51]

Pate testified: "There's no final say as to what an individual would do under all circumstances. . . . It's evident this drill sergeant did drink some vodka [the investigation did not conclude that his drinking was responsible for his conduct] and I assume that it was against the regulations—the conditions under which he did it. I don't know. I think maybe I would take a stripe away from him for a thing like that. It's a fairly serious thing.

"As to the remaining part of it—it's a little fuzzy and hazy to me just what transpired. But I suspect I would probably have transferred him away for stupidity . . . I would probably have written in his Service Record Book that under no conditions would this sergeant ever drill recruits again. I think I would let it go at that. That's not a final answer, I know."[52]

But Pate's testifying had the potential to upset the arrangement the Marine Corps Headquarters had worked out with the key Congressional leaders:

Meanwhile, in Washington, Pate's appearance at the trial was causing considerable turmoil. Colonel Hittle, the congressional liaison officer, received a number of calls from incensed members of Congress demanding an explanation of Pate's action. This was a delicate issue, because only congressional expectations that Pate would clean up the Parris Island mess had precluded a full-scale investigation of Marine recruit training. Should Congress lose faith in the Commandant, an investigation was still possible. Hittle was careful in his reply to these queries: 'The Commandant said what he did because he thought it was the right thing to say. And he's bending over backwards not to prejudice the case for McKeon."[53]

Berman, however, instead of attacking the Marine Corps, became its defender of traditional Marine Corps values. He controlled the trial from the beginning to end realizing the trial was only a part of a complicated legal process; in defending McKeon, that public opinion was important in the outcome of the trial in the defense of McKeon.

One of the most brilliant moves by the defense was to call retired Marine Corps Lieutenant General Lewis "Chesty" Puller, who had been awarded the Navy Cross five times and was the greatest living legend of the Corps at that time.

> Defense counsel Thomas P. Costello, who was assisting Berman, was McKeon's brother-in-law, called from New York to Puller's home in Virginia, telling him, "General, McKeon needs help that only you can give. Are you willing to testify for him?"
>
> Puller's response was, "I don't know McKeon, but he's not what interests me. If what I read in the papers is true, it's the Marine Corps that needs help. I'll do anything I can for the Corps. What is it you want?"
>
> He was told, "We want you to talk about Marine training and tradition—that's all. Nothing about McKeon. They know your record and what you stand for. You can work out the details with Berman."
>
> General Puller said, "All right. If the Secretary of the Navy orders me to active duty to testify, I'll do it. I don't see how I can refuse."
>
> Mrs. Puller interjected, "Lewis, for heaven's sake, stay out of this mess. We've had so much trouble and controversy in our career. Can't we have a little peace for a change?"
>
> Puller responded, "Dear, I'm not picking a fight. I don't give a damn about the Drill Instructor himself. The important thing is the Marine Corps. If we let 'em, they'll tear it to pieces. Headquarters won't speak up. It's my duty to do it."[54]

Marines had been writing Puller from many parts of the country since the opening of the case. Hank Adams, his Guadalcanal companion, had called from California to express concern for the future of the Corps. "They're going to give us the works over the loss of these six unfortunate boys," he said, "but I notice the Air Force has killed a hundred and sixteen men in the past month, from published notices of crashes, and not one word has been said in protest."[55]

After his courtroom appearance, the *New York Times* reported: "A living legend came back to Parris Island today. He is Lieutenant General Lewis B. (Chesty) Puller, retired, the most decorated and revered of living Marines.... The appearance of the stubby, tenacious man with the face of an English bulldog and the chest of a pouter pigeon brought the largest crowd yet to the schoolhouse.... Ramrod-straight, his uniform blouse ablaze with ribbons, the general sat in the witness chair and testified in a drill-field voice.

*Berman* in his direct questioning: How long were you in Korea?
*General Puller:* About nine months.
*Berman*: Were you in combat?
*General Puller:* Yeah.
*Berman*: Were you decorated?
*General Puller:* Yeah.
*Berman*: Without going into your other decorations, isn't it true that you have received five Navy Crosses?
*General Puller:* Correct. (Berman asked Puller to point out the decoration.)
Berman asked his opinion of the Marine Corps' mission.
*General Puller:* The definition of military training is success in battle. In my opinion that is the only objective of military training. It wouldn't make any sense to have a military organization on the backs of the American taxpayers with any other definition. I've believed that ever since I've been a Marine.
*Berman*: What is the most important element of that training?
*General Puller:* I'll quote Napoleon. He stated that the most important thing in military training is discipline. Without discipline an army becomes a mob.
*Berman*: Now, then, in that context, can you tell us whether you have an opinion, based again on your experience, as to whether or not the train-

ing in discipline is for all situations confined to lesson plans, or syllabi or training regulations?

*General Puller:* No. The training of a basic Marine is conducted almost entirely outside—in the field, on the drill ground, on the rifle range—that kind of work. The Marine gets an idea of how the Marine Corps is run during this training, but his training is outside work.

*Berman*: Can you tell us, General, of the things you learned here as a recruit?

*General Puller:* Well, the main thing—that I have remembered all my life—is the definition of *esprit de corps*. Now my definition—the definition I was taught, that I've always believed in—is that *esprit de corps* means love for one's military legion, in my case the United States Marine Corps. I also learned that this loyalty to one's Corps travels both ways, up and down.

*Berman*: Now, General, I want you to assume that what is the evidence in this case is a fact. That on a Sunday evening a drill instructor took a platoon that was undisciplined and lacked spirit and on whom he'd tried other methods of discipline. And that for purposes of teaching discipline and instilling morale he took that platoon into a marsh or creek—all the way in front of his troops—would you consider that oppression?

*General Puller:* In my opinion it is not.

*Berman*: Can you state an opinion as to whether leading troops is a good practice?

*General Puller:* Any kind of commander or leader is not worth his salt if he does not lead his troops under all conditions.

Berman reviewed the story of the tragic march into the creek and asked Puller a longer question on the same point, on the training and discipline of troops.

*General Puller:* In my opinion the reason American troops made out so poorly in the Korean War was mostly due to lack of night training. And if we are going to win the next war I say that from now on fifty per cent of the training should be devoted to night training.

*Berman:* So, in your opinion, was this act of this drill instructor in leading his troops, under those conditions and for that purpose, good or bad military practice?

*General Puller:* Good. From what I read in the papers yesterday of the testimony of General Pate before this court, that he agrees and regrets that this man was ever ordered tried by general court-martial.[56]

> After Puller's testimony the Court took a recess. Upon return, Berman, with thirty-three witnesses standing by, rested his

case. With favorable testimony of the Commandant and the Corps' greatest living hero, any trial lawyer must have the sense, the feel, when you have made your case and stop while you are ahead and winning.

Berman never expected a complete acquittal, but was successful in his objective of minimizing the damage. The investigation did not conclude he was drunk, only that he had been drinking. The decision of the trial court found McKeon guilty of involuntary manslaughter by simple negligence and of drinking in the enlisted barracks. He was found not guilty of the more serious offenses: manslaughter by culpable negligence, oppression and drinking in the presence of a recruit. He was sentenced to reduction in rank to private, nine months of hard labor. The nine months was limited to time already served.[57]

On May 2, Staff Sergeant Matthew McKeon learned, unfortunately through an article in the *New York Times*, that he was being relieved from his assignment at Parris Island. This was the first information about his impending transfer that reached him because of the implication of negligence, incompetence, or malfeasance. Thus, his career would end on this dark note. In 1959, 3 years after the tragedy, he received an honorable discharge for medical disability.[58]

Another outcome was the transfer of Major General Burger. Fleming commented:

> This was an inevitable decision given the realities of the political climate facing the Marine Corps in Washington, and the continued press attention to Parris Island. Someone had to get the ax, even if it had to be Pate's personal friend, Joe Burger ... who apparently had no inkling of impending relief of command. The final result of all the efforts was that the Marine Corps was to have time to correct the recruit training problems. There was no Congressional investigation of the alleged abuses at Parris Island. It appeared attention would be on McKeon now being described as the underdog, and press pressure increased.[59]

The Marine Corps had brought in some of its most talented officers to salvage the valuable Marine Corps Recruit Training unit, Lieutenant General Merrill Twining and two future Commandants, Generals David M. Shoup and Wallace Greene, Jr.

Correcting the recruit training problems was going to require institutional reform, and reform moves slowly in a large organization. Commandant Charles Krulak had a perspective on change. "One of the things learned from my father [Lieutenant General Victor Krulak] was four years may seem a long time, but in reality it is short. If you think of the Marine Corps as a big ocean-going vessel, and you're the CO of that vessel, and you say, 'right full rudder,' you start that rudder turning, that ship doesn't turn for a long, long time. If it's a big oil tanker, it just takes forever to turn. That's the way the Marine Corps is. If you think that you can turn on a dime, you're crazy."[60]

When Brigadier General Wallace M. Greene, Jr., arrived at Parris Island in the aftermath of Ribbon Creek, he found 10 recruits in the hospital with broken jaws.[61] He later described a similar incident in a letter to Colonel Robert D. Heinl, Jr., which Fleming relates:

> A drill instructor made a recruit stand at attention while the instructor struck him repeatedly, breaking his jaw. When the recruit fell to the deck, the drill instructor kicked him time after time. This was not an isolated incident—Bob, this was a common, everyday treatment which fortunately did not always put the recruit in the hospital.[62]

Although the recruit training improved, there were continued abuses by some drill instructors in spite of Greene's efforts. The needed changes were not going to be accomplished overnight, and he did not believe the Marine Corps could maintain its public support if these abuses continued and became public, which would inevitably lead to a congressional investigation.

After time, Greene became progressively frustrated with the increasingly less emphasis and attention to the recruit problem and lack of support from the Marine Corps Headquarters with its failure to provide him with the help he needed; particularly not sending him a qualified public relations officer he needed under his authority to accomplish the mission and assigned to him.[63]

An exceptional leader, Greene proceeded with his initiatives to preserve the stature of the Marine Corps. He had visits by civilian groups to observe the training, supplying them with copies of his speeches which spelled his objectives and the policies to be implemented to accomplish them; Boy Scout troops were given the opportunity to visit; certain dignitaries were permitted to use the golf course; parents could visit, but preferably after graduation; reporters were welcome and could get interviews with Greene.

These, and other actions by Greene, were very successful, and his openness paid off.[64]

Greene needed favorable press to get the word out to the American people about the reforms he was implementing. An Associated Press reporter, Ben Price, was assigned to cover the Parris Island beat. He was a competent and highly regarded reporter who was going to report the truth as he observed it, but he did have a hidden agenda.

The abuse problems improved but still continued. Price learned of them and reported on them, and as a prominent reporter for the Associated Press, his stories were frequently on the front page of many American papers. He did not hesitate to be critical or to report any abuses that came to his attention. The articles he wrote were critical, and as a result Greene's staff proceeded to cut off certain privileges that Price had enjoyed: use of the telephone (requiring him to use a public telephone); access to the home addresses of Marines facing court-martial; and his photographer's use of the base photographic laboratory.

Greene described Price's articles as "twisted . . . news to a degree highly detrimental to the Marine Corps and the public interest."[65]

It got progressively worse when Price published an article on March 9, 1957, alleging the drill instructors were not following orders that prohibited mistreatment of recruits; some claimed that thumping was need to train recruits, but Price stated, "The great majority of the DIs was obeying the regulations because they were good Marines."[66]

Greene countered with allegations of subversion in the interviews by Price, which created a furor with Associated Press and resulted in Commandant Pate telling Greene, "For heaven's sake, say nothing again that will alienate the press."[67]

Pate had lunch with Price to consider an amicable way to end the turmoil over the way Greene was reacting to the Price articles.

In a letter dated March 20, 1957, Pate stated that Greene's actions "put me in a very embarrassing position that I am having trouble wiggling out of."[68]

The same letter informed Greene he was to be reassigned from Parris Island to command Camp Lejeune and ordered him to stay away from the drill instructors.[69] He was essentially being relieved for cause for unsatisfactory performance.

His fitness report, signed on March 1, 1957, gave Greene a rating of "outstanding," except only "excellent" in administrative duties and rated "not observed" in endurance and presence of mind.[70] It was certainly an unfavorable report and would normally be a career-ender for future promotion.

Although furious with such a marginal efficiency report, he returned it on March 24, 1957, not taking the opportunity of checking the block to challenge it. He wrote an angry letter he never sent to the Commandant to demand a Court of Inquiry, but instead, did a "reasoned" letter to General Pate to present his side of the controversy with Price, but it didn't change Pate's decision.

The controversy ultimately subsided with the press backing off. Greene left with his wife for Camp Lejeune in the family car, having had a farewell party in the officer's club and leaving the post through a double line of saluting Marines.[71]

If one didn't know Marine Corps history, one would indeed conclude this effectiveness report was a career-ender assignment for Greene, particularly if he was passed over for promotion to Major General when the next board met (which he was not); but he became Commandant on January 1, 1964, obviously rising above the report.

Asked to summarize this incident in assessing accountability, the leadership required to resolve it, and the lessons learned, Commandant Carl Mundy said: "The Corps tends, periodically, to drift in and out of those type 'abuses,' but there are sometimes causes for it that may be attributable, even, to senior leadership. The most poignant example of that is the days when General E.E. Anderson, the Assistant Commandant, wanted to keep the four stars Lyndon Johnson had bestowed on his favorite, and his personal choice to be the 24th Commandant—Lew Walt—and to become the 'youngest' and 'first aviator' to become Commandant.

"To do that, by the law that enabled President Lyndon B. Johnson to promote Walt from Lieutenant General to General, the Corps had to stay at an end-strength of 200,000 or better, and so in the Cushman/Anderson regime, the informal 'word' to the recruiting service was: 'If it walks and talks, send it to a recruit depot and let them sort it out'—but, implicitly, 'keep the numbers above 200,000.' This was also the period when Robert McNamara thrust upon the Armed Services 'Project 100,000.'

"Together, these resulted in the Army and Marine Corps taking in murderers, drug addicts, and mental groups that were classified 'four' but that were probably 'fives' or 'sixes.' Getting these dregs through recruit training required Marine NCO DIs to deal with gangsters, racists, and intelligence levels unable to grasp instruction, and if they became abusive in trying to deal with these dregs daily, it may be understandable as much as indicative. In other words, it may be that the 'System'—and the senior leadership—were more at fault than the NCOs upon which discipline was vested.

"And it was ultimately General Bob Barrow, first at Parris Island, then as DC/S Manpower, and ultimately, as Commandant, who set things straight.

"The point should be, Greene or Barrow and even others dealt with the problem. In either instance, while your draft offers a bit of qualification as to the Marine Corps seeking to build men, it may be desirable to balance it a bit more.

"In my own case, since I underwent Basic Training in the 1954–1956 timeframe, every one of the examples cited—plus others—but less broken jaws—are ones I experienced in officer candidate training. We viewed them more as a passage to manhood and enduring lessons in discipline than corporal punishment, and as lessons in discipline that endure with those of my class though today. The 'S—Bird' in my platoon who 'sneaked a smoke' outside the Quonset hut after hours and was caught and then caused to put the bucket over his head and smoke a whole pack of Camels under it deserved, in the eyes of his peers, what he got for breaking very explicit rules.

"The drill sergeant who imposed the punishment did so professionally—not corporally—with my whole platoon assembled at attention while he reminded us that to 'light up' at night in combat when 'word' had been passed not to smoke was to give enemy gunners a target onto which to direct mortar and artillery fire with the probable results of not just killing the 'S—Bird' who broke the rule, but more important, of killing a lot of other Marines, and/or neutralizing as combat effective squad, platoon, or company. We 'got it,' and not one of us felt sorry for the 'S—Bird.'

"Similarly, as we stood at attention while 'Goettge Bugs'—the equivalent of Parris Island sand fleas at Quantico—crawled into our ears and noses, the teaching point by the Platoon Sergeant again emphasized that in combat, a Marine who slapped at mosquitoes, sand fleas, or whatever kind of bug, risked making a sound that could give away a position to enemy fire.

"To be sure, there was some pure, harassing, 'punishment'—usually group, rather than individual—but it came, for example, when we were 'slouching' at something. If we were sluggish during close order drill, 'skylarking,' or 'getting short' near the end of training, that was the time when we would be halted and told to 'get 'em out there!'—which meant extended arms with M–1s on fingertips while shoulders ached while the Drill Sergeant lectured us on the fact that Marines who get lazy or careless get other Marines killed. Harsh as they may have been, we carried the emblazoned recollection of these lessons onward into the Corps for those of us who remained, but also into the executive offices of America in which so many

Marines have succeeded over the years—like Jim Baker, Bill Donaldson, George Schultze, Hugh McColl, Fred Smith, Tom Monahan, and a hundred other successful executives in business and government who cite, repeatedly, their success as attributable to the 'fiery forge' of their early days in the Marine Corps.

"The point is this, that there have been abuses over time, and whatever they might be attributable to and however badly some of them need to be corrected, there is a counterbalance. We, who underwent the training of the time, emerged with a well-taught understanding from a DI that 'to break discipline and rules can result, in combat, in casualties at best, and defeat, at worst'—and these lessons have stuck with millions of young men and women through lives and careers. Members of the press and other Americans who have not walked through that forge would never understand that.

"I make no excuses for the McKeon incident at Ribbon Creek, but if that is to be a focus in the book, it needs, I believe, additional emphasis on the fact that boys have been developed into men through 'fiery forges' over time. I even recall being inspired reading Leon Uris's *Battle Cry* by the toughness and challenge of 'Boot Camp' he painted."[72]

## The Ski Lift Tragedy

On February 3, 1998, in the small town of Cavalese in the high peaks of Italy's Dolomite Mountains, a U.S. Marine Corps EA–6B Prowler jet cut a supporting cable that sent a ski gondola plummeting to the ground. It killed all 20 people on board, 11 men and 9 women. The dead included three Italians, two Americans, two Poles, four Belgians, seven Germans, one Dutch national, and the car operator. No one aboard the aircraft was injured, and the aircraft sustained only minor damage to its underside with cable burns along the side indicating it chipped the cable from above.

The EA–6B Prowler jet involved was a four-seat electronic warfare aircraft. The crew of four were all Marine captains: pilot Richard J. Ashby; navigator Joseph Schweitzer; and electronic countermeasures operators Chandler P. Seagroves and William L. Ramey II. Only the pilot could control the aircraft. The mission was to monitor and block electronic frequencies and jam enemy radar to provide continuous presence and protection with electronic measures to allied operations in Bosnia.

The EA–6B aircraft was based in Cherry Point, North Carolina. It was at Aviano on temporary duty, and the crews rotated every 6 months. Its training mission was to fly low, to evade radar detection, and fast, so it could climb rapidly if necessary. It was estimated that on this training mission, the aircraft was flying 600 miles an hour at 270 feet above ground.

Any incident resulting in deaths of innocent civilians is tragic, but this created very serious anger among our NATO allies and jeopardized relations with our NATO partners in Italy.

General Charles C. Krulak was Commandant when this incident occurred. He reflected in his oral history: "This was one of the most difficult issues that the Marine Corps had to face during my tenure as a Marine Commandant. An issue that wasn't associated with warfighting or the budget. It was just a very tough time because it lasted for months."

"It would have been a lot worse had we not, from the very beginning, made it totally open to everybody. The greatest example of that, I think, were the Article 32 investigation and the court-martial itself. There were hundreds of news media there on the first day of the Article 32 and the first day of the first court-martial. Hundreds, foreign and domestic. We made a conscious decision that this would be the most open hearing ever been held by any Service. We believed that the only way that we could come out of this tragedy would be if we, as a Marine Corps, said we were going to give you, whether you are an Italian press or a U.S. press, total visibility on everything that is happening. You can judge whether the United States Marine Corps does the right thing. We went to the extent that we opened up the hearing room to the press. Overflow press were placed in a tent where we fed in live video and sound of what was going on in the hearing room. We put in the tent and in the hearing room, a public affairs officer who was also a lawyer. If the press had any questions they reviewed hard data from a lawyer who could speak with some authority."[73]

General Timothy A. Peppe, commander at the Aviano airbase, suspended low-altitude flights by U.S. military aircraft until the causes of the Italian accident were determined. The Italian defense ministry said Colonel Orfeo Durigon, an air security expert and commander at the Aviano base, was Italy's representative on the commission set up by the U.S. Air Force to investigate the accident. Prodi, who returned from a visit to Estonia, spoke by telephone with U.S. President Bill Clinton who expressed his condolences and ensured that Italian authorities would be fully involved in the investigation into the tragedy.[74]

General Krulak dispatched Major General Michael P. DeLong, Deputy Commander of the U.S. Marine Forces, Atlantic, to head up an investigation of the mishap. In addition to investigating the mishap, he was to recommend what, if any, legal proceedings should be required.

Before investigation of the accident, it was too early to know whether courts-martial would result.

General Charles C. Krulak did not prejudge the incident, stating he would wait until the investigations were complete, but he promised: "If there's accountability to be had, there will be accountability." Discussions went back and forth to determine jurisdiction on who was to hear the matter as provided and interpreted by the Status of Forces Agreement. It was decided the United States had jurisdiction rather than the Italian courts.

With its forces stationed throughout the world, the United States has to be careful that emotion-filled incidents like this do not prevent execution of a fair and balanced investigation and trial. The court-martial trial was held at Camp Lejeune, North Carolina. Measures were taken to ensure a fair and balanced due process; there was not going to be a whitewash of the investigation and hearing, nor a search for a scapegoat.

Captain Ashby, the pilot, was charged with manslaughter, negligent homicide, damage to military property, damage to private property, and dereliction of duty based upon the allegation that the aircraft was flying too fast and too low through the valley, specifically alleging flying at 600 knots at an altitude of 270 feet in violation of speed and altitude restrictions.

Lieutenant General Peter Pace, the Marine Corps commander, determined that the seriousness of the charges and the availability of the evidence warranted that Captain Schweitzer, the navigator, should face the same charges as Ashby and in addition, both should be charged with obstruction of justice and conspiracy to obstruct justice at a general court-martial. If convicted of criminal negligence, each defendant could be sentenced to a total of 200 years in prison, 10 years for each death.

According to a newspaper report: "The little-known National Imagery and Mapping Agency (NIMA) was responsible for the map used by the pilots on this mission. . . . NIMA was established in 1996 to succeed the Defense Mapping Agency because in the Gulf War it was not providing up-to-date intelligence. To cope with this problem there was major reorganization that brought together the expertise of eight small government agencies from the CIA and the Pentagon with the U.S. mapmakers so that our military would have real up-to-date and timely information. There were conflicts between the military cartographers and the intelligence analysts. With the merger, many of the experienced people retired early or transferred out."[75]

CIA Director James Woolsey, who opposed the NIMA consolidation, commented: "They just lost too many senior people and had a hard time getting everything organized. I think it was a mistake to move the CIA analysts out of the CIA and put them into what was essentially a complete defense agency. Since its inception, the NIMA was subjected to budget and staff cutbacks which had taken a toll on the agency. The NIMA report that studied its aeronautical program after the accident stated that 'clerical personnel lack the technical training or managerial skills to remain competent in the field of information gathering.'"[76]

Retired Admiral Bobby Ray Inman, USN (Ret.), formerly director of the National Security Agency, contended that NIMA, as well as its predecessor, never had enough money to do its job. "Essentially," he said, "with intelligence, you get what you pay for."

According to a newspaper report:

> The defense for the crew members focused on failures of the Marine Corps chain of command, including a faulty map given to the aviators, and the fact that the crew was instructed they could fly as low as 1,000 feet instead of a 2,000-foot restriction.
>
> The defense argued that there were deficiencies in training and numerous communications failings within the Marine Corps and between the Marines and the Air Force, which was supposed to provide information for the Marine squadrons rotating through Aviano Air Base, Italy. Furthermore, the Defense Department's National Imagery and Mapping Agency supplied a chart that did not show the 30-year-old cableway.[77]

Jeff Edwards, a retired Navy Lieutenant Commander, investigated the accident for the defense team representing the Marine Corps aviators. To prepare his case, Edwards had conferences with three NIMA analysts in St. Louis and commented, "None could explain how NIMA ensured the accuracy of the charts." He had earlier written a memo, on November 20, 1998, that concluded: "It sends chills down my spine to think I relied on this information to keep me from hitting a tower or other obstruction. NIMA's chart did not show the gondola cable, but the Italian aviation map did show the cable. The investigation of the incident revealed that 'the Italian Charting Authority suggested ... this incident would not have occurred if the pilots had been provided with the Italian equivalent which depicted the cableway.'"[78]

At the court martial, Captain Ashby described the crash itself. "I thought, this wire is going to go through the canopy, and I thought, 'We're dead,' that's what I thought." He said he tried to push the plane's nose down and to squat down in his seat—impossible since he was strapped in it—so the cable would not slice through the canopy and hit him in the head. It was too late to have much effect, but he said, "It seemed like it lasted forever to me, timewise. I just kind of braced for this big crash," he said, but "basically nothing happened at that point."

It was not until hours later, Captain Ashby said, at a military hospital where he and the three other crew members had been taken, that he knew anyone on the ground had died. "Basically, after we finished our checkups, getting our blood pulled, as we finished, they put us in this central waiting room in the hospital," he said. "When they turned the TV off, that's when I got kind of, really worried. I mean I was already worried; that's when I became aware there was probably something more to this they don't want us to know."

Captain Ashby's lawyer, Frank Spinner, asked him how he reacted when the squadron commander, Colonel Richard Muegge, told the crew what had happened. The captain's answer was not audible as his voice broke with emotion. (Colonel Muegge was later relieved of command because of lapses in connection with the accident.)

At other times, Captain Ashby sparred vigorously with the prosecutor, Major Daugherty. "I'm accepting responsibility, sir," the captain said. But he added, "There's a difference between responsibility and criminal responsibility, sir."[79]

The prosecutor goaded Captain Ashby about why he had not seen a church in the valley where he was supposed to make a turn. Major Daugherty asked why the mapmakers put churches on the chart, if not for navigation. "I don't know why they mark them, sir, I'd rather have them mark the cableway than the church," the accused pilot replied.

Captain Ashby also described rocking his plane's wings, as he entered the valley, to see the river below. That would have the effect of confusing his radar altimeter, defense witnesses said. Defense experts said the radar altimeter could have been confused if the plane dipped one wing and the belly pointed to a distant mountain.

Prosecutor Major Daugherty pointed out that while the crew believed the minimum altitude allowed was 1,000 feet, investigators found a document in the cockpit showing it was 2,000. But Ashby asserted that he and his navigator, Schweitzer, had planned the flight from information in a folder that they were told had all the relevant information. "We flew it professionally, we briefed it professionally, and we did it to the best of our abilities," Captain Ashby asserted.[80]

On March 4, 1999, it was announced that all but one of the charges against Captain Ashby were dropped, but not the charge of obstruction of justice. He was sentenced to 6 months in jail and dismissed from the Marine Corps. The Marine Corps issued a statement following the acquittal verdict of Captain Richard Ashby on March 4, 1999:

> The Marine Corps released the following statement regarding today's acquittal of Captain Richard Ashby. Ashby was the pilot of the EA–6B Prowler aircraft that sliced through the cables suspending a ski gondola February 3, 1998, at a resort near Cavalese, Italy. He was tried by court-martial at Marine Corps Base, Camp Lejeune.
>
> From the very beginning, the Marine Corps has emphasized that our purpose was to determine the truth, to ensure the integrity of the judicial process, and to hold individuals accountable if they were found to be criminally liable. This court-martial proceeding allowed us to do just that. The evidence of this case was examined thoroughly by the members of the court, who carefully weighed all the facts and came to a determination. The proceedings were open for all to scrutinize, and draw their own conclusion about the fairness of the military judicial process. The Marine Corps continues to feel deeply about all those whose lives were forever altered by this tragedy.

The acquittal on the manslaughter charges sparked outrage in Italy and across Europe. On March 5, 1999, Secretary of Defense William Cohen made a statement to reporters about the acquittal and diplomatic relations with Italy: "It's a very emotional decision I think right now but we have strong ties. But our relationship goes very deep and very long so I expect it will continue. . . . Everyone still feels the heartfelt grief that we want to share with the families who suffered the loss of their loved ones. This was a very difficult case and all I can say is it was open, it was fair in terms of the process itself and they came to the conclusion that there was not criminal misconduct. And I can't second guess that." On his arrival in Naples, Cohen spoke by phone with Italian Defense Minister Carlo Scognamiglio. "We had a good conversation," he said. "He understands the situation. He thanked me for giving him a personal recitation of the facts. . . . Our relationship is still strong."[81]

Originally, Captain Schweitzer was charged with manslaughter and the other charges against Ashby, but those charges were dropped when Ashby was acquitted of the manslaughter charges. The investigation revealed that Schweitzer had filmed part of the flight just before the jet cut the wires of the ski lift. It was not an official taping as part of the mission but only a "have video" taken by the crew.

While the Marine Corps wanted to be sure of a thorough and fair investigation, it would not tolerate any lack of integrity. Schweitzer admitted burning the tapes, and he pled guilty to obstruction of justice and conspiracy for the burning of a videotape.

On April 2, 1999, the jury concluded its deliberation at Camp Lejeune and sentenced Schweitzer to a dismissal from the Marine Corps. It was the equivalent of a dishonorable discharge. The sentence required the approval of the commander, Lieutenant General Peter Pace. Schweitzer's attorney, Dave Beck, unsuccessfully requested a reduction in penalty.

When General Krulak was asked why he thought there was acquittal on the manslaughter charges, he responded: "Better lawyers, better lawyers. The government has got to prove them guilty. They put in a lot of things; their radar altimeter; the testimony of the pilots; the fact that the gondola wasn't on the map. All these things, though not central to the argument, caused enough doubt so that the pilots were found not guilty of manslaughter. The fact that the radar altimeter didn't work—again, the reality was we tested it and it did work. But even if it didn't work, the rules stated that if an altimeter was faulty, the aircraft was to immediately climb to 2,000 feet. The pilots claimed that they thought that the height restriction was 1,000 versus 2,000 feet. The reality is different, for in the cockpit itself they found documentation that said 2,000 feet. There are just a lot of things. But there was so much controversy swirling that the defense made a good case. That's the way the Uniform Code of Military Justice and our legal system works. You are innocent until you are proven guilty.

"The openness in the way the trial was conducted was significant in the impact the incident had on the Marine Corps. The lawyer would explain what was going on. It made a major difference. On the first day there were hundreds of people. By the end of the third day, there were only about five or six. The press, which could have just been devastating to the Marine Corps, was in fact pretty fair. We would be unhappy with a specific decision but the bottom line was, it was completely open to the public.

"Were they flying recklessly? The court said no. I'm not the court. I say when you are flying 150 miles an hour above the speed limit, when you are flying and you hit a cable that is 1,700 feet below your minimum altitude, and you had just done a barrel roll within two minutes of hitting that cable, yes, I would say they were flying recklessly.

"I absolutely felt no pressure from the President of the United States, from the Secretary of State, from the Secretary of Defense, from the Secretary of the Navy, absolutely zero pressure. If I had felt pressure, I think my track record would have shown that I would have told them to get stuffed! My entire effort was to find out really happened and have justice be done. Do the right thing. The bottom line is when the first press came out on the trial, the lead article in the *Washington Post*, the most liberal of all papers, applauded the Marine Corps' handling of this case. People may disagree with the verdicts. People disagree with verdicts in many cases. That's not the issue. The issue is was it done right? Was there a trial? Was all the evidence made available? Yes! Did we try to cover up anything? The answer was no![82]

"The important aspect of the investigation was to learn what caused the accident, not to find a scapegoat, and to identify procedures that needed to be taken to prevent it from happening again. U.S. low-level flying in Italy was immediately suspended. Italy and the United States made a change in procedure: units not permanently based in Italy—like the aircrew that caused the accident—would not be allowed to carry out low-level flights unless specifically authorized by the Italian Defense Ministry. A panel was established for much closer coordination between the American and Italian military to include the submission of a daily report on intended flights by the United States. At the time, Italy played a major role in the military campaign over Kosovo. Flight safety rules and procedures were established to ensure that training and operational flights can take place over Italy by U.S. planes, in a safe manner and in a way that would prevent this type of accident again. A United Press International article on April 16, 1999, stated that the report signed by Italian Defense attaché Brigadier General Pino Bernardis 'concludes that the accident was caused by air crew error and that supervisory error occurred within the air crew chain of command.'"[83]

It is interesting that the four-star generals being studied here understood the importance of accountability as more junior officers, and certainly as they went up in rank and responsibility.

As lieutenant colonel on an exercise at Iwo Jima, Commandant Krulak had a potential tragedy for which he accepted responsibility: "It was General Steele and Colonel Esau's belief that in all probability the most likely use of Marines was to be in some kind of evacuation mission and so that's what we did. At Iwo Jima, Beach Guard, we were the first battalion to land in battalion strength on Iwo Jima since the war, and it was a very emotional event.

"I made a terrible mistake at Beach Guard that almost cost the life of one of my Marines. We had left Hawaii and had been traveling to the Pacific and, although we were doing a lot of PT on board the ship, it's never the same as the reality of being on the ground and humping gear, et cetera. So we had landed on Iwo Jima and did the exercise and it was very successful and I had my Marines stack arms and then called the MAU commander and asked him if he would let me take the battalion to the top of Mount Suribachi. We had come all the way to Iwo Jima and it would have been a crime not to go on Suribachi. He said, 'Yes, go.' We started moving to Suribachi. It was a hot day and they don't call it the sulphur island for nothing. I mean it has active sulpha vents and the island itself is hot. I did a lousy map recon, because as the crow flies from the airfield to Suribachi is nothing, but to get there you do a twist and turn to get past little hills and not so little hills. We hadn't been using enough water so that when we got to the top of Mount Suribachi, we had a near casualty who almost died and, in fact, we had to medevac him off the top of Suribachi itself. At the time, I thought he was dead. And I don't think I've ever felt worse about anything. I was not worried about my career, but about my absolute lack of sensitivity to time, distance, heat, and the lack of water. I was so focused on this battalion's opportunity to climb to the top of Mount Suribachi and to give each one of my Marines that unbelievable experience, that I almost cost a Marine's life. Most of the Marines didn't even know it happened, so they were just emotionally touched by being on Suribachi and tears flowing and all that. But the reality is we almost killed a Marine because I had done poor planning and forgotten many of the basics. On the way back we took it very slowly. We settled into our camp, spent the night there and evacuated off the next day and, at that point, found out that the Marine was going to be okay. You're a lieutenant colonel in the Marine Corps and you're still making PFC mistakes. A lesson to be learned here is you need to really understand what ship board life is like and the impact it has on the physical condition of your people. You can never forget the basics."

General Tony Zinni described an incident involving a mishap of one of his Marines: "I had an experience in Okinawa with a machinegun fire incident. This company commander was conducting a live fire range over the weekend, and he wanted to do an envelopment exercise, lay down a base of fire. There was nothing that precluded him from doing this. But the way the range was laid out and the envelopment he was going to do ended up firing out of the range. Some of the rounds went into a small Okinawan village. It didn't do any damage. It was way at the end of the range. There was an investigation, and the investigation found that there wasn't enough guidance in the range regs, but it was critical of this officer for his decision.

"I was bothered by this. There was a push to relieve him of his command. I didn't think that was right, and I thought that we had not given him enough information to do this type of operation. So I went to the Commanding General Norm Smith and I said if you want to hold somebody responsible—and the commands above him wanted to but were really out to get ahead by doing so, to show the Japanese that we would take action.

"I said, 'First of all, this company commander was training on a weekend. He had his company out there trying to do the right thing, and he's a damn good company commander.' The range regs were too vague, they gave insufficient guidance.

"He probably didn't make the best decision in the world. If he had analyzed that range a little bit more, he would have seen that that envelopment may not have been the best thing to do, but things were not real clear, but it may not have been the best idea. He was caught up in the training, and he made the decision.

"I said, 'Look, this guy learned something from this, and nobody got hurt. I have my obligation as the regimental commander. I obviously didn't prepare him well enough if he went out there and did this, so it's my fault.' I said, 'If somebody has to be relieved, you relieve me and not this company commander. If you relieve this company commander, you're going to have to relieve me, too.'

"So General Smith said, 'You know, you've put me in a tough spot, because the powers that be really want to take action against this company commander.'

"I said, 'Look, I'm not making an idle offer. I'm responsible.'

"He [General Smith] obviously didn't relieve me, didn't relieve the company commander, he said, 'Well, make sure he understands what he did.'

"General Smith took the heat, too. The relationships with the Okinawans were always very strained, because of a lot of training incidents and things that were happening. So it was always delicate, politically.

"But I went back and, of course, everybody found out what had happened. That I was at fault—relieved me. I didn't tell anybody, but everybody found out what happened. I think the point is not having a 'zero defects' mentality. You know, there are obviously killer things that can go wrong that are going to ruin a career, obviously, culpable negligence or criminal negligence, or something so drastic in its outcome and consequence that you can't avoid it.

"But absent that, if someone is trying to do the right thing, if you look at it and they're using their best judgment, if they're learning from it, you have to allow them some room to make those mistakes. You can't have the 'zero defects' mentality where you kill everybody.

"Sometimes a commander has got to stand in the way of that spear. You've got to be willing to take it on yourself, because that's what your troops expect from you, that you would support them. I didn't do that to gain any more respect or admiration or anything else. It was the right thing to do in my mind.

"You couldn't fake it out there. You were doing a disservice to your troops, yourself and the mission by not telling it like it was. If it was screwed up, you had better say it was screwed up, because it was expected of you. Your peers would chastise you for not stepping up and accepting the responsibility. Your subordinates would lose respect for you if you didn't."

Zinni was asked: "How far did that company commander go? Did he still make a career?"

"Yes," he replied, "he's still in. This incident was not a career-ender. I wouldn't let it be. I wrote his fitness report."[84]

Willingness to take the blame is part of a leader's character. In none of the incidents described in this chapter was there any attempt to avoid accepting responsibility or to find a scapegoat to blame to take pressure off the senior leadership.

To be successful as a leader, particularly when the span of your responsibilities grows, you must delegate. But while you can delegate authority, you cannot delegate responsibility. Commandant Krulak summed it up: "As a Marine you are expected to take responsibility for yourself and to assume responsibility for others. . . . accountability is the proof of whether or not you've been responsible. . . . accountability is what the nation expects of our Corps."

Chapter 11

# "Miracles Must Be Wrought if Victories Are to Be Won": Character and Leadership

## Initiative

In his book *First to Fight: An Inside View of the U.S. Marine Corps*, Lieutenant General Victor H. Krulak wrote:

> The space separating defeat and victory is often very small, and the more powerful assailant does not always prevail. "The battle, sir," said Patrick Henry, "is not to the strong alone; it is to the vigilant, the active, the brave." Most often, the ingredients of victory are initiative, resourcefulness, adroitness, and improvisation.
>
> The Greeks before the walls of Troy were the weaker by far. But they created the Horse, which erased the difference between weak and strong, and Greece triumphed.
>
> The American colonists at Princeton had little hope of matching, much less exceeding, the British strength. Yet they won by improvisation. Leaving campfires to flicker in the night, the Americans in fact broke camp and surprised and routed the more powerful British.
>
> At Cannae, Chancellorsville, the Plains of Abraham, and Attu, one of the contestants made his tactical or strategic point by deception and improvisation.
>
> Improvisation has been a way of life for the Marines. Examples extend all the way from conversion of native Central American

livestock and canoes into military transportation to use of a home window air conditioner in Vietnam to keep the electronics systems in a complex aircraft operational. But few improvisations are more impressive than their figuring our how to drop bombs accurately in the dark or their contriving to land at Inchon, Korea, in 1950 without the forces, means, or time to do the job.[1]

Commandant Lemuel C. Shepherd, Jr., commented: "In battle you can't always do things by the book. You've got to take initiative in combat. Take chances when the opportunity arises to gain a victory." He described the advantage our military forces had in World War II in the Pacific by having initiative when the Japanese soldier did not: "The Japanese soldiers didn't use their initiative a great deal. I know they didn't nor did they exploit their advantages when they had a chance. I don't think they were imaginative fighters. They were sturdy. They can live on practically nothing—a little rice. They were good fighters, but when a Japanese soldier was ordered to hold a position he stayed there. There were very few Japanese prisoners ever taken. I think that at the beginning of the war, the Japs made very remarkable advances—down through the Malay Peninsula, Singapore, and all through the South West Pacific islands—and they built up a reputations of being wonderful jungle fighters.

"It's a myth that the Jap was a super jungle fighter. I found in my experience that our Marines were better jungle fighters than the Japs were. We just dispelled this theoretical superiority of the Jap as a jungle fighter. They were cunning. They were determined. And they were painstaking in their digging—they were always digging and organizing the ground, but they certainly didn't have much imagination, and I don't think that their units were too effective. But they were good fighters; there wasn't any question about that."[2]

Examples of the initiative of senior Marine Corps leaders abound. When Sailors on liberty in foreign countries engaged in disorderly conduct and got into fights, often it was the Marine Corps MPs that kept things under control. Commandant Barrow reflected: "At the end of World War II, the Sixth Fleet put ashore between 3,000 and 7,000 sailors a night in cities with back pay and no inhibitions. At a briefing, the senior commanders expressed concern. The shore patrol was a job no one wanted and got passed around. I raised my hand to the commodore and the senior Marine colonel and said, 'Do you want this to work right? Make me the shore patrol officer for every damn liberty port.'

"So they looked like they could have just about died of appreciation. 'Gosh, Barrow, that's good. You mean you will do this at every . . . at every port?' I said, 'I will do it at every port. I just want some conditions. I want some people assigned to me permanently. I don't care what their regular duties are. They could be from other ships and places, but I want to do some screening. I want a small cadre that knows how to go into a place and set up communications, get a little motor pool going, and to learn the layout of the land, liaison with the local police, learn what places are bad and which are good, and we have a little set procedure. It all happens like that and you don't have to educate people. I'll be in charge.'

"It was a great success. We came out of the Mediterranean with, at that time, the lowest shore patrol incidents, only twelve to be exact, and none of them were major, for the entire cruise. We got a lot of accolades. We did what anybody who'd think about it would do. We knew the way to deal with these people, particularly if you had the experience of dealing with them. You don't wait for the guy that's got some beer in him to be a problem and then you end up having to fight him or separating him from some problem that he's deeply emerged in. You blanket this whole community with shore patrol; if a man had too much to drink, which is the root cause of most problems, we whisked him back to the ship before he got into trouble. We helped him. We were looked upon as friendly cops. Those guys didn't want to get in trouble. They wanted to get back and they did what we asked them to do. So the climate of helping out other people was what did it. It was a nice experience."[3]

After the Republic of North Korea invaded South Korea on June 25, 1950, Lieutenant Colonel Ray Davis was given command of 1st Battalion of the 7th Marines. He used incredible initiative to form the 7th Marine Regiment. According to Davis:

> When the war started the 7th Marine Regiment didn't exist. It had been deleted after World War II, and we needed to form a new regiment. When I arrived at Camp Pendleton in August 1950, [Colonel Homer L.] Litzenberg, commanding officer of the 7th Marines, asked for me and told me that I had five days to form a new 1st Battalion, get it on a ship, and get to war.
>
> Without initiative I would be leaving for Inchon, Korea, with less than half an infantry battalion. I did what had to be done in this, and many other, situations during my career. Fortunately there came a convoy of trucks into my Tent Camp Two,

mainly hauling equipment. I told four of my senior officers to commandeer one truck each, start driving around the many acres of Camp Pendleton, and ask every group of Marines they saw, "Anybody want to go to Korea?" Soon truckloads of Marine "volunteers" came back into Tent Camp Two. All in all, we fulfilled our 800-troop requirement in this innovative manner—in just eight hours of "recruiting!"

Davis also illustrated leadership as well as initiative:

We used the first two of five days just gaining the men, their equipment, and their administrative records. The third and fourth days were spent firing their rifles, practicing small unit tactics, and hiking in the rough Pendleton hills. Soon they were on buses heading for San Diego and the good ship USS *Okanogan*. This was a Navy assault transport built for a 1,500-man Marine Infantry Battalion with all of its supporting units, such as artillery, plus weapons and equipment.

After 18 days at sea and a brief stop in Japan, we landed at Inchon Harbor, as the reserve battalion of the 1st Marine Division's reserve regiment, the 7th Marines. The 5th Marines of Lieutenant Colonel Ray Murray had hit Wolmi-do Island off Inchon, the Division's left flank of the amphibious assault. Chesty Puller, in command of the 1st Marines, hit the right flank over the beach walls.

We had not relaxed for the 18-day sea voyage. We trained small units as hard as we could, day and night, during the trip. In addition to firing our rifles at every target we could find from the fantail of the *Okanogan*, we fired machineguns, mortars, rocket launchers, and threw hand grenades at every piece of trash, orange crates, or whatever the ship's crew would toss overboard for us. At first naturally these Navy folks were aghast to hear my operational desires, but they really entered into the innovative scheme. We had over two weeks of good, solid training for Marines who were super-motivated. This was no game; they were going to war at Inchon, the port city to Seoul, the capital of South Korea. It had been overrun by North Korean troops on 25 June 1950.

It was the same way on land. We did not simply go for a stroll through the countryside while in the mobile rear as reserve. We hit every hill enroute to and around Seoul as if it were still covered with enemy—which the 5th and 1st Marines had mostly cleared out. Our tactics were better every day—and night—by the time we crossed the Han River and were given the mission of moving after the enemy who headed north from Seoul.[4]

General Tony Zinni described an occasion when he used initiative as a junior officer. One night at the officers' club bar, some of the officers were talking about a riot in the guard house. Zinni had had a few beers, and told the group at the club, "I can handle the problems we've got here."

His regimental commander learned of his comments and said to Zinni, "I heard you think you can get the guard to handle the situation. Good, you're now the new guard company commander. You've got free rein. You can set up the guard any way you want. Take a day and decide what you want and get back to me with what you propose."

Zinni wanted 100 volunteers of different races who were all over 6 feet tall and weighed at least 200 pounds. He was given permission to recruit anyone he thought would be a good member of the guard team. Zinni raised the volunteers and was pleased that a large number of the group were African-Americans, Hispanics, and other minorities. As one of the chief enlisted leaders, he selected an African-American gunnery sergeant whom he described as a "model Marine" who had assignments as a drill instructor, was a superb marksman, and had taught at the Corps Physical Fitness Academy. A second senior NCO he selected weighed 250 pounds, was an expert in martial arts with a third degree black belt in judo, and was the Marine Corps heavyweight judo champion. Zinni had two lieutenants, one black and the other Jewish. He wanted to illustrate how such a diverse collection of Marines could work together. The morning physical training sessions were very visible to the entire camp to impress all with their size, strength, and condition.

Human nature being what it is, the guard unit was tested with demonstrations and challenging confrontations. There were still stabbings, cuts and bruises, and gang threats. One of Zinni's cleverest moves was to spray the troublemakers during a riot with an indelible ink so those inmates who led the disturbance could be identified after the riot came under control.

Zinni established the opportunity for the inmates to discuss their issues; in doing so, he was able to sort out who the weak commanders were and found that they had the most difficulty maintaining control and thus the largest number of Marines in the guard house for discipline violations. He organized human relations classes to improve, among other things, race relations. It didn't happen overnight, but Zinni's initiative and leadership resulted in bringing the riots, demonstrations, and discipline problems under control.[5]

General Ray Davis gave some sound advice on initiative: "There is often a fine line between a medal and a court-martial." If an officer is afraid that he might make a mistake during a show of initiative, he will be reluctant to be innovative. The fear of making a mistake within the officer and NCO ranks is unhealthy and can be disastrous to the readiness of the Marine Corps.

Many of the senior generals in this study addressed their positions on initiative and the possibility of mistakes. General Oliver Prince Smith, who commanded the Marine Division in the Korean War, supported his staff, expecting and receiving maximum effort from them: "I don't want an officer on my staff who never makes an error or mistake because I will strongly suspect that he isn't doing anything or that he is blaming his mistakes on someone else."[6]

One of General Holland M. Smith's long-time staff members said of the general, "Few will know that he often threw the protective cloak of his authority and position around an erring subordinate who he knew to be capable of rising above his mistakes."[7]

Commandant Robert H. Barrow emphasized that:

> we must do more to develop the teacher and scholar relationship spoken of in the Marine Corps Manual. Our younger officers and men realize that they are very much in a learning role and that a peacetime training atmosphere is one in which mistakes can be made and corrected without the consequences often imposed by war. Accordingly, seniors should be especially mindful of the need to be patient, to make allowances for error, to evaluate and explain, and to be reasonable and tactful in making corrections. As stated in the May 1971 *Marine Leader*, "Inertia and lack of aggressiveness are more reprehensible than mistakes or errors in judgment."
>
> While it is essential that we require our young officers and men to adhere to high standards of performance and conduct,

this requirement should not lead to a state of absolute conformity. Within the precept of our standards, we should encourage individualism, imagination, and bold initiative.[8]

One of the best messages on the importance of initiative and mistakes made in being innovative came from Commandant Alfred Gray in *Warfighting*:

> Marine Corps doctrine demands professional competence among its leaders. As military professionals charged with the defense of the nation, Marine leaders must be true experts in the conduct of war. They must be men of action and of intellect both, skilled at "getting things done" while at the same time conversant in the military art. Resolute and self-reliant in their decisions, they must also be energetic and insistent in execution.
>
> The military profession is a thinking profession. Officers particularly are expected to be students of the art and science of war at all levels—tactical, operational, and strategic—with a solid foundation in military theory and a knowledge of military history and the timeless lessons to be gained from it.
>
> Leaders must have a strong sense of the great responsibility of their office; the resources they will expend in war are human lives.
>
> The Marine Corps' style of warfare requires intelligent leaders with a penchant for boldness and initiative down to the lowest levels. Boldness is an essential moral trait in a leader, for it generates combat power beyond the physical means at hand. Initiative, the willingness to act on one's own judgment, is a prerequisite for boldness. These traits carried to excess can lead to rashness, but we must realize that errors by junior leaders stemming from over-boldness are a necessary part of learning. We should deal with such errors leniently; there must be no "zero defects" mentality. Not only must we not stifle boldness or initiative, we must continue to encourage both traits in *spite of mistakes*. On the other hand, we should deal severely with errors of inaction or timidity. We will not accept lack of orders as justification for inaction; *it is each Marine's duty to take initiative as the situation demands*.

Critiques are an important part of training because critical self-analysis, even after success, is essential to improvement. Their purpose is to draw out the lessons of training. As a result, we should conduct critiques immediately after completing the training, before the memory of the events has faded. Critiques should be held in an atmosphere of open and frank dialogue in which all hands are encouraged to contribute. We learn as much from mistakes as from things done well, so we must be willing to admit and discuss them. Of course, a subordinate's willingness to admit mistakes depends on the commander's willingness to tolerate them. Because we recognize that no two situations in war are the same, our critiques should focus not so much on the actions we took as on why we took those actions and why they brought the results they did.[9]

Often, officers articulate in strong terms how restricted they felt because of a lack of latitude or authority, while others believe that they had full latitude to do whatever was necessary; if something was not proscribed by law or regulation, they figured it was within their authority. Better to ask forgiveness than ask for permission. An officer who wants a risk-free environment normally will not (and should not) rise very high in rank and responsibility. A leader can and should learn from mistakes. Mistakes are a fact of life in any endeavor.

But there are caveats regarding younger officers and the use of initiative. A junior officer does not know enough or have the experience to be a division commander. Before a younger officer moves out too much, he needs the feel, the experience, the judgment that come through a period of time of learning his job. Part of the learning process is for senior officers to truly delegate authority downward and provide the latitude for learning and the inevitability of making mistakes.

An officer can just sit back and take whatever comes into the office or his unit that can be handled easily. But to be given increasing responsibility, he should go out and stir things up. The best officer in the Marine Corps is the officer who goes out and looks for challenges. When you expose yourself by using initiative you are going to make some mistakes, but you will also accomplish a lot more. When an officer showing initiative has honorable intentions, was looking out for his people, was fighting to improve their quality of lifestyle and their contribution to making a better Marine Corps, to improve readiness, always trying hard, giving the job the best effort, then mistakes can be and are acceptable.

## The Role of Faith

Commandant Lejeune wrote in his memoir: "I often wonder why the religious side of the soldiers' lives is not more often described. Surely it is a theme worthy of the genius of those having the gift of expressing beautiful thoughts in exquisite poetry or in noble prose."[10]

Throughout the history of the Marine Corps, its leaders have been among the most religious of any institution in this country. They were and are deeply devout, and their belief in and reliance on God are an integral part of their desire to serve in a profession in which their lives and the lives of those they lead are constantly on the line in service and love for God and country. Their faith carries them through many of the lonely challenges they have as leaders, particularly in combat, but equally important in the development of Marines: enlisted, NCOs, and officers.

General Lejeune expressed the support he got from his belief in God upon his selection to command the Army's 2[d] Division in France during World War I:

> All the senior officers of the Division came in to congratulate me. Somehow, I don't feel at all elated, but I am sobered by the task before me, the necessity of making good, the responsibility for the well-being and the lives of 28,000 officers and men, and, greatest of all, the fact that my acts may in some critical moment have a decisive effect in winning or losing a battle. Every night of my life, I pray to God to take from my heart all thought of self or personal advancement, and to make me able to do my full duty as a man and as a General towards my men and my country.[11]

> While interesting myself wholeheartedly in the military training of the Division, I deemed my highest duty to be the welding of all its units into a harmonious whole, and the kindling and fostering of a division spirit, or esprit which would animate the hearts of all its officers and men.

> There is no substitute for the spiritual in war. Miracles must be wrought if victories are to be won, and to work miracles men's hearts must be afire with self-sacrificing love for each other, for their units, for their division, and for their country. If each man knows that all the officers and men in his division are animated with the same fiery

> zeal as he himself feels, unquenchable courage and unconquerable determination crush out fear and death becomes preferable to defeat or dishonor.
>
> Fortunate indeed is the leader who commands such men, and it is his most sacred duty to purify his own soul and to cast out from it all unworthy motives, for men are quick to detect pretense or insincerity in their leaders, and worse than useless as a leader is the man in whom they find evidences of hypocrisy or undue timidity, or whose acts do not square with his words.... It is indeed true that in war the spiritual is to the material as three or even four to one.[12]

General Lejeune described the religious services held in France when he was visited by Secretary of the Navy Daniels and his wife:

> On Easter morning, we attended an unusual service in a theater located in a Second Division town. Every seat was taken by a soldier, a marine, or a welfare worker. On the stage were Secretary Daniels (a Methodist), a Catholic chaplain, a Presbyterian chaplain, and I (an Episcopalian). The Presbyterian chaplain said the prayers, the men sang the hymns, the Catholic chaplain read a chapter from the Bible, and Mr. Daniels preached the sermon.[13]

General Lejeune commented on the role of the spiritual and that it was first the chaplains who provided it. He wrote about:

> a young man who graduated from the Virginia Theological Seminary only a year or two before we entered the war. His father, Bishop Arthur Lloyd, suggested that he apply for appointment as a chaplain in the Army. He declined to do so, but enlisted instead, saying that he was too young to be a chaplain, and that he believed he would have greater influence among the men if he were a private soldier. He went overseas and served with a combat company, and regularly, on the nights before going into battle, he held communion service, and every man in his company, whether he were Catholic, Protestant, or Jew, joined in the service and took communion. Young Lloyd came home a physical wreck from the effects of

poison gas, but valiantly continued his ministry until the end, which came two or three years after his return from the war.[14]

Of obvious importance of the role of God in our military leadership is the chaplain. I discussed the chaplain's role and responsibility with Chaplain Captain Eli Takesian, USN (Ret.), who commented: "In every instance, regardless of conditions, the basic spiritual requirements of a chaplain's holy ordination remain constant, in war as in peace." He went on to say that the statement has been made within their calling that chaplains "bring God to people, and people to God," that "chaplains are, or should be, the spiritual bearers of faith, hope, compassion, and healing."

Lieutenant General Victor Krulak had an abiding faith that he believed was necessary for a military man who makes sacrifices. He had a very perceptive insight into the role of faith: "Survival is not enough. You don't fight just to survive. You fight for a purpose, and the purpose probably has some emotion as well as realism in it, and you know that the odds of survival are something less than 100 percent, and that there has to be a Providence that helps to make the decision that will preserve you and those around you.

"If you regard it as a mechanical product of learning all about the profession and just being able, as setting up a computer program, to turn on the current and press a few buttons to get it started, then the whole emotion of being a commander is lost. You might just as well have a computer for a commander, to make your decisions."[15]

Concerning the role of faith in his life as a Marine, Commandant Charles C. Krulak said, "My belief in the Living God played a significant role in my life as a Marine. I became a Christian while attending the U.S. Army Command and General Staff College and from that moment on, Christ played a major role in almost every decision I made . . . as a husband, father, and Marine officer. The more senior I became, the more time I spent on my knees. I did NOT pray for Chuck Krulak. . . . I prayed for those in the Chain of Command, I prayed for wisdom in making decisions, I prayed for my Marines, and I prayed for the Marine Corps. I did not evangelize, but I was not afraid to let people know where I stood regarding my religion. While Commandant, I am sure that the vast majority of my Marines knew that I was a Christian. No major decision was made by me as Commandant that I did not pray about first. I am not ashamed about that fact. Knowing all of the living Commandants, I am convinced that each of them shared a deep sense of faith and that my beliefs were not unique."[16]

Krulak recounted an episode during the Saipan campaign during World War II. General Holland M. Smith came ashore just a couple of hours after the landing had started and saw a little barbed wire enclosure that held three bedraggled Japanese prisoners who had no water or shade. Smith told one of the guards, "Tell your commanding officer that I want this corrected." Responding to a comment that the prisoners were the enemy, "He drew himself up and he said, 'We're civilized. We're decent. We're God-fearing men, and that's the way we must behave. We're not savages.'" Krulak continued, "Well, I feel that very strongly. War's a paradox of brutalities, but over it all, there has to be a faith that you and I are doing the right thing, that you're being guided in your decisions by some force that's far greater than any textbook that you've seen, else you just wouldn't have the courage to make the decision."

General Krulak further said in describing Smith: "Smith was a tremendously spiritual man, willing to be regarded as a practicing Christian and anxious to do the things that a practicing Christian is supposed to do. He had a warm feeling for everyone around him, whether it was his clerk or his orderly, or his aide or his cook."[17]

General Smith, according to his aide Captain Mac Asbill, had a special fondness for the clergy, and some of his best friends were Catholic priests. He told a story of one of these priests who early in the war wanted to join a Marine Raider battalion that was planning a dangerous mission. Smith thought it too risky and would not allow him to go. The priest then spoke to the Raiders, induced them to pray that he be allowed to join them, and then told the general that if he were not allowed to go, the faith of 1,500 Marines would be destroyed. The general told him he could go.[18]

Commandant Lemuel C. Shepherd, Jr., provided an insight into the role of God and faith: "I felt very strongly about the spiritual. I felt that we needed the help of the Almighty to carry us on in this war that we were fighting for Christianity. The fact that we had landed [on Guam during World War II] on Easter Sunday morning had somewhat of a spiritual effect, and I felt that it was only with God's help that we were able to overcome the adversities with which we were faced. Being a religious man myself, I gave full support in every possible way to my chaplains. I attended services regularly. I always supported my chaplains and addressed a chaplains' convention in Chicago after the war.

"In battle is when men need spiritual help. In combat there is only one person who can help you and that is God. I recall distinctly during the battle for Guam—I think it was near the close of the campaign—when I was returning from a visit with the troops. I came to a gathering of men in a clearing in a dump of woods and I stopped to see what was going on there. The men were from the 4th Marines and they were having a service. The men had asked the chaplain if he would conduct this service, to thank Almighty God for the victory they had attained during the past several days. It was near the end of the campaign, up by Ritidian Point, northern tip of Guam. It had just been captured and the battle was more or less over. The men had called the chaplain and asked him if he would conduct services, to thank Almighty God for sparing their lives in the campaign.

"So I think the men—to put it very simply—I'm sure they derived great spiritual benefit from the chaplains and they helped to win the campaign. I gave my chaplains full support in everything they did—going to church—I'd always go to Sunday services wherever we were stationed for any length of time. I'd see that chapels were built and services conducted. I attended service, at least one or two every Sunday during training periods and also during battles whenever I was able to do so."

Shepherd's oral history interviewer asked him: "Were you generally satisfied with the type of chaplain that served you? Were they prepared for this type of thing?" He responded: "Well, I'll tell you, some were and some were not always well prepared, for instance whenever a chaplain joined my division, I would talk to him personally, and I said, 'Now, chaplain, I want you to get out with the men in battle. Your job is to be up there with the front line troops and to give the spiritual help that they require whenever possible and with the Romanists to conduct the last rites for the dying and severely wounded. Furthermore you can do a great deal by being with wounded and writing a note to the man's parents saying, 'I just talked to your son, he has a wound but he's going to come through it all right. He's going to get well, and he just asked me to tell you he is all right.' I said, 'Your place is at the front, not sitting in some headquarters command post.' I insisted on their performing not just their religious duties, but a type of, you might call it, Red Cross duty, by being up in the dressing stations, behind the front lines. I didn't actually require them to be on the front line, but in the dressing stations, the first aid stations behind the lines, to administer the last rites in case of the seriously wounded, talk to the men, give them special help and write letters and things of that nature. As a whole, I impressed upon the chaplains to get up there close to the fighting.

"A chaplain was just one of the command. Therefore, they had to be in physical and mental condition to march and to see men die and to carry on their religious devotions in the field which was foreign to many who had only been in some little parish where all they had to do was to call on their parishioners and preach a sermon."[19]

When fighting to take Guadalcanal, Chesty Puller was very sensitive and conscious of the care of the bodies of his dead Marines. His biographer Burke Davis wrote:

> Dr. Smith [Dr. Edward L. Smith, Jr., one of the unit's physicians] noted in his diary that Puller seemed more concerned over losses: "He has become almost fanatical in his desire to see that the men are properly cared for. If a man's body is lost he is greatly disturbed, and frets about the time lost before he can recover the body and give it a decent burial. Not an outwardly religious man himself, he encourages divine services to be held frequently on the front lines for the men who want them. He would much sooner give services himself than not to have any." Puller was often dissatisfied with a chaplain's talk to the men and would grumble: "Maybe it's time I tried my hand. I think I could do better." Dr. Smith thought he would have been the island's best chaplain, and wrote in open admiration: "Whatever he says is sincere. I have never seen an officer with so little bluff."[20]

Puller believed in leading from the front, and he expected the same of his chaplains. During combat in the Pacific, Burke Davis described Puller's attitude toward chaplains in performing their responsibilities:

> A regimental chaplain came to Puller's tent one night in December. "Colonel, I want you to get out an order for me."
>
> "I can't get you an order. See Colonel Frisbie, he's your man."
>
> "I'm afraid of him."
>
> "His bark's worse than his bite. If you have a reasonable request, he'll help you. What's on your mind? Maybe I can give a hand."
>
> "Well. I want you to prohibit all these good Protestant boys from joining the Catholic Church."
>
> "Holy smoke, man, we can't do that! If they're deserting you, there must be a reason. If you fellows would get down to work like the Catholic chaplains, you'd have no trouble."

The disgruntled minister went away.[21]

Puller had another confrontation with the same chaplain while traveling in the combat area visiting his troops:

> The patrol rode the last few miles into the camp at Cape Gloucester. As Puller jumped from a truck he was confronted by an outstretched hand—it was his acquaintance, the Protestant chaplain who had complained of Catholic inroads on New Guinea. Puller was in no mood to befriend him.
>
> "Where've you been all this time?"
>
> "Why, I've been here doing my best to help out."
>
> "You weren't up where the fighting was. I think I'll prefer charges against you for being absent from your regiment."
>
> "Colonel, I was with the medical battalion, aiding the wounded. We worked around the clock."
>
> "They've got a chaplain of their own. Your place was with the fighting men—your own battalion. You remember our little talk about Protestant boys joining the Catholics? Well, conduct like yours is one reason for it. They see those priests doing their duty and see you evading it. I can't work up much sympathy for you."[22]

General Lewis W. Walt, who was the senior Marine Commander in the Vietnam War, provided his thoughts on the role of the chaplain in his book *Strange War, Strange Strategy*:

> It would be presumptuous for me to explain the role of the ministry in Vietnam. That has been done in large part by Chaplain John O'Connor and I hope by others who can equally illuminate the role of the military chaplain in the vortex of war. What I have to say is addressed only to the type of man we, the soldiers, have come to expect from the men of God of all faiths who accompany us. It is one small part of the reason we hold them in such respect and seek them out for relief from our own travail.[23]

General Walt gave an example of why he believed so strongly in the chaplain's role in combat:

> M Company made contact early, with one platoon engaged, and the chaplain moved forward toward the fight, calm and confident, attending the wounded with dignity and priestly demeanor, administering last rites to the dead as he found them on the battlefield—words of faith and dignity above the sound of battle. Soon the execution of his office as a chaplain brought him to the forefront of the fight, where he used his young strength to pull or carry wounded and dead men into the shelter of a fold of ground, into a little temporary chapel only feet away from the slashing bullets, but sanctified for a moment at least by his presence and faith.[24]

In personal discussions with Commandants, I asked them about their faith. Commandant Kelley told me, "One should never confuse 'faith' as exclusively related to religion. I view it in a much broader context. In that regard, let me make two points. First, I do not and never have worn my religious beliefs on my sleeve. I am an orthodox and devout Christian who believes that actions prove more than words. Second, almost six decades ago I took a solemn oath to support and defend our Constitution—a document which clearly delineates the separation of church and state. From the beginning of my service to our country, I have been influenced by the teachings of the Augustinian Fathers of Villanova University—that the two most important words in life, regardless of one's religion, are honesty and integrity. For without a strict adherence to both, everything else becomes hollow to meaningless. So, rather than talking about 'faith' in a religious context, I prefer to think about my personal adherence to 'standards of right behavior.'

"I have always found it interesting to note that the officer corps of our military establishment is held to the highest standards of right behavior. I believe that it is a product of humility, honesty, moral courage, trust, and allegiance manifested by honorable men and women.

"It is fitting, I believe, that for 230 years Marines have been influenced and motivated by two simple Latin words—*Semper Fidelis*—Always Faithful. So, when I think of 'faith' I also think of 'faithful' and then ask: 'Wouldn't it be a wonderful world if each of us were *Semper Fidelis* to a God of our choosing, to our beloved nation, to our family, and to each other?'"[25]

Commandant Mundy answered questions about faith: "I have been a Christian since early childhood, so it follows naturally that faith has played a part in my entire life. I never faced a crisis, difficult situation, or difficult decision without asking for help from the Almighty. Nor have I ever doubted that the successes in my life and career were not achieved alone. I certainly experienced failures and made mistakes along the way, and tough as they sometimes were, faith always played a part in getting me through them."[26]

Commandant Mundy made an excellent point keeping in mind that chaplains are Naval personnel in that they must meet Marine Corps standards to be effective. Mundy reflected: "The thing I used to tell chaplains in my guidance was, 'Remember that you lead a very unusual flock here and that what might work in the First Baptist Church in Sumter, South Carolina, is not necessarily going to work with Marines. You have to inspire Marines not only because they are going to be saved when they go to heaven, but you also have to fire them up and send them into battle, and you have to understand that they will look at you and perhaps listen to your sermon, but they are also checking out the length of your trousers while you are talking, and they are looking at your haircut, and if your belly is hanging over your belt or if your belt is too short, whatever it is, Marines are going to judge you. Unique. Sailors will not, soldiers will not. But Marines will. So you have to relate to us.'"[27]

In putting into perspective the roles of religion and the chaplain, an article by Captain Eli Takesian, USN (Ret.), provides excellent insights. As a 19-year-old enlisted man in 1951, Takesian was shipped to Korea with the 14th Replacement Draft. He recalled:

> Beset by spiritual and philosophical conflicts, I went to the battalion chaplain and opened my gut, innocently, sincerely, asking about God, justice, war, killing, etc. The chaplain's bland response was a litany of pat answers and, finally, an invitation to join his denomination. He seemed safely insulated by religious dogma, catechisms and systems. Whatever the case, I left his presence empty, dejected, feeling that he had neither heard nor understood. This negative experience manifested positive results years later, especially in Vietnam, where troops posed the same kinds of gut-wrenching questions I had asked in Korea. What I knew, I shared. When uncertain, I would say something like, "I don't know the answer, but let's talk about the question." It helped them. It helped me. To be receptive to,

and honest with, the young Marine who shares from the depths is basic ministry.[28]

In 1970, as Colonel P.X. Kelley took command of 1st Marines in Vietnam, he gave specific instructions to Chaplain Takesian: "Chaplain, since you have ecclesiastical training and experience, I need not pretend to tell you how to do your job. But I have an absolute imperative. Every Marine in this regiment will have access to spiritual ministry; therefore, I expect our chaplains to be with the troops, in the field where they are most needed. Whether a Marine attends religious services is his choice; but he will be given the opportunity. Should human obstacles get in the way of this mandate, tell me. I will address the matter personally."[29]

Chaplain Takesian wrote an article entitled "Preparing for Combat" in which he provided guidelines:

> Chaplains who faithfully serve troops now are developing vital relationships. As good shepherds they know their people; and their people know them by *name*. Identification is important. Sincerity is crucial. Marines have a way of chewing up and spitting out phony-baloney chaplains. Conversely, they cling to chaplains they deem authentic and who truly care.
> 
> When I first reported to 3d Battalion, 5th Marines [in 1967], troops talked incessantly about *their* chaplain, Vic Krulak [one of Lieutenant General Victor Krulak's sons, a Marine Corps chaplain]. They idolized him. Why? Because, they said, Chaplain Krulak was always with them in the field as trusted priest and friend. He gained their confidence the old-fashioned way: he earned it! Although Vic Krulak had transferred from the battalion well before my arrival, his spiritual presence remained.
> 
> "Walk your talk" and "practice what you preach" are apt clichés. Combat offers chaplains ample opportunity to live out their sermons about faith, courage, charity, sacrifice, etc. Most chaplains I knew in Vietnam walked the second mile, faithfully. However, in my opinion, some failed to walk the first, doing their utmost to keep from going to the field. Actions speaking louder than words, their sermons were hollow and their talk cheap. The troops knew it, and responded with cold silence and, in private, with verbal scorn.[30]

Renewal begins when a combat operation ends. Focus is on the dead, the wounded, the grieving. Memorial services are held back at the base camp. Following an operation, my highest priority was to visit casualties in hospitals, whenever possible, before they were flown home. Since the unit commander had occasional access to a helicopter, I often accompanied him to distant hospitals. I delivered mail to the wounded and greetings from guys in the outfit. After I returned from making such calls, troops would gather round and ask questions.

Bonds are so tight that, whenever buddies are killed, troops have a tough time shaking grief. Some swear to never again risk making friends. Yet when replacements report aboard, the brotherhood solidifies, immediately. No words can adequately describe the mystical bond of Marines in combat.[31]

## Delegation

Commandant Alfred M. Gray, Jr., was asked about the challenges he was given by senior people to whom to carry out various tasks: "Did you feel that they had delegated to you and had an appreciation for your ability, giving you additional responsibilities?"

He answered: "They never got in my way. I never had a cap put on me in terms of responsibilities, what I wanted to do, never, from the time I was a young guy until the time I was Commandant. In other words, they were leaders who believed in delegating—they delegated to you. They just turned me loose. They figured I knew what I had to do and what it took to get it done."[32]

Commandant Carl E. Mundy, Jr., who was conscious of the importance of delegating, said, "You cannot make every decision in the Marine Corps. You have good people around you, let them run it. . . . The difficulty is not making every decision yourself. Now, indeed we profess from the earliest stages of our leadership training to delegate authority, let the subordinates act, take responsibility for what they do but don't get in their way in trying to tell them specifically what to do. That is all good philosophy and it is all good in practice but indeed it is difficult to sit still and let others do it."[33]

General Mundy's philosophy on delegation was based on trust. "The willingness," he said, "to empower subordinates. It sounds like currently popular top-quality leadership or whatever we choose to term it. But that is to place trust in people, and then going back to the accountability, to be accountable for what they do. This is right out of maneuver warfare, it is right out of Deming management or anything else, but it is the willingness to say, 'Go for it,' and then the willingness, when he or she does not make it, to say, 'I didn't make it. It's not them. I didn't. I lead this outfit. I'm responsible for what goes on around here. Hang that horse around my neck.'"[34]

Commandant Mundy was very appreciative of those who sought responsibility. He commented that the strength of General Walter E. Boomer, USMC, who was his Assistant Commandant from 1992 to 1994, was as a "superb manager and a superb leader. He is a superb officer, but one of his strengths is his management ability. He wanted to take a more active role in doing what one might presume to be the chief of staff where we want him to run the staff. He did not want minor decisions coming to me as they had. I appreciated that the Commandant doesn't have time to be involved in everything. And Walt, rightfully, I think, saw that he would handle the day-to-day operations of the Marine Corps and would send me up fairly tight packages to make a decision on, much as one would use a chief of staff."[35]

Commandant Mundy's oral history interviewer commented on his delegating policy "that General Mundy provided broad guidance, but that General Krulak drove the agenda, again noting that you did all this with the Commandant's approval."

Krulak responded to that: "That does a disservice to General Mundy. I was probably General Mundy's Russ Appleton [a colonel Krulak relied heavily on as Commandant]. I think that he and I had a Vulcan mind meld, that he was very comfortable with giving me commander's intent. It was my responsibility to go back to him regularly and tell him what I was doing to carry out his guidance. He was comfortable with the arrangement. I doubt if any Commandant has ever gotten weekly feedback from one of his generals. There were times when he would pick up the phone and say, 'Go slow here' or 'Speed up there.' Most of the time there would be some comment like, 'Keep on whirling, young Dervish!' Sometimes I would not hear back from him, and on occasion he would email to me, 'I know you think I'm probably not reading these. I am. Silence is consent.'"[36]

Commandant General Charles C. Krulak commented in his oral history: "General Zinni was probably one of the great operational commanders in the Marine Corps. He is a brilliant officer and spent a lot of time at Quantico teaching, so he had a firm foundation on the tactical, operational, and strategic levels. He spent a lot of time observing and understanding operations other than war. He was comfortable in that environment. And so I tried to keep out of his way and let him. He was very effective. I let him run the show and he did a magnificent job."[37]

"If you have a mission that you've assigned a unit within the Marine Corps, give them not just the weapons and the numbers and the stuff to accomplish the mission, but give them the space they need to accomplish it also."[38]

Delegation in effective leadership is expected to go down to even enlisted troops. Commandant Krulak encouraged what he called "power down." He explained: "The real warriors of the 21st century will be our [noncommissioned officers]. You and I remember Vietnam—when that corporal and sergeant would take a patrol out every night, leaving the lines at 2000 and coming back at 0400. Sometimes they would have contact. We were trusting corporals to do that. Now, in peacetime, they need a lot of supervisors. We are going into an environment that we have got to put the trust back into that young officer and NCO. We are going to be working very hard on that. I call him the 'strategic corporal.'

"In World War II, Korea, and Vietnam, the young Marine could be the world's greatest hero, but he really had no strategic impact. In future wars, tremendous capability and lethality will be in the hands of the young corporal. Combine that with the immediate 'CNN effect,' and it turns some of those actions into strategic actions. That young NCO needs to be highly trained because what he does or fails to do may literally impact on national policy."[39]

Chesty Puller's biographer wrote about an incident that clearly showed that he delegated:

> When he returned to base, Puller and the troops got a commendation from General McDougal for these actions—and the young captain also got a replacement, one Bill Lee, who had earlier served three years in Nicaragua, and had been pleading for a chance to return. Lee was a tall, muscular athlete from Haverhill, Massachusetts, who had been sixteen years in the Corps and was conditioned by years of playing fullback on the team of a coal-burning battleship and by boxing and pulling an oar on a crew.
>
> Puller unhesitatingly chose him to help direct Company M, and Lee found him an ideal commander: "He never really gave me orders. He just told me what Headquarters wanted, asked

me if I knew the country, and to get up the men we needed. He was a common sense officer, and you always knew where you stood with him. When he was displeased about something I'd done, he never chewed me out as so many inexperienced officers would have done. He would say, 'If I'd been doing that, I'd have done it this way,' and that would be the end of it. We got on like brothers. Most important of all, he was not green when he first came to Nicaragua. Haiti had taught him jungle fighting, and he took to the new country like a native."[40]

Colonel Charles Cooper was the Marine Corps' aide to Admiral David L. MacDonald (Chief of Naval Operations, 1963–1969) and related a very challenging responsibility that was delegated to him. He wrote in his book *Cheers and Tears: A Marine's Story of Combat in Peace and War*:

> Most Americans are familiar with the name Admiral Hyman G. Rickover. Some have called him "the father of the nuclear Navy." Others who knew him personally and had to deal with him called him a royal pain in the ass. A strongly opinionated, driving, and irascible figure, he was promoted to the rank of rear admiral by direction of Congress. He was promoted to full admiral, again by direction of Congress, at the age of 73 and remained on active duty until he was forcibly retired at age 82. With his congressional power base, he was beholden to no one but himself. Nevertheless, he did have to do business within the Navy. He dominated and controlled the entire nuclear construction program. He was 64 years old when the following incident took place.
>
> Admiral McDonald felt that Rickover's personal management style was the opposite of what was generally accepted as leadership. He was also upset that the nuclear program's super high standards were "raping the rest of the Navy"—absorbing most of its top talent. He didn't like the man personally, but realized that he had to deal with him and at least try to tone down some of his wild demands on the personnel system.
>
> One morning Admiral Mac asked me to stay after the lineup, and had me take a seat. He told me that he had given Ike Kidd instructions that whenever Admiral Rickover, who always dialed his own calls, called our office, his call was to

be transferred to me, the Marine Aide. No one else was to talk with him. Absolutely no one! Then the Admiral looked a bit conspiratorial and said, "Charlie, you're well aware of how pushy, demanding, and unreasonable Hyman Rickover is with everyone. He expects to preempt God himself, to see me on demand. I'm tired of his impolite, abrasive style, and you're going to help me teach him a lesson." This was getting interesting. He continued, "You're the only member of my staff that I can rely on to carry out these explicit orders. Marines understand orders. Whenever he calls and wants to see me, no matter what my schedule says, I want you to be extremely polite and invite him to come over right away. Then, after he arrives, I want you to make damn sure he waits at least one hour before you let him cross that entrance to my office. At least one hour! Do you understand?" Yes, I understood this almost unbelievable order: I had become the "Rickover Aide," as my office mates dubbed me. Never once did I fail in this sacred mission. Mine was the unpleasant chore of having to stay with Admiral Rickover the first few times he went through this "humility drill," as we aides called it. He would storm about the reception room, telling me what a bunch of idiots the former CNOs had been, what screwed up outfits the Navy, the Naval Academy, the Navy Department, and the CNO staff all were. But he gradually learned that he was going to waste at least a full hour every time he came over. We saw a lot less of Admiral Rickover once he understood that.[41]

Part of a leader's success in delegating is to determine to whom to delegate. Commandant Robert H. Barrow provided some important wisdom on delegating: "If you want to get something done, you'd better look for the best person to do it, which is a pretty simple formula; don't pick the next one who comes through the door."[42]

Commandant Barrow considered that there were times when there was not enough of the delegation that was needed to develop future leaders. He commented:

Some of our junior officers and NCOs experience a lack of challenge in their assignments in comparison with expectations. This may be a result of inflated expectations, but often it is a result of over-direction and supervision by a senior who feels compelled to cover himself and ensure a task is completed to his precise satisfaction, or by failure of the senior to realize the full capabilities and potential of his junior. As an example, in my view there are few things more demoralizing to a young staff officer (indeed any staff officer) than the nitpicking senior who feels obliged to massage and recast every piece of staff work that crosses his desk. As I look back through the years, some of my least favorite Marines have been the eager but cautious staff officers who worked out their anxieties on the papers produced by their juniors.[43]

In an article entitled "The Care of the Need of Young Officers," Colonel Louis Metzger provided some valuable advice on delegating:

Let's let lieutenants be officers and actually command. No formation should be assembled or dismissed by an officer. Working parties, unless unusual circumstances dictate, should be NCOs. Let the NCOs do the job they are there for and gain experience and prestige thereby. Officers should be officers and not super sergeants.... Too many lieutenants are leaving the Corps because many of their seniors neglect to tell them what it's all about.

Delegating to subordinates inspires them to give their best. They do not want to disappoint such a leader, to violate his trust in them. The leader keeps aware of what they are doing, for he always monitors what is going on but without getting bogged down in detail.

How far you go up the ladder in the military depends upon your ability to delegate. You certainly come to understand quickly in large units that you cannot do it all yourself.

Delegation of authority, but never responsibility, is clearly necessary. You can't do it all yourself and be successful as your responsibilities increase. The commander who effectively communicates his vision for an operation and defines the end state of the operation, or what critical missions must be accomplished to achieve success, gives his subordinate leaders the opportunity to exercise their own individual initiative to ensure the success of the operation. Even if the original plan that was developed is no longer viable, subordinate leaders must be able to adapt and modify, then execute a new plan based on the current situation, knowing that they are still working within the framework the higher commander formulated.

Delegation is more than sparing the energy of the overworked leader. It is a vital aspect in developing the leadership growth of subordinates. Within our military, it is a senior officer's obligation to develop the younger generation of officers for the future. One of the most appreciated acts of a leader is to give a person a job and let him do it. The subordinate will not let down the trust and confidence in him, which instills loyalty in both directions.

**Chapter 12**

# "The Marine Way of Life": The Pattern for Success

The senior Marine Corps generals in this study were essentially self-appointed leaders because they had a characteristic possessed by very few: the desire for command and the willingness to work toward that goal of achieving and succeeding in it. There are many officers who *think* they want command but who are not willing, either consciously or subconsciously, to expend the effort required. There are some who get command and lose it because they are incompetent and fail, or because they are unwilling after learning what it entails to undertake what can be its awesome responsibilities.

## Desire to Lead

This discussion raises a question that needs answering: What does command entail? To be a successful commander requires a willingness to devote 24 hours a day, 7 days a week, to your command. This will often mean that your family will have to take a secondary role to the mission. In addition, there must be a willingness for the commander and his family to live in a goldfish bowl, since their actions are closely observed by contemporaries, subordinates, and superiors. The commander must be willing to learn, teach, cope with stress, and live with the basic and often elementary fundamentals necessary to develop the unit and still believe his talents for "bigger things" not being wasted. He must like to be with young people and to live with their energy and the problems they create. The commander must be able to delegate and be willing to accept the responsibility for any failure of his subordinates. Command is complex, and the commander must be able to simultaneously handle training, maintenance, tests, administration, inspections, communications, messes, supply, athletics, discipline, job proficiency, awards, and public relations.

Even the most senior generals must be able to take orders, for no leader is ever really in a position of not having to answer to someone or to some group. The commander must be willing to compete with other units without losing the spirit of cooperation and the fact that all the individual units together make up a whole team. Often he is expected to accomplish the impossible with inadequate means. If things go wrong, the successful commander accepts the responsibility, even though the failure might rest with his staff, subordinates, or higher headquarters. He must be able to do the best he can with whatever he has, which on occasions might be very little. He must be able through hard work and leadership to create a superior unit with average manpower. It is the commander's job to inspire subordinates to put out the maximum.

The responsibility for the failure of a unit or mission rests with the commander. He must realize that failure results in his relief from command. Command requires a man who can physically and emotionally cope with the responsibility and strain without losing his effectiveness and his patience. Often, the compensation is only personal satisfaction since there is generally very little reward or glory, particularly in time of peace. Often it is only intrinsically rewarding. And the reward for your efforts may go to a superior rather than to the man most responsible for the performance of the unit or the accomplishment of the mission.

When one stops to consider the overwhelming tasks, the sacrifice, the pressure, the responsibility, the hard work, and the just and unjust criticism faced by the commander a second question arises: Why seek command? Here are the reasons given by some senior Marine leaders in this study.

General Lejeune was working for Commandant George Barnett at Marine Corps Headquarters in Washington as a colonel from January 1, 1915, to August 24, 1916, and as a brigadier general from August 29, 1916, until September 10, 1917. He reflected on a conversation with the Commandant:

> I insisted on being relieved . . . and told him I wanted a change to duty with troops . . . a command at the front. . . . my soul was filled with an indescribable yearning for the opportunity for service overseas. The bleaker the military situation . . . the more intense was my desire to give myself fully to the great cause in which our country was engaged.

As it was happening, Lejeune said he was excited by the prospect of a command of a combat unit:

> I have always taken great pride in the fact that for three weeks I was privileged to command the 64$^{th}$ Brigade.

> Personally, I can never cease to be grateful for the opportunity which was given me to give all my strength, all my mind, all my energy, and my very soul to the carrying out of the great duty with which I was entrusted. It was a tremendous strain and a great responsibility, but a never-to-be-forgotten experience, an experience which I value more highly than great riches, or pomp, or power.
>
> I have done my duty to the best of my ability and have had no thought of pleasure or comfort or advancement, but only the passionate, intense desire to carry through to a victorious end.[1]

When the United States entered World War I, Commandant Vandegrift was a lieutenant involved in the Banana Wars. His first fight, however, was not with the Germans, but with Marine Corps Headquarters to receive an opportunity for command at the front. He described this as time as "the most frustrating period of my life." As a "regular soldier," he said he had spent his adult life working, studying, and training for the supreme moment to serve in combat (command), but that he was being shunted aside despite the most ingenious attempts and pathetic appeals directly to the Commandant to send him over to Europe, which he was not able to achieve. He reflected in his memoir:

> Man's only refuge in such moments is personal philosophy: The big one, the war to end wars, had come and gone and I had missed it. This was a personal calamity of tremendous proportions, but there it was and wishing wasn't going to change a thing. In December new orders arrived—I sailed for America, where I was to become an instructor in the Officers Basic School at Quantico.[2]

When asked why he sought command, Commandant Kelley said: "I wanted to be the guy who's making decisions. I honestly believed I could make a contribution."

General Gray's answer to the same question was: "I really enjoyed the opportunity to help grow people, grow the generals, grow the young officers, grow the young enlisted Marines. I got the chance to do some things for people. I could counsel and guide Marines, guide them through by example. My big message was always, 'Don't let anything ever stop you from taking care of your people; don't ever stop listening to them.'"[3]

General Mundy related, "There's no doubt that any officer worth his salt aspires to command. Leadership—command—is what being an officer is all about. It's a privilege of the military profession. I've known few fellow Marine officers who spent their time wishing for a desk job instead of leading Marines."[4]

Commandant Krulak responded to the question, "Why did you seek command?" by saying: "First off, I never thought in terms of 'Command' ... I thought in terms of 'Stewardship.' When given a Command, I looked at myself as having been given 'stewardship' of the organization and the people within that organization. I actively sought Command because I felt that when I became a Marine, I became an 'Officer of Marines—Leader of Men and Women.' The essence of being a Marine Officer is to lead young Marines—and to do that is to Command. Command is challenging ... it is demanding ... it is mentally and physically taxing ... and it is fun!! Command provides a means of influencing young lives in a positive manner. Command is a means of repaying the Corps for the privilege of being a Marine."[5]

Commandant Jones once stated: "When I became a battalion commander, I really felt I had achieved everything I wanted to do in the Marines. I was able to successfully avoid every staff job. I was never an S3, I was never an S2, never an S4. I commanded four or five companies."[6]

General Ray Davis reflected on his career and commented:

> I think my career pattern was largely by accident, a very favorable one in that every time a war started I seemed almost overdue to join the forces and head out. I was always among the first to go. I went right out to Guadalcanal and later to Korea. I was at Inchon landing and was at Chosin reservoir. These are not things you plan except you do have to have a desire to be involved to be in these things and you have to make your desires known. When there is an opportunity, you have to tell your boss that this is exactly what you want to do and prevail in an argument with him to let you go.[7]

In his book *Battle Ready*, written with General Zinni, Tom Clancy related:

> When Zinni checked into the 2ᵈ Marine Division, he fought off the personnel officer's kindly attempt to give him a break after his two tough Vietnam tours and life-threatening wounds.

> He didn't want an undemanding staff job; he wanted to go to a rifle company, where the action was—the heart of the Marine Corps. You don't get more central to Marine identity.
>
> Zinni was delighted. He was to get command of his sixth company; and it was a rifle company.[8]

The first command is a high point in a Marine's career. A young Marine receiving his orders to command can taste the excitement. Life becomes intense, charged with a purpose. The privileges, such as they are, in view of his obligations are almost ridiculously small. Observing your superior ranking officers, you may realize a desire for command, saying to yourself, "I can do that better than that guy."

A junior officer should be constantly expanding his interests, growing older and wiser with meaningful experience, wanting the satisfaction of accomplishments. How you do in command affects your future potential. A good commander is capable of doing what he is asked and produces good results. A Marine must aspire to be the best lieutenant, the best captain, the best leader in each promotion. If successful, each cumulative command equips you for more responsible commands.

It takes years to earn higher command. It is an apprenticeship that pays off: If you want to continue up in the chain of command, you must want and accept more and more responsibility.

One of the most meaningful insights about command was from Navy Admiral Paul David Miller, who was raised by a Chief Petty Officer stepfather: "Command is for the Marine who loves responsibility, that is one of the challenges of leadership. It's yours twenty-four hours a day. Command is an assignment that you were totally responsible for all the activities within that unit. There is an intrinsic reward; it is satisfying a need to be able to project a certain amount of order and discipline to yield results. That's your reward, that you did it, to want bigger and bigger responsibilities. To seek it, but it was not ambition, but the challenge of taking on the toughest responsibilities."

## Selflessness

Commandant Lejeune learned early in his career that selflessness was required to be a successful Marine Corps leader:

> My father in our conversations frequently referred to the obligation of service which I would assume when I became

identified with the Navy [referring to his entrance as a midshipman at the Naval Academy]. He impressed on me the fact that I was about to become an officer of the United States Government, that I would owe the Government my undivided allegiance, and that it would be my duty to serve it honorably and faithfully in peace, and to defend it loyally and courageously in war against its enemies, both foreign and domestic. His words were stored away in my memory and they have often recurred to my mind during the more than forty-four years that have elapsed since I entered the service of the United States.[9]

He was saying goodbye to his father before embarking on his first assignment, and reflected in his *Reminiscences*:

We reached Ravenswood in ample time for the train, and I can see my father's face now and hear his voice, which was broken with emotion, as he said to me just as the train moved out, "Goodbye my dear son; goodbye."

My mind was filled with serious thoughts for a while, but I was young—just past twenty-one—physically powerful, and constitutionally lighthearted, so it was not surprising that my thoughts in time reverted to eager anticipation of the adventures ahead, or that my responsibilities should sit very lightly on my shoulders. In fact, I was filled with the joy of living. I am glad to say, however, that in a few years I began to realize that there was a serious side to life, that duty should come before pleasure, and that every man owed a debt to corps and country which it was his highest privilege pay.[10]

In World War I, Lejeune was impressed with the selflessness and leadership of a French Army officer:

General Brese, as well as the Army and Corps Commanders, were very cordial and friendly. In fact, all the French general officers whom I met were free of what we call "side." They seemed to be without conceit, or egotism, and I could observe no evidences of personal ambition among them. All appeared to be entirely intent on driving the enemy army from the soil of their beloved country and in saving *la belle France* from subjugation by their hereditary foes.

They were exemplars, too, of true democracy; their attitude towards the French soldiers being in no sense one of superiority, but always that of a father towards his son. Similarly, there was a delightful atmosphere of camaraderie between the Generals and their aides and other junior officers on unofficial occasions. All seemed to talk at once, and one man's opinion was as good as another's without regard to the rank of the officers engaged in the argument or conversation. Where all were so exquisitely courteous, it appeared to be impossible for anyone to take offense. When a stranger like myself expressed his views, however there was instant silence, and all listened intently until his flow of language ceased, when the senior, if he differed with him, would reply that the General is right, but that under such and such different conditions, such and such ought to be done.[11]

Lejeune also pointed out that selflessness—the term he used was "forgetfulness of self"—was the attitude of the U.S. Army and the Marine Corps during the war:

Finally a strange flag proudly fluttered to the breeze on the heights and the heights and the battlements of the Rhine. It was a beautiful flag, a flag emblematic of freedom and liberty, a flag beloved of more than one hundred million people, a flag brought to the Old World from the New by the most splendid army that had ever marched and fought under any flag, anywhere, at any time! Such were our convictions. It was a proud day for America, not only because of the glorious victory that had been achieved, of which the crossing of the Rhine was the symbol, but also because in none of our hearts was there a vestige of the lust of conquest. None of us coveted one foot of European or any other foreign soil. All of us desired only to do our full share of the task, which we had undertaken, and then to return home empty-handed.

While the Marine Corps Expeditionary Force, when landed in a foreign country, is primarily intended to protect the lives and property of American citizens residing there during periods of disorder; it is also intended to benefit and not to oppress the inhabitants of the country where it is serving. This altruistic conception of the duties of Marines was constantly impressed on the officers and men stationed abroad, with the result that the good will of the law abiding people with whom they were associated was gained and peace and good order were restored and maintained.[12]

The Marine Corps is dependent on the confidence and the affection of the American people for its maintenance and support. The realization of this fact induced the Commandant to endeavor, both by precept and example, to influence officers and men to so conduct themselves as to gain and keep the good opinion and the friendship of the good Americans with whom they might come in contact.[13]

Early in his career Lejeune contemplated leaving the Marine Corps, but he did not because of his father's reasoning and pointing out the importance of service:

> I talked much to my father about leaving the Service and talking up some other occupation or profession. He advised me strongly not to resign at that time, saying that I ought to take advantage of the opportunity to see something of the world, thereby broadening my mind; and that after two years on board ship I would be better able to determine whether or not I desired to make the Navy my life vocation. I agreed that this advice was sound, but decided to save a part of my pay each month, which savings, added to the year's pay I would receive if I elected to leave the Service at the end of the six year course, would go far toward enabling me to get a start in civil life.

Fortunately for the Marine Corps and our country, Lejeune remained for 37 years and had a meaningful, long-lasting impact on the character and leadership of the Corps.

Commandant David M. Shoup, in a message to the Marine Corps Association on January 1, 1960, commented: "Throughout our long history, Marines have never had an easy time of things. We never will. Ours is a profession which calls for self-sacrifice, dedication, and a deep sense of duty." This, he said, was "the Marine way of life."

Commandant Leonard F. Chapman, Jr., in an annual message in 1969 on the "State of the Corps," said: "The achievements which have been made in the past year by the Marine Corps have been realized through the sacrifice, complete dedication, and great personal courage of the individual Marine."

Commandant Robert H. Barrow said: "I think there are two things that motivate a young man to want to become a Marine, both of them probably in his subconscious mind: One is he wants to prove his manliness. . . . Second, the Marine Corps is not a religion, but it's sort of religious-like. And I believe that self-denial is the basis of all religious life. People really want to believe in something, make a commitment, a sacrifice. So they come to us and they make a sacrifice. They give up all that long hair and their funny clothes and their loud music and their civilian kind of freedom—to be a Marine. They make a commitment."[14]

In his birthday message on November 10, 1988, Commandant Alfred M. Gray, Jr., commented to all his Marines on the meaning of selflessness:

> "The Marine Corps has no ambition beyond the performance of its duty to its country. Its sole honor derives from that recognition which cannot be denied to a Corps of Marines who have sought for themselves little more than a life of hardship and the most hazardous assignments in battle." These inspiring thoughts of General Clifton B. Cates, our 19th Commandant, sufficed for generations who fought in Korea, Vietnam, and countless other locations in the succeeding 39 years, and whom we emulate today. The quality of a Marine's performance resides in a state of mind. Only when every Marine understands that he is first a rifleman will we field the combined arms teams capable of deploying to do what the nation demands. We are warriors first and foremost. Our physical and mental being must be concentrated on enhancing within ourselves what we call the warrior virtues: courage, integrity, intelligence, and concerned leadership. Our predecessors understood and possessed these virtues. If they had not, they would not have triumphed in battle at Belleau Wood, Iwo Jima, the Chosin Reservoir, or throughout the I Corps tactical zone of Vietnam. . . . the Marines continue to march throughout the globe asking for so little and doing so much.

Commandant Carl E. Mundy, Jr., was asked what he considered the 10 most important traits for the Marine Corps officer to have. On the top of his list, he placed selflessness: "Selflessness, I think, is dedication to the organization above self. I wrote about that in *Leading Marines,* and I think that that is a very fundamental factor for a leader, because if others see that you truly believe in the organization above your own self-interests, they will emulate that and they will follow you because they will know that your interest is the welfare of them, because they are the organization."[15]

Commandant Charles C. Krulak provided excellent insight into selflessness: "When you're in the military, active duty, you willingly give up many of your rights. You give up the right to live where you want to live. You execute your orders and go where people want you to go. You give up your right to not get shot at. You give up your right to speak out on political issues. You give up your right to campaign and you do that freely. But when you retire after having fought for and served the Constitution of the United States, you pick up the rights you so willingly put aside. I never felt bad about it. As a matter of fact, I question those who would watch their country and their military have the opportunity to choose between two people, one of them who represented eight years of degrading of the military combat effectiveness and another who said I'm going to reverse that degradation and not speak up. To me it was a lack of moral courage and a lack of doing what is right for the nation. When you're on active duty you keep your council to yourself. But when you're retired, not only do you have the right but also you need to execute that right."[16]

Frugalness was part of selflessness in a Marine's life between the wars and in the immediate postwar period. Commandant Barrow told me: "We had a Depression-bred crew of Marines in Korea and World War II who did things for themselves. . . . this was very common to see Marines, peace and war, sitting on the edge of their bunks or foxhole or whatever sewing their web gear together. These were lean years. We who lived through the hardship, the frugalness; there was a paucity of just about everything except will, a determination to do whatever we had, however little that may be. There was no paucity of spirit, wile, comradeship, and camaraderie. But it made for a stronger Corps that comes from the fact that we didn't have a lot of other things. We were drawn closer together. We were paid inadequately, so there was no quest for material things. We tended to make our own amusement, our own fun, in a little close-knit community. For job satisfaction and motivation, the Corps stresses a higher purpose than the individual's specific assignment. It is inspired by the Marine relating his work to the purpose of the Marine Corps, service to country, service with the best. Along with this, there is the development of greater camaraderie flourishing on the job, at the club, on the playing field, and in their homes."[17]

A few stories of selfless service illustrate this common Marine value. Commandant Shepherd gave up a significant higher command opportunity in his earlier career, illustrating that selflessness can be exemplified in loyalty to your unit at the expense of a position of greater responsibility. He recalled a wartime experience he had: "About this time the Marine Corps formed the Defense Battalions for deployment on various key islands in the Western Pacific. I had a chance to command one of these battalions. I turned it down. The hardest decision had to make was when General Marston asked me if I would like to be the regimental commander of the 6th Marines which was leaving for New Zealand. It was a great, great temptation, because the 6th Marines was a formed regiment ready to go out and fight. I've forgotten what happened to the commander at the time.

"But I reluctantly said, 'No, General, I can't do it. I've organized the 9th Marines from scratch. I've worked with the officers, I've worked with the men, I can't let them down. I can't just walk out on this fine group of officers and enlisted men with whom I have worked so hard, who believe in me. I can't do it.' I was dedicated to these young men who had responded to my training wholeheartedly. We had worked up a regimental spirit, a battalion spirit, and I did not feel that I should walk off and leave them. I'd trained that regiment and I wanted to fight with them in combat. The 9th Marines was a very fine organization and I have always been proud to have commanded it, which left the states during the first part of January, 1943."[18]

Selflessness and courage are not limited to the battlefield. One of the most magnificent illustrations of selflessness was that of General Merritt A. Edson, USMC, who as a colonel received the Medal of Honor for leading the 1st Marine Raider Battalion that was so prominent in the assault and seizure of Tulagi. His heroism and selflessness went beyond combat to the battlefield of Washington bureaucracy.

In the postwar dispute over reorganization, a bill was introduced in Congress in 1947 that would have permitted the Secretary of Defense, rather than Congress, to determine the missions of the various Services. The Marine Corps saw this bill as a threat to its continued existence as a fighting force. Corps leaders were concerned that a hostile Secretary, by administrative action, could relegate them to nothing more than routine guard duty at Navy posts. An order was issued prohibiting active duty Naval and Marine officers from testifying against the bill. General Holland M. Smith commented that his former chief of staff, General "Red Mike" Edson, sacrificed his career and resigned from the Corps in a noncombat act of courage in order to speak against the efforts to destroy the Corps.[19]

Edson, according to General Holland:

> with the iron firmness and calm which had won him his Medal of Honor, submitted his request for immediate retirement and headed for Capitol Hill. In trenchant testimony, Edson, hero of the Ridge, took the legislation to pieces as General Vandegrift, under administrative pressure, was no longer able to do.... In sacrificing a brilliant career for what he believed was right, General Edson had attained great results. Through his efforts, through those of a devoted nucleus of former Marines and Marine friends in Congress, and most of all through unwavering support of the American people, the Marine Corps—for the time being—was safe.[20]

Commandant Krulak gave an excellent description of the selflessness of his Assistant Commandant, General "Butch" Neal, to his oral history interviewer, who asked him: "In September you chose a new Assistant Commandant, General Richard I. Neal. How did you go about selecting your Assistant Commandant? Why General Neal?"

Krulak responded: "That was the best personnel decision I made as the Commandant other than when I brought Russell Appleton in ... but I brought Russ in before I was the Commandant. I didn't know General Butch Neal very well. In 1993 we were both young generals in the Manpower Department. At the time, as we discussed, I was the Director of Personnel Management and a two-star select. He was the Director of Manpower Policy as a one-star. I always thought he was a cocky bantam rooster. I knew he was smart. I didn't know whether we'd get along very well. He seemed to me, whenever I was around him, as kind of flip. As I looked at potential relief for Rich Hearney, I wanted to move people on, so it couldn't be a Christmas or a Blades. I looked at the aviators and the ground as well as my desire to get an additional CINC position. I knew we had two great players for CINCs, Butch Neal and Tony Zinni. I asked Russ Appleton to go down to visit Butch Neal at Central Command and talk about Chuck Krulak and about Butch Neal and about our relationship. Russ was very up front. He relayed to General Neal my concerns that we had always had a kind of a friendly rivalry during our careers. I was concerned that this might carry over into the CMC/ACMC relationship.

"General Neal told Appleton: 'He's misread me: I'm as loyal as anybody could ever be. If you question that, ask several of my bosses.'

"I got a hold of General Benny Peay [J.H. Binford Peay], U.S. Army, who was CINCCENT at that time, and Peay said, 'Butch Neal is the greatest thing since sliced bread. You'll love him to death.'

"So we brought him up and everything that everybody ever said about Butch Neal was true. In fact, they didn't say enough. Butch Neal was a magnificent Marine, just a great Marine officer, a magnificent leader, smart as a whip, unbelievable moral courage. He could have been the Commandant or could have been the CINC for U.S. Central Command. He could have been the Chairman of the Joint Chiefs of Staff. He is that talented. He became an unbelievable strong right arm. He became like, I'm sure, Stonewall Jackson was to Robert E. Lee. He just was everything that an Assistant Commandant could be to a Commandant. He fought some of the really tough fights! He's fought the fraternization fight. He fought the adultery fight. He helped fight the gender integrated recruit training fight. He sat on the JROC. He dominated the JROC. He outsmarted everybody. He helped me by supporting me at our off sites. He helped me behind the scenes by smoothing rough feelings that I might have made with my generals. His loyalty was unquestioned . . . in a good way, in every good way you could expect. He pumped me up when I was feeling down. He befriended me and my wife. His wife befriended us. Any crappy little job he'd do. He expected no grandiose accolades, medals. He did it for the good of the Marine Corps.

"One of the great disappointments for Butch was not making CINCCENT. That would have crushed most people, but not Butch. It hurt him for about a day. The next day, he came in 110 percent, just the same way as he always did. Butch Neal was as much a part of the 31st Commandancy as anybody. He was just a phenomenal general officer. When he departed, after two years as the Assistant Commandant, he did so, once again, sacrificing because he knew that if he didn't leave, we wouldn't get the upward movement of the aviators. So he stepped down at the very end, he was the ultimate in selflessness."[21]

There is a conflict in today's Marine Corps between selfless service and what had been labeled "careerism." In the military personnel decisions, either by Marine Corps Headquarters personnel policy or personal preference or ambition, the officer corps has become involved in the planning of their own career: what needs to be done for promotion, what assignments they desire, particularly those they believe will best further their career, what schools they seek. Several Commandants have strived hard to change this.

Commandant David M. Shoup was concerned and did something about it. His obituary in the *Marine Corps Gazette* said:

Part of General Shoup's plan for combat readiness included curtailing the politicking within the Corps. He knew how "teams" were formed to enhance the position of senior officers and advance the careers of junior officers. He had seen officers plan a succession of assignments under seniors who would further their careers and help them avoid career-killing mistakes. All that was stopped. He halted "ticket punching" and directed personnel planners to assign "jobs commensurate with demonstrated potential for future assumption of greater responsibilities." He reminded all hands that the Fleet Marine Force was the main reason for the Corps' existence and that assignments to the FMF would include a cross-section of Marines.[22]

This effort was made, but the careerism has continued over the years. Barrow, who became Commandant 16 years later, expressed his concern over Marines personally being involved in their career assignments: "This business of negotiating with your monitor that goes on now so much, some of which I disapprove of, didn't exist in my day. Indeed, there's a whole cult of officers who took great pride in the fact that they never talked to their monitors and they never saw their cases. I never went to Washington. I have never looked at my records. I have never talked to my monitor because I'll go wherever they send me. Of course, that's right down the monitor's alley because if everybody would be a non-complainer you could send them just anywhere."

Then he said he had observed assignment policy change: "So now they negotiate. One of the first things you do in your new duty station is to start negotiating for your next duty station. It's the damndest thing I've ever seen. 'We have this for you. We have that.' 'No, I don't want that. What about this?'"[23]

Commandant Gray's career was one of selfless service. He told me: "If you were worried about getting ahead in the military or getting promoted, you would have never done what I did. I didn't care about getting promoted or I wouldn't have stayed in Vietnam a long time, turned down schools, or anything else I did."[24]

General Gray further expressed his strong feelings on careerism. In an article in the *Marine Corps Gazette* in October 1987 entitled "The Art of Command," he stated:

> We have, in my view, too much careerism creeping into the officer corps of Marines. What do I mean by careerism?

Officers who worry more about themselves and how they are going to get ahead than they do about the people they are privileged to lead. General Kelley spoke to officers for three years on this topic. We let him down and obviously haven't done enough about it. We are going to continue the effort; we're going to stamp out careerism in our Corps.[25]

General Anthony Zinni put careerism into perspective as he viewed it. In an article published in the *Washington Post* around April 2000, the author quotes some younger Army officers stating senior leaders would place subordinates under the bus in a heartbeat to protect or advance their careers. I asked Zinni to comment on whether there appeared to be that perception among younger Marine Corps officers and on how senior leaders can ensure this attitude does not grow.

Zinni responded: "This whole issue becomes one of careerism, and I think when you end up with an all-volunteer force, when you end up with a military that's very popular and so recruiting and retention are not generally big issues, although there are times they become so, the competition is so hard and so strict the ability to choose between competitive people with good records and great service becomes more difficult.

"It generates two problems. One, the military makes everything a competition. You have to compete for schools, you have to compete for promotion, you have to compete for choice assignments, and command. That competition generates a sense of careerism where people are looking out for their own futures because it's a highly competitive environment, and to self-manage their careers. This becomes evident to subordinates that they seem preoccupied with this.

"I think the Services have to change this approach. We have to have a system where you just go out there and do your job, we'll make the decisions on your assignments, and we'll make the decisions on your ability to move up. We'll give you the opportunities; you just go out and prove yourself. That's the system we have to create instead of everything being a competition, everything being a test, and then the onus is put on you to make sure you've got through and you've gotten everything done to be even eligible for promotion, assignments, school opportunities.

"We sort of force this personal ambition on officers who would rather not do it. I mean the vast majority of people I know find it distasteful, but they find themselves stuck with it. Even if they have the best motivation. Listen to people that don't talk about the next move in terms of a promotion, they talk about it as the next opportunity to command, or the next opportunity to be with troops.

"We've got to encourage that kind of positive thinking, and we don't. I think the system is broad and it encourages careers. That's been the problem."

I asked General Zinni: "What would you say was the most impressive act of selfless service you've ever witnessed in your career?" He responded: "Well, you know, I would have to go back, I mean I've been in a number of wars, or so-called wars, but I would to back to my time in Vietnam as a company commander. It was my second tour, it was toward the end of the U.S. military presence there, there were no illusions amongst my Marines about the military being popular, or the war being popular or to even understanding why we were there.

"Yet on battlefields I saw these troops, the day I was wounded, I saw my Marines, I had a number wounded and killed, that were willing to or courageous enough to put their lives on the line, and they were not doing it for some sort of patriotic cause or anything else. They were doing it for each other.

"To me, it really marked the strength of the Marine Corps, the strength of the camaraderie and their reliance on each other, and a kind of cohesion and that sense of camaraderie that can be built up in a unit. To me that's the ultimate selflessness is for your buddy in the next fighting foxhole."[26]

The Marine is not the only one who must be selfless. There is considerable selflessness on the part of the family. Hard work and long hours are not difficult for a dedicated leader. Indeed, it may not even be considered work. He can justify the sacrifice on his part and that of his family because he is serving God and country, but often the family can pay a price, sometimes a very heavy price. Commandant Barrow provided an example: "I know I was not a good father. So what's new? A lot of Marines have not been good fathers, if you mean by that, not being able to devote a lot of time during those formative years, whether boy or girl, of growing up. But I didn't spend a lot of time with my children doing things that, typically, a father would do—go away for the weekend, and picnic, or go to the beach, or hike, or do things like that. I just didn't have time for it. So thank God I had a wife who was not only a wonderful mother, but one who could pick up many of the things that a father would normally do."[27]

Many in the civilian population are not aware of the selflessness and sacrifice of a career officer's family in the Marine Corps. General Ray Davis' wife Knox told this story about their tour at Quantico:

When the massive releases began after World War II ended, most of our friends were Reservists who were soon to be released. Many good friends that we really liked were departing with few to be left except the Regulars. I went to a big party, four tables of bridge. One of the wives of a reservist said "Horrors! Do you all know that Knox is the only one who is staying in?" That's one out of 16 women, you know—16 women! I went home and I told Ray the things I'd heard: "You're living off the government, you have no initiative, you're afraid you can't get a job." All these things so often heard in those days, I told Ray. And I said you are going to get out, you're just going to get out of this Marine Corps, that's all there is to it. I'll go back to teaching school, if necessary.

So Ray sat me down and said: "Well, you couldn't teach school, because we have our sons Gilbert and Miles." Then he reviewed many reasons why the Marine Corps was his chosen profession. And I told him: "All right, I will stay in with you, and you'll never hear that from me again." He's heard a lot of other things, but not that. I never one time after that complained about being in the Marine Corps.

General Davis continued:

Having made a final decision to stay in the Corps, Knox and I would say good-bye to our soon-to-be-civilian friends and settled into life at Quantico.

I received orders to the First Provisional Marine Brigade on Guam. Guam was one of the combat islands in the Pacific, and with the war recently over, there were no family accommodations. I would be separated from my family again.[28]

General Mundy reflected about family selflessness for a Marine: "When our Service hymn, the 'Marine Hymn,' is played, Linda [his wife] will stand. But when the 'Marines Hymn' is played, her thumbs will go along the seams of her skirt, and she will stand to attention out of pride in the Marine Corps.

"I think that Linda understood . . . she came from a generation in which we sent the men off to war, and it was the duty of those who remained behind to bear the loneliness and to bear the burdens and to keep the morale up at the front.

"I could tell when Linda's spirits were down a little bit at home, from letters, or in later years, tapes that we would exchange. And she would complain about the car when it broke down and she could not get it fixed, or some teacher was not doing well by our children or something like that. But she bore her responsibility—that responsibility being to bear the loneliness, and so on—totally. Never did she say to me, 'Look, I want you out of there to come home and carry your half of this burden here, or your majority of this burden.' So she understood that. The other thing about her is that . . . you have mentioned that we were childhood sweethearts. We joined the church together. We were fourth graders. I pulled her pigtails. I had known her for a long, long time. In part, perhaps, in growing up together and in maturing together and then in partnering and getting married, Linda knew me, and she knew literally what . . . she knew the drum beat that was in my inner being.

"She knew her responsibilities. . . . you know, all of us are mothered, by our mothers and/or by our wives. We are inspired; we are told to stand up and try it again, and so on, and Linda fulfilled that role with me and still does to this day.

"She is the classic . . . for me to say military wife, I would say yes, but for me to say she is the classic American lady whose primary role in life was twofold. One was to support her husband in whatever way it took to do it, and the other one—and I am not putting these necessarily in order—the other one was to raise her children and instill them with values.

"What she was able to do, probably more than me, because I was gone a lot of the time, but the fact that we have two sons in the Marine Corps today, that is not unique. I mean, there are people who have more kids in the Marine Corps than we have, and there are a lot of people that have sons in the Marine Corps.

"But Linda instilled in our children their father's pride in what he was, probably more than I did, and I think that they would tell you that. I think all three of them would tell you that.

"So, no, Linda Sloan Mundy never even hinted to me that I should get out, and indeed, in those moments when I would falter or when we would be at home on leave, you know, when I was a captain or something, and we would watch . . . our friends were now moving into brick homes, getting established, and running for office in the town or something like that, becoming leaders in the community, and I would have a flittering, 'Gee whiz, what if I got out and came back here, and we would not be living in

Whiskey Gulch with the pipes running down the wall or something; why don't I do that?'

"But, really, Linda would listen, and Linda would never, ever interrupt and jump in and say, 'No, you don't want to do that.' But over the next day or so, Linda would put me back on course and would say, 'Well, why don't we go back to Quantico and think about that for a while?' And, of course, as soon as I got back to Quantico, that thought left my mind. Or when I was ready to quit, any time, any job, or anything, Linda would always just say, 'Well, let's think about it for a day or two.' Or she would say nothing, and a day or two later, she would say something that put me back on course.

"So she has truly been inspirational, and this is not just the classic testimonial of give your wife a bouquet of flowers when you retire or change command and say something nice about her. But, indeed, she is, I am sure, not unique, but she is certainly classic among what a military wife and mother should be."[29]

General Charles Krulak gave an account on the role of selflessness of the wife that pulls it all together and produces a message to all Marine officers that should be a guideline for their entire career. It was made by Major General Richard C. Shulze, who to Krulak was the conscience of the Marine Corps.

General Shulze had returned from a meeting with the Commandant and Krulak reflected that after "an hour he came back upstairs. I could see he was visibly shaken. He walked into his office, so after a while I went into his office and asked if he was alright. He responded, 'Well, something very interesting just happened. . . . The Commandant offered me three stars. . . . I turned him down.'

"I exclaimed, 'What? You turned down three stars?' 'Yes.'

"By that time I was in for a dime, in for a dollar, so I asked, 'Why did you turn him down?' He gave me some personal information about his family and how it was just something that, at this time, he could not do. And because of that, because he had turned down this promotion, he said he was going to retire. All I could say was, 'Please don't.' I mean I loved him, so I was walking out and was almost to the door.

"General Shulze said, 'Chuck, come here for a minute.' I turned around and I walked back. He said, 'You need to understand that sooner or later, the Marine Corps is going to break your heart.' I said, 'What do you mean by that?'

"He replied, 'Just that. That sooner or later it's going to break your heart. If you're a captain and don't get selected to major, this precious institution is going tell you to go home. If you're a major and don't make lieutenant colonel, this precious institution at the twenty-year mark is going to tell you to go home, if you're a lieutenant colonel at twenty-six years or a colonel at thirty, even if you're the Commandant of the Marine Corps, sooner or later the institution is going to tell you to go home.'

"'Now, if during all of the time you're a Marine, you show your family, both in word and more important in action, that they are number one, that your career is not the most important thing, but your family is the most important, then when the time comes that you need to put Marine Corps first because there's an IG inspection coming up or because you've got to work ten hours to get ready or because you've got to go to Okinawa or you've got to go to war, your family's going to be supportive because all along they've known that they are number one to you. More importantly, when the time comes for the Marine Corps to break your heart and you walk out that door, you can look to your left and your wife is going to be there with you. You can hold her hand and walk off into the sunset knowing that you put part of your life behind you, but you're going ahead. However, if for whatever reason, you've put the Marine Corps in front of your family, then when you ask for the extra sacrifice of the family, you're going to get some problems from your family. But more importantly, when it comes time for you to leave because the Marine Corps has 'broke your heart,' you will look to your left and your wife may be there physically, but don't expect her to be there emotionally.'

"They were very powerful words and I've never forgotten them. And I often related that story as Commandant. I would normally tell that story to send signals to my officers, my enlisted, that the family comes first. That those people who are successful in their married life are going to be great Marines. Those who have problems in their married life normally are the ones who end up having difficulty in the Marines! If you've got a well-oiled machine operating in the family side, you're going to have a well-oiled machine in the Marine side as well. It was a great lesson I learned from the conscience of the Marines."[30]

## Retirement

The strongest and most consistent pattern in the character and leadership of the senior generals in this study is their love of the Marine Corps and their Marines. It is so well stated by Commandant John A. Lejeune in his memoir:

> My term of office as Major General Commandant, U.S. Marine Corps will expire on March 5, next. On that date I shall still

have ahead of me twenty-two months' active service before being transferred to the retired list by operation of law. Many of my friends have urged me to allow them to interest themselves in endeavoring to secure my reappointment. I am exceedingly grateful to them. To be Commandant of the Marine Corps is the highest honor that can come to any Marine. However, I shall have had my full share of service in that office on March 5 and I shall then relinquish it voluntarily and cheerfully.

I shall always look back on the more than eight years that I have been Commandant as years that have been full of the joy of service, and I shall always remember with much pride the great privilege that has been mine, of being connected with the administrations of President Wilson, President Harding and President Coolidge, and of being associated with the members of the committees of Congress which have had jurisdiction over Marine Corps legislation and appropriations.

My interest in the great Corps in which I have served my country for nearly thirty-nine years will continue unabated, and I shall keep in close touch with its activities and with its officers and men not only during the remainder of my active service, but throughout the remaining years of my life as well.[31]

Commandant Alexander A. Vandegrift wrote in his memoir:

On the last day of December I accompanied General Gates to the Secretary of the Navy's office where I read my orders to retirement and received an unexpected star on my Distinguished Service Medal. Sullivan swore in Gates and we returned to Headquarters. I took leave of my staff, the Headquarters Battalion, and the crack Marine Barracks troops who kindly provided an honor guard, and the Marine Band.

I was in two minds about leaving because that is only human if you have served something you love for nearly forty years. In those years I saw my Corps expand for service in World War I. I saw it wither away during the doldrums after. I saw it grow to nearly half a million men in World War II. I had since fought its demise.

I was proud to command some of the finest troops the world has ever seen. My men came from every walk of life, almost every race and creed. Welded together, organized into splendid regiments, divisions and corps, and filled with the esprit traditional to the Marines, these young men who fought in Pacific campaigns from Guadalcanal to Okinawa left a rich heritage for their Corps and for their country. A grateful nation should never forget what they did. To the names of Valley Forge, Lexington, Concord, Gettysburg, Shiloh, San Juan Hill, Belleau Wood, St. Mihiel and the Argonne they added Guadalcanal, Bougainville, Tarawa, Saipan, Tinian, Guam, Peleliu, Iwo Jima and Okinawa.

These proud names spelled sublime sacrifice. To those who fought so splendidly, to those who fell and to the scarred survivors, I can speak only the immortal words of John: "Greater love hath no man than this, that a man lay down his life for his friends."[32]

General Robert E. Cushman, Jr., was asked about retirement: "How did you feel about this, emotional?" He responded: "No, I'm not the emotional type, really, on things like that. No, I just looked back on the 44 years as being something I'd do all over again. I enjoyed it."[33]

Commandant Lewis H. Wilson was asked by his oral historian "to sum up your 38 years of active duty, looking back, what are the high points? The greatest satisfactions? What are the low points?" Wilson responded: "Well, that is a big order. I certainly have given it no specific thought nor do I have any notes. I can, without emotion, say that my years as a Marine have been delightful and personally rewarding indeed. I believe that if I were a student at Millsaps College today, and having achieved whatever success I have, that I would still become a Marine."[34]

On Friday evening, June 29, 1979, at a parade at Marine Barracks, Washington, Commandant Robert H. Barrow assumed command of the Marine Corps from Commandant Wilson. He recalled of that occasion: "It didn't take much to make me happy during my Marine Corps career. I was just happy to be a Marine and happy with the whole situation and where I found myself, but that was a special happiness, special for me because I had a lot of family and friends, all of my immediate family, some from my hometown; it was just a happy occasion."[35]

I asked Commandant Paul X. Kelley: "What were your thoughts at retirement of the meaning of your career, of your service to God and country?" He responded: "When I saw my retirement in the near future, I made a promise to myself that I would not be a 'General Emeritus' hanging around the Pentagon. Rather, I wanted to see what different service I could give to my country. President George H.W. Bush asked if I would like to be the sixth Chairman of the American Battle Monuments Commission. During this appointment I served two and one-half years under President Bush, during which the Commission was responsible for the site selection, groundbreaking, and design of the Korean War Veterans Memorial and two and one-half more years were served under President Clinton. During this period the Commission did all of the legislative work leading up to the establishment of the long overdue World War II Memorial. Shortly after his inauguration in 2001, President George W. Bush reappointed me as Chairman of the Commission, and for the next three years we built and then dedicated that memorial. Since my father had died while on active duty during that war, it was a moving experience to be a part of this magnificent tribute to our Greatest Generation. But, as I said to those assembled at my retirement parade in 1987: 'As I take my first 30-inch step into retirement tonight, all I ask is that you remember me as a Marine who tried.'"[36]

Commandant Carl E. Mundy, Jr., answered the same question by saying, "When I walked out of the historic home of the Commandants, in uniform for the last time, to relinquish command of the Marine Corps, I thought to myself that I might not miss being the Commandant very much; but I would miss a lot, and probably for the rest of my life, getting up each morning, looking at the Eagle, Globe, and Anchor on my uniform as I dressed, and then spending another day in the company of Marines— the band of brothers and sisters I had come to know and cherish over a lifetime of being among them. I didn't think much about what would come after the Corps. I knew there would be opportunities, adventures, and money, but somehow, I also knew that whatever they were, they would never come close to the red stripe down my leg.

"I decided to try to become a Marine at age six, and never wanted to be anything else. In any category I can measure, the Corps took me as a young man, and made me far more than I would ever have been in any other profession. It gave me the highest decoration I will ever wear: the Marine Emblem. It made me a general, and a Commandant, but the most lasting satisfaction it ever bestowed was the privilege of leading Marines, calling myself one of them, and ultimately being responsible for the Corps—and that's a satisfaction that will be with me for the rest of my life.

"At his retirement ceremony, one of the colorful characters of our Corps, 'Big Foot' Brown, made the comment, 'Dear God, how I wish I could go back and do it all over again.' I wish I had thought of those words first, because that pretty well says it all."[37]

General Holland M. Smith, at the peak of his career, wrote to a friend, "My love of the Marine Corps is exceeded only by my loyalty to my country." On another occasion he commented: "As I approach the setting sun of my career, I am grateful to God that I have had long service in our magnificent Marine Corps."[38]

Lieutenant General Victor H. Krulak commented about his retirement: "It appeared to be a prudent time and a proper relief could be available, I realized it was time to retire. And I did it without any rancor. You might say that an individual would have a right to just a nickel's worth of bitterness having been told by the Commandant that the letter was signed, recommending that [I] be the Commandant. But somehow it didn't happen. It may sound a little bit idealistic, but the truth of the matter is that the Marines did just a hell of a lot for me. When I became a second lieutenant, my real objective in life was to get to be a major so that I wouldn't have to wear puttees. Well, I got a hell of a lot further than that. When I was sick or wounded they looked after me. I never had a bad job in all of my 34 years. . . . I look back on it now as a most rewarding experience, and really end the whole deal feeling in the Marine Corps debt."[39]

General Ray Davis was asked by his oral history interviewer: "How would you sum up your years in the Marine Corps?" He responded: "I wouldn't know how to do any better. I don't have any misgivings anywhere. How could you, going from a poor country boy in Georgia up to four stars in the most elite organization in the world. There's just no way that I could imagine any major misgivings about that.

"The things that you miss the most are the people. You know that the Marine Corps family is such a collection of totally outstanding people. Check off just the people I admire most, like Greene and Chapman and Walt and Chaisson, Masters and Buse and Nickerson, I could just go on and on. Exposure to General Krulak was a gain for me. I'm not associated with those kinds of people anymore. Even in my job here, where I was involved with the presidents of Southern Bell, Georgia Power Company, the gas company, the banks—involved with them very frequently. There is not that quality of great family relationship that we had in the Marine Corps, both for me and for my family.

"So, that's what we really miss, being out of it. Again, it was great; I gave it everything I had. I can't look back and see a single time when I took my pack off to coast."[40]

Lieutenant General Chesty Puller did not want to retire and could have had more years of service, but was forced to for medical reasons. After a social function following retirement, he returned to his home in Saluda, Virginia, and that evening his wife Virginia Puller found him pensive and distracted. They sat on a screened porch, looking out into the dusk lit by fireflies. She asked him: "Lewis, is there anything you'd wish for, now that it's all over?" He replied, "Well, I'd like to do it all over again. The whole thing." She sighed. He went on: "And more than that—more than anything—I'd like to see once again the face of every Marine I've ever served with."[41]

In correspondence with the author, Commandant Charles C. Krulak wrote, "What were my thoughts (at my retirement) regarding the meaning of my career in service to our country as a Marine? I had been a Marine ... if not in fact, certainly in my mind for my entire life. I had grown up in the Corps and had never really known anything else but the Corps. With that in mind, many might have thought that I would not be able to make the adjustment to life without the Marine Corps. Nothing could be further from the truth. I left the Corps with an undying sense of gratitude for having been afforded the honor to serve my country, in peace and war. The Marine Corps gave me far more than I ever gave the Marine Corps. . . . perhaps the greatest gift was to allow me to serve my country with selfless men and women at my side. As I left the Parade Deck at 8$^{th}$ and I, I didn't leave the Corps behind and I didn't leave my Marines behind. Both are with me today. They are tucked in a very special place in my soul and whenever I need a lift, I just peek into that special place and I am rejuvenated. No Marine ever leaves the Corps. . . . they might retire, but they never leave."[42]

Part of Commandant Krulak's "presentation on retirement" was entitled "A Farewell to the Corps:"

> From my earliest days, I was always awed by the character of the Marine Corps, by the passion and love that inspired the sacrifices of Marines like my father and his friends. As a young boy, I admired the warriors and thinkers who joined our family for a meal or a visit ... Marines like "Howlin Mad" Smith, Lemuel C. Shepherd, Gerald C. Thomas, and Keith B. McCutcheon. I wondered about the source of their pride, their selflessness, and their sense of purpose. Now, at the twilight of my career, I understand those Marines. I know that they were

driven by love for the institution to which they had dedicated their lives and by the awesome responsibility they felt to the Marines who shared their devotion and sacrifice. Today, that same motivation burns deep within the heart of each of us. The ethos of our Corps, purchased so dearly by these heroes of old, reaches into our souls and challenges us to strive tirelessly for excellence in all that we do. It profoundly influences the actions of every Marine who has ever stood on the yellow footprints at our recruit depots or taken the oath as an officer of Marines.

The ethos of our Corps is that of the warrior. It is defined by two simple qualities . . . our two touchstones. The first is our Touchstone of Valor. When we are summoned to battle, we don our helmets and flak jackets; we march to the sound of the guns; we fight and we win—guaranteed. The second is our Touchstone of Values. We hold ourselves and our institution to the highest standards . . . to our core values of Honor, Courage, and Commitment. These two touchstones are inextricably and forever linked. They form the bedrock of our success and, indeed, of our very existence.

The words of my father ring as true today as when he first wrote them over 50 years ago: "We exist today—we flourish today—not because of what we know we are, or what we know we can do, but because of what the grassroots of our country believes we are and believes we can do. . . . The American people believe that Marines are downright good for the country; that the Marines are masters of a form of unfailing alchemy which converts unoriented youths into proud, self-reliant stable citizens—citizens into whose hands the nation's affairs may safely be entrusted. . . . And, likewise, should the people ever lose that conviction as a result of our failure to meet their high—almost spiritual—standards, the Marine Corps will quickly disappear."

May God bless each and every one of you and may God bless our Corps!

The lives and careers of the senior Marine generals examined in this volume reveal a pattern for success that is available to every officer—indeed, to every person. Success, up to the limits of one's innate abilities, is available to all who dedicate themselves to their career, who are willing to work long and hard to prepare themselves, who recognize and develop the high character necessary to successful leadership, who love their fellow humans and show concern for their well being, and who can communicate with other officers in a manner that inspires confidence and devotion to duty.

# Notes

## Chapter 1

1. Major General John A. Lejeune, USMC, *Marine Corps Gazette* 8, no. 4 (December 1923), 2–3.
2. General Paul X. Kelley, USMC, testimony before the Senate Armed Forces Committee, February 5, 1987.
3. Author interview with General Paul X. Kelley, USMC (Ret.), June 3, 2005.
4. Author interview with General Alfred M. Gray, Jr., USMC (Ret.), October 27, 2004.
5. Commandant Leonard F. Chapman, Jr., USMC (Ret.), unpublished speech.
6. Author correspondence with General Carl E. Mundy, Jr., USMC (Ret.), December 18, 2004.
7. Author interview with General James L. Jones, USMC, July 21, 2001.
8. General Charles C. Krulak, USMC (Ret.), oral history with Dr. David B. Crist, 143.

## Chapter 2

1. General Robert H. Barrow, USMC (Ret.), oral history with Brigadier General Edwin H. Simmons, USMC (Ret.) and Dr. Edgar F. Puryear, Jr., June 24, 2004.
2. Major General John A. Lejeune, USMC (Ret.), *The Reminiscences of a Marine* (Philadelphia: Dorrance and Company, 1930), 199.
3. Ibid., 219–220.
4. Ibid., 241.
5. Merrill L. Bartlett, *Lejeune: A Marine's Life, 1867–1942* (Annapolis: U.S. Naval Institute Press, 1996), 121.
6. Ibid., 128–129.
7. Ibid., 129.
8. Ibid., 131–132, 139–141.
9. Ibid., 139–141.
10. Lejeune, 471–472.
11. General A.A. Vandegrift, USMC (Ret.), *Once a Marine: The Memoirs of General A.A. Vandegrift, United States Marine Corps* (New York: Ballantine Books, 1966), 86–87.
12. Ibid., 218.
13. T. Holcomb to Admiral H.R. Stark, November 9, 1940, November 24, 1940; Holland M. Smith Papers, Quantico, VA; Norman Varnell Cooper, "The Military Career of General Holland M. Smith, USMC," PhD dissertation, University of Alabama, 1974, 135–136.
14. General Clifton B. Cates, USMC (Ret.), oral history with Brigadier General Edwin H. Simmons, USMC (Ret.), April 26, 1973, 205–210.
15. General Lemuel C. Shepherd, Jr., USMC (Ret.), oral history with Benis M. Frank, 473–478.
16. General Carl E. Mundy, USMC (Ret.), oral history with Brigadier General Edwin H. Simmons, USMC (Ret.), 79.
17. William C. Westmoreland, *A Soldier Reports* (Garden City, NY: Doubleday, Inc., 1976), 166–167.
18. General Lewis W. Walt, USMC (Ret.), *Strange War, Strange Strategy: A General's Report on Vietnam* (New York: Funk and Wagnalls, 1970), ix–x.
19. Mundy, 79.
20. Author interview with Admiral James L. Holloway III, USA (Ret.), July 18, 2001.
21. Lieutenant General Victor H. Krulak, USMC (Ret.), oral history with John T. Mason, 214–223.
22. General Robert E. Cushman, Jr., USMC (Ret.), oral history with Benis M. Frank, 394–400.

[23] Ibid.
[24] "Dispute Embroils Marines," *The Washington Post*, April 10, 1975.
[25] Ibid.
[26] Cushman, 402–404.
[27] Mundy, 12.
[28] General Louis H. Wilson, Jr., USMC (Ret.), oral history with Brigadier General Edwin H. Simmons, USMC (Ret.), 463.
[29] Cushman, 403–405.
[30] *U.S. News and World Report*, May 6, 1975, and May 12, 1975.
[31] *The Washington Post*, May 6, 1975.
[32] Cushman, 406–408.
[33] Wilson, 376.
[34] Ibid., 462–463.
[35] Ibid., 39.
[36] Ibid., 336.
[37] Barrow, 2–11.
[38] Ibid.; author interview with General Robert H. Barrow, USMC (Ret.), June 24, 2004.
[39] Author interview with General Alfred M. Gray, Jr., USMC (Ret.), October 27, 2004.
[40] Author interview with General Carl M. Mundy, USMC (Ret.), March 5, 2004; Mundy oral history, 582–590.
[41] Ibid.
[42] General Charles C. Krulak, USMC (Ret.), oral history with Dr. David B. Crist, 19; author interview with General Krulak.
[43] Ibid., 140.
[44] Ibid., 134.
[45] Ibid.
[46] Ibid., 135.
[47] Ibid., 155.
[48] Author interview with General Charles C. Krulak, USMC (Ret.), July 5, 2005.
[49] Author interview with General James L. Jones, USMC (Ret.), July 21, 2001.
[50] Ibid.
[51] Lyric Wallwork Winik, "We Can Help Shape the World," *Parade*, January 19, 1993.

## Chapter 3

[1] Major General John A. Lejeune, USMC (Ret.), *The Reminiscences of a Marine* (Philadelphia: Dorrance and Company, 1930), 33.
[2] Ibid., 30.
[3] Ibid., 30–31.
[4] Ibid., 36.
[5] Ibid., 44–45.
[6] Ibid., 52.
[7] Ibid., 58.
[8] Ibid., 60.
[9] Those who failed a course based on a combination of daily grades and the final exam, barring a reexam offered by the Academic Board, were dismissed from the Academy for "academic reasons." A reexam, if offered, was taken within a few days after appearance before the Academic Board. Failure of the reexam, barring the granting of a re-re-exam by the Board, resulted in dismissal also. In some instances, midshipmen who were deemed to be so deserving, were "turned back" to the USNA Class behind them.
[10] Ibid., 37.
[11] Ibid., 90–91.

[12] Ibid., 93–96.

[13] General A.A. Vandegrift, USMC (Ret.), *Once a Marine: The Memoirs of General A.A. Vandegrift, United States Marine Corps* (New York: Ballantine Books, 1966), 27.

[14] General Clifton B. Cates, USMC (Ret.), oral history with Benis M. Frank, 3–5.

[15] Ibid.

[16] General Lemuel C. Shepherd, Jr., USMC (Ret.), oral history, 287–293.

[17] Charles T. Jones and R. Manning Ancell, eds., *Four Star Leadership for Leaders* (Mechanicsburg, PA: Executive Books, 1997), 153–155.

[18] General Robert E. Cushman, Jr., USMC (Ret.), oral history with Benis M. Frank, 101–102.

[19] General Louis H. Wilson, USMC (Ret.), oral history with Brigadier General Edwin H. Simmons, USMC (Ret.), 384–391.

[20] General Robert H. Barrow, USMC (Ret.), oral history with Brigadier General Edwin H. Simmons, USMC (Ret.), 33–58.

[21] Author interview with General Paul X. Kelley, USMC (Ret.), June 13, 2005.

[22] Author interview with General Alfred M. Gray, Jr., USMC (Ret.), October 27, 2004 and oral history with Brigadier General Edwin H. Simmons, USMC (Ret.).

[23] Author interview with General Carl E. Mundy, Jr., USMC (Ret.), March 5, 2004; June 24, 2004; July 5, 2004; August 9, 2004; October 27, 2004.

[24] Author interview with General Charles C. Krulak, USMC (Ret.), December 21, 2004; General Charles C. Krulak, USMC, oral history with Dr. David Crist, 1–8.

[25] Author interview with General James L. Jones, USMC, July 31, 2001.

[26] Burke Davis, *Marine: The Life of Lt. Gen. Lewis B. "Chesty" Puller, USMC* (Boston, MA: Little, Brown, 1962), 20, 24.

[27] Ibid.

[28] Ibid.

[29] Lowell Thomas, *Old Gimlet Eye: The Adventures of Smedley D. Butler* (New York: Farrar and Rinehart, 1933), 7–10.

[30] General Holland M. Smith, USMC (Ret.), and Perry Finch, *Coral and Brass* (Washington, DC: Zenger Publishers, 1949).

[31] General Raymond Davis, *The Story of Ray Davis* (Varina, NC: Research Triangle Publishing, 1995), 29.

# Chapter 4

[1] General A.A. Vandegrift, USMC (Ret.), *Once a Marine: The Memoirs of General A.A. Vandegrift, United States Marine Corps* (New York: Ballantine Books, 1964), 217–218.

[2] Author interview with General Paul X. Kelley, USMC (Ret.).

[3] General Carl E. Mundy, Jr. USMC (Ret.), oral history with Brigadier General Edwin H. Simmons, USMC (Ret.), 666.

[4] General Charles C. Krulak, USMC (Ret.), oral history with Dr. David B. Crist.

[5] Mundy, oral history.

[6] Krulak, oral history.

[7] General Raymond G. Davis, USMC (Ret.), oral history with Benis M. Frank.

[8] Major General John A. Lejeune, USMC (Ret.), *The Reminiscences of a Marine* (Philadelphia: Dorrance and Company, 1930), 323.

[9] General Robert H. Barrow, USMC (Ret.), oral history with Brigadier General Edwin H. Simmons, USMC (Ret.).

[10] Jeter A. Isely and Philip A. Crowl, *The U.S. Marines and Amphibious War: Its Theory and Its Practice in the Pacific* (Princeton: Princeton University Press, 1951), 5.

[11] Ibid., 5.

[12] The above is a summary of the Gallipoli Campaign in Isely and Crowl.

[13] James D. Hittle, "Sea Power and a National General Staff," U.S. Naval Institute *Proceedings* 79 (October 1949), 135–143, 1091–1103; Holland M. Smith, "Amphibious Tactics," *Marine Corps Gazette*, June 1945–March 1947; Isely and Crowl, 4.
[14] Lieutenant General Victor H. Krulak, USMC, *First to Fight* (Annapolis, MD: Naval Institute Press, 1984), 72–75.
[15] Major General John A. Lejeune, USMC, *Marine Corps Gazette* 8, no. 4 (December 1923), 243.
[16] Vandegrift, 60–61.
[17] Krulak, 76–79.
[18] Ibid.
[19] Major General Eli K. Cole, USMC, "Joint Overseas Operations," U.S. Naval Institute *Proceedings* (1929), 927–929.
[20] Ibid.
[21] Isely and Crowl, 31.
[22] Colonel Robert H. Dunlap, USMC, *Marine Corps Gazette* 6, no. 3 (1921), 237.
[23] Ibid.
[24] Krulak, 79–80.
[25] Cole, 927–929.
[26] Ibid.
[27] Krulak, 75–76.
[28] Ibid., 79–82.
[29] General Lemuel Shepherd, USMC (Ret.), oral history with Benis M. Frank, 268–270.
[30] Norman Varnell Cooper, "The Military Career of General Holland M. Smith, USMC," PhD dissertation, The University of Alabama, 1974, 139–141.
[31] Cooper, 139–141.
[32] Smith, 79–80.
[33] Captain Charles J. Moore, USN, oral history, 825–827; Cooper, 206.
[34] Smith, 205.
[35] Ibid.
[36] R.K. Turner to T. Holcomb, October 13, 1943, Holcomb papers; Cooper, 202; Lejeune, *Marine Corps Gazette* (December 1923), 243.
[37] Major General John A. Lejeune, USMC, U.S. Naval Institute *Proceedings* (October 1926), 1865–1867.
[38] Cole.
[39] Vandegrift, 254.
[40] Krulak, 220.
[41] Colonel Rufus H. Lane, USMC, "The Mission and Doctrine of the Marine Corps," *Marine Corps Gazette* (1923).
[42] Fleet Admiral Ernest J. King, *Fleet Admiral King: A Naval Record* (New York: W.W. Norton, Inc., 1952), 321–322.
[43] Isely and Crowl, 3
[44] Vandegrift, 17–18.
[45] Ibid., 232–234.
[46] Ibid., 234–235.
[47] Isely and Crowl, 342.
[48] Buell, 236.
[49] Forrest C. Pogue, *George C. Marshall: Organizer of Victory* (New York: The Viking Press, 1973), 449; General George C. Marshall in a memorandum for Admiral King, November 22, 1944; Cooper, 405–406.
[50] S. Jarman to R.C. Richardson, Jr., June 23, 1944, Exhibit J, Buckner Report; Cooper, 336; Smith, 172.
[51] Buell, 306–307.
[52] Smith, 176.

⁵³ C.G. USAF CPA, memo to CINCPAC, December 27, 1943; Turner papers; Cooper, 259–260.
⁵⁴ Ibid.
⁵⁵ Ibid.
⁵⁶ Holland M. Smith to A.A. Vandegrift, January 6, 1944, in Holland M. Smith (henceforth HMS) papers, Auburn; Cooper, 261–262.
⁵⁷ Holland M. Smith to A.A. Vandegrift, February 11, 1944.
⁵⁸ Ibid.
⁵⁹ Buell, 307.
⁶⁰ *The New York Times*, July 20, 1944, 7.
⁶¹ HMS press release, October 27, 1948; Cooper, 385–386.
⁶² Buckner Board Report, 3, 10; Cooper, 386–388.
⁶³ Holland, 179–180.
⁶⁴ Vandegrift, 265.
⁶⁵ R.C. Smith comment, Exhibit M, and Testimony Exhibit A and D, Buckner Report; Cooper, 387–389.
⁶⁶ Cooper, 407–408.
⁶⁷ Nimitz, 309.
⁶⁸ Vandegrift, 265.
⁶⁹ Potter, 307.
⁷⁰ Cooper, 379.
⁷¹ Ray Richards, "Army General Relieved in Row over Huge Marine Loses," *San Francisco Examiner*, July 8, 1944, 15; Cooper, 378–379.
⁷² Sherrod, "An Answer," 18; Cooper, 401–402.
⁷³ Holland M. Smith to CINCPAC, October 11, 1944, and transcript of disc recording of interview with R.C. Smith, June 19, 1944; HMS papers, Quantico; Cooper, 403.
⁷⁴ CNO to Chief of Staff, U.S. Army, Ser. 003233, 6 November 1944, copy in Turner papers; the assertion of the 27th Division historian that King approved Nimitz's recommendation is incorrect: Love, 27th Division, 669; Cooper, 404.
⁷⁵ Draft copy of a letter from Admiral Ernest J. King to Admiral Chester W. Nimitz, November 8, 1944, King papers, Operational Archives; Cooper, 405.
⁷⁶ HMS to A.A. Vandegrift, October 11, 1944, HMS papers, Auburn; Cooper, 403.
⁷⁷ HMS to A.A. Vandegrift, February 4, 1944, HMS papers, Auburn; Cooper, 267.
⁷⁸ HMS to A.A. Vandegrift, July 15, 1944, HMS papers, Auburn; Cooper, 341.
⁷⁹ HMS to A.A. Vandegrift, July 18, 1944, HMS papers, Auburn; Cooper, 341.
⁸⁰ Vandegrift, 323.
⁸¹ Christopher M. Jones, "The Role of Politics and the Survival of the V–22 Osprey," *Journal of Political and Military Land Sociology* 21, no. 3 (Summer 2001).
⁸² Ibid.
⁸³ Associated Press, April 11, 2000.
⁸⁴ Associated Press, June 11, 2002.
⁸⁵ *The Washington Post*, December 13, 2000.

## Chapter 5

¹ Major General John A. Lejeune, USMC (Ret.), *The Reminiscences of a Marine* (Philadelphia: Dorrance and Company, 1930), 307–308. Emphasis added.
² Ibid., 379–380.
³ Ibid., 277–278.
⁴ Ibid., 436.
⁵ Ibid., 346–347.
⁶ Burke Davis, *Marine! The Life of Lt. Gen. Lewis B. (Chesty) Puller, USMC* (Boston: Little, Brown and Company, 1962), 204–205.

[7] Ibid., 118.
[8] Ibid., 198.
[9] Ibid., 194–195.
[10] Ibid., 195.
[11] General Raymond G. Davis, USMC (Ret.), oral history with Benis M. Frank, 1978, 132.
[12] Ibid., 59.
[13] Ibid. Emphasis added.
[14] Ibid., 51.
[15] General A.A. Vandegrift, USMC (Ret.), *Once A Marine: The Memoirs of General A.A. Vandegrift, United States Marine Corps* (New York: Norton Books, 1964), 58.
[16] Ibid., 180.
[17] Ibid., 150
[18] Ibid., 182.
[19] Ibid., 287.
[20] General Lewis W. Walt, USMC (Ret.), *Strange War, Strange Strategy: A General's Report on Vietnam* (New York: Funk and Wagnalls, 1970), 33, 38.
[21] Charles T. Jones and R. Manning Ancell, eds., *Four-Star Leadership for Leaders* (Mechanicsburg, PA: Executive Books, 1997), 25–26.
[22] Ibid.
[23] Ibid.
[24] General Robert H. Barrow, USMC (Ret.), oral history with Brigadier General Edwin H. Simmons, USMC (Ret.), 478.
[25] Ibid., 485–489.
[26] Ibid., 29.
[27] Ibid., 36–37.
[28] Ibid., 48.
[29] General Charles Krulak, USMC (Ret.), oral history with Dr. David B. Crist, 276.
[30] Ibid., 45, 99–100.
[31] Ibid.
[32] Tom Clancy with General Anthony Zinni, USMC (Ret.), and Tony Koltz, *Battle Ready* (New York: G.P. Putnam's Sons, 2004), 53.
[33] Ibid., 131–134.
[34] Ibid., 49.
[35] Author interview with General Anthony Zinni, USMC (Ret.), December 17, 2003.
[36] Author interview with General James L. Jones, USMC (Ret.), July 31, 2001.
[37] Wilson, 463–464.
[38] Walt, ix.
[39] Lejeune, 464.
[40] General Carl E. Mundy, USMC (Ret.), oral history with Brigadier General Edwin H. Simmons, USMC (Ret.), 164.
[41] Ibid.
[42] Ibid., 437.
[43] General Robert H. Barrow, USMC (Ret.), oral history with Brigadier General Edwin H. Simmons, USMC (Ret.), 41–42.
[44] Ibid., 68.
[45] Vandegrift, 66.
[46] Vandegrift, 77.
[47] Davis.
[48] Ibid., 290.
[49] Jones.

## Chapter 6

[1] Major General John A. Lejeune, USMC (Ret.), *The Reminiscences of a Marine* (New York: Arno Press, 1979), 414–415.

[2] Burke Davis, *Marine! The Life of Lt. Gen. Lewis B. (Chesty) Puller, USMC* (Boston: Little, Brown and Company, 1962), 80–81, 171.

[3] Ibid., 171.

[4] General A.A. Vandegrift, *Once a Marine: The Memoirs of General A.A. Vandegrift, United States Marine Corps* (New York: Ballantine Books, 1966), 208–209.

[5] Marine Corps Operations, 3,365; Norman Varnell Cooper, "The Military Career of General Holland M. Smith, USMC," PhD dissertation, University of Alabama, 1974, 362–363.

[6] G.B. Erskine to Commandant Marine Corps, December 22, 1950, Comment and Monography File, USMC History Archives; General Robert E. Hogaboom, Papers, Marine Corps Museum, Quantico, VA; Hogaboom, oral history, 213; Cooper, 363.

[7] Carl W. Hoffman, *The Seizure of Tinian* (Washington, DC: Historical Division Headquarters, U.S. Marine Corps, 1951), 21–22; George Carroll Dyer, *The Amphibians Came to Conquer: The Story of Admiral Richmond Kelly Turner*, 2 vol. (Washington, DC: U.S. Government Printing Office, 1972), vol. 2, 954.

[8] Mac Asbill, Jr., Notes on Holland M. Smith. Historical Division, Headquarters, U.S. Marine Corps, Washington, DC; Cooper, 365–367.

[9] Hoffman, 22–23; Cooper, 367.

[10] Hoffman, 23–24; Admiral Harry W. Hill, USN, Papers Archives, Naval History Division, Washington Navy Yard, Washington, DC, 534; R.E. Hogaboom to Commandant Marine Corps, January 22, 1951; Hogaboom papers; E.D. Forrestal, *Admiral Raymond A. Spruance, USN: A Study in Command* (Washington, DC: U.S. Government Printing Office, 1966), 152; Cooper, 367.

[11] Davis, 338.

[12] General Lemuel C. Shepherd, Jr., USMC, oral history, 155–156.

[13] General Lewis H. Wilson, Jr., USMC (Ret.), oral history with Brigadier General Edwin H. Simmons, USMC (Ret.), History and Museums Division Headquarters, U.S. Marine Corps, Washington, DC, 1988, 457.

[14] General Robert H. Barrow, USMC (Ret.), oral history, 69–71.

[15] General Charles C. Krulak, USMC (Ret.), oral history, 27.

[16] General Lewis H. Wilson, Jr., oral history, 354–362.

[17] Oral history, General Carl E. Mundy, Jr., USMC (Ret.), with Brigadier General Edwin H. Simmons, USMC (Ret.), History and Museums Division Headquarters, U.S Marine Corps, Washington, DC, 2000, 711.

[18] Ibid.

[19] Barrow, 202.

[20] Krulak, 46.

[21] Ibid.,163–165.

[22] Vandegrift, 254–255.

[23] Ibid., 239. Emphasis added.

[24] General Clifton B. Cates, USMC (Ret.), oral history with Benis M. Frank, 215–216.

[25] Lieutenant General Charles C. Cooper, USMC (Ret.), with Richard E. Goodspeed, *Cheers and Tears: A Marine's Story of Combat in Peace and War* (Reno, NV: Wesley Press, 2002), 123.

[26] Vandegrift, 215.

[27] Ibid., 193–194.

[28] Davis, 71–72.

[29] Ibid., 333.

[30] Mundy, 609–610.

[31] Major General Donald M. Weller, USMC (Ret.), interview with Dr. Norman Varnell Cooper, February 2, 1973; Cooper, 402.

[32] Tom Clancy with General Anthony Zinni, USMC (Ret.), and Tony Koltz, *Battle Ready* (New York: G.P. Putnam's Sons, 2004), 142.

## Chapter 7

[1] General Michael W. Hagee, USMC, "The Marine Corps Professional Reading Program," *Marine Corps Gazette* 89, no. 4 (April 2005).
[2] "Raising the Mental Bar," *Marine Corps Gazette* 89, no. 4 (April 2005).
[3] General Holland M. Smith, USMC (Ret.), and Percy Finch, *Coral and Brass* (Washington, DC: Zenger Publishing Co., Inc., 1949), 29.
[4] General A.A. Vandegrift, USMC (Ret.), *Once a Marine: The Memoirs of General A.A. Vandegrift, United States Marine Corps* (New York: Ballantine Books, 1966), 25, 31.
[5] General Robert H. Barrow, USMC (Ret.), oral history with Brigadier General Edwin H. Simmons, USMC (Ret.), and author interview, June 24, 2004.
[6] Author interview with General Alfred M. Gray, USMC (Ret.), August 26, 2004.
[7] Burke Davis, *Marine! The Life of Lt. Gen. Lewis B. (Chesty) Puller, USMC* (Boston: Little, Brown and Company, 1962), 15–16.
[8] Ibid., 17–18.
[9] Ibid., 22–23.
[10] Ibid., 40.
[11] Ibid., 123.
[12] Ibid., 141.
[13] Ibid., 357.
[14] "Living with a Legend," *Leatherneck*, June 1985, 20–22.
[15] General Raymond G. Davis, *The Story of Ray Davis, USMC (Ret.)* (Varina, NC: Research Triangle Publishing, 1955), 73.
[16] Ibid., 196.
[17] Author interview with General Anthony Zinni, USMC (Ret.).
[18] Tom Clancy with General Anthony Zinni, USMC (Ret.), and Tony Koltz, *Battle Ready* (New York: G.P. Putnam's Sons, 2004), 136.
[19] Author interview with General Carl E. Mundy, Jr., USMC (Ret.).
[20] Author interview with Gray.
[21] E.B. Potter, *Nimitz* (Annapolis: Naval Institute Press, 1976), 383.
[22] Author interview with Gray.
[23] General Carl E. Mundy, Jr., USMC (Ret.), oral history with Brigadier General Edwin H. Simmons, USMC (Ret.), 18.

## Chapter 8

[1] Major General John A. Lejeune, USMC (Ret.), *The Reminiscences of a Marine* (New York: Arno Press, 1979), 178.
[2] Ibid., 284–286.
[3] Ibid., 129.
[4] General A.A. Vandegrift, USMC (Ret.), *Once a Marine: The Memoirs of General A.A. Vandegrift, United States Marine Corps* (New York: Ballantine Books, 1966), 28–29.
[5] Ibid., 236–237.
[6] Ibid., 42.
[7] Ibid., 65.
[8] General Clifton B. Cates, USMC (Ret.), oral history with Benis M. Frank.
[9] General Lemuel C. Shepherd, Jr., USMC (Ret.), oral history with Benis M. Frank, 19.
[10] Ibid., 422.
[11] Ibid., 351–353.

[12] Ibid., 367–368.
[13] Ibid., 428–429.
[14] Ibid., 439–440.
[15] Ibid., 438.
[16] Ibid.
[17] Ibid.
[18] Ibid.
[19] Ibid.
[20] General Louis H. Wilson, USMC (Ret.), oral history interview with Brigadier General Edwin H. Simmons, USMC (Ret.), 411.
[21] Ibid., 120.
[22] General Robert H. Barrow, USMC (Ret.), oral history interview with Brigadier General Edwin H. Simmons, USMC (Ret.), 6–17.
[23] Ibid.
[24] Author interview with General Paul X. Kelley, USMC (Ret.).
[25] General Carl E. Mundy, Jr., USMC (Ret.), oral history with Brigadier General Edwin H. Simmons, USMC (Ret.), 84.
[26] Ibid., 86.
[27] Ibid., 87.
[28] Ibid., 248.
[29] Ibid., 673.
[30] Author interview with Mundy.
[31] Ibid.
[32] Ibid.
[33] Author interview with General Charles C. Krulak, USMC (Ret.).
[34] Ibid.
[35] Ibid.
[36] Author interview with Mundy, March 5, 2004.
[37] Ibid.
[38] Burke Davis, *Marine! The Life of Lt. Gen. Lewis B. (Chesty) Puller, USMC* (Boston: Little, Brown and Company, 1962), 97, 100.
[39] E.B. Potter, *Nimitz* (Annapolis: Naval Institute Press, 1976), 160.
[40] General Raymond G. Davis, USMC (Ret.), *The Story of Ray Davis* (Varina, NC: Research Triangle Publishing, 1995), 38.
[41] Charles T. Jones and R. Manning Ancell, eds., *Four Star Leadership for Leaders* (Mechanicsburg, PA: Executive Books, 1997), 23–24. Emphasis added.
[42] General Raymond G. Davis, USMC (Ret.), oral history with Benis M. Frank, 108.
[43] Ibid., 109.
[44] Ibid., 72.
[45] Ibid., 249.
[46] Ibid., 264.
[47] Author interview with Jones.
[48] Lejeune, 59–60.
[49] Ibid., 99–100.
[50] Vandegrift, 36–37.
[51] Ibid., 32–33.
[52] Barrow, oral history, 62–65.
[53] Author interview with General Alfred M. Gray, Jr., USMC (Ret.), October 8, 2008.
[54] Author interview with Kelley.
[55] Author interview with Mundy.
[56] Author interview with Krulak.
[57] Davis, *Marine!* 55.

⁵⁸ Ibid., 48–49.
⁵⁹ "They Never Faltered or Fell Back," U.S. Naval Institute *Proceedings* (November 2003), 50.
⁶⁰ Lieutenant General Charles G. Cooper, USMC, *Cheers and Tears: A Marine's Story of Combat in Peace and War* (Reno, NV: Wesley Press, 2002), 20.
⁶¹ Lowell Thomas, *Old Gimlet Eye: Adventures of Smedley D. Butler* (New York: Farrar and Rinehart, Inc., 1933), 10.

## Chapter 9

¹ Norman Varnell Cooper, "The Military Career of General Holland M. Smith, USMC," PhD dissertation, University of Alabama, 1974, 289.
² Clifton La Bree, *The Gentle Warrior: General Oliver Prince Smith, USMC* (Kent, OH: Kent State University Press, 2000), x.
³ Ibid., 169.
⁴ General A.A. Vandegrift, USMC (Ret.), *Once a Marine: The Memoirs of General A.A. Vandegrift, United States Marine Corps* (New York: Ballantine Books, 1966), 271–273.
⁵ Burke Davis, *Marine! The Life of Lt. Gen. Lewis B. (Chesty) Puller, USMC* (Boston: Little, Brown and Company, 1962), 172.
⁶ La Bree, 23.
⁷ Vandegrift, 185.
⁸ Vandegrift, 181, 206–209.
⁹ Major General John A. Lejeune, USMC (Ret.), *The Reminiscences of a Marine* (New York: Arno Press, 1979), 116.
¹⁰ General Raymond G. Davis, USMC (Ret.), *The Story of Ray Davis* (Varina, NC: Research Triangle Publishing, 1995), 7.
¹¹ General Charles C. Krulak, USMC (Ret.), oral history with Dr. David B. Crist, and interview with Edgar F. Puryear, Jr., 141–142.
¹² Lejeune, 433.
¹³ General Clifton B. Cates, USMC (Ret.), oral history with Benis M. Frank, 29.
¹⁴ Wilson, 400–401.
¹⁵ Cooper, 80.
¹⁶ Mundy.
¹⁷ Charles T. Jones and R. Manning Ancell, eds., *Four Star Leadership for Leaders* (Mechanicsburg, PA: Executive Books, 1997).
¹⁸ Davis, *The Story of Ray Davis*, 178–179.
¹⁹ Author interview with General Robert H. Barrow, USMC (Ret.).
²⁰ Davis, *Marine!* 118–119.
²¹ Ibid., 361–362.
²² Barrow, 55–56.
²³ Davis, *The Story of Ray Davis*, 76.
²⁴ Cooper, 87–88.
²⁵ Krulak, 200–201. Emphasis added.
²⁶ Cooper, 288.
²⁷ Ibid., 288–289.
²⁸ Barrow, 592–594.
²⁹ Ibid., 28–29.
³⁰ Ibid., 52–53.
³¹ Ibid.
³² Krulak, 226.
³³ General Lewis W. Walt, USMC (Ret.), *Strange War, Strange Strategy: A General's Report on Vietnam* (New York: Funk and Wagnalls, 1970), x.
³⁴ Ibid.

³⁵ La Bree, 45.
³⁶ Krulak, 193.
³⁷ Davis, *The Story of Ray Davis*, 179.
³⁸ Tom Clancy with General Anthony Zinni, USMC (Ret.), and Tony Koltz, *Battle Ready* (New York: G.P. Putnam's Sons, 2004), 59.
³⁹ Lejeune, 433.
⁴⁰ Cooper, 313.
⁴¹ General Lemuel C. Shepherd, Jr. USMC (Ret.), oral history with Benis M. Frank, 243–245.
⁴² Cooper, 160.
⁴³ Krulak, 275.
⁴⁴ Ibid.
⁴⁵ LaBree, x.
⁴⁶ Davis, *Marine!* 163–164.
⁴⁷ Krulak, 211.
⁴⁸ Clancy, Zinni, and Koltz, 155.
⁴⁹ Cooper, 48–49.
⁵⁰ Author interview with General Robert H. Barrow, USMC (Ret.), June 24, 2004.
⁵¹ Author interview with General Anthony Zinni, USMC (Ret.), December 17, 2003.
⁵² Author interview with General Paul X. Kelley, USMC (Ret.).
⁵³ Ibid.
⁵⁴ Author interview with Captain Eli Takesian, CHC, USN (Ret.).
⁵⁵ Charles Osgood, *Osgood on Speaking* (New York: Morrow and Company, Inc., 1988), 25.
⁵⁶ Kelley.
⁵⁷ Alfred M. Gray, Jr., Fleet Marine Force Manual 1: *Warfighting* (Washington, DC: United States Marine Corps, 1989), 12; author interview with General Alfred M. Gray, Jr., USMC (Ret.), October 8, 2008.
⁵⁸ Lejeune, 77.
⁵⁹ Ibid., 374–375.

## Chapter 10

¹ General A.A. Vandegrift, USMC (Ret.), *Once a Marine* (New York: Ballantine Books, 1964), 44.
² General Carl E. Mundy, Jr., USMC (Ret.), oral history with Brigadier General Edwin H. Simmons, USMC (Ret.), 52, and author interview, December 18, 2004.
³ General Robert H. Barrow, USMC (Ret.), oral history with Brigadier General Edwin H. Simmons, USMC (Ret.), March 20, 1992, 4–12.
⁴ Ibid.
⁵ Author interview, correspondence, and telephone conversations with General Paul X. Kelley, USMC (Ret.).
⁶ Author interview with Chaplain Eli Takesian, USN.
⁷ Kelley interviews.
⁸ Ibid.
⁹ Secretary of Defense Caspar Weinberger, press statement on the Long Commission Investigation Report, December 23, 1983.
¹⁰ Caspar Weinberger, letter to Bill Nichols, dated January 9, 1984.
¹¹ General Paul X. Kelley, USMC, letter to Bill Nichols, dated January 10, 1984.
¹² Takesian interview.
¹³ Press statement, December 27, 1983.
¹⁴ Ronald Reagan, *An American Life* (New York: Simon and Schuster, 1990).
¹⁵ Ibid.
¹⁶ Mike O'Callighan, editorial in the *Las Vegas Sun*, December 21, 1983.
¹⁷ Kelley interviews.
¹⁸ Author interview with General James L. Jones, USMC (Ret.), July 31, 2001.

19 Ibid.
20 Ibid.
21 Mundy oral history, 473.
22 Ibid.
23 Ibid., 474.
24 Author interview with General Carl E. Mundy, Jr., USMC (Ret.), December 18, 2004.
25 Mundy oral history, 474–475.
26 Ibid., 476–477.
27 Ibid., 462–477.
28 General William C. Westmoreland, USA, *A Soldier Reports* (New York: Doubleday and Company, Inc., 1976), 375.
29 Ibid., 376.
30 W.R. Peers, *The My Lai Inquiry* (New York: W.W. Norton and Company, 1979), 223.
31 Westmoreland, 377.
32 Author interview with Lieutenant General Charles G. Cooper, USMC (Ret.).
33 Ibid.
34 Ibid.
35 Ibid.
36 Ibid.
37 Mitchell Paige, *A Marine Named Mitch* (New York: Vantage Press, 1975), 15.
38 Ibid.
39 Keith Fleming, *The U.S. Marine Corps in Crisis: Ribbon Creek and Recruit Training* (Columbia: University of South Carolina Press, 1988), 17–18.
40 Lieutenant General Wallace M. Greene, Jr., letter to Colonel Robert D. Heinl, Jr., November 19, 1960.
41 Fleming, 25.
42 Ibid., 27.
43 Ibid., 40–41.
44 Ibid.
45 Ibid., 41.
46 Ibid., 42.
47 Ibid., 52–53.
48 James M. McCarthy, "The Man Who Helped Sergeant McKeon," *Life Magazine*, August 13, 1956, 59.
49 Ibid.
50 Ibid.
51 Lieutenant Colonel Duane L. Faw, memo to Commanding General, Marine Corps Recruiting Depot Parris Island, dated June 30, 1956, copy in Personal Papers Collection, Greene Papers, box 43, folder 9, Marine Corps Historical Center, Washington, DC; Fleming, 76.
52 Fleming.
53 Ibid., 81.
54 Ibid., 83.
55 Ibid., 84.
56 Burke Davis, *Marine! The Life of Lieutenant General Lewis B. (Chesty) Puller, USMC* (Boston: Little, Brown and Company, 1962), 380–381.
57 Ibid., 382–384.
58 Fleming, 53.
59 Ibid.
60 Author interview with General Charles C. Krulak, USMC (Ret.), December 21, 2004.
61 Fleming, 27.
62 Ibid.
63 Ibid., 101–102.

⁶⁴ Ibid., 102–105.
⁶⁵ Brigadier General W.M. Greene, Jr., letter to General R. McPate, March 8, 1956, copy in Greene Papers 42–1; Fleming, 104–105.
⁶⁶ Brigadier General W.M. Greene, Jr., letter to General R. McPate, March 9, 1956, copy in Greene Papers 43–8; Fleming, 107.
⁶⁷ General R. McPate, letter to Brigadier General W.M. Greene, Jr., March 12, 1957, copy in Greene Papers 41–2.
⁶⁸ General R. McPate, letter to Brigadier General W.M. Greene, Jr., March 30, 1957, copy in Greene Papers 42–1.
⁶⁹ Ibid.
⁷⁰ Fleming, 108–109.
⁷¹ Ibid.
⁷² Mundy interview.
⁷³ General Charles C. Krulak, USMC (Ret.), oral history, 248.
⁷⁴ *Agence France Press*, February 4, 1948.
⁷⁵ *The Virginia Pilot*, February 6, 1998.
⁷⁶ *The Christian Science Monitor*, May 27, 1999.
⁷⁷ Ibid.
⁷⁸ Ibid.
⁷⁹ *The New York Times*, February 27, 1999.
⁸⁰ Ibid.
⁸¹ Secretary of Defense William Cohen, press conference, March 5, 1999.
⁸² Krulak oral history, 248–249.
⁸³ Ibid., 51.
⁸⁴ Author interview with General Anthony Zinni, USMC (Ret.), December 17, 2003.

# Chapter 11

¹ Lieutenant General Victor H. Krulak, USMC (Ret.), *First to Fight: An Inside View of the U.S. Marine Corps* (Annapolis: Naval Institute Press, 1984), 111.
² General Lemuel C. Shepherd, Jr., USMC (Ret.), oral history with Benis M. Frank, 168, 239–241.
³ General Robert H. Barrow, USMC (Ret.), oral history with Brigadier General Edwin H. Simmons, USMC (Ret.), 352–354.
⁴ General Raymond G. Davis, USMC (Ret.), *The Story of Ray Davis* (Varina, NC: Research Triangle Publishing, 1995), 97–98
⁵ Tom Clancy with General Anthony Zinni, USMC (Ret.), and Tony Koltz, *Battle Ready* (New York: G.P. Putnam's Sons, 2004), 121–126.
⁶ Clifton La Bree, *The Gentle Warrior: General Oliver Prince Smith, USMC* (Kent, OH: Kent State University Press, 2001), 106.
⁷ General Holland M. Smith, USMC (Ret.), and Percy Finch, *Coral and Brass* (Washington, DC: Zenger Publishing Co., Inc., 1948).
⁸ General Robert H. Barrow, USMC (Ret.), *Marine Corps Gazette* 65 (March 1981), 28.
⁹ General Alfred M. Gray, Jr., USMC (Ret.), *Warfighting* (New York: Doubleday, 1994), 58–59, 63.
¹⁰ Major General John A. Lejeune, USMC (Ret.), *The Reminiscences of a Marine* (Philadelphia: Dorrance and Company, 1930), 440.
¹¹ Ibid., 301.
¹² Ibid., 307.
¹³ Ibid., 440.
¹⁴ Ibid.
¹⁵ Lieutenant General Victor Krulak, USMC (Ret.), oral history with John T. Mason, Jr., 56–59.
¹⁶ Author interview with General Charles C. Krulak, USMC (Ret.), July 5, 2006.

17 Ibid., 46.
18 Norman Varnell Cooper, "The Military Career of General Holland M. Smith, USMC," PhD dissertation, University of Alabama, 1974, 294.
19 Shepherd, 225–228.
20 Burke Davis, *Marine! The Life of Lieutenant General Lewis B. (Chesty) Puller, USMC* (Boston: Little, Brown and Company, 1962), 148.
21 Ibid., 188–189.
22 Ibid., 201–202.
23 General Lewis W. Walt, *Strange War, Strange Strategy: A General's Report on Vietnam* (New York: Funk and Wagnalls, 1970), 50.
24 Ibid., 151.
25 Author interview with General Paul X. Kelley, USMC (Ret.), June 13, 2005.
26 Author interview with General Carl E. Mundy, Jr., USMC (Ret.), December 18, 2004.
27 Mundy, 667–668.
28 Captain Eli Takesian, CHC, USN (Ret.), "Ministering to Marines in a Sustained Combat Environment," *Marine Corps Gazette*, February 2001.
29 Ibid.
30 Ibid.
31 Ibid.
32 Author interview with General Alfred M. Gray, Jr., USMC (Ret.), October 27, 2004.
33 Mundy, 163.
34 Ibid., 675.
35 Ibid., 391.
36 General Charles C. Krulak, USMC (Ret.), oral history with Dr. David B. Crist, 103.
37 Ibid., 130.
38 Ibid., 25.
39 Author interview with General Charles C. Krulak, USMC (Ret.), December 21, 2004.
40 Davis, 61.
41 Lieutenant General Charles G. Cooper, USMC (Ret.), *Cheers and Tears: A Marine's Story of Combat in Peace and War* (Reno, NV: Wesley Press, 2002), 126.
42 Barrow, oral history, 579.
43 General Robert H. Barrow, USMC (Ret.), *Marine Corps Gazette* 65 (March 1981), 28.

## Chapter 12

1 Major General John A. Lejeune, USMC (Ret.), *The Reminiscences of a Marine* (Philadelphia: Dorrance and Company, 1930), 247, 409.
2 General A.A. Vandegrift, USMC (Ret.), *Once a Marine: The Memoirs of General A.A. Vandegrift* (New York: Ballantine Books, 1966).
3 Author interview with General Alfred M. Gray, Jr., USMC (Ret.), October 27, 2004.
4 Author correspondence with General Carl E. Mundy, Jr., USMC (Ret.), March 5, 2004.
5 Author correspondence with General Charles C. Krulak, USMC (Ret.), November 6, 2006.
6 Author interview with General James L. Jones, USMC (Ret.), July 21, 2001.
7 Charles T. Jones and R. Manning Ancell, eds., *Four-Star Leadership for Leaders* (Mechanicsburg, PA: Executive Books, 1997), 23.
8 Tom Clancy with General Anthony Zinni, USMC (Ret.), and Tony Koltz, *Battle Ready* (New York: G.P. Putnam's Sons, 2004), 128.
9 Lejeune, 34.
10 Ibid., 52.
11 Ibid., 275.
12 Ibid., 428; Gray interview, October 8, 2008.
13 Lejeune, 465.

[14] *U.S. News and World Report*, September 10, 1979; author interview with General Robert H. Barrow, USMC (Ret.).
[15] General Carl E. Mundy, Jr., USMC (Ret.), oral history with Brigadier General Edwin H. Simmons, USMC (Ret.), 674.
[16] General Charles C. Krulak, USMC (Ret.), oral history with Dr. David B. Crist, 28.
[17] Author interview with General Robert H. Barrow, USMC (Ret.).
[18] General Lemuel C. Shepherd, Jr., USMC (Ret.), oral history with Benis M. Frank, 43.
[19] Robert Debs Heinl, USMC, *Soldiers of the Sea* (Baltimore, MD: The Nautical Aviation Publishing Company of America, 1991), 517–518.
[20] Ibid.
[21] Charles Krulak, oral history.
[22] Obituary of General David M. Shoup, USMC, *Marine Corps Gazette*, March 1983, 13–14.
[23] General Robert H. Barrow, USMC, (Ret.), oral history with Brigadier General Edwin H. Simmons, USMC (Ret.), 357.
[24] Gray interview.
[25] Alfred M. Gray, Jr., "The Art of Command," *Marine Corps Gazette*, October 1987, 18.
[26] Author interview with General Anthony Zinni, USMC (Ret.), December 17, 2007.
[27] Barrow interview, June 24, 2004.
[28] General Raymond G. Davis, USMC (Ret.), *The Story of Ray Davis* (Varina, NC: Research Triangle Publications, 1995), 82.
[29] Mundy, oral history, 671.
[30] Charles Krulak, oral history.
[31] Lejeune, 484.
[32] Vandegrift, 331–332.
[33] General Robert E. Cushman, Jr., USMC (Ret.), oral history with Benis M. Frank.
[34] General Louis H. Wilson, Jr., USMC (Ret.), oral history with Brigadier General Edwin H. Simmons, USMC (Ret.).
[35] General Robert H. Barrow, USMC (Ret.), oral history with Brigadier General Edwin H. Simmons, USMC (Ret.), 37.
[36] Author correspondence with General Paul X. Kelley, USMC (Ret.), January 13, 2005.
[37] Mundy correspondence, December 18, 2004.
[38] Letter from General Holland M. Smith, USMC, to A.A. Vandegrift, February 4, 1944.
[39] Lieutenant General Victor H. Krulak, USMC (Ret.), oral history with John T. Mason, Jr.
[40] General Raymond G. Davis, USMC (Ret.), oral history with Benis M. Frank, 264–265.
[41] Burke Davis, *Marine! The Life of Lieutenant General Lewis B. (Chesty) Puller, USMC* (Boston: Little, Brown and Company, 1962), 373.
[42] Krulak correspondence.

# About the Author

Edgar F. Puryear, Jr., is a professor emeritus at Georgetown University, where he taught from 1983 to 2000, and has served as a scholar in residence at National Defense University. Over the last 45 years he has lectured on military character and leadership at numerous American military institutions and installations. He currently practices law in Madison, Virginia.

Dr. Puryear is the author of *Nineteen Stars: A Study in Military Character and Leadership* (Presidio Press, 1978); *Stars in Flight: A Study in Air Force Character and Leadership* (Presidio Press, 1981); *George S. Brown, General, U.S. Air Force: Destined for Stars* (Presidio Press, 1983); *American Generalship: Character is Everything: The Art of Command* (Presidio Press, 2001); and *American Admiralship: The Moral Imperatives of Naval Command* (Naval Institute Press, 2005).

www.ingramcontent.com/pod-product-compliance
Lightning Source LLC
Chambersburg PA
CBHW082102230426
43671CB00015B/2589